Handbook of Latent
Semantic Analysis

Handbook of Latent Semantic Analysis

Edited by

Thomas K Landauer
Danielle S. McNamara
Simon Dennis
Walter Kintsch

Routledge
Taylor & Francis Group

NEW YORK AND LONDON

First published 2007 by
Lawrence Erlbaum Associates, Inc.

This edition published 2011 by Routledge

Routledge
Taylor & Francis Group
711 Third Avenue
New York, NY 10017

Routledge
Taylor & Francis Group
2 Park Square, Milton Park
Abingdon, Oxfordshire OX14 4RN

First issued in paperback 2014

Routledge is an imprint of the Taylor and Francis Group, an informa business

Cover design by Tomai Maridou

Cover art "Round About," 1998, 48" x 48", Oil Paint and Roofing
Tar on Denim, by Randy McNamara

Library of Congress Cataloging-in-Publication Data

Handbook of latent semantic analysis / edited by Thomas K Landauer ...
[et al.].
   p. cm. — (University of Colorado Institute of Cognitive Science series)
   Includes bibliographical references and index.
ISBN 978-0-8058-5418-3 — 0-8058-5418-5 (cloth : alk. paper)
ISBN 978-1-4106-1534-3 — 1-4106-1534-0 (E Book)
1. Semantics—Data processing. 2. Semantics—Mathematical models. 3.
   Semantics—Psychological aspects.   I. Landauer, Thomas K
P325.5.D38H36   2006
410'.151—dc22   2006014971
                                                                  CIP

ISBN 13: 978-0-8058-5418-3 (hbk)
ISBN 13: 978-1-138-00419-1 (pbk)

Contents

PART II: LSA IN COGNITIVE THEORY

PART III: LSA IN EDUCATIONAL APPLICATIONS

PART VI: CONCLUSION

Preface

WHAT IS THIS BOOK FOR?

This volume, *Handbook of Latent Semantic Analysis*, celebrates the theoretical and practical contributions of latent semantic analysis over the past 15 years. These chapters, written by the leading investigators using LSA, provide the research community with a seminal volume on this revolutionary technique. The first editor, Tom Landauer, was the project leader of the team that developed LSA in the late 1980s. Since the time that LSA was first proposed, there has been an explosion of research and applications involving LSA. LSA has become both a widely debated theoretical model and a widely used cognitive tool. A search for latent semantic analysis in *Science Citation Index* reveals hundreds of published journal articles, most of which appeared in the last 3 years. In addition, the LSA Web site that provides access to the computational tools has received 7.8 million hits since April 2001.

Nonetheless, although there has been substantial interest in LSA, there remain many misconceptions about the technical and theoretical underpinnings of the technique and how it can be appropriately used. Here we provide a definitive volume to which one can turn to gain a more thorough understanding of LSA. The first section, Introduction to LSA: Theory and Methods, provides the theoretical and mathematical foundations of LSA, as well as basic information on how to use LSA. The second section, LSA in

Cognitive Theory, provides examples of how LSA can be used to test theories of cognition and to better understand cognitive phenomena. The third and fourth sections, LSA in Educational Applications and Information Retrieval and HCI Applications of LSA, provide examples of how LSA can be used in the real world. The fifth section describes ways in which LSA has been extended to meet a wider array of problems and questions. Our goal is to provide clear directives to researchers concerning the situations when LSA will be the optimal technique to be used, and when it may not be.

Thus, this volume provides readers with valuable information about the rationale and theory underlying LSA, basic information about how to use LSA, implications of LSA for cognitive theories, and examples of how LSA has been applied to practical problems. We hope this volume provides necessary information and guidance about LSA and the examples of how LSA has been used in practical applications will give others insight into how they too can make use of what it offers. We further hope that discussion of its theoretical assumptions, as well as current alternatives to LSA, will lead to further developments of methods for extracting meaning from text. We believe that LSA provides a road to meaning, and this destination will be reached by communicating LSA to the research community.

WHAT IS LATENT SEMANTIC ANALYSIS?

Latent semantic analysis (LSA) is a theory and method for extracting and representing the meaning of words. Meaning is estimated using statistical computations applied to a large corpus of text (Landauer & Dumais, 1997). The corpus embodies a set of mutual constraints that largely determine the semantic similarity of words and sets of words. These constraints can be solved using linear algebra methods, in particular, singular value decomposition. LSA has been shown to reflect human knowledge in a variety of ways. For example, LSA measures correlate highly with humans' scores on standard vocabulary and subject matter tests; it mimics human word sorting and category judgments; it simulates word–word and passage–word lexical priming data; and it accurately estimates passage coherence. In addition, LSA has found application in a number of areas, including selecting educational materials for individual students, guiding online discussion groups, providing feedback to pilots on landing technique, diagnosing mental disorders from prose, matching jobs with candidates, and facilitating automated tutors.

LSA Is a Technique for Analyzing Text

Before the advent of LSA, extracting meaning from text involved significant human intervention—legions of coders spending hours rewriting text in formal notation. LSA analyses demonstrated that a great deal of what is conveyed by a text can be extracted automatically using the tools of linear algebra. LSA provides not only that information explicit in the text, but also the underlying or latent meaning of the text —an advance that has had profound implications across a broad array of application areas.

LSA Is a Theory of Meaning

Whereas LSA was developed as a practical technique, it also makes novel and hotly contested conjectures about the nature of meaning. The theory postulates that the meaning of a text is largely conveyed by the words from which it is composed. The order in which the words appear is important in some specific cases, but it is not as critical in determining meaning as the words themselves. Furthermore, the theory underlying LSA arguments concerns the developmental acquisition of word meanings. Some theories of vocabulary acquisition posit an incremental process that proceeds by composing the elements of sense experience. In contrast, according to LSA, meaning is acquired by solving an enormous set of simultaneous equations that capture the contextual usage of words.

LSA Is a New Approach to Cognitive Science

Finally, LSA exemplifies a new approach to cognitive science. Rather than focusing on dissecting the minutiae of laboratory experiments, LSA attempts to account for the data produced by real participants in real tasks. One task of cognitive science, it argues, should be to account for what most people do most of the time. The use of large text corpora to test cognitive theories is radically altering our assumptions and our approaches to answering questions in cognitive science.

HOW DID THIS VOLUME COME ABOUT AND WHO DO WE HAVE TO THANK?

This volume was preceded in May 2004 by a workshop at the University of Colorado. We met there to discuss our research and to find common ground among researchers using LSA. In that respect, the workshop was immensely useful and illuminating. It was also fun. The workshop was funded by the Institute of Cognitive Science at University of Colorado and the Institute for Intelligent Systems at the University of Memphis; we are grateful for the institutes' support of such research endeavors. We are also grateful to many individuals who helped to organize that workshop, including the staff of the Institute of Cognitive Science and the many student volunteers who helped make the conference both pleasant and successful. We further thank the chapter reviewers for their dedication to the field. Although the chapters were reviewed primarily by the contributors to this volume, we also thank Mina Johnson-Glenberg and Daniel Navarro for helping with the review process. Finally, we are most grateful to those who contributed their chapters to this volume. Without the work that they have conducted to use, explore, and understand LSA and in turn to better understand human cognition, this volume most certainly would not have been possible. We thank them for the research they are conducting and for their contributions to this volume.

We also thank Randy McNamara for the artwork that graces the cover of this book. Randy McNamara has an MFA from Indiana University, has won numerous awards, and has shown extensively on the east and west coast, most recently at Gallery 825 in Los Angeles. Randy McNamara presently resides in Los Angeles with his wife and two young sons.

—Danielle McNamara
—Walter Kintsch
—Simon Dennis
—Tom Landauer

REFERENCES

Landauer, T. K., & Dumais, S. T. (1997). A solution to Plato's problem: The Latent Semantic Analysis theory of acquisition, induction and representation of knowledge [Electronic version]. *Psychological Review, 104*(2), 211–240.

I

Introduction to LSA
Theory and Methods

1

LSA as a Theory of Meaning

Thomas K Landauer

Pearson Knowledge Technologies and University of Colorado

The fundamental scientific puzzle addressed by the latent semantic analysis (LSA) theory is that there are hundreds of distinctly different human languages, every one with tens of thousands of words. The ability to understand the meanings of utterances composed of these words must be acquired by virtually every human who grows up surrounded by language. There must, therefore, be some humanly shared method—some computational system—by which any human mind can learn to do this for any language by extensive immersion, and without being explicitly taught definitions or rules for any significant number of words.

Most past and still popular discussions of the problem focus on debates concerning how much of this capability is innate and how much learned (Chomsky, 1991b) or what abstract architectures of cognition might support it—such as whether it rests on association (Skinner, 1957) or requires a theory of mind (Bloom, 2000).

The issue with which LSA is concerned is different. LSA theory addresses the problem of exactly how word and passage meaning can be constructed from experience with language, that is, by what mechanisms—instinctive, learned, or both—this can be accomplished.

Carefully describing and analyzing the phenomenon has been the center of attention for experimental psychology, linguistics, and philosophy. Other areas of interest include pinpointing what parts of the brain are most heavily involved in which functions and how they interact, or positing functional modules and system models. But, although necessary or useful, these approaches do not solve the problem of how it is possible to make the brain, or any other system, acquire the needed abilities at their natural scale and rate.

This leads us to ask the question: Suppose we have available a corpus of data approximating the mass of intrinsic and extrinsic language-relevant experience that a human encounters, a computer with power that could match that of the human brain, and a sufficiently clever learning algorithm and data storage method. Could it learn the meanings of all the words in any language it was given?

The keystone discovery for LSA was that using just a single simple constraint on the structure of verbal meaning, and a rough approximation to the same experience as humans, LSA can perform many meaning-based cognitive tasks as well as humans.

That this provides a proof that LSA creates meaning is a proposition that manifestly requires defense. Therefore, instead of starting with explication of the workings of the model itself, the chapter first presents arguments in favor of that proposition. The arguments rest on descriptions of what LSA achieves and how its main counterarguments can be discounted.

THE TRADITIONAL ANTILEARNING ARGUMENT

Many well-known thinkers—Plato, Bickerton (1995), Chomsky (1991b), Fodor (1987), Gleitman (1990), Gold (1967), Jackendoff (1992), Osherson, Stob, and Weinstein (1984), Pinker (1994), to name a few—have considered this *prima facie* impossible, usually on the grounds that humans learn language too easily, that they are exposed to too little evidence, correction, or instruction to make all the conceptual distinctions and generalizations that natural languages demand. This argument has been applied mainly to the learning of grammar, but has been asserted with almost equal conviction to apply to the learning of word meanings as well, most famously by Plato, Chomsky, and Pinker. Given this postulate, it follows that the mind (brain, or any equivalent computational system) must be equipped with other sources of conceptual and linguistic knowledge. This is not an entirely unreasonable hypothesis. After all, the vast majority of living things come equipped with or can develop complex and important behavioral capabilities in isolation from other living things. Given this widely accepted assumption, it would obviously be impossible for a computer using input only from a sample of natural language in the form of unmodified text to come even close to doing things with verbal meaning that humans do.

THE LSA BREAKTHROUGH

It was thus a major surprise to discover that a conceptually simple algorithm applied to bodies of ordinary text could learn to match literate humans on tasks that if done by people would be assumed to imply understanding of the meaning of words and passages. The model that first accomplished this feat was LSA.

LSA is a computational model that does many humanlike things with language. The following are but a few: After autonomous learning from a large body of representative text, it scores well into the high school student range on a standardized multiple-choice vocabulary test; used alone to rate the adequacy of content of expository essays (other variables are added in full- scale grading systems; Landauer, Laham, & Foltz, 2003a, 2003b), estimated in more than one way, it shares 85%–90% as much information with expert human readers as two human readers share with each other (Landauer, 2002a); it has measured the effect on comprehension of paragraph-to-paragraph coherence better than human coding (Foltz, Kintsch, & Landauer, 1998); it has successfully modeled several laboratory findings in cognitive psychology (Howard, Addis, Jing, & Kahana, chap. 7 in this volume; Landauer, 2002a; Landauer & Dumais, 1997; Lund, Burgess, & Atchley, 1995); it detects improvements in student knowledge from before to after reading as well as human judges (Rehder et al., 1998; Wolfe et al., 1998); it can diagnose schizophrenia from what patients say as well as experienced psychiatrists (Elevåg, Foltz, Weinberger, & Goldberg, 2005); it improves information retrieval by up to 30% by being able to match queries to documents of the same meaning when there are few or no words in common and reject those with many when irrelevant (Dumais, 1991), and can do the same for queries in one language matching documents in another where no words are alike (Dumais, Landauer, & Littman, 1996); it does its basic functions of correctly simulating human judgments of meaning similarity between paragraphs without modification by the same algorithm in every language to which it has been applied, examples of which include Arabic, Hindi, and Chinese in their native orthographic or ideographic form; and when sets of all LSA similarities among words for perceptual entities such as kinds of objects (e.g., flowers, trees, birds, chairs, or colors) are subjected to multidimensional scaling, the resulting structures match those based on human similarity judgments quite well in many cases, moderately well in others (Laham, 1997, 2000), just as we would expect (and later explain) because text lacks eyes, ears, and fingers.

I view these and its several other successful simulations (see Landauer, 2002a; Landauer, Foltz, & Laham, 1998) as evidence that LSA and models like it (Griffiths & Steyvers, 2003; Steyvers & Griffiths, chap. 21 in this volume) are candidate mechanisms to explain much of how verbal meaning might be learned and used by the human mind.

ABOUT LSA'S KIND OF THEORY

LSA offers a very different kind of account of verbal meaning from any that went before, including centuries of theories from philosophy, linguistics, and psychology. Its only real predecessor is an explanation inherent in connectionist models but unrealized yet at scale (O'Reilly & Munakata, 2000). Previous accounts had all been in the form of rules, descriptions, or variables (parts of speech, grammars, etc.) that could only be applied by human intercession, products of the very process that needs explanation. By contrast, at least in programmatic goal, the LSA account demands that the only data allowed the theory and its computational instantiations be those to which natural human language users have access. The theory must operate on the data by means that can be expressed with mathematical rigor, not through the intervention of human judgments. This disallows any linguistic rule or structure unless it can be proved that all human minds do equivalent things without explicit instruction from other speakers, the long unattained goal of the search for a universal grammar. It also rules out as explanations—as contrasted with explorations—computational linguistic systems that are trained on corpora that have been annotated by human speakers in ways that only human speakers can.

This way of explaining language and its meaning is so at odds with most traditional views and speculations that, in Piaget's terminology, it is hard for many people, both lay and scholar, to accommodate. Thus, before introducing its history and more of its evidence and uses, I want to arm readers with a basic understanding of what LSA is and how it illuminates what verbal meaning might be.

BUT WHAT IS MEANING?

First, however, let us take head-on the question of what it signifies to call something a theory of meaning. For a start, I take it that meaning as carried by words and word strings is what allows modern humans to engage in verbal thought and rich interpersonal communication. But this, of course, still begs the question of what meaning itself is.

Philosophers, linguists, humanists, novelists, poets, and theologians have used the word "meaning" in a plethora of ways, ranging, for example, from the truth of matters to intrinsic properties of objects and happenings in the world, to mental constructions of the outside world, to physically irreducible mystical essences, as in Plato's ideas, to symbols in an internal communication and reasoning system, to potentially true but too vague notions such as how words are used (Wittgenstein, 1953). Some assert that meanings are abstract concepts or properties of the world that exist prior to and independently of any language-dependent representation. This leads to assertions that by nature or definition computers cannot create meaning from data; meaning must exist first. Therefore, what a computer creates, stores, and uses cannot, *ipso facto*, be meaning itself.

A sort of corollary of this postulate is that what we commonly think of as the meaning of a word has to be derived from, "grounded in," already meaningful primitives in perception or action (Barsalou, 1999; Glenberg & Robertson, 2000; Harnad, 1990; Searle, 1982). In our view ("our" meaning proponents of LSA-like theories), however, what goes on in the mind (and, by identity, the brain) in direct visual or auditory, or any other perception, is fundamentally the same as what goes on in any other form of cognition and has no necessary priority over other sources of knowledge, such as—in particular—autonomous manipulations of strings of words that convey abstract combinations of ideas such as imaginary numbers. Of course, strings of words must somehow be able to represent and convey both veridical and hypothetical information about our inner and outer worlds; otherwise, language would not be very useful. Certainly, that is, much perceptual experience must map onto linguistic expressions. And many linguistic expressions must map onto perceptual experience. However, once the mappings have been obtained through the cultural evolution of a language, there is no necessity that most of the knowledge of meaning cannot be learned from exposure to language itself. The highly developed verbal-intellectual feats of Helen Keller, and the more modest but still near normal knowledge and communication accomplishments of most congenitally blind people—including the correct use of color and shape words—would be impossible (Keller, 1905; Landau & Gleitman, 1985).

This puts the causal situation in a different light. We may often first learn relations of most words and passages to each other from our matrices of verbal experiences and then attach them to perceptual experience by embedding them in the abstract word space. Take the example of geographical maps. A map of England's cities can be constructed from a relatively small set of measured point-to-point distances projected onto the surface of a sphere. You can understand the geography of England simply by viewing the map. I can tell you that Cambridge is North of London and Oxford north of Cambridge, and you can then tell me that Oxford is north of Cambridge (from the map, not the logic).

It is important to understand that in LSA, as in a map, the coordinates are arbitrary. North and south are conventionally used for the earth, but the relation of any point to any other would be just as well located by any other set of nonidentical axes. LSA axes are not derived from human verbal descriptions; they are underlying points in a coordinate system, in LSA's case, one that relates meanings to each other. LSA's theory of meaning is that the underlying map is the primitive substrate that gives words meaning, not vice versa. By contrast, artificial intelligence (AI) ontologies, such as WordNet and CYC, start with intuitive human judgments about relations among words, the output of the mechanism LSA seeks to provide.

In LSA, words do not have meanings on their own that define the axes, words get their meanings from their mapping. Nonetheless, it is sometimes possible to rotate the space so that at least some words, as discrete points, fall near common, not necessarily orthogonal, axes so that word names can be associated with them to yield intuitive interpretation. Some other LSA-like systems have been built to maximize such intuitiveness (Griffiths & Styvers, 2003).

ON THE EPISTEMOLOGICAL NATURE OF LSA

Now a map is not the thing itself; it is an abstraction from which much more can be induced—an infinite number of point-to-point distances computed by triangulation from earlier established points—than is possible with only raw perceptual experiences of the real thing, say from walking around England's green and pleasant land. Just so, language maps perceptions and actions onto the physical world, and vice versa, but does very much more by supporting induction of an infinite number of meanings of words and word combinations. It is, according to LSA, almost entirely the relations that are represented and activated by words and collections of words that create verbal meaning. And it is primarily these abstract relations that make thinking, reasoning, and interpersonal communication possible. Qualitatively, this proposal shares much with the ideas of Wittgenstein (1953), but as we will see, LSA transforms them into a concrete and testable mathematical theory.

However, there is another noteworthy difference between many abstract theories and LSA. The difference concerns the unique nature of the phenomenon with which LSA deals. Memory and language are not physical objects, they are properties of an information-processing system. Their nature is only present in information storage, organization, and control. Thus, LSA is not only a mapping technique that is not the real thing—a computer, not a brain—it is a real thing in the same sense as thought is a real thing. It not only models, it does some of the same things. In this way, it is a bit unusual as a model. Bohr's model of the atom is a marvel of physical explanation, but it cannot actually build physical molecules. Model airplanes or ships can be faithful representations, even fly or sail, but they cannot transport people or cargo. Even most mathematical models in psychology have the same limitation, some neural nets being exceptions.

OTHER MEANINGS

Word meanings are not the only form of meaning. Complex relations among perceptions and actions must be entities of a highly similar sort, the kind shared by nonverbal and preverbal animals and infants. And these "primitive" meanings must also have learned interrelations with verbal meaning that places at least some on the same cognitive map as words. Integrating perceptions into the map also changes the meanings of words and passages. This is an almost self-evident necessity that is fully consistent with our claim that most relations among verbal meanings can be learned from language experience alone. As we shall see, the success of LSA is incontrovertible evidence of this. Our later description of cross-language retrieval by LSA also suggests a mechanism by which the mapping between perception and language might be constructed.

Just as creation of geographical maps from a small number of observations allows induction of greatly more relations, if the meaning of verbal expressions is a structure of the same sort, then most word–word and word–perception relations should be inducible from measures of a small subset of such relations. The question of how this is done can be approached by finding computable models that can accomplish the same thing. LSA is one such model.

LSA IS NOT A COMPLETE MODEL OF LANGUAGE

Lest the scope of our argument be misunderstood, let me make it clear before going on that LSA is not a complete theory of language or meaning. It does not take into account word order by which the meaning of sentences or the implications of sentence and paragraph order are altered. Without human help, it often does not adequately represent the variability of meanings conveyed by predication, anaphora, metaphor, modification, attachment, quantification, logical or mathematical propositions, or negations. These are important issues in language understanding that have not yet been reduced to the kinds of explanation we desire. This fact, however, does not mean that the theory is wrong, only that it does not cover all aspects of language. The analogy of accounting for the trajectory of a falling leaf comes to mind. Thus, contra Popper, constructing examples of sentence-to-sentence similarities for which a model does not match human judgments well (Glenberg & Robertson, 2000) does not falsify the theory. Nor does it show that the general approach to language modeling will not succeed. Indeed, new approaches to modeling the modification of meaning by word order may not be too long in coming. A good start on the latter problem is represented by Dennis's SP model (chap. 3 in this volume, 2005).

All this aside, however, estimates of the relative amount that word order and word choice contribute to overall meaning of a sentence or paragraph suggest that the latter carries the lion's share, on the order of 80%–90% (Landauer, 2002a, and later.)

ABOUT INTUITIVE REVULSION TO LSA

Undoubtedly, however, this approach to the question will fail to satisfy many from the other camps. They will still feel that, at best, computers can only artificially mimic or mirror the real thing, not actually be it themselves. We have no strong quarrel with such a position. LSA is a theory—not reality itself—at least in so far as the particular mathematics it uses are unlikely to be the same. Nonetheless, the fact that LSA can do many of the things that humans do almost indistinguishably from humans means that it must in part be isomorphic to the real thing—whatever it is. Thus, we believe that a successful computational model, even if incomplete, supplies a better foundation for progress in explaining the phenomena of language and meaning than do purely verbal philosophical arguments from which simulations of human performance cannot be constructed without contributions from the knowledge of language that is to be explained.

In any event, however, such arguments do not overly concern us. LSA as a theory of meaning has aimed primarily at a more restricted, empirical, and pragmatic domain for explaining the nature of meaning. We are interested in how to get a machine to do useful things with language even if not the same things in exactly the same way. The question is how experience can be used to learn how to use words and strings of words to do what humans do. It is because LSA can do so that we think it provides a promising theory about how language works. Because by any sensible interpretation, adequate use of words requires knowledge of verbal meaning and LSA makes adequate use of words, LSA must have such knowledge too.

A REVIEW TO HERE

Let me review what I have argued so far. LSA demonstrates a computational method by which a major component of language learning and use can be achieved. It is in that sense that LSA is a theory. It is specifically a theory of meaning because it offers an explanation of phenomena that are ordinarily considered to be manifestations of meaning—the expression, comprehension, and communication of ideas and knowledge in words and passages of words. It offers an explicit theory about the nature of word and passage meaning and its acquisition and application. It makes possible computer systems that accomplish a wide range of cognitive tasks performed by humans, and often does them essentially as well. This makes its basic mechanism, or something much like it, a candidate for explaining the corresponding human abilities. LSA is a theory about an essential aspect of language, not of everything about language. However, its successes encourage hope that more complete theories in the same spirit, say with additional cooperating mechanisms based on instinct or learning, are possible.

MORE ABOUT THE MISSING PIECES OF THE PUZZLE

However, consider somewhat further the matter of how word order and grammar affect meaning—important influences that unsupplemented LSA ignores. For simplicity, I will sometimes lump together under the term *syntax*, many of the ways in which differences in word order are involved in linguistic descriptions of its effects on meaning: including word class requirements, constituent combination, and higher order sentence structures (see Wikipedia). Note, however, that not all the ways in which grammar and syntax work are excluded by LSA. The combinations of words that best produce a passage meaning must have the right tenses, number, determiners, and so forth. It is only those differences that require differential word order that are at stake.

Given the long and almost exclusive concentration of linguistic research and theory on these factors, how can LSA do so well without them? People in over 2,000 cultures have learned hundreds of easily distinguishable languages, any one of which is almost incomprehensible to speakers of any of the others. Some scholars (Bickerton, 1995; Chomsky, 1991a, 1991b; Fodor, 1987; Gold, 1967; Pinker, 1994) think that the heart of this mystery is the wide variety of grammars governing how different classes of words and the ordering of words in an utterance give rise to differences in meaning (the meaning of words usually treated as a primitive).

This is an important unsolved problem despite long and sophisticated attempts. The principal attack has been to search for an innately given skeleton that is easily transmuted into that for a given language by exposure to a small sample of its use, somewhat as songbirds learn their songs. Unfortunately, we do not know of any detailed mechanism by which this could actually work (even in song birds), much less an algorithm that can accomplish the feat. However, we believe that an even more important but tractable problem (as LSA's success without word order suggests) is how people learn the meaning of all the words in their language. English is probably the champion, having many millions of sometimes-used words of which a well-educated adult must have reasonable command of the meaning of around 100,000. Following Plato (and some others in between), Chomsky

(1991a, 1991b) has averred that this is simply impossible because the exposure to words in informative contexts is manifestly much too limited. Thus, he (and others) have concluded that infants must start out with all the possible concepts needed in any human environment and simply learn names to go with a large number of them. Thus, the acquisition of meaning for words is finessed, the meanings preexist in all of us—supposedly learning names for all of concepts takes very little new knowledge, just as picking the right grammar supposedly does. In both cases, I find such claims unsatisfactory, given the difference, say, between the concepts needed by a Chinese rice farmer, a French biochemist, and an Inuit seal hunter, and between the strongly interrelated use of grammars to combine them into meaningful utterances. But that is not my major complaint about the hypothesis. The most unacceptable part is the basis of the hypothesis, which in a nutshell can be expressed as such: "I cannot imagine any way that all the concepts and words could be learned with the evidence available." Before a problem is solved, people often cannot imagine a solution. That humans have a species special instinctive capacity for language, as argued by Pinker (1994) and others (e.g., Ridley, 1994), is unexceptionable, but does not answer the more interesting question of how the instinct works.

Thus, I do not argue that humans have no innate knowledge relevant to language. Without experience, centipedes and foals can walk, and bees can navigate; surely humans come ready for the cognitive tasks that all humans must perform. From worms to humans, the brain/mind must be extremely flexible, able to adapt dramatically when so required. Learning a particular vocabulary of tens of thousands of words must be one of those situations.

What is needed, then, is a mental mechanism that actually can learn language from the available evidence. Presumably, this must be a previously unknown mechanism because the theories of learning previously available to world-class thinkers like Chomsky (1991a, 1991b), Fodor (1987), Skinner (1957), Pinker (1994), and Pylyshyn (1980), did not suffice. Such a mechanism must instantiate a computation that can do what's needed.

To bring this to an end, let me summarize: LSA provides one way to do very much of what's needed. LSA falls short of what human minds can do in several ways, some quite important. But, the really important thing it does do is provide a computational theory of what word and passage meaning is and how it can be acquired from the evidence available to an ordinary human. The theory is proposed not only as an idealization or abstraction of the actual mechanism, but as a computational information-processing mechanism that actually performs many of the same functions. However, it is not claimed that its computational method is the same as nature's except at a higher level of abstraction that includes it as an example. What is claimed to be the same as human's is the general kind of function computed.

THE COMPUTATION EMPLOYED BY LSA

Finally, assuming that readers are now willing to grant the possibility that LSA qualifies as a theory of meaning—even if they still object to the way we have operationalized the term—we are ready to see what LSA is and how it does what it does. The description will still be a high-level conceptual account, the real math left for Martin and Berry (chap. 2 in this volume) and other sources (Berry, Dumais, & O'Brien, 1995; Deerwester, Dumais, Furnas, Landauer, & Harshman, 1990).

The most important foundation for LSA, especially given the way we have introduced the problem, is the power of exploiting mutual constraints. LSA rests on a single conceptually simple constraint, that the representation of any meaningful passage must be composed as a function of the representations of the words it contains. This constraint, somewhat generalized, goes under the name of "compositionality." The particular compositional constraint imposed by LSA is that representations of passages be sums of its representations of words. Basic algebra gives the most familiar example of how this constraint supplies the inductive power needed. Consider these two simultaneous equations: $A + 2B = 8$ and $A + B = 5$.

As all algebra students know, neither equation alone tells the value of either A or B, but the two together tells both. In the very same way, in LSA the meaning of a passage of text is the sum of the meanings of its words. In mathematical form:

$$\text{meaning passage} = \Sigma(m_{\text{word 1,}}\ m_{\text{word 2,}} \cdots m_{\text{word } n}). \qquad \textbf{1.1}$$

Thus, LSA models a passage as a simple linear equation, and a large corpus of text as a large set of simultaneous equations. (The mathematics and computations, singular value decomposition, by which the system is usually solved, are spelled out by Berry, 1992, and Martin & Berry, chap. 2 in this volume.) The constraint-satisfaction approach is also used by Dennis and by Steyvers and Griffiths (chaps. 3 and 21, respectively, in this volume), but with different constraints. To create an LSA representation of word meanings that satisfies this condition, one first secures a large (ideally, but never completely) representative sample of the language experience of people that is typical in content and size to that experienced by people whose language is to be captured in the model. Ideally, this would include all natural exposures to and uses of language, including their perceptual, physiological, and mind/brain contexts. This being unavailable, we have used the best approximation that we can find and fit into a computer, a large corpus of text that has been sampled so as to represent what a normal human would have read. (Landauer & Dumais, 1997, estimated that up to 80% of the words known to a college freshman would have been met only in print, and those met in speech would almost all have been met many times in print as well.) This is called a training corpus, which then divides the corpus of text into segments that carry (ideally again) full and coherent meanings, typically paragraphs. From this, one constructs a matrix with a row for each unique word type and a column for each passage; the cells contain (an information-theoretic transform of) the number of times that a particular word type appears in a particular passage.

As should be apparent from this description, the solution for any one word may depend on the solution of many other words; indeed, changing any one could, in principle, change every other. Therefore, successful simulation of human word and passage meaning can depend strongly on giving it a sufficiently large and representative text corpus to learn from, just as humans need vast experience to learn their languages. Hart and Risley (1995) estimated from large-scale systematic observations that an average child hears around six million word tokens per year. In practice, we have usually found that corpora containing from 10^7 to 10^{10} words of text divided into 10^5 to 10^9 paragraphs with 10^5 to 10^6 different word types—amounts of language experience roughly equivalent to that of children to highly literate adults—produce good results.

This produces a set of 10^5 to 10^9 simultaneous linear equations. Leaving out many important details, this system of simultaneous equations is solved for the meaning of each word-type and each passage, with a solution in which every paragraph conforms to the additive equation given earlier. Because the sample of paragraphs is very large and representative, we can be reasonably sure that new meaningful paragraphs will conform to the same function. Success in applications, such as scoring novel essays, confirms this expectation.

The solution is in the form of a set of vectors, one for each word and passage, each vector having typically 200–500 elements—factors or dimensions—in a "semantic space." The meaning of any new passage is computed by vector addition of the word vectors it contains. The similarity of meaning of two words is measured as the cosine (or dot product or Euclidean distance, depending on the application) between the vectors, and the similarity of two passages (of any length) as the same measure on the sum or average of all its contained words. Note carefully the important difference between this process and methods that measure the relative frequency of local co-occurrence to estimate the similarity of meaning of words. For example, Lund & Burgess, 1996.

DIMENSION REDUCTION AND ITS IMPORTANCE

I have glossed over the fact that the vectors representing words and passages usually have 200–500 elements rather than 3 or 10,000. It is actually a matter of critical importance to the success of LSA and of other similar methods (Erosheva, Fienberg, & Lafferty, 2004; Griffiths & Steyvers, 2003; Steyvers & Griffiths, chap. 21 in this volume). Consider again the mapping of geographical points. Suppose you measured the distances between, say, Oslo, Baghdad, and Sydney, and tried to plot them all on the same straight line. They would not fit together. If you try to do it in two dimensions, it gets much better, but still with gross distortions. Using three dimensions—a globe—you get quite close, ignoring elevations, which would take yet another dimension. Suppose now that you now plotted the same positions in one more dimension, say new measures in feet instead of miles. It would be of limited help, yielding greater accuracy than might be needed. A better solution is to find a dimensionality for which the resolution is optimized for your purposes, for example, for words to make near synonyms such as "car" and "automobile" much but not exactly the same, unrelated concepts such as "philosophy" and "automobile" not at all, and distantly related words such as "football" and "algebra" only slightly.

Here is another kind of explanation. With enough variables, every object is different from any other. For too few, all objects can easily be the same. Consider the vectors | a m r c | and | a m x b |. They are different by two components. If we drop the last two components, they are identical. If we drop just the last component, they are more nearly the same than initially. The effect is much like squinting just the right amount to make two different faces look the same while still looking like faces. If we want a graded similarity function relating words and passages that varies from little to much in a helpful way, we need an intermediate number of dimensions. (Note that it would not do to simply have different granularity on a single dimension because of the mapping problem described earlier.)

Something analogous happens in LSA. Here we want the amount of resolution in the model to match the resolution in human word and passage meanings. Optimal dimension reduction is a common workhorse in analysis of complex problems in many fields of science and engineering. One way of showing its immense importance in LSA is what happens when the original word by paragraph matrix is reconstructed from the reduced dimensional representation—estimating each now by distances from others. Suppose the initial matrix for a corpus has 500 million cells—each containing the number of times one of 50,000 unique word types appears in a particular one of 100,000 paragraphs. Over 99.9% of the cells will turn out to be empty. This makes the comparison of word or paragraph meanings quite chancy. However, after dimension reduction and reconstruction, every cell will be filled with an estimate that yields a similarity between any paragraph and any other and between any word and any other.

This is an extremely powerful kind of induction. It is what accounts for LSA's advantage over most current methods of information retrieval, which rely on matching literal words (or words that have been stemmed or lemmatized or to be equivalent to a few others). It is also what accounts for its ability to measure the similarity of two essays that use totally different words, and for all of the other properties of LSA that defy the intuition that learning language from language is impossible.

ABOUT CO-OCCURRENCE AND LSA

Sometimes people misunderstand the mechanism by which LSA represents similarity of word meanings as counting the relative number of times that two words appear in the same sentences or passages. Whereas LSA starts with a kind of co-occurrence, that of words with passages, the analysis produces a result in which the fact that two words appear in the same passage is not what makes them similar. As in all simultaneous equation problems, it is the degree to which they have the same effects on their summed values wherever they occur in meaningful passages that is measured in the result. Indeed, in a study (Landauer, 2002a) of a large random sample of word pairs, the correlation between LSA-measured word pair similarities (cosines and several alternate contingency metrics) and the number of times they appeared in the same passage was only a little higher than that with the number of times they appeared separately in different passages, which, by the common notion of co-occurrence, should make them more different, not more similar. In a way, the result is the opposite of word meaning coming from co-occurrence. LSA learns about the meaning of a word from every meeting with it and from the composition of all the passages in which it does not occur. It is only after learning its meaning by SVD and dimension reduction that its relation to all other words can be computed.

Consider also that the fact that two words that appeared in the same sentence would not be very good evidence that they had the same meaning because there would often be more expressive value in using two different words. On the other hand, it might be evidence that they were related to the same topic, and thus reflecting their choice by the author because the meanings of each helped to add up to the desired meaning of the whole, a different direction of causation for local co-occurrence.

Similarly, sometimes the mechanism of LSA has been attributed to indirect co-occurrences: **A** does not occur in the same passage as **B**, but both occur in some third passage, or more elaborately that local co-occurrences are percolated up a hierarchical or other network structure to connect with other words. This seems a quite unlikely mechanism to me. If direct local co-occurrence is not much more effective than separate occurrences, then indirect chains between words do not look promising. In any event, no such model has had the success of LSA, and LSA does not work that way.

It follows the same kind of arguments that the number or proportion of literal words shared between two passages is not the determinant of their similarity in LSA, as is illustrated later.

EXAMPLES OF LSA PROPERTIES

Here are a few more examples of what LSA accomplishes. Results are stated in cosines (which for vectors are ordered in the same manner as correlations). Cosine values can range between –1 and 1, but in practice rarely go below 0 for word–word, passage–passage, or word–passage similarities. Randomly chosen pairs of words from the same corpus as the example have a mean of about .03 and a standard deviation of about .08.

Next are some phrase and sentence cosine similarities where there are no shared words. These examples are selected, not typical, but of a sort that occurs often enough to make a large difference in the model's ability to simulate human similarity judgments:

"Several doctors operated on a patient"
"The surgery was done by many physicians " (cosine = .66)

"A circle's diameter":
"radius of spheres" (cosine = .55)
"music of the spheres" (cosine = .03)

Next are a few examples of what LSA accomplishes, first some typical word–word cosine similarity measures, presented in Table 1.1. Note that when LSA computes a meaning vector for a whole passage, the identities of the literal words of which it was composed are lost. The computation is a one-way function that cannot be reversed. It is possible to search for a set of words that will capture the gist of the meaning by adding up to near the same total. These are not necessarily the words initially used, and of course word order cannot be recovered at all, although one could usually construct a new syntactically correct passage with a highly similar overall meaning. The situation is analogous to human memory for text; a short time after reading a sentence or paragraph, people remember the gist of what they have read but loose the exact wording, a phenomenon known since Bartlett (1932). LSA's paragraph meanings are a form of gist.

WORD SENSES

As follows from the basic additive linear function of LSA, the vector representation of a unique word type is the average effect that it has on the meaning of paragraphs in which it occurs. (It also results from the effects of paragraphs in which it does not appear, but we will ignore that here for sim-

TABLE 1.1
Typical Word–Word Cosine Similarity Measures

Word Pair	Cosine
thing–things	.61
man–woman	.37
husband–wife	.87
sugar–sweet	.42
salt–NaCl	.61
cold–frigid	.44
mouse–mice	.79
doctor–physician	.61
physician–nurse	.76
go–went	.71
go–going	.69
going–gone	.54
should–ought	.51
kind–unkind	.18
upwards–downwards	.17
clockwise–counterclockwise	.85
black–white	.72
she–her	.98
he–him	.93
junk–garbage	.37
sun–moon	.28
sun–earth	.46
moon–earth	.40
Nebraska–Kansas	.87
Nebraska–Florida	.25
Kansas–Florida	.24

plicity.) A word vector thus carries all of its "senses"—all the different ways in which it has been used weighted by the relative magnitude of its effects in each paragraph in which it has occurred. Conversely, all of the contextually determined meanings of a word enter into the meaning of a paragraph. There are no separate representations for separate senses of a word type. The notion of disambiguating a word by sense before interpreting a passage containing it—for which a great deal of effort has been spent in computational linguistics—has no place in the LSA theory. Instead of prior disambiguation, the context in which it appears determines its contribution to meaning. Paragraph meaning is usually not unnaturally distorted by this mechanism for two reasons. First, the proportion of a word's various merged meanings is equal to the importance it gains from the meanings of all its occurrence and nonoccurrences. Thus, it will convey most strongly the right meaning for just those paragraphs in which it occurs. If one broke a word's meaning into discrete components (which we would not do because LSA treats the meaning as a continuous whole), and multiplied the resulting components by their frequency over the whole corpus, then the overall amount of conflict between components would usually be small. In other words, because strong aspects of meaning occur most often and are most likely to be right for their context when they do, and weak aspects do the converse, the average effect of "ambiguity" is small. Only when two aspects of a word's meaning are nearly equally strong (occur in equally important roles over equal numbers of paragraphs with very different meanings) will great conflict arise. Second, to the extent that an aspect of a word's meaning is unrelated to the rest of a paragraph in which it occurs, it is orthogonal to the paragraph's meaning to the same degree, and therefore acts only as noise.

To test this hypothesis, I studied LSA representations of multiple-sense words as defined by WordNet (Fellbaum, 1998; Landauer, 2002b). Every strongly multiple-sense word that we examined had significant similarity (cosine) to the text of each of its senses as defined in WordNet (with all forms of the word deleted from the definition.) Here is an example:

"*Swallow*"—"The process of taking food into the body through the mouth by eating." cosine = .57
"*Swallow*"—"Small long winged songbird noted for swift graceful flight and the regularity of its migrations." cosine = .30

However, there are exceptions to this picture within sentences. Sometimes word meanings affect each other. One example is in predication. In "My surgeon is a butcher" and "My butcher is a surgeon," different aspects of the meaning of a word are selected by differences in word order. Another example occurs in some metaphorical expressions, such as "His wife is the staysail of his life." Such phenomena—cases where a word does not correctly distinguish between meanings or lends only part of its meaning to a passage according to LSA—appear to occur much more frequently in linguistics books than in ordinary text. Nevertheless, they surely need explanation. Kintsch (1998, 2000, 2001, chap. 5 in this volume) has shown how LSA can help to construct explanations of this phenomenon.

For "My butcher is a surgeon" versus "My surgeon is a butcher," a set of n nearest neighbors to "butcher" in the semantic space are chosen. Vectors for words among them that are sufficiently similar to "surgeon" are added to that for "surgeon." As a result, the sentence meaning emphasizes the aspects of the meaning of "butcher" that are also contained in "surgeon," but not vice versa. Kintsch has incorporated this idea into his construction integration (CI) model, giving the process an iterative settling effect that improves its outcome. The algorithm is tested by comparing the original and modified sentences with words or expressions that carry the meaning that was not in the receiving word previously and should have been magnified in the resulting sentence vector, for example "precise." Unfortunately, to date, the choice of which is the predicate and which the object still depends on human judgments. Artificial intelligence parsers go some distance here, but neither are good enough to do the job nor free of human intervention.

(Note here that strong word order effects are almost entirely within sentences. When LSA is used to measure the similarity of multisentence passages, word order effects become of less and less consequence because of the rapidly increasing dominance of word choice, as described later.)

Set phrases or idioms pose a different problem with a more obvious solution. Many such expressions may be thought of as patterns of words on their evolutionary way to condensing to a single word. Such patterns can be detected by the fact that they occur much more often than they would if the words were independent. These are commonly called collocations, and their identification has been done by several different statistical approaches. Once identified, collocations can be collapsed into a single word vector for participation in LSA space training. Adding such an algorithm is *ex cathedra* for LSA, but retains its spirit by eschewing direct aid from human knowledge of word meanings.

EVALUATIONS AND PROOFS

The initial demonstrations (Landauer & Dumais, 1997) of LSA's ability to simulate human word meaning made use of a standardized vocabulary test, Educational Testing Service's TOEFL (Test of English as a Second Language). The test presents a target word and four alternative words and asks the student to choose the one whose meaning is most similar. LSA was trained on a corpus of size and content approximating that of an average American college freshman's lifetime reading, based on a sampling by Touchstone Applied Science Associates (TASA) of books used in K–12 schools and found in their libraries. LSA took the same test and got as many right as successful applicants to U.S. colleges from non-English-speaking countries. Further simulations showed that the rate at which LSA acquired vocabulary as a function of the amount of language exposure closely approximated the rate of vocabulary growth of American children, approximately 10 words a day as measured by average gains over a year. Moreover, just as is true for student learners, only 2 or 3 of the 10 words newly correct each day had been encountered during the last 24 hours. In LSA, the improvement came instead from the entailment of every word's relation to every other. Word meaning knowledge is not all or none, but grows gradually, not showing itself outwardly until good enough and in the right context with the right measuring instrument.

Recently, there have been several reports of models of different kinds that excel LSA on the same set of TOEFL items, getting as many as 90% correct, far better than the average student as well. These have all depended on having a much larger potential corpus to learn from, for example, the entire Internet, and searching it anew for the answer to each question. These models are of interest for practical applications such as data mining, and as different search techniques by which human memory might conceivably be used in performing the task. They also show convincingly that word meaning is latent in the evidence of experience and can be extracted from natural linguistic data. However, they do not speak to the question of whether such models can explain the human ability because they use more data than a typical human could have, and, especially, because they search for answers in a database after being given the question rather than answering from previously acquired knowledge. The fair comparison here, college applicants using the Internet to answer TOEFL items, would not be theoretically interesting for present purposes. Moreover, these models do not explain how words combine to form meaningful utterances, therefore nothing about meaning as construed here.

SYNTAX AGAIN

Some authors have also characterized LSA as a "bag-of-words" technique. This is true in the narrow sense that the data it uses does not include word order within passages. However, what the words are and what the model does with the words is critically different from the keyword or "vector space models" of current search engines with which the sobriquet of "bag-of-words method" is usually associated. In these techniques, query-to-document similarities are based on counting and weighting pair-wise word identities. The measurement of similarity of passages suggests throwing scrabble chips bearing words into bags of two different colors and counting (in some sophisticated way, of course) how many blue chips bear the same words as red chips. The result is just a value of the match in literal comparisons, no representation is first formed of the meaning of the things being compared, and there is no constraint on what words can be in the same bag. This is not a very appealing analog of the human process, much more like the naïve strawman notion of machine models of language attacked by Searle (1982) in his famous Chinese room allegory. By contrast, LSA accounts for the effects of all the words in each of the documents, matching or not, and such that their overall similarities match human judgments of semantic similarities. The LSA constraint that the combination of words in a "bag" add up to a meaningful passage for all passages in a very large sample of language gives a strong constraint on the content of a "bag." Thus, my fear that the use of "bag-of-words" for LSA significantly distorts its understanding for unwary readers.

BABEL AND THE EQUIVALENCE OF LANGUAGES

The severe dimension reduction from the original representation by, say, 100,000 words to 300 factors is an inductive step that forces the resulting vectors to drop unimportant detail to capture optimum levels of similarity. This process can be applied as easily to any language in which there are meaningful wholes composed of discrete meaningful units, be they French words or Chinese ideographs. This property is what has made it possible to automatically build LSA search engines with almost equal ease in Hindi, Arabic, Japanese, and Hebrew, as in those with Roman orthography. Non-English systems have also included German, English, Spanish, Italian, Swahili, and Latvian. It also makes it possible to build search engines in which passages composed in very different forms of meaning conveyance, such as Roman letters and Chinese ideographs, can be evaluated for similarity of meaning essentially as easily as passages all in one language.

All languages so far tried can be aligned with any other so that paragraphs in one have the same meaning as the other to nearly the same degree as those translated by expert human translators. Among other interesting things, this seems to confirm the belief that all languages are in some fundamental way the same. Because all languages must represent substantially the same set of meaning relations, they must also represent substantially the same relations among words. Importantly, however, in LSA the sameness is not given by observation of the phenomenon but by a well-specified computation that creates the equivalence.

The secret is again the common compositional constraint; in all languages, the parts add up to paragraph meanings. If two passages mean the same thing, then their summed vectors will be the same. Note the central importance of paragraphs (used in the general sense of a set of words with unitary meaning) as the determining unit of meaning. Informal support for paragraph meaning as the objective function of the learning model comes from observation of the normal units of discourse in which people write and converse, as appears in research corpora, and is taught as the optimal unit for a complete idea in composition classes.

Note now that the solution of the system of linear equations is unique only up to linear transformation and there are therefore an infinite number of solutions. Thus, even if two individuals had almost identical experience, small variations and differences in their LSA-like brains might result in quite different solutions, as might different languages.

How then can people understand each other? The theoretical answer is that every solution would approximate a linear transform of every other, and a mechanism exists by which we align the transformation that takes an individual's semantic space to some particular language's statistically canonical cultural form. The LSA answer, of course, is that closely matching a small fraction of my words and utterances with yours will drag the rest of the structure with it, as in aligning two maps by overlaying just two points (see Goldstone & Rogosky, 2002, for a related computational technique).

An LSA-based developmental hypothesis might go like this. Babies first learn a primitive embedding structure of word–word relations by hearing words in multiple verbal contexts, then gradually add mutually consistent words and word groups to an evolving mini structure of meaningful interrelations. Such growth will resemble that of a crystal; immersed in the medium of words and passages, new words will attach where meaningful combinations are ready to use them, and new ability to understand word combinations will emerge as more words take their places.

Word and passage meanings should start out quite ill or fuzzily defined because of the sparseness of possible embeddings. Early vocabulary should consist primarily of words of the highest frequency in the child's attentionally filtered verbal experiences. Most of this would come from the ambient speech to which they are exposed (Hart & Risley, 1995).

Ambient language exposure consists primarily of utterances by competent speakers in phrases, sentences, and paragraphs, which the child can begin to understand slowly and again fuzzily. By LSA, the quality of the representation of words and paragraphs will increase in a mutually reinforcing iterative process. As simulated by LSA, the lion's share of this incremental growth will be hidden from easy detection. Learning to construct meanings of words and passages are tightly coupled and follow a similar course. Eventually, there will be a sufficient core to support vocabulary growth at the 10 per day observed to pass the TOEFL threshold at age 12. Note that the points at which this process includes perceptual and motor context (again for both positive and nonoccurrence effects) are continuous, simultaneous, and intermingled with language experience from the beginning. The meaning of "tree" becomes better defined as a better place for it is constructed in the semantic space, and a better place is constructed as the learner has more experiences containing and not containing a perceptual tree.

In an unpublished pilot study, Dumais and I examined the trajectory of LSA word neighborhood changes during early learning. This was done by substituting nonsense words for actual words with increasing numbers of occurrences. At first, a word had many word neighbors of modest similarity, mimicking the early errors of overgeneralization that children make. Then there was a contraction to a small number of more tightly clustered neighbors, and finally to an again larger number, but with both closer neighbors and presumably neighbors that matched the multiple senses of the words—although the last property was not investigated at the time.

In Landauer and Dumais (1997), a hypothetical course of language experience is presented for a child to learn what "hurts" means when uttered by its mother. The new knowledge arises from the word's embedding in other utterances that put it near the child's own learned representation of "hurts," which by the cultural conversion presented previously, makes it the same as the mother's. This would also be the explanation of Quine's famous objection to association as the mechanism of word learning (Quine, 1960; see also Bloom, 2000). A perceived object fits into a visual/semantic space by its LSA similarities to things already there (see Edelman, 1998, 1999; Valentine, Abdi, & Otoole, 1994).

Much the same mechanism is taken advantage of in the (proprietary and successful) cross-language information retrieval method described earlier. The system creates separate semantic spaces that share a relatively small number of documents that are known to have close to the same meaning, for example, translations or news accounts of the same event from different language sources. It places those known to be alike in the same relation to one another in a new joint semantic space, then moves the rest in the same way. This never places a document or word type from one language exactly in the same place as any from another (in English and Chinese a "component" usually has no very similar vector in the other language). Most words considered to correspond in bilingual dictionaries will tend to be quite close to each other, and documents that have been carefully translated will be very close to each other.

This also yields an explanation of why the best way to learn a new language is by immersion; a small number of common words, a small amount of direct instruction and experience and/or of hearing foreign words or passages in situations where it is obvious how the meaning would be expressed in L1 will support alignment of L1 and L2. It also mirrors the common intuition that different languages do not map perfectly onto one another, and there may often be no way to express the same idea exactly in a different language.

Moreover, if the relations among percepts—both innate and experiential—were organized in the same manner, it would take only a comparatively few correlations of perceptual and linguistic experience to make all their connections fall in line to a close approximation. A Helen Keller could put unseen and unheard objects and language together on the sole basis of correlations between touch, smell, and taste stimuli along with a very brief early history of normal perceptual-language associative experience (Keller, 1905).

Because everybody shares experiences with many other people, statistics will insure that there is good, if imperfect, agreement across members of a community. This would happen by a process of consensus promoted by both interpersonally engaged and ambient conversation (and, recently, newspapers, popular songs and books, movies, and television), so that semantic knowledge and abstract ideas will recursively feed on themselves. Of course, each person's understanding of the meaning of a word will still be slightly different, in ways ranging from minute to large, for example, if one person has read a word only in one "sense" and someone else has read it only in another.

Such a process remains to be simulated in detail to see if it would have the power and reach needed, but at least conceptually it provides a possible solution to a chronic philosophical problem referred to as publicity, how people share meanings as they must.

One piece of supporting simulation data was reported by Landauer and Dumais (1997). The rate of acquisition of new word knowledge was simulated as an accelerating function of the number of words previously encountered. Whereas a simulated 50-year-old reader would learn a new word in two encounters, it would take a 20-year-old person eight chances. Of course, a person's total vocabulary follows a typical S-shaped growth curve, the rate of growth first increases, then slows down as the number of unknown types encountered decreases.

The LSA prediction is that vocabulary should grow in each individual by embedding words both old and new in large, common, and increasingly stable semantic space, allowing people of all ages to continue to improve their sharing of meanings with others. The principal evidence supporting this expectation is that addition of new paragraphs to an LSA information retrieval system requires less and less frequent re-computation of the space to give words and passages appropriate meanings. After learning from a large corpus, newly encountered words can be "folded in," that is, placed at the average point of all the paragraphs in which they occur without re-computing the SVD, thus obeying the fundamental LSA constraint. Unless there has been a relatively large addition, say greater than 20%, of new words or a significant change in the corpus domain, the difference between this way of adding vocabulary and that of recomputing the SVD is negligible.

FINAL WORDS ABOUT WORD ORDER AND MEANING

LSA's successes would seem utterly impossible if word order played as dominant a role in the actual use of verbal meaning as it does in the science of linguistics. How can this be explained? Here are three approaches: See if we can estimate just how much is missing by ignoring word order, try to put bounds on the relative contributions of word combinations and word order to passage meaning, consider what other roles the omnipresence of word order conventions in many languages might play.

It is worth noting that many, perhaps most, languages are not nearly as fussy about word order as English, and their informal speakers are not nearly as fussy as their teachers and theorists. One reason is that some of the information carried by syntax in English is carried in some other languages by a greater variety of differential word forms and affixes that index the sentential roles of words rather than order dependant combinations.

An informal example may help intuition. Readers will have little trouble figuring out what the following word string means:

["order syntax? much. ignoring word Missed by is how"]

Scrambled sentences and passages are often fairly easy to understand, even without laborious reconstruction. By first getting the topical gist from the combination of words, then rearranging most of the words to grammatically correct and empirically probable orders, one can usually recover the original form of an utterance, at least modulo differences that do not affect meaning. It is not always trivial to construct a paragraph that when randomized defeats general gist understanding or leaves serious ambiguities in the mind of the reader. Even double, missing, and incorrectly placed negations and modifiers, as well as outright sentential contradictions in paragraphs, frequently go unnoticed by readers (Kintsch, 1998), and their lack often does not appreciably alter the meaning of the text for the reader. The LSA interpretation is that the meaning of a passage being the average of many words, the effect of a few deviant meanings may sometimes have little effect on the whole.

We can go beyond this qualitative argument to a quantitative estimate in the following way. We used LSA alone in a linear ordering algorithm to place a large set of essays on a line such that the 300-dimensionality similarities between them were minimally distorted. We then compared this ordering to one based on average scores for the same essays given independently by two expert humans. Finally, we measured the amount of shared information in the scoring of the essays (a) by the two human experts—presumably based on all they could extract from all aspects of the writing, including syntax—and (b) between the scoring by LSA and the humans. The measure used was mutual information (also known as cross-entropy). This measures the amount, in information-theoretic bits, by which the uncertainty (entropy) in one source can be reduced by knowing the other. The result was that the human–human mutual information was .90 and the average machine–human was .81. That is, the machine, on average, shared 90% as much information with each of two human experts as the experts shared with each other. This gives us a first rough estimate that 10% of information in multisentence texts that is used by humans comes from word order. It would be hazardous to make too much of this result without replication and confirming extensions, but it is evident that at least in judging essay content quality, the opportunity to use word order does not greatly improve expert performance.

The next approach is more abstract. For convenience, assume that a typical well-educated adult English speaker knows 100,000 words well enough to understand their contributions to the meaning of sentences (see Landauer & Dumais, 1997), and an average sentence contains 20 words. The number of possible combinations of words in a sentence is then $100,000^{20}$, the number of information-theoretic bits $\log_2 (100,000)^{20} = 332$ bits. The number of possible orders of 20 words is 20!, the number of bits $\log_2 (20!) = 61$ bits. The total maximum information in a 20-word sentence is thus $332 + 61 = 393$, of which $61/393 = 15.4\%$ is from word order. If we add in the corresponding amounts for a series of sentences in a paragraph or essay, then the situation gets even more lopsided because possible word combinations multiply across multiple sentences and paragraphs, whereas the number of permutations only add, word order effects being almost exclusively within sentences. Thus, this approach comes interestingly close to the first one, with 10%–15% of information in English text from word order.

In many of the practical applications of LSA, people have joined it with statistical models of word order. These methods, which are the workhorses of modern speech recognition systems (Rosenfeld, 1996), model language by computing the frequency with which sequences of word—n-grams—usually 2–5 in length, appear in large corpora of representative text. Such models can be somewhat more powerful when applied to text than to speech because in text what follows can affect the comprehension of what came before, whereas in real-time speech processing the previous words are too soon gone. Nonetheless, about all they have been made to do is to tell us is how likely it is that the observed order of words is expectable in general or in a certain domain or from a certain source. Nonetheless, they can provide yet another hint about the limits of the effect of word order. In an unpublished 1996 pilot study, Noah Coccaro and I selected random 10-word sentences from the *Wall Street Journal*. The order of words in each sentence was then randomly scrambled. Finally, we tried to recover the original order by using n-gram probabilities from a large *Wall Street Journal* corpus to find the word order that had the highest probability. About half of the sentences were perfectly recovered, another quarter sufficiently that no change in meaning resulted, the rest with minor ambiguities.

Finally, let us speculate a bit on why English, and to a lesser extent other language speakers, bother themselves, their listeners, students, and editors so closely and insistently about adhering to conventional patterns. Please note that I am not asserting that word order is not important to meaning; it clearly is. What I wish to point out, however, is that its role in verbal meaning may have been overestimated, and thus the importance of word combination underappreciated.

Clearly, one source of the ubiquity of word order conventions is a matter of style, like wearing skirts or ties or serving the dessert before or after the cheese. Another is plain cultural habit. One of your ancestors one day started usually putting adjectives before nouns, and her children learned *n*-gram probabilities from her. Read some literature or science from the mid-19th century (Darwin is nice for the purpose), and you often find the word order consistent but consistently different from Pinker's. To what extent did formal English evolve a more efficient way to represent and convey meaning through word order, and to what extent was there just the same sort of evolutionary cultural drift as there was in hats, driven in the same way as Peacock's tails?

I think fashion and habit are part of the story, but there is yet another reason to use conventional word order even supposing it had no influence on meaning. The reason is increased efficiency and accuracy for speaker, hearer, reader, and thinker. Such an efficiency would accrue to almost any conventional word order. To illustrate this, imagine a language that was totally without word order conventions. To say anything you would just choose a set of words and string them together in any order. This language would require a rather huge number of words, but many real languages, such as German, are more forgiving about word order than English, and some encryption schemes employ orderless code blocks. This is accomplished by using more complex words—making the building blocks carry more information—and partly by more flexible conventions. Given a partially order-free language—for example, only within sentences—you would soon find that if you put your words in alphabetic order when speaking or writing your hearers or readers would make fewer mistakes in understanding; you would thereby have created an error-correcting coding scheme. Note that you would also think, speak, and understand faster and more accurately because each word would cue the next.

The proposal, then, is that conventional (rule governed maybe, but I prefer experiential and statistically shaped) word order provides a communicative advantage. Extending the speculation, the universal grammar or UR syntax that Chomsky and followers have sought is a natural consequence of agreeing on what kinds of meanings should come after which others to make talking more effective, and various interacting groups have stumbled on and evolved various ways to do it. Unfortunately, linguistic theory has yet to find a computational theory that can simulate that evolutionary process or the passing of its result from old to young through exposure to language.

The critical problem of utterance production—speaking or writing—raises its intransigent head here. LSA theory and systems are not designed to simulate or explain this essential property of language. The theory says that passages that are emitted should obey the constraint, but this is of limited help. What mechanism could manage to emit words, sentences, and paragraphs that do that? Some unknown (to LSA, but partially described by phenomenon-level linguistic theories and rules) computation must insure that utterances usually create comprehensible word strings.

In addition, the meanings expressed in sequential mathematical and logical statements are not in LSA's theoretical purview, but models of them can nevertheless profit from using LSA as a component. For example, "John hit Mary" might be decomposed in some propositional form in which much of the meaning is order free, for example [a hitting < {[John, Marry]} < (hitter: John)]. However, there is still order in deciding who is the hitter. Kintsch's work with predication, metaphor, and analogy models (chap. 5 in this volume) takes this tack, marrying LSA to automatically represent individual word meanings with syntactic models that are effective but rely on help from human coding.

As with every other scientific theory, LSA succeeds by abstracting only a limited range of phenomena to explain from the enormous complexity of nature. LSA offers one explicit and computable mechanism for an essential and previously inexplicable component of language, how the meanings of words and passages can be acquired from experience. Perhaps LSA's success for this component will encourage new research into how other important properties of language that must arise from normal experience—the syntax of one's language in particular—do so.

SOME FINAL PHILOSOPHICAL AND PSYCHOLOGICAL MUSINGS

The property of LSA that a passage of words on being understood, turns into a something that cannot be turned back into its words is familiar to both intuition and experimental psychology. Kintsch calls this the transition from text base to situation model. The abundant psychological evidence is that people are hard-pressed to recall verbatim what they have read a few occupied minutes earlier, but can recognize it as familiar when seen again. More wonderfully, they retain information that the text conveyed and can recognize it in hundreds of disguises and use it in hundreds of ways: to paraphrase, to reason from, to piece together with others of the same, to criticize and praise. More recent research has shown that knowledge of the original words is not completely lost; give a subject a choice of those that were there or not and they will do quite well. LSA at least shadows this. Even though the exact words are irretrievably mingled into something else, a word originally there is much like the new whole. We have built algorithms that can generate small sets of words, either the originals

or others, that carry the core of the original meaning, such that added together they produce a vector nearly identical to the original.

However, the fact that passage-meaning vectors, and even whole essay
vectors—which are essentially sums of passage meanings—cannot be
turned back into words has interesting implications. We may think of a passage vector as an unexpressed idea. Consider the everyday introspective
experience that a meaning is there before it becomes words. This is demonstrated by our claims that we cannot find words to express an idea, that we
did not mean what we said, and by our ability to edit a passage to make it
express more nearly what we meant.

Words themselves are discreet isolates. What are they when combined
and forgotten? Have they lost their individuality? LSA suggests an answer.
First, let us observe that people rarely speak isolated words, they usually
speak and understand groups of words, and typically groups of words larger
than a sentence, more akin to paragraphs (this is another reason that constructing paragraph meaning is so important in LSA). A number of interesting conjectures spring from this observation. First, we may suppose that the
comprehension of a new sentence or passage consists not only of the addition
of word meanings but also of similar nonverbal vectors, including perceptual records, retrieved from memory. Thus, reading comprehension would
be enriched by the recovery and incorporation of associated information.

Perhaps unconscious thoughts of all kinds are just "untranslatable" vectors derived from perceptual experience and discourse, additive combinations of different passages that cannot be unpacked into strings of words.
Might not such "nonverbal" thoughts nevertheless constitute an important
part of cognition? Surely the content of articles and books read long ago still
influences thought, decision, and action even though the individual words
are not recoverable. Perhaps the residues of condensed unverbalizable, but
nevertheless influential, memories play a very large role in both our conscious and unconscious life, biasing verbally expressible thoughts, feeding
unverbalizable ones and their expression in emotion and action. Maybe
falling in love relies on a match of untranslatable vectors, which is why a
matching verbal checklist does not always equal romantic chemistry.
Kintsch (1974) made great progress in this same direction by proposing that
word strings were turned into a form of logical propositions for storing in
memory, a strategy often adopted in artificial intelligence. In these approaches, however, literal words or equivalent discrete symbols arranged
in structured formats still carry the meaning. What is proposed here is not
that such representations do not exist, but that much of cognition may consist of LSA-like representations that carry and combine meanings in a very
different way.

Other phenomena of mind seem to find possible explanations in this
manner. Where do thoughts and new ideas come from, from additive com-

binations of other thoughts all verbally inexpressible or only partly so? From the averaged vectors of two or more words that do not correspond to any single word? How about the unverbalizeable emotional storms of depression and anxiety, the word-salads of schizophrenics? Are meaning vectors making trouble without being able to speak? How about the mysterious origins of insights, intuitions, sudden solutions to math problems? Are meaning vectors doing wonders without telling? Think about consciousness. Maybe some of what we think of as not conscious is just stuff we cannot talk to ourselves about even though it may be quite full of complex meanings. Maybe the "meanings" of sunsets, thunderstorms, gestures, or of supernatural beliefs, irrational fears, Freud's unconscious wishes, automatic actions, unintentional learning, the search for the meaning of life, can all find new explanations in the dynamics of verbally inexpressible LSA-like vectors.

IN SUM

LSA demonstrates a computational method by which a major component of language learning and use can be achieved. It is in that sense that it is a theory. It is specifically a theory of meaning because it applies to and offers an explanation of phenomena that are ordinarily considered to be manifestations of meaning: the expression, comprehension, and communication of ideas and facts in words and passages of words. It makes possible computer systems that accomplish a wide range of cognitive tasks performed by humans, and often does them essentially as well and with the same detailed performance characteristics. This makes its basic mechanism, or something equivalent to it, a candidate for explaining the corresponding human abilities. The research strategy and program that the LSA community follows is well described by Stokes in *Pasteur's Quadrant* (1997). Start with a practical problem, do the science needed to understand what's going on and how to fix it, test your understanding and its completeness by whether you succeed and how you fail: iterate.

LSA's initiating event was people's difficulties in finding services they wanted in the Bell System Yellow Pages. Observational experimentation discovered that the cause was that there were always many more words with related meanings that searchers tried than indexers indexed (Furnas, Landauer, Gomez, & Dumais, 1987). The solution was to find a way for a computational model to learn word meanings from vast amounts of exposure to text, just as humans do, so that it could tell when an inquiring person's words meant nearly enough the same thing as its. The tests were manifold, some abstracted controlled laboratory experiments, many more by building software systems that had to understand the degree to which two words or passages had the same meaning. The model did surprisingly well, underwriting many useful inventions, insights into the nature of verbal meaning (word choice more important relative to word order than previously suspected), new theoretical conceptions of how language might work (passage meaning as a sum of word meanings), and realizations of where the theory is incomplete or falls short (accounting for the effects of word order, analogy, inference, generation of meaningful language). What LSA can do has pointed to a new path in the study and engineering of meaning.

ACKNOWLEDGMENTS

Research was supported by the NSF, AFRL, ARI, ONR, DARPA, IES, McDonnell Foundations. Thanks to Touchstone Applied Science Associates.

REFERENCES

Barsalou, L. (1999). Perceptual symbol systems. *Behavioral and Brain Sciences, 22,* 577–660.
Bartlett, F. C. (1932). *Remembering.* Cambridge, England: Cambridge University Press.
Berry, M. W. (1992). Large scale singular value computations. *International Journal of Supercomputer Applications, 6*(1), 13–49.
Berry, M. W., Dumais, S. T., & O'Brien, G. W. (1995). Using linear algebra for intelligent information retrieval. *SIAM: Review, 37*(4), 573–595.
Bickerton, D. (1995). *Language and human behavior.* Seattle, WA: University of Washington Press.
Bloom, P. (2000). *How children learn the meaning of words.* Cambridge, MA: MIT Press.
Chomsky, N. (1991a). Linguistics and adjacent fields: A personal view. In A. Kasher (Ed.), *The Chomskyan turn* (pp. 3–25). Oxford, England: Blackwell.
Chomsky, N. (1991b). Linguistics and cognitive science: Problems and mysteries. In A. Kasher (Ed.), *The Chomskyan turn* (pp. 26–53). Oxford, England: Basil Blackwell.
Deerwester, S., Dumais, S. T., Furnas, G. W., Landauer, T. K., & Harshman, R. (1990). Indexing by latent semantic analysis. *Journal of the American Society for Information Science, 41*(6), 391–407.
Dennis, S. (2005). A memory-based theory of verbal cognition. *Cognitive Science, 29*(2), 145–193.
Dumais, S. T. (1991). Improving the retrieval of information from external sources. *Behavior Research Methods, Instruments and Computers, 23*(2), 229–236.
Dumais, S. T., Landauer, T. K., & Littman, M. L. (1996). Automatic cross-linguistic information retrieval using Latent Semantic Indexing. In SIGIR'96 - Workshop on Cross-Linguisitic Information Retrieval, (pp. 16–23).
Edelman, S. (1998). Representation is representation of similarity. *Behavioral and Brain Sciences, 21,* 449–498.
Edelman, S. (1999). *Representation and recognition in vision.* Cambridge, MA: MIT Press.
Elvevåg, B., Foltz, P. W., Weinberger, D. R., & Goldberg, T. E. (2005). *Quantifying incoherence in speech: An automated methodology and novel application to schizophrenia.* Manuscript submitted for publication.

Erosheva, E., Fienberg, S., & Lafferty, J. (2004). Mixed-membership models of scientific publications. *Proceedings of the National Academy of Sciences, 97*(2), 11885–11892.

Fellbaum, C. (1998). Introduction. In C. Fellbaum (Ed.), *WordNet: An electronic lexical database* (pp. 1–19). Cambridge, MA: MIT Press.

Fodor, J. A. (1987). *Psychosemantics.* Cambridge, MA: MIT/Bradford.

Foltz, P. W., Kintsch, W., & Landauer, T. K. (1998). Analysis of text coherence using latent semantic analysis. *Discourse Processes, 25,* 285–307.

Furnas, G. W., Landauer, T. K., Gomez, L. M., & Dumais, S. T. (1987). The vocabulary problem in human–system communication. *Communications of the Association for Computing Machinery, 30*(11), 964–971.

Gleitman, L. R. (1990). The structural sources of verb meanings. *Language Acquisition, 1,* 3–55.

Glenberg, A. M., & Robertson, D. A. (2000). Symbol grounding and meaning: A comparison of high-dimensional and embodied theories of meaning. *Journal of Memory and Language, 43,* 379–401.

Gold, E. M. (1967). Language identification in the limit. *Information and Control, 10,* 447–474.

Goldstone, R. L., & Rogosky, B. J. (2002). Using relations within conceptual systems to translate across conceptual systems. *Cognition, 84,* 295–320.

Griffiths, T., & Steyvers, M. (2003). Topic dynamics in knowledge domains. *Proceedings of the National Academy of Sciences, 101*(Suppl. 1), 5228–5235.

Harnad, S. (1990). The symbol grounding problem. *Physica D, 42,* 335–346.

Hart, B., & Risley, T. R. (1995). *Meaningful differences in the everyday experience of young American children.* Baltimore: Paul H. Brookes.

Jackendoff, R. (1992). *Languages of the mind.* Cambridge: Bradford/MIT Press.

Keller, H. (1905). *The story of my life.* New York: Doubleday, Page & Company.

Kintsch, W. (1974). *The representation of meaning in memory.* Hillsdale, NJ: Lawrence Erlbaum Associates.

Kintsch, W. (1998). *Comprehension: A paradigm for cognition.* New York: Cambridge University Press.

Kintsch, W. (2000). Metaphor comprehension: A computational theory. *Psychonomic Bulletin and Review, 7,* 257–266.

Kintsch, W. (2001). Predication. *Cognitive Science, 25,* 173–202.

Laham, D. (1997). Latent semantic analysis approaches to categorization. In M. G. Shafto & P. Langley (Eds.), *Proceedings of the 19th Annual Meeting of the Cognitive Science Society* (p. 979). Mawhwah, NJ: Lawrence Erlbaum Associates.

Laham, D. (2000). *Automated content assessment of text using latent semantic analysis to simulate human cognition.* Unpublished doctoral dissertation, University of Colorado, Boulder.

Landau, B., & Gleitman, L. (1985). *Language and experience: Evidence from the blind child.* Cambridge, MA: Harvard University Press.

Landauer, T. K. (2002a). On the computational basis of cognition: Arguments from LSA. In B. H. Ross (Ed.), *The psychology of learning and motivation* (pp. 43–84). New York: Academic Press.

Landauer, T. K. (2002b). Single representations of multiple meanings in latent semantic analysis. In D. Gorfein (Ed.), *On the consequences of meaning selection* (pp. 217–232). Washington, DC: American Psychological Association.

Landauer, T. K., & Dumais, S. T. (1997). A solution to Plato's problem: The latent semantic analysis theory of the acquisition, induction, and representation of knowledge. *Psychological Review, 104*(2), 211–240.

Landauer, T. K., Foltz, P. W., & Laham, D. (1998). Introduction to latent semantic analysis. *Discourse Processes, 25*, 259–284.

Landauer, T. K., Laham, D., & Foltz, P. W. (2003a). Automated essay assessment. *Assessment in Education: Principles, Policy and Practice, 10*(3), 295–308.

Landauer, T. K., Laham, D., & Foltz, P. W. (2003b). Automated scoring and annotation of essays with the Intelligent Essay Assessor. In M. D. Shermis, & J. Burstein (Eds.), *Automated essay scoring: A cross-disciplinary perspective* (pp. 87–112). Mahwah, NJ: Lawrence Erlbaum Associates.

Lund, K., & Burgess, C. (1996). Producing high-dimensional semantic spaces from lexical co-occurrence. *Behavioral Research Methods, Instruments, and Computers, 28*, 203–208.

Lund, K., Burgess, C., & Atchley, R. A. (1995). Semantic and associative priming in high-dimensional semantic space. In J. D. Moore & J. F. Lehman (Eds.), *Cognitive sciences society* (pp. 660–665). Pittsburgh, PA: Lawrence Erlbaum Associates.

O'Reilly, R., & Munakata, Y. (2000). *Computational explorations in cognitive neuroscience: Understanding the mind by simulating the brain.* Cambridge, MA: MIT Press.

Osherson, D., Stob, M., & Weinstein, S. (1984). Learning theory and natural language. *Cognition, 17*, 1–28.

Pinker, S. (1994). *The language instinct.* New York: HarperCollins.

Pylyshyn, Z. W. (1980). Computation and cognition: Issues in the foundations of cognitive sciences. *Behavioral and Brain Sciences, 3*(1), 111–169.

Quine, W. O. (1960). *Word and object.* Cambridge, MA: MIT Press.

Rehder, B., Schreiner, M. E., Wolfe, M. B. W., Laham, D., Landauer, T. K., & Kintsch, W. (1998). Using latent semantic analysis to assess knowledge: Some technical considerations. *Discourse Processes, 25*, 337–354.

Ridley, M. (1994). *The Red Queen: Sex and the evolution of human behavior.* London: Penguin.

Rosenfeld, R. (1996). A maximum entropy approach to adaptive statistical language modeling. *Computer Speech and Language, 10*, 187–228.

Searle, J. R. (1982). The Chinese room revisited. *Behavioral and Brain Sciences, 5*, 345–348.

Skinner, B. F. (1957). *Verbal behavior.* East Norwalk, CT: Appleton-Century-Crofts.

Stokes, D. E. (1997). *Pasteur's quadrant: Basic science and technological innovation.* Washington, DC: Brookings Institution Press.

Valentine, D., Abdi, H., & Otoole, A. (1994). Categorization and identification of human face images by neural networks: A review of linear autoassociative and principal component approaches. *Journal of Biological Systems, 2*, 412–423.

Wittgenstein, L. (1953). *Philosophical investigations.* Oxford, England: Blackwell.

Wolfe, M. B. W., Schreiner, M. E., Rehder, B., Laham, D., Foltz, P. W., Kintsch, W., et al. (1998). Learning from text: Matching readers and text by latent semantic analysis. *Discourse Processes, 25*, 309–336.

2

Mathematical Foundations Behind Latent Semantic Analysis

Dian I. Martin
Small Bear Technical Consulting, LLC

Michael W. Berry
University of Tennessee

Latent semantic analysis (LSA) is based on the concept of vector space models, an approach using linear algebra for effective yet automated information retrieval. The vector space model (VSM) was developed to handle text retrieval from a large information database where the text is heterogeneous and the vocabulary varies. One of the first systems to use a traditional VSM was the System for the Mechanical Analysis and Retrieval of Text (SMART; Buckley, Allan, & Salton, 1994; Salton & McGill, 1983). Among the notable characteristics of the VSM, used by SMART, is the premise that the meaning of documents can be derived from its components or types. The underlying formal mathematical model of the VSM defines unique vectors for each type and document, and queries are performed by comparing the query representation to the representation of each document in the vector space. Query-document similarities are then based on concepts or similar semantic content (Salton, Buckley, & Allan, 1992).

LSA is considered a truncated vector space model that represents types and documents in a particular high-dimensional type-document vector space. The truncated VSM, VSM_k, used in LSA, uncovers the underlying or "latent" semantic structure in the pattern of type usage to define documents in a collection. As mentioned in chapter 1 (Landauer, this volume), a document is defined as the sum of the meaning of its types. By using the truncated singular value decomposition, LSA exploits the meaning of types by removing "noise" that is present due to the variability in type choice. Such noise is evidenced by polysemy (multiple meanings for one word) and synonymy (many words describing the same idea) found in documents (Deerwester, Dumais, Furnas, Landauer, & Harshman, 1990; Furnas, Landauer, Gomez, & Dumais, 1987). As a result, the similarity of documents is no longer dependent on the types they contain, but on the semantic content; therefore, documents deemed relevant to a given query do not necessarily contain the types in the query (Dumais, 1991; Letsche & Berry, 1997).

This chapter describes the vector space model and the mathematical foundations that LSA is based on both in broad concepts for readers seeking general understanding and finer detail for readers interested in the specifics. Creating the vector space model for latent semantic analysis is discussed first, which is a theoretical explanation of how a type-by-document input matrix derived from a document collection is decomposed into a vector space of type and document vectors by the singular value decomposition (SVD). It is by using the truncated SVD that LSA obtains the meanings of types and documents. In the next section, the actual computation of the vector space for LSA is described in fine detail. The computation required to convert an input matrix into vectors is complex, and this section is for those readers interested in understanding the sophisticated mathematical calculations of the "Lanczos algorithm with selective reorthogonalization" that is used to build the type and document vectors. Then, use of the truncated vector space model for LSA is covered. This section describes the basic manipulations of the vector space. Subsequent chapters of this volume describe, in detail, the many interesting and important applications that use the vector space model of LSA.

CREATING THE VECTOR SPACE MODEL
FOR LATENT SEMANTIC ANALYSIS

The Input Matrix

To create a vector space model for latent semantic analysis, a type-by-document matrix must first be constructed. The rows of the input matrix are comprised of types, which are the individual components that make up a document. Typically, these individual components are terms, but they can be phrases or concepts depending on the application. The columns of the input matrix are comprised of documents, which are of a predetermined size of text such as paragraphs, collections of paragraphs, sentences, book chapters, books, and so on, again depending on the application. A document collection composed of n documents and m types can be represented as an m by n type-by-document matrix $\mathbf{A}$. Often $m >> n$, the number of types is greater than the number of documents, however, there are cases where this is reversed and $n >> m$, for example, when collecting documents from the Internet (Berry & Browne, 2005; Berry, Drmac, & Jessup, 1999). Initially, each column of the matrix $\mathbf{A}$ contains zero and nonzero elements, a_{ij}. Each nonzero element, a_{ij}, of the matrix $\mathbf{A}$ is the frequency of ith type in the jth document. A small example of a document collection and its corresponding input type-by-document matrix with type frequencies can found in Tables 2.1 and 2.2 (Witter & Berry, 1998). In this example, documents are the actual title, consisting only of italicized keywords. Documents labeled M1–M5 are music-related titles, documents labeled B1–B4 are baking-related titles, and no document has more than one occurrence of a type or keyword.

A weighting function is generally applied to the each nonzero (type frequency) element, a_{ij}, of $\mathbf{A}$ to improve retrieval performance (Berry & Browne, 2005; Dumais, 1991). In retrieval, the types that best distinguish particular documents from the rest of the documents are the most important; therefore, a weighting function should give a low weight to a high-frequency type that occurs in many documents and a high weight to types that occur in some documents but not all (Salton & Buckley, 1991). LSA applies

TABLE 2.1
Titles for Topics on Music and Baking

Label	Titles
M1	*Rock* and *Roll Music* in the 1960's
M2	Different *Drum Rolls*, a Demonstration of Techniques
M3	*Drum* and Bass *Composition*
M4	A Perspective of *Rock Music* in the 90's
M5	*Music* and *Composition* of Popular Bands
B1	How to Make *Bread* and *Rolls*, a *Demonstration*
B2	*Ingredients* for Crescent *Rolls*
B3	A *Recipe* for Sour*dough Bread*
B4	A Quick *Recipe* for Pizza *Dough* using Organic *Ingredients*

Note. Keywords are in italics.

TABLE 2.2
The 10 x 9 Type-by-Document Matrix With Type Frequencies Corresponding
to the Titles in Table 2.1

Types	Documents								
	M1	M2	M3	M4	M5	B1	B2	B3	B4
Bread	0	0	0	0	0	1	0	1	0
Composition	0	0	1	0	1	0	0	0	0
Demonstration	0	1	0	0	0	1	0	0	0
Dough	0	0	0	0	0	0	0	1	1
Drum	0	1	1	0	0	0	0	0	0
Ingredients	0	0	0	0	0	0	1	0	1
Music	1	0	0	1	1	0	0	0	0
Recipe	0	0	0	0	0	0	0	1	1
Rock	1	0	0	1	0	0	0	0	0
Roll	1	1	0	0	0	1	1	0	0

both a local and global weighting function to each nonzero element, a_{ij}, in order to increase or decrease the importance of types within documents (local) and across the entire document collection (global). The local and global weighting functions for each element, a_{ij}, are usually directly related to how frequently a type occurs within a document and inversely related to how frequently a type occurs in documents across the collection, respectively. So, $a_{ij} = $ local(i, j) * global(i), where local(i, j) is the local weighting for type i in document j, and global(i) is the type's global weighting (Dumais, 1991; Letsche & Berry, 1997). Local weighting functions include using type frequency, binary frequency (0 if the type is not in the document and 1 if the type is in the document), and log of type frequency plus 1. Global weighting functions include normal, gfidf, idf, and entropy, all of which basically assign a low weight to types occurring often or in many documents. A common local and global weighting function is log-entropy. Dumais found that log-entropy gave the best retrieval results, 40% over raw type frequency (Dumais, 1991). The local weighting function of log (type frequency + 1) decreases the effect of large differences in frequencies. Entropy, defined as 1 +

$$\sum_j \frac{p_{ij} \log_2 (p_{ij})}{\log_2 n} \text{ where } p_{ij} = \frac{tf_{ij}}{gf_i}, tf_{ij} = \text{type frequency of type } i \text{ in document}$$

j, and gf_i = the total number of times that type i appears in the entire collection of n documents, gives less weight to types occurring frequently in a document collection, as well as taking into account the distribution of types over documents (Dumais, 1991). A more detailed description of the local and global weighting functions can be found in Berry and Browne (2005) and Dumais (1991). Table 2.3 has the local and global weighting function log-entropy applied to each nonzero type frequency in the type-by-document matrix given previously in Table 2.2.

Typically, the type-by-document input matrix **A** is considered sparse because it contains many more zero entries than nonzero entries. Each document in the collection tends to only use a small subset of types from the type set. Usually, only about 1% or less of the matrix entries are populated or nonzero (Berry & Browne, 2005). In the small example in Tables 2.2 and 2.3, approximately 25% of the matrix entries are nonzero.

Decomposition of Input Matrix Into Orthogonal Components

Once the input matrix **A** is created, it is transformed into a type and document vector space by orthogonal decompositions in order to exploit truncation of the vectors. Transforming a matrix by using orthogonal decompositions, or orthogonal matrices, preserves certain properties of the matrix, including the norms, or vector lengths and distances, of the row and column vectors that form the $m \times n$ type-by-document input matrix **A**. Specifically, orthogonal matrix decompositions preserve the 2-norm and the Frobenius norm of matrix **A** (Golub & Van Loan, 1989; Larson & Edwards, 1988).

TABLE 2.3
The 10 × 9 Weighted Type-by-Document Matrix Corresponding to the Titles in Table 2.1

Types	Documents								
	M1	M2	M3	M4	M5	B1	B2	B3	B4
Bread	0	0	0	0	0	.474	0	.474	0
Composition	0	0	.474	0	.474	0	0	0	0
Demonstration	0	.474	0	0	0	.474	0	0	0
Dough	0	0	0	0	0	0	0	.474	.474
Drum	0	.474	.474	0	0	0	0	0	0
Ingredients	0	0	0	0	0	0	.474	0	.474
Music	.347	0	0	.347	.347	0	0	0	0
Recipe	0	0	0	0	0	0	0	.474	.474
Rock	.474	0	0	.474	0	0	0	0	0
Roll	.256	.256	0	0	0	.256	.256	0	0

What is an orthogonal matrix? An orthogonal matrix is one with the property of $Q^T Q = I$, where Q is an orthogonal matrix, Q^T is the transpose of matrix Q (the rows and columns of Q are the columns and rows of Q^T), and I is the identity matrix:

$$Q^T Q = \begin{bmatrix} 1 & 0 & \cdots & 0 & 0 \\ 0 & 1 & 0 & & 0 \\ \vdots & 0 & \ddots & \ddots & \vdots \\ 0 & & \ddots & 1 & 0 \\ 0 & 0 & \cdots & 0 & 1 \end{bmatrix} \qquad \textbf{2.1}$$

If Q is comprised of n column vectors, that is, $Q = [\mathbf{q}_1, \mathbf{q}_2, \ldots, \mathbf{q}_n]$, then for every pair of vectors $(\mathbf{q}_i, \mathbf{q}_j)$, taking the dot product $\mathbf{q}_i^T \mathbf{q}_j = 0$ if $i \neq j$ and $\mathbf{q}_i^T \mathbf{q}_j \neq 0$ if $i = j$. If two vectors satisfy the property that the dot product $\mathbf{q}_i^T \mathbf{q}_j = 0$ if i $\neq j$, then they are said to be orthogonal. Taking this a step further, an orthogonal matrix is also orthonormal. Each vector $\mathbf{q}_i$ is orthonormal if the length of $\mathbf{q}_i = 1$, denoted by $\| \mathbf{q}_i \| = 1$, which means $\mathbf{q}_i^T \mathbf{q}_i = 1$. Because the vectors $[\mathbf{q}_1, \mathbf{q}_2, \ldots, \mathbf{q}_n]$ in matrix Q are orthonormal, they point in totally different directions, forming 90-degree angles between each and every vector. Moreover, the vectors in Q from an orthonormal basis for a vector space, meaning every vector in the vector space can be written as a linear combination of vectors $[\mathbf{q}_1, \mathbf{q}_2, \ldots, \mathbf{q}_n]$. More specifically, the vectors $[\mathbf{q}_1, \mathbf{q}_2, \ldots, \mathbf{q}_n]$ span the vector space and are linearly independent, that is, $c_1 \mathbf{q}_1 + c_2 \mathbf{q}_2 + \ldots + c_n \mathbf{q}_n = 0$ if and only if the scalars $c_i = 0$ (Golub & Van Loan, 1989).

There is more than one method for decomposing the type-by-document matrix A into orthogonal components. One method is the QR factorization, which is described in detail in Berry and Browne (2005) and Berry et al. (1999), another method called the ULV low-rank orthogonal decomposition is described in detail in Berry and Fierro (1996), and yet another method called the semi-discrete decomposition (SDD) is described in detail in Kolda and O'Leary (1998). Whereas all these methods are viable options, the most popular method used by LSA to decompose the type-by-document input matrix A is the singular value decomposition (SVD). The SVD is generally the chosen orthogonal matrix decomposition of input matrix A for various reasons. First, the SVD decomposes A into orthogonal factors that represent both types and documents. Vector representations for both types and documents are achieved simultaneously. Second, the SVD sufficiently captures the underlying semantic structure of a collection and allows for adjusting the representation of types and documents in the vector space by choosing the number of dimensions (more on this later). Finally, the computation of the SVD is manageable for large datasets, especially now with current computer architectures (including clusters and symmetric multiprocessors; Berry & Martin, 2005).

The SVD for a $m \times n$ type-by-document input matrix **A** as described earlier, with the rank (number of vectors in the basis of the column space or the vector subspace spanned by the column vectors) of **A** = r, is defined as follows:

$$\mathbf{A} = \mathbf{U}\Sigma\mathbf{V}^{\mathrm{T}} \qquad\qquad 2.2$$

where **U** is an orthogonal matrix ($\mathbf{U}^{T}\mathbf{U} = \mathbf{I}_m$), **V** is an orthogonal matrix ($\mathbf{V}^{T}\mathbf{V} = \mathbf{I}_n$), and Σ is a diagonal matrix ($\Sigma = \mathrm{diagonal}(\sigma_1, \sigma_2, ..., \sigma_n)$) with the remaining matrix cells all zeros [Golub & Van Loan, 1989]). The first r columns of the orthogonal matrix **U** contain r orthonormal eigenvectors associated with the r nonzero eigenvalues[1] of $\mathbf{AA}^{T}$. The first r columns of the orthogonal matrix **V** contain r orthonormal eigenvectors associated with the r nonzero eigenvalues of $\mathbf{A}^{T}\mathbf{A}$. The first r diagonal entries of Σ are the nonnegative square roots of the r nonzero eigenvalues of $\mathbf{AA}^{T}$ and $\mathbf{A}^{T}\mathbf{A}$. The rows of matrix **U** are the type vectors and are called left singular vectors. The rows of **V** are the document vectors and are called right singular vectors. The nonzero diagonal elements of Σ are known as the singular values (Berry, Dumais, & O'Brien, 1995).

Truncation of Orthogonal Components

A pictorial representation of the SVD of input matrix **A** and the best rank-k approximation to **A** can be seen in Figure 2.1 (Berry et al., 1995; Witter & Berry, 1998). Given the fact that **A** can be written as the sum of rank 1 matri-

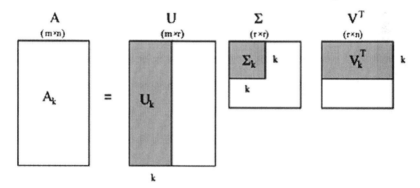

Figure 2.1.   Diagram of the truncated SVD.

---

[1]As defined in Larson and Edwards (1988), an eigenvector and eigenvalue of the matrix **A** satisfy $\mathbf{Ax} = \lambda\mathbf{x}$, where **x** is an eigenvector and λ is its corresponding eigenvalue. Two properties of eigenvectors and eigenvalues that play a role in the SVD computation are that all eigenvalues of a symmetric matrix ($\mathbf{B}^{T} = \mathbf{B}$) are real, and the eigenvectors associated with each distinct eigenvalue for a symmetric matrix are orthogonal.

ces (Björck, 1996): $A = \sum_{i=1}^{r} u_i \sigma_i v_i^T$, r can be reduced to k to create

$A_k = \sum_{i=1}^{k} u_i \sigma_i v_i^T$. The matrix $\mathbf{A}_k$ is the best or closest (distance is minimized)

rank k approximation to the original matrix $\mathbf{A}$ (Björck, 1996; Berry & Browne, 2005; Berry et al., 1995; Berry et al., 1999). The matrix $\mathbf{A}_k$ ($\mathbf{A}_k = \mathbf{U}_k \mathbf{\Sigma}_k \mathbf{V}_k^T$) is created by ignoring or setting equal to zero all but the first k elements or columns of the type vectors in $\mathbf{U}$, the first k singular values in Σ, and the first k elements or columns of the document vectors in $\mathbf{V}$. The first k columns of $\mathbf{U}$ and $\mathbf{V}$ are orthogonal, but the rows of $\mathbf{U}$ and $\mathbf{V}$, the type and document vectors, consisting of k elements are not orthogonal. By reducing the dimension from r to k, extraneous information and variability in type usage, referred to as "noise," which is associated with the database or document collection is removed. Truncating the SVD and creating $\mathbf{A}_k$ is what captures the important underlying semantic structure of types and documents. Types similar in meaning are "near" each other in k-dimensional vector space even if they never co-occur in a document, and documents similar in conceptual meaning are near each other even if they share no types in common (Berry et al., 1995). This k-dimensional vector space is the foundation for the semantic structures LSA exploits.

Using the small document collection from Table 2.1 and its corresponding type-by-document matrix in Tables 2.2 and 2.3, the SVD can be computed and truncated to a two-dimensional vector space by reducing the rank to $k = 2$. Table 2.4 shows the SVD of the example type-by-document matrix given in Table 2.3. The values in the boldface cells in the type matrix $\mathbf{U}$, the document matrix $\mathbf{V}$, and the diagonal matrix of singular values Σ are used to encode the representations of types and documents in the two-dimensional vector space.

Figure 2.2 shows a rank-2, $k = 2$, plot of the types, represented by squares, and documents, represented by triangles, in the music and baking titles collection. Each point represents a type or document vector, a line starting at the origin and ending at a defined type or document point. The (x, y) pair is defined by $x =$ first dimension or column of matrix $\mathbf{U}$ or $\mathbf{V}$ multiplied by the first singular value and $y =$ second dimension or column of matrix $\mathbf{U}$ or $\mathbf{V}$ multiplied by the second singular value for type and document points, respectively. Looking at the vectors for the types and documents, the types most similar to each other and the documents most similar to each other are determined by the angles between vectors (more on this in the Querying subsection). If two vectors are similar, then they will have a small angle between them. In Figure 2.2, the documents M4, "A Perspective of Rock Music in the 90's," and M1 "Rock and Roll Music in the 1960's" are the closest documents to document M3, "Drum and Bass Composition," and yet they share no types in common. Similarly, the type vector for "music" is closest

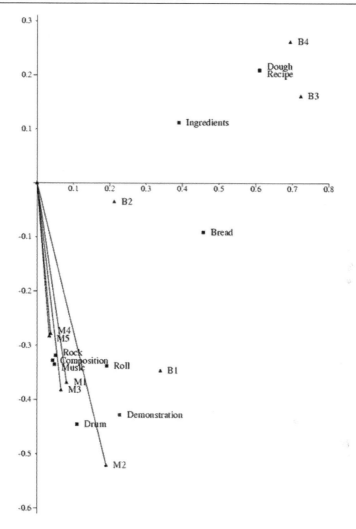

Figure 2.2. The rank-2 LSA vector space for the music/baking titles collection.

to type vectors "rock" and "composition," however, the next closest type vector corresponds to the type vector for "drum." This similarity is notable because "music" and "drum" never co-occur in the same document.

The best selection of rank or number of dimensions to use in the space remains an open question. In practice, the choice for k depends on empirical testing. For large datasets, empirical testing shows that the optimal choice for the number of dimensions ranges between 100 and 300 (Berry et al., 1999; Jessup & Martin, 2001; Lizza & Sartoretto, 2001). As stated previously, whatever the choice for k, the rank-k matrix, $\mathbf{A}_k$, constructed by the truncated SVD factors,

TABLE 2.4
The SVD of the Weighted Type-by-Document Matrix Represented in Table 2.3

Matrix U-Type Vectors

Bread	.42	−.09	−.20	.33	−.48	−.33	.46	−.21	−.28
Composition	.04	−.34	.09	−.67	−.28	−.43	.02	−.06	.40
Demonstration	.21	−.44	−.42	.29	.09	−.02	−.60	−.29	.21
Dough	.55	.22	.10	−.11	−.12	.23	−.15	.15	.11
Drum	.10	−.46	−.29	−.41	.11	.55	.26	−.02	−.37
Ingredients	.35	.12	.13	−.17	.72	−.35	.10	−.37	−.17
Music	.04	−.35	.54	.03	−.12	−.16	−.41	.18	−.58
Recipe	.55	.22	.10	−.11	−.12	.23	−.15	.15	.11
Rock	.05	−.33	.60	.29	.02	.33	.28	−.35	.37
Roll	.17	−.35	−.05	.24	.33	−.19	.25	.73	.22

Matrix Σ-Singular Values

1.10	0	0	0	0	0	0	0	0	
0	.96	0	0	0	0	0	0	0	
0	0	.86	0	0	0	0	0	0	
0	0	0	.76	0	0	0	0	0	
0	0	0	0	.66	0	0	0	0	
0	0	0	0	0	.47	0	0	0	
0	0	0	0	0	0	.27	0	0	
0	0	0	0	0	0	0	.17	0	
0	0	0	0	0	0	0	0	.07	
0	0	0	0	0	0	0	0	0	

Matrix V-Document Vectors

M1	.07	−.38	.53	.27	.08	.12	.20	.50	.42
M2	.17	−.54	−.41	.00	.28	.43	−.34	.22	−.28
M3	.06	−.40	−.11	−.67	−.12	.12	.49	−.23	.23
M4	.03	−.29	.55	.19	−.05	.22	−.04	−.62	−.37
M5	.03	−.29	.27	−.40	−.27	−.55	−.48	.21	−.17
B1	.31	−.36	−.36	.46	−.15	−.45	.00	−.32	.31
B2	.19	−.04	.06	−.02	.65	−.45	.41	.07	−.40
B3	.66	.17	.00	.06	−.51	.12	.27	.25	−.35
B4	.63	.27	.18	−.24	.35	.10	−.35	−.20	.37

produces the best approximation to the type-by-document input matrix **A**, always. Keep in mind that this does not equate to the optimal number dimensions to use in certain applications; meaning one should not always use the first 100–300 dimensions. For some applications it is better to use a subset of the first 100 or 300 dimensions or factors (Landauer & Dumais, 1997).

COMPUTING THE VECTOR SPACE MODEL FOR LATENT SEMANTIC ANALYSIS

Solving an Eigenproblem

Computing the reduced dimensional vector space for a given type-by-document input matrix is a nontrivial calculation. Given a realistic, large $m \times n$ type-by-document matrix **A** where $m \geq n$, computing the SVD becomes a problem of finding the k largest eigenvalues and eigenvectors of the matrix $\mathbf{B} = \mathbf{A}^T\mathbf{A}$. Finding the eigenvectors of **B** produces the document vectors (recall from the Decomposition of Input Matrix into Orthogonal Components subsection the columns of orthogonal matrix **V** in the SVD are the eigenvectors of **B**), and finding the eigenvalues of **B** produces the singular values (the nonnegative square roots of the eigenvalues of **B**). The type vectors are produced by back multiplying, $\boldsymbol{U}_k = A V_k \Sigma_k^{-1}$. If $n > m$, there are more documents than types, then computing the SVD is reduced to finding the k largest eigenvalues and eigenvectors of $\mathbf{B} = \mathbf{AA}^T$. In this case, finding the eigenvectors of **B** produces the type vectors (recall from the Decomposition of Input Matrix into Orthonal Components subsection the columns of orthogonal matrix **U** in the SVD are the eigenvectors of **B**), and again finding the eigenvalues of **B** produces the singular values (the nonnegative square roots of the eigenvalues of **B**). As with type vectors in the previous case, the document vectors are produced by back multiplying, $V_k = A^T U_k \Sigma_k^{-1}$. To summarize, given the symmetric matrix **B**, which is created from the sparse input matrix **A**, the objective is to find the k largest eigenvalues and eigenvectors of **B**. Thus, the SVD computation is based on solving a large, sparse symmetric eigenproblem (Berry, 1992; Golub & Van Loan, 1989).

Basic Lanczos Algorithm

The Lanczos algorithm is proven to be accurate and efficient for large, sparse symmetric eigenproblems where only a modest number of the largest or smallest eigenvalues of a matrix are desired (Golub & Van Loan, 1989; Parlett & Scott, 1979). The Lanczos algorithm, which is an iterative method and most often used to compute the k largest eigenvalues and eigenvectors of $\mathbf{B}$, actually approximates the eigenvalues of $\mathbf{B}$ (Berry & Martin, 2005).

The Lanczos algorithm involves the partial tridiagonalization of matrix $\mathbf{B}$, where a tridiagonal matrix is defined as follows:

$$T = \begin{bmatrix} \alpha_1 & \beta_1 & 0... & 0... \\ \beta_1 & \alpha_2 & \beta_2 & 0... \\ ... & ... & ... & ... \\ 0... & 0 & \beta_{v-1} & \alpha_v \end{bmatrix} \qquad 2.3$$

where $\mathbf{T}_{ij} = 0$ whenever $|i-j| > 1$ (Parlett, 1980). A tridiagonal matrix $\mathbf{T}$ is considered unreduced if $\beta_i \neq 0$, $i = 1, \dots , v - 1$. A sequence of symmetric tridiagonal matrices $\mathbf{T}_j$ is generated by the algorithm with the property that eigenvalues of $\mathbf{T}_j$ are progressively better estimates of $\mathbf{B}$'s largest (or smallest) eigenvalues (Berry, 1992). These eigenvalues emerge long before tridiagonalization is complete, before the complete v × v tridiagonal matrix is produced. There are important reasons for transforming matrix $\mathbf{B}$ to an unreduced tridiagonal matrix. First, eigenvalues and eigenvectors of $\mathbf{T}$ can be found with significantly fewer arithmetic operations than for $\mathbf{B}$. Second, every symmetric matrix $\mathbf{B}$ can be reduced to $\mathbf{T}$ by a finite number of elementary orthogonal transformations ($\mathbf{Q}^T\mathbf{B}\mathbf{Q} = \mathbf{T}$). Finally, as long as $\mathbf{T}$ is unreduced, $\mathbf{T}$'s eigenvalues are distinct; there are not multiple eigenvalues with the same value (Parlett, 1980).

Step 1 of the Lanczos algorithm is to tridiagonalize the symmetric matrix $\mathbf{B}$. To compute $\mathbf{T}_j = \mathbf{Q}^T\mathbf{B}\mathbf{Q}$, define the orthogonal matrix $\mathbf{Q} = [\mathbf{q}_1, \mathbf{q}_2, \dots , \mathbf{q}_j]$ where the vectors $\mathbf{q}_i$, known as the Lanczos vectors, are orthonormal vectors. To reduce $\mathbf{B}$ to a tridiagonal matrix step by step, the vectors for $\mathbf{Q}_j$ and the entries of $\mathbf{T}_j$ are computed one column at a time by the following the basic Lanczos recursion (Parlett, 1980; Parlett & Scott, 1979):

1. Generate a random vector $\mathbf{q}_1$ such that it is orthonormal ($\|\mathbf{q}_1\| = 1$).
2. Define $\beta_0 \equiv 0$ and $\mathbf{q}_0 \equiv 0$.
3. Recursively do the following for $j = 1, 2, \dots , l$:

$r_j = \mathbf{B}\mathbf{q}_j - \mathbf{q}_{j-1}\beta_{j-1}$;

$\alpha_j = \mathbf{q}_j^T r_j = \mathbf{q}_j^T \times (\mathbf{B}\mathbf{q}_j - \mathbf{q}_{j-1}\beta_{j-1}) = \mathbf{q}_j^T \mathbf{B}\mathbf{q}_j$,

where $\mathbf{q}_j^T \mathbf{q}_{j-1}\beta_{j-1} = 0$ due to orthogonality;

$r_j = r_j - \mathbf{q}_j\alpha_j$;

$\beta_j = \|r_j\|$, where $\|r_j\|$ is the vector length of r_j;

$\mathbf{q}_{j+1} = \dfrac{r_j}{\beta_j} = \dfrac{r_j}{\|r_j\|}$, where $\mathbf{q}_{j+1}$ becomes orthonormal.

To determine α_j, r_j, β_j and $\mathbf{q}_{j+1}$, at each step only β_j, $\mathbf{q}_{j-1}$, and $\mathbf{q}_j$ are needed. There are two things to observe about the computations in the Lanczos algorithm. First, by mathematical induction, it can be proven that the vectors $\mathbf{q}_i$ are uniquely determined by $\mathbf{B}$ and $\mathbf{q}_1$ (Parlett, 1980). Second, the vector $\mathbf{q}_{j+1}$ ($= \mathbf{B}\mathbf{q}_j - \beta_{j-1}\mathbf{q}_{j-1} - \alpha_j\mathbf{q}_j$), before normalizing or dividing by $\beta_j = \parallel r_j \parallel$ to make its vector length equal to one, is built on the previous vectors $\mathbf{q}_{j-1}$ and $\mathbf{q}_j$; therefore, the next Lanczos vector $\mathbf{q}_{j+1}$ is obtained by orthogonalizing $\mathbf{B}\mathbf{q}_j$ with respect to $\mathbf{q}_{j-1}$ and $\mathbf{q}_j$ (Berry, 1992; Berry & Martin, 2005). This guarantees the orthogonality of vectors $\mathbf{q}_j$ in the matrix $\mathbf{Q} = [\mathbf{q}_1, \mathbf{q}_2, \dots, \mathbf{q}_j]$, and the normalizing of each Lanczos vector guarantees that the vectors $\mathbf{q}_j$ are orthonormal. Given these two observations, the vectors in $\mathbf{Q}_j$ form the orthonormal basis for a subspace known as a Krylov subspace (Golub & Van Loan, 1989; Parlett, 1980). A Krylov subspace is defined by the span of $\{\mathbf{q}_1, \mathbf{q}_2, \dots, \mathbf{q}_j\}$ = span of $\{\mathbf{q}_1, \mathbf{B}\mathbf{q}_1, \dots, \mathbf{B}^{j-1} \mathbf{q}_1\}$. Therefore, the span of $\{\mathbf{Q}_j\}$ is a Krylov subspace for the matrix $\mathbf{B}$. The Lanczos procedure can be viewed as a technique for computing orthonormal bases for the Krylov subspaces at different j steps and for computing an orthogonal projection of $\mathbf{B}$ onto these subspaces (Berry, 1992).

Step 2 of the Lanczos algorithm is to examine the eigenvalues for $\mathbf{T}_j$ at various steps j to see if they are good approximations to the eigenvalues of $\mathbf{B}$. This is done by diagonalizing the tridiagonal matrix $\mathbf{T}_j$ and finding its eigenvalues and eigenvectors (remember an eigenvalue λ_k and its corresponding eigenvector $\mathbf{x}_k$ associated with $\mathbf{T}_j$ satisfy $\mathbf{T}_j\mathbf{x}_k = \lambda_k\mathbf{x}_k$). Let $\mathbf{T}_j = \mathbf{S}_j\Theta_j\mathbf{S}^T_j$, where $\mathbf{S}_j = [\mathbf{s}_1, \dots, \mathbf{s}_j]$ is a $j \times j$ orthogonal matrix and $\Theta_j = \text{diag}(\theta_1, \dots, \theta_j)$ is a diagonal matrix. The eigenvalues, $\lambda_k = \theta_k$ ($k = 1, 2, \dots, j$), and eigenvectors, $\mathbf{x}_k = \mathbf{Q}_j\mathbf{s}_k$ ($k = 1, 2, \dots, j$), of $\mathbf{T}_j$ are produced by the following derivation:

$$\text{since } \mathbf{Q}^T_j\mathbf{B}\mathbf{Q}_j = \mathbf{T}_j = \mathbf{S}_j\Theta_j\mathbf{S}^T_j$$
$$\text{then } (\mathbf{Q}_j\mathbf{S}_j)^T\mathbf{B}(\mathbf{Q}_j\mathbf{S}_j) = \Theta_j \text{ or}$$
$$\mathbf{B}(\mathbf{Q}_j\mathbf{S}_j) = \Theta_j(\mathbf{Q}_j\mathbf{S}_j).$$

2.4

An eigenpair $(\lambda_k, \mathbf{x}_k)$ for $\mathbf{T}_j$ is known as a Ritz pair, where the eigenvalue λ_k is called a Ritz value, and the eigenvector $\mathbf{x}_k$ is called a Ritz vector (Golub & Van Loan, 1989; Parlett, 1980). These Ritz pairs are the best set of approximations to the desired eigenpairs of $\mathbf{B}$ (Parlett, 1980). The accuracy of these approximations has been studied in great depth by Kaniel and Saad (Berry, 1992; Parlett, 1980), and they conclude that the eigenvalues of $\mathbf{T}_j$ are good approximations to the extreme, largest or smallest, eigenvalues of $\mathbf{B}$. This accuracy is determined by examining the residual norm, $\parallel \mathbf{B}\mathbf{x}_k - \lambda_k\mathbf{x}_k \parallel$, of each Ritz pair. The residual norm can be calculated without constructing $\mathbf{x}_k$ ($k = 1, 2, \dots, j$) by simply taking the bottom elements of the normalized eigenvectors, $\mathbf{s}_k$ $(k = 1, 2, \ldots , j)$, of $\mathbf{T}_j$ (Parlett, 1980). If the accuracy of an eigenvalue of $\mathbf{T}_j$ is sufficient, then step 3 of the Lanczos algorithm is to compute the eigenvectors, $\mathbf{x}_k$ $(k = 1, 2, \ldots , j)$, of $\mathbf{T}_j$. Once an accepted eigenpair of $\mathbf{B}$ is determined, a singular vector and singular value have been found. This is considered step 4 of the Lanczos algorithm. If $\mathbf{B} = \mathbf{A}^\mathrm{T}\mathbf{A}$, then a right singular vector has been found, and if $\mathbf{B} = \mathbf{AA}^\mathrm{T}$ then a left singular vector has been found. Table 2.5 outlines the basic steps of the Lanczos algorithm for computing the sparse SVD of input matrix $\mathbf{A}$.

Lanczos Algorithm With Selective Reorthogonalization

Theoretically, it is easy to prove (and as already explained) that the basic Lanczos recursion guarantees orthogonality among all vectors in matrix $\mathbf{Q}$ $= [\mathbf{q}_1, \mathbf{q}_2, \ldots , \mathbf{q}_j]$ by only orthogonalizing the current Lanczos vector with the previous two Lanczos vectors (Parlett, 1980). However, in using finite-precision arithmetic, the Lanczos procedure suffers from the loss of orthogonality in the Lanczos vectors. This leads to "numerically multiple" eigenvalues, the same eigenvalue calculated multiple times, and unwanted eigenvalues of $\mathbf{T}_j$. There are a few options for dealing with these problems. One is to use total reorthogonalization where every Lanczos vector is orthogonalized against all previously generated Lanczos vectors. This approach requires a great deal of storage and many arithmetic operations and can complicate the Lanczos process. Another option is to disregard the loss in orthogonality among Lanczos vectors and deal with these problems directly, but in practice it is difficult to keep track of unwanted or "numerically multiple" eigenvalues. Currently, the best option for remedying these problems is to use selective reorthogonalization of the Lanczos vectors, which is known as the "Lanczos algorithm with selective reorthogonalization" (Berry, 1992; Parlett, 1980; Parlett & Scott, 1979). In

TABLE 2.5
Lanczos Algorithm for Computing the Sparse SVD

1. Use the basic Lanczos recursion to generate a sequence of symmetric tridiagonal matrices, $\mathbf{T}_i$ $(i = 1, 2, \ldots, p)$.

2. For some $j \leq p$, compute the eigenvalues of $\mathbf{T}_j$. Determine which eigenvalues of $\mathbf{T}_j$ are good approximations to the eigenvalues of $\mathbf{B}$.

3. For each accepted eigenvalue, or Ritz value, λ_k compute its corresponding eigenvector, or Ritz vector, $\mathbf{x}_k$, where $\mathbf{x}_k = \mathbf{Q}\mathbf{s}_k$. The set of Ritz pairs are used as an approximation to the desired eigenvalues and eigenvectors of matrix $\mathbf{B}$.

4. For all accepted eigenpairs $(\lambda_k, \mathbf{x}_k)$ compute the corresponding singular vectors and values for type-by-document input matrix A.

this method, the Lanczos vectors are periodically reorthogonalized against the previous ones whenever a threshold for mutual orthogonality is exceeded (Berry & Martin, 2005). In a comparison study among several algorithms, it was found that the Lanczos algorithm using selective reorthogonalization was the fastest method for computing k of the largest singular vectors and corresponding singular values (Berry, 1992). With a recent parallel/distributed implementation of the Lanczos algorithm using selective reorthogonalization, the capacity to handle larger data collections, and thus input matrices, is now feasible (Berry & Martin, 2005). The time and storage burden of transforming a type-by-document input matrix into singular vectors and values has been reduced, increasing the suitability of this algorithm for computing the SVD.

USING THE VECTOR SPACE MODEL FOR LATENT SEMANTIC ANALYSIS

Querying

Once a reduced rank, or k-dimensional, vector space for types and documents has been produced, finding types and documents close to a given query becomes a simple process. A query is represented in the k-dimensional vector space much like a document; therefore, it is referred to as a *pseudo-document* (Deerwester et al., 1990). A query is the weighted sum of its type vectors scaled by the inverse of the singular values, this individually weights each dimension in the k-dimensional type-document vector space. A query can be represented by

$$query = q^T U_k \Sigma_k^{-1} \qquad 2.5$$

where $\mathbf{q}^T$ is vector containing zeros and weighted type frequencies corresponding to the types specified in the query. The weighting is determined by applying one of the weighting functions described in the Input Matrix subsection.

Once a pseudo-document is formed and projected into the type-document space, a similarity measure is used to determine which types and documents are closest to the query. The cosine similarity measure is commonly used, and the cosine angle between the query, or pseudo-document, and each of the documents or types is computed. The cosines and the corresponding documents or types are then ranked in descending order; thus, the document or type with the highest cosine with the query is given first. Once the ranked list is produced, documents or types above a certain threshold are then deemed relevant (Letsche & Berry, 1997).

Referring back to the small music/baking titles collection example given in the Creating the Vector Space Model for Latent Semantic Analysis section, the query "Recipe for White Bread" can be computed as a pseudo-document and projected into the rank-2 space in Figure 2.2. Calculating the cosines of the query vector with each document vector, a ranked list of the largest cosines is shown in Table 2.6. Given a cosine threshold of greater than .80, documents B2, B3, B1, and B4 are the most relevant. Document B2, "Ingredients for Crescent Rolls," is found to be the most relevant to the query "Recipe for White Bread," even though this document has no types in common with the query.

One way to enhance a query and thereby retrieve relevant documents is to apply a method known as relevance feedback (Salton & Buckley, 1990). Given the query and the initial ranked list of documents and their corresponding cosines with the query, relevance feedback allows users to indicate which documents they think are relevant from the initial list. The query with the incorporation relevance feedback is represented by

$$query = q^T U_k \Sigma_k^{-1} + d^T V_k \qquad\qquad 2.6$$

where d^T is a vector whose elements specify which documents to add to the query (Letsche & Berry, 1997). Again, this query is matched against the documents to obtain a ranked list of documents.

There are three sorts of comparisons that can be done in the vector space: comparing two types, comparing two documents, and comparing a type to a document. By definition, a query is considered a document, a pseudo-document; therefore, the comparison between two documents is the same as comparing a pseudo-document and a document. The same is true when comparing a document and a type. The analysis on these three types of comparisons was first described in Deerwester et al. (1990) and is presented here.

To find the degree of similarity between type i and type j, the dot product between row vectors in A_k is examined. Given the reduced matrix $A_k = U_k \Sigma_k V_k^T$, the dot product between any two type vectors reflects the similar-

TABLE 2.6
Results for the Query "Recipe for White Bread" Using a Cosine Threshold of .80

Document	Cosine
B2: Ingredients for Crescent Rolls	.99800
B3: A Recipe for Sourdough Bread	.90322
B1: How to make Bread and Rolls, a Demonstration	.84171
B4: A Quick Recipe for Pizza Dough using Organic Ingredients	.83396

ity of types in the document collection. Therefore, if the (square) similarity matrix to obtain all the type-to-type dot products is defined as

$$\mathbf{A}_k\mathbf{A}_k^T = \mathbf{U}_k\mathbf{\Sigma}_k\mathbf{V}_k^T \, (\mathbf{U}_k\mathbf{\Sigma}_k\mathbf{V}_k^T)^T = \mathbf{U}_k\mathbf{\Sigma}_k\mathbf{V}_k^T \, \mathbf{V}_k\mathbf{\Sigma}_k\mathbf{U}_k^T = \mathbf{U}_k\mathbf{\Sigma}_k\mathbf{\Sigma}_k\mathbf{U}_k^T \qquad 2.7$$

then the dot product between any two types is the dot product between row i and j of $\mathbf{U}_k\mathbf{\Sigma}_k$. Therefore, to perform a comparison in k-dimensional vector space between any two types, the type vectors scaled by the singular values are used to compute the similarity measure regardless of whether the similarity measure used is the cosine, Euclidean distance, or some other measure.

The comparison of two documents follows the same analysis. To determine the degree of similarity between two documents, the dot product between column vectors is examined. Given the reduced matrix $\mathbf{A}_k = \mathbf{U}_k\mathbf{\Sigma}_k\mathbf{V}_k^T$, the dot product between any two document vectors indicates the extent to which two documents have similar type patterns or type meanings. If the (square) similarity matrix to compute all the document-to-document dot products is created by

$$\mathbf{A}_k^T\mathbf{A}_k = (\mathbf{U}_k\mathbf{\Sigma}_k\mathbf{V}_k^T)^T\mathbf{U}_k\mathbf{\Sigma}_k\mathbf{V}_k^T = \mathbf{V}_k\mathbf{\Sigma}_k\mathbf{U}_k^T \, \mathbf{U}_k\mathbf{\Sigma}_k\mathbf{V}_k^T = \mathbf{V}_k\mathbf{\Sigma}_k\mathbf{\Sigma}_k\mathbf{V}_k^T \qquad 2.8$$

then the dot product between any two documents is the dot product between row i and j of $\mathbf{V}_k\mathbf{\Sigma}_k$. Therefore, to do a comparison between any two documents, or a document and a pseudo-document, the document vectors, or pseudo-document vector, scaled by the singular values are used to compute the similarity measure.

The comparison between a type and a document is different than the comparison between any two types or any two documents. In this case, the comparison is analyzed by looking at an element of $\mathbf{A}_k$. Remember that the reduced rank matrix is defined as $\mathbf{A}_k = \mathbf{U}_k\mathbf{\Sigma}_k\mathbf{V}_k^T$, and the element a_{ij} of $\mathbf{A}_k$ is obtained by taking the dot product of row vector $\mathbf{i}$ in $\mathbf{U}_k$ scaled by $\sqrt{\mathbf{\Sigma}_k}$ and the row vector $\mathbf{j}$ in $\mathbf{V}_k$ scaled by $\sqrt{\mathbf{\Sigma}_k}$. Thus, following the same procedure as with types and documents, when computing a comparison, regardless of similarity measure used, between a type and a document or pseudo-document, the corresponding type vector and document vector scaled by the square root of the singular values are needed.

Updating

The ability to add new types and documents to the reduced rank type-document vector space is important because the original information in the document collection oftentimes needs to be augmented for different contextual or conceptual usages. One of three methods, "folding-in," recomputing the SVD, or SVD-updating, described in Berry et al. (1995) is generally used when updating or adding new types or documents to an existing vector space. However, to date, there is no optimal way to add information to an existing type-document space that is more accurate than recomputing the k-dimensional vector space with the added information while directly and accurately affecting the underlying latent structure in the document collection.

The simple way of handling the addition of types and documents is to "fold" types or documents into the k-dimensional vector space. The "folding-in" procedure is based on the existing type-document vector space. As with querying, to fold-in a document, a pseudo-document is built. A new document, d, is folded into the existing k-dimensional vector space by projecting d onto the span of the current type vectors by computing $d_{new} = d^T U_k \Sigma_k^{-1}$. The vector $\mathbf{d}$, representing a document, contains zero and nonzero elements where the nonzero elements correspond to the type frequencies contained in the document adjusted by a weighting function described in the Input Matrix subsection. Similarly, to fold a new type vector, $\mathbf{t}$, into an existing k-dimensional vector space, a projection of $\mathbf{t}$ onto the space of the current document vectors is computed by $t_{new} = tV_k \Sigma_k^{-1}$. In this case, the vector $\mathbf{t}$ contains zero and nonzero elements where the nonzero elements are weighted elements corresponding to the documents that contain the type. Both the vectors of $\mathbf{d}_{new}$ and $\mathbf{t}_{new}$ are added to the vector space as another document and type, respectively. This method is a quick and easy way to add new types and documents to a vector space, but by no means does it change the existing type-document vector space. Essentially the new types and documents have no effect on the underlying semantic structure or meanings of types and documents.

The best way to produce a k-dimensional type-document vector space with new types and documents playing a role in the meanings of types and documents is to reproduce the type-by-document matrix with the added types and documents, recompute the SVD, and regenerate the reduced rank vector space. The exact effects of adding those specific types or documents are reflected in the vector space. Of course, the expense of this method is time. Although time efficient ways of calculating the SVD are being developed, recomputation is still computationally intensive (Berry & Martin, 2005).

One algorithm that has been proposed in literature as an alternative to folding in and recomputing the SVD is the SVD-updating algorithm (Berry et al., 1995). Performing the SVD-updating technique requires three steps: adding new documents, adding new types, and correcting for changes in type weightings. All steps use the reduced rank vector space, $\mathbf{A}_k$, to incorporate new types or documents into the existing type-document space by exploiting the previously computed singular vectors and values. This technique is definitely more difficult and more computationally complex than folding-in, but it does guarantee the orthogonality of vectors among the existing and new type and document vectors. Although the SVD-updating technique does try and mimic the effects of new types and documents on the underlying semantic structure, it will deviate somewhat from the actual recomputation of the reduced rank space using the same data because the update is based on $\mathbf{A}_k$ and not an original type-by-document matrix $\mathbf{A}$ (Berry et al., 1995). An updating method, which is guaranteed to match the results of a recomputed SVD, is given in Zha and Simon (1999).

Downdating

Following the same argument as updating, the ability to remove types and documents from a reduced rank vector space is also important because there are times when the original information in a document collection needs to be diminished for different contextual and conceptual usages. Again there are three methods—"folding-out," recomputing the SVD, or "downdating the reduced model" method—used in downdating or removing a type or document from an existing vector space. However, as with updating, to date there is no way to remove information from an existing type-document space that accurately affects the underlying semantic structure of a document collection and is more expedient than recomputing the original k-dimensional vector space.

The simplest method for removing information from a type-document vector space is "folding-out" of types or documents. This technique simply ignores the unwanted types and documents as if they were absent from the vector space and thus the document collection. The types and documents are no longer used in comparisons.

Of course, the method of removing types or documents from a document collection, reproducing the type-by-document matrix, recomputing the SVD, and regenerating the k-dimensional vector space is always an option. Recreating the type-document vector space with certain types and documents removed is definitely the most accurate in showing the effects of the removed information on the underlying semantic structure of the original database. As stated in the Updating subsection, this requires computational complexity and time.

One other algorithm, described in Witter and Berry (1998), called downdating the reduced model (DRM), tries to reflect the change that removing types and documents has on the reduced rank vector space without recomputing the SVD as a new type-by-document vector space. This technique involves three steps: removing a type, removing a document, and updating type weights from the reduced rank vector space $\mathbf{A}_k$. The previously calculated singular vectors and values are used in downdating the vector space. This algorithm approximates the effects that removing types and documents have on the reduced rank vector space, and it maintains orthogonality among the existing and new type and document vector columns. The DRM method is not as accurate as recomputing the vector space, but it is more accurate than folding-out. But likewise it is also computationally more time efficient than recomputing the vector space but much slower that folding-out.

CONCLUSIONS

Latent semantic analysis (LSA) uses a reduced rank vector space model to exploit the latent semantic structure of type-document associations. As evidenced by this chapter, creating, calculating, and using the reduced rank vector space model is nontrivial and based on sophisticated numerical algorithms. The mathematical foundations laid out in this chapter are the basis for which the applications of LSA are built on. The remaining chapters of this volume describe the various LSA applications and manipulations that exploit the reduced rank vector space model and structure.

REFERENCES

Berry, M. W. (1992). Large sparse singular value computations. *International Journal of Supercomputer Applications, 6,* 13–49.

Berry, M. W., & Browne, M. (2005). *Understanding search engines: Mathematical modeling and text retrieval* (2nd ed.). Philadelphia: SIAM.

Berry, M. W., & Drmac, Z., & Jessup, E. (1999). Matrices, vector spaces, and information retrieval. *SIAM Review, 41,* 335–362.

Berry, M. W., Dumais, S., & O'Brien, G. (1995). Using linear algebra for intelligent information retrieval. *SIAM Review, 37,* 573–595.

Berry, M. W., & Fierro, R. (1996). Low-rank orthogonal decompositions for information retrieval applications. *Numerical Linear Algebra With Applications, 3,* 301–327.

Berry, M. W., & Martin, D. (2005). Principle component analysis for information retrieval. In E. Kontoghiorghes (Series Ed.), *Statistics: A series of textbooks and monographs: Handbook of parallel computing and statistics* (pp. 399–413). Boca Raton, FL: Chapman & Hall/CRC.

Björck, Å. (1996). *Numerical methods for least squares problems.* Unpublished manuscript, Linköping University, Linköping, Sweden.

Buckley, C., Allan, J., & Salton, G. (1994). Automatic routing and ad-hoc retrieval using SMART: TREC 2. In D. Harman (Ed.), *Proceedings of the Second Text Retrieval Conference TREC-2* (National Institute of Standards and Technology Special Publication No. 500–215, pp. 45–56). Gaithersburg, MD: NIST.

Deerwester, S., Dumais, S., Furnas, G., Landauer, T., & Harshman, R. (1990). Indexing by latent semantic analysis. *Journal of the American Society for Information Sciences, 41,* 391–407.

Dumais, S. (1991). Improving the retrieval of information from external sources. *Behavior Research Methods, Instruments, and Computers, 23*, 229–236.

Furnas, G., Landauer, T., Gomez, L., & Dumais, S. (1987). The vocabulary problem in human–system communication. *Communications of the ACM, 30*, 964–971.

Golub, G., & Van Loan, C. F. (1989). *Matrix computations* (2nd ed.). Baltimore: Johns Hopkins Unversity Press.

Jessup, E., & Martin, J. (2001). Taking a new look at the latent semantic analysis approach to information retrieval. In M. W. Berry (Ed.), *Computational information retrieval* (pp. 121–144). Philadelphia: SIAM.

Kolda, T. G., & O'Leary, D. P. (1998). A semi-discrete matrix decomposition for latent semantic indexing in information retrieval. *ACM Transactions on Information Systems, 16*, 322–346.

Landauer, T., & Dumais, S. (1997). A solution to Plato's problem: The latent semantic analysis theory of acquisition, induction, and representation of knowledge. *Psychological Review, 104*, 211–240.

Larson, R., & Edwards, B. (1988). *Elementary linear algebra.* Lexington, MA: Heath.

Letsche, T., & Berry, M. W. (1997). Large-scale information retrieval with latent semantic indexing. *Information Sciences, 100*, 105–137.

Lizza, M., & Sartoretto, F. (2001). A comparative analysis of LSI strategies. In M. W. Berry (Ed.), *Computational information retrieval* (pp. 171–181). Philadelphia: SIAM.

Parlett, B. (1980). *The symmetric eigenvalue problem.* Englewood Cliffs, NJ: Prentice-Hall.

Parlett, B., & Scott, D. (1979). The Lanczos algorithm with selective reorthogonalization. *Mathematics of Computation, 33*, 217–238.

Salton, G., & Buckley, C. (1990). Improving retrieval performance by relevance feedback. *Journal of the American Society for Information Sciences, 41*, 288–297.

Salton, G., & Buckley, C. (1991). Automatic text structuring and retrieval—experiments in automatic encyclopedia searching. *Proceedings of the 14th Annual International ACM SIGIR Conference on Research and Development in Information Retrieval*, pp. 21–30.

Salton, G., Buckley, C., & Allan, J. (1992). Automatic structuring of text files. *Electronic Publishing, 5*, 1–17.

Salton, G., & McGill, M. (1983). *Introduction to modern information retrieval.* New York: McGraw-Hill.

Witter, D., & Berry, M. W. (1998). Downdating the latent semantic indexing model for conceptual information retrieval. *The Computer Journal, 41*, 589–601.

Zha, H., & Simon, H. (1999). On updating problems in latent semantic indexing. *SIAM Journal of Scientific Computing, 21*, 782–791.

3

How to Use the LSA Web Site

Simon Dennis
University of Adelaide

Many researchers and students interested in applying latent semantic analysis (LSA) become daunted by the complexities of building spaces and applying those spaces to new problems. In an effort to provide a simpler interface, the University of Colorado built the LSA Web site (http://lsa.colorado.edu).[1] The Web site contains several precomputed semantic spaces and tools to manipulate those spaces in a number of ways. This chapter provides an overview of the site and describes some of the issues that you will need to be aware of in order to use the site correctly. Like any model, poor results can be obtained from LSA if parameters are not set appropriately. We will highlight some of the most common errors and give advice on how to use the site to generate the best results.

In the discussions in this chapter, we will assume that you have a basic understanding of the mechanics of LSA and are familiar with terms such as cosine, psuedodoc, and so on. If this is not the case, then before proceeding you should read chapter 2 in this volume on the mathematical foundations of LSA.

Figure 3.1 shows the home page of the LSA Web site. On the left-hand side is a main menu, which provides fast links to the main areas of the Web

---

[1]Special thanks is due to Darrell Laham, who was responsible for the initial creation of the site, and to Jose Quesada and Dian Martin, who have been responsible for the maintenance of the site.

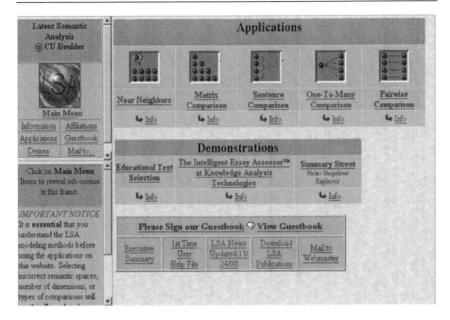

Figure 3.1.   The home page of the LSA Web site at http://www.lsa.colorado.edu

site. On the right-hand side are the applications, a series of demonstrations of LSA in action in some applied settings and a list of links to auxiliary functions such as the site guestbook and a list of LSA publications. This chapter focuses on the applications. First, however, we need to consider two issues that will be relevant regardless of which application you employ, namely, how to choose a semantic space and how many factors to select.

SPACES AND FACTORS

When using LSA, a key decision is the nature of corpus that should form the basis of the semantic space. Some aspects of this decision are obvious. Clearly, one must use a space that is likely to contain the terms that will be used in the application (including choosing a space based on the correct language). LSA simply ignores any terms that did not appear in the corpus from which it was constructed, so any semantic distinctions that rely on these terms will be lost.

Some other issues are more subtle. As a rule of thumb, the larger the space the more likely it is that it will contain sufficient knowledge to triangulate the meaning of relevant terms. However, sometimes the general meanings of terms are not the ones that are appropriate in a specific setting. For instance, if one is interested in assessing medical student essays on the circulatory system, it is most likely the case that the term "heart" should refer to the organ that pumps blood. In general usage, however, it is more common for the term "heart" to refer to courage and compassion. For these purposes, it is more appropriate to use a corpus constructed from texts relating to the area of interest. The appendix outlines the semantic spaces that are available on the LSA Web site. These include both English and French spaces taken from a number of genres, subject areas, and grade levels. You should look through this list to familiarize yourself with the different options. If none of these are sufficiently similar to the material that you will be dealing with, then it may be necessary to construct your own space. The next chapter outlines this process.

A second issue that arises in all applications of LSA is the number of factors that should be employed. We have found that, in general, about 300 factors seems to work well, and it is rare that fewer than 50 factors gives good results. For example, Figure 3.2 shows performance (corrected for guessing) on 80 retired items from the synonym component of the Test of English as a Foreign Language (TOEFL; Landauer & Dumais, 1997). In this task, applicants to U.S. universities from non-English-speaking countries choose from four alternatives the one that is closest in meaning to a stem word. To simulate this task with LSA, the cosine between the stem word and each of the alternatives is calcualted and the alternative with the highest cosine is chosen. Note that the performance as a function of the number

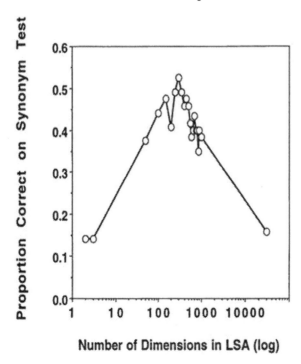

Figure 3.2. Performance on the TOEFL vocabulary task as a function of the number of factors employed.

of dimensions employed peaks at about 300 dimensions. However, the number of dimensions that produces best performance interacts with the task and the size of the space, so experimentation is often called for.[2]

THE APPLICATIONS

There are five main applications supplied by the LSA Web site:

1. Nearest neighbor: Returns a list of the terms in the LSA space that are closest to a target text.
2. Matrix comparison: Compare a set of texts against each other.
3. Sentence comparison: Submit a sequence of texts and receive the cosines between each adjacent pair (used for calculating textual coherence).
4. One to many comparison: Compare a target text against a set of texts (used for vocabulary testing and essay grading).
5. Pairwise comparison: Submit a sequence of texts and receive the cosines between each pair.

The following sections consider each in turn, pointing out the tasks that can be achieved using the application and discussing the associated parameters.

Nearest Neighbors

The nearest neighbor application returns a list of the terms in the given LSA space that are most similar to a given term and the corresponding cosines to the target term. Figure 3.3 shows the nearest neighbor application and Table 3.1 shows the results for the term "dog."

As with all of the applications, you must select a semantic space and the number of factors to employ (the maximum number of factors available will be used if you leave this field blank). In addition, the nearest neighbor application allows you to select how many terms will be returned and set a cutoff for the frequency of these terms. When deciding on the placement of term vectors, the LSA algorithm attempts to place each vector as well as it can given the occurrence information it has from the corpus. If a term appears very infrequently (i.e., it is a very low frequency word or perhaps a typographical mistake), then its position will be very close to the terms that hap-

---

[2]This problem is also discussed in the next chapter. Note that reducing the number of dimensions in an existing space is equivalent to creating a new space with the reduced number of dimensions.

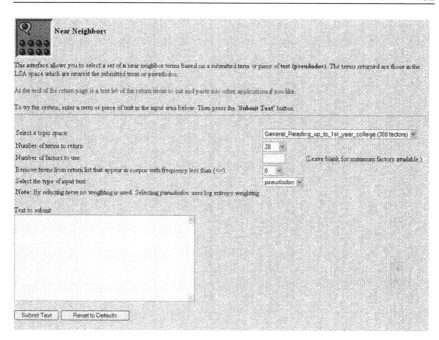

Figure 3.3.   The nearest neighbor tool.

TABLE 3.1

Results From the Nearest Neighbor Application for the Term "Dog" With the Frequency Cutoff Set to 10

LSA Similarity	Term
.99	dog
.86	barked
.86	dogs
.81	wagging
.80	collie
.79	leash
.74	barking
.74	lassie
.72	kennel
.71	wag

pen to appear in the one document in which it appears, despite the fact that the evidence that it should appear in this location is not strong. Consequently, these terms will often appear quite high in the nearest neighbor lists, despite the fact that they are unlikely to be the terms of interest. The frequency cutoff mechanism allows you to filter these terms from the output. Typically, you would set this to about five, but again it depends on your objectives in using LSA and experimentation may be called for. Finally, the nearest neighbor results will be influenced by weighting that is employed. By default, the application is set to pseudodoc, which means that log entropy weighting and inverse singular values are employed (see chap. 2). This is usually the most appropriate for nearest neighbor comparisons, but is also possible to set the weighting to term, which does not employ weighting.

A final warning that applies across the tools is that long word lists may receive a time out error due to the limited capacity of the server. If possible, reduce the size of these before submitting them to the tool. If this is not possible, then you may have to consider setting up your own space as outlined in the next chapter.

Matrix Comparison

The matrix application is designed to allow you to quickly obtain all comparisons of a set of terms or texts. Figure 3.4 shows the matrix application and Table 3.2 shows the results that are returned if the terms "dog," "cat,"

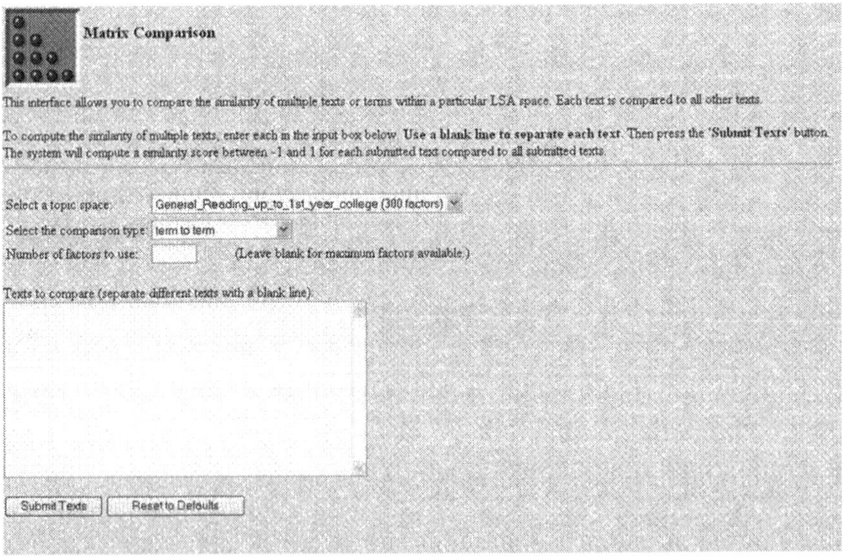

Figure 3.4.   The matrix tool.

TABLE 3.2
Results From the Matrix Application for the Terms "Dog," "Cat," "Puppy,"
and "Kitten"

Document	Dog	Cat	Puppy	Kitten
dog	1	0.36	0.76	0.28
cat	0.36	1	0.38	0.61
puppy	0.76	0.38	1	0.43
kitten	0.28	0.61	0.43	1

"puppy," and "kitten" are submitted. When entering the items to be compared, you must leave a blank line between each term or text. The only parameter that needs to be set other than the space and number of factors parameters is the kind of comparison—"term to term" or "document to document." As in the nearest neighbor application, this parameter controls whether log entropy weighting is used. When "term to term" is set, no weighting is used. When "document to document" is set, all items are log entropy weighted.

Sentence Comparison

To comprehend a text, readers must form a connected representation of the content. The ability to do this is heavily influenced by how well the concepts in the text are related to each other—the coherence of the text. Many factors contribute to coherence, but Foltz, Kintsch, and Landauer (1998) found that by taking the mean of the cosines of the LSA vectors representing successive sentences in a text, one could approximate empirical data on coherence. The sentence comparison application achives this task. Figure 3.5 shows the application and Table 3.3 shows the results when the nursery rhyme "Incy Wincy Spider" is submitted. The application indicates the cosine between each successive pair of sentences and provides the mean and standard deviation of these values. Note that unlike the matrix application, the sentence comparison application does not require you to separate sentences with blank lines. Simple punctuation is used to segment the text.

One to Many Comparison

The one to many application takes a single text and compares it to a number of other texts. Figure 3.6 shows the application. The primary text is input into the first text box and the comparison texts are entered into the second text box separated by blank lines. Table 3.4 shows a typical output.

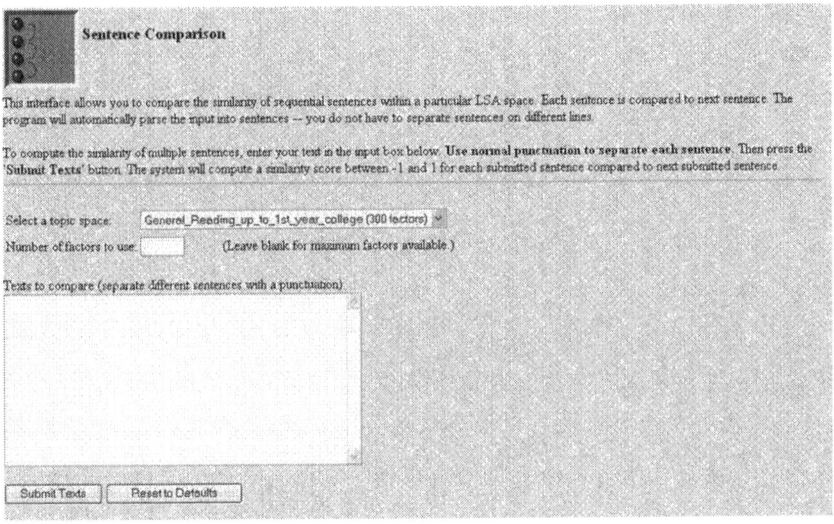

Figure 3.5. The sentence comparison tool.

TABLE 3.3
Results From the Sentence Comparison Application for the Nursery Rhyme
"Incy WincySpider"

COS	SENTENCES
	1: Incy wincy spider climbed up the water spout.
.24	
	2: Down came the rain and washed the spider out.
.91	
	3: Out came the sunshine and dried up all the rain.
.20	
	4: So incy wincy spider climbed up the spout again.

Note. Mean of the Sentence to Sentence Coherence is .45. Standard deviation of the Sentence to Sentence is .32.

In function, this application is similar to the matrix comparison application. However, there are a couple of additional facilities that have been included in this application that may prove useful. First, in addition to making "term to term" and "document to document" comparisons, you can also make "term to document" and "document to term" comparisons. In the former case, the primary text will not be weighted, but the comparison texts will be. In the later case, the reverse is true.

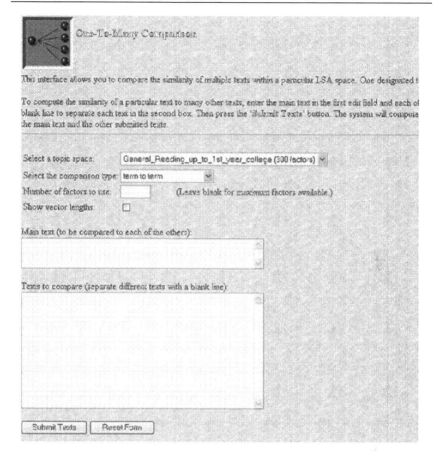

Figure 3.6. The one to many tool.

Second, the tool allows you to generate vector lengths (see Table 3.4). Vector lengths give an indication of the amount of information that is encoded by a text and they can be useful in determining the importance of individual terms or subtexts to the meaning vector associated with a larger text.

Finally, you will note that in the example (Table 3.4), the term "kiten" was misspelled. As outlined previously, LSA ignores such terms and in this tool gives the warning: "WARNING: The word kiten does not exist in the corpus you selected. Results can be seriously flawed. Consult the documentation before proceeding." You should be especially careful when interpreting results when important terms may not have played a role in the construction of the meaning of the text (Landauer, 2002).

The one to many tool is the one that is used for many demonstrations of LSA. For instance, the one to many tool can be used to answer multiple-choice synonym tests like the Test of English as a Foreign Language

TABLE 3.4
Results From the One to Many Application

Texts	Vector Length
dog	3.36
cat	1.88
puppy	.70
kiten	.00

(TOEFL; see Landauer & Dumais, 1997) by putting the target into the first textbox and the choice options into the second textbox. The option that has the highest cosine would be the one chosen.

Of all of the demonstrations of the capabilities of LSA, perhaps the most startling and most controversial is its ability to mark essay questions (Landauer & Dumais, 1997). Using the one to many tool, one can simulate essay assessment by putting the summary to be graded into the first textbox and putting prescored essays into the second textbox. A score can be assigned by taking the mean of the scores that were assigned to the essays that are most similar to the target essay. Such an exercise would be useful in understanding the LSA component of essay scoring mechanisms. One should be aware, however, that current essay grading software incorporates a great deal of additional information beyond the LSA cosines and so performance in current commercial systems that employ LSA will be significantly better than this exercise might suggest.

Pairwise Comparison

The final application is the pairwise tool (Fig. 3.7), which allows you to submit a list of texts separated by blank lines and returns the comparisons of each of the pairs. Table 3.5 shows the output from the application. Note that unlike the sentence comparison application in which sentence one is compared to sentence two, sentence two to three, and so on, in the parwise tool sentences one and two are compared, then three and four, and so on. As with the one to many tool, the pairwise tool allows you to specify "term to term," "document to document," "term to document," and "document to term" comparisons.

CONCLUSIONS

The LSA Web site was created by the staff at the University of Colorado to allow researchers and students to investigate the properties of LSA. Many

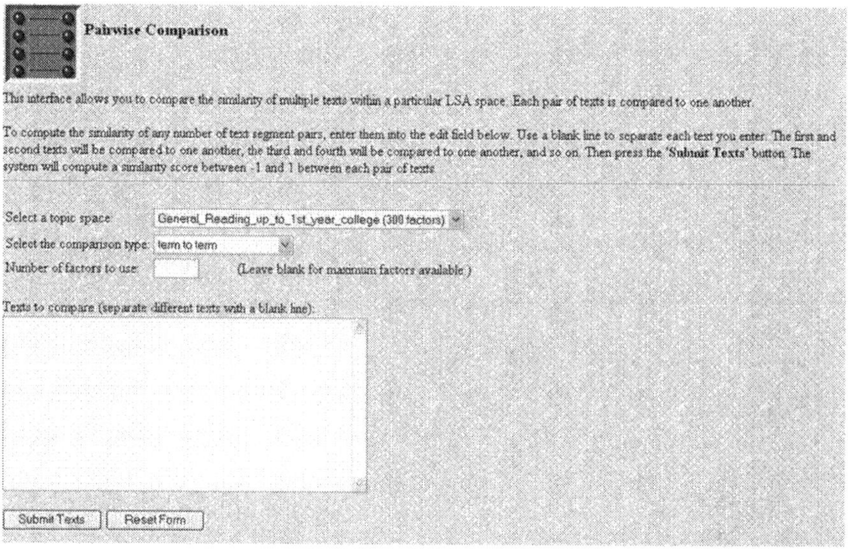

Figure 3.7.   The pairwise tool.

TABLE 3.5
Results From the Pairwise Application

Texts	Cat
dog	.36
Texts	Kitten
puppy	.43

of the common tasks that one would like to accomplish with LSA are possible through the Web site. However, if one wishes to create spaces on the basis of corpora that are not included on the site or one needs to be able to generate comparisons more rapidly than is possible with a shred resource like the Web site, then it will be necessary to create your own spaces. The process for achieving this is outlined in the next chapter.

REFERENCES

Foltz, P. W., Kintsch, W., & Landauer, T. K. (1998). The measurement of textual coherence with latent semantic analysis. *Discourse Processes, 25*, 285–308.

Landauer, T. K. (2002). On the computational basis of learning and cognition: Arguments from lsa. In N. Ross (Ed.), *The psychology of learning and motivation* (Vol. 41, pp. 43–84). New York: Academic Press.

Landauer, T. K., & Dumais, S. T. (1997). A solution to plato's problem: The latent semantic analysis theory of the acquisition, induction, and representation of knowledge. *Psychological Review, 104*, 211–240.

APPENDIX
AN OUTLINE OF AVAILABLE SEMANTIC SPACES

Literature

The literature space is composed of English and American literature from the 18th and 19th century (English = 294 works; American = 444 works). This space is a collection of literary text taken from the project Gutenberg page. The space is composed of 104,852 terms and 942,425 documents, with 338 dimensions. The total number of words is 57,092,140.

Literature With Idioms

Literature with idioms is the same space, but with a different parsing. The words in each of the idioms has been combined into a single token, so that the meaning of the idiom can be separated from the meanings of the individual words. The corpus has been created with 500 factors.

Encyclopedia

This space contains the text from 30,473 encyclopedia articles. There are 60,768 unique terms. There are 371 saved dimensions. Studies show that the optimum dimensionality for this collection is usually 275–350.

Psychology

This space contains the text from three collegelevel psychology textbooks with each paragraph used as a document. There are 13,902 documents and 30,119 unique terms. There are 398 saved dimensions. Optimum dimensionality appears to be approximately 300–400.

Small Heart

This small space contains the text from a number of articles about the heart. Each document is a sentence of an article.

French Spaces

There are 8 French semantic spaces:

- Francais-Monde (300) contains 6 months (January to June of "Le Monde" newspapers, 1993). It contains 20,208 documents, 150,756 different unique words, and 8,675,391 total words.
- Francais-Monde-Extended (300) contains 6 other months (July to December of "Le Monde" newspapers, 1993).
- Francais-Total (300) is the concatenation of Francais-Monde (300) + Francais-Livres (300).
- Francais-Livres (300) contains books published before 1920: 14,622 documents, 111,094 different unique words, and 5,748,581 total words.
- Francais-Livres1and2 (300) contains books published before 1920 + recent books. Livres1and2 is 119,000 documents.
- Francais-Livres3 (100) is smaller and contains only recent literature with idioms. Livres3 is 26,000 documents.
- Francais-Contes-Total (300) contains traditional tales as well as some recent tales. This semantic space is used to study recall or summary of stories by children and adolescents.
- Francais-Production-Total (300) contains texts written by children from 7 to 12 years in primary school in Belgium and France. There are 830 documentss and 3,034 unique terms. This space was created using a stop list of 439 common words. There are 94 saved dimensions.

General Reading Space

These spaces use a variety of texts, novels, newspaper articles, and other information, from the Touchstone Applied Science Associates, Inc. (TASA) corpus used to develop *The Educator's Word Frequency Guide*. We are thankful to the kind folks at TASA for providing us with these samples.

The TASA-based spaces break out by grade level—there are spaces for 3rd, 6th, 9th, and 12th grades, plus one for "college" level. These are cumulative spaces, that is, the 6th-grade space includes all the 3rd-grade documents, the 9th-grade space includes all the 6th and 3rd, and so forth.

The judgment for inclusion in a grade-level space comes from a readability score (DRP—degrees of reading power scale) assigned by TASA to each sample. DRP scores in the TASA corpus range from about 30 to about 73. TASA studies determined what ranges of difficulty are being used in different grade levels, for example, the texts used in 3rd-grade classes range from 45–51 DRP units. For the LSA spaces, all documents less than or equal to the maximum DRP score for a grade level are included, for example, the 3rd-grade corpus includes all text samples that score <= 51 DRP units. Following are the specifics for each space:

name	*grade*	*maxDRP*	*#docs*	*#terms*	*#dims*
tasa03	3	51	6,974	29,315	432
tasa06	6	59	17,949	55,105	412
tasa09	9	62	22,211	63,582	407
tasa12	12	67	28,882	76,132	412
tasaALL	college	73	37,651	92,409	419

The breakdown for samples by academic area (in tasaALL):

	samples	*paragraphs*
Language Arts	16,044	57,106
Health	1,359	3,396
Home Economics	283	403
Industrial Arts	142	462
Science	5,356	15,569
SocialStudies	10,501	29,280
Business	1,079	4,834
Miscellaneous	675	2,272
Unmarked	2,212	6,305
Total	37,651	119,627

4

Creating Your Own
LSA Spaces

Jose Quesada
Warwick University

Although many researchers use LSA today, not that may run their own SVDs (single value decompositions) to create their own spaces. There are several reasons for this: (a) A public Web site exists that is sufficient for most uses of LSA, and the group at the University of Colorado, Boulder, has had programmers that are able to do some "extra jobs" when researchers requested features not available in the Web site. (b) On some occasions, it is difficult to collect a representative corpus of text. (c) There are memory requirements: Current SVD methods place the entire matrix in memory to invert it (see Martin & Berry, chap. 2 in this volume). That places a significant bottleneck in the size of the LSA analyses that one can run, and was the main reason why LSA analyses could not be run on personal computers. However, nowadays the memory bottleneck is no longer an issue, because a consumer-level PC can be configured with more than enough memory to run a large SVD. (d) Computer expertise is required. Traditionally, computers with a memory large enough to run SVD ran UNIX. Also, the numerical computation support needed for large SVDs was available only under machines using UNIX. Not that many people in psychology had the expertise needed to run or desire to learn that operating system, not available on personal computers. Linux had been available for PCs since the early 1990s, but its user base was small. This situation has changed. On one hand, both apple and IBM-compatible PCs have reached a point where UNIX-based operating systems (OS) are available and mainstream (MacOS-X and Linux, respectively). Most of the classical and current work on LSA takes place on UNIX machines. One reason is that the UNIX philosophy is text-oriented: The fact that UNIX relies on a command line interface where small utilities are chained together makes it ideal to process text. Another reason is that in the past, machines with memories large enough to carry out LSA analyses were large mainframes. Nowadays, LSA analyses can be performed on personal computers under any operating system. However, learning UNIX will help any researcher that is interested in working with text. This chapter focuses on implementations of SVD programs for this OS. The researcher that still opts for staying within a Microsoft Windows framework can, however, still make use of several commercial alternatives (Matlab, Mathematica, R, general programming languages) that will be described later.

The main objective of this chapter is to de-mystify the process of creating your own LSA space. All that is required is general knowledge of a programming language (described later) and an off-the-shelf computer system. The chapter is divided into software-related issues and theoretical issues. The fist section presents the advantages and problems posed by all the different alternatives in the software world to run an SVD. The second section focuses on decisions regarding selecting the number of dimensions, the proper corpus, and weighting schemes (see Landauer, chap.1 in this volume, for an introduction of these terms). These are software independent. The third section concludes the discussion.

SOFTWARE-RELATED ISSUES

There are three basic steps to creating a LSA space and work with it: parsing text, computing an SVD, and manipulating the vectors so one can compute similarities between the passages in which one is interested. The ideal situation may be for one to perform the three of them with the same tool. However, a combination of tools may prove to be better than a single one, because it affords more flexibility. For example, a programming environment A may be very well suited to parse text, but not for handling matrices and vectors. The opposite may be true for the programming environment B. In that situation, it might be advantageous to combine A and B. This section presents a review of some current possibilities to carry out the three steps.

Parsing Text

Parsing is breaking the input text stream into useable tokens or units, usually words. There are many decisions and issues to address when breaking a text into tokens. To name a few: filtering (i.e., removing HTML tags), common words (i.e., remove or not remove common words), word length (i.e., How long do you want to allow words to be? Do you want to truncate or not the words that exceed the limit?), keep or not keep punctuation marks, numbers, and so forth, and document boundaries (i.e., What delimiter signifies a document boundary?). For example, we may decide that we are not interested in punctuation marks and numbers. Then, strings such as "18-hole" would be parsed as "hole" and strings such as "end" would be parsed as "end". Some natural language processing (NLP) libraries (e.g., GATE, http://www.gate.ac.uk/) provide functions to perform different types of parsing. Unfortunately, there is no universally accepted way to parse text, so different packages differ in the options they offer and the output they produce. This is important because the same corpus parsed with slightly different parser parameters will render different LSA spaces. It is highly encouraged that researchers compare their parsing with older ones when trying to replicate previous experiments.

At this point, it is important to introduce the distinction between types and tokens. A type is the class (e.g., word) that the parser uses as unit, and a token is each occurrence of that class. For example, in the sentence "I have one brother and one sister," the type "one" is represented by two tokens. The number of types in the corpus is usually the largest dimension in our word × context matrix, and thus it will determine the largest number of dimensions that we can ask in the SVD program (although it could be the number of documents; see Martin and Berry, chap. 2 in this volume). An obvious first step in text analysis is to compute a frequency table (i.e., how many tokens there are per type in the corpus). Frequency counts will depend on the parsing decisions. For example, words separated by a hyphen (e.g., high-quality) would be counted as one or two words depending on our decision to make the hyphen a valid character. Note that all the posterior processing (context-type matrix computation, weighting, SVD, etc.) will be determined by the parsing. This is important because one of the most common problems when trying to replicate previous work is to reproduce the parsing exactly. This constitutes an exercise in reverse engineering unless the original parser used and a detailed list of the parameters is available.

The remainder of this section explains several possible choices to parse text, commenting on the advantages and disadvantages of each.

Using a Specialized Language With Regular Expressions. A regular expression (abbreviated as regexp, regex, or regxp) is a string that describes or matches a set of strings, according to certain syntax rules. For example, the regular expression "a*" matches all strings that start with the letter "a." A good option is to use a specialized language for the parsing. Perl (http://www.perlfoundation.org/) is probably the best at this job, although any language that implements regular expressions is suitable. There are advantages to using a general language such as Perl: Perl has a gigantic standard library. The Comprehensive Perl Archive Network (CPAN) contains thousands of libraries for text-related tasks, plus some other tasks such as talking to databases, crawling the Web, and so on. Crawling the Web, parsing the text, and talking to databases are three tasks that are very related to corpus compilation. Having an appropriate corpus is a prerequisite for creating an LSA semantic space. In addition, Perl provides excellent support through mailing lists, books, and online tutorials. Perl is very popular in the NLP community, so chances are that somebody has solved the problem you face before you and has posted the solution. Finally, Perl is multi-platform, available in mostly any known platform.

Perl was originally designed to parse text, although it has outgrown this purpose. The disadvantages of using Perl for parsing are hard to find. One of them is (a) speed (as it is an interpreted language). (b) Perl scripts tend to be hard to maintain; in fact, Perl is the only language the author knows that has a book on the sole topic of increasing the maintainability of code (Scott, 2004). And (c), Perl is most efficient for small projects; coordinating different people to work on a large-scale application is normally better done on a language with strict typing and a more exigent implementation of object-oriented (OO) ideas. All these comments are also applicable to newer scripting languages such as Ruby and Python, which are designed explicitly as OO languages.

Using Telcordia Tools: mkey[pindex]. Telcordia is the company (formerly Bell communication research, or Bellcore) that originally developed latent semantic indexing (LSI), and patented it for information retrieval. Telcordia requests that researchers fill out a form acknowledging that this technology cannot be used for commercial purposes before they share this software. It can be obtained from http://lsi.research.telcordia.com/[1] The Telcordia tools are UNIX-only. They are designed with the UNIX philosophy in mind (small tools that do only one thing, very well, and can be concatenated together to do more complex tasks).

The best way to explain the basic mkey flags is to use an example. The following line is one possible use of the tool:

mkey -k10000 -c stop-list -l 2 -m 20 -M100000 docs.rawForm >
docs.parsed

---

[1]A majority of the published work has been done with the Telcordia tools. Even new researchers who recently started doing LSA work have used those. However, at the time of this writing, the Web site mentioned did not have the tools available. I ignore if Telcordia has changed the distribution policy. I opted for keeping the tools in the chapter because of their historical importance and value as reference.

The "-k10000" allows 10,000 unique words to be used; "-l 2" eliminates words of length less than 2; the "-m 20" truncates words of length greater than 20; and the "-M100000" allows a maximum line length of 100,000 characters.

Mkey can use a stop-list, which is a list of words that will not be included in the results. This list is indicated by the use of the -c flag followed by the name of a file containing the stop words. The file should contain one word per line. The Telcordia tools come with an example stop-list, but there are many other available on the Web. One can specify function words (high-frequency words that carry little meaning) in that list. Most uses of LSA do not require a stop-list as appropriate weighting will reduce the influence of high-frequency words.

Note that some of the parsing options are designed to reduce the number of types (e.g., truncating long words or removing very short words). This is a vestigial influence of the design decisions made in the time mkey was created to optimize very smalls amounts of memory. None of these decisions has psychological, or practical, relevance nowadays. The Telcordia tools write a file called RUN_SUMMARY with all the options used in the parsing, so replicating old parsings should be easy.

Using General Text Parser (GTP).   GTP (Giles, Wo, & Berry, 2003) replicates the mkey parsing for backward compatibility. GTP could be considered the reference program for LSA analyses because it is a rewrite of the older Telcordia suite in a more modern way. It is a very large program. Contrary to what its name indicates, GTP is not only a parser: It actually can run an SVD at the end of the process. GTP is 100% C++ code .[2]

GTP "has increased in the number of command line arguments to an almost unbearable point. Even expert users have a difficult time keeping all the options straight. A wordy dialogue about each option would be as unbearable as the number of options available" (Giles et al., 2003, p. 460). However, the chapter by Giles et al. documents very well all the options available, files written, and so forth. The reader is referred to that chapter for a more extensive description of the features available.

GTP has the following advantages: (a) It has compact source code, because the program is only one application that encompasses all the needed functionality to parse the text (and even run the SVD). (b) GTP provides good debugging and error handling. (c) GTP is actively maintained by the authors. (d) There is java version that comes with a graphical user interface.

However, GTP has some shortcomings. It uses the operating system's sort command. Sort is a UNIX utility that takes input (e.g., text) and returns a

---

[2]A new java version has been developed. The JAVA version includes a graphical user interface (GUI) that helps solve the problems with the multitude of command line options of previous versions.

sorted list. Thus, it is exposed to any known problems of this tool. In some operating systems, sort may create large temporary files. Although the error handling is better than the one in the Telcordia tools, there are still several situations in which interpreting GTP errors may be difficult.

An important warning should be issued against using 8-bit characters. Both the Telcordia tools and GTP are sensitive to this problem. If your text contains accents or any other special characters, then the Telcordia tools and GTP will not be able to use it. It is recommended to remove it during the parsing.

Using Matlab and the Text to Matrix Generator Library (TMG; Zeimpekis & Gallopoulos, 2004).   Matlab (MathWorks, 2004) is a common tool to manipulate matrices. However, Matlab's text processing capabilities are reduced. TMG is a Matlab toolbox that was designed to mimic the parsing that is standard in the information retrieval conferences such as the Text REtrieval Conference (TREC). This just happens to be the parsing described in the previous section. There are several advantages to using TMG: (a) All the steps (parsing, SVD, vector handling) can take place within the same environment: Matlab. (b) TMG has a graphical user interface. (c) Matlab's sparse matrix package makes all the matrix operations really easy. One can normalize, apply weights, and so forth with simple commands.

There are some disadvantages associated with TMG. It does not have as many options for manipulating text as some other parsers. In addition, at this moment, the software has not been tested with large corpora such as TASA, and several errors are possible.

Using R (R-foundation Team, 2004).   R is an environment and programming language for statistical computation. It includes a set of Tools for Textual Data Analysis (TTDA library; Muller, 2004) designed for corpus processing in R. The advantages of using R for parsing are many. One has access to many recently developed statistical techniques (e.g., support vector machines, Bayesian networks, etc.). This is because many of the statistic departments where new ideas are developed use R, so the best way to use the most modern, up-to-date approach to statistics is to use R as well. R also implements regular expressions, making it easy to process text. Moreover, there is an excellent mailing list on R, where experts answer problems and post their solutions.

There are also disadvantages of parsing within R. R (like Matlab) is a matrix-oriented programming language and was not designed from the bottom-up to process text. For example, R places all objects in memory, and this might be a limitation when working with large amounts of text. Also, R has a steep learning curve. Finally, the TTDA library is still in initial stages, so it might not be as reliable as more seasoned tools.

In summary, the options to parse text for an LSA analyses are very diverse. Most of the work done in the past with LSA used proprietary UNIX tools, but currently many packages and programming languages offer the features needed to parse text. The tools used in the past determine the parsing that should be done today if the experimenter wants to compare her results with those published.

Computing an SVD

There are two ways of performing an SVD once we have an adequate parsing of the corpus: implementing your own, or using one of the existing programs. Implementing a new program for sparse SVD is not recommended, because thorough testing is required. A number of warnings should be issued about computing SVDs. They have been particularly relevant when working using GTP/pindex, but should be considered when using any other method.

Checking the Existence of Empty Documents in the Corpus. If the program finds a document that, after filtering, has no words in it, it will still add a column with all zero frequencies to the words-contexts matrix. This may change the SVD solution obtained. It is advised to remove all empty documents. Empty documents may not be obvious to detect. They may appear, for example, when the string used as document separator is repeated accidentally, and when a document contains no valid keywords after the parser traverses it (due to stop lists, character exclusion list, etc).

The Number of Dimensions That Are Requested Is Not Necessarily the Number of Dimensions That the Program Returns. Some researchers may be surprised finding that their LSA spaces do not contain exactly the same number of dimensions that were requested. This is due to the nature of the Lanczos algorithm (see Martin and Berry, chap. 2 in this volume). Corpora with more dimensions than the number requested can be easily fixed by removing the extra dimensions, so it is always better to generate spaces with more dimensions than needed, and then use only a smaller number.

Creating the Space Is Normally an Iterative Process. Generating a new space is an elaborate, time-consuming process. The experimenter often tries several combinations of parameters (e.g., number of dimensions, parsing options, and weighting) when creating a space. The final goal of explaining behavioral data that serve as a benchmark for the model may be obtained with different approaches, so one should be ready to run more than one SVD on the same dataset.

The next step for this section is to describe the possibilities for getting SVDs on sparse matrices.

Mathematica (Wolfram Research, 2004). Version 5 and higher of Mathematica include methods for singular value decomposition on sparse arrays. Mathematica is a mainly symbolic environment, which is not exactly what is needed, but its numerical capabilities are certainly improving with newer versions and make it a solid alternative. As always, external libraries that run SVDs efficiently can be linked.

Matlab (MathWorks, 2004). After version 6, sparse matrices are supported. The implementation of sparse SVDs in Matlab does not use the Lanczos algorithm. Alternative packages based on the Lanczos method can be found (e.g., PROPACK; Larsen, 2000).

R (The R Foundation, Open Source). It can be linked to LAPACK and other sparse matrices libraries. R provides a sparse library called sparseM (Koenker & Ng, 2004). However, it seems to be in state of development and no new updates have been seen in the last year. There seems to be a faction of R contributors that plans to write an alternative one, with different design decisions. It thus seems to be advisable to just wait and see what happens with R and sparse matrices. Given that the R community is very active, there could be changes in the near future that make R a strong alternative. Linking external libraries is possible as well.

GTP and Pindex (Part of the Telcordia Tools). This is the original software developed at Bell Labs to perform SVDs for information retrieval. It is based on the public domain LAPACK library, but has been refined over time. Pindex is operating system specific, and it will only run under UNIX. Pindex uses system calls and pipes to bind together a large collection of smaller programs that do the parsing and SVD on a specified corpus. The program in charge of the parsing, mkey, has been described in the previous section. Pindex is not maintained and poorly documented. However, most of the current LSA work at the University of Colorado, Boulder, is still performed using pindex. GTP is a C++ version of pindex. In the case of GTP, the sources are available, there is documentation, and it is maintained. GTP can do the parsing and the SVD, or one can parse the corpus independently, create a sparse matrix, and use GTP to run an SVD on it. For details on its use and concrete options, see Giles, Wo, and Berry (2003, Table 27.2). Today, the reference SVD package is GTP. The spaces that are accessible to the general public have all been created with the University of Tennessee implementation of the Lanczos SVD algorithm in GTP/pindex (see later). For a complete description of the Lanczos method of running an SVD on sparse matrices, see Parlett (1998) and Martin and Berry (chap. 2 in this volume). For reference on the options available and general overview of its use, see Giles, Wo, and Berry (2003).

Operating With Vectors

Creating the space is the first step in using LSA. Once the space is created, much of the experimenter's time is spent performing operations on the vectors. Several design decisions can be made depending on the experimenter's needs. For example, one can place all the vectors in memory if the operations concern the entire space (e.g., nearest neighbor operations). In other circumstances, it will be best to leave the vectors on disk and read them only when they are needed (e.g., when we are interested in comparing a few pairs only). These different approaches can save a lot of computation time.

The "Telcordia" Suite.   This suite, constructed in the late 1980s, contains several utilities to handle vectors. For example, *Syn* compares sets of vectors using cosines or Euclidean distances, *tplus* combines several vectors into one (what is called a *pseudodoc*) by averaging or summing over them, and *getkeydb* converts from words to unique ids (rows in the matrix). The reader is referred to the manual pages for additional information on these tools' functionality. These tools read vectors from disk and thus may not be optimal for speed sensitive operations. They are very flexible research tools due to the ease with which they can be combined together using UNIX pipes. The tools are only available on UNIX and include little error handling.

Matlab, Mathematica, and R.   Matlab, Mathematica, and R are all matrix-oriented programming languages. Once the SVD result matrices are in Matlab format, all the vector operations are trivial. The standard is to place all vectors in memory, although it is always possible to read them sequentially from disk or use the available interfaces to relational databases.

SOFTWARE-INDEPENDENT (THEORETICAL) ISSUES

This second section reviews the most common issues on the creation of LSA spaces: the selection of the corpus, weighting, and dimension optimization.

Size, Properties of the Corpus

In a very strict sense, a corpus is part of the hypothesis that the experimenter tests. Implicitly, it is assumed that the contents of the average participant's memory must be some reflection of that corpus. Because of that, corpus selection is a very important part of the process of creating an LSA space. There are two common errors that are easily committed when creating LSA spaces:

    1. To use a very small corpus. One can use general corpus statistics to determine what is an appropriate corpus size. According to Zipf's law (1949), the frequency of use of the nth-most-frequently-used

word in any natural language is approximately inversely proportional to n. If this is true, there must be an asymptote in the distribution. We could use this fact as an additional rule to determine corpus size: One has a corpus big enough when, for any new learning experience added, the probability of adding a new type is so low that is negligible. In other words, we can interpret any new utterance as a function of our collection of previously seen types, without having to add new ones.

2. To use a non-representative corpus. As an extreme example, an experimenter could imagine to create a corpus of 19th-century literature to represent the knowledge of his undergraduate participants. Such a space would not be representative of these students, however.

An interesting property of corpus-based theories of cognition (e.g., LSA) is that they cannot be tested independently of the corpus. Imagine that we collect a corpus, run an SVD on it, and use the resulting space to predict human similarity judgments between certain words. Imagine that the model does not explain the data very well. Is it that the model's processes are unrealistic, or is it that the corpus is not very representative? In this situation, those two factors are confounded. A possible solution is to test the same model with different corpora and different tasks. If the model explains the judgments' variance across different situations, then we have more convincing evidence of the psychological reality of the model.

Weighting

LSA uses a transformation of the raw frequency of word-context coocurrence (see, e.g., Landauer & Dumais, 1997) that is called weighting. The objective is to diminish the influence of words that are extremely frequent and that do not carry much meaning. These are called function words (e.g., "the," "a"). Different weighting schemes have been tried with different success. The most common weighting scheme is the log of the local term frequency and the inverse of the entropy of the term in the corpus. This weighting scheme gets substantial improvements in both information retrieval applications (e.g., Dumais, 1991, chap. 16 in this volume; Harman, 1986) and cognitive modeling (e.g., Landauer & Dumais, 1997).

$$P_{ij} = \frac{keyLocalFrequency}{keyGlobalFrequency} \qquad \textbf{4.1}$$

$$localWeight = \log_2(keyLocalFrequency + 1) \qquad \textbf{4.2}$$

$$globalWeight = 1 + \frac{\sum_j^{ncontexts} P_{ij} * \log_2 P_{ij}}{\log ncontexts} \qquad 4.3$$

The previous expression (inverse entropy) gives more weight to words that convey more information. It takes values between 0 and 1, being smaller for higher entropy terms. The inverse entropy measure estimates the degree to which observing the occurrence of a component specifies what context it is in; the larger the entropy of a key is, the less information its observation transmits about the places it has occurred, so the less usage-defined "meaning" it has.

To illustrate this fact, imagine a corpus with 1,000 passages. Imagine the very extreme case of a key i that appears once in each passage (thus P_{ij} = .001). Then, knowing that we have the key i in a new passage, A, in which we are interested, the presence of key i does not help us much in telling apart the meaning of this passage. This fact is reflected in the weighting that key i gets: 0.

$$P_{ij} = \frac{1}{1000} = .001 \qquad 4.4$$

$$GlobalWeight = 1 + \frac{\sum_1^{1000} .001 * \log_2 .001}{\log_2 1000} = 1 + \frac{1000 * \frac{1}{1000} * (\log_2 1 - \log_2 1000)}{\log_2 1000} = 1 - 1$$

The final weight for each key is the multiplication of the local weight and the global weight. For an empirical comparison of different weighting functions, see Harman (1986).

Number of Dimensions

Determining the number of dimensions of a statistical model is a crucial problem. In multidimensional scaling (MDS), there is a measure of "goodness of fit" called stress. If one plots number of dimensions and stress, then there is usually a decreasing function that can be used as a guide to select the optimum dimensionality: This is called the elbow rule, because one looks for the "elbow" in the curve (Cox & Cox, 2001). However, several researchers show that there is an optimum dimensionality for LSA spaces (e.g., Dumais, 2003, Fig. 2; Landauer & Dumais, 1997, Fig. 3). LSA does not seem to show a monotonic decreasing curve as MDS. The peaked profile that LSA usually shows is common with other statistical models where dimensionality is a free parameter, with the optimal model being detailed enough to capture the information available in the dataset, but not so complex as to be fitting noise.

There is currently no method for automatically selecting the optimum dimensionality of LSA spaces. However, in related algorithms, some advances have been made. Model selection has been applied to MDS by Lee (2001). Model selection has also been applied to principal component analysis (PCA; Minka, 2001). Note that in both the MDS and the PCA cases, probabilistic formulations of the algorithms were created to apply the model complexity ideas. A probabilistic formulation of LSA (e.g., pLSI; Blei, Ng, & Jordan, 2001; Hofmann, 1999) produced the family of topics models (Steyvers & Griffiths, chap. 21 in this volume). In the topics models, Griffiths and Steyvers (2004) proposed a method to automatically select the number of topics, which are the equivalent to LSA dimensions.

A standard practice to select the dimensionality is to use some external validation criterion, such as performance of humans in an certain task. Researchers manipulate systematically the number of dimensions and validate the "behavior" of the resulting space against human data. For example, Landauer and Dumais (1997) found that a dimensionality of around 300 was the best for solving the TOEFL test, and plenty of other experiments have confirmed that there must be is some interval (around 100–1,500; e.g., Landauer, 2002) where most tasks are performed optimally. However, that is not necessarily the case. For example, Laham (personal communication) showed that in an LSA space for the Myers corpus (using the textbook by Myers, 1995), the accuracy solving a psychology test increased with dimensions.

There are at least three reasons to argue against general procedures to determine the optimal dimensionality. (a) The optimal dimensionality is task dependent. That is, a space may perform best at task A with dimensionality n, but the optimal dimensionality for task B may be different from n. (b) The optimal dimensionality is content dependent. Remember that LSA postulates that the collection contains a representative sample of the experience of a single human. The collection can be biased toward a particular type of knowledge. Then, two corpora representative of two people may be radically different in contents, and there is no reason to believe that the dimensionality of the spaces that best describe them is similar. (c) The optimal dimensionality is size dependent: big (encyclopedia-like) versus small (smallheart[3]) spaces have completely different properties. In Fig-

---

[3]Smallheart is a subcorpus containing articles from an encyclopedia that are about the heart. It is available online at http://www.lsa.colorado.edu. From now on, all the corpus that we refer to by name are both available online and documented in the "semantic spaces" section of the Web site.

Dimensionality

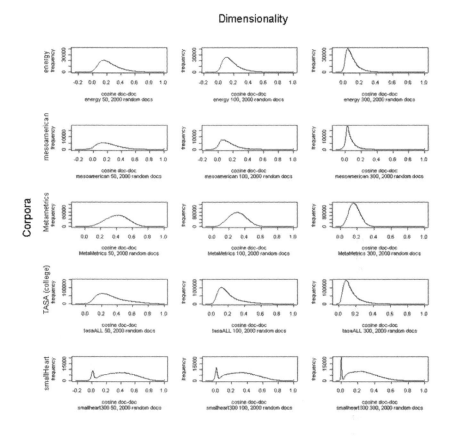

Figure 4.1.   Distribution of cosines in the document to document space at dimensions 50, 100, 300 for different corpora.

ure 4.1, it can be seen that in general higher dimensionality implies smaller mean cosine and smaller variance too. The graph shows large corpora, such as TASA (3 M. words) and MetaMetrics (2 Billion words), and small corpora of a few thousand words: Mesoamerican, Energy, and smallheart (see the LSA Web site for descriptions). Small corpora are more sensitive to isolated groups of objects that are similar only to themselves, and not to the rest of the corpus. For example, in the smallheart corpus there is a spike of cosines around zero. They correspond to a small set of documents that are not about the heart, but about the manatee (South American aquatic mammal) that were probably placed in that corpus by accident. These documents form a cluster of their own, and the cosines between all other documents and these are really small.

CONCLUDING REMARKS

This chapter has reviewed the current software options to perform three steps involved in creating LSA spaces: parsing the text, computing an SVD, and operating with vectors. A number of problems and general observations have been commented on the processes. There are other dimensionality reduction techniques, reviewed in the chapter by Hu, Cai, Wiemer-Hastings, Graesser, and McNamara (chap. 20 in this volume). Some of the problems described in this chapter are common in those other techniques. For example, the parsing issues are important for the topics model (Steyvers & Griffiths, chap. 21 in this volume).

This chapter tried to demystify the process of creating an LSA space. If more researchers can create and use LSA spaces, chances are that novel statistical theories can be put forward and compared with LSA using the same corpora.

REFERENCES

Blei, D., Ng, A. Y., & Jordan, M. I. (2001). Latent dirichlet allocation. In T. K. Leen, T. G. Dietterich, & V. Trestp (Eds.), *Advances in Neural Information Processing Systems 13*, (pp. 601–608). Cambridge, MA: MIT Press.

Cox, T. F., & Cox, M. A. A. (2001). *Multidimensional scaling*. London: Chapman & Hall.

Dumais, S. (1991). Improving the retrieval of information from external sources. *Behavior Research Methods, Instruments and Computers, 23*(2), 229–236.

Dumais, S. (2003). Data-driven approaches to information access. *Cognitive Science, 27*(3), 491–524.

Giles, J. T., Wo, L., & Berry, M. W. (2003). GTP (general text parser) software for text mining. In H. Bozdogan (Ed.), *Statistical data mining and knowledge discovery* (pp. 455–471). Boca Raton, FL: CRC press.

Griffiths, T. L., & Steyvers, M. (2004). Finding scientific topics. *Proceedings of the National Academy of Sciences, 101*, 5228–5235.

Harman, D. (1986). An experimental study of the factors important in document ranking. In *Association for computing machinery conference on research and development in information retrieval*. New York: Association for Computing Machinery.

Hofmann, T. (1999). Probabilistic latent semantic indexing. *Proceedings of 22nd Annual International ACM SIGIR Conference on Research and Development in Information Retrieval*, 50–57.

Koenker, R., & Ng, P. (2004). SparseM (R-package; Version 0.54) [Computer software]. Vienna, Austria: The R foundation.

Landauer, T. K. (2002). On the computational basis of learning and cognition: Arguments from LSA. In N. Ross (Ed.), *The psychology of learning and motivation* (Vol. 41, pp. 43 – 84). New York: Academic Press.

Landauer, T. K., & Dumais, S. T. (1997). A solution to Plato's problem: The latent semantic analysis theory of the acquisition, induction, and representation of knowledge. *Psychological Review, 104*, 211–240.

Larsen, R. M. (2000). Lanczos bidiagonalization with partial reorthogonalization (PROPACK; Version 2.1) [Computer program]. Avavilable from http://soi.stanford.edu/~rmunk/PROPACK/

Lee, M. D. (2001). Determining the dimensionality of multidimensional scaling representations for cognitive modeling. *Journal of Mathematical Psychology, 45*(1), 149–166.

MathWorks. (2004). *Matlab*. Natick, MA: The MathWorks.

Minka, T. P. (2001). Automatic choice of dimensionality for PCA. In S. Becker, S. Thrun, & K. Obermayer, (Eds.), *Advances in Neural Information Processing Systems 15* (pp. 598–604). Cambridge, MA: MIT Press.

Muller, J.-P. (2004). Tools for textual data anaylsis (R-package; Version 0.1.1) [Computer tools]. Available from http://wwwpeople.unil.ch/jean-pierre.mueller/

Myers, D. G. (1995). *Psychology* (5th ed.). New York: Worth Publishers.

Parlett, B. N. (1998). *The symmetric eigenvalue problem* (2nd ed.). Philadelphia: SIAM.

Scott, P. (2004). *Perl Medic: Transforming legacy code*. Reading, MA: Addison-Wesley.

Team, R. D. C. (2004). R: A language and environment for statistical computing (Version 2.0). Vienna, Austria: R Foundation for Statistical Computing.

Wolfram Research, I.. (2004). Mathematica (Version 5.0). Champaign, IL: Wolfram Research.

Zeimpekis, D., & Gallopoulos, E. (2004). Text to matrix generator (Version 3) [Computer toolbox]. Available from http://scgroup.hpclab.ceid.upatras.gr/scgroup/Projects/TMG

Zipf, G. K. (1949). *Human behaviour and the principle of least-effort*. Cambridge, MA: Addison-Wesley.

II

LSA in Cognitive Theory

5

Meaning in Context

Walter Kintsch
University of Colorado

How is meaning represented in the mind? More specifically, how is the meaning of words represented in the mind? LSA gives a straightforward answer: as vectors in the semantic space. The trouble is, this answer seems to be patently false. Words often have more than one meaning and different senses. How can a single vector deal with this complexity?

The literature on word meanings is huge and ranges from philosophy to linguistics to psychology.[1] It is not possible to do more here than to situate LSA within that complex landscape. Broadly speaking, we can distinguish two approaches to the representation of meaning: *mental lexicon* approaches that list word meanings like a huge dictionary in the mind, and *generative* approaches that construct meaning out of certain elements (e.g., semantic markers or LSA vectors) via some sort of composition rules.

The mental lexicon can be thought of as a list (possibly structured) of definitions of word meanings and senses. Some words have different meanings, like *bark* in *dogs bark* and *bark of a tree*, that are unrelated semantically; most words have different senses when they are used in different contexts that are related yet distinct, like the senses of *run* in *horses run* and *colors run*.

---

[1] Actually, philosophers tend to talk about the meaning of concepts, not words, just as psychologists are more likely to study concept formation than vocabulary acquisition. Here we focus, like linguists, on word meanings instead. How to get to concepts from words is yet another problem.

What form the definitions of meanings and senses take varies: They might be expressed in some formal language (logic, or logic-like), or they may be intuitively derived general phrases (as in a common dictionary or in WordNet), or they may be prototypes (e.g., Rosch, 1978), perceptual or other. WordNet provides a good example of what a mental lexicon might look like. WordNet lists word meanings and senses in the English language, defines these meanings with a general phrase and some illustrative examples, and links them to semantically related terms (Fellbaum, 1998; Miller, 1996). This is all done by hand coding. For example, *calf* has two meanings in WordNet, both nouns; one is identified as *young domestic cattle*, the other as *muscular back part of shank*; *bite* has only a single meaning but 2 grammatical forms and 10 distinct senses; *bark* has three different meanings and two grammatical forms, all with several senses. WordNet is an extremely valuable resource for language research, but it should not be regarded as a model for the mental representation of word meanings.

There are two basic problems with the mental lexicon in all its forms: It is static and it relies on hand coding. Word meanings are fluid and flexible. Language changes, and different individuals use language in somewhat different ways. Indeed, words can be used creatively in novel ways and still be understood. To model word meanings, they must be embedded in a system that evolves dynamically. Furthermore, there is an unavoidable element of arbitrariness in listing meanings and senses. Even if each is constructed by a well-specified algorithm (as in some prototype models), just how many meanings and senses need to be distinguished? There are 40 senses listed in WordNet for the verb *run*; whereas most informed judges would agree on most of them, one could argue with some of the distinctions made, or propose additional ones. And how many perceptual prototypes would be needed to define the concept *run*?

Given these limitations of the mental lexicon approach, linguists, philosophers, and psychologists have long been interested in a generative system where meanings can be constructed dynamically in some principled way. However, it has not been easy to make this idea work. Three classes of generative models can be distinguished: semantic elements models, semantic relations models, and family resemblance models.

Suppose there existed a table of semantic elements from which all meanings could be constructed via well-defined composition rules, much as all substances can be reduced to combinations of the chemical elements. This idea seems to have an irresistible appeal for philosophers and linguists. Thus, Katz and Fodor (1963) elegantly but inadequately decompose the meaning of *bachelor* into the semantic markers +*male*, +*adult*, and −*married*. Apart from the fact that these three markers fail to define the full meaning of *bachelor*, are they really semantic elements −*male* and *adult* seem reasonable candidates, but *married*? In any case, such questions cannot be settled by intuition, but require some principled account and to date nobody has ever come up with anything like an adequate list of semantic primitives, comparable to the table of chemical elements. There have been various attempts to get around this problem, for example, by distinguishing between *defining features* and ad hoc *characteristic features* that are invented as needed (Smith, Shoben, & Rips, 1974), or by introducing probabilistic features (Smith & Medin, 1981), but no comprehensive feature-based model of word meanings has ever been devised. A related approach relies on elementary semantic relations, rather than semantic elements. Collins and Quillian (1969) used the IS-A relation to construct semantic hierarchies, but other relations would also have to be considered. More recently, Pustejowski (1996) used this approach successfully, but his system seems restricted to the intersection between syntax and semantics and does not provide full definitions of word meanings.

If explicit definitions of word meanings are so hard to come by, then the alternative is to define meaning implicitly, by its relations to other words. In LSA, the meaning of a word is not defined, but situated with respect to all other words in the semantic space. Meaning, for LSA, is a relation among words. In such a relational system, one cannot talk about the meaning of a word in isolation; words have meaning only by virtue of their relations to other words—meaning is a property of the system as a whole. (We discuss later how this verbal web of semantic relationships is related to perception and action, the real world we live in.) The notion that the meaning of a word (or concept) depends on its relation with other words (concepts) in the system is an old one and widely shared in linguistics (e.g., the interdependent terms of Saussure, 1915/1959), philosophy (e.g., the incommensurability of concepts belonging to different ontologies in Kuhn, 1962), computer science (e.g., the semantic nets of Quillian, 1967), and psychology (e.g., in terms of associative nets), although it is by no means without its detractors (e.g., Fodor, 1998). Goldstone and Rogosky (2002) provide an informative discussion of the feasibility of the "conceptual web" approach to meaning.

What needs to be shown is that LSA indeed provides a workable framework for the representation of word meanings, despite the seemingly fatal flaw that it conflates all meanings and senses of a word into a single vector. The predication model of Kintsch (2001) was designed to address this problem.

PREDICATION

LSA computes a context-free vector for the meaning of each word. Different meanings and different senses of a word are all lumped together in this vector. The meaning of *bark*, in LSA, is right between the *tree* and the *dog*. By itself, therefore, LSA does not provide an account of the polysemy of words, nor is LSA, in its present form, a complete theory of semantics. It models the associative basis of semantics, but some semantic phenomena require additional theoretical mechanisms. Ideally, one ought to be able to combine the basic semantic space that LSA provides with other existing models of cognitive processing to arrive at a more encompassing semantic theory. An account of how word senses/meanings emerge in context can be obtained in this way, by combining LSA with the constraint-satisfaction model of discourse comprehension of Kintsch (1998). The idea is simple in principle: Take the context-free word vector from LSA and embed it into its discourse and semantic context, generating a spreading activation network that selects context appropriate information, which is then used to calculate a context appropriate word sense/meaning.

More specifically (for details, see Kintsch, 2001), consider simple predication sentences of the form Argument-Predicate (e.g., Noun-Verb, Noun-is-Adjective, or $Noun_1$-is-$Noun_2$). A simple syntactic parse is needed at that point to tell LSA which word is the argument and which is the predicate. Let **A** be the vector of the argument, and **P** the vector of the predicate. What we want to do is to generate a sense of **P** that is appropriate for argument **A**. Let us assume that people comprehend word meanings in context in much the same way as they comprehend text, by integrating word meaning and context through a spreading activation process, as in the construction-integration model of text comprehension of Kintsch (1998). Kintsch (2001) proposed the following algorithm. Construct a network of words consisting of A, P, and the n (e.g., $n = 100$) closest neighbors (words) of **P** in the LSA space. Connect all the neighbors of P to both **P** and **A** by a link whose strength is equal to the cosine between the neighbor and **P** or **A**, respectively (i.e., a measure of their relatedness to **A** and **P**). Link all neighbors with each other with negative link strengths, in such a way that the sum of all positive and all negative links has the same absolute value. Activation spread in such a network will tend to concentrate in **A** and **P** and in those neighbors of **P** that have relatively strong links to **A**. In other words, the argument **A** selects those words from the semantic neighborhood of **P** that it is related to, suppressing other aspects of **P**. Take the k ($k = 5$ in the simulations) most strongly activated neighbors of **P** and combine their vectors with **P** to compute a sense of **P** and in the context of A, P_A.

There are two ways for this algorithm to fail. First, the network may not settle; that is, no stable solution that fits both **A** and **P** can be found (there is no guarantee that a network with negative links must reach a stable state). Second, the network may settle, but **A** becomes deactivated (because the neighborhood of the predicate is unrelated to the argument); in this case, too, no solution that satisfies both **A** and **P** can be found.

To illustrate how the predication model works, consider the sentence, *The horse runs*. What we want to do is to compute a vector that represents the meaning of *run* in the context of *horse runs*. What predication does it to let the argument *horse* select among the neighbors of the predicate *run* those that are related to *horse*. In Figure 5.1, only three neighbors of *run* are shown, but in actual applications this number would be higher, for example, 100. All neighbors are related to *run*, by definition, but only one—*come*—is related to *horse*. Thus, spreading activation in this simple network will result in the asymptotic activation values shown in Figure 5.2. Predication then

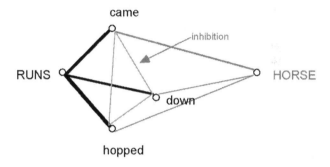

Figure 5.1. An illustration of how predication works for the sentence *The horse runs*. Three neighbors of the predicate *run* are shown; the width of the links between words indicates the value of the cosine between them.

ACTIVATION VALUES:

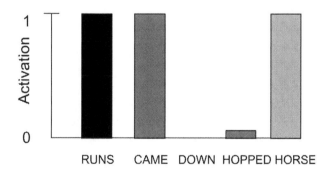

Figure 5.2. Spreading activation in the network shown in Figure 5.1 yields the following asymptotic activation values for the nodes in the network.

computes the vector for *run* in the context of *horse* as the vector sum of *run* and *come* weighted by their activation values (note that this is merely an oversimplified illustration).

Now consider the sentence *The color runs*. Figures 5.3 and 5.4 illustrate how predication calculates the vector for *run* in the context of *color runs*. The outcome is different this time, and *down* is the neighbor of *run* selected to modify its meaning.

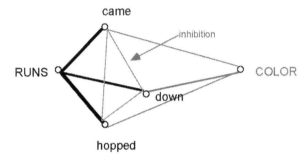

Figure 5.3.   An illustration of how predication works for the sentence *The color runs*. Three neighbors of the predicate *run* are shown; the width of the links between words indicates the value of the cosine between them.

ACTIVATION VALUES:

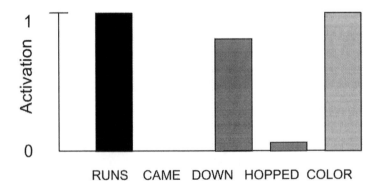

Figure 5.4.   Spreading activation in the network shown in Figure 5.3 yields the following asymptotic activation values for the nodes in the network.

How much the meaning of a word changes when it is used in context de-pends on exactly how word and context are related. For example, consider the sense of *house* that is constructed in the context of yard, as in *house yard*. According to predication, there is not much of a change at all: The first four closest neighbors of *house* are the same as for *yard*, and therefore the sense of *house* in the context of *yard* remains pretty much unchanged. But now con-sider *house of representatives*. If house is predicated about *representatives*, it changes its meaning a great deal, because *representatives* selects rather dis-tant items from the neighborhood of *house*, which when combined with the *house* vector change its meaning quite dramatically. As another example, consider how the meaning of *long* is affected by three different contexts. For *long time*, there is really no change—*long* is used in its dominant context; *yard long* is already a little more unusual, but *yard* still selects four fairly close neighbors of *long*; for *long story*, there is quite dramatic meaning change, because *story* picks out neighbors of *long* that are fairly remote and hence significantly alter the vector for *long*. It is instructive to compare the sense of *long* in *long story* with intuitive landmarks: Words related to the dominant meaning of long (e.g., *yard, distance,* or *measure*) have a lower co-sine with $long_{story,}$ whereas words such as *book, time,* or *talk* become more closely related—in agreement with human intuitions about what *long* means in this context. Moreover, the predication model allows us to com-pute a quantitative measure of meaning changes in context in terms of the average rank of the words from the semantic neighborhood of the predicate that are selected by an argument. For *long time*, the rank change is 0; for *yard long*, the change is 2.4; and for *long story*, the rank change is 15.8.

The predication model, which combines LSA and contextual constraint satisfaction, successfully simulates a number of semantic phenomena, in-cluding asymmetries and context dependencies in similarity judgments, causal inferences (Kintsch, 2001), as well as metaphor comprehension (Kintsch, 2000, 2001; Kintsch & Bowles, 2002) and analogy solution (Mangalath, Quesada, & Kintsch, 2004). The emergence of context appro-priate word senses/meanings can also be modeled in this way.

POLYSEMY

Figure 5.5 gives an example of how the predication model deals with polysemy. In the example shown, the homonym *mint* is employed in three different sentences, in each with a different meaning: *Mint is flavored candy, Mint are leaves of a plant,* and *Banks mint coins.* Thus, three different vectors can be constructed for *mint*, by predicating *flavored candy, leaves of a plant,* or *banks coins* about *mint*. To get an idea whether these contextual vectors actu-ally capture the meaning changes of *mint* when it is used in these different contexts, one can compare them with intuitively plausible associates of *mint* in each context: *Chocolate* for the *candy* context, *stem* for the *plant* context, and *money* for the *bank* context. The unmodified *mint* vector is similar to all three associates, its cosine with *chocolate, stem,* and *money* being .37, .20, and .36, respectively. Interestingly, these three words are not associated with each other, despite the fact that they all are similar to *mint* (an impossible configuration in two dimensions, but feasible in a high-dimensional space): *stem–money,* and *stem–chocolate* have cosines of –.01 and .03, respectively, whereas *chocolate–money* is slightly elevated (.14)—undoubtedly reflecting the fact that *chocolate* costs *money.* The relationships of the contextually modified *mint* vectors to these three associates are shown in Figure 5.5. Predication seems to successfully catch the meaning changes of *mint* as it used in these three sentences, in that the contextually constructed meaning of *mint* behaves as expected: *Mint-as-candy* is only associated with *chocolate, mint-as-plant* is only associated with *stem,* and *mint-as-verb* is only associated with *money.* To show that the predication model can account for polysemy more generally, we fit the model to experimental results that have been reported in the literature.

Two recent experimental studies have shown that word senses are highly context dependent—a result taken by their authors to require that the different word senses must be distinguished in the mental lexicon: "Local" representations of all the senses of a word are said to be needed in the

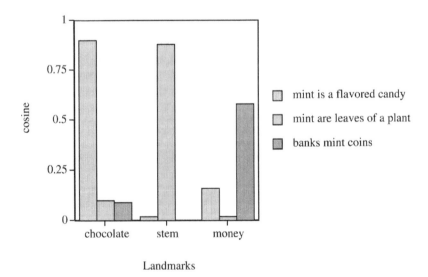

Figure 5.5.   The cosine between three landmark associates of *mint* (*chocolate, stem,* and *money*) when *mint* is used in three different sentence contexts, each with a different meaning (after Kintsch, 2001).

mental lexicon to account for these experimental results. Instead, we show that a model that has only a single, "global" representation for a word (the LSA-vector) can account for these data, if it is supplemented by a mechanism that enables it to generate contextually appropriate modifications of the global word meaning (the predication model).

In the first study to be analyzed here, Klein and Murphy (2001; Exp. 1) employed a recognition memory paradigm to find out how polysemous words are perceived. Subjects studied phrases such as either *wrapping paper* or *daily paper*, which were followed in the test phase by *shredded PAPER*; subjects had to decide whether they had seen the capitalized word before. The critical manipulation involved the repetition of phrases in which words were used in the same sense or in a different sense. Two phrases were created for each sense, as in

Sheets of material	*Newspaper*
wrapping paper	daily paper
shredded paper	liberal paper

There were three repetition conditions in this experiment: Either the same phrase was repeated (e.g., *wrapping paper* followed by *wrapping PAPER*), or a consistent sense phrase was repeated (e.g., *wrapping paper* followed by *shredded PAPER*), or an inconsistent sense phrase was repeated (e.g., *wrapping paper* followed by *daily PAPER*).[2] The results are shown in Table 5.1. Same phrases were recognized best, consistent sense phrases were second best, and inconsistent sense phrases were least well recognized. In their Experiment 2, a sense–nonsense judgment was used with similar phrases. When a phrase was repeated with a consistent word sense, subjects were 96% correct; when a phrase was repeated with an inconsistent word sense, subjects were correct only 87% of the time. Reaction times mirrored those

TABLE 5.1
Percent Correct Recognition in Experiment 1 of Klein and Murphy (2001) for Three Experimental Conditions and Cosines for the Experimental Materials in Those Conditions

	Same Phrase	Same Sense	Different Sense
Percent recognition of test word	79%	64%	56%
Cosine between study phrase and test phrase	1.00	.62	.44

[2]This experiment is a variation on the classical encoding specificity study of Tulving and Thomson (1973).

results. The authors conclude that concepts must be represented locally, for if they were represented globally, repetitions should be equally helpful, whether or not they are consistent.

A reinterpretation of their data in terms of LSA and the predication model is straightforward, however: Consistent phrases are more similar to each other and hence benefit more from repetition than inconsistent phrases. Thus, the cosine between the consistent *wrapping paper–shredded paper* is .85, but the cosines between the inconsistent *wrapping paper–daily paper* and *shredded paper–daily paper* are .71 and .67, respectively. Klein and Murphy (2001) used 24 item quadruples, as in the previous example, in their Experiment 1.[3] The cosines between the 96 prime and target phrases were computed according to the predication model. Calculations failed in nine cases. In these instances, the LSA knowledge space (the *General Reading Space* available at http://lsa.colorado.edu), which represents the knowledge that typical high school students might have acquired through reading by the time they graduate, was inadequate. For instance, LSA could not figure out the meaning of phrases like *liberal paper*, or *underage drinker.*[4] The average cosine for consistent prime target pairs and inconsistent pairs are also shown in Table 5.1. The difference is statistically significant by sign-test, $p < .001$, as well as t-test, $t(21) = 4.53$, $p < .001$. Thus, we can conclude that the results of Klein and Murphy reflect standard similarity effects and do not contradict global representations—as long as we can generate emergent context-specific word senses.

The second study to be discussed here is similar to the Klein and Murphy work in that it argues for the necessity of local representations of word meanings. We shall show, once again, that LSA-cum-predication provides a reasonable alternative account of their data. But this study also raises another question that needs to be considered carefully, because it concerns a major limitation of LSA, as well as all purely verbally based representations of meaning.

PERCEPTUAL REPRESENTATIONS

LSA constructs its semantic space from a purely verbal input. Human meaning is based on much more: Perception, action, emotion all play a role, in addition to the verbal component. For LSA, *mint* is a symbol that stands in certain relationship to other symbols, as represented by the semantic space. For people, *mint* is that, but it also is a real plant that looks and tastes in a familiar way; the word *mint* refers to an object in the world—the world

---

[3]I thank Klein and Murphy for providing me with their experimental materials.

[4]It is not clear how much typical high school students know about *liberal paper*; they certainly know about *underage drinker*—but not from their reading, illustrating an important difference between what LSA can know and what people know.

in which we live, perceive, and act is linked to the world of words. Not only that, but the real world is primary and the verbal system is derivative. Animals live in a meaningful world without words. A complete theory of meaning must include perceptual/action representations.

In face of the obvious significance of nonverbal representations, the role of verbal information in word meanings is sometimes being denigrated. Barsalou (1999) argues that all meaning representations are basically perceptual. Glenberg and Robertson (2000) claim that purely verbal approaches, such as LSA, are misleading and deceptive. Such arguments, however, greatly underestimate the power of words. There is more to meaning than words, but words provide an image of the world that is rich and subtle, not merely an insipid caricature of the perceptual world. To make this point, we first show that LSA, with the help of predication, can explain the experimental results of Salomon and Barsalou (2001), who claimed that their data require not only local meaning representations, but also that these representations had to be perceptual, not verbal, in character. We demonstrate first, that global presentations that are contextually modified provide a reasonable alternative account, and the purely verbal LSA-based system mirrors many of the features of the perceptual world investigated in their experiment. We do not deny the importance of perceptual representations for human cognition, we merely want to point out that language evolved to mirror the world we live in, and does so quite well.

Salomon and Barsalou (2001) note that there are perceptual differences between different word senses. For instance, *butterfly wings* and *bee wings* look different and hence two quite distinct senses of wing might be involved; but *wasp wings* and *bee wings* look much the same, and hence there would be no need to distinguish separate word senses. Salomon and Barsalou's results support these claims. Thus, the question arises, to what extent a purely verbal representation—that is, LSA—can capture that perceptual information; if language is a mirror of the mind, then it should be sensitive to the perceptual differences between *bee wings* and *butterfly wings*.

Salomon and Barsalou (2001) performed a priming study, where participants first verified either a concept-property pair like *wasp wing* or *butterfly wing* and then a target pair like *bee wing*. The perceptually similar *wasp wing* significantly primed *bee wing*, but the perceptually dissimilar *butterfly wing* did not. Furthermore, Salomon and Barsalou showed that perceptual similarity mattered in this case, because there were no priming differences between items that were conceptually similar or dissimilar when there was no perceptual difference. In the case of our example, *butterfly body* and *wasp body* primed *bee body* equally well—presumably, because the bodies of a wasp, bee, and butterfly look more or less alike, unlike their wings.

Salomon and Barsalou's experimental materials consisted of quadruples, such as the following:

Perceptual differences:
Same form: *wasp wing → bee wing*
Different form: *butterfly wing → bee wing*
No perceptual differences:
Similar concepts: *wasp body → bee body*
Dissimilar concepts: *butterfly body → bee body*

They performed two experiments, one with a long and one with a short
interstimulus interval. Their results are shown in Table 5.2, averaged over
ISI. They concluded, first, that perceptual similarity mattered, over and
above general conceptual similarity. Second, they claimed that their data
provide evidence for local, rather than global, representations.

Language—in the form of a language-based system like LSA—can capture the pattern of these results. LSA has indirectly encoded some of the
perceptual information needed to know that *wasp wing* and *butterfly wing*
are really quite different, whereas *wasp body* and *butterfly body* are not. If we
compute a vector for *wasp wing, butterfly wing,* and *bee wing,* using the predication procedure described earlier, we can compute how close to each other
these vectors are in the LSA space. For instance, the cosine between *wasp
wing* and *bee wing* is .66, whereas the cosine between *butterfly wing* and *bee
wing* is only .48. Hence, *wasp wing* could be expected to be a better prime for
bee wing than *butterfly wing*. On the other hand, both *wasp body* and *butterfly
body* are equally close to *bee body* in the LSA space. The cosines are .94 and
.91, respectively—LSA really can't tell the difference between these
concepts (and neither can most of us).

More formally, cosines were computed (using the predication algorithm) between all pairs of phrases in Table 1 of Salomon and Barsalou

TABLE 5.2
Average Similarity Ratings on a 7-Point Scale and Mean Verification Times
for Expts. 1 and 2 of Salomon and Barsalou (2001)

	Critical Conditions (Wing in the Example)		Control Conditions (Body in the Example)	
	Same Form (wasp-bee)	Different Form (butterfly-bee)	Similar Concept (wasp-bee)	Dissimilar Concept (butterfly-bee)
Rated similarity	6.1	2.7	6.4	4.4
Verification time	810 ms	900 ms	790 ms	760 ms
Cosine	.70	.39	.72	.50

(2001). The average cosines for the four priming conditions of Salomon and Barsalou are shown in Table 5.2. Table 5.2 also shows the average similarity ratings between same-form and different-form phrases given by Salomon and Barsalou's subjects. Note that the Salomon and Barsalou data are averages over two experiments with slightly different procedures and materials (but rather similar results), whereas the cosines are computed on only the seven examples given in Salomon and Barsalou (their Table 1, which includes examples of materials from both experiments).

With only 7 items, statistical analyses do not have much power, but they confirm that LSA predicts priming results much like those reported by Salomon and Barsalou. The statistical analysis in the original paper focuses on the contrast between the average of columns 1, 3, and 4 in Table 5.2 against column 2 (coefficients 1, –3, 1, 1). This contrast is significant in an analysis of variance of the verification times reported by Salomon and Barsalou, as well as in an analysis of the cosines as computed here, $F(1, 18) = 8.51, p < .01$. A sign test for the same contrast is also significant, $p < .05$. On the other hand, there was no statistically significant difference between similar and dissimilar concepts in the experimental results. In the cosine analysis, there is a difference as shown in Table 5.2, but smaller than in the critical condition and not significant statistically. Thus, the LSA cosines follow more closely the similarity ratings of Salomon and Barsalou's subjects than the verification times. Item similarity—whether subject ratings as reported by Salomon and Barsalou or LSA cosines—is thus not perfectly correlated with verification times.

The point of this reanalysis is not to argue that Salomon and Barsalou's subjects did not use perceptual representations in making their decisions; there is every reason to believe that they did. What is interesting is that a purely verbal representation of word meanings—LSA—mirrors perceptual differences in their main features, if not in their entirety. Language evolved to talk about perception, action, and emotion; it is not surprising that verbal representations reflect these domains with considerable accuracy. Furthermore, perception is not the only source of knowledge. A lot of words we learn about through other words, from reading.[5]

The analyses reported here support the argument that data such as those of Salomon and Barsalou (2001) and Klein and Murphy (2001) do not necessarily require us to assume a mental lexicon with local lexical representations. To represent each word sense and each word meaning in a mental lexicon sounds straightforward, but it raises a host of intractable problems when one tries to do so. Klein and Murphy present an excellent discussion of these issues in their work. Thus, it is nice to have an alternative: Word

---

[5]It has been estimated (Landauer & Dumais, 1997) that people learn between three to four times as many words from reading than from oral language.

meanings can be represented by a context-free vector as in LSA, and their different senses and meanings can be generated in context. Thus, they are emergent rather than pre-stored, which has important consequences for the kind of research questions future investigators need to ask. Note that we are not only advocating a generative approach to meaning, but that the predication algorithm actually models the emergence of word senses and meanings in context, something that, to our knowledge, no other model has as yet achieved.

At the risk of redundancy, let me repeat: We are not claiming that LSA, with or without predication, is a fully adequate theory of meaning, or that any theory based on purely verbal data could be. People surely use nonverbal as well as verbal representations.[6] We are merely claiming that verbal representations reflect more of the world of perception and action than Barsalou and Glenberg suppose.

LSA is all words; how might one link the words and perception/action? The LSA vectors do not refer to anything in the real world. Instead, the representation that LSA generates is a map of meanings. Maps do not represent meaning directly, but relationships among meanings—what is where relative to each other. In the terminology of Shepard (1987), they are second-order isomorphisms (in contrast to first-order isomorphisms, e.g., a picture, feature system, or dictionary definition, which attempt to capture meaning directly). The measurement of meaning, thus, is more like derived than direct measurement in physics: A direct measure of, for example, distance in terms of meters or miles is a primitive function calculated from real variables (meters), whereas a derivative measure calculates distance as a function of velocity (an intensity-direction vector) and travel time. Both types of measurement have their uses. Derivative length measures are by no means unusual—it is the only possible way to measure distance between stars, for instance.

It is obvious that human knowledge is not purely verbal as LSA is. However, so far an actual system that integrates the perceptual and verbal domains has not yet been constructed. The difficulty of doing so seems to lie primarily in the coding of perceptual stimuli appropriate for computer analysis and faithful to the human experience. ASCI code serves us well for words, but pictures or sounds, not to mention touch or feelings, are another matter. There appears to be no in principle difficulty here, but practical problems that so far have stymied research progress. However, progress is being made in this area. Edelman (1998) has already described a second-order representation for object recognition based on dimension reduction in a manner not unlike LSA. Landauer (2002) has explored further how an

---

[6]But, even for perceptual scene representations, symbolic representations that tend to be invariant across image-based details generally dominate image-based information (Sanocki, 2003).

LSA-like system could generate mental representations in the perceptual domain. Rogers et al. (2004) present a parallel distributed network that associates (via backpropagation) visual descriptions of objects with their names, thus generating a high-dimensional semantic space. Concepts are represented as points in this space, thus integrating verbal and visual information.

Instead of a system that integrates the perceptual and verbal domains, it might be possible to explore the possibility of constructing a purely verbal system (like LSA) and a purely visual system (e.g., a scaled-up version of Edelman, 1998) and then coordinating the two systems. Landauer (chap. 1 in this volume) has discussed how two semantic spaces for different languages can be aligned to allow for cross-language information retrieval. Goldstone and Rogosky (2002) have shown how two symbolic systems (like Reader A's semantic space and Reader B's semantic space) can be put into correspondence simply on the basis of their within-system similarity relations. They also have shown, however, that although an intrinsic account of meaning is feasible, extrinsic information when combined with the intrinsic information can greatly improve the correspondence.

Thus, the fact that LSA is based only on verbal information is a limitation of LSA, but not a fatal flaw. Verbal systems, including LSA, ought to be seriously considered as models of mental representation, for they have significant advantages over first-order isomorphisms. As shown here, they avoid some of the intractable issues that arise from local representations of word senses and meanings. Verbal representations do not have to be local to allow for polysemy, and Landauer and Edelman make the same claim for perceptual representations. Furthermore, as Goldstone and Rogosky (2002) point out, we do not have to choose between intrinsic and extrinsic accounts of meaning—the two approaches are not mutually exclusive but are, in principle, perfectly compatible.

ACKNOWLEDGMENTS

This research was supported by Grant EIA-0121201 from the National Science Foundation. I thank José Quesada, who wrote the predication program used here, as well as the members of the LSA Research Group for their helpful discussions.

REFERENCES

Barsalou, L. E. (1999) Perceptual symbol systems. *Behavioral and Brain Sciences, 22,* 577–660.
Collins, A. M., & Quillian, M. R. (1969). Retrieval from semantic memory. *Journal of Verbal Learning and Verbal Behavior, 8,* 240–247.

Edelman, S. (1998). Representation is representation of similarities. *Behavioral and Brain Sciences, 21,* 449–498.

Fellbaum, C. (Ed.). (1998). *WordNet: An electronic lexical database.* Cambridge, England: Cambridge University Press.

Fodor, J. (1998). *Concepts: Where cognitive science went wrong.* Oxford, England: Oxford University Press.

Glenberg, A. M., & Robertson, D. A. (2000). Symbol grounding and meaning: A comparison of high-dimensional and embodied theories of meaning. *Journal of Memory and Language, 43,* 379–401.

Goldstone, R. L., & Rogosky, B. J. (2002). Using relations within conceptual systems to translate across conceptual systems. *Cognition, 84,* 295–320.

Katz, J. J., & Fodor, J. A. (1963). The structure of semantic theory. *Language, 39,* 170–210.

Kintsch, W. (1998). *Comprehension: A paradigm for cognition.* New York: Cambridge University Press.

Kintsch, W. (2000). Metaphor comprehension: A computational theory. *Psychonomic Bulletin and Review, 7,* 257–266.

Kintsch, W. (2001). Predication. *Cognitive Science, 25,* 173–202.

Kintsch, W., & Bowles, A. R. (2002). Metaphor comprehension: What makes a metaphor difficult to understand? *Metaphor and Symbol, 17,* 249–262.

Klein, D. E., & Murphy, G. L. (2001). The representation of polysemous words. *Journal of Memory and Language, 45,* 259–282.

Kuhn, T. (1962). *The structure of scientific revolutions.* Chicago: University of Chicago Press.

Landauer, T. K. (2002). On the computational basis of learning and cognition: Arguments from LSA. In B. H. Ross (Ed.), *The psychology of learning and motivation* (pp. 43–84). New York: Academic Press.

Landauer, T. K., & Dumais, S. T. (1997). A solution to Plato's problem: The latent semantic analysis theory of acquisition, induction and representation of knowledge. *Psychological Review, 104,* 211–240.

Mangalath, P., Quesada, J., & Kintsch, W. (2004, August). *Analogy making: A computational model based on LSA.* Paper presented at the Cognitive Science Society, Chicago.

Miller, G. A. (1996). *The science of words.* New York: Freeman.

Pustejowsky, J. (1995). *The generative lexicon.* Cambridge, MA: MIT Press.

Quillian, M. R. (1967). Word concepts: A theory and simulation of some basic semantic capabilities. *Behavioral Science, 12,* 410–430.

Rogers, T. T., Ralph, M. A. L., Garrard, P., Bozet, S., McClelland, J. L., & Hodges, J. R. (2004). Structure and deterioration of semantic memory: A neuropsychological and computational investigation. *Psychological Review, 111,* 205–235.

Rosch, E. (1978). Principles of categorization. In E. Rosch & B. Lloyd (Eds.), *Cognition and categorization* (pp. 27–48). Hillsdale, NJ: Lawrence Erlbaum Associates.

Salomon, K. O., & Barsalou, L. W. (2001). Representing properties locally. *Cognitive Psychology, 43,* 129–169.

Sanocki, T. (2003). Representation and perception of scenic layout. *Cognitive Psychology, 47,* 43–86.

Saussure, F. (1959). *Course in general linguistics* (W. Baskin, Trans.). New York: McGraw-Hill. (Original work published in 1915)

Shepard, R. N. (1987). Toward a universal law of generalization for psychological science. *Science, 237,* 1317–1323.

Smith, E. E., & Medin, D. L. (1981). *Categories and concepts.* Cambridge, MA: Harvard University Press.

Smith, E. E., Shoben, E. J., & Rips, L. J. (1974). Structure and process in semantic memory: A feature model for semantic decision. *Psychological Review, 81,* 214–241.

Tulving, E., & Thomson, D. M. (1973). Encoding specificity and retrieval processes in episodic memory. *Psychological Review, 80,* 352–373.

6

Symbolic or Embodied Representations: A Case for Symbol Interdependency

Max M. Louwerse

University of Memphis

Over the last decade, the debate regarding embodied versus symbolic representations in language comprehension has dominated areas within the cognitive sciences (Barsalou, 1999; Glenberg, 1997; Kintsch, 1998; Lakoff & Johnson, 1999; Landauer & Dumais, 1997). At the center of the debate is the question of whether language comprehension is primarily symbolic or whether it is fundamentally linked to embodied (perceptual and motor) mechanisms. Advocates of either side of the spectrum have polemically presented their views (Barsalou, 1999; Fodor, 1980; Glenberg & Robertson, 2000; Harnad, 1990; Lakoff & Johnson, 1999; Pylyshyn, 1984; Searle, 1980). These discussions often give the impression that language comprehension involves either symbol processing or embodied simulation. The current study replaces this with the question to what extent language comprehension is symbolic and embodied. It is hard to imagine that logical reasoning or mathematics could exist without any form of symbolic processing. At the same time, it is hard to imagine how visual rotation and spatial orientation tasks can operate without any form of perceptual processing. It is therefore very likely that symbolic and embodied processes go together in language

107

comprehension. This study will therefore not adopt an eliminative view[1] (Goldstone & Barsalou, 1998) that rules out a symbolic (or for that matter embodied) representation, but instead will adopt an integrative view that assumes some relationship exists between language and perception. The nature of the relationship between embodied and symbolic representations thereby is the central question. This study will argue for symbol interdependency, a dependency of symbols on other symbols and dependency of symbols on embodied experiences. The mechanism behind symbol interdependency can be represented by statistical models like latent semantic analysis.

PREDOMINANTLY EMBODIED THEORIES

According to embodied approaches of meaning, symbols (e.g., words) always have to be grounded to a referent in the physical world. A theory emphasizing the link between symbol and reality is obviously not new. De Saussure (1916), for instance, already argued that a linguistic sign (what we will call "symbol") is composed of a signifier (the acoustic image) and a signified (the mental representation of an external reality). That is, the basis of linguistic and nonlinguistic comprehension lies in the sensorimotor experiences of actions. With every word we read or hear, we are grounding that word in our perceptual experiences. For instance, we understand the word "eagle" differently when reading the sentence, "The ranger saw the eagle in the sky," than when we read, "The ranger saw the eagle in the nest" (Zwaan, Stanfield, & Yaxley, 2002), because we generate different embodied representations of the two sentences.

Recently, a large body of empirical evidence has accumulated, suggesting that perceptual variables affect conceptual processing. For instance, comprehenders' motor movements match those described in the linguistic input. Klatzky, Pellegrino, McCloskey, and Doherty (1989) showed that the comprehension of verbally described actions (e.g., the phrase "picking up a grape") was facilitated by preceding primes that specified the motor movement (e.g., grasp). Glenberg and Kaschak (2002) found similar evidence measuring how much the sensibility of a sentence is modified by physical actions. When subjects read sentences like "Mark gave you a pen" and used a congruent action (press a button close to the body of the subject) reaction times were lower than when an incongruent action (press button away from the body of the subject) was applied. Kaschak et al. (2004) presented subjects with sentences describing motion in a particular direction (e.g.,

---

[1] It is important to note here again that most symbolic and embodied approaches are not eliminative. For instance, symbolic approaches do not rule out perceptual experience (Kintsch, 1998; Landauer, 2002) and embodied approaches do not exclude symbolic representations (Barsalou, 1999; Zwaan, 2004).

"The storm clouds rolled in") and simultaneously presented dynamic black and white stimuli matching or mismatching the direction described in the sentence (up, down, toward, away). Again, response times were faster for the matching cases than for the mismatching ones.

Zwaan et al. (2002) measured response times for pictures matching the content of sentences and pictures that did not. For instance, they used sentences about a nail being pounded either into the wall or into the floor. Response times for pictures matching the sentence (e.g., vertically oriented nail for sentence in which nail pounding into the floor) were faster than mismatching pictures, leading to the conclusion that subjects simulated the scenes described in the sentence. Similarly, Zwaan and Yaxley (2003) showed that spatial iconicity affects semantic judgments (the word "attic" presented above the word "basement" resulted in faster judgments than the reverse iconic relationship), suggesting that visual representations are activated during language comprehension (see also Boroditsky, 2000; Fincher-Kiefer, 2001; Matlock, Ramscar, & Boroditsky, 2005).

Three theories of embodiment are currently most prominent in the field of discourse psychology (Pecher & Zwaan, 2005): Glenberg's (1997) *indexical hypothesis*, Zwaan's (2004) *immersed experiencer framework*, and Barsalou's (1999) *perceptual symbols theory*. According to all three theories, knowledge is not transduced into (amodal) symbolic representations, but instead into modality-specific states (e.g., visual states). For instance, the indexical hypothesis states that comprehenders index words and phrases to actual objects or analogical perceptual symbols, generate affordances of these objects or perceptual symbols, and then mesh these affordances using syntax. We understand the sentence, "John used his shoe to hit the mosquito," by considering all possible things one can do with a shoe, such as walking and hitting. Of all these affordances that are generated, we then select the relevant one based on the syntagmatic information (one does not walk mosquitoes, but one can hit them).

Despite the overwhelming evidence for embodiment in comprehension, there are a number of questions that remain unanswered. If words are directly related to perceptual representations (e.g., images) representing those words, which in turn activate affordances of these perceptual representations, language does not seem to be an efficient communicative tool. First, it would require considerable learning and memory resources to activate perceptual information in even the simplest language task. An utterance of a few sentences would result in a combinatorial explosion of representations in various modalities. Such an explosion of options is not an impossible way to communicate, but certainly not an efficient one. Second, a direct relationship between symbol and perceptual representation makes it difficult to communicate about imaginative things and abstract objects. For instance, it is difficult to think of the embodied representations that are activated in reading this chapter. Third, with a direct link between word and embodied representation, it is not straightforward to explain language acquisition. Does a child need to learn the link between each word and its representation? If so, it is difficult to explain why children rarely attend to the word the adult talks about (Bloom, 2000). Finally, why do humans have language and other species do not? After all, other species are embodied and have the vocal tracts to communicate, but do they not have the sophisticated communicative system that humans have? These issues do not warrant the conclusion that language processing is not embodied, but at least suggest that embodiment is unlikely to be the whole story.

PREDOMINANTLY SYMBOLIC THEORIES

Predominantly symbolic theories assume conceptual representations are typically nonperceptual. That is, mental representations are autonomous symbolic representations. It is not surprising that the autonomy of symbolic representations became particularly popular around the cognitive revolution in the 1950s with the various information-processing theories based on computational models, including predicate calculus, script and schema theories, and connectionism. A typical example of symbolic representations is propositional representations (i.e., the mental sentences that form idea units). As a shorthand notation, these propositions generally consist of predicates and arguments (Kintsch, 1974, 1998). A proposition like HIT(JOHN, MOSQUITO) represents a hitting event where the agent *John* hits the object/patient *mosquito*. There is some experimental evidence for the psychological reality of these mental sentences (Bransford & Franks, 1971; Kintsch & Keenan, 1973; Wanner, 1975). Various other psychological symbolic models have been proposed to describe how human memory is organized both semantically and schematically (Collins & Quillian, 1969; Minsky, 1975; Quillian, 1966; Rumelhart & Ortony, 1977; Schank & Abelson, 1977; Smith, Shoben, & Rips, 1974). These proposals for knowledge representation formed the origin of complex computational implementations, including frame representation language (FRL), knowledge representation language (KRL; Bobrow & Winograd, 1977; Fikes & Kehler, 1985), and Cyc (Lenat & Guha, 1989). According to all these symbolic approaches, mental representations must be amodal because we cannot have an internal homunculus that can look at modality-specific mental images in our mind (Pylyshyn, 1973). Furthermore, if symbol systems can approximate human language comprehension performance well, then they must at least have some validity in modeling human language processing (Landauer & Dumais, 1997).

Three symbolic computational models of language processing are currently most prominent in the field of discourse psychology: Lund and Burgess's (1996) hyperspace analog to language (HAL), Griffiths and Steyvers' (2004) topics model, and Landauer and Dumais' (1997) latent semantic analysis (LSA). All three are statistical corpus-based techniques for representing world knowledge by estimating semantic similarities between the latent semantic structure of terms and texts. Within the scope of this book, we refrain from a redundant description of LSA.

LSA is undoubtedly the model that has received the most attention and is most widely used in computational psycholinguistic research. It automatically grades essays (Landauer, Foltz, & Laham, 1998). It performs equally well as students on the Test of English as a Foreign Language (TOEFL) tests (Landauer & Dumais, 1997), measures the coherence of texts (Foltz, Kintsch, & Landauer, 1998; McNamara, Cai, & Louwerse, chap. 19 in this volume), and classifies authors and literary periods (Louwerse, 2004). Recently, LSA has also been used in Coh-Metrix (Graesser, McNamara, Louwerse, & Cai, 2004; Louwerse, McCarthy, McNamara, & Graesser, 2004), a web-based tool that analyzes texts on over 50 types of cohesion relations and over 200 measures of language, text, and readability. LSA has also been used in intelligent tutoring systems like AutoTutor and iSTART (Graesser et al., 2000; McNamara, Levinstein, & Boonthu, 2004). LSA is able to understand metaphors (Kintsch, 2000), and can assist in problem solving (Quesada, Kintsch, & Gomez, 2002). The current volume provides sufficient evidence for the variety of LSA's cognition-based applications.

In fact, the performance of LSA is so impressive that some have argued LSA's potential as a model of language comprehension (Landauer, 2002, chap. 1 in this volume; Landauer & Dumais, 1997; Louwerse & Ventura, 2005). However, the enthusiasm for LSA as a model of a mechanism of human comprehension should be downplayed by the fact that LSA is not embodied (Glenberg & Robertson, 2000). LSA presumably cannot differentiate between drying your feet with a t-shirt (acceptable) and drying your feet with glasses (unacceptable). LSA presumably cannot "understand" how laptops can be used to protect oneself from an attack, but napkins cannot. Although it is indeed hard to argue that LSA is embodied, the question can be raised as to what extent symbols have to be grounded and how this grounding process takes place.

SYMBOL INTERDEPENDENCY

Embodiment theories (Barsalou, 1999; Glenberg, 1997; Pecher & Zwaan, 2005; Searle, 1980; Zwaan, 2004) have argued that symbols must be grounded before they can have any meaning. Because the mechanism of LSA does not allow for grounding of symbols, LSA cannot subsequently be a model of language understanding. Landauer (2002; chap. 1 in this volume) has argued that if sensory information were to be added to the LSA space, LSA could become an embodied system. Although it seems feasible that higher order relationships can emerge from sensory data, the question should be raised as to whether the problem of symbol grounding in LSA requires that sensory information is added to the training corpus. Does a direct relation between symbolic and embodied representations exist?

In fact, Deacon (1997) has argued that the relationship between symbol and embodied representation is of a secondary nature. His answer to the question concerning why humans have language and other species do not explains that humans have the symbolic mind for it. Deacon argues that humans have the mental ability to represent complex abstract entities of meaning and the relations between these entities. Other species simply do not have that capacity, although some approach it (e.g., chimpanzees). Deacon's proposal of the special mental abilities humans have is a model of symbolic transduction, loosely based on Peirce's (1923) theory of signs. Peirce identifies three different kinds of signs: icons, indices, and symbols. Icons are mediated by a similarity between the sign and the object it refers to, like a portrait representing a person. There is a physical similarity between the portrait and what it represents (the person). Indices are mediated by contiguity between sign and object, like smoke indicating fire. An index represents an association of correlation between icons. It needs to be learned that where smoke is, there is fire. In fact, if we were to live in an environment with continuous smoke, but no fire, then we would lose this indexical association. The third level of representation is symbolic. Symbols are mediated by an arbitrary, conventional relationship between sign and object, like wedding rings being symbols of marriage. A symbol is a relationship between icons, indices, and other symbols.

Different levels of interpretation can now be formed based on the hierarchical relationships of this classification. Indexical relationships consist of iconic relationships. For instance, the iconic relationship between the icon smoke and what this icon represents needs to be associated with the icon fires and what this icon represents. Note that indexical relationships are temporally and spatially contiguous. If they do not occur at the same time in the same place, then the relationship disappears. This is different for symbolic relationships: They occur outside time and space and exist by means of convention. Most animals are able to form iconic and indexical relationships, but they cannot reach the higher order symbolic relationships. Only humans can, because of their unique brain structure (Deacon, 1997).

Deacon's hierarchy of relationships is not straightforward and allows for different interpretations. What follows is one such interpretation: A sign can be an icon, index, or symbol. It is therefore not the case that a word is a symbol. It can be an icon, as is the case with onomatopoeias like "oink," an index as in deictic expressions like "there," or symbol like "morning." Let's consider a child learning the meaning of words. The child first sees the icon of a dog and what that icon represents, the sheepdog walking around in the house. By the time the child is about a year old it is able to associate the word "dog" it has frequently heard with the icons of that particular dog. Note that the word "dog" solely means this one particular sheepdog walking around in the house: There are strict temporal and spatial constraints. By the time the child gets older, different indexical relationships ("dog" for his sheepdog, "dog" for the neighbor's Labrador, "dog" for his uncle's Dachshund) become the symbol "dog." Note that the symbol "dog" represents the various indexical relationships, but also the relationships between the various symbols. That is, by being able to build the hierarchy of indexical relations, the child is able to build interdependencies between symbols. In Deacon's (1997) words, "The correspondence between words and objects is a secondary relationship, subordinate to a web of associative relationships of a quite different sort, which even allows us to reference to impossible things" (p. 90).

The ability to build these higher order relationships is certainly not unique for language comprehension and production. For instance, it can also be found in logic and reasoning where relationships operate at a higher, more abstract level. Interestingly, this higher order relationship can be found in an ability that children need prior to learning language: theory of mind, the ability to ascribe mental states that are often not directly observable to themselves and to others (Bloom, 2000).

Symbol interdependency provides a cognitive mnemonic device. Information gets recoded. Comprehenders do not have to activate every single detail of the indexical relationship of iconic relations of icons representing objects, but can use a simple shorthand. In a neural-network fashion, all nodes related to these symbols—including indices and icons—get some activation, but for default communicative purposes not enough to be processed in working memory. Symbols can therefore always be grounded in our experience of the physical world, but in language comprehension they do not always have to be grounded. Much of their meaning can come from relations to other symbols. That is, in default conversation and reading setting, comprehenders do not ground each and every word they encounter. When a situation arises where such grounding is desirable, comprehenders do not take the short-cut of relying on the meaning from other symbols, but also use embodied representations.

Symbol interdependency argues that symbols are built onto embodied representations and that interrelations between symbols can capture meaning to a large extent, although not completely. This would lead to the prediction that language, being built onto embodied representations, should be able to capture some of the relations. LSA would be a good tool to reveal these relations.

EMBODIMENT AND LSA

Various studies have raised doubts about the claim that LSA cannot capture embodied representations (Kintsch, chap. 5 in this volume; Louwerse, Hu, Cai, Ventura, & Jeuniaux, in press). In a number of studies, Louwerse et al. showed that LSA simulates categorization and prototypicality reasonably well, replicating Collins and Quillian (1969) and Rosch (1973). Furthermore, they showed that LSA ranks concepts of time in a temporally appropriate order. This is true for days of the week, moths of the year, and other concepts of time, like seconds, minutes, and hours. Louwerse et al. (in press) also showed that by just using higher order co-occurrences, LSA correlates with real distances between places, independent of the type of city (U.S. cities or world cities), corpus (TASA or encyclopedia), or language (English or French). Louwerse et al.'s method differed in one important respect from other methods: They did not compare one word to another word, but instead looked at the interrelations of words belonging to a semantic field.

A similar method can be applied to Glenberg and Robertson's (2000) study that showed LSA cannot reveal embodied relations. Glenberg and Robertson gave a compelling case against LSA and in favor of embodiment theory by selecting sentences like the following:

1. *Setting*: After wading barefoot in the lake, Erik needed something to get dry.
2. *Related*: He used his towel to dry his feet.
3. *Afforded*: He used his shirt to dry his feet.
4. *Non-afforded*: He used his glasses to dry his feet.

The authors showed that LSA cosines for the comparison between target sentence and setting sentence could not distinguish between non-afforded and related/afforded sentences. In other words, for LSA the related/afforded sentence was the same as the non-afforded one. Sensibility and envisioning data from human subjects, however, did show a difference between related/afforded and non-afforded sentences with lowest scores for the latter. Glenberg and Robertson (2000) thus drew the conclusion that LSA cannot capture the meaning of novel situations, whereas humans can.

According to the symbol interdependency hypothesis, symbols can be grounded and in peculiar cases of novel situations are likely to be grounded. But the symbol interdependency hypothesis also states that language is structured according to embodied experiences and that LSA should therefore be able to capture the meaning of the novel situations. According to the same symbol interdependency hypothesis, words elicit meaning through associations with other words. That is, the semantic relationship between text units (e.g., words) is not dependent on the relation between these two units, but on the interdependency of these units in relation to a web of interdependent units. In other words, instead of comparing the relation between the sentence (1) (setting) and a target sentence like (4) (non-afforded target) in the previous example, the symbols interdependent on (1) and those interdependent on (4) should be compared. Here, this is operationalized as follows. First, the relevant words in each of the three target sentences were selected, in the previous example dry, towel, shirt, and glasses, using the Touchstone Applied Science Associates (TASA) corpus. Similar to Glenberg and Robertson's (2000) study, distinguishing concepts were chosen (e.g., "dry," "towel," "shirt," "glasses") rather than the full sentences. For each of these distinguishing four concepts, the five nearest LSA neighbors (words most similar to the target words) were selected. In the example, the near neighbors for "glasses" are "glasses," "bifocals," "eyeglasses," "spectacles," and "nearsighted." As a working hypothesis, these five words together form the closest interdependencies between each target word. Next, for the four groups, each consisting of five words, a similarity matrix was computed. These matrices were each supplied to an ALSCAL algorithm to derive a multidimensional scaling (MDS) representation of the stimuli (Kruskall & Wish, 1978). That is, the matrix of LSA cosine values was translated into a matrix of Euclidean distances. This matrix is compared with arbitrary coordinates in an n-dimensional space. The coordinates are iteratively adjusted such that the Kruskall's stress is minimized and the degree of correspondence maximized. Coordinates on a one-dimensional scale for each matrix were saved and used for comparison purposes.

As expected, no significant differences were found between the related and the afforded sentences, $t(32) = 1.47, p = .15$. An expected difference was found between the related sentences and the non-afforded sentences, $t(32) = 3.44, p < .01$, with the related sentences yielding higher scores, $M = .13, SD = .87$, than non-afforded sentences, $M = -.80, SD = .69$. Unexpectedly, the afforded and non-afforded sentences only resulted in a marginally significant difference, $t(32) = 1.70, p = .09$, but with the expected pattern, $M = -.32$, $SD = .93$ and $M = -.80, SD = .69$. A correlation between the non-afforded sentence and the setting (dry–glasses), however, showed a strong negative correlation, $r(18) = -72, p < .01$, suggesting that these are furthest away in a Euclidean distance. An explanation for not finding a significant difference may lie in the dimensionality. Because of the comparison, the number of dimensions was limited to 1, despite high stress and low R^2. Furthermore, several of the items were homonyms (e.g., glasses) or syntactically ambiguous (e.g., dry).

When the MDS coordinates were compared with Glenberg and Robertson's sensibility and envisioning ratings, a positive correlation was found, $r(54) = .328, p = .01; r(54) = .31, p = .02$, respectively. Means are presented in

Table 6.1. Although these results may not be conclusive, they at least raise doubts about the claim that LSA cannot model embodied relations.

CONCLUSIONS

The results of the various simulations presented in this study and other studies (e.g., Kintsch, chap. 5 in this volume; Louwerse et al., in press) do not yield a final conclusion that symbolic systems do not represent perceptual information, but instead conclude that symbols can convey embodied information. This is what we have called the symbolic interdependency hypothesis: Symbolic relations exist between indexical relationships and ultimately iconic relationships, as well as between other symbols. Symbols are thereby interdependent abstract systems of meaning that are occasionally grounded in the comprehender's iconic experience of the world, and symbolic systems are structured after these iconic relations. Algorithms like LSA allow us to reveal some of these relations. This study has shown that by taking near neighbors of target words, embodied relations that are presumably hidden for LSA can in fact be unraveled.

The interdependency of symbols allows us to ground some words without the necessity to ground others, providing comprehenders with a convenient mnemonic support for language processing. That perception and cognition structure language is not surprising. If language was at some point used by our ancestors as a tool to convey perceptual experiences, then the tool was likely conveniently shaped to fit the objects it must operate on (Anderson, 2005). The fact that language consists of phrasal structures (Chomsky, 1957), subjects always precede objects (Greenberg, 1963), and categories are determined by the way we perceive the structure of the world (Rosch, 1978), are clear examples how thought structures language.

But what about the rich empirical evidence that activation of language leads to activation of perceptual information? This study has argued that symbols can be (and are occasionally) grounded in perceptual experiences, but do not always have to be. It has thereby replaced the question of

TABLE 6.1
MDS Coordinates and Glenberg and Robertson (2000) Findings

	MDS Coordinates	Sensibility Ratings	Envisioning Ratings
Related	.15 (.85)	6.02 (.85)	6.13 (.76)
Afforded	−.40 (.96)	4.41 (1.13)	4.92 (1.15)
Non–afforded	−.71 (.77)	1.31 (.56)	1.47 (.74)

Note. Standard deviations between parentheses.

whether language comprehension is symbolic or embodied by the question to what extent language comprehension is both symbolic and embodied.

ACKNOWLEDGMENTS

This research was supported by grant NSF-IIS-0416128 to the author. Any opinions, findings, and conclusions or recommendations expressed in this material are those of the author and do not necessarily reflect the views of NSF.

The TASA corpus used was generously provided by Touchtone Applied Science Associates, Newburg, NY, who developed it for data on which to base their Educators Word Frequency Guide.

REFERENCES

Anderson, J. R. (2005). *Cognitive psychology and its implications*. New York: Worth.

Bobrow, D. G., & Winograd, T. (1977). An overview of KRL-0, a knowledge representation language. *Cognitive Science, 1*, 3–46.

Barsalou, L. W. (1999). Perceptual symbol systems. *Behavior and Brain Sciences, 22*, 577–660.

Bloom, P. (2000). *How children learn the meanings of words*. Cambridge, MA: MIT Press.

Boroditsky, L. (2000). Metaphoric structuring: Understanding time through spatial metaphors. *Cognition, 75*, 1–28.

Bransford, J. D., & Franks, J. J. (1971). The abstraction of linguistic ideas. *Cognitive Psychology, 2*, 331–350.

Chomsky, N. (1957). *Syntactic structures*. The Hague: Mouton.

Collins, A., & Quillian, M. (1969). Retrieval time from semantic memory. *Journal of Verbal Learning and Verbal Behavior, 8*, 240–248.

Deacon, T. (1997). *The symbolic species: The co-evolution of language and the human brain*. London: Allen Lane.

Fikes, R. E., & Kehler, T. (1985). The role of frame-based representation in knowledge representation and reasoning. *Communications of the ACM, 28*, 904–920.

Fincher-Kiefer, R. (2001). Perceptual components of situation models. *Memory and Cognition, 29*, 336–343

Fodor, J. A. (1980). Methodological solipsism considered as a research strategy in cognitive psychology. *Behavioral and Brain Sciences, 3*, 63–109.

Foltz, P. W., Kintsch, W., & Landauer, T. K. (1998). The measurement of textual coherence with latent semantic analysis. *Discourse Processes, 25*, 285–307.

Glenberg, A. M. (1997). What memory is for. *Behavioral and Brain Sciences, 20*, 1–55.

Glenberg, A. M., & Kaschak, M. (2002). Grounding language in action. *Psychonomic Bulletin and Review, 9*, 558–565.

Glenberg, A. M., & Robertson, D. A. (2000). Symbol grounding and meaning: A comparison of high-dimensional and embodied theories of meaning. *Journal of Memory and Language, 43*, 379–401.

Goldstone, R., & Barsalou, L. W. (1998). Reuniting perception and conception. *Cognition, 65*, 231–262.

Graesser, A. C., McNamara, D. S., Louwerse, M. M., & Cai, Z. (2004). Coh-Metrix: Analysis of text on cohesion and language. *Behavior Research Methods, Instruments, and Computers, 36,* 193–202.

Graesser, A. C., Wiemer-Hastings, P., Wiemer-Hastings, K., Harter, D., & Person, N., & the TRG. (2000). Using latent semantic analysis to evaluate the contributions of students in AutoTutor. *Interactive Learning Environments, 8,* 128–148.

Greenberg, J. H. (1963). Some universals of grammar with particular reference to the order of meaningful elements. In J. H.Greenberg (Ed.), *Universals of language* (pp. 73–113). Cambridge, MA: MIT Press.

Griffiths, T., & Steyvers, M. (2004). Finding scientific topics. *Proceedings of the National Academy of Sciences, 101,* 5228–5235.

Harnad, S. (1990). The symbol grounding problem. *Physica D, 42,* 335–346.

Kaschak, M. P., Madden, C. J., Therrriault, D. J., Yaxley, R. H., Aveyard, M. E., Blanchard, A. A., et al. (2004). Perception of motion affects language processing. *Cognition, 94,* B79–B89.

Kintsch, W. (1974). *The representation of meaning in memory.* Hillsdale, NJ: Lawrence Erlbaum Associates.

Kintsch, W. (1998). *Comprehension: A paradigm for cognition.* New York: Cambridge University Press.

Kintsch, W. (2000). Metaphor comprehension: A computational theory. *Psychonomic Bulletin and Review, 7,* 257–266.

Kintsch, W., & Keenan, J. (1973). Reading rate and retention as a function of the number of propositions in the base structure of the text. *Cognitive Psychology, 5,* 257–274.

Klatzky, R. L., Pellegrino, J. W., McCloskey, D. P., & Doherty, S. (1989). Can you squeeze a tomato? The role of motor representations in semantic sensibility judgments. *Journal of Memory and Language, 28,* 56–77

Kruskal, J. B., & Wish, M. (1978). *Multidimensional scaling.* Beverly Hills, CA: Sage University Series.

Lakoff, G., & Johnson, M. (1999). *Philosophy in the flesh: The embodied mind and its challenge to Western thought.* New York: Basic Books.

Landauer, T. K. (2002). On the computational basis of learning and cognition: Arguments from LSA. In N. Ross (Ed.), *The psychology of learning and motivation* (Vol. 41, pp. 43–84). San Diego, CA: Academic Press.

Landauer, T. K., & Dumais, S. T. (1997). A solution to Plato's problem: The latent semantic analysis theory of acquisition, induction, and representation of knowledge. *Psychological Review, 104,* 211–240.

Landauer, T. K., Foltz, P. W., & Laham, D. (1998). An introduction to latent semantic analysis. *Discourse Processes, 25,* 259–284.

Lenat, D. B., & Guha, R. V. (1990). *Building large knowledge-based systems.* Reading, MA: Addison-Wesley.

Louwerse, M. M. (2004). Semantic variation in idiolect and sociolect: Corpus linguistic evidence from literary texts. *Computers and the Humanities, 38,* 207–221.

Louwerse, M. M., Hu, X., Cai, Z., Ventura, M., & Jeuniaux, P. (in press). The embodiment of amodal symbolic knowledge representations. *International Journal of Artificial Intelligence Tools.*

Louwerse, M. M., McCarthy, P. M., McNamara, D. S., & Graesser, A. C. (2004). Variations in language and cohesion across written and spoken registers. In K. Forbus, D. Gentner, & T. Regier (Eds.), *Proceedings of the 26th Annual Meeting of the Cognitive Science Society* (pp. 843–848). Mahwah, NJ: Lawrence Erlbaum Associates.

Louwerse, M. M., & Ventura, M. (2005). How children learn the meaning of words and how LSA does it (too). *Journal of Learning Sciences, 14*, 301–309.

Lund, K., & Burgess, C. (1996). Producing high-dimensional semantic spaces from lexical co-occurrence. *Behavior Research Methods, Instrumentation, and Computers, 28*, 203–208.

Matlock, T, Ramscar, M., & Boroditsky, L. (2005). The experiential link between spatial and temporal language. *Cognitive Science, 29*, 655–664.

McNamara, D. S., Levinstein, I. B. & Boonthum, C. (2004). iSTART: Interactive strategy trainer for active reading and thinking. *Behavioral Research Methods, Instruments, and Computers, 36*, 222–233.

Minsky, M. (1975). A framework for representing knowledge. In P. Winston (Ed.), *The psychology of computer vision* (pp. 211–277). New York: McGraw-Hill.

Pecher, D., & Zwaan, R. A. (Eds.). (2005). *Grounding cognition: The role of perception and action in memory, language, and thinking*. New York: Cambridge University Press.

Peirce, C. S. (1923). *The collected papers of Charles Sanders Peirce* (C. Hartshorne, P. Weiss, & A. Burks, Eds.). Cambridge, MA: Harvard University Press.

Pylyshyn, Z. W. (1973). What the mind's eye tells the mind's brain: A critique of mental imagery. *Psychological Bulletin, 80*, 1–24.

Pylyshyn, Z. W. (1984). *Computation and cognition: Towards a foundation for cognitive science*. Cambridge, MA:MIT Press.

Quesada, J. F., Kintsch, W., & Gomez, E. (2002). A computational theory of complex problem solving using Latent Semantic Analysis. In W. D. Gray & C. D. Schunn (Eds.), *Proceedings of the 24th Annual Conference of the Cognitive Science Society* (pp. 750–755). Mahwah, NJ: Lawrence Erlbaum Associates.

Quillian, M. (1966). *Semantic memory*. Cambridge, MA: Bolt, Beranek, & Newman.

Rosch, E. (1973). Natural categories. *Cognitive Psychology, 4*, 328–350.

Rosch, E. (1978). Principles of categorization. In E. Rosch & B. B. Lloyd (Eds.), *Cognition and categorization* (pp. 27–48). Hillsdale, NJ: Lawrence Erlbaum Associates.

Rumelhart, D., & Ortony, A. (1977). The representation of knowledge in memory. In R. Anderson, R. Spiro, & W. Montague (Eds.), *Schooling and the acquisition of knowledge* (pp. 99–135). Hillsdale, NJ: Lawrence Erlbaum Associates.

Saussure, F. de. (1916). *Cours de linguistique générale [Course in general linguistics]*. Lausanne: Payot.

Schank, R. C., & Abelson, R. P. (1977) *Scripts, plans, goals and understanding: An inquiry into human knowledge structures*. Hillsdale, NJ: Lawrence Erlbaum Associates.

Searle, J. R. (1980). Minds, brains, and programs. *Behavioral and Brain Sciences, 3*, 417–57.

Smith, E. E., Rips, L. J., & Shoben, E. J. (1974). Semantic memory and psychological semantic. In G. H. Bower (Ed.), The psychology of learning and motivation, 8, 1–45. New York: Academic Press.

Wanner, E. (1975). *On remembering, forgetting, and understanding sentences*. The Hague: Mouton.

Zwaan, R. A. (2004). The immersed experiencer: Toward an embodied theory of language comprehension. In B. H. Ross (Ed.), *The psychology of learning and motivation* (Vol. 43, pp. 35–62). New York: Academic Press.

Zwaan, R. A., Stanfield, R. A., & Yaxley. R. H. (2002). Do language comprehenders routinely represent the shapes of objects? *Psychological Science, 13,* 168–171.

Zwaan, R. A., & Yaxley, R. H. (2003). Spatial iconicity affects semantic-relatedness judgments. *Psychonomic Bulletin and Review, 10,* 954–958.

7

Semantic Structure and Episodic Memory

Marc W. Howard
Bing Jing
Syracuse University

Kelly M. Addis
Indiana University

Michael J. Kahana
University of Pennsylvania

A central function of episodic memory is to form and utilize associations between items experienced at nearby times. In addition to these newly formed episodic associations, subjects enter the laboratory with a great deal of knowledge about verbal stimuli. Studying the relation between episodic and preexisting, or semantic, associations can help shed light on the processes that lead to episodic retrieval. One prominent view is that episodic memory and semantic memory are separate memory systems (Tulving, 1983, 2002), and that semantic and episodic cues compete during memory retrieval. This competition would predict a reciprocal relation between the efficacy of episodic and semantic cues in predicting episodic retrieval.

For decades, the difficulty in measuring the complex network of preexisting associations among words handicapped researchers seeking to understand the relation between episodic and semantic memory. Until very recently, researchers were forced to rely on subjective judgments in measuring the effects of semantic similarity on episodic recall (e.g., Romney, Brewer, & Batchelder, 1993; Schwartz & Humphreys, 1973). Unfortunately, the combinatorics of directly measuring relations among tens of thousands of words renders this approach extremely difficult to accomplish for verbal learning experiments that use random lists of words. The recent development of computational methods to estimate semantic similarity has created new opportunities for examining the interaction between semantic and episodic associations. This chapter reports results derived from computational estimates of semantic similarity, in particular, latent semantic analysis (LSA; Landauer & Dumais, 1997), which estimates semantic similarity by extracting information about the contexts in which words appear, coupled with conditional analyses of recall transitions.

CONDITIONAL ANALYSES OF TRANSITIONS IN FREE RECALL

LSA can be used to measure the effect of semantic associations on episodic recall (Howard & Kahana, 2002b). We will describe the ability of conditional measures of semantic and temporal factors to illuminate the complexity of learning. We will also review another computational method for assessing word similarity, the word association space (WAS; Steyvers et al., 2004) derived from free association norms, and compare its properties to those of LSA. We start by introducing methods for conditional analyses of transitions in free recall.

Conditional Analyses of Temporal Factors Using the Lag–CRP

In free recall, subjects recall as many items from a list as possible without experimenter-imposed constraints on the order of recall. By observing the transitions from one recall to the next as the subject searches through his memory of the list, we can learn about the structure of memory. This chapter looks at two classes of variables that affect recall transitions: semantic similarity and temporal proximity. Kahana (1996) developed a measure, the *conditional response probability* as a function of lag, or lag–CRP, to describe the effect of temporal proximity on episodic recall transitions. Temporal proximity between two items in a list can be measured by lag, the difference in their serial positions. The lag–CRP measures the probability of recall transitions of various temporal lags.

Recall transitions measured with the lag–CRP show evidence for two effects: contiguity and asymmetry. Contiguity means that recall transitions between nearby items in the list are more likely than recall transitions between distant items in the list; and asymmetry means that forward recall transitions are more likely than backward recall transitions. Both of these properties can be seen illustrated for a wide variety of data in Figure 7.1. The ubiquity of contiguity and asymmetry (Kahana, 1996; Howard & Kahana, 1999; Kahana & Caplan, 2002; Kahana, Howard, Zaromb, & Wingfield, 2002) suggests that they are a very general property of episodic memory for items learned in series. Because it characterizes the fundamental nature of temporal associations, the lag–CRP has also proven to be an important tool in developing models of free recall memory (Howard, Fotedar, Datey, & Hasselmo, 2005; Howard & Kahana, 2002a; Howard, Kahana, & Wingfield, in press).

In calculating the lag–CRP, a probability is estimated for recall transitions of each possible lag. In estimating these event probabilities, we divide the number of times the event occurs by the number of times the event could have occurred. A concrete example should help to illustrate this process. Consider the following list: *"absence hollow pupil river darling campaign helmet."* Let's suppose that a subject recalls the words *"river, campaign, darling,"* in that order. The first pair of recalls, *river–campaign* is associated with a lag of +2 because *campaign* was two positions after *river* in

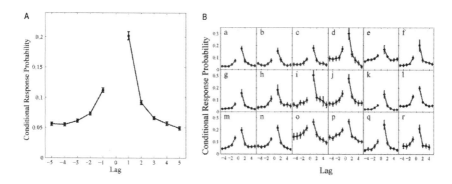

Figure 7.1.   Temporally-defined associations in free recall. Each panel shows the probability of recalling a word from serial position i + lag immediately following recall of serial position i—that is, the conditional response probability (CRP) as a function of lag. A. Lag–CRP averaged across 18 different experiments. B. Lag–CRP curves from the following studies: a. Murdock (1962) (LL 20, 2 s). b. Murdock (1962) (LL 30, 1 s). c. Murdock and Okada (1970). d. Kahana et al. (2002) (Exp. 1). e. Howard and Kahana (1999) (Exp. 2). f. Murdock (1962) (LL 20, 1 s). g. Murdock (1962) (LL 40, 1 s). h. Murdock and Metcalfe (1978) (LL 20, 5 s/item). i. Howard and Kahana (1999) (Exp. 1, delayed). j. Kahana et al. (2002) (Exp. 2). k. Roberts (1972). l. Zaromb et al. (in press, Exp. 1). m. Zaromb et al. (in press, Exp. 2). n. Thapar et al. (unpublished). o. Kimball and Bjork (2002). p. Kimball, Bjork, and Bjork (2001). q. Kahana and Howard (2005, massed condition). r. Kahana et al. (2005).

the list. The numerator for lag +2 would be incremented. The denominators for lags –3 to +3 would all be incremented. For the second recalled pair, *campaign–darling,* the numerator for –1 would be incremented because *darling* was presented one position before *campaign.* The denominators for lags –5 to +1 would be incremented, with the exception of lag –2, which would have been an erroneous response because *river* was already recalled. In averaging over retrievals, lists, and subjects, we arrive at an approximation of the conditional probability of recalling items at that lag.

Howard and Kahana (1999) used the lag–CRP to measure temporally-defined associations between items in continuous distractor free recall (CDFR). In CDFR, a distractor task intervenes between each item presentation. The duration of the interitem distractor task is referred to as the interpresentation interval (IPI). A distractor task also follows the last item in the list prior to the recall test. The duration of the interval following the last item is referred to as the retention interval (RI). Howard and Kahana (1999, Exp. 2) showed that despite changes in the IPI ranging from 0 to 16 s, there was no significant change in the shape of the lag–CRP curves. This finding is not simply a consequence of reduced attention given to the distractor; the 16 s RI was enough to severely disrupt the recency effect in the 0 s IPI condition. Initially, the finding that the lag–CRP persists across a delay long enough to disrupt the recency effect seems paradoxical; as the absolute strength of temporal connections between items decreases, there is little or no effect on the lag–CRP. This paradox, however, is only apparent. The lag–CRP is a relative measure that determines the probability of recalling an item at a particular lag, given that *some* recall transition is made. As the IPI increases, the overall number of items recalled decreases, but the relative probability of making recall transitions to various lags is unaffected. Howard and Kahana (1999) showed that these data were inconsistent with a description based on the Raaijmakers and Shiffrin (1980) search of associative memory (SAM) model, the dominant model of serial position effects in free recall at the time.

Conditional Analyses of Semantic Factors Using LSA

The basic approach of analyzing recall transitions in the lag–CRP can be generalized from lag to any relevant stimulus dimension. The LSA–CRP (Howard & Kahana, 2002b) measures the effect of LSA $\cos \theta_{ij}$ on individual recall transitions. Howard and Kahana (2002b) examined the LSA–CRP for a continuous distractor free recall study (Howard & Kahana, 1999). They found that the LSA–CRP for high values of $\cos \theta_{ij}$ was about twice as large as that for lower values of $\cos \theta_{ij}$—LSA had a highly significant effect on recall transitions in free recall. Surprisingly, they also found that as the length of the interitem distractor increased, presumably weakening the strength of temporal associations, the effect of cos θ_{ij} on recall transitions decreased. This finding suggests a deep relation between episodic and semantic associations.

In calculating the lag–CRP, we estimated a probability for transitions to each possible lag. Lag is a discrete variable that only takes on certain values. To perform a similar analysis with LSA cos θ_{ij}, a continuous variable, we must first choose some way to discretize cos θ_{ij}. Howard and Kahana (2002b) took the distribution of observed cos θ_{ij} values for the pairs within the pool of words used in this experiment (see Fig. 7.5a) and formed 100 bins with equal numbers of members. Figure 7.2a shows typical pairs in these bins and their corresponding cos θ_{ij}. For each pair of recalled words, there is some cos θ_{ij} and some corresponding cos θ_{ij} bin between the just-recalled word and each other available word in the list. As with the lag–CRP, the LSA–CRP estimates the probability of making recall transitions that fall in each cos θ_{ij} bin.

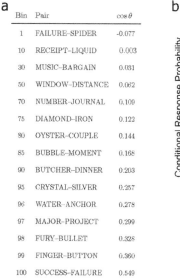

Bin	Pair	cos θ
1	FAILURE–SPIDER	-0.077
10	RECEIPT–LIQUID	0.003
30	MUSIC–BARGAIN	0.031
50	WINDOW–DISTANCE	0.062
70	NUMBER–JOURNAL	0.109
75	DIAMOND–IRON	0.122
80	OYSTER–COUPLE	0.144
85	BUBBLE–MOMENT	0.168
90	BUTCHER–DINNER	0.203
95	CRYSTAL–SILVER	0.257
96	WATER–ANCHOR	0.278
97	MAJOR–PROJECT	0.299
98	FURY–BULLET	0.328
99	FINGER–BUTTON	0.360
100	SUCCESS–FAILURE	0.549

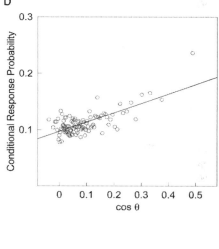

Figure 7.2. Semantic associations in free recall. a. Word pairs drawn from selected cos θ_{ij} bin. Only very high bins predominantly contain pairs with obvious semantic relations. b. The LSA–CRP shows the probability of successively recalling words from different cos θ_{ij} bins. Each pair of words in the word pool used in the experiment has a value of cos θ_{ij} associated with it. This distribution was divided into 100 bins containing equal numbers of pairs, so that each pair was associated with a bin. Each time a word was recalled, each potentially-recalled word has a similarity to the just-recalled word and is thus associated with a bin. The left panel shows probability of recall as a function of the average cos θ_{ij} in each bin. Figure 7.2b reprinted from "When does semantic similarity help episodic retrieval?" by M. W. Howard and M. J. Kahana, 2002, *Journal of Memory and Language, 46,* pp. 85–98, copyright © 2002, with permission from Elsevier.

The following example illustrates the calculation of the LSA–CRP. Suppose the subject studied the list *absence hollow pupil river darling campaign helmet* and recalled the words *"river, campaign,* and *darling,"* in sequence. For the first pair of recalled items, we find that the cos θ_{ij} between *river* and *campaign* falls into bin 41. We therefore increment both the numerator and denominator associated with bin 41. In addition to recording information about the observed event, we also need to keep track of the other possible events that could have been observed at that recall transition. If we have 100 cos θ_{ij} bins and a list with 12 items, not all of the bins could have been observed on any particular recall transition. Accordingly, we calculate the cos θ_{ij} bin between *river* and all the potentially recalled words in the list and increment the corresponding denominators. For instance, because *river–absence* falls into bin 65, we increment the denominator associated with bin 65. Because *river–hollow* falls into bin 53, we increment the denominator associated with bin 53, and so on. We then move on to the next pair of recalled items, *campaign–darling.* This recall would be analyzed in the same manner as *river–campaign,* with the exception that *campaign–river* would be excluded from the denominator because the already recalled item *river* would have been an erroneous response at that output position.[1]

Figure 7.2b shows the LSA–CRP calculated for data from Experiment 2 of Howard and Kahana (1999). To quantify the general trend of the relation between recall transitions and LSA cos θ_{ij}, we calculated a regression line for the recall probability across the 100 cos θ_{ij} bins for each subject as in Howard and Kahana (2002b). The line in Figure 7.2b represents the average (across subjects) regression. According to this regression, the conditional probability of recalling an available item with a very high cos θ_{ij} is about twice that of an available item with a cos θ_{ij} near zero. Even after excluding the 20 highest cos θ_{ij} bins, the regression of recall probability on cos θ_{ij} remained significant. This illustrates LSA's ability to capture relatively subtle semantic relations and the relevance of these relations for episodic recall (Howard & Kahaba, 2002b).

Insight Into the Relation Between Episodic and Semantic Cues

The foregoing subsections have described a common framework based on conditional analyses of recall transitions to assess the influence of temporal and semantic factors on recall order in the free recall task. Armed with these

---

[1]We have recently become aware of a discrepancy between the published LSA–CRP analyses (Howard & Kahana, 2002b) and the description above. In the analyses published in Howard & Kahana (2002b), the process of excluding already-recalled words from the denominator extended to words that were recalled but after the present pair of recalls. This discrepancy did not induce a systematic discrepancy across LSA bin, so the conclusions of Howard and Kahana (2002b) remain valid, but the numerical values of the LSA–CRP are not correct. All of the results in the present chapter (including Fig. 7.2b) were calculated with the correct analysis.

methods, we can begin to ask questions about the relation between episodic and semantic cues on episodic retrieval. One possibility is that episodic and semantic memory rely on distinct memory systems (Tulving, 1983, 2002). In this case, one might expect that at retrieval subjects rely on some combination of semantic and episodic cues. In this case, episodic and semantic factors on retrieval would be inversely related to each other.

Using the LSA–CRP to measure the effect of semantic similarity on recall transitions using LSA, Howard and Kahana (2002b) examined how the effect of semantic similarity is modulated by temporal variables in two sets of analyses of the continuous distractor free recall data from Experiment 2 of Howard and Kahana (1999). In the first of these analyses, Howard and Kahana (2002b) calculated an LSA–CRP separately for transitions at each of several values of | lag |, collapsing over forward and backward transitions. This enabled them to look at how the effect of semantic similarity on output order interacted with the effect of temporal distance. Howard and Kahana (2002b) found that in delayed free recall, with the IPI set to zero, there was a larger effect of LSA cos θ_{ij} on retrieval transitions when the words in question were also presented at small values of | lag |. That is, when the IPI was zero, there was a larger effect of semantic similarity between words that shared a strong temporal relation. However, in the three conditions in which the IPI was non-zero, the interaction was not different from zero and was significantly smaller than the effect observed with an IPI of zero. Even an IPI as short as 2 s was sufficient to disrupt the interaction. This finding is consistent with the idea that it is necessary to discover the semantic relations between words during encoding (Glanzer, 1969) and it is easier to coactivate words that were presented close together in time. The presence of an interitem distractor, even a brief one, would presumably be sufficient to disrupt these active encoding processes.

The foregoing analysis did not support the hypothesis that episodic and semantic memory are reciprocally related components of memory retrieval in an episodic memory task. In addition to this analysis, Howard and Kahana (2002b) calculated an LSA–CRP separately for each condition of Experiment 2 of Howard and Kahana (1999). These conditions vary on the value of IPI, ranging from 0 s to 16 s. Increasing the IPI would be expected to result in a decrease in the strength of temporally-defined associations between items. Indeed, the overall number of recalled items drops dramatically as the IPI increases. If episodic and semantic associations compete with each other to determine recall order, then one might expect the decrease in the strength of temporal associations to be accompanied by an increase in the effect of semantic similarity, as measured by the LSA–CRP. In fact, Howard and Kahana (2002b) found exactly the opposite—as the IPI increased from 0 s to 16 s, the slope of the regression line relating the CRP to LSA cos θ_{ij} decreased. This finding enables us to reject the hypothesis that episodic and semantic memory systems compete for resources in episodic retrieval. Rather, they appear to support each other such that semantic cues have the largest effect on retrieval when episodic cues are also strong.

CONDITIONAL LSA ANALYSES WITH LEARNING

To examine the relation between semantic and temporal factors during learning, we analyze changes in semantic and temporal organization over learning trials from a study of temporal retrieval effects reported by Klein, Addis, and Kahana (2005). In the FR–Varied condition, subjects performed free recall on a list of words that was presented in a different random order on each of five study–test cycles. In this condition, the temporal associations between words are changing from trial to trial as presentation order changes. The repetition of the words over trials may allow a general increase in the strength of temporal associations, but this increase would be diffuse, as competing associations are formed on each successive trial. In the FR–Constant condition, the list was repeated in the same order on each cycle. In this condition, the strength of temporal cues should also increase with learning. Moreover, one might expect that the relative strength of the temporal associations would remain fixed over learning due to the fact that the list is presented in a consistent order each time. These two conditions should place different pressures on temporal and semantic factors as learning progresses.

Results

Figure 7.3a shows lag–CRPs for the FR–Constant (top) and FR–Varied (bottom) conditions. Subjects showed increased use of temporal associations across trials in the FR–Constant condition, but decreased use of temporal associations across trials in the FR–Varied condition. Figure 7.3b shows LSA–CRPs, calculated with 100 cos θ_{ij} bins for the same data. In the FR–Varied condition, the LSA–CRP appears to grow more pronounced over learning trials, whereas the LSA–CRP appears largely unchanged across trials in the FR–Constant condition.

To assess these visual impressions more quantitatively, we computed summary statistics to describe the effect of temporal and semantic factors on their respective CRPs. To derive a summary statistic for temporal factors, we fit the power function $CRP = A\text{lag}^{-B}$ to the forward ($1 \leq \text{lag} \leq 5$) and backward ($-5 \leq \text{lag} \leq -1$) components of the lag–CRP (Kahana et al., 2002). We took the (across-subjects) average exponent B of the power function fits as a measure of the modulation of the lag–CRP by lag. We took the average slope of a linear regression of LSA–CRP to cos θ_{ij} for each bin fit to each individual subject's data as measure of cos θ_{ij}'s effect on recall transitions.

Figure 7.3c shows forward and backward lag exponents averaged across subjects for each condition. A 2 (direction) × 2 (condition) × 5 (trial) repeated measures analysis of variance (ANOVA) showed main effects of direction [($F(1, 11) = 14.98$, $MSe = 0.86$, $p < .005$], condition [$F(1, 11) = 69.13$, $MSe = 0.90$, $p < .001$], and trial [$F(4, 44) = 12.17$, $MSe = 0.09$, $p < .001$]. There were also significant interactions between direction and condition [$F(1, 11) = 17.39$, $MSe = 0.39$, $p < .005$] and, critically, between condition and trial [$F(4, 44) = 23.68$, $MSe = 0.15$, $p < .001$]. Neither the interaction between direction and trial [($F(4, 44) = 1.07$, $n.s.$], nor the three-way interaction between direction, condition, and trial [$F(4, 44) = 1.33$, $n.s.$] approached significance. When considering just the FR–Constant condition, there was a significant effect of direction [$F(1, 11) = 18.56$, $MSe = 1.03$, $p < .005$], and a significant effect of trial [$F(4, 44) = 3.41$, $MSe = 0.13$, $p < .02$], but no interaction between

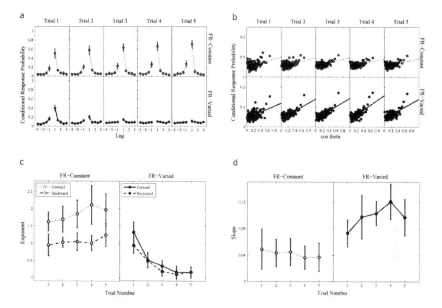

Figure 7.3. Changes in temporal and semantic associations with learning. Each panel shows data from two experimental conditions. In the FR–Constant condition, the word list was presented in the same order on each learning trial. In the FR–Varied condition, the list was presented in a new random order on each learning trial. In all cases, error bars reflect 95% confidence intervals. a. Temporally-defined associations remain largely unchanged with learning in the FR–Constant condition, whereas they rapidly diminish in the FR–Varied condition. b. Semantic associations remain relatively constant across learning trials in the FR–Constant condition, whereas they increase markedly in the FR–Varied condition. c. The exponents of power function fits to the forward and backward components of the lag–CRPs shown in (a) demonstrate a modest increase in the effect of temporal associations in the FR–Constant condition, but a dramatic decrease in the FR–Varied condition. d. Regression slopes of the LSA–CRP (b) are relatively constant across trials in the FR–Constant condition. In contrast, there is an increase in the slope over trials in the FR–Varied condition. Data from Klein, Addis, and Kahana (2005).

direction and trial [$F(4, 44) = 1.05$, $n.s.$]. The FR–Varied condition showed a significant effect of trial [$F(4, 44) = 36.91$, $MSe = 0.11$, $p < .001$], but no effect of direction [$F(1, 11) = 2.20$, $n.s.$].

These analyses indicate that, whereas the effect of temporal factors on retrieval—as measured by the lag–CRP with lag calculated relative to the most recent list presentation—decreases with learning in the FR–Varied condition, it increases with learning when the lists are repeated in a constant order. In the FR–Constant condition, although the strength of temporal associations can be assumed to increase across trials, the lack of a significant interaction between direction and trial indicates that the asymmetry in temporally-defined associations does not change over trials. This finding is particularly challenging for theoretical accounts of the lag–CRP: Although the discrepancy between the lag–CRP for adjacent lags and remote lags grew over time, the discrepancy between the lag–CRP for forward and backward recall transitions did not.

The analysis of average LSA slopes confirmed our qualitative impressions. A 2 (condition) × 5 (trial) repeated measures ANOVA showed a significant main effect of condition [$F(1, 11) = 24.4$, $MSe = .004$, $p < .001$], no main effect of trial [$F(4, 44) = 1.98$, $n.s.$], and a significant interaction [$F(4, 44) = 4.23$, $MSe = 0.001$, $p < .01$]. This interaction was driven by an increase in slope with trial in the FR–Varied condition [$F(4, 44) = 5.728$, $MSe = 0.001$, $p < .005$]. There was no effect of trial on the LSA–CRP slope in the FR–Constant condition [$F(4, 44) < 1$, $n.s.$].

Discussion

The changing influence of semantic and episodic cues across learning trials, as already described, appears inconsistent with the hypothesis that semantic and episodic cues strictly compete during retrieval. In the FR–Constant condition, it seems reasonable to assume that the strength of temporal associations among list items increases with learning. Even though the list was presented in a consistent order on each trial, temporal factors did not come to completely dominate recall transitions. For instance, the lag–CRP from the FR–Constant condition did not come to resemble the type of lag–CRP function one would expect from serial recall, in which the vast majority of list items are recalled at a lag of +1 (Klein et al., 2005). Even as the effect of lag on retrieval increased over learning trials, the regression slope of the LSA–CRP did not decrease significantly, as one would expect if there were an inverse relation between episodic and semantic factors. Even more puzzling, the pattern we observed previously—increased semantic effects when temporal cues were strong (Howard & Kahana, 2002b)—was also not observed here: As temporal cues increased in strength with learning, there was no corresponding increase in the effect of semantic similarity on retrieval.

In the FR–Varied condition, the effect of semantic similarity increased over learning trials while the lag–CRP flattened. At first glance, it appears that these results from the FR–Varied condition provide straightforward support for the hypothesis of an inverse relation between temporal and semantic factors on retrieval, but on closer examination it is not so obvious that this is the lesson provided by these data. Although the lag–CRP decreased over learning trials in the FR–Varied condition, it should be noted that lag was calculated based on the most recent list presentation. It might be more accurate to say that when the list was presented in multiple orders, there is a decrease over trials in the relative importance of the most recent presentation order to specifying the temporal associations between list items. It should also be noted that the increase in the effect of semantic similarity with learning in the FR–Varied condition confirms that the increase in subjective organization (Tulving, 1966) observed with learning is accompanied by an increase in the effects of semantic similarity on retrieval transitions (Schwartz & Humphreys, 1973).

Although we can reject the hypothesis that temporal and semantic factors exhibit a simple inverse relation during episodic retrieval, the hypothesis that the effect of semantic similarity is greatest when temporal cues are strongest was also not supported by the results of the FR–Constant condition. As summarized in Table 7.1, increasing the length of the IPI in continuous distractor free recall reduced both overall recall probability and subjects' reliance on semantic associations (Howard & Kahana, 2002b). The same manipulation did not significantly alter subjects' reliance on temporally-defined associations in choosing items to recall (Howard & Kahana, 1999, 2002b). Here we showed that when words were learned with a vari-

TABLE 7.1
The Complex Relation Between Temporal and Semantic Factors in Free Recall

Manipulation	Increasing IPI	Learning Trials	
Condition	CDFR	FR–Varied	FR–Constant
Recall probability	-	+	+
Temporal associations	=	-	+
Semantic associations	-	+	=

Note. The column labeled "Increasing IPI," where IPI is an abbreviation for interpresentation interval, refers to results reported by Howard and Kahana (2002b). CDFR stands for continuous–distractor free recall. The columns labeled "FR–Varied" and "FR–Constant," where FR stands for free recall, refer to results originally reported in Klein et al., (2005) and here. A table entry with a plus sign indicates that the experimental manipulation heading the column resulted in an increase in the dependent measure labeling the row. A minus sign indicates a decrease in the dependent measure, while an equal sign indicates no effect.

able order of presentation across trials, probability of recall increased along with the effect of semantic relatedness on memory retrieval, while the effect of temporal proximity decreased (Figure 7.3, solid). However, when lists were learned in a consistent order, although probability of recall still increased, the effect of temporal factors increased while the effect of LSA cos θ_{ij} on output order remained constant (Figure 7.3, dashed). Taken together, these three sets of findings illustrate a more complex relation between temporal and semantic factors in episodic recall than has previously been appreciated. Our ability to describe these processes is largely a consequence of the methodological advantage of being able to assess semantic similarity between large numbers of pairs of words without the time or expense of subjective ratings. The next section discusses the potential for other computational methods of assessing semantic similarity to measure output order in free recall.

WAS AND LSA

The preceding work demonstrates that LSA, especially when combined with conditional measures of memory retrieval, provides a valuable tool in the experimental study of memory. This, of course, does not preclude the possibility that other computational measures may also provide useful experimental tools for studying the effects of semantic structure on episodic memory performance. This section discusses semantic associations measured with the word association space (WAS; Steyvers et al., 2004), another computational method that has successfully been used to describe the effects of semantic factors on episodic memory performance.

WAS: Word Association Space

LSA constructs a semantic representation from two main components. First, information about word co-occurrence in naturally occurring text is extracted. Second, this information is provided as input to a singular value decomposition (SVD) step that performs dimensional reduction. Recent computational measures developed by Steyvers and colleagues (Griffiths & Steyvers, 2002, 2003; Steyvers et al., 2004) have explored variations on both of these major aspects of LSA. Although we will not conduct conditional analyses with it here, the topics model (Griffiths & Steyvers, 2002, 2003; Steyvers & Griffiths, chap. 21 in this volume) warrants some discussion here. The topics model attempts to capture the semantic relations between words by hypothesizing that a body of text, such as the TASA corpus often used to construct LSA spaces, is generated from a set of discrete topics. These topics function something like latent variables. The conditional probabilities of observing a particular word in a particular topic, as well as the probability that each context contains a particular topic are then adjusted to best predict the observed corpus. The topics model, like LSA, takes in information about word co-occurrence but uses different mathematical techniques to estimate relations between words. In contrast, WAS (Steyvers et al., 2004) uses mathematical techniques similar to those used in LSA but with a very different source of input information.

WAS starts with an associative matrix constructed from free association norms collected at the University of South Florida (USF Norms; Nelson, McEvoy, & Schreiber, 2004). These norms have provided a valuable experimental tool in evaluating the role of semantic factors on item recognition (Nelson, Zhang, & McKinney, 2001), cued recall (Nelson & Zhang, 2000), and extralist cued recall (Nelson, Bennett, Gee, Schreiber, & McKinney, 1993). In particular, the USF norms have proven useful in revealing the importance of indirect word associations in guiding episodic recall (Nelson, Bennett, & Leibert, 1997; Nelson, McKinney, Gee, & Janczura, 1998).

The calculation that results in the WAS space operates on the normed probability A_{ij} of responding with word j when probed with word i. Steyvers et al. (2004) started with a symmetric measure of associative strength generated from the free association matrix:

$$S_{ij}^{(1)} := A_{ij} + A_{ji}.$$

They supplemented this with a measure that included indirect associations, which prior studies have shown affect extralist cued recall performance (Nelson et al., 1997; Nelson & McEvoy, 2000):

$$S_{ij}^{(2)} := S_{ij}^{(1)} + \Sigma_k S_{ik}^{(1)} S_{kj}^{(1)}.$$

The associative matrix, $\mathbf{S}^{(1)}$ or $\mathbf{S}^{(2)}$, is then decomposed using singular value decomposition yielding a representation with reduced dimensionality. Steyvers et al. (2004) also evaluated a version of WAS that performed multidimensional scaling (MDS) on a path length derived from the free association norms. Because the SVD solution typically outperformed, or showed equivalent performance to that of the MDS solution, and because of the formal similarity of the SVD solution to LSA, we will only examine WAS–SVD here, and will refer to it simply as WAS.

Scalar Measures of WAS and Memory Performance Measures

In order to illustrate the utility of WAS as an experimental tool, Steyvers et al. (2004) examined the correlation between WAS $\cos \theta_{ij}$ and judgments of remembered semantic similarity between a probe word and a study list, extralist cued recall performance, and extralist intrusions in free recall. These correlations were compared to correlations calculated using $S_{ij}^{(1)}$ and $S_{ij}^{(2)}$, as defined previously, as well as LSA cos θ_{ij}. In all three cases, WAS cos θ_{ij} showed a stronger correlation with performance than LSA cos θ_{ij}. We will discuss the recall results of Steyvers et al. (2004) in more detail here.

In extra-list cued recall, a list is presented for study (e.g., Nelson et al., 1998; Tehan & Humphreys, 1996). An associate of one of the list words is then presented as a cue for that target list word. Steyvers et al. (2004) took a large set of cue–target pairs and correlated the various scalar semantic measures with the probability that each cue evoked its target across lists and subjects. They found that WAS showed a slightly higher correlation than the raw associative strengths. For instance, the correlation for $\mathbf{S}^{(2)}$ was approximately .5, whereas the correlation for the cos θ_{ij} from the vector space calculated from $\mathbf{S}^{(2)}$ retaining 400 dimensions was .55. However, both of these numbers were considerably higher than the correlation observed for LSA cos θ_{ij}, which was about .3 (right panel of Figure 2, Steyvers et al., 2004).

The free recall data examined by Steyvers et al. (2004) was originally reported by Deese (1959), who found that lists with a particular construction yield high rates of intrusion of particular items. For instance, when presented with the list *dream pillow bed tired* ... , subjects were as likely to recall the word *sleep* as they were to recall words that were actually presented. Steyvers et al. (2004) correlated the probability of intruding a non-presented target item with the average similarity of that item to the presented list items using the various scalar measures mentioned previously. Although they found that the correlation between WAS cos θ_{ij} and the probability of an intrusion was much higher than that of LSA cos θ_{ij}, the correlation for both was much lower than that for the raw free association measures $\mathbf{S}^{(1)}$ and $\mathbf{S}^{(2)}$. This superiority is perhaps not surprising insofar as Deese (1959) constructed these lists using free association norms. In order to shed further light on the differences between WAS and LSA as measures of the effect of semantic similarity on episodic retrieval, we will calculate conditional analyses for LSA and WAS for the free recall data on which the LSA–CRP was developed (Howard & Kahana, 1999, 2002b).

Conditional Analyses With WAS

We were provided with a set of 400-dimensional WAS vectors derived from $S^{(2)}$ for the 421-word subset of the pool used in Howard and Kahana (1999) for which free association norms are available. We used these WAS vectors to calculate cos θ_{ij} for each pair of items in the subset and calculated a WAS–CRP precisely analogous to the LSA–CRP described earlier for the data from Experiment 2 of Howard and Kahana (1999). Missing pairs were ignored in these analyses. To ensure that any discrepancies between these and prior analyses were not a consequence of the missing words, we recalculated the LSA–CRP with only the 421 words for which WAS vectors were available. As an exploratory method, we also calculated a CRP using the inner product rather than cos θ_{ij} for each LSA and WAS. All of these analyses were calculated using both 10 and 100 bins. Although the results were comparable, it is our opinion that the results with 100 bins are more illuminating, so the focus is on these here.

Both LSA and WAS showed a definite increase in the CRP with increasing semantic similarity for both cos θ_{ij} and inner product (see Fig. 7.4). All of these measures of semantic similarity hold some merit for describing the effect of semantic similarity on episodic recall. The average of the LSA cos θ_{ij} regressions yielded a slope of .17 ± .05 (95% confidence interval). The aver-

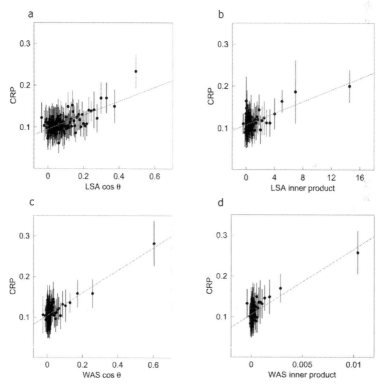

Figure 7.4. Semantic associations measured using LSA and WAS. a. CRP computed using the cos θ_{ij} calculated from LSA. b. CRP computed using the inner product calculated from LSA. c. CRP computed using the cos θ_{ij} calculated from WAS. d. CRP computed using the inner product calculated from WAS. Note that the scales on the x-axes in (b) and (d) are not directly comparable. The error bars are 95% confidence intervals.

age of the WAS cos θ_{ij} regressions yielded a slope of .28 ± .08 (95% confidence interval). Although the average slope was considerably larger for WAS cos θ_{ij} than for LSA cos θ_{ij}, it is extremely difficult to interpret this result because LSA and WAS distribute cos θ_{ij} very differently across pairs. This can be seen informally by comparing the density of points along the cos θ_{ij} axis in Figure 7.4a versus c. Figure 7.4c, representing the WAS cos θ_{ij} CRP, shows a relatively wide gap between the highest cos θ_{ij} and the rest of the distribution. This is because bin 100 contains a wider range of WAS cos θ_{ij} values. The difference in the distribution of these variables makes it difficult to directly compare the efficacy of LSA and WAS as measures of the effect of semantic factors on episodic recall. Further, as we shall see shortly, the various measures under consideration here have different sensitivities to word frequency. We will discuss the effect that the shape of the distributions and sensitivity to word frequency have on the suitability of both WAS and LSA for various applications.

To help clarify these issues, Figure 7.5 shows distributions of LSA and WAS cos θ_{ij} and inner product on log–log coordinates. In generating the distributions, the word pool was first split into high- and low-frequency halves. The distribution of pairs composed of two high-frequency words are shown in grey; the distribution of pairs composed of two low-frequency words are shown in black. From these distributions, we can infer several properties of these measures. First, LSA cos θ_{ij} is distributed differently than the other measures, showing a broad peak and a curved tail in log–log coordinates. The other distributions (with the exception of the LSA inner product high-frequency distribution) show an approximately linear tail on log–log coordinates, suggesting a power law tail to the distribution.

These differences in the shape of the distributions make it extremely difficult to interpret analyses that summarize the effect of semantic similarity with a single scalar measure. An advantage of the conditional approach used here is that it enables us to examine the properties of these measures without obscuring differences in the shape of the distribution that would skew, for instance, average cos θ_{ij} of adjacent recalls.

LSA cos θ_{ij} is also distinctive from the other distributions by virtue of its sensitivity to word frequency. Whereas the other distributions are shifted to the right for the high-frequency pairs (grey line), the low-frequency pairs actually have a higher average cos θ_{ij} than the high-frequency pairs. This pattern is reversed for the other measures, especially prominently for the LSA inner product. This suggests that variation in LSA cos θ_{ij} is anticorrelated with the normative frequency of the words for which cos θ_{ij} is being calculated. This analysis also suggests that the WAS cos θ_{ij} and inner product of a pair are weakly correlated with the word frequency of the members of the pair and that LSA inner product should be strongly corre-

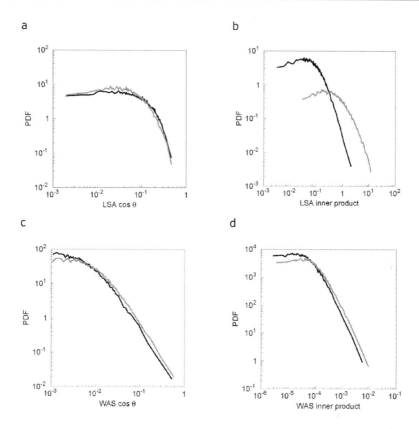

Figure 7.5.   The effect of word frequency on the distribution of LSA and WAS similarity. A 421-word subset of the Toronto Noun Pool was split into high-frequency and low-frequency subsets by a median split with Kučera–Francis word frequency. As a consequence, LSA inner product is much greater for high-frequency pairs than for low-frequency pairs era–Francis word frequency. This figure shows the distribution of similarity scores derived from LSA or WAS in log–log coordinates. The black lines show distributions for pairs taken from the low-frequency subset; the grey lines show distributions for pairs from the high-frequency subset. a. LSA cos θ_{ij} is lower for high-frequency pairs than for low-frequency pairs. This suggests that, with respect to the angular distribution of vectors, high-frequency words are not clustered, but are distributed more like corners of a box. b. LSA inner product. In LSA, vector length is correlated ($r \approx .6$) with Kučera–Francis word frequency. As a consequence, LSA inner product is much greater for high-frequency pairs than for low-frequency pairs. c. WAS cos θ_{ij}. In contrast to the LSA cos θ_{ij} distributions, the WAS cos θ_{ij} distributions contain many more very low-similarity pairs. Also in contrast to LSA cos θ_{ij}, WAS cos θ_{ij} is higher for high-frequency pairs than low-frequency pairs. This suggests that in WAS high-frequency words are clustered in a central region of the space. d. WAS inner product. Like the LSA inner product, the WAS inner product shows a separation between high-frequency pairs and low-frequency pairs such that high-frequency pairs have a higher inner product. These distributions are not as widely separated as those for LSA inner product.

lated with the word frequency of the members of the pair. Each of these measures provides some degree of sensitivity to word frequency. Depending on what one wants to measure in a particular experiment, sensitivity to word frequency may or may not be a desirable property. It is perhaps worth noting that the weighting function employed in LSA specifically tries to minimize the importance of high-frequency words. However, the fact that the LSA inner product is strongly correlated with word frequency but does not show a CRP vastly different from the other measures suggests that the CRPs of the other measures are not strongly influenced by word frequency.

SOME FINAL THOUGHTS

We have discussed ways to assess the roles of newly-formed episodic and preexisting semantic associations in determining episodic recall performance. We briefly reviewed conditional analyses of temporal factors in free recall and the extension of these measures to semantic factors using LSA cos θ_{ij}. These conditional analyses described a complex relation between episodic and temporal factors in free recall (Table 7.1). We reviewed the finding that the effect of semantic factors on recall decreased as the duration of the delay between list items, or IPI, was increased (Howard & Kahana, 2002b). We examined the effect of learning on temporal and semantic factors using two presentation schedules. When words were repeated in a random order across learning trials, the effect of temporal factors—at least with reference to the most recently presented list—decreased dramatically, whereas the effect of semantic factors, as illustrated by the LSA–CRP, increased dramatically. This finding is consistent with previous results on the relation between temporal and semantic factors during learning (Schwartz & Humphreys, 1973). However, when the items were presented in a consistent order on each study–test cycle, the effect of temporal factors increased while the effect of semantic factors remained approximately constant. These findings present something of a puzzle for models of temporal and semantic factors in episodic recall.

Do episodic and semantic associations result from a common source? If they do, retrieved temporal context would be a strong candidate. LSA and the topics model both ultimately describe a word in terms of the contexts in which it appears. Contextual retrieval is also a key feature of two recent models of episodic memory. Dennis and Humphreys (2001) used retrieved context as the central mechanism for a model of episodic recognition memory. This model predicted that words that occur in many contexts should be harder to recognize than words that occur in few contexts, with word frequency controlled. This prediction has been confirmed (Steyvers & Malmberg, 2003). The temporal context model (TCM; Howard & Kahana, 2002a; Howard et al., 2005) exploits contextual retrieval to describe newly formed associations in episodic recall. Because TCM describes context as a combination of patterns retrieved by items, it may be possible to describe something not too dissimilar to the contextual mixing performed by both LSA and the topics model. Kwantes (2005) has recently built a model that captures some aspects of semantic meaning from a framework built on MINERVA, a model that was developed to describe episodic memory performance. A description of the interactions between temporal and semantic factors in episodic recall will be an essential step in developing a unified model of episodic and semantic learning.

ACKNOWLEDGMENTS

The authors wish to acknowledge support from NIH grants MH069938 to MWH and MH55687 to MJK. Mark Steyvers generously provided the WAS vectors used here. We thank both Mark Steyvers and Simon Dennis for useful discussions concerning this work. We thank Per Sederberg and Jonathan Miller for careful study of the analysis code used to generate the LSA–CRP in Howard and Kahana (2002b). We thank Sridhar Iyer for programming support.

REFERENCES

Deese, J. (1959). On the prediction of occurrence of particular verbal intrusions in immediate recall. *Journal of Experimental Psychology, 58*, 17–22.

Dennis, S., & Humphreys, M. S. (2001). A context noise model of episodic word recognition. *Psychological Review, 108*, 452–478.

Glanzer, M. (1969). Distance between related words in free recall: Trace of the STS. *Journal of Verbal Learning and Verbal Behavior, 8*, 105–111.

Griffiths, T., & Steyvers, M. (2002). A probabilistic approach to semantic representation. In W. Gray and C. Schunn (Eds.), *Proceedings of the 24th Annual Conference of the Cognitive Science Society* (pp. 381–386). Austin, TX: Cognitive Science Society.

Griffiths, T., & Steyvers, M. (2003). Prediction and semantic association. In S. Becker, S. Thrun, & K. Obermayer (Eds.), *Advances in Neural Information Processing Systems 15* (pp. 11–18). Cambridge, MA: MIT Press.

Howard, M. W., Fotedar, M. S., Datey, A. V., & Hasselmo, M. E. (2005). The temporal context model in spatial navigation and relational learning: Toward a common explanation of medial temporal lobe function across domains. *Psychological Review, 112*(1), 75–116.

Howard, M. W., & Kahana, M. J. (1999). Contextual variability and serial position effects in free recall. *Journal of Experimental Psychology: Learning, Memory, and Cognition, 25*, 923–941.

Howard, M. W., & Kahana, M. J. (2002a). A distributed representation of temporal context. *Journal of Mathematical Psychology, 46*, 269–299.

Howard, M. W., & Kahana, M. J. (2002b). When does semantic similarity help episodic retrieval? *Journal of Memory and Language, 46*, 85–98.

Howard, M. W., Kahana, M. J., & Wingfield, A. (in press). Aging and contextual binding: Modeling recency and lag-recency effects with the temporal context model. *Psychonomic Bulletin and Review.*

Kahana, M. J. (1996). Associative retrieval processes in free recall. *Memory and Cognition, 24,* 103–109.

Kahana, M. J., & Caplan, J. B. (2002). Associative asymmetry in probed recall of serial lists. *Memory and Cognition, 30,* 841–849.

Kahana, M. J., Dolan, E. D., Sauder, C. L., & Wingfield, A. (2005). Intrusions in episodic recall: Age differences in editing of overt responses. *Journal of Gerontology: Psychological Sciences, 60,* 92–97.

Kahana, M. J., & Howard, M. W. (2005). Spacing and lag effects in free recall of pure lists. *Psychonomic Bulletin & Review, 12,* 159–164.

Kahana, M. J., Howard, M. W., Zaromb, F., & Wingfield, A. (2002). Age dissociates recency and lag-recency effects in free recall. *Journal of Experimental Psychology: Learning, Memory, and Cognition, 28,* 530–540.

Kimball, D. R., & Bjork, R. A. (2002). Influences of intentional and unintentional forgetting on false memories. *Journal of Experimental Psychology: General, 131*(1), 116–130.

Kimball, D. R., Bjork, R. A., & Bjork, E. L. (2001, July). *Retrieval inhibition can increase or decrease false memories.* Paper presented at International Conference on Memory III, Valencia, Spain.

Klein, K. A., Addis, K. M., & Kahana, M. J. (2005). A comparative analysis of serial and free recall. *Memory and Cognition, 33*(5), 833–839.

Kwantes, P. J. (2005). Using context to build semantics. *Psychonomic Bulletin and Review, 12*(4), 703–710.

Landauer, T. K., & Dumais, S. T. (1997). Solution to Plato's problem: The latent semantic analysis theory of acquisition, induction, and representation of knowledge. *Psychological Review, 104,* 211–240.

Murdock, B. B. (1962). The serial position effect of free recall. *Journal of Experimental Psychology, 64,* 482–488.

Murdock, B. B., & Metcalfe, J. (1978). Controlled rehearsal in single-trial free recall. *Journal of Verbal Learning and Verbal Behavior, 17,* 309–324.

Murdock, B. B., & Okada, R. (1970). Interresponse times in single-trial free recall. *Journal of Verbal Learning and Verbal Behavior, 86,* 263–267.

Nelson, D. L., Bennett, D. J., Gee, N. R., Schreiber, T. A., & McKinney, V. M. (1993). Implicit memory: Effects of network size and interconnectivity on cued recall. *Journal of Experimental Psychology: Learning, Memory, and Cognition, 19*(4), 747–764.

Nelson, D. L., Bennett, D. J., & Leibert, T. W. (1997). One step is not enough: Making better use of association norms to predict cued recall. *Memory and Cognition, 25,* 785–796.

Nelson, D. L., & McEvoy, C. L. (2000). What is this thing called frequency? *Memory and Cognition, 28*(4), 509–522.

Nelson, D. L., McEvoy, C. L., & Schreiber, T. A. (2004). The University of South Florida free association, rhyme, and word fragment norms. *Behavior Research Methods, Instruments and Computers, 36*(3), 402–407.

Nelson, D. L., McKinney, V. M., Gee, N. R., & Janczura, G. A. (1998). Interpreting the influence of implicitly activated memories on recall and recognition. *Psychological Review, 105,* 299–324.

Nelson, D. L., & Zhang, N. (2000). The ties that bind what is known to the recall of what is new. *Psychonomic Bulletin and Review, 7*(4), 604–617.

Nelson, D. L., Zhang, N., & McKinney, V. M. (2001). The ties that bind what is known to the recognition of what is new. *Journal of Experimental Psychology: Learning, Memory, and Cognition, 27*(5), 1147–1159.

Raaijmakers, J. G. W., & Shiffrin, R. M. (1980). SAM: A theory of probabilistic search of associative memory. In G. H. Bower (Ed.), *The psychology of learning and motivation: Advances in research and theory* (Vol. 14, p. 207–262). New York: Academic Press.

Roberts, W. A. (1972). Free recall of word lists varying in length and rate of presentation: A test of total-time hypotheses. *Journal of Experimental Psychology, 92,* 365–372.

Romney, A. K., Brewer, D. D., & Batchelder, W. H. (1993). Predicting clustering from semantic structure. *Psychological Science, 4,* 28–34.

Schwartz, R. M., & Humphreys, M. S. (1973). Similarity judgments and free recall of unrelated words. *Journal of Experimental Psychology, 101,* 10–15.

Steyvers, M., & Malmberg, K. J. (2003). The effect of normative context variability on recognition memory. *Journal of Experimental Psychology: Learning, Memory, and Cognition, 29*(5), 760–766.

Steyvers, M., Shiffrin, R. M., & Nelson, D. L. (2004). Word association spaces for predicting semantic similarity effects in episodic memory. In A. Healy (Ed.), *Experimental cognitive psychology and its applications: Festschrift in honor of Lyle Bourne, Walter Kintsch, and Thomas Landauer* (pp. 237–249). Washington, DC: American Psychological Association.

Tehan, G., & Humphreys, M. S. (1996). Cuing effects in short-term recall. *Memory and Cognition, 24*(6), 719–732.

Tulving, E. (1966). Subjective organization and effects of repetition in multi-trial free-recall learning. *Journal of Verbal Learning and Verbal Behavior, 5*(2), 193–197.

Tulving, E. (1983). *Elements of episodic memory.* New York: Oxford University Press.

Tulving, E. (2002). Episodic memory: From mind to brain. *Annual Review of Psychology, 53,* 1–25.

Zaromb, F. M., Howard, M. W., Dolan, E. D., Sirotin, Y. B., Tully, M., Wingfield, A., et al. (in press). Temporally-based false memories in fee recall. *Journal of Experimental Psychology: Learning, Memory, and Cognition.*

8

A Semantic Space for Modeling Children's Semantic Memory

Guy Denhière
Université de Provence

Benoît Lemaire
Université de Grenoble

Cédrick Bellissens
University of Memphis

Sandra Jhean-Larose
IUFM de Paris, and Université de Vincennes

In contrast to many LSA semantic spaces in the literature, which are based on domain-specific corpora, we chose to build a general child corpus intended to model children's semantic memory (Denhière, Lemaire, Bellissens, & Jhean-Larose, 2004), and to offer a layer of basic semantic associations on top of which computational models of children's cognitive processes can be designed and simulated (Lemaire, Denhière, Bellissens, & Jhean-Larose, in press).

DEVELOPMENTAL DATA

We possess little direct information on the nature and the properties of the semantic memory of the children from 7 to 11 years old (Cycowicz, 2000; De Marie & Ferron, 2003; Howe & Courage, 2003; Murphy, McKone, & Slee, 2003; Towse, Hitch, & Hutton, 2002). However, we can refer to studies relating to the vocabulary acquisition for this period of cognitive development to build an approximation of children's semantic memory and to work out a corpus corresponding roughly to oral and written linguistic materials that a 7- to 11-year-old child is exposed to (Lambert & Chesnet, 2002; Lété, Springer-Charolles, & Colé, 2004).

From a theoretical point of view, the question: "How do children learn the meaning of words?" has received different kinds of answers. Bloom (2000) argued that the mind does not have a module for language acquisition and the processes of association and imitation are not sufficient to explain word learning that requires rich mental capacities: conceptual, social, and linguistic, which interact in complicated ways. As Gillette, Gleitman, Gleitman, and Lederer (1999, p. 171) pointed out, "lexical, and syntactic knowledge in the child, far from developing as separate components of an acquisition procedure, interact with each other, and with the observed world in a complex, mutually supportive, series of bootstrapping operations." In connectionist modeling of language acquisition (see Elman, 2004; Shultz, 2003), Li, Farkas, and Mac Whinney (2004) developed DevLex, a self-organizing neural network model of the development of the lexicon, designed to combine the dynamic learning properties of connectionist networks with the scalability of representive models such as HAL (Burgess & Lund, 1997) or LSA (Landauer & Dumais, 1997). Finally, as Louwerse and Ventura (2005) emphasized, children likely do not learn the meaning of words through learning words, but through different forms of discourse, and by understanding their relation in context. In consequence, these authors assume that "LSA is how all language processing works, and that LSA can be considered a model of how children learn the meaning of words" (p. 302). From these points of view, whatever the complexity of the processes implicated in language acquisition, it should be possible to reproduce different states of meaning acquisition by estimating two things: the mean normative vocabulary of children, and the written data to which children are exposed. Then it should be possible to construct corpora trained in a model that take into account complex interaction of usage contexts.

One has estimated the quantitative aspects of vocabulary development. Landauer and Dumais (1997) wrote that "it has been estimated that the average fifth-grade child spends about 15 minutes per day reading in school, and another 15 out of school reading books, magazines, mail, and comic books (Anderson, Wilson, & Fielding, 1988; Taylor, Frye, & Maruyama,

1990). If we assume 30 minutes per day total for 150 school days, and 15 minutes per day for the rest of the year, we get an average of 21 minutes per day. At an average reading speed of 165 words per minute, which may be an overestimate of natural, casual rates, and a nominal paragraph length of 70 words, they read about 2.5 paragraphs per minute, and about 50 per day" (p. 217).

Ehrlich, Bramaud du Boucheron, and Florin (1978) estimated the mean vocabulary of two French children (n = 538) in four scholar grades (from second through fifth), and from four social and economic classes (senior executives, medium ranking executives, employees, and workers) by using a judgment task of lexical knowledge (scaled in five levels, from "never heard" to "I know that word very well, and I use it frequently"), and a definition task ("tell all the senses of that word"). The verbal materials were made of 13,500 root words (63% substantives, 17% verbs, and 20% adjectives, and adverbs) assumed to be representative to a general adult vocabulary (first-year college students). Then, the 13,500 root words were judged by 150 adults on a five level scale, and the 2,700 better known and more frequently used words were taken to make part of the experimental materials submitted to children to test the extent of their vocabulary as a function of age and social and economic classes. The results showed that the number of totally unknown root words decreased by about 4,000 from second through fifth grade, the number of very well-known root words increased by only 900, and the number of medium known root words increased by about 3,000. According to the authors, the frequently used vocabulary does not vary so much over primary school grades, but children are learning a lot of new words that, for the most part, they are unlikely to use (Ehrlich et al., 1978). The meaning knowledge level of substantives and verbs were equivalent whatever the age of the children, and were higher than knowledge level of adjectives and adverbs. Finally, the mean vocabulary was larger for favored classes (i.e., a mean difference of 600 words between the two extreme classes), and these differences kept the same over the four scholar grades. Moreover, after the results from the definition task, the vocabulary of the children was enriched by approximately 1,000 root words each school grade, with the increase from second through fifth grade at about 3,000 (Ehrlich et al., 1978).

More recently, Biemiller (2001, 2003; Biemiller & Slonim, 2001) presented results that confirmed most of the pioneer results of Ehrlich et al. (1978). In short, Biemiller and Slonim (2001), referring to the Dale and O'Rourke's Living Word Vocabulary (1981), estimated that in the second grade the mean normative vocabulary was 5,200 root words, increasing to approximately 8,400 root words by fifth grade. This reflects acquiring about 2.2 words per day from ages 1 through 8 (end of grade two), and 2.4 words per day from ages 9 through 12. In other words, an average child learns between 800 and 900 root words a year, a figure that is close to the one obtained by Anglin (1993).

There is evidence that the vocabulary is acquired in largely the same order by most children. Biemiller et al. (2001) found that when vocabulary data are ordered by children's vocabulary levels rather than their grade level, they can clearly identify ranges of words *known well* (above 75%), words *being acquired* (known between 25%, and 74%), and words *little known*. At any given point in vocabulary acquisition, a child is likely to be learning root words from about 2,000 to 3,000 words in a sequence of from13,000 to 15,000 words. This makes the construction of a "vocabulary curriculum" plausible. Unfortunately, although these findings imply the existence of a well-defined sequence of word acquisition, a complete sequential listing of the 13,000–15,000 root words expected at the level of 12th grade cannot now be furnished (for more details, see Biemiller, 2003, 2005).

OUR CORPUS

Various kinds of written data children are exposed to have to be represented in our corpus. We gathered texts for a total of 3.2 million words. We could have gathered many more texts, but we are concerned with cognitive plausibility. Our goal was to build a semantic space that reproduces as close as possible the verbal performances of a 7- to 11-year-old child. Moreover, we are not only concerned with mimicking the representation of the semantic memory, but also its development, from raw written data to the semantic representation of words. Therefore, the type and size of the input are important factors.

Children are exposed to various kinds of written data: storybooks, schoolbooks, encyclopedias, and so on. It is very hard to estimate the proportion of each source to the total exposure to print. Actually, the main problem is that children have been exposed to language long before they can read: They learn the meaning of some words through exposure to speech, not to mention the perceptual input. This is a well-known limitation of LSA (Glenberg & Robertson, 2000), but it is less of a problem with adult corpora. Indeed, the proportion of words learned from reading is much higher for adults than for children. Therefore, we need to take this problem into account in the design of child corpora by trying to mimic this kind of input. We could have used spoken language intended for children, but these kinds of data are less formal than written language and thus harder to process. We ended up by gathering children's productions, a kind of language that is closer to basic spoken language than stories or textbooks. In addition, we decreased the significance of textbooks, and the encyclopedia, because these sources of information affect the children's knowledge base after they have learned to read. Altogether, the child corpus consists of stories and folktales written for children (~1. 6 million words), children's own written productions (~800,000 words), reading text-books (~400,000 words), and a children's encyclopedia (~400,000 words).

The size of the corpus is another important factor. It is very hard to estimate how many words we process every day. It is not easy to estimate this number from the literature because, as we mentioned earlier, most studies are based either on just root words or on the number of words children know, and not those to which they were exposed. Then, according to Landauer and Dumais' (1997) estimate, we consider a relevant corpus size to be tens of millions of words for adults, and several million words for children around 10 years of age. The size of the corpus we are presenting in this chapter is 3.2 million words. After processing this corpus by LSA, we compared it with human data.

COMPARISON OF SEMANTIC SIMILARITIES WITH HUMAN DATA

In order to validate the specific child semantic space *Textenfants*, we used four more additionally constraining tests: association norms, semantic judgments, a vocabulary test, and memory tasks. First, we investigated whether our semantic space could account for word associations produced by children who were provided with words varying in familiarity. Therefore, the first test compares the performances of *Textenfants* on French verbal association norms recently published by de La Haye (2003). Second, we compared the performances of *Textenfants* with second- and fifth-grade children's judgments of semantic similarity between couples of words extracted from stories. Third, we tested whether our semantic space is able to represent definitions. Like Landauer et al. (1998) did with the TOEFL test, we compared LSA scores to performances of four groups of children. The task consisted in choosing the correct definition from a set of four definitions (correct, close, distant, and unrelated). We believe that this test is more constraining than the first one because definitions could be either words, phrases, or sentences, but no dictionary was part of this corpus. Fourth, we used the semantic space to assess the children's performances of recall and summarization. We revisited results of nine prior experiments, and compared the number of propositions recalled to the cosine measure between the source text, and the text produced by each participant. To the extent that these are correlated, *Textenfants* can be used to assess verbal protocols without resorting to the tedious propositional analysis.

Association Norms

The first experiment is based on verbal association norms (de La Haye, 2003). Because previous results are based on children from grades 2 to 5, our interest here concerns the 9-year-old norms. Two-hundred stimulus printed words (144 nouns, 28 verbs, and 28 adjectives) were provided to 100 9-year-old children. For each word, participants had to write down the first word that came to their mind. The result is a list of words, ranked by frequency. For instance, given the word *eau* (*water*), results are the following:

- boire (*drink*): 22%
- mer (*sea*): 8%
- piscine (*swimming pool*): 7%
- ...
- vin (*wine*): 1%
- froid (*cold*): 1%
- poisson (*fish*): 1%

This means that 22% of the 9-year-old children provided the word *boire* (*drink*) when given the word *eau* (*water*). This value can be used as a measure of the strength of the association between the two words. These association values were compared with the LSA cosine between word vectors: We selected the three highest ranked words, as well as the three lowest ranked (vin, froid, poisson in the previous example). We then measured the cosines between the stimulus, and the highest ranked, the second highest, the third highest, and the mean cosine between the stimulus word, and the three lowest ranked. Results are presented in Table 8.1.

Student *t*-tests show that all differences are significant ($p < .05$). This means that our semantic space is not only able to distinguish between the strong and weak associates, but can also discriminate the first ranked from the second ranked, and the latter from the third ranked.

The correlation with human data is also significant, $r(1,184) = .39, p < .01$. Actually, two factors might have decreased this value. First, although we tried to mimic what a child has been exposed to, we could not control the frequencies with which each word occurred in the corpus. Therefore, some words might have occurred with a low frequency, leading to an inaccurate

TABLE 8.1
Mean Cosine Between Stimulus Word and Various Associates
for 9-Year-Old Children

Words	Mean Cosine With Stimulus Word
Highest-ranked words	.26
2nd highest-ranked words	.23
3rd highest-ranked words	.19
3 lowest-ranked words	.11

semantic representation. When the previous comparison was performed on the 20% of words with lower LSA weights (those words for which LSA has the most knowledge), the correlation was much higher, $r(234) = .57, p < .01$.

The second factor is the agreement among participants: When most children provide the same answer to a stimulus word, there is high agreement, which means that both words are very strongly associated. However, there are cases when there is almost no agreement: For instance, the first three answers to the word *bruit* (*noise*) are *crier* (*to shout;* 9%), *entendre* (*to hear;* 7%), and *silence* (*silence;* 6%). It is not surprising that the model corresponds better to the children's data in case of a high agreement, because this denotes a strong association that should be reflected in the corpus.

In order to select answers whose agreement was higher, we measured their entropy. When we selected 20% of the items with the lowest entropy, the correlation increased, $r(234) = .48, p < .001$.

We also compared these results with the several adult semantic spaces, a literature corpus, and four French newspaper corpora. Results are presented in Table 8.2. Despite much larger sizes, all adult semantic spaces correlate worse than the children's semantic space with the data of the participants in the study. Statistical tests show that all differences between the children model and the other semantic spaces are significant ($p < .03$). All these results show that the degree of association between words defined by the cosine measure within the semantic space seems to correspond quite well to children's judgments of association.

Semantic Judgments

A second test consisted of comparing *TextEnfants* with two groups of 45 children's results (Grade 3 vs. Grade 5) in a semantic distance judgment task. We asked participants to judge on a 5-point scale the semantic similar-

TABLE 8.2
Correlations Between Participant Child Data and Different Kinds of Semantic Spaces

Semantic Space	Size (in Million Words)	Correlation With Children Data
Children	3.2	.39
Literature	14.1	.34
Le Monde (1993)	19.3	.31
Le Monde (1995)	20.6	.26
Le Monde (1997)	24.7	.26
Le Monde (1999)	24.2	.24

ity between two words extracted from a story used in the Diagnos™ tests (Baudet & Denhière, 1989). For each of the seven stories selected, all the possible noun-noun couples were constructed ("giant-woman," "forest-woman," "house-woman," etc.), and had to be judged. For each couple, we obtained an average similarity value for each grade that we compared with LSA cosines for the two words of the couples. The judgments were significantly correlated between the two groups of children (ranged from .80 to .95 as function of stories), and correlations between LSA cosines, and as shown in Table 8.3, children's judgments were significant for all but one ("Giant" story).

In conclusion, the degree of association between words (test 1), and the semantic distance between concepts (test 2), defined by the cosine measure within the semantic space *TextEnfants* fit quite well to children's productions and judgments.

Vocabulary Test

The third experiment is based on a vocabulary test composed of 120 questions (Denhière, Thomas, Bourguet, & Legros, 1999). Each question is composed of a word and four definitions: the correct one, a close definition, a distant definition, and an unrelated definition. For instance, given the word *pente* (*slope*), translations of the four definitions are:

- Tilted surface which goes up or down (correct).
- Rising road (close).
- Vertical face of a rock or a mountain (distant).
- Small piece of ground (unrelated).

TABLE 8.3
Correlations Between LSA Cosines and Children's Semantic Similarity
Judgments

Texts	Grade 3	Grade 5	Couples (N)
Giant	.22	.21	66
Donkey	.24*	.22*	105
Truck	.28*	.25*	66
Chamois	.34*	.40**	55
Clowns	.48**	.50**	56
Lion	.55**	.63**	66
Bear cub	.55**	.58**	91

*p < .05, **p < .01.

Participants were asked to select what they thought was the correct definition. This task was performed by four groups of 30 children from second, third, fourth, and fifth grades. These data were compared with the cosines between a given word, and each of the four definitions. Altogether, 116 questions were used because the semantic space did not contain four rarely occurring words.

Figure 8.1 displays the average percentage of correct, close, distant, and unrelated answers for the second and fifth grades. The first measure we used was the percentage of correct answers. It is .53 for the model, which is exactly the same value as for the second-grade children. Except for unrelated answers, the model data generally follow the same pattern as the children's data. When restricted to the 99 items that LSA had encountered frequently in the corpus (weight < .70), results of the model fall in-between the percent correct for second and third-grade children.

We also investigated a possible effect of corpus lemmatization. French uses more word forms than English. This fact could reduce the power of LSA because there might be less opportunity to encounter relevant contexts. Replacing all words by their lemma could therefore improve the representation of word meaning: Instead of having N_1 paragraphs with word P_1, N_2 paragraphs with word P_2, ... N_p paragraphs with word P_n, we could have $N_1 + N_2 + ... + N_p$ paragraphs with word P, which could be better from a statistical point of view. All forms of a verb are therefore represented by its infinitive, all forms of a noun by its nominative singular, and so forth. We used the Brill tagger on French files developed by the CNRS–ATILF laboratory at Nancy, France, as

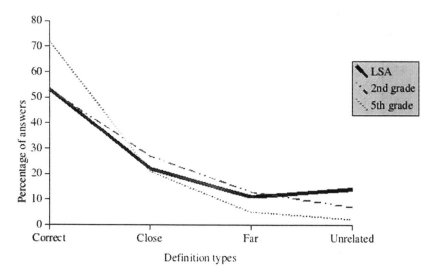

Figure 8.1.   Percentage of answers for children and model data.

well as the Namer lemmatizer. However, results were worse than before when all words were lemmatized. Verb lemmatization also resulted in no improvement. Hence, lemmatization proved to be of no help in the present case.

Then, we modified the lemmatizer in order to lemmatize only verbs, and found better results, almost exactly corresponding to the second-grade data. This can be due to the fact that verb lemmatization groups together forms that have the same meaning. However, the different forms of a noun do not have exactly the same meaning. For instance, *flower* and *flowers* are not arguments of the same predicates. In our semantic space, the cosine between *rose* and *flower* is .51, whereas the cosine between *rose* and *flowers* is only .14. *Flower* and *flowers* do not occur in the exact same contexts. Another example can be given from the neighbors of *bike* and *bikes*. First, three neighbors of *bike* are *handlebar*, *brakes*, and *pedals*, whereas the first three neighbors of *bikes* are *motorbikes*, *trucks*, and *cars*. *Bike* and *bikes* do not occur either in the same contexts. Therefore, representing them by the same form probably confuses LSA.

Memory Tasks

The last experiment is based on recall or summary tasks (Thomas, 1999). Three groups of children (mean age of 8.3 years old), and six groups of adolescents (between 16 and 18 years old) were asked to read a text and write out as much as they could recall, immediately after reading or after a fixed delay of one week. For three of these groups, participants were asked to write a summary. We used seven texts. We tested the ability of the semantic representations to estimate the amount of knowledge recalled. This amount is classically estimated by means of a propositional analysis: First, the text as well as each participant production are coded as propositions. Then, the number of text propositions that occur in the production is calculated. This measure is a good estimate of the information recalled from the text. Using our semantic memory model, this amount of recall is given by the cosine between the vector representing the text, and the vector representing the participant production.

Table 8.4 displays all correlations between these two measures. They are all significant ($< .05$), and range from .45 to .92, which means that the LSA cosine applied to our children's semantic space provides a good estimate of the text information recalled, whatever the memory task, recall or summary, and the delay.

In an experiment with adults, Foltz (1996) has shown that LSA measures can be used to predict comprehension. Besides validating our model of semantic memory, this experiment shows that an appropriate semantic space can be used to assess text comprehension more quickly than propositional analysis, which is a very tedious task.

TABLE 8.4
Correlations Between LSA Cosines and Number of Propositions Recalled for
Different Texts

Texts	Task	Number of Participants	Correlations
Hen	Immediate recall	52	.45
Dragon	Delayed recall	44	.55
Dragon	Summary	56	.71
Spider	Immediate recall	41	.65
Clown	Immediate recall	56	.67
Clown	Summary	24	.92
Bear cub	Immediate recall	44	.62
Bull	Delayed recall	23	.69

CORPUS STRATIFICATION FOR DEVELOPMENTAL STUDIES

The corpus presented so far contains the kind of texts a child is exposed to, but it does not reproduce the order in which texts are processed over a child's life. Actually, it would be very valuable to have a corpus in which paragraphs are sorted according to the age they are intended for, which would make it possible to obtain a corpus for virtually any age. Comparing the model of semantic memory (or any processing model based on it) with data from children would be much more precise. In addition, it would then be possible to simulate the development of semantic memory.

We proceeded in two steps: First, we gathered more texts that were intended for a specific age and, second, we sorted every paragraph of each category according to a readability measure.

Gathering Texts for Specific Age

We defined four age levels: 4–7, 7–11, 11–18, and adults (over 18). The goal was to build a well-rounded semantic space that includes lexical, encyclopedic, and factual information. Lexical information is given by dictionaries. Encyclopedic information is provided by handbooks and encyclopedia. Factual information is obtained from stories and novels. For each age level, we therefore collected French texts in each of the following categories: children's written productions, dictionary, encyclopedia, textbooks, and stories or novels. Each level is included in the next one. Level 1 is therefore composed of productions from 4- to 7-year-old children, a dictionary, an encyclopedia, first-grade reading textbooks, and stories for 4- to 7-year-old children. Level 2 is composed of all the texts of level 1, plus productions from 7- to 11-year-old children, a dictionary, an encyclopedia, reading texts, and stories for 7- to 11-year-old children, and so on. For adults, the daily newspaper *Le Monde* was used in place of textbooks.

Sorting Paragraphs According to a Readability Measure

In order to be more precise, all paragraphs of a given level were sorted according to the age they best correspond to. We relied on a readability measure defined by Mesnager (1989, 2002), which has been carefully standardized. This measure is based on the percentage of difficult words and the mean length of sentences. Difficult words are those that are not part of a list of 32,000 French common words. We computed the readability measure for every paragraph of each category. As a rough test, we found that for each information source, the mean measure for level N was higher than the mean measure for level $N - 1$, *which is satisfactory.*

APPLICATIONS OF THE MODEL OF SEMANTIC MEMORY

This section presents two applications of this model of semantic memory. The first one consists of comparing the relationships between co-occurrence frequency and LSA similarities. The second one aims at linking this model of semantic memory to a model of comprehension based on the construction-integration model designed by Kintsch (1988, 1998).

Studying the Development of Semantic Similarities

The semantic similarity of two words (or, stated differently, their associative strength) is classically reduced to their frequency of co-occurrence in language: The more frequently two words appear together, the higher their similarity. This shortcut is used as a quick way of estimating word similarity, for example, in order to control the material of an experiment, but it also has an explanatory purpose: People tend to judge two words as similar because they were exposed to them simultaneously. Undoubtedly, the frequency of co-occurrence is correlated with human judgments of similarity (Spence & Owens, 1990). However, several researchers have questioned this simple relation (Bellissens & Denhière, 2002; Burgess, Livesay, & Lund, 1998). The goal of this simulation is to use our semantic space to study the relation between co-occurrence and similarity.

An ideal method to study the relation between co-occurrence and similarity would consist of collecting all of the texts subjects have been exposed to and then comparing their judgments of similarity with the co-occurrence parameters of these text—a task that is obviously impossible. One could think of a more controlled experiment by asking participants to complete similarity tests before and after text exposure. The problem is that the mental construction of similarities through reading is a long-term cognitive process, which would probably not be apparent over a short period. It is also possible to count co-occurrences in representative corpora, but that would give only a global indication a posteriori. Thus, we would learn nothing about the direct effect of a given first- or second-order co-occurrence on semantic similarity. It is useful to know precisely the effect of direct and high-order co-occurrences during word acquisition. Assume a person X who has been exposed to a huge set of texts since learning to read. Let S be the judgment of similarity of X between words W1 and W2. The questions we are interested in are:

- What is the effect on S of X reading a passage containing W1 but not W2?
- What is the effect on S of X reading a passage containing W1, and W2?
- What is the effect on S of X reading a passage containing neither W1 nor W2, but words co-occurring with W1 and W2 (second-order co-occurrence)?
- What is the effect on S of X reading a passage containing neither W1 nor W2, but third-order co-occurring words?

Our simulation follows the evolution of the semantic similarities of 28 pairs of words over a large number of paragraphs, according to the occurrence values. We started with a corpus size of 2,000 paragraphs. We added one paragraph, ran LSA on this 2001-paragraph corpus, and, for each pair, computed the gain (positive or negative) of semantic similarity due to the new paragraph, and checked whether there were occurrences, direct co-occurrences, or high-order co-occurrences of the two words in the new paragraph. We then added another paragraph, ran LSA on the 2002-paragraph corpus, and so on. Each new paragraph was simply the following one in the original corpus. More precisely, for each pair X-Y, we put each new paragraph into one of the following categories:

- Occurrence of X but not Y.
- Occurrence of Y but not X.
- Direct co-occurrence of X and Y.
- Second-order co-occurrence of X and Y, defined as the presence of at least three words that co-occur at least once with both X and Y in the current corpus.
- Third-or-more-order co-occurrence, which forms the remainder (no occurrence of X or Y, no direct co-occurrence, no second-order co-oc-

currence). This category represents three-or-more co-occurrences because paragraphs whose words are completely neutral with X and Y
(i.e., they are not linked to them by a high-order co-occurrence relation) do not modify the X-Y semantic similarity.

We stopped the computation at the 13,637th paragraph. A total of 11,637
paragraphs were thus traced. This experiment took 3 weeks of computation
on a 2 GHz computer with 1.5 Gb of RAM. As an example, Figure 8.2 describes the evolution of similarity for the two words *acheter (buy)* and
magasin (shop). This similarity is −.07 at paragraph 2,000, and increases to
.51 at paragraph 13,637. The curve is quite irregular: There are some sudden
increases and decreases. Our next goal was to identify the reasons for these
variations.

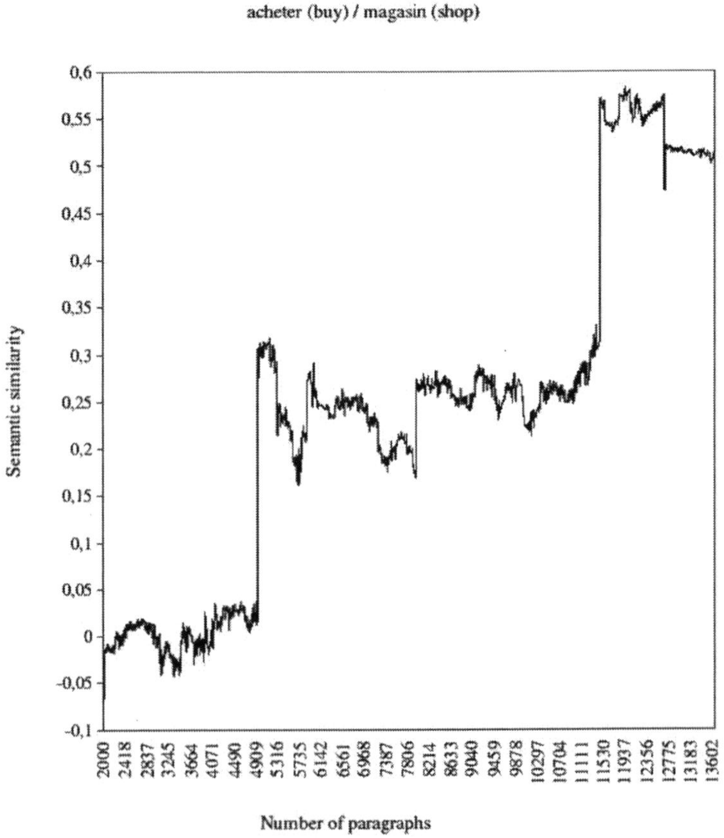

Figure 8.2. Similarity between *acheter (buy)* and *magasin (shop)* as a function of the
number of paragraphs in the corpus.

For each pair of words, we partialed out the gains of similarity among the different categories. For instance, if the similarity between X and Y was .13 for the 5,000-paragraph corpus, and .15 for the 5,001-paragraph corpus, we attributed the .02 gain in similarity to one of the five previous categories. We then summed up all gains for each category. Because the sum of the 11,637 gains in similarity is exactly the difference between the last similarity and the first one, we ended up with a distribution of the total gain in similarity among all categories. For instance, for the pair *acheter (buy)-magasin (shop)*, the .58 [.51 – (–.07)] total gain in similarity is partialed out in the following way: –.10 due to occurrences of only *acheter (buy)*, –.19 due to occurrences of only *magasin (shop)*, .73 due to the co-occurrences, .11 due to second-order co-occurrences, .03 due to third-or-more-order co-occurrences.

This means that the paragraphs containing only *acheter (buy)* contributed all together to a decrease in similarity of .10. This is probably due to the fact that these occurrences occur in a context that is different to the *magasin (shop)* context. In the same way, occurrences of *magasin (shop)* led to a decrease in the overall similarity. Co-occurrences tend to increase the similarity, which is expected, and high-order co-occurrences contribute also to an increase.

We performed the same measurement for all 28 pairs of words. These pairs were selected from the 200 items of the association task presented earlier, and their first-ranked associated word, as provided by children. We kept only words that appeared at least once in the first 2,000 paragraphs in order to have the same number of semantic similarities for all pairs. Average results are the following: –.15 due to occurrences of the first word, –.19 due to occurrences of the second word, .34 due to the co-occurrences, .05 due to second-order co-occurrences, .09 due to third-or-more-order co-occurrences.

First of all, we found pairs of words that never co-occur [e.g., *farine(flour)-gâteau(cake)*], even though their semantic similarity increases. Another result is that, except in a few cases, the gain in similarity due to a co-occurrence is higher than the total gain in similarity. This result occurs because of a decrease due to occurrences of only one of the two words (–.15, and –.19). In addition, high-order co-occurrences play a small but significant role: They tend to increase the similarity (.14 in total).

Modeling Text Comprehension on the Basis of the Semantic Memory Model

In a second application, we use our semantic memory model as a component of a fully automatic model of text comprehension, based on the construction-integration model (CI; Kintsch, 1998), a predication mechanism (Kintsch, 2001), and a model of the episodic buffer. This model is implemented in a Perl program that takes as input a text divided into propositions (Lemaire, Denhière, Bellissens, & Jhean, in press). Figure 8.3 shows the general architecture.

Let us explain the flow of information, which is an operational approximation of the CI model. Each proposition is considered in turn. First, the LSA semantic space (also called semantic memory) is used to provide terms that are semantically similar to the propositions and their components, thus simulating the process by which we automatically activate word associates in memory while reading. A fixed number of associates is provided for the predicate, but also for each of the arguments. For instance, given the proposition *carry(truck, food)* corresponding to the sentence *The truck is carrying bikes*, our semantic space provides the terms *transport, kilometers,* and *travel* for the proposition, the terms *car, garage,* and *vehicle* for the argument *truck,* and the terms *motorbikes, trucks,* and *cars* for the argument *bikes.* Associates for the arguments are simply the terms whose cosine with the arguments in the semantic space is higher. Associates for the predicate require a bit more calculation because only those that are close enough (beyond a

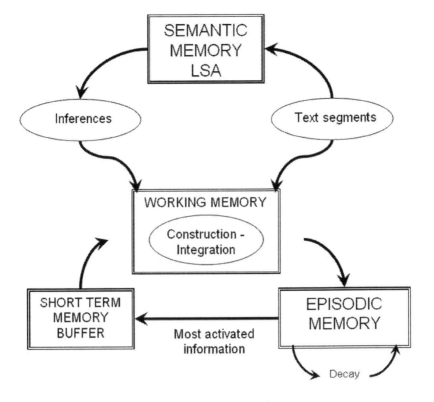

Figure 8.3.   Architecture of the model of text comprehension.

given threshold) to at least one of the arguments are kept. This algorithm comes from Kintsch's predication model (Kintsch, 2001). In our example, the three associates *transport, kilometers,* and *travel* were kept because they are similar enough to the *truck* or *bikes.*

Not all associates are relevant within the context, but this is not a problem because the next phase will rule out those that are not related to the current topic. Actually, all the terms in working memory (none for the first sentence) are added to the current proposition, and all its associates. As we will explain later, relevant propositions coming from episodic memory can also be added. All of these terms and propositions are processed by the construction/integration phase of Kintsch's model. The LSA semantic space is used once more to compute the similarity weights of links between all pairs of terms or propositions. For instance, the weight of *truck/bikes* is . 67, the weight of *carry(truck, bikes)/travel* is .16, and so on. Next, a specific spreading activation mechanism is used to give activation values to terms according to the weight of their connection with other terms. Those that are the most strongly linked to other terms will receive high activation values. For instance, the term *garage* in the previous example is weakly linked to all other terms or propositions. Therefore, this term will be given a low association value and will be dropped out.

The most highly activated items are stored in working memory. Three strategies are available: a fixed number of items is selected, following Baddeley's model (2000); or a maximum sum of activation is defined, which is distributed among the items (Just & Carpenter, 1992); or only those items whose activation values are above a given threshold are selected.

Selected elements will be added later to the next proposition and its associates. They are also stored in episodic memory. This memory is the list of all terms or propositions already encountered, either because they were part of text propositions, or because they were provided by semantic memory as associates. Terms or propositions are attached to an activation value in episodic memory. This value is initially their activation value in working memory, but a decay function lowers this value over time. This activation value is increased each time a new occurrence of a term or proposition is stored in episodic memory. Both values are then combined according to functions we will not explain here. What is important is that elements in episodic memory can be recalled by the construction phase in case they are similar enough to the current proposition. The semantic space is then used once more to compute similarities and to decide whether or not elements in episodic memory are recalled. This last process simulates the fact that there was a digression in the text, leading to the fact that the previous propositions were dropped out from working memory. When the digression ends, these propositions will be recalled from episodic memory because they will be similar again to the current propositions. However, if the digression lasts too long, the decay function will have greatly lowered the activation values of the first propositions, and they will not be recalled any more.

Here is an English translation of a simulation we performed with the children semantic space *Textenfants*. Consider the following text: *The gardener is growing his roses. Suddenly, a cat meows. The man throws a flower at it.*

The First Proposition Is Grow (Gardener, Roses).   Terms that are neighbors of *grow* but also close to *gardener* or *roses* are: *vegetable, vegetables, radish.* Neighbors of *gardener* are: *garden, border, kitchen garden* (one word in French). Neighbors of *roses* are: *flowers, bouquet, violets.* LSA similarities between all pairs of words are computed. After the integration step, working memory is:

- *grow (gardener, roses)* (1.00)
- *grow* (.850)
- *gardener* (.841)
- *border* (.767)
- *garden* (.743)
- *roses* (.740)
- *flowers* (.726)

The Second Proposition Is Meow (Cat).   Because the second sentence is not related to the first one, no terms appear to be gathered from episodic memory. Terms that are neighbors of *meow* but also close to *cat* are: *meows, purr.* Neighbors of *cat* are *meow, meows, miaow.* They are added to working memory. LSA similarities between all pairs of words are computed. After the integration step, working memory is:

- *meow* (cat) (1.00)
- *grow (gardener, roses)* (.967)
- *cat* (.795)
- *meow* (.776)

All terms related to the first sentence (*border, garden,* . . .) were removed from working memory, because the second sentence is not related to the first one. However, the entire proposition is still there.

The Third Proposition Is Throw (Man, Flower).   *Flowers, bouquet, roses,* and *violets* are back to working memory, because they are close to the argument *flower.* Terms that are neighbors of *throw* but also close to *man* or *flower* are: *command, send, Jack. Man* is too frequent for providing good neighbors; therefore, the program did not consider it. Neighbors of *flower* are: *petals, pollen, tulip.* LSA similarities between all pairs of words are computed. After the integration step, working memory is:

- *flower* (1.00)
- *flowers* (.979)
- *petals* (.978)
- *grow(gardener, roses)* (.975)
- *roses* (.974)
- *violets* (.932)
- *bouquet* (.929)
- *throw(man, flower)* (.917)
- *tulip* (.843)
- *pollen* (.832)

To sum up, the LSA semantic space is used three times: first, to provide associates to the current proposition and its arguments; second, to compute the weights of links in the construction phase; and, third, to compute similarities between the current proposition and the episodic memory items for their possible reactivation in working memory.
The main parameters of that model are:

- The minimal and maximal weight thresholds for terms, in order to only consider terms for which LSA has enough knowledge.
- The number of associates provided by the LSA semantic space.
- The similarity threshold for the predication algorithm.
- The strategy for selecting items in working memory after the integration step.
- The decay, and updating functions of episodic memory.

This program can be used with any semantic space, but, when combined with the semantic space described in this chapter, it should be very useful for the study of children's text comprehension.

CONCLUSIONS

This chapter presented a semantic space that is designed to represent children's semantic memory. It is based on a multisource corpus composed of stories and tales, children's productions, reading textbooks, and a children's encyclopedia. Our goal is to build a general semantic space as opposed to domain-specific ones. Results of the four tests we performed (comparison with association norms, semantic judgments, vocabulary test, recall, and summary tasks) are promising (Denhière & Lemaire, 2004). The next step is to simulate the development of this semantic memory in order to reproduce developmental changes in performance on these tests among children from ages 4 to 7 years old to adolescence. One of the goals would be to reproduce the effect of prior knowledge on text comprehension

(Caillies, Denhière, & Jhean-Larose, 1999; Caillies, Denhière, & Kintsch, 2002). The semantic space we constructed was linked to a comprehension model derived from the construction-integration model (Kintsch, 1998). Like the CI model, our model uses semantic memory to activate the closest neighbors of the current concept or proposition, to select the most relevant elements, and to keep the most activated in working memory. In addition, several models of short-term memory are implemented, and an episodic buffer is used to store ongoing information and provide relevant prior items to working memory. Our current work consists in adding a long-term working memory (Ericsson & Kintsch, 1995) and a generalization process of episodic memory traces (Bellissens, & Denhière, 2004; Denhière et al., 2004).

ACKNOWLEDGMENTS

The authors would like to thank Eileen Kintsch, Walter Kintsch, and an anonymous reviewer for their comments on a previous version of this chapter.

REFERENCES

Anderson, R. C., Wilson, P. T., & Fielding, L. G. (1988). Growth in reading, and how children spend their time outside of school. *Reading Research Quarterly, 23*, 285–303.

Anglin, J. M. (1993). Vocabulary development: A morphological analysis. *Monographs of the Society for Research in Child Development, 58*, 1–165.

Baddeley, A. D. (2000). The episodic buffer: A new component of working memory? *Trends in Cognitive Science, 4*, 417–423.

Bellissens, C., & Denhière, G. (2002). Word order or environment sharing: A comparison of two semantic memory models. *Current Psychology Letters, 9*, 43–60.

Bellissens, C., & Denhière, G. (2004). Retrieval structure construction during reading: Experimentation, and simulation. In K. Forbus, D. Gentner, & T. Regier (Eds.), *Proceedings of the 26th Annual Meeting of the Cognitive Science Society* (pp. 91–95). Mahwam, NJ: Lawrence Erlbaum Associates.

Biemiller, A. (2001). Teaching vocabulary. Early, direct, and sequential. *Perspectives, 26*, 15–26.

Biemiller, A. (2003). Vocabulary: Needed if more children are to read well. *Reading Psychology, 24*, 323–335.

Biemiller, A. (2005). Size, and sequence in vocabulary development: Implications for choosing words for primary grade vocabulary instruction. In A. Hiebert & M. Kamil (Eds.), *Teaching, and learning vocabulary: Bringing research to practice* (pp. 223–242). Mahwah, NJ: Lawrence Erlbaum Associates.

Biemiller, A., & Slonim, N. (2001). Estimating root word vocabulary growth in normative, and advantaged populations: Evidence for a common sequence of vocabulary acquisition. *Journal of Educational Psychology, 93*, 498–520.

Bloom, P. (2000). *How children learn the meanings of words.* Cambridge, MA: MIT Press.

Burgess, C., & Lund, K. (1997). Modeling parsing constraints with high dimensional context space. *Language and Cognitive Processes, 12,* 1–34.

Burgess, C., Livesay, K., & Lund, K. (1998). Explorations in context space: Word, sentences, discourse. *Discourse Processes, 25,* 211–257.

Caillies, S., Denhière, G., & Jhean-Larose, S. (1999). The intermediate effect: Interaction between prior knowledge, and text structure. In H. Van Oostendorp & S. R. Goldman (Eds), *The construction of mental representation during reading* (pp. 151–168). Mahwah, NJ: Lawrence Erlbaum Associates.

Caillies, S., Denhière, G., & Kintsch, W. (2002). The effect of prior knowledge on understanding from text: Evidence from primed recognition. *European Journal of Cognitive Psychology, 14,* 267–286.

Cycowicz, Y. M. (2000). Memory development, and event-related brain potential in children. *Biological Psychology, 54,* 145–174.

Dale, E., & O'Rourke, J. (1981). *The living word vocabulary.* Chicago: World Book/Childcraft International.

De La Haye, F. (2003). Normes d'association verbale chez des enfants de 9, 10 et 11 ans et des adultes [Verbal association norms for 9, 10, 11 year old children]. *L'Année Psychologique, 103,* 109–130.

DeMarie, D., & Ferron, J. (2003). Capacities, strategies, and metamemory: Tests of a three-factor model of memory development. *Journal of Experimental Child Psychology, 84,* 167–193.

Denhière, G., & Lemaire, B. (2004). A computational model of children's semantic memory. In K. Forbus, D. Gentner, & T. Regier (Eds.), *Proceedings of the 26th Annual Meeting of the Cognitive Science Society* (pp. 297–302). Mahwah, NJ: Lawrence Erlbaum Associates.

Denhière, G., Lemaire, B., Bellissens, C., & Jhean-Larose, S. (2004). Psychologie cognitive et compréhension de texte: Une démarche théorique et expérimentale [Cognitive psychology and text comprehension: A theoretical and experimental approach]. In S. Porhiel & D. Klingler (Eds.), *L'unité Texte* (pp. 74–95). Pleyben: Perspectives.

Denhière, G., Thomas, H., Bourget, M., & Legros, D. (1999). *Quatre savoirs fondamentaux à faire acquérir pour vaincre les illettrismes* [Acquiring four basic knowledge areas to overcome illiteracy]. Ministère de l'emploi et de la solidarité. Paris: GPLI.

Ehrlich, S., Bramaud du Boucheron, G., & Florin, A. (1978). *Le développement des connaissances lexicales à l'école primaire* [A lexical database for primary school children]. Paris: Presses Universitaires de France.

Elman, J. (2004). An alternative view of the mental lexicon. *Trends in Cognitive Science, 8,* 301–306.

Ericsson, K. A., & Kintsch, W. (1995). Long-term working memory. *Psychological Review, 102,* 211–245.

Foltz, P. W. (1996). Latent semantic analysis for text-based research. *Behavior Research Methods, Instruments, and Computers, 28,* 197–202.

Gillette, J., Gleitman, H., Gleitman, L., & Lederer, A. (1999). Human simulations of vocabulary learning. *Cognition, 73,* 135–176.

Glenberg, A. M., & Robertson, D. A. (2000). Symbol grounding, and meaning: A comparison of high-dimensional, and embodied theories of meaning. *Journal of Memory, and Language, 43,* 379–401.

Howe, M. L., & Courage, M. L. (2003). Demystifying the beginnings of memory. *Developmental Review, 3,* 17–21.

Just, M. A., & Carpenter, P. A. (1992). A capacity theory of comprehension: Individual differences in working memory. *Psychological Review, 99,* 122–149.

Kintsch, W. (1998). *Comprehension: A paradigm for cognition.* Cambridge, England: Cambridge University Press.

Kintsch, W. (2001). Predication. *Cognitive Science, 25,* 173–202.

Lambert, E., & Chesnet, D. (2002). NOVLEX: Une base de données lexicales pour les élèves du primaire [A lexical databasefor primary school children]. *L'Année Psychologique, 2,* 215–235.

Landauer, T. K., & Dumais, S. T. (1997). A solution to Plato's problem: The latent semantic analysis theory of the acquisition, induction, and representation of knowledge. *Psychological Review, 104,* 211–240.

Landauer, T. K., Foltz, P. W., & Laham, D. (1998). Introduction to latent semantic analysis. *Discourse Processes, 25,* 259–284.

Lemaire, B., Denhière, G., Bellissens, C., & Jhean-Larose, S. (in press) A computational model for simulating text comprehension, *Behavior Research Methods.*

Lété, B., Springer-Charolles, L., & Colé, P. (2004). MANULEX: A grade-level lexical database from french elementary-school readers. *Behavior Research Methods, Instruments, and Computers, 36,* 156–166.

Li, P., Farkas, I., & Mac Whinney, B. (2004). Early lexical development in a self-organizing neural network. *Neural Networks, 17,* 1345–1362.

Louwerse, M. M., & Ventura, M. (2005). How children learn the meaning of words, and how LSA does it (too). *Journal of the Learning Sciences, 14*(2), 301–309.

Mesnager, J. (1989). Lisibilité des livres pour enfants: Un nouvel outil? [Children's books readability: A new tool?] *Communications et Langage, 25,* 17–31.

Mesnager, J. (2002). Pour une étude de la difficulté des textes: la lisibilité revisitée [A study of text difficulty: Readability revisited]. *Le Français aujourd'hui, 137,* 29–42.

Murphy, K., McKone, E., & Slee, J. (2003). Dissociations between implicit, and explicit memory in children: The role of strategic processing, and the knowledge base. *Journal of Experimental Child Psychology, 84,* 124–165.

Shultz, T. (2003). *Computational developmental psychology.* Cambridge, MA: MIT Press.

Spence, D. P., & Owens, K. C. (1990). Lexical co-occurrence, and association strength. *Journal of Psycholinguistic Research, 19,* 317–330.

Taylor, B. M., Frye, B. J., & Maruyama, G. M. (1990). Time spent reading, and reading growth. *American Educational Research Journal, 27,* 351–362.

Thomas, H. (1999). *Diagnostic du fonctionnement cognitif, évaluation dynamique et remédiation. Pour une approche interdisciplinaire* [Diagnosis of cognitive operation, dynamic assessment and remediation: In need of an interdisciplinary approach]. Unpublished doctoral dissertation, Université de Provence.

Towse, J. N., Hitch, G. J., & Hutton, U. (2002). On the nature of the relationship between processing activity, and item retention in children. *Journal of Experimental Child Psychology, 82*, 156–184.

9

Discourse Coherence
and LSA

Peter W. Foltz
*Pearson Knowledge Technologies and
New Mexico State University*

Coherence is a concept that describes the flow of information from one part of a discourse to another. A number of approaches to modeling coherence have been developed, focusing on such factors as discourse modeling (e.g., Grosz, Joshi, & Weinstein, 1995; Mann & Thompson, 1988), the effects of coherence on comprehension (e.g., Kintsch, 1988, 1998; Lorch & O'Brien, 1995), and techniques for automated segmentation of discourse (e.g., Choi, Wiemer-Hastings & Moore, 2001; Hearst, 1997). All of these approaches must make certain decisions about what aspects of discourse are used in the modeling of coherence. Discourse coherence is composed of many aspects, ranging from lower level cohesive elements in discourse such as coreference, causal relationships, and connectives, up to higher level connections between the discourse and a reader's mental representation of it. For all coherent discourse, however, a key feature is the subjective quality of the overlap and transitions of the meaning as it flows across the discourse. LSA provides an ability to model this quality of coherence and quantify it by measuring the semantic similarity of one section of text to the next.

Although LSA has primarily been used at a "document" level, in which one compares one document to another or compares queries to documents, it can be used equally well for comparing any textual unit within a document to the next unit within the same document. This approach provides the advantage of automating the measurement of coherence and permits its application to modeling the effects of coherence in discourse. This chapter addresses how LSA can be applied to measuring discourse coherence. It examines at what level of discourse LSA measures coherence, how to use various LSA-based measures of coherence, and how these measures tie in to theoretical models of discourse processing. Finally, it describes a range of different types of discourse coherence to which LSA has been applied. These discourse types include approaches to predicting comprehension of written text, analyses of textbooks, predicting team performance from discourse, and measuring severity of clinical disorders through analyzing spoken interviews.

WHAT IS DISCOURSE COHERENCE?

Whereas there has been a lot of research on discourse coherence, what is surprising in the research literature is how often the term *coherence* is used but not operationally defined. This is likely due to the fact that coherence is a more subjective concept; we know it when we see it, but we cannot always describe it. Thus, much research has focused on trying to identify the factors that encompass coherence. Consulting dictionaries and writing guidelines does show that there is some consistency in their views of coherence. Wordnet's definitions of coherence, are "the state of cohering or sticking together" and "the logical and orderly and consistent relation of parts" (http://www.wordnet.princeton.edu/perl/webwn). These definitions match well with those found in other standard dictionaries. Writing guides that focus more on training writers state: "Coherence is the unifying element of good writing" (http://www.elc.polyu.edu.hk/elsc/material/Writing/coherenc.htm) and "The most convincing ideas in the world, expressed in the most beautiful sentences, will move no one unless those ideas are properly connected" (http://www.webster.commnet.edu/grammar/transitions.htm).

Coherence can also be examined at a higher level in which it is not just between a reader and the text, but between people involved in discourse and whatever medium they use for communicating; "coherence, broadly defined, is that which in a discourse connects utterances with utterances, utterances with people, and people with other people. It is, in short, the 'glue' of text and conversation" (Erickson, 2002). Thus, coherence is not just a within text factor, but can be examined in any type of discourse by a single person or by multiple people as well as how the discourse interacts with the context. Put together, the previous definitions all capture the idea that the discourse be able to hold together based on some consistent understanding of the relationships among the discourse items.

The fact that coherence is so often defined in broad terms stems from the fact that coherence is comprised of so many factors (e.g., Sanders, Spooren, & Noordman, 1992). These factors occur both in the text and in the reader's mind and all combine and interact to create the subjective feeling in the reader of the text "holding together." For example, in order for readers to understand discourse, it must be assembled in memory as a consistent representation. To do this, readers must apply knowledge and strategies in processing discourse to create this representation. The readers' strategies include using coreference, making causal connections, using syntactic signals, drawing inferences, and applying their background knowledge. Thus, coherence is a function of the ability to use different strategies to assemble and link disparate pieces of information to each other and to prior knowledge (see Lorch & O'Brien, 1995). In this manner, coherence gets at the topicality, referentiality, and logic of how the information holds together in a reader's mind.

The concept of coherence can be distinguished from that of "cohesion," which typically refers to surface features of the text that help the reader link both within and across sentences (e.g., Halliday & Hassan, 1976). Cohesion typically includes such features as reference, substitution, ellipsis, conjunction, repetition, and pronouns. Thus, the key distinction between coherence and cohesion can be thought of a distinction of discourse levels, where *cohesion* focuses more on the effect of the choice of individual words for linking sentences locally, whereas *coherence* focuses more on the effect those words have on the flow of meaning within and across the whole document. Coherence, therefore, captures aspects of long range dependencies, which shows how any part of the text must "hang together" with the other parts. Although more of a global measure than cohesion, coherence can still be measured at different levels, examining how it flows from one unit of text to the next, where a unit could be a sentence, paragraph, or larger text section.

HOW DOES LSA REPRESENT COHERENCE?

In order to measure coherence with LSA, one can represent individual text sections as vectors in a semantic space. As the discourse moves from one section to the next, one can compute the cosine from each text section vector to the next. Thus, discourse coherence in LSA can be thought of as measuring movements in a high-dimensional space. The size and direction of these movements indicate how quickly the discourse moves to a new topic. Generally, highly coherent discourse should have very small movements, represented by greater cosines, whereas less coherent discourse will have smaller cosines.

By solely using LSA for computing coherence, the focus of analysis is primarily on the flow of the LSA-derived meaning, and ignores a large number of linguistic, logical, and rhetorical factors in text, as well as knowledge and context that may not have been present in the text. Many of these factors have been examined elsewhere in both theoretical models and in applications that measure coherence or discourse structure. For example, Morris and Hirst (1991) used hand coding of thesaural relations to identify chains of related words across sentences. Breaks in these lexical chains tended to indicate structural elements in the text, such as changes in topics and the writer's intentional structure (e.g., Grosz & Sidner, 1986). Computational models have included use of lexical co-occurrence, context vectors and term distribution to do subtopic structuring (Hearst, 1997; Kaufmann, 1999), the use of centering theory (e.g., Grosz et al., 1995) for computing coherence metrics (Barzilay & Lapata, 2005; Karamanis, Poesio, Mellish, & Oberlander, 2004; Miltsakaki & Kukich, 2000), and segmenting based on rhetorical structure (Marcu, 2000).

Although there are a large number of factors that can be considered in determining coherence, to some extent many of these factors are correlated. For example, a causal connective can be considered a lower level syntactic device, but the use of causal connectives can improve the flow of meaning, because writers may still repeat or use related terms across causally connected sentences. Thus, LSA can capture some degree of causal connections, although indirectly. The Coh-Metrix approach (see McNamara, Cai, & Louwerse, chap. 19 in this volume) incorporates a number of these factors using measures, including using LSA, to produce overall metrics of referential cohesion. The present chapter focuses just on LSA-based measures. It is not claimed that LSA should be a lone measure, nor is it a complete model of human's coherence relations; instead, this chapter illustrates the degree to which LSA can capture effects of coherence relations independently of other measures.

Depending on the goals of measurement, a number of factors from the text can be varied to determine differing aspects of coherence. The next section describes some of these factors. Later, examples are given of their usage.

Size of Unit of Analysis

Discourse analysis can examine coherence at the individual word level up to paragraph or document levels. One critical issue is what size unit of text is to be measured. The granularity of measurement can be adjusted by measuring the similarity of one word, sentence, paragraph, or chapter to the next. Sentence-to-sentence coherence will provide measures of how well individual concepts are being described at a fairly granular level and can be applied to detecting more local breaks in flow. For example, this approach can detect if two sentences appear to be wholly unrelated. Paragraph-to-paragraph coherence, on the other hand, provides some measure of how well the general concepts that are being covered flow across the document. At this level, one could locate places in which the flow of an idea seems to end and a new idea is introduced. This approach can be instrumental for identifying groups of paragraphs that can be segmented into individual topics.

As the size of granularity for a text unit decreases, the variability in measurement becomes greater. For example, a paragraph-to-paragraph analysis will tend to provide a fairly narrow range of cosines, with lower cosines indicating greater topic shift. On the other hand, a sentence-to-sentence analysis will have much greater variability in cosines from one segment to the next, because there is less meaning conveyed in a sentence as compared to a paragraph. Thus, a low cosine between two sentences could be due to cohesion factors that are not being considered by LSA (e.g., the use of the word "Therefore"), or it could be due to less topic overlap.

Whereas this greater variability suggests that measuring coherence at a sentence level is suboptimal, there are a number of solutions. One is to use sentence-to-sentence coherence to get an overall measure of a text's coherence by averaging the cosines of the transitions for each sentence. A second solution for the greater variability in the analysis of more granular text units is to use a moving window. A moving window compares one group of sentences to the next group of sentences continuously across the whole text. For instance, one can compute a single vector for sentences k, $k + 1$, and $k + 2$, and then compare that to a vector for sentences $k + 3$, $k + 4$, and $k + 5$. This approach has the effect of smoothing differences that may be due to individual variations in one sentence and tends to capture effects of longer range dependencies (e.g., over three sentences) rather than just one. Thus, by varying the size of the moving windows, it is possible to vary the degree to which LSA is measuring more local or global coherence effects.

Physical Distance in Documents

The previous examples all assume that coherence is measured by examining similarity of adjacent text sections. However, one can also choose text sections that vary in their physical distance within a document. For example, comparing two paragraphs that are separated by several intervening paragraphs can provide a measure of how well an idea is persisting across the discourse (i.e., Was the author still talking about the same concept N paragraphs later? To what extent does the author move from one topic to the next?). This approach is referred to as "lag coherence." One can also compare each text section to the document as a whole in order to characterize how well it fits in with the overall discourse. Text sections that have lower cosine with the overall document will tend to be those that are less central to the overall themes of the document. The aforementioned approaches can equally be applied to spoken discourse. One can compute the similarity of one person's utterance to the next utterance said by another person, or to an utterance said t seconds later. This can capture effects of the extent to which a person is having an overall influence on the conversation.

Overall, applying these approaches has permitted a range of interesting theoretical findings, as well as useful applications within spoken and written discourse. Outlined next is some of the research that has been done applying these approaches.

MEASURING COHERENCE IN TEXTS

As an educational application, LSA can be used for measuring the comprehensibility and readability of texts. Over the past 40 years, there has been considerable effort dedicated to modeling the effects of a text on comprehension. Coherence is a critical factor in comprehensibility (see Lorch & O'Brien, 1995; McNamara, Kintsch, Songer, & Kintsch, 1996). Nevertheless, modeling it has often relied on using hand-crafted methods (e.g., Britton & Gulgoz, 1991). Although propositional models of text have been shown to be effective at predicting readers' comprehension (e.g., Kintsch, 1988, 1998), a problem with the approach is that in-depth propositional analysis is time consuming and requires a considerable amount of training. Although semi-automatic methods of propositional coding (e.g., Turner & Greene, 1978) require a little less effort, the degree of effort is still significant and limits the size of the text that can be analyzed. Thus, most texts analyzed and used in reading comprehension experiments have been small, typically from 50 to 500 words, and almost all are under 1,000 words. Automated methods, such as readability measures (e.g., Flesch, 1948; Klare, 1963), provide another characterization of the text; however, they do not correlate well with comprehension measures (Britton & Gulgoz, 1991; Kintsch & Vipond, 1979). Thus, whereas the coherence of a text can be measured, it has often involved considerable effort.

Foltz and colleagues (Foltz, 1996; Foltz, Kintsch, & Landauer, 1998) used LSA to measure the coherence of texts developed by McNamara et al. (1996) in order to determine the role of LSA-based coherence on comprehension. The McNamara et al. study used four texts that systematically varied in their coherence at both macro- and microlevels. Foltz et al. computed the average sentence-to-sentence cosine for each of the texts and used it as a measure of coherence. The predicted coherence correlated strongly with that of readers' comprehension scores on text-based questions, but more standard word overlap measures were not strongly correlated.

Sentence-to-sentence provides a fairly local measure in smaller texts, but one can also generate more global statistics of large texts. Foltz et al. (1998) further reported using section-to-section coherence to measure how quickly textbooks move from one topic to the next. In this analysis, they computed the average of the cosines for all paragraphs that were separated by N intervening paragraphs in a 3,500 paragraph introductory psychology textbook. By varying the number of intervening paragraphs, there is a remarkably regular function with the semantic similarity of paragraphs falling off exponentially as a function of their distance in the text (see Fig. 9.1). The results further show that paragraphs that were, on average, 200 paragraphs away from each other, as measured linearly in the book, still had slightly greater cosines than any two randomly chosen paragraphs. Although paragraphs that were separated by 200 intervening paragraphs were separated by approximately two chapters, there is still some slightly greater than chance level of similarity. This indicates that the book author has ordered the information in such a way that there are very long range dependencies in terms of how one piece of textual information relates to others.

In addition, Foltz et al. (1998) found that applying this analysis to different textbooks could provide indications of the difficulty of the textbooks. For example, textbooks that professors thought were more difficult tended to have lower overall coherence. Figure 9.2 shows the average coherence

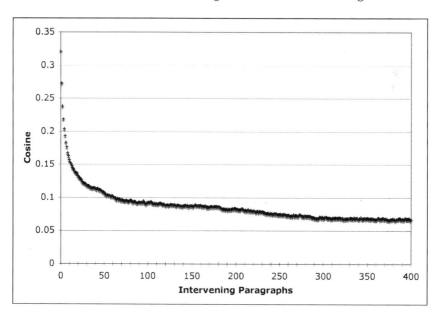

Figure 9.1.   Average cosine based on the number of intervening paragraphs.

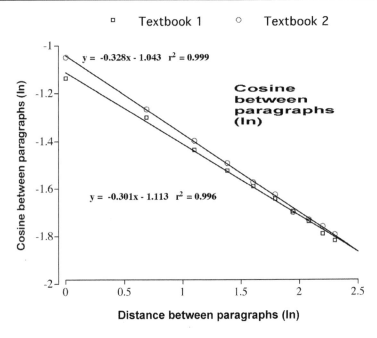

Figure 9.2.   Average log cosine as a function of log distance between paragraphs for two textbooks.

from one paragraph to the next as a function of their number of intervening paragraphs in two introductory psychology textbooks, in which one was generally considered to be more difficult than the other. The results can be interpreted in the following way: The more coherent text is one in which new topics are introduced without as much of a coherence gap as exists in the less coherent text. Thus, this approach appears to be highly robust at measuring the effects of these coherence relationships among topics across large documents.

Discourse Segmentation

Across a discourse, breaks in coherence can serve as markers for changes in topic. Thus, measuring coherence can be used for automatically determining where one segment of information ends and another starts. Document segmentation has a range of applications, including areas of information retrieval, discourse structuring (Hearst, 1997; Hearst & Plaut, 1993; Slaney & Ponceleon, 2001), and automated summarization (Raynar, 1999).

The general approach of using LSA for measuring the similarity of adjoining text passages also permits more detailed examination of conceptual coherence; for example, detection of places in a text where coherence breaks down because the author has purposely changed topics or subtopics, voice or diction, written poorly or oddly, and so on. By adjusting the granularity of what is being compared, one can locate more global or local topic shifts.

Two examples of such analyses are given in Figures 9.3 and 9.4. Figure 9.3 illustrates how the method can reveal erratic changes in topic between

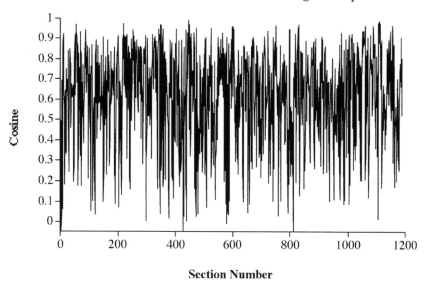

Figure 9.3.   Coherence between each section of text to the next in a large book.

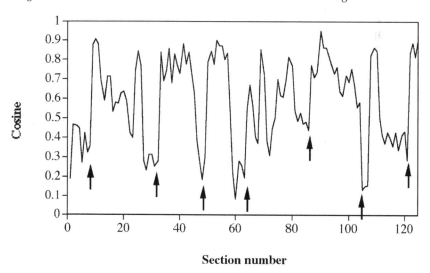

Figure 9.4.   Coherence (cosine) between sections of text with breaks between chapters indicated with arrows.

short sections of text across a very large book by computing the similarity of each text section to the next. In this case, text sections were defined by using the author's heading structure in the text (typically 5–10 paragraphs). Figure 9.4 zooms in on the first 130 sections of the book. The arrows on the figure indicate the places in the text that represent breaks between chapters. Note that it can show systematicity of changes between chapters as one might expect. At the end of chapters, there tends to be a general drop in coherence between one chapter and the next. Nevertheless, not all places with minimum cosines are chapter breaks, but they may still indicate changes in the author's topic within the chapter, or may represent other types of text, such as unusual anecdotes that are not highly coherent to the original text.

Foltz et al. (1998) performed a segmentation analysis on an introductory textbook at the paragraph level. Using a sliding window of 10 paragraphs, the average cosine between any two adjacent paragraphs within chapters was .43 (SD = .14), and the average cosine between paragraphs at chapter breaks was .16. Thus, generally, the coherence between paragraphs at chapter breaks was significantly lower than the overall coherence of the text ($p <$ .001). By choosing all coherence breaks that have a cosine two standard deviations below the mean (i.e., < .15), the method identified 9 out of the 18 breaks that were actual breaks between chapters. However, at the same time, it detected 31 other coherence breaks in the text that had a cosine of two standard deviations below the mean. Thus, although the method correctly identified half the breaks, it had false alarms on a number of other places in the text that were not chapter breaks.

More recently, Choi et al. (2001) examined LSA for segmentation of documents at the sentence level. Using a test-bench of a set of hand-segmented news articles, Choi and colleagues compared an LSA-based algorithm against a term-overlap vector-based model. They found that the LSA metric was twice as accurate as the vector-overlap model at locating the appropriate segments in news articles. Slaney and Ponceleon (2001) similarly computed LSA-based similarity among text sections, but used the coherence in order to regenerate a hierarchical organization of the text. In this work, they used a Gaussian window and varied the segment size of analysis from sentence-width to half the document length. This approach tends to filter out high spatial frequencies that may be due to idiosyncrasies of language as opposed to true document segments. The velocity of the trajectory in this smoothed LSA space was used to identify segment boundaries and the range of their scopes. Based on the identified segments and their scopes, they were able to develop effective hierarchical segmentations of documents.

Overall, the results for segmentation suggest that LSA can measure components of coherence to detect segments. Using moving windows and varying the window size as done in Slaney and Poncelon (2001) can help detect the different levels of coherence that may be within the discourse. With more development, such methods can also be used to characterize and assess more global organizational issues such as the optimal order for introducing ideas or sequencing sections or chapters. Additional measures may need to be included in order to improve the sensitivity of detection of section breaks. Thus, a hybrid approach incorporating LSA, lower level cohesive factors, and measurement of rhetorical structure may improve overall segmentation.

Coherence in Student Essays

Evaluation of student writing often involves assessing both how well a student covers a topic and how coherently the student has linked the ideas within the essay. Miltsakaki and Kukich (2000) have used centering theory (Grosz et al., 1995) for detecting shifts in the local focus of essays and found that it contributed significantly to the accuracy of computer-scored essays. Thus, coherence measures can be useful in automated essay scoring. LSA has also been applied for scoring essays, both examining the coherence between sentences and the coherence of sentences to the essays as a whole. Interestingly, for the typical 150–500 word essays, better essays often tend to have low coherence, because a student must cover multiple facets or examples in a short span of text. Additional details on applying LSA for essay scoring are discussed in this volume (see Landauer, Laham, & Foltz, 2003).

Team Dialogues

Although much of the coherence research has focused on written discourse, LSA can also be applied to spoken discourse. In spoken discourse, an extra dimension of measurement is added because one can not only measure the internal coherence of what someone says, but one can also measure how coherent what one person says is to the next person. This can be used as the basis for characterizing the flow of ideas between participants in conversations as well as idea flow within a particular speaker's discourse.

Communication between team members provides a rich source of data that can serve as indications of the knowledge and competencies of the individuals and the team, the amount of team situation awareness, and indications of team performance problems. Nevertheless, assessment of teams has been hindered by the fact that the verbal communication among team members is difficult to collect and analyze. Prior attempts at coding the content of communication have shown promise (see, e.g., Bowers, Jentsch, Salas, & Braun, 1998), but have relied on tedious hand-coded techniques or have used limited data such as frequencies and durations of communications. Thus, automated techniques of modeling team communications provide the promise of quickly judging team performance and permitting feedback to teams both in training and in operations.

In an experiment designed to measure team cognition and communication, teams of three people flew simulated missions in an unmanned air vehicle simulator (UAV; see Gorman, Foltz, Kiekel, Martin, & Cooke, 2003; Kiekel, Cooke, Foltz, Gorman, & Martin, 2002; Martin & Foltz, 2004). A set of 67 transcripts was collected from 11 teams, each of which completed 7 missions. The task comprised a three-team member task in which each team member is provided with distinct, although overlapping, training; has unique, yet interdependent roles; and is presented with different and overlapping information during the mission. The overall goal was to fly the UAV to designated target areas and to take acceptable photos at these areas. Throughout the CERTT Lab UAV-STE missions, an objective performance measure was also calculated to determine each team's effectiveness at completing the mission.

A variety of automated analyses of the transcripts have been performed in order to determine how well they can predict team performance. Foltz (2005), Martin and Foltz (2004), and Gorman et al. (2003) describe how LSA-based methods similar to essay scoring can be used to predict overall performance. In this method, the semantic similarity of whole transcripts are compared against other transcripts to predict performance. The results indicated that the LSA estimated performance scores correlated strongly with the actual team performance scores ($r = .76$, $p < .01$).

As part of the project, work has focused on measuring the coherence of the teams using LSA. Gorman and colleagues (Gorman et al., 2003; Kiekel et al., 2002) measured the amount of topic shifting during missions by computing the average similarity among team member utterances over different lags (e.g., 2 to 35 utterances away in the dialogue). As in Foltz et al. (1998), they found a similar pattern that the cosines decreased exponentially with greater lags. They then used the slope of the exponential function to measure the amount of topic shifting within teams, with lower slopes, indicating more topical variation. They found that, on the initial missions, teams used more topic shifting, but as they gained experience, they made a qualitative shift to a more stable coherence, reflecting both a more constrained vocabulary and more consistent shifts of topics. Thus, the approach shows that LSA-based coherence analyses can be equally applied to spoken dialogues and can be used to determine how well individual team members work together.

Coherence in Clinical Dialogues

Whereas team dialogue can indicate abnormal coherence patterns in teams, one can similarly use LSA to detect abnormal patterns of communication in clinical patients. In schizophrenia, for instance, the fundamental problem

of linking ideas together in a meaningful manner comprises the very definition of "thought disorder." The disturbance in the structure, organization,
and coherence of thought makes patient discourse difficult to comprehend.
Because the detection of a patient's verbal self-presentation as elicited in a
clinical interview is an essential diagnostic tool in psychiatry, being able to
measure this disruption in coherence has the promise of providing tools to
detect thought disorder as well as to understand the underlying
relationship between thought disorder and semantic processing.

In a series of studies, Elvevåg, Foltz, Weinberger, and Goldberg (2006)
have analyzed the coherence of discourse created by both schizophrenic patients and normal individuals that served as controls. Using a set of clinical
interviews of both patients and normal controls, a series of LSA-based measures were tested to measure the coherence in the discourse and predict the
presence and severity of schizophrenia. For example, a measure was computed that determined the similarity of a patient's response to the interviewer's questions and how it deviated from the interviewer's response over
time. There was a significant correlation between this similarity measure and
trained clinicians who rated the interviews on the degree of "tangentiality"
(how the participant's responses tended to stay or go off the topic; $r = .44, p <$
.01). In a second measure, a moving window was used to compute the coherence of patient and control responses to questions. As the size of the windows were increased (up to 8 words in a window), the measures became
sensitive to discriminating patients with high and low levels of thought disorder. For example, although there was no significant difference between
controls and patients for coherence with a window of two words to the next
two words, there was a significant difference for windows of seven or eight
words. This indicates that at higher levels of discourse planning, coherence
breaks down in to a greater extent for the schizophrenic patients.

Incoherent discourse, with a disjointed flow of ideas, is a cardinal symp-
tom in numerous psychiatric and neurological conditions. The results of
the studies on clinical interviews suggest that LSA can be used as a tool for
automatically rating clinical interviews based on their coherence. In addition, such measures help to validate the cognitive models of schizophrenia
that examine the role of coherence in patient dialogue. Nevertheless, many
potential extensions to this research on other clinical populations and other
types of interviews remain to be investigated.

HOW TO COMPUTE COHERENCE USING THE LSA
WEB SITE

The Web site, http://www.LSA.colorado.edu, provides a number of ways
of computing coherence. The link to "Sentence Comparison" permits users
to enter a text and compute the cosine between each sentence and the next.

The system automatically parses the text into sentences, using periods, question marks, and exclamation marks as delimiters and then returns the cosine between each adjoining sentence, as well as the mean and standard deviation of all sentences.

However, one often wants to compare units other than sentences to compute coherence (e.g., paragraphs, sections, or words). Whereas there is no specific facility for this, it can be accomplished using the "Matrix Comparison" link. Each text unit needs to be separated by a blank line from the next and then the whole text is pasted into the text box. The resulting matrix can be viewed or pasted into a spreadsheet document. The cosine for the coherence of each section to the next can be found directly above the diagonal of the matrix (e.g., column 2, row 1; column 3, row 2, etc.) In order to compute lag coherence (i.e., coherence when separated by intervening text sections), one can extract the elements of the matrix corresponding to the lag. For example, at a lag of 2, one extracts column 3, row 1, then column 4, row 2, and so forth.

There is no direct facility on the Web site for performing moving windows of coherence that encompasses multiple sections. Thus, in order to perform an analysis with a moving window, one must first revise the text to be analyzed so that it has multiple sections grouped into larger sections of the desired window size. For example, to analyze the coherence at the word level of the sentence *John walked to the store to buy some bread* with a window size of 2, one would want to compare the following texts.

John walked → to the
walked to →the store
to the→store to
the store→to buy
...

This could be accomplished by creating each of the two word pairs separated by blank lines and then pasted in to the matrix comparison web page. One would then extract the cosines from the cells for each of the pairs that were needed.

Once the cosines have been extracted from the matrix, additional analyses can be performed on them, including computing means and standard deviations as well as performing smoothing functions (e.g., Gaussian functions, moving averages). Additional details on using the Web site are provided in this volume.

CONCLUSIONS

Discourse comprehension is a complex cognitive process, so modeling coherence can require taking into account many different aspects of language processing. Nevertheless, LSA-based analyses of coherence perform well at measuring effects related to coherence, such as predicting comprehension, segmenting documents, and finding differences in spoken coherent and less coherent discourse. An LSA-based analysis determines coherence entirely based on the derived semantic relatedness of one text unit to the next. Thus, it is making a coherence judgment based on the extent to which two text units are discussing a semantically related topic or have words whose meaning is related. The method, however, is not performing any syntactic processing or parsing of the text, nor taking into account higher level organizational or rhetorical factors. For example, within any unit of text, it does not take into account the order of the words. Furthermore, it does not take into account some of the features typically analyzed in cohesion (e.g., Halliday & Hasan, 1976), such as pronominal reference, substitution, or ellipsis. It also ignores linking clauses and signals (e.g., *therefore*, *since*) and does not detect originality.

Despite its sole focus on semantic similarity, it is important to note how well LSA succeeds at automatically modeling effects of coherence. Although it does not take into account syntactic features, the analysis of the semantic features provide considerable strength in prediction. For example, LSA is still able to model aspects of Halliday and Hasan's notion of cohesion through lexical reiteration, synonymy, and hyponymy. In addition, it goes beyond this level in determining coherence based on semantic relatedness due to terms tending to occur in similar contexts. Thus, even when a sentence uses syntactic signals of coherence, it is likely that there will be semantic signals of coherence in the sentences as well.

In LSA, repeating the same sentence would result in a text that would be judged highly coherent (although, to a human, not very interesting). Therefore, although readers need coherence in a text, for learning to occur there must be at least some change in the semantic content across the text sections. Indeed, the degree of optimal coherence in a discourse is highly dependent on the information in the discourse and the reader. People with different amounts of knowledge will benefit differently from different levels of coherence (e.g., McNamara et al., 1996). So, whereas LSA can compute coherence metrics, it is still dependent on the context in order to determine whether the computed coherence can be considered high or low.

One critical aspect of LSA's analysis is its ability to compute coherence at much more global levels of discourse than is done by a number of other automated coherence analyses. For instance, many other coherence analyses instead tend to focus on local sentence-to-sentence links. However, by using moving window techniques and computing lag coherence, LSA is able to track changes in information that are separated by many document sections. Thus, one of LSA's great strengths is its ability to model long-range dependencies and topic shifts across the discourse. Because of this, it is well suited for analyzing large documents as well as verbal communication among people interacting.

As described in this chapter, LSA works over a wide range of different types of discourse and on different levels of granularity, including spoken utterances, sentences, paragraphs, and document sections. The results suggest that LSA is accounting for general aspects of relationships within semantic memory that correspond to human notions of how discourse should "stick together." Based on LSA representation, a coherent text should be a "leisurely stroll" through a high-dimensional space in which each step to the next section or topic should not require large changes in direction or large jumps.

There is a wide range of applicability of LSA-based coherence analyses to areas such as educational assessment, monitoring of spoken communication, and document design and analysis. For educational and document design applications, it can be used for automated measurement of books for readability, identifying information gaps in texts, automated topic segmentation, finding the optimal ordering of text units for training, and automatically adjusting training material to maintain the appropriate reading and knowledge levels. For monitoring spoken communication, it can be used to diagnose disorders, monitor teams, and adjust feedback to teams based on judged performance.

In order to develop such applications, additional research questions about the nature of coherence will need to be addressed. For example, it will be important to determine the most important factors for modeling coherence and how those factors vary depending on the type of discourse and context. In order to develop more optimized learning, it will be important to determine the correct size steps for a leisurely (coherent) stroll through any text. Initial research in both team performance and for student essays suggests on that there is a U-shaped function between coherence and performance. We see performance degradation at high and low levels of coherence with the best performance somewhere in the middle. These findings suggest that there are optimal levels of coherence for different types of discourse, tasks, and people. By examining varying domains and tasks, we may be able to determine what would be the appropriate level of coherence for different readers based on the type of text, the domain, and the reader's background knowledge.

Finally, despite accounting for a number of discourse factors, LSA is not the sole or the ultimate model of coherence. There are many aspects LSA is not designed to model, for example, pronouns, anaphora, and pragmatics. Thus, there are a number of other discourse and knowledge factors that can be included in concert with LSA analyses to create a hybrid model of coherence. By leveraging off of the strength of each type of measure, such a model can provide a more robust accounting for the effects of coherence. Nevertheless, LSA effectively models aspects of semantic similarity very well on its own.

REFERENCES

Barzilay, R., & Lapata, M. (2005). Modeling local coherence: An entity-based approach. *Proceedings of the 43 Annual Meeting of the Association for Computational Lingusitics*, 141–148.

Bowers, C. A., Jentsch, F., Salas, E., & Braun, C. C. (1998). Analyzing communication sequences for team training needs assessment. *Human Factors, 40*, 672–679.

Britton, B. K., & Gulgoz, S. (1991). Using Kintsch's computational model to improve instructional text: Effects of repairing inference calls on recall and cognitive structures. *Journal of Educational Psychology, 83*, 329–345.

Choi, F., Wiemer-Hastings, P., & Moore, J. (2001). Latent semantic analysis for text segmentation. In L. Lee & D. Harman (Eds.), *Proceedings of the 2001 Conference on Empirical Methods in Natural Language Processing* (pp. 109–117). Philadelphia: Association for Computational Lingusitics.

Elvevåg, B., Foltz, P. W., Weinberger, D. R., & Goldberg, T. E. (2006). *Coherence and incoherence in speech*. Manuscript submitted for publication.

Erickson, T. (2002). *Discourse architectures: Designing and visualizing computer-mediated conversation. Call For Participation: A Chi 2002 Workshop*. Retrieved March 6, 2005, from http://www.visi.com/~snowfall/DA_DiscourseArch02CFP.html

Flesch, R. F. (1948). A new readability yardstick. *Journal of Applied Psychology, 32*, 221–233.

Foltz, P. W. (1996). Latent semantic analysis for text-based research. *Behavior Research Methods, Instruments and Computers, 28*(2), 197–202.

Foltz, P. W. (2005). Tools for enhancing team performance through automated modeling of the content of team discourse [Electronic version]. *Proceedings of HCI International Conference*.

Foltz, P. W., Kintsch, W., & Landauer, T. K. (1998). The measurement of textual coherence with latent semantic analysis. *Discourse Processes, 25*, 285–307.

Gorman, J. C., Foltz, P. W., Kiekel, P. A., Martin, M. A., & Cooke, N. J. (2003). Evaluation of latent semantic analysis-based measures of communications content [Electronic version]. *Proceedings of the 47th Annual Human Factors and Ergonomic Society Meeting*.

Grosz, B., Joshi, A. K., & Weinstein, S. (1995). Centering: A framework for modeling the local coherence of discourse. *Computational Linguistics, 21*(2), 203–225.

Grosz, B., & Sidner, C. (1986). Attention, intentions and the structure of discourse. *Computational Linguistics, 12*(3), 175–204.

Halliday, M. A. K., & Hasan, R. (1976). *Cohesion in English*. London: Longman.

Hearst, M., (1997). TextTiling: Segmenting text into multi-paragraph subtopic passages. *Computational Linguistics, 23*(1), 33–64.

Hearst, M. A., & Plaut, C. (1993). Subtopic structuring for full-length document access. *Proceedings of the 16th Annual International ACM SIGIR Conference on Research and Development in Information Retrieval*, 59–68.

Karamanis, N., Poesio, M., Mellish, C., & Oberlander, J. (2004). Evaluating centering-based metrics of coherence for text structuring using a reliably annotated corpus. *Proceedings of the 41st Annual Meeting of the Association for Computational Linguistics*, 391–398.

Kaufmann, S. (1999). Cohesion and collocation: Using context vectors in text segmentation. *Proceedings of the 37th annual meeting of the Association for Computational Linguistics*, 591–595.

Kiekel, P. A., Cooke, N. J., Foltz, P. W., Gorman, J., & Martin, M. (2002). Some promising results of communication-based automatic measures of team cognition. *Proceedings of the Human Factors and Ergonomics Society 46th Annual Meeting*, 298–302.

Kintsch, W. (1988). The role of knowledge in discourse comprehension: A construction-integration model. *Psychological Review, 2*, 163–182.

Kintsch, W. (1998). *Comprehension: A paradigm for cognition.* New York: Cambridge University Press.

Kintsch, W., & Vipond, D. (1979). Reading comprehension and readability in educational practice and psychological theory. In L. G. Nilsson (Ed.), *Perspectives on memory research* (pp. 329–365). Hillsdale, NJ: Lawrence Erlbaum Associates.

Klare, G. R. (1963). *The measurement of readability.* Ames, IA: Iowa University Press.

Landauer, T. K., Laham, D., & Foltz, P. W. (2003). Automated scoring and annotation of essays with the Intelligent Essay Assessor. *Assessment in Education, 10*(3), 295–308.

Lorch, R. F., Jr., & O'Brien, E. J. (Eds.). (1995). *Sources of coherence in reading.* Hillsdale, NJ: Lawrence Erlbaum Associates.

Mann, W. C., & Thompson, S. A. (1988). Rhetorical structure theory: Toward a functional theory of text organization. *Text, 8*, 243–281.

Marcu, D. (2000). *The theory and practice of discourse parsing and summarization.* Cambridge, MA: MIT Press.

Martin, M., & Foltz, P. W. (2004, May). Automated team discourse annotation and performance prediction using LSA. *Proceedings of the Human Language Technology and North American Association for Computational Linguistics Conference (HLT/NAACL)*, 97–100.

McNamara, D. Kintsch, E., Songer, N. B., & Kintsch, W. (1996). Are good texts always better? Interactions of text coherence, background knowledge, and levels of understanding in learning from text. *Cognition and Instruction, 14*, 1–43.

Miltsakaki, E., & Kukich, K. (2000). The role of centering theory's rough-shift in teaching and evaluation of writing skills. *Proceedings of the 38th Annual Meeting of the Association for Computational Linguistics*, 408–415.

Morris, J., & Hirst, G. (1991). Lexical cohesion computed by thesaural relations as an indicator of the structure of text. *Computational Linguistics, 17*(1), 21–48.

Raynar, J. C. (1999). Statistical models for topic segmentation. *Proceedings of the 37th Annual Meeting of the Association for Computational Linguistics*, 357–364.

Sanders, T. J. M., Spooren, W. P. M., & Noordman, L. G. M. (1992). Toward a taxonomy of coherence relations. *Discourse Processes, 15*, 1–35.

Slaney, M., & Ponceleon, D. (2001). Hierarchical segmentation: Finding changes in a text signal. *Proceedings of the SIAM Text Mining 2001 Workshop*, 6–13.

Turner, A. A., & Green, E. (1978). Construction and use of a propositional textbase (MS No. 1713). *Selected Documents in Psychology, 8*(58).

10

Spaces for Problem Solving

Jose Quesada
Warwick University

What if the mechanisms that have been proposed for learning the semantics of natural languages are more general, and some other aspects of high-level cognition could be explained appealing to the same principles. Landauer and Dumais (1997) anticipated that the representational approach taken in LSA is not necessarily reduced to word events, and other complex activities (described as a sequence of events) could be explained using the same assumptions. Quesada, Kintsch, and Gomez (2005) presented latent problem-solving analysis (LPSA) as a theory of representation in experienced problem solving that adopts the idea that complex activities are represented similarly to how we represent semantics. The basic idea is as follows. Consider that the events of interest are states of a system instead of words, and the contexts in which they appear are trials instead of documents. Then, co-ocurrence information between events and trials can be used to infer the relationship between them and represent the constraints of the problem. What LPSA proposes is that problem spaces are constructed from experience with the environment alone. The same inference mechanism could be used to learn the semantics of different problem-solving domains. In problem-solving domains, there are a high number of weak relations between tokens (tokens representing states of the system or actions to control it). Any event in a system (either an action or a state) is a "word" in traditional LSA parlance, and each context (e.g., a trial in an experiment, or a landing in a flying simula-

185

tor) is the equivalent to a document. Then, one can construct a matrix of events by trials as a starting point for the inference algorithm (in this case, singular value decomposition, SVD). This matrix is very sparse, and as one can infer from the long tails of the distributions presented in Figure 10.1, most events do not occur but in a few contexts.

I shall illustrate these ideas with some examples of complex problem-solving tasks. Consider the complex, dynamic task Firechief (Omodei & Wearing, 1993, 1995). In this problem, participants have to extinguish a forest fire by allocating trucks and helicopters with mouse commands. Every time a participant performs an action, it is saved in a log file as a row containing action number, command (e.g., drop water or move)

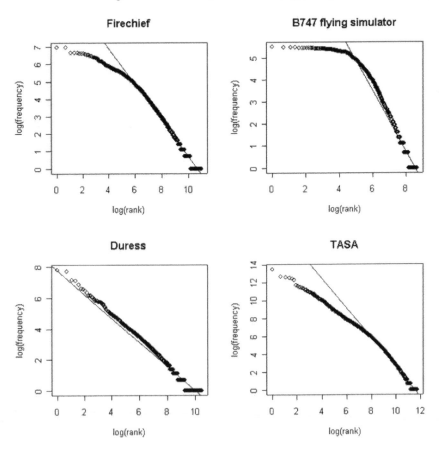

Figure 10.1.   Different frequency-rank curves for three complex problem-solving tasks, and one corpus of text (TASA). Even though the curves do not perfectly follow Zipf's law, they show that in the three problem-solving domains, as in the language corpus, there are very few popular events and a large majority of low frequency events.

or event[1] (e.g., a wind change or a new fire), current performance score, appliance number, appliance type, position, and landscape type. Most of these variables are not continuous, but on a nominal scale, such as "type of movement." For more information on the structure of the log files, see Omodei and Wearing (1995).

LPSA can be trained on a corpus of thousands of trials collected from participants playing Firechief in different experimental conditions. Each trial is a log file of about 300 actions. Actions are created by concatenating the different numeric and nominal attributes that define them. In the Firechief case, the corpus was composed of 360,199 actions in 3,441 trials. Among them, only 57,565 were different actions, which means that on average each action appears 6.25 times in the corpus. Note that LPSA represents only the information that actual people interacting with the system experienced, not all possible actions in this problem. The coocurrence matrix is then submitted to singular value decomposition (SVD) and recreated using only a small fraction (e.g., 100–300) of the dimensions. The resulting space is a problem space for Firechief.

As another example, consider the Duress task (e.g., Christoffersen, Hunter, & Vicente, 1997). Dual Reservoir System Simulation (Duress) is a thermal-hydraulic scenario that was designed to be representative of industrial processes. In this system, all variables are continuous. Duress has two redundant feedwater streams that can be configured to supply water to either, both, or neither of two reservoirs. Participants control 8 valves and 2 heaters to satisfy the goals of the system: to keep each of the reservoirs at a prescribed temperature (e.g., $40°C$ and $20°C$, respectively) and to satisfy the current water output demand (e.g., 5 liters per second and 7 liters per second, respectively). The system is determined by the laws of conservation of mass and energy, and its state can be described using 34 variables. Running a SVD on the Duress state-context matrix using several years of logs produces a problem space. Duress spaces also contain a few thousand events, but in this case they are system states, a subset of the 34 rounded continuous variables. Rounding the value of continuous variables ensures that the number of types is not excessive and the average token repetition is close to natural languages. Applying the same logic of an SVD decomposition of a trial by state matrix produces a metric space that can serve as a good approximation for a human problem space for Duress.

In these two examples, we can see that the events used to train the model can be either actions or states (they convey the same information). Also, we can see that the variables that define the system can be continuous or discrete: For LPSA, the relevant information is the coocurrence relationships

---

[1]Events are generated by the system, whereas actions are generated by the user. Events are also lines in the log file. Only 1%–2% of the lines in a log file are events.

between the token these variable values form and the contexts in which they appear.

Note that the knowledge extracted from experience is not explicitly represented as rules. For example, when working with Duress, LPSA does not infer the laws of conservation of mass and energy nor represent these laws directly as rules, but as fuzzy relations between past states of the system. In a later section, I show how these constraints as represented in LPSA are sufficient to mimic human similarity judgments and predict future states with accuracy. Of course, people also extract rules (e.g., Anderson & Lebiere, 1998) and build models of the relations between variables (e.g., Glymour, 2001) explicitly when interacting with their environments. What I propose is that both the associative (LPSA-like) and the rule-based systems work in parallel helping each other. In fact, many theorists in cognitive science propose that our mind is separated into two such systems (e.g., Evans & Over, 1996; Kahneman, 2003; Sloman, 1996, 2002; Stanovich, 2004).

Stanovich and Cunningham (1991) review a collection of theories that propose two different systems of reasoning. He grouped them as system1 and system 2. System1 is characterized as automatic, unconscious, and relatively undemanding of computational capacity. System 2 is controlled, reflected in IQ tests, rule-based, and involved in analytical cognition. The tasks that pertain to system1 are highly contextualized, whereas system 2 tends to decontextualize (abstract) problems. The two systems can produce contrary solutions to the same situation. Stanovich (1991) is concerned with the evolutionary interpretation of the two systems and their relevance to arguments about rational behavior.

Sloman (1996) tagged the two components "associative system" and "rule-based system." He used similarity-based thought and temporal similarity relations to draw inferences and make predictions that resemble those of a sophisticated statistician: "Rather than trying to reason on the basis of an underlying causal or mechanical structure, it constructs estimates based on underlying statistic structure. Lacking highly predictive causal models, this is the preferred mode for many forecasters, such as weather and economic ones" (Sloman, 1996, p. 4). In pilots, for example, the underlying causal or mechanical structure can be present, but, after extensive experience, it can be easier for them to operate using the statistical structure that they have extracted during practice. Thus, the organism faces important induction problems that can be solved in different ways. For some situations, the "rule-based" system provides advantages, whereas in others it is the automatic, associative system that dominates induction.

The key step for induction in LPSA is the reduction of the dimensionality of the space. Imagine a hypothetical problem-solving task that, when performed from the beginning to the end in one of the N possible ways, traverses 300 states. To make it a really simple example, let us assume that every state is described using six dichotomous variables (2^6 = 64 possible states). Because we have 300 states in our sample of performance, there are $64^{300} = 7_E541$ possible paths in this task. Every sample would be represented as a matrix of 6 × 300 = 1,800 values. After the dimension reduction used in LPSA, every sample would be represented as a vector of only 100–300 values.

The areas where LPSA has been applied differ from the traditional problem-solving domains, such as puzzles that have been used widely in psychology. Puzzles are aimed at system 2, whereas system1 is best studied in the context of realistic, semantically rich tasks.

I propose that both language and complex solving use the same system of representation (multidimensional spaces) and inference mechanism (dimension reduction). Problem-solving domains show similar distributional properties to each other and to language. Figure 10.1 shows frequency distributions for three complex problem-solving tasks and one language corpus, TASA. When the log of the frequency of each type is plotted against the log of its rank, the result is close to a straight line. This implies a power law relation between rank of the item's frequency and actual frequency in the corpus (Zipf, 1949). Even though both the problem-solving corpora and the TASA language corpus show departures from a perfect power law, the distributions show that there are very few high-frequency types and very long tail, low-frequency types.

Of course, there are many ways in which these frequency curves could exist as a consequence of different systems of representation. However, considering language and complex problem solving as two examples of a common representational system has advantages. First, it integrates language semantics with some types of problem solving in which one has to learn a large vocabulary of action-states. As we will see in this chapter, LPSA is an existence proof demonstrating the possibility of a formalism that describes a varied sample of complex tasks. Second, it has an easy evolutionary explanation that our representational system could be adapted to this particular situation. If events in the environment (no matter what they are: words, faces, cities, etc.) are distributed in a similar way, with many nonfrequent events, and a selected few that are highly frequent, then it is rational to represent them using a common system.

Of course, I do not try to suggest that metric spaces learned from raw co-occurrence data can explain representation in all types of problem-solving and decision behavior. I view LPSA as an associative, intuitive system that works in collaboration with a conscious, rule-based system. People use both systems in different degrees depending on the problems they face. I focus here on the knowledge that can be obtained using co-occurrence type context only. However, there are other possibilities in a corpus-based approach to cognitive representation. Frequency (occurrence) and joint frequency (co-occurrence) are two of the simplest statistics that can be derived from a corpus. Future proposals may use more fine-grained assumptions to infer structured representations from distributional information.

The other chapters in this book are examples of how a corpus-based approach to cognition is useful in the areas of semantics and language comprehension. The next sections argue that this corpus-based approach to cognitive representation holds promise for the areas of problem solving and decision making.

First, I review some issues in the literature and how LPSA addresses them. Second, I review the experiments and simulations that present evidence for LPSA assumptions in the problem-solving domain. Third, the discussion and conclusions are presented.

SOME THEORETICAL ISSUES IN PROBLEM SOLVING AND LPSA SOLUTIONS

I have presented the basics of the LPSA theory and its relations to LSA. This theory was developed as a response to four theoretical issues in the field of problem solving. This section presents these issues, why they are important and unaddressed by current theories, and how LPSA tries to address them.

The Recursive Definition of Problem Spaces

From the very early attempts of the general problem solver (GPS; Newell & Simon, 1963) to the more contemporary approaches to expert and novice comparisons, the problem-solving tasks selected for study have had a remarkable importance in shaping theory. However, as the field adopted new tasks, new theories needed to be proposed. Particularly distressing was the fact that each task generated an independent theory, often poorly specified by a flow diagram, and thus different results could barely be integrated: "Theorists seem simply to write a different theory for each task" (Newell, 1980, p. 694). Newell proposed that the integrative metatheory could be built around the problem space hypothesis: "The fundamental organizational unit of all human goal-oriented symbolic activity is the *problem space*" (Newell, 1980, p. 696).

The concept of problem space has been central to theory construction in the field of problem solving.[2] This concept has been used widely and differ-

---

[2]However, the problem space is a surprisingly ill-defined concept that has been changed and reworked in successive works by its own proponents (Newell, 1980, 1990) and by others (e.g., Laird, Rosenbloom, & Newell, 1986; see Quesada, unpublished, appendix J for a review of different attempts of definition). Because most researchers in problem solving use it, it has been stretched and adapted in different ways to cover new situations, and some authors (e.g., Burns & Vollmeyer, 2000) have issued warnings about this.

ent researchers have interpreted it in different ways. It is natural that a useful concept experiences many incarnations in psychology. However, the definition and origin of problems spaces are often vague and mysterious. One contribution of the distributional approach to problem solving advocated here is that problem spaces are derived empirically from experience. In most theories of representation in problem solving, the problem spaces are hypothesized by experimenters, not derived automatically by an unsupervised procedure. Newell (1980) pointed out that one of the major items on the agenda of cognitive psychology is to banish the homunculus (little man residing "elsewhere" that is responsible of all the marvelous things that have to be done to create the system's behavior). The homunculus is present in the classical problem-solving theory at least in one place: the intelligent creation of the problem space. This argument is circular: The generation of problem spaces is a symbolic cognitive task, and therefore it must be performed by means of a problem space. LPSA provides a solution to break this recursive explanation: The problem spaces are derived automatically from experience, there is no need for an intelligent agent in their creation.

The Increasing Importance Given to Content (Semantics) in Problem Solving Required a Way to Model Content

In the 1960s and 1970s, the problem-solving studies were oriented to the detection and testing of general heuristics (e.g., means–end analysis) by which a person could reduce search in a problem space (Newell & Simon, 1972). The possibility of an algorithm that could solve a very general class of problems was contemplated in programs such as the GPS (Newell & Simon, 1963). The idea that several problems could be abstracted away, removing any content to leave a common formal skeleton, was appealing. As research progressed, the ideal of a GPS drifted away. Two formally equivalent versions of the same problem with different cover stories could make the solution times vary enormously (Kotovsky & Fallside, 1989; Kotovsky, Hayes, & Simon, 1985; Kotovsky & Simon, 1990). If the representations and methods were the same, then why would the two problems be so different in difficulty?

At about the same time, evidence on why content matters in problem solving emerged within the expertise literature. Experts could have extraordinary abilities that were restricted to a particular domain, being unable to extrapolate them to domains that were seemingly related (e.g., Adelson, 1984; Ericsson, Krampe, & Tesch-Römer, 1993; Ericsson & Staszewski, 1989). It seemed that what experts were capitalizing on was not better general purpose search heuristics so much as domain-specific knowledge (e.g., Chase & Simon, 1973). That is, the advantage of experts is tied to the semantics of the domain. LPSA offers a way of capturing the semantics of the domain in a formal way. It also explains how different domains can be represented using the same formalism. In LPSA, every event carries meaning because its representation is computed in relation to past experiences with other events.

Tasks Are Not Representative of Real-Life Situations

Most experimenters during the 1970s and 1980s used simple tasks, such as the Tower of Hanoi, missionaries and cannibals, and so on, to study problem solving in laboratory situations. However, many real-life situations have certain characteristics that are not captured by these tasks. Many real tasks are (a) *dynamic*, because early actions determine the environment in which subsequent decision must be made, and features of the task environment may change independently of the solver's actions; (b) *time-dependent*, because decisions must be made at the correct moment in relation to environmental demands; and (c) *complex*, in the sense that most variables are not related to each other in a one-to-one manner. In these situations, the problem requires not one decision, but a long series, and these decisions are, in return, completely dependent on one another. For a task that is changing continuously, the same action can be definitive at moment *t1* and useless at moment *t2*. However, traditional, experimental problem-solving research has focused largely on tasks (e.g., anagrams, concept identification, puzzles, etc.) that are not representative of the features already described. Several researchers have started working on a set of computer-based, experimental tasks that are dynamic, time-dependent, and complex, called *microworlds*, and the area of thinking and reasoning that deals with them has been called complex problem solving (CPS). I have discussed two examples of *microworlds*, Firechief and Duress. To test LPSA, I have chosen tasks that are representative of real-world tasks, and have the characteristics mentioned earlier. Thus, in addition to the laboratory tasks, I have used a real-world task, a high-fidelity landing simulator.

No Common Representational Assumptions for Different Tasks: One Task, One Theory of Representation

This problem was also raised by Newell (1980). Certain modelers tend to analyze tasks in a way that is mostly dictated by their intuition of how people proceed when interacting with the environment. For example, Lee and Anderson (2001) used a simplified air traffic controller task (ATC) in a controlled lab situation; they used three levels of description: the unit-task level, the functional level, and the keystroke level. However, Lee and Anderson (2001) used no learning or representation theory to generate such decompositions: "[Our] task decomposition does not depend on any particular theory of skill acquisition. Rather, it solely relies on a pretheoretical task analysis" (p. 273). Although this decomposition may be well motivated and valid for the task at hand, there is no attempt to abstract a task representation that can be used in more than that particular task. In psychology, the investigation of how people represent and interact with the problem-solving tasks is called task analysis. Is task analysis the way to find common representational assumptions for different tasks? Schraagen, Chipman, and Shute (2000) review 20 papers, and each of those presents on average several techniques for task analysis. These techniques include verbal protocol analysis, interviews, elaborated knowledge elicitation methods, similarity judgments, analytical descriptions of the task such as manuals, and so on. It seems evident that there are no integrated theories about the task, nor are there consistent criteria for accepting or rejecting a particular task analysis. The distributional approach that LPSA exemplifies appears to propose a common measure for CPS tasks that can be applied to a wide variety of tasks, as we have already seen in the introduction.

TESTING LPSA IN PROBLEM SOLVING

LSA was tested mainly by proving that the model could do some higher cognition task as well as humans (e.g., solving a synonym test; Landauer & Dumais, 1997). In our testing of LPSA, we (Quesada et al., 2005) have followed the same approach. However, we have also tested some basic assumptions of the metric spaces that LPSA proposes as problem spaces.

Human Similarity Judgments

People can evaluate the similarity between problem-solving solutions. This is a skill that most people practice overtly in their daily life. Sometimes we have to compare other people's solutions to problems. For example, a teacher grading two student essays of the same test must compare them to each other, and maybe to an ideal essay that she would produce. Chess players study and compare the solutions (moves) of masters in difficult games as part of their training. Personnel selection departments compare the solutions of employees solving their daily projects for promotion.

If the model captures people's intuitions on similarity, then LPSA cosines for pairs of trials should correlate with human judgments of similarity. One of the simplest experiments that can be done to test LPSA is to select a few pairs of trials. Quesada, Kintsch, and Gomez (2005) did just that using Firechief. The videos were selected from a corpus of 1,000 trials collected in past experiments with Firechief. LPSA was trained in the same corpus. All the trials had identical landscape, initial conditions, and events (fire appearances, wind changes). That is, the variance in every two videos was due only to participant interventions and their interaction with the system rules.

Quesada, Kintsch, and Gomez (2005) presented experienced participants with eight pairs of videos and were asked to assign a number from 0 to 100 for each pair reflecting the similarity of the two items in the pair. Participants could play the videos as many times as they wanted. Their similarity judgments correlated .94 with the LPSA cosines for these trials.

Testing for Asymmetry

In LPSA, problem spaces are metric spaces. That is, similarity is represented as a metric distance, and it is symmetrical. However, Tversky (1977) demonstrated that in certain circumstances, human similarities are asymmetrical (e.g., the similarity of China to Korea is not the same as Korea to China). If problem-solving spaces are metric spaces, then there must be no asymmetries in the similarity judgments for trials. Quesada, Gonzalez, and Vakunov (in preparation) designed experiments in which participants watched a screen with two replay videos played simultaneously, A and B. The A video was the reference video: Participants had to focus on it, consider its characteristics, and make similarity judgments of the other video B with respect to the reference one. The instructions emphasized the importance of the reference video, asking them to use the A video as their comparison point, and make every judgment relative to it.

Twenty pairs were sampled from the 380 possible permutations of 20 videos taken two by two, and another 20 pairs were obtained by reversing the original pairs: That is, the A video was the former B video, and vice versa. Participants were told that people vary in the way they solve the task and that we wanted them to express the similarity of the two videos numerically (1–100). The same design was tested with two different complex problem-solving tasks: Firechief and the water purification plant (WPP) task (see, e.g., Gonzalez, Lerch, & Lebiere, 2003).

Quesada et al. (in preparation) were not able to find any reliable asymmetries in any of these two tasks. At least at the trial level, similarity judgments of replay videos for this kind of problem-solving situations are symmetrical. The failure to find the asymmetry could be due to the fact that Quesada et al. used very different materials from those used by Tversky (1977). However, Aguilar and Medin (1999) failed to replicate Tversky (1977) using the same design and type of materials in several experiments, which points in the direction that asymmetries in human similarity comparisons are small and may be hard to obtain. In any case, these results agree with the idea that people may represent problem-solving situations within the metric constraints imposed by LPSA.

Context Effects

Another assumption of metric models challenged by Tversky (1977) was that of context independence. Tversky found that adding additional elements to a comparison of two elements may change the perceived similarity between the two elements. Concretely, the extra elements would increase the salience of some features and tip the balance of importance that was obtained when the two items were alone, with no context. Tversky and Gati (1978, study 3) showed relevant context effects as well with countries as stimuli. Medin, Goldstone, and Gentner (1993, exp. 1) found that context can determine what features of an item are considered. In their experiment, people compared triplets of artificial, simple stimuli. The advantage of these stimuli is that they differ in only a few features. The open question is: Can one find the same context effects using highly complex problem-solving videos? Quesada et al. (in preparation) presented people with sets of four videos that could be played simultaneously. Participants had to rearrange four balls in a square; each ball represented a video. So the closer the balls were, the more similar they considered the problem solutions in the videos (Goldstone, 1994). Quesada et al. (in preparation) used the average similarity judgments in the symmetry experiment (average of A → B and B → A) as distances to select the stimuli for the context experiment.

Using these distances, Quesada et al. (in preparation) calculated the closest neighbor of each of the 20 videos. Then, they created a list of random quintuplets [A B C P Q]. C was the target, A and B were two items with random similarities to C. P was the closest neighbor of A and Q was the closest neighbor of B. This design mimics those used before with countries (e.g., Tversky, 1977; Tversky & Gati, 1978, study 4) and schematic faces (Tversky, 1977). However, Quesada et al.'s (in preparation) study differs from the studies that used artificial stimuli with separable dimensions. In problem-solving tasks such as Firechief and Duress, it is very difficult for people to find natural separable dimensions. Most changes are continuous and multifaceted in these tasks. Quesada et al. (in preparation) found no systematic context effects in judging similarities of problem-solving episodes. Although this is only indirect evidence, it seems that the LPSA assumption of context independence hold at least while watching videos in the two complex tasks explored.

Expertise Effects

LPSA can be used to model expertise effects. LPSA is a fully specified computational model that combines the advantages of two major expertise theories: long-term working memory (LTWM; Ericsson & Kintsch, 1995) and the constraint-attunement hypothesis (CAH; Vicente & Wang, 1998). A description of these two theories and how they relate to LPSA follows.

Current theories disagree on what are the most relevant factors that contribute to expertise. The LTWM theory claims that working memory has two different components: a short-term working memory (STWM), which is available under any condition, but of very limited capacity, and a long-term memory (LTWM), which is available only in the domain where one is an expert, but provides unlimited capacity. Thus, the LTWM theory breaks the dichotomy between STWM and long-term memory (LTM). STWM accounts for working memory in unfamiliar activities but does not appear to provide sufficient storage capacity for working memory in skilled complex activities. LTWM is acquired in particular domains to meet specific demands imposed by a given activity on storage and retrieval. LTWM is task specific. Intense practice in a domain creates retrieval structures: associations between the current context and some parts of LTM that can be retrieved almost immediately without effort. The contents of working memory act as the center of a focus that activates other contexts from LTM that are related to them thanks to the retrieval structures. A retrieval structure is defined as an abstract, hierarchical knowledge structure used to organize cues used in the encoding and retrieval of information. LTWM theory proposes that LTWM is generated dynamically by the cues that are present in short-term memory. During text comprehension, for example, where the average human adult is an expert, retrieval structures retrieve propositions from LTM and merge them with the ones derived from text.

The retrieval structures have to be proposed *ex professo* for each domain for which the theory is to be applied. For example, the retrieval structure that chess masters use to encode and retrieve chess information was proposed to be a chessboard (Ericsson & Kintsch, 1995, p. 237).[3] On the other hand, the retrieval structure that a waiter uses for memorizing orders is assumed to be a spatial description of the table.[4] This situation is less than optimal, as when one defines a retrieval structure for each task, one is falling

---

[3]There are other process theories of expertise that also propose the concept of retrieval structure, such as the elementary perceiver and memorizer model (EPAM, e.g., Richman, Staszewski, & Simon, 1995), but I have omitted them from the discussion for brevity. In EPAM, the concept of retrieval structure has changed with the theory. In chess situations, it was also supposed to be a chess board, although reimplementations such as CHREST (Gobet, 1993) proposed that the retrieval structure had two components: what Gobet called "Hypothesis," the longest set of which is the pattern containing the largest quantity of information up to that point, and an "internal representation," which was a schematic representation of the chess board. For expert digit memorization, the retrieval structure proposed was treelike, with chunks of size three, four, and five (running times) and an algorithm that assembled the structure recursively.

[4]The retrieval of the similar contexts in text comprehension was not formalized until Kintsch (1998) proposed how to use the combination of LSA and CI for that. Formalization of the retrieval structures in LTWM for other tasks have not been proposed by the authors (although see Gobet, 2000a).

victim of the problem "one task, one theory" described earlier (Newell, 1980). In LTWM (at least the first instantiation of 1995) the retrieval structures are specific for each task and different from each other; in some cases, the retrieval structures have a hierarchical component, whereas in some other cases there is a strong spatial component; this lack of definition has been criticized as "vague" by Gobet (1998), among others.

LTWM, like most theories of expertise, is a process theory. That is, it specifies the psychological mechanisms that explain the problem solving: It is a theory of "how." An alternative view is the constraint-attunement hypothesis (CAH; Vicente & Wang, 1998), which is a product (i.e., input-output) theory of expertise, where the question to answer is "what" conditions are needed to observe expertise effects, rather than "how." The CAH theory proposes an important distinction between *intrinsic* and *contrived* tasks. *Intrinsic* tasks are definitive features of the domain of expertise, for example, blindfolded chess, memorizing dinner orders, and memorizing digits. A *contrived* task is one that is not part of the domain of expertise, but designed to fulfill some experimental purposes. For example, chess players just play chess, and remembering random chess configurations is not part of the task. Vicente and Wang consider that most of the tasks used in the memory expertise literature are *contrived*, not *intrinsic*, and hence are not explained by LTWM and other process theories. In CAH, environmental constraints are represented by the abstraction hierarchy. This is a hierarchy of means–ends relations that each experimenter must construct by hand for each task. The main proposal of the CAH is that the amount of structure in the environment determines how large the expert's advantage can be, and that these constraints can be represented by the abstraction hierarchy.

Quesada (unpublished, chap. 6) used the data from a 6-month long, six-participant experiment reported in Christoffersen, Hunter, and Vicente (1996, 1997, 1998) to generate an "LPSA-simulated expert" with 3 years of experience with the DURESS problem.

To test the "LPSA-simulated expert" created after averaging the experience of the six participants, the reference task selected was prediction. Prediction plays a very important role in humans' interaction with the environment. Some scientists argue that many features of the cognitive system (e.g., representation, memory, and categorization) can be conceptualized as tools that help to predict the next states of an organism's environment (e.g., Anderson, 1990).

The methodology that Quesada (2004, chap. 6) used was to test how well a prediction could be generated using the nearest neighbors of a target slice of behavior. For example, in a trial of Duress, how much of the end can be predicted using the information from the beginning of a control episode? Or, when we are reading a passage of text, how much of the information contained at the end can an experienced reader anticipate? To implement this idea, one possibility is to define a cutting point that divides the predicting and predicted parts of the passage, and manipulate their sizes while evaluating the quality of the prediction. For brevity, assume that the cutting point we define is the point that leaves three quarters of the trial behind.

The model could predict the last quarter of any trial using the first three quarters with an average accuracy of .8 (expressed in the cosine between the last and predicting blocks). When the system was given an experience of only 6 months, the predictions fell down to less than .3. If the system is trained with 3 years of practice in an environment with no constraints (i.e., not governed by rules of conservation of mass and energy), then the predictions were (as expected) very bad, and comparable to the novice level. LPSA's explanation for these results unifies CAH and LTWM. LPSA can explain both amount of practice effects (main tenant of LTWM) and amount of environmental structure effects (main tenant of CAH). At the same time, LPSA can be considered a computational implementation of the retrieval structures that LTWM proposes.

What is a retrieval structure in our theory? In LPSA, the retrieval structure is implemented as the closest area in the problem space to the situation at hand. If the current context is represented as a point in this space, then the retrieval structure is an area of close points that are retrieved from memory when the situation is analyzed. Note that these retrieval structures are created empirically from the statistics of the environment in LPSA, and thus they are not a priori. The procedure to define the retrieval structures in text comprehension situations is the same as the one for the very different situation of problem solving in the thermodynamic task, which is certainly an advantage of the theory because the retrieval structures do not change with the task to be modeled.

Another line of evidence for LPSA as a theory of expertise comes from *landing technique assessment*. Quesada et al. (2005) used a high-fidelity flying simulator to collect 400 landings where the landing conditions were manipulated systematically, and created a vector space with them. Two instructors evaluated the landing, one of them sitting in the copilot seat, and the other one watching plots of relevant variables in real time (complete- and reduced-information raters, respectively).

The reason for this different exposure to information was to use the knowledge of the raters to filter the variables of interest from the more than 10,000 available in a landing flying simulator! The reduced-information expert plotted only 6 variables, and even with this incredibly small set he could rate landing technique just fine. Thus, the LPSA model was trained with the variables that the reduced-information rater used in his plots to evaluate the landing technique. Then, the nearest neighbors of any new landing were used to generate automatic ratings. Each new landing acted as a probe to retrieve past landings that were similar to it. The grade for a new landing was simply the weighted average of the grades retrieved for its neighbors.

Quesada et al. (2005) created several corpora modifying the number of dimensions (100, 150, 200, 250, 300, 350, and maximum dimensionality, 400) and the number of nearest neighbors used to estimate the landing ratings (from 1 to 10). Another manipulation was the inclusion or exclusion of a time tag, and the type of weighting scheme used (log entropy vs. none). This way, the possible combinations of levels were $(7 \times 10 \times 2 \times 2) = 240$. For each of these combinations of levels, Quesada et al. (2005) used leave-one-out cross-validation to calculate the ratings for the landing excluded. The estimated ratings for each of the 400 landings were then correlated with the real ratings. The combination of levels that best correlated with both humans was selected, and that was the corpus with 200 dimensions, 5 Nearest Neighbors, no weighting, and no time tagging.

The average agreement between human raters was not very high (correlation of only .48). However, this correlation is in line with others reported for the following: Clinical Psychologists (.41), Stockbrokers (<.40), Grain Inspectors (.62), and Pathologists (.50; Shanteau, 2001, p. 237, Table 13.3).

The ratings that the model generated agreed with both humans .46 and .39, respectively, about as much as the two human graders agreed with each other (.48).

One of the LPSA assumptions is that experienced humans perform dimension reduction to represent their environments. The equivalent model (5 nearest neighbors, no weighting, no time stamping) without performing dimension reduction (i.e., using 400 dimensions, which is the shortest dimension of the matrix) correlates with humans (on average for all criteria) only .26, which can be interpreted as evidence for dimension reduction in the representation.

CONCLUSIONS

Problem solving, mental models, and reasoning are explanatory concepts employed in cognitive science to account for performance in complex tasks. LPSA shows that simple ideas, such as similarity-based processing and pattern matching, could have a role even in cognitively complex tasks.

LPSA assumes that representation takes place in a space that has fewer dimensions than the external (distal stimuli) space represented. Thus, the representation is simpler than the represented world. Chater and collaborators (e.g., Chater, 1999; Chater & Vitanyi, 2003) present a view of a cognitive system that compresses data, simplifying the representations. This compression may be lossy (i.e., the system partly throws away information in the process), but the resulting representation may be more adaptive (i.e., it may predict future states of nature better, or produce better inferences, because accidental, inessential information is not present).

LPSA also assumes that humans retrieve past experiences most similar to the current one automatically. The response to the current situation (e.g., in grading a landing) occurs partially because the ratings of past landing that are similar to this one "come to mind," and the response is a composite of those ratings.

This automatic retrieval of past situations takes place at the same time that people use more effortful processes to solve the task. We propose that both the associative (LPSA) and the rule-based systems work in parallel helping each other, and that people use one or the other more depending on the situation at hand. In complex, dynamic tasks like the ones described here, we propose that the associative system is used often.

LPSA provides the means for modeling the constraints in different domains in a comparable manner. What we propose is to use large, naturalistic corpora of problem-solving activity to generate problem space representations. The particular representation that LPSA generates is a metric space via dimension reduction. The great advantage of LPSA is that it can deal with truly complex problem-solving tasks, and with large corpora that provide realistic estimates of human problem-solving behavior.

To conclude this chapter, we would like to use Simon's (1981) parable of the ant and the beach. Simon (1981) wondered why the path that an ant describes when walking on a beach is so complex, and how this complexity can be ascribed to the ant. However, he continued, it could be the case that the complexity is in the beach itself. In other words, the cognitive system's complexity can be a reflection of the structure of the environment (Anderson, 1990, 1991). A formal description of the constraints of this environment can very well be the best approximation to the cognitive representation that the mind uses. We view LPSA as a computational description of the beach obtained by analyzing the paths of thousands of ants.

ACKNOWLEDGMENTS

I would like to thank Walter Kintsch, my PhD advisor and coauthor in the papers on which this chapter is derived, for extensive support and editing comments. Simon Dennis provided insights at different times while I was writing the materials for my dissertation. The simulator and expert time was possible thanks to a grant supported by the European Community Access to Research Infrastructure Action of the Improving Human Potential Program under contract number HPRI-CT-1999-00105 with the National Aerospace Laboratory (NLR). This research was also supported by Grant EIA - 0121201 from the National Science Foundation, and by an ESRC Postdoctoral Fellowship Award PTA-026–27-0716.

REFERENCES

Adelson, B. (1984). When novices surpass experts—the difficulty of a task may increase with expertise. *Journal of Experimental Psychology-Learning Memory and Cognition, 10*(3), 483–495.

Aguilar, C. M., & Medin, D. L. (1999). Asymmetries of comparison. *Psychonomic Bulletin and Review, 6*(2), 328–337.

Anderson, J. R. (1990). *The adaptive character of thought.* Hillsdale, NJ: Lawrence Erlbaum Associates.

Anderson, J. R. (1991). Is human cognition adaptive? *Behavioral and Brain Sciences, 14*(3), 471–517.

Anderson, J. R., & Lebiere, C. (1998). *The atomic components of thought.* Mahwah, NJ: Lawrence Erlbaum Associates.

Burns, B. D., & Vollmeyer, R. (2000). Problem solving: Phenomena in search for a thesis. In L. R. Gleitman & A. K. Joshi (Eds.), *Proceedings of the Cognitive Science Society Meeting* (pp. 627–632). Mahwah, NJ: Lawrence Erlbaum Associates.

Chase, W. G., & Simon, H. A. (1973). The mind's eye in chess. In W. G. Chase (Ed.), *Visual information processing* (pp. 215–281). New York: Academic Press.

Chater, N. (1999). The search for simplicity: A fundamental cognitive principle? *Quarterly Journal of Experimental Psychology Section a-Human Experimental Psychology, 52*(2), 273–302.

Chater, N., & Vitanyi, P. (2003). Simplicity: A unifying principle in cognitive science? *Trends in Cognitive Sciences, 7*(1), 19–22.

Christoffersen, K., Hunter, C. N., & Vicente, K. J. (1996). A longitudinal study of the effects of ecological interface design on skill acquisition. *Human Factors, 38,* 523–541.

Christoffersen, K., Hunter, C. N., & Vicente, K. J. (1997). A longitudinal study of the effects of ecological interface design on fault management performance. *International Journal of Cognitive Ergonomics, 1,* 1–24.

Christoffersen, K., Hunter, C. N., & Vicente, K. J. (1998). A longitudinal study of the impact of ecological interface design on deep knowledge. *International Journal of Human–Computer Studies, 48*(6), 729–762.

Ericsson, K. A., & Kintsch, W. (1995). Long-term working memory. *Psychological Review, 102*(2), 211–245.

Ericsson, K. A., Krampe, R. T., & Tesch-Römer. (1993). The role of deliberate practice in the acquisition of expert performance. *Psychological Review, 100*(3), 363–406.

Ericsson, K. A., & Staszewski, J. J. (1989). Skilled memory and expertise: Mechanisms of exceptional performance. In D. Klahr & K. Kotovsky (Eds.), *Complex information processing: The impact of Herbert A. Simon* (pp. 235–267). Hillsdale, NJ: Lawrence Erlbaum Associates.

Evans, J. S. B. T., & Over, D. E. (1996). *Rationality and reasoning.* Hove, England: Psychology Press.

Glymour, C. (2001). *The mind's arrows: Bayes nets and graphical causal models in psychology.* Boston: MIT Press.

Gobet, F. (1998). Expert memory: A comparison of four theories. *Cognition, 66*(2), 115–152.

Goldstone, R. (1994). An efficient method for obtaining similarity data. *Behavior Research Methods, Instruments, and Computers, 20*, 381–386.

Gonzalez, C., Lerch, F. J., & Lebiere, C. (2003). Instance-based learning in dynamic decision making. *Cognitive Science, 27*, 591–635.

Kahneman, D. (2003). A perspective on judgment and choice—mapping bounded rationality. *American Psychologist, 58*(9), 697–720.

Kotovsky, K., & Fallside, D. (1989). Representation and transfer in problem solving. In D. Klahr & K. Kotovsky (Eds.), *Complex information processing: The impact of Herbert A. Simon* (pp. 69–108). Hillsdale, NJ: Lawrence Erlbaum Associates.

Kotovsky, K., Hayes, J. R., & Simon, H. A. (1985). Why are some problems hard? Evidence from Tower of Hanoi. *Cognitive Psychology, 17*(2), 248–294.

Kotovsky, K., & Simon, H. A. (1990). What makes some problems really hard: Explorations in the problem space of difficulty. *Cognitive Psychology, 22*(2), 143–183.

Laird, J., Rosenbloom, P., & Newell, A. (1986). *Universal subgoaling and chunking.* Boston: Kluwer.

Landauer, T. K., & Dumais, S. T. (1997). A solution to Plato's problem: The latent semantic analysis theory of the acquisition, induction, and representation of knowledge. *Psychological Review, 104*, 211–240.

Lee, F. J., & Anderson, J. R. (2001). Does learning a complex task have to be complex? A study in learning decomposition. *Cognitive Psychology, 42*, 267–316.

Medin, D. L., Goldstone, R. L., & Gentner, D. (1993). Respects for similarity. *Psychological Review, 100*(2), 254–278.

Newell, A. (1980). Reasoning, problem solving, and decision processes: The problem space as a fundamental category. In R. Nickerson (Ed.), *Attention and performance VII* (pp. 693–718). Cambridge, MA: Harvard.

Newell, A. (1990). *The unified theories of cognition.* Cambridge, MA: Harvard University Press.

Newell, A., & Simon, H. A. (1963). GPS: A program that simulates human thought. In E. A. Feigenbaum & J. Feldman (Eds.), *Computers and thought* (pp. 279–293). New York: McGraw Hill.

Newell, A., & Simon, H. A. (1972). *Human problem solving.* Englewood Cliffs, NJ: Prentice-Hall.

Omodei, M. M., & Wearing, A. J. (1993). Fire Chief (Version 2.3). University of Melbourne.

Omodei, M. M., & Wearing, A. J. (1995). The fire chief microworld generating program: An illustration of computer-simulated microworlds as an experimental paradigm for studying complex decision-making behavior. *Behavior Research Methods, Instruments and Computers, 27*, 303–316.

Quesada, J. F. (2004). *Latent problem aolving Analysis (LPSA): A computational theory of representation in complex, dynamic problem solving tasks.* Unpublished doctoral dissertation, Granada, Spain.

Quesada, J. F., Gonzalez, C., & Vakunov, P. (in preparation). *Testing symmetry and context effects in similarity judgments for complex problem solving solutions.* Unpublished manuscript.

Quesada, J. F., Kintsch, W., & Gomez, E. (2005). *Latent problem solving analysis (LPSA): A theory of representation in complex problem solving*. Manuscript submitted for publication.

Richman, H., Staszewski, J., & Simon, H. A. (1995). Simulation of expert memory using EPAM IV. *Psychological Review, 102*(2), 305–330.

Schraagen, J. M., Chipman, S., & Shute, V. J. (2000). State-of-the-art review of cognitive task analysis techniques. In J. M. Schraagen, S. Chipman, & V. L. Shalin (Eds.), *Cognitive task analysis* (pp. 467–487). Mahwah, NJ: Lawrence Erlbaum Associates.

Shanteau, J. (2001). What does it mean when experts disagree? In E. Salas & G. Klein (Eds.), *Linking expertise and naturalistic decision making* (pp. 229–244). Mahwah, NJ: Lawrence Erlbaum Associates.

Simon, H. A. (1981). *The sciences of the artificial*. Cambridge, MA: MIT Press.

Sloman, S. (2002). Two systems of reasoning. In T. Gilovich, D. Griffin, & D. Kahneman (Eds.), *Heuristics and Biases: The psychology of intuitive judgment* (pp. 379–396). Cambridge, MA: Cambridge University Press.

Sloman, S. A. (1996). The empirical case for two systems of reasoning. *Psychological Bulletin, 119*(1), 3–22.

Stanovich, K. E., & Cunningham, A. E. (1991). Reading as constrained reasoning. In J. R. Sternberg & P. A. Frensch (Eds.), *Complex problem solving: Principles and mechanisms* (pp. 3–61). Hillsdale, NJ: Lawrence Erlbaum Associates.

Stanovich, K. E. (2004). *The robot's rebellion: Finding meaning in the age of Darwin*. Chicago: University of Chicago Press.

Tversky, A. (1977). Features of similarity. *Psychological Review, 84*(4), 327–352.

Tversky, A., & Gati, I. (1978). Studies of similarity. In E. Rosh & B. B. Lloyd (Eds.), *Cognition and categorization* (pp. 79–98). Hillsdale, NJ: Lawrence Erlbaum Associates.

Vicente, K. J., & Wang, J. H. (1998). An ecological theory of expertise effects in memory recall. *Psychological Review, 105*, 33–57.

Zipf, G. K. (1949). *Human behaviour and the principle of least-effort*. Cambridge MA: Addison-Wesley.

III

LSA in Educational Applications

11

Assessing and Improving Comprehension With Latent Semantic Analysis

Keith Millis
Joseph Magliano
Katja Wiemer-Hastings
Stacey Todaro
Northern Illinois University

Danielle S. McNamara
University of Memphis

Assessing and improving reading comprehension are crucial goals for educators and psychologists alike. Students across the nation have great difficulty in comprehending what they read. It is therefore important that educators are able to identify students at risk for failing, and to have some procedure available to help students improve their comprehension. Assessment and intervention go hand in hand. To know whether a student has trouble understanding a passage, one must identify whether the student had successfully performed any number of processes related to reading (e.g., word recognition, inferencing, making connections between the current and prior sentences, etc.). And to improve a student's comprehension, it is likely that the intervention address at least a subset of those same reading processes.

This chapter summarizes some research that we have conducted that uses LSA to assess reading comprehension. We also discuss research that we have done that uses LSA to give feedback to readers as they read with the goal that they become better readers.

ASSESSING COMPREHENSION

Currently, educators usually rely on multiple-choice tests to assess their students' comprehension. In multiple-choice tests, the student reads a passage before answering multiple-choice questions about that passage. This time-honored tradition offers several advantages: easy administration and scoring, low costs, and high reliability. Despite the advantages, there are certain limitations to multiple-choice tests. One is that they often do not accurately tap the cognitive representations and mechanisms that underlie learning. For example, to understand implicit relations in connected discourse, the reader must generate bridging inferences that conceptually link explicit ideas. However, most multiple-choice tests provide only a summary statistic of overall comprehension, rather than scores reflecting bridging ability or other component processes of comprehension (except perhaps, a vocabulary score). More importantly, multiple-choice tests measure comprehension after the student reads the text. Consequently, the tests are limited in accurately measuring inferential activities and reading strategies that occur during reading (Carver, 1992; Farr, Pritchard, & Smitten, 1990; Hanna & Oaseter, 1980; Katz, Lautenschlager, Blackburn, & Harris, 1990). A third limitation is that these tests tap surface knowledge (e.g., particular words or phrases) gained from a text rather than the deep understanding that leads to long-term learning (e.g., Shapiro & McNamara, 2000). Indeed, students often adopt special test taking strategies, such as reading the questions first before searching the text for answers (Farr et al., 1990). As a consequence, the student may answer the question correctly, yet fail to understand the text at a deep level.

Our research makes use of latent semantic analysis (LSA) to address three limitations of standard postreading comprehension measures. First, LSA allows online comprehension assessment; second, the measures are easily and automatically calculated; and, third, the comprehension measures reveal deep comprehension processes (Magliano & Millis, 2003; Shapiro & McNamara, 2000). In our research, we have readers tell us what they are thinking about while they read a text. These thoughts are called verbal protocols. Verbal protocols, together with LSA, provide an alternative to standard measures such as multiple-choice tests for assessing reading comprehension. This alternative arises from the assumptions that (a) the verbal protocols produced while reading a sentence (or immediately thereafter) capture the thoughts of the reader during (and not after) comprehension, (b) the protocols reflect the nature of the person's understanding, and (c) LSA can classify the protocols on understanding by comparing the protocols to texts representing different types or levels of understanding. Although the use of verbal protocols has led to lively debates within experimental psychology (cf. Ericsson & Simon, 1993; Nisbett & Wilson, 1977), verbal protocols are now commonly assumed to reveal thoughts in short-term memory that are codeable in language (Ericsson & Simon, 1993; Pressley & Afferbach, 1995). Using LSA to classify verbal protocols on the extent to which the reader understands the text is advantageous because verbal protocols are tedious and time consuming to hand code. Moreover, expert knowledge is needed to identify and classify the units of language of interest.

OVERVIEW OF APPROACH

In the studies to be reported in this chapter, participants read texts one sentence at a time on a computer screen. After specific sentences, they are asked to either say aloud or type into the computer their thoughts regarding their "understanding of the sentence in regard to the text as a whole." Admittedly, the instruction is a bit vague, but we did not want to affect their natural responses by giving detailed examples. They are also told that there is no right or wrong answer. Their response comprises the verbal protocol for that sentence. The computer then computes the semantic similarity between the protocol and several "semantic benchmarks" using LSA. Semantic benchmarks are fixed texts associated with that sentence that convey different types of reading strategies that might be exhibited at that sentence (Millis, Magliano, Wiemer-Hastings, & McNamara, 2001). They are functionally similar to "ideal answers" to questions in Graesser's AutoTutor (see Graesser et al., chap. 13 in this volume) in that the magnitude of the LSA cosines between the verbal protocol and each of the benchmarks are taken to be indicators of conceptual understanding.

There are various constraints on which the architecture of this approach can be successful. One is the extent to which the content of the semantic benchmarks captures a person's level of understanding. This is quite challenging because readers can say a wide variety of things to any given sentence. They might restate the sentence, elaborate the sentence, combine ideas across sentences, reveal a personal anecdote, type in a metacognitive statement (e.g., "Oh, I thought so"), or exhibit a combination of strategies. In addition, the success of using our LSA-based system to measure comprehension depends on the assumption that skilled and less-skilled comprehenders will produce recognizably different content in their protocols. For example, it would be ideal, if for a given sentence, skilled comprehenders always say X and less-skilled comprehenders always say Y, and that X and Y are semantically dissimilar from one another.

Theories of discourse comprehension have posited two assumptions that have guided us on what to look for in the verbal protocols that would discriminate between skilled and less-skilled comprehenders. One is that better readers are more likely than poor readers to reactivate text that is causally related to the current sentence. That is, better readers actively construct a text representation that is guided by the causal structure of the text. When they read a sentence, they attach the ideas from the current sentence to causal antecedents in the prior text representation (Graesser, Singer, & Trabasso, 1994). The second is that better readers are more likely than poor readers to establish inferences based on their world knowledge, which links the current text representation to the theme of the text (Trabasso & Magliano, 1996). Better readers use their world knowledge to actively understand the text.

We have used these theoretical considerations to guide the construction of the semantic benchmarks. In most of the research to be described in this chapter (except when otherwise noted), we compared verbal protocols to three semantic benchmarks: the *current sentence, prior causally relevant sentences,* and *world knowledge.* The current sentence benchmark contained content words from the current sentence: nouns, verbs, adjectives, and adverbs. The prior causally relevant sentence benchmark contained the content words from sentences that were identified by a hand-conducted causal analysis to be causal antecedents to the current sentence (see Trabasso, van den Broek, & Suh, 1989). Theoretically, these benchmarks represent the ideas that skilled readers should be reactivating as they read the current sentence. The world knowledge benchmarks represented elaborations associated with each sentence. The words comprising this benchmark were empirically derived from a question-answering task and were not in either of the other two benchmarks. Although relevant knowledge could be identified by LSA from similar passages in a background corpus, we have not as yet done so.

Can LSA identify the source of the information contained in a verbal protocol? That is, can the cosines between a verbal protocol and the benchmarks reveal whether the verbal protocol contained information from the current sentence or from causal antecedents? A study by Magliano, Wiemer-Hastings, Millis, Muñoz, and McNamara (2002) addressed this question by having students supply self-explanations after reading sentences of expository texts suitable for college freshman. Self-explanations (McNamara et al., chap. 12 in this volume; McNamara, 2004; McNamara, Levinstein, & Boonthum, 2004) are verbal protocols that express an attempt by the reader to explain the current sentence in the context of the passage by using various reading strategies, such as paraphrasing, bridging, elaborating, predicting, using logic and common sense. The self-explanations from Magliano et al. (2002) were coded on the extent that they elaborated the current sentence, revealing the use of the strategies. Self-explanations that merely restated or paraphrase the current sentence were coded as "sentence-focused." Sentence-focused explanations do not provide any new information beyond the current sentence. Self-explanations that included a concept from an immediately prior text sentence were coded as "local-focused." Local-focused explanations might include an elaboration of a concept mentioned in the current or immediately prior sentence, but there is no attempt to link the current sentence to the theme of the text. Self-explanations that linked the sentence to the theme of the text with world knowledge were coded as "global-focused." Global-focused explanations tend to use multiple reading strategies, and indicate the most active level of processing. Table 11.1 gives examples of self-explanations to sentence 13 of the text "Stages of Thunderstorm Development," which is presented in the appendix, the benchmarks associated with that sentence, and the LSA cosines between them.

As expected, Magliano et al. (2002) found a correspondence between the self-explanations and the source of information contained in them. For ex-

TABLE 11.1
Example Self-Explanations and Semantic Benchmarks to the Sentence 13 of the Text "Stages of Thunderstorm Development" (See the Appendix)

Self-Explanation Category	Example Self-Explanations	Current Sentence Benchmark	Prior Text Benchmark	World Knowledge Benchmark
		Hour size precipitation amount becomes updraft support	Cloud release develops start storm	Fall hold down heavy
Sentence-focused:	The updraft cannot support the amount of precipitation after an hour.	.75	.08	−.06
Local-focused:	Eventually, there is too much moisture and hailstones and the system gets too heavy.	.18	.22	.24
Global-focused:	Thunderstorms only last for about an hour because since the rain is so heavy, the air cannot continue to rise.	.33	.41	.32

ample, the left-hand side of Figure 11.1 displays the proportion of clauses within each type of self-explanation as classified by human judges. It also displays the source of the clauses in terms of whether the main content of the clause came from the current sentence or prior text and/or world knowledge. Explanations classified as sentence-focused consisted almost exclusively of content from the current sentence, and very little from prior text or world knowledge. In contrast, global-focused self-explanations contained more content from prior text and/or world knowledge than from the current sentence. But, more importantly, the same pattern emerged on the cosines that were generated between the self-explanations and the semantic benchmarks (see the right-hand side of Fig. 11.1). These data suggest that LSA can "identify" the source of information in verbal protocols, enabling it to serve as a proxy for human raters.

DO LSA COSINES PREDICT COMPREHENSION?

Our LSA-based approach to measuring comprehension has produced very encouraging results. Before we describe these results, let us first outline what we mean by "comprehension." The goal of comprehension is to generate a coherent representation of the discourse and, in particular, the situations and events depicted in the discourse. Discourse psychologists refer to the representation of the situations as the "situation model" of the text. Although the situation model is based on the explicit ideas mentioned in the discourse, it includes reader-generated inferences about temporal, causal, and spatial attributes of the entities, protagonists, and events mentioned in

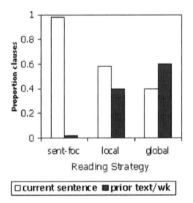 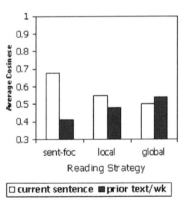

Figure 11.1.   The percentage of clauses in verbal protocols judged by humans to contain information from either the current sentence and prior text or world knowledge (left) and LSA cosines between the verbal protocols and current sentence and prior text or world knowledge benchmarks (right) as a function of general reading strategy.

the text. The situation model is incrementally built across time, as each clause is read and as inferences pertaining to that clause are generated. In narratives, the situation model includes the location and goals of the protagonists. In expository texts, the situation model would ideally include the ideas underlying the exposition—what the author is describing. It is clearly out of our scope to use LSA to account for all of these processes. Our goal has been more restricted, namely, to assess the extent to which the reader is focusing on information from the text and world knowledge that is directly relevant to the ideas expressed by the current sentence.

Narrative Text

Magliano and Millis (2003) tested whether LSA could be used to assess the comprehension of simple narrative text. In their study, college students "thought aloud" to selected sentences in very simple fairy tales, and read others silently. The students were grouped into skilled and less-skilled comprehenders based on their performance on the Nelson-Denny test of comprehension. To measure how well they comprehended the stories, students in Study 1 answered questions about them and students in Study 2 recalled them. For each student, mean cosines were computed between each verbal protocol and the current sentence (i.e., the sentence to which the participants' had thought aloud), and the prior causally relevant sentences (as determined by a hand-coded causal analysis). In this case, the text sentences served as semantic benchmarks.

The LSA cosines between the verbal protocols and the benchmarks predicted measures of comprehension when submitted to regression analyses. Three predictors were included in the equations, including two LSA benchmarks (LSA current sentence, LSA prior causal sentence) and Nelson-Denny scores. There were three regression equations, one predicting performance on the True–False questions, one predicting recall from the passages to which the participants thought aloud, and one predicting recall from the passages that were read silently. The standardized coefficients (beta weights) are shown in Table 11.2. The LSA cosines were predictive in all three equations. The negative slope for the LSA cosine for the current sentence indicates that greater similarity between the verbal protocols and the current sentence is associated with decreased comprehension. In contrast, the positive direction of the prior causal sentence predictor indicates that comprehension increased when the verbal protocols were similar to causally related antecedent sentences. Performance on the Nelson-Denny test contributed significantly only to the prediction of recall of the silently read passages.

There are three noteworthy points to these results. First, the direction of the LSA beta weights is consistent with theories of comprehension.

TABLE 11.2
Beta Weights From Regression Analyses to Predict Comprehension of Narrative
Texts Including LSA Cosines and the Nelson-Denny Test of Comprehension

Predictor Variable	Dependent Variable		
LSA Benchmark	True–False Questions	Recall (Think Aloud Passages)	Recall (Silently Read Passages)
LSA current sentence	−.61*	−.36**	−.22*
LSA prior causal sentence	.36**	.58**	.47**
Nelson-Denny	.02	.11	.23*
R^2	.38**	.45**	.38**

*p < .05, **p < .01.

Namely, a coherent representation is achieved when the reader attempts to conceptually link the current sentence with the causal structure of the text (Trabasso et al., 1989). Second, the finding that the LSA cosines predicted recall for stories that were silently read indicates the cosines generalize to narrative text read in a more externally valid setting. That is, few competent readers externalize their thoughts as they read a story. Generalization is especially important for a future comprehension test using this procedure. Third, the LSA-based cosines were more predictive of the comprehension measures than was the Nelson-Denny, thus highlighting the utility of this procedure to uncover comprehension processes.

Expository Text

To test whether LSA could account for the comprehension of more difficult expository text, we had 75 undergraduate psychology students attending Northern Illinois University read one of two expository texts on the computer, and after reading each sentence, type in their thoughts at that moment in time. One passage described the origins of coal, and the other described medical problems associated with heart disease (modified from McNamara, Kintsch, Songer, & Kintsch, 1996). After completing both passages, they were given a comprehension test of the material. The comprehension test consisted of eight short answer questions. One-half of the questions were constructed to measure the explicit ideas mentioned in the text, whereas the other half were constructed to measure inferences thought to be included in the situation model. The score for each answer was the percentage of propositions that human raters had judged to be matches with the propositions needed for an ideal answer. The percentages for each question type were summed, creating a score for the textbase and for the situation model. The score for the textbase and situation model questions were 2.31 (SD = .77) and 1.46 (SD = .61), respectively. The bivariate correlation between the textbase and situation model scores was .43, indicating a shared variance of 18%. Students also took the Nelson-Denny test of comprehension.

To examine whether the cosines predicted readers' comprehension of expository text, the cosines between what they had typed in after each sentence and the two benchmarks (current sentence, prior causal text), and their Nelson-Denny scores were entered into three regression equations, one for each type of comprehension score (textbase, situation model, total). The prior causal text contained content words from causal antecedent sentences that had to be at least two sentences prior to the current sentence. Thus, the prior text benchmark words represented "distal causes." The standardized regression coefficients (beta weights) are shown in Table 11.3. The results were very similar across the three equations and to the results obtained with narrative texts. The cosines for the distal causes were consistently significant. The positive slope for this variable indicates that the more semantically similar participants' self-explanations were to the distal causes for the current sentence, the more questions they answered correctly. The slope for the current sentence benchmark was statistically significant for performance on the textbase questions and the overall score. The negative slope for this variable indicated that the more semantically similar the self-explanation was to the current sentence, the more poorly participants did in answering the textbase questions, but not the situation model questions. This result suggests that performance on the textbase questions

TABLE 11.3

Beta Weights From Regression Analyses to Predict Comprehension of Expository Texts Including LSA Cosines and the Nelson-Denny Test of Comprehension

Predictor Variable	Dependent Variable		
LSA Benchmark	*Textbase*	*Situation Model*	*Total*
LSA current sentence	−.61*	−.36	−.59*
LSA distal causes	.58**	.59**	.69**
Nelson-Denny	.25*	.30**	.32**
R^2	.20**	.20**	.28**

was more closely tied to the reader's focus on the current sentence rather than on distal causes.

DOES THE TYPE OF BENCHMARK MATTER?

The LSA benchmarks thus far discussed have represented information from current and prior causal sentences. They were chosen to capture the extent to which the reader links the current sentence representation to causal antecedents mentioned in the prior text. However, verbal protocols can reveal and be categorized on other processes as well. One is general reading strategies conveyed by self-explanations that were briefly described earlier in this chapter—namely, sentence-focused, local, and global strategies (see Magliano et al., 2002; McNamara et al., chap. 12 in this volume). These general reading strategies represent the extent to which the reader actively elaborates the current sentence with the prior text, the theme of the text, and world knowledge. Another process is to identify the use of more specific reading strategies, such as paraphrasing, bridging, and generating elaborations. Paraphrasing occurs when the self-explanation contains a restatement of the current sentence. Bridging occurs when the self-explanation contains a connection between the current sentence and a prior sentence. An elaboration occurs when the self-explanation contains an idea that was not mentioned in the text.

We have recently compared three different types of benchmarks on their utility for classifying verbal protocols on the general and specific strategies that they may reveal (Millis et al., 2004). The first type is referred to as *content words*; these are the benchmarks that we have discussed earlier representing three sources of information: the current sentence, prior text, and world knowledge (see Table 11.1). The second is called *exemplars*. The exemplars for a given sentence include three examples of sentence-focused, local-focused, and global-focused strategies that were previously collected and coded as good examples of the three categories. For example, the protocol "The updraft cannot support the amount of precipitation after an hour" was used as a sentence-focused benchmark for sentence 13 of the thunderstorm text. The third type is *strategy* benchmarks. The content of these benchmarks represent different types of reading strategies that could be displayed for that sentence. For example, the protocol "The surging of warm and moist air add to the height of the cloud" served as a bridging benchmark for sentence 13 in that it explains why the precipitation becomes too heavy for the updraft. There were up to three benchmarks representing paraphrases of the current sentence, bridges that could be made at that sentence, and elaborations that had been made at that sentence. The exemplar and strategy benchmarks were taken from hand-coded protocols previously collected.

Students in this study read and provided self-explanations to each sentence of two expository texts. Cosines were computed between each self-explanation and the benchmarks. There were up to 21 cosines altogether—3 for content words, 9 for exemplars that included 3 for each global strategy (sentence-focused, local, and global), and approximately 9 for specific strategies that included 3 for each particular strategy (i.e., paraphrases, bridges, and elaborations), although some sentences produced fewer than 3 bridges or elaborations. The mean cosine for benchmarks representing each strategy was computed. This resulted in 9 cosines for each self-explanation: 3 for content words, 3 for exemplars, and 3 for strategies.

Human judges categorized the self-explanations on general and specific reading strategies. The interjudge reliability on a subset of self-explanations was adequate, Kappa = .80. Using a randomly chosen half of the self-explanations,[1] Millis et al. (2004) predicted the type and presence of general and specific reading strategies from the cosines and the length of the self-explanation (log number of words). We computed a series of discriminant analyses for this task because discriminant analysis predicts group membership, and in this case, the type of general reading strategy (i.e., sentence-focus, local, global) and specific reading strategy (i.e., presence or absence of a paraphrase, bridge, or elaboration) is analogous to group membership. We then used signal detection to assess the accuracy of prediction for each reading strategy. A d' was computed for each strategy based on hits and false alarms. For example, a hit for a sentence-focused strategy occurred when both the discriminant analysis and human judges assigned the self-explanation to that category. A false alarm for sentence-focused strategy occurred when the discriminant analysis categorized the self-explanation as a sentence-focus strategy, but the human judged it as either a local or a global strategy.

The d's for each strategy are shown in Figure 11.2. The magnitude of the d's ranged from .89 to 1.54 (chance performance equals zero). McNamara et al. (chap. 12 in this volume) reports similar values, but has improved classification when word-based algorithms are added to the LSA cosines. Nevertheless, the magnitude is less important than the pattern across benchmarks because the goal is to compare types of benchmarks. The d's for general strategies in Figure 11.2 are the mean of the d's for local and global strategies. Across all types of benchmarks, the d's for sentence-focused ($M = 1.50$) and global ($M = 1.21$) general reading strategies were much higher than for local strategies ($M = .63$), indicating that the approach is most suitable for identifying self-explanations that are either minimal or complete with multiple strategies.

---

[1]The other half was used to test the coefficients obtained from the first half, but these data are not reported here because they do not directly address differences among benchmarks.

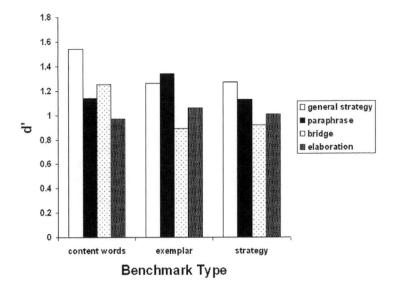

Figure 11.2.   d's as function of type of benchmark and strategy.

The d's indicate some differences among the different types of benchmarks in their utility for classifying reading strategies. In regard to identifying general strategies, the content words produced d's that were .28 higher than the exemplar and strategy approaches. Generally, the content words did better than exemplars and strategy benchmarks, except that the exemplars did slightly better than the content words in correctly identifying paraphrases and elaborations. From a practical consideration, this is advantageous because the content words' benchmarks were by far the easiest to construct.

IMPROVING COMPREHENSION: CAN FEEDBACK AFFECT GENERAL STRATEGY USE?

Given that we have been able to predict general strategies using LSA, it is important to consider whether it can be used to improve comprehension. A starting point is whether feedback based on the classification of self-explanations affects the use of the strategies. Feedback plays a crucial role in improving learning, inferencing, and in computer-assisted learning environments and intelligent tutoring systems (Winne, Graham, & Prock, 1993). The chapter by McNamara et al. (chap. 12 in this volume) discusses a much more elaborate system than what is presented here, but both provide feedback based on typed-in self-explanations. In this study, we were interested in whether feedback based on an LSA-based classification of general reading strategies would be effective in producing a change in the quality of their self-explanations, as evaluated by the system. If feedback does increase the quality, then this would not only provide further support that LSA can be used to assess comprehension, but that LSA could be used to improve comprehension.

METHODS

Undergraduate psychology students at Northern Illinois University ($N = 87$) were given a brief tutorial on self-explaining text. In this tutorial, they were told about how self-explanations can increase comprehension, and were given examples of self-explanations that varied on quality, and also examples of paraphrases, bridges, and elaborations. They were specifically told that although paraphrasing provides a good first start to a self-explanation, effective self-explanations include multiple strategies. They were then instructed to evaluate a computerized tutor meant for students to practice generating self-explanations. The interface of the tutor was fairly simple. It consisted of three textboxes: one in which the text would appear one sentence at a time, one in which the participants were told to type their self-explanation, and one in which the tutor gave feedback to the students. Students in the feedback conditions (see later) were also asked to rate the appropriateness or the quality of the feedback using a 1 (inappropriate) to 6 (very appropriate) Likert-type scale. This task was meant to increase the plausibility of their task, namely, to evaluate the tutor. Because of time restrictions, participants only self-explained one of two expository texts, "The Origins of Coal" or "Heart Problems."

The participants were randomly assigned to one of four conditions. In a *no-feedback* condition, the participants did not receive any feedback on their self-explanations. In a *general-only* condition, they only received feedback consisting of one word (e.g., "Ok") based on the general quality of their self-explanation. In a *full* condition, they received general feedback and also feedback on using particular strategies, if they were identified. An example of full feedback would be: "Good. I'm pleased to see that you are bridging here." In order to maximize the naturalness of the feedback, the computer randomly picked one out of six responses for each strategy. In a *random* condition, the computer gave full feedback based on randomly generated values between 0 and 1.0. Examples of feedback are listed in Table 11.4.

The type of feedback within the feedback conditions was based on the classification of the self-explanation. The cosines obtained with the content word benchmarks (current sentence, prior causal sentences, and world knowledge), along with the number of words in the self-explanation were entered into a weighted linear equation that produced a predicted general reading strategy (text focused, local, global). The weights were computed

TABLE 11.4
Computer Feedback as a Function of Self-Explanation Category

Self-Explanation Category	Computer Feedback
General quality:	
Text-focused	"OK"
Local	"Good"
Global	"Excellent"
Specific strategy:	Sample Feedback
Paraphrase	"I believe you are rephrasing the sentence for the most part." or "Are you primarily paraphrasing the sentence?" etc.
Bridge	"I like it when you connect your thoughts with a previous sentence." or "I'm pleased to see that you are bridging here." etc.
Elaboration	"It looks to me that you are drawing upon what you know." or "I like it when you tie in what you know into the self explanation." etc.

from a discriminant analysis that was conducted on an independent data set. The computer gave the feedback "Ok," "Good," "Excellent" to classified text-focused, local, and global self-explanations, respectively. In the general feedback condition, this was the extent of the feedback. However, in the full feedback condition, additional feedback was given if the computer identified any specific strategy based on rules using the magnitude and pattern of the cosines. These threshold values were determined empirically from the prior independent data set. For example, the self-explanation was coded as a paraphrase if the cosine for current sentence was greater than .80, and if the cosines for prior text and world knowledge were both lower than .15. The self-explanation was coded as including a bridge if the cosine for prior text was greater than .40, and an elaboration if the cosine for world knowledge was greater than .37.

RESULTS

Accuracy of Classifications

Two humans independently classified the self-explanations from 16 participants as either being text-focused, local, or global on general quality. These were coded from 1 to 3, respectively. The reliability of the judges was adequate, $r = .79$ (alpha = .91). The correlations between the raters and the computerized classifications were .70 and .75. Therefore, the classifications based on LSA agreed with the human judges roughly to the extent that they agreed with one another.

The Effect of Feedback on Overall Quality

For each participant, the computerized classifications of text-focused, local, and global self-explanations were assigned scores of 1, 2, and 3, respectively. A mean quality score was computed for each participant by averaging these scores. The averaged quality scores were analyzed using a 4 (feedback condition) × 2 (text) between-participants ANOVA. The main effect of condition was significant, $F(3, 79) = 3.67, p < .05$. The mean quality scores for no-feedback, random, general-only, and full were 1.72 ($SD = .63$), 1.85 ($SD = .50$), 2.17 ($SD = .65$), and 2.12 ($SD = .56$), respectively. Post-hoc comparisons indicated that the no-feedback conditions received significantly lower quality scores than the general-only and full conditions, but not the random condition. There was also a main effect of text, $F(1, 79) = 4.91, p < .05$. The mean for the heart and coal passages were 2.1 and 1.8, respectively. The condition by text interaction was not significant, $F(1, 79) = 2.41, p < .10$.

The Effect of Feedback on Using Effective Strategies

For each participant, we computed the percentage of self-explanations of each type. The percentages for bridging and elaborative inferences were combined because these two strategies were described to the participants as being effective strategies, whereas paraphrasing was described as merely a beginning to self-explaining. These values were submitted to a 2 (strategy type) × 4 (feedback condition) × 2 (text) mixed ANOVA with strategy as the within-participants factor. The only significant result was a strategy by condition interaction, $F(3, 79) = 3.72, p = .05$. The interaction is shown in Figure 11.3. As feedback became more complete, paraphrasing decreased whereas bridging and elaborating increased. Indeed, when there was no feedback, there was no statistical difference between the occurrences of paraphrasing and bridging or elaborative inferences ($p < .70$). In the presence of random feedback, the difference was marginally significant ($p = .06$); however, the difference was highly significant for general and full feedback ($p < .001$).

The Effect of Feedback on Appropriate Ratings

A mean appropriateness rating was computed for each participant in the feedback conditions. The means for the random, general, and full condi-

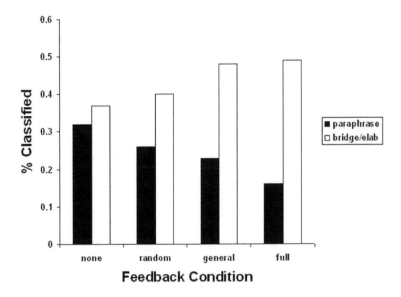

Figure 11.3. The percentage of paraphrases and bridges or elaborations in self-explanations classified by tutor under four feedback conditions.

tions were 4.7, 4.3, and 4.5, respectively. There were no significant effects when the means were submitted to ANOVA.

Summary of Feedback Study

In summary, feedback as determined by LSA cosines between the self-explanations and semantic benchmarks improved the quality of the self-explanations. Feedback in the general and full conditions elicited more effective general reading strategies than having no feedback. The same was true for specific reading strategies. Paraphrasing decreased whereas bridging and elaborations increased with feedback. Interestingly, there was no difference between the general and full conditions on general and specific reading strategy usage, suggesting that one word (e.g., "Good") was just as effective as one word with additional information (e.g., "Good. I like it when you bring up prior text."). Perhaps participants inferred the additional information in the general condition from the content of the feedback that they were given. Random feedback improved self-explanations somewhat and participants were seemingly unaware that the feedback was not appropriate. This finding is not too surprising given that random feedback will be correct by chance roughly one third of the time. However, the result also indicates that the participants showed little metacognitive awareness of their strategy use with respect to the appropriateness of the feedback.

CONCLUSIONS

The use of LSA to assess comprehension offers several advantages over standard multiple-choice tests. First, the verbal protocols that LSA categorizes are snapshots of the comprehender's mind during comprehension. Second, LSA analyses of verbal protocols reveal the use of different types of reading strategies, such as paraphrasing, bridging, and elaborating. Third, using these classifications to provide feedback to the reader improves the quality of the self-explanations. Fourth, producing a verbal protocol in the manner that we have does not have the "feel" of taking a traditional pen-and-paper test, partly because the student is told that there is no right or wrong answers. This might reduce lowered performance due to test anxiety and "stereotype threat" (e.g., Steele & Aronson, 1995).

We should point out that we have had encouraging results with LSA, despite the fact that others in this volume have reported difficulty when using short texts. With short texts, replacing one word might lead to very different cosines. In our case, the texts are benchmarks and self-explanations. We can only speculate as to why we have been relatively successful. One reason might be that most of our research is correlational in which many items are averaged, thereby reducing the effect of outliers. Classifying self-explanations into discrete reading strategy categories has been more challenging. For example, McNamara et al. (chap. 12 in this volume) reports that various word-based algorithms must be added to LSA cosine in order to achieve a satisfactory level of classification. The feedback study described earlier also used a classification procedure, but in that study the classification of the self-explanations was probably just good enough so that the feedback content could change the quality of the self-explanations.

In conclusion, our results indicate that LSA can be used successfully to predict comprehension, assess overall reading strategies, and identify specific reading strategies in verbal protocols. These results provide encouraging directions for assessing deep level comprehension using an online and automatic measure. Moreover, the LSA-based system can be used to generate feedback to the reader, which in turn improves strategy use. Thus, LSA based measures can be used to not only assess comprehension, but also to improve it.

REFERENCES

Carver, R. P. (1992). What do standardized tests of reading comprehension measure in terms of efficiency, accuracy, and rate? *Reading Research Quarterly, 27*, 346–359.

Ericsson, K. A., & Simon, H. A. (1993). *Protocol analysis: Verbal reports as data.* Cambridge, MA: MIT Press.

Far, R., Pritchard, R., & Smitten, B. (1990). A description of what happens when an examinee takes a multiple-choice reading comprehension test. *Journal of Educational Measurement, 27*, 209–226.

Graesser, A. C., Singer, M., & Trabasso, T. (1994). Constructing inferences during narrative text comprehension. *Psychological Review*, 101, 371–395.

Hanna, G. S., & Oaster, T. R. (1980). A new tool for measuring and understanding individual differences in the component processes of reading comprehension. *Journal of Educational Psychology*, 93, 103–128.

Katz, S., Lautenschlager, G., Blackburn, A., & Harris, F. (1990). Answering reading comprehension items without passages on the SAT. *Psychological Sciences*, 1, 122–127.

Magliano, J. P., & Millis, K. K. (2003). Assessing reading skill with a think-aloud procedure and latent semantic analysis. *Cognition and Instruction*, 21, 251–284.

Magliano, J. P., Wiemer-Hastings, K., Millis, K. K., Muñoz, B. D., & McNamara, D. (2002). Using latent semantic analysis to assess reader strategies. *Behavior Research Methods, Instruments, and Computers*, 34, 181–188.

McNamara, D. S. (2004). SERT: Self-explanation reading training. *Discourse Processes*, 1–38.

McNamara, D. S., Kintsch, E., Songer, N. B., & Kintsch, W. (1996). Are good texts always better? Text coherence, background knowledge, and levels of understanding in learning from text. *Cognition and Instruction*, 14, 1–43.

McNamara, D. S, Levinstein, I. B., & Boonthum, C. (2004). iSTART: Interactive strategy training for active reading and thinking. *Behavior Research Methods, Instruments, and Computers*, 36, 222–233.

Millis, K. K., Kim, H. J., Todaro, S. Magliano, J. P., Wiemer-Hastings, K., & McNamara, D. (2004). Identifying reading strategies using latent semantic analysis: Comparing semantic benchmarks. *Behavior Research Methods, Instruments, and Computers*, 36, 213–231

Millis, K. K., Magliano, J. P., Wiemer-Hastings, K., & McNamara, D. (2001). Using LSA in a computer-based test of reading comprehension. In J. D. Moore, C. Luckhardt-Redfield, & W. L. Johnson (Eds.), *Artificial intelligence in education: AI-ED in the wired and wireless future: Vol. 68. Frontiers in artificial intelligence and applications* (pp. 583–585). Amsterdam: IOS Press.

Nisbett, R. E., & Wilson, T. D. (1977). Telling more than we can know: Verbal reports on mental processes. *Psychological Review*, 84, 231–259.

Pressley, M., & Afflerbach, P. (1995). *Verbal protocols of reading: The nature of constructively responsive reading*. Hillsdale, NJ: Lawrence Erlbaum Associates.

Shapiro, A. M., & McNamara, D. S. (2000). The use of latent semantic analysis as a tool for the quantitative assessment of understanding and knowledge. *Journal of Educational Computing Research*, 22, 1–36.

Steele, C. M., & Aronson, J. (1995). Stereotype threat and the intellectual test performance of African Americans. *Journal of Personality and Social Psychology*, 69, 797–811.

Trabasso, T., & Magliano, J. P. (1996). How do children understand what they read and what can we do to help them? In M. Grades, P. van den Broek, & B. Taylor (Eds.), *The first R: A right of all children*, (pp. 160–188). New York: Columbia University Press.

Trabasso, T., van den Broek, P., & Suh, S. (1989). Logical necessity and transitivity of causal relations in the representation of stories. *Discourse Processes*, 12, 1–25.

Winne, P. H, Graham, L., & Prock, L. (1993). A model of poor readers' text-based inferencing: Effects of explanatory feedback. *Reading Research Quarterly*, 28, 53–66.

APPENDIX

Stages of Thunderstorm Development

1. All thunderstorms have a similar life history.
2. Thunderstorms start with the development of large cumulonimbus clouds.
3. The development of these clouds requires warm, moist air.
4. As this warm, moist air is lifted, it releases sufficient latent heat to provide the buoyancy necessary to maintain it's upward flight.
5. This process is facilitated when there are high surface temperatures.
6. As such, thunderstorms are most common in the late afternoon and early evening.
7. However, surface temperature alone is not sufficient for the growth of towering cumulonimbus clouds.
8. Fueled by only surface temperatures, at best the cloud would be small and evaporate in 1–15 minutes.
9. The development of large cumulonimbus clouds requires a continual supply of warm, moist air.
10. Each new serge of warm, moist air rises higher than the last.
11. This processes continually adds to the height of the cloud.
12. When these updrafts reach speeds up to 60 miles per hour, they are capable of supporting hailstones and great amount of precipitation.
13. Usually, within an hour the amount and size of precipitation becomes too much for the updraft to support.
14. One part of the cloud develops a downdraft.
15. Rain begins to fall.
16. These downdrafts can also cause gusty winds.
17. It is during this stage that lightening usually occurs.
18. Eventually downdrafts dominate throughout the cloud.
19. The cooling effect of falling precipitation coupled with the influx of colder air aloft mark the end of the thunderstorm activity.
20. Although the life span of a cumulonimbus cell is only about an hour, a storm can develop new cells as it moves.

12

Evaluating Self-Explanations in iSTART: Comparing Word-Based and LSA Algorithms

Danielle S. McNamara
University of Memphis

Chutima Boonthum
Irwin Levinstein
Old Dominion University

Keith Millis
Northern Illinois University

Interactive strategy training for active reading and thinking (iSTART) is a web-based application that provides young adolescent to college-age students with self-explanation and reading strategy training (McNamara, Levinstein, & Boonthum, 2004). Although untutored self-explanation—that is, explaining the meaning of text to oneself—has been shown to improve text comprehension (Chi, Bassok, Lewis, Reimann, & Glaser, 1989; Chi, de Leeuw, Chiu, & LaVancher, 1994), many readers explain text poorly and gain little from the process. iSTART is designed to improve students' ability to self-explain by teaching them to use reading strategies such as comprehension monitoring, making bridging inferences, and elaboration. In the final phase of training, students practice using reading strategies by typing self-explanations of sentences from science texts. The computational challenge is to provide appropriate feedback to the students concerning their self-explanations. To do so requires capturing some sense of both the meaning and quality of the self-explanation. LSA is an important component in that process. Indeed, an important contribution of LSA is that it allows researchers to automatically capture meaning in text (see also, E. Kintsch et al., chap. 14 in this volume; Graesser et al., chap. 13 in this volume). Interpreting text is critical for intelligent tutoring systems, such as iSTART, which are designed to interact meaningfully with, and adapt to, the users' input. One question, however, regards the extent to which LSA enables or enhances the accuracy of self-explanation evaluation in iSTART. Thus, in this chapter, we compare various systems of self-explanation evaluation that differ in terms of whether the algorithms are word-based, incorporate LSA, or use a combination of algorithms. Because we want to increase the number of texts available for practice in iSTART, we sought to develop evaluation systems that required less human preparation of the included texts, so an important characteristic of the systems discussed is the amount of "hand-coding" required. This chapter describes iSTART and our evaluation of these feedback systems.

iSTART: THE INTERVENTION

iSTART is modeled after a human-delivered reading strategy intervention called self-explanation reading training (SERT; McNamara, 2004; McNamara & Scott, 1999; O'Reilly, Best, & McNamara, 2004). SERT training can be administered to a small group of students in about 2 hours. It consists of three phases, an introduction with definitions and examples of self-explanation and six reading strategies, a demonstration of the strategies by a student on a videotape, and practice using the strategies with science texts. The six reading strategies include (a) comprehension monitoring, being aware of understanding; (b) paraphrasing, or restating the text in different words; (c) elaboration, using prior knowledge or experiences to understand the text (i.e., domain-specific knowledge based inferences); (d) logic or common sense, using logic to understand the text (i.e., domain-general knowledge based inferences); (e) prediction, predicting what the text will say next; and (f) bridging, understanding the relation between separate sentences of the text. During the introduction phase, a description of the strategy and examples of self-explanations using the strategies are provided. Comprehension monitoring is presented as a strategy that should be used all of the time. Paraphrasing is presented as a basis or jumpstart for self-explanation, but not as means for self-explaining text because it does not go beyond the text. The remaining strategies are various forms of inferences (i.e., domain specific, domain-general, predictive, and bridging) that improve the students' ability to make sense of difficult text.

Although SERT has been found to be effective both in terms of improving comprehension scores and course performance (McNamara, 2004; McNamara & Scott, 1999; O'Reilly, Best, & McNamara, 2004), there are scale-up problems in administering SERT with human tutors to students in many classrooms. First, it is expensive to provide and train the tutors. Second, the delivery of training may vary from one class to the next, despite best efforts to maintain consistency. Third, human tutors cannot be made accessible to all students who need it. Finally, the training is delivered to students in groups and therefore cannot be tailored to the individual needs of the learner.

iSTART alleviates these shortcomings while at the same time providing comprehension gains equivalent to SERT (Magliano et al., 2005; O'Reilly, Sinclair, & McNamara, 2004; O'Reilly, Best, & McNamara, 2004). Because iSTART is web-based, it has the potential to make the training available to any school in the country with Internet access. Furthermore, as an automated tutoring system, it can deal with students individually, which affords them self-paced learning. Automated tutors can also keep track of students' performance and provide adaptive scaffolding. Web-based systems can also be easily accessed outside the classroom, which potentially increases the time that students can spend on training. Finally, systems that incorporate pedagogical agents and automated linguistic analysis can engage the student in interactive dialog and thereby induce an active learning environment (e.g., Bransford, Brown, & Cocking, 2000; Graesser, Hu, & Person, 2001; Graesser, Hu, & McNamara, 2005; Graesser et al., chap. 13 in this volume; Louwerse, Graesser, Olney, & the Tutoring Research Group, 2002).

In iSTART, pedagogical agents instruct trainees in the use of self-explanation and other active reading strategies to comprehend the meaning of text while they read. It consists of three modules, including an introduction, a demonstration, and a practice module. The introduction module presents reading strategy concepts in the form of a classroom discussion among three animated characters (an instructor and two students) that interact with each other, provide information, pose questions, and give explanations and examples of the reading strategies. These characters are full-body figures with heads that are slightly exaggerated to make mouth movements and facial expressions more visible. The characters speak using a text-to-speech synthesizer. Their speech is audible and appears as text in a speech bubble. They possess a repertoire of gestures and can move about the screen. The interactions between the characters vicariously simulate the active processing necessary to learn the strategies. After each section of the introduction, the students complete brief multiple-choice quizzes to assess their learning of the strategies. The quizzes are designed as learning tools to guide the student to a better understanding of each SERT strategy by providing hints, prompts, and explanations for incorrect choices.

In the demonstration module, one animated character (Merlin) guides the trainees in analyzing the explanations produced by a second animated character (Genie). Genie (representing a student) reads aloud each sentence from a science text and produces a self-explanation that appears both in spoken form and as text in a box on the web page. Merlin continues by asking the student using the program to indicate which strategies Genie employed in producing his self-explanation. Merlin follows up by asking the student to identify and locate in the text box the various reading strategies contained in Genie's self-explanation. Merlin may follow up further by asking the trainee to identify the sentence referenced from the text when Genie uses a bridging strategy. Merlin then gives Genie verbal feedback on the quality of his self-explanation. This feedback mimics the interchanges that the student will encounter in the practice module. For example, sometimes Merlin states that the self-explanation is too short, prompting Genie to add to his self-explanation. Of course, Merlin also gives the trainee feedback, for example, applauding a correct identification.

In the practice module, Merlin plays coach to the trainees and provides feedback to them while they practice self-explanation using the repertoire of reading strategies. The goal is to help the student acquire the skills necessary to integrate knowledge from various sources to understand a target sentence. This knowledge may come from something they have read in the passage (e.g., the previous sentence), general knowledge, or domain knowledge. For each sentence, Merlin reads the sentence aloud before asking the student to self-explain it by typing a self-explanation. Merlin gives feedback, sometimes asking the student to modify unsatisfactory self-explanations. Once the self-explanation is satisfactory, Merlin asks the student to identify what strategies were used and where they were used in the explanation. As in the demonstration module, Merlin sometimes follows up by asking the student to identify an earlier sentence to which the self-explanation referred. Then Merlin provides general feedback. During this phase, the agent's interactions with the trainee are moderated by the quality of the explanation. For example, more enthusiastic feedback is given for longer, more relevant explanations, whereas increased interactions and support are provided for shorter, less relevant explanations.

The feedback that a student receives depends on algorithms that evaluate the characteristics and quality of the student's self-explanation. Clearly, the feedback is more appropriate when the algorithms successfully interpret the student's input. The focus of this chapter is on the algorithms used to evaluate the self-explanations and thus guide feedback during training.

iSTART: DESCRIPTION OF FEEDBACK SYSTEMS

iSTART was intended from the beginning to employ LSA to determine appropriate feedback. The goal was to develop benchmarks for each of the SERT strategies relative to each of the sentences in the practice texts and to use LSA to measure the similarity of a trainee's explanation to each of the benchmarks. Each benchmark is simply a collection of words, in this case, words chosen to represent each of the strategies (e.g., words that represent a bridge to a prior sentence). However, while work toward this goal was progressing, we also developed a preliminary "word-based" system to provide feedback in our first version of iSTART (see McNamara et al., 2004). The original word-based system included several hand-coded components. This is referred to as *WB1-Assoc* in Table 12.1, which stands for *word-based one, with associated words*. For example, for each sentence in the text, the "important words" were identified by a human expert and a length criterion for the explanation was manually estimated. Important words were generally content words that were deemed important to the meaning of the sentence. For each important word, an association list of synonyms and related terms was created. The lists were created by examining dictionaries and existing protocols as well as by human judgments of what words were likely to occur in a self-explanation as associations to each important word. In essence, the association list was meant as a stand-in for LSA until the LSA components were completed.

A trainee's explanation was analyzed by matching the words in the explanation against the words in the sentence and words in the corresponding association lists. A formula based on the length of the sentence, the length of the explanation, the length criterion, the number of matches to the important words, and the number of matches to the association lists produced a rating of 0 (inadequate), 1 (barely adequate), 2 (good), or 3 (very good) for the explanation.

The rating of 0, or inadequate, was based on a series of filtering criteria that assessed whether the explanation was too short, too similar to the original sentence, or irrelevant. Length was assessed by a ratio of the number of words in the explanation to the number in the target sentence, taking into consideration the length criterion. Similarity was assessed in terms of a ratio of the sentence and explanation lengths and the number of matching important words. If it was close in length with a high percentage of word overlap, then the explanation was deemed too similar to the target sentence. Relevance was assessed from the number of matches to important words in the sentence and words in the association lists. If the explanation failed any of these three criteria, then the trainee was given feedback corresponding to the problem and encouraged to revise the self-explanation.

The systems we consider in this chapter also include a metacognitive filter that searches the trainees' explanations for patterns indicating a description of the trainee's mental state, such as "now I see ... " or "I don't understand this at all." Whereas the main purpose of the filter is to enable the system to respond to such nonexplanatory content when appropriate, we also used the same filter to remove "noise," such as "What this sentence is saying is ... " from the explanation before further processing. We have examined the effectiveness of the systems with and without the filter and found that they all perform slightly better with than without it. Thus, the systems in this chapter all include the metacognitive filter.

This first word-based system required a great deal of human effort per text, primarily because of the need to create an association list for each important word. However, because we envisioned a scaled-up system adaptable to many classrooms, we needed a system that required relatively little manual effort per text. One obstacle was the need to manually identify the important words in each sentence and to create the association lists. Therefore, we replaced the lists of important and associated words with a list of content words (nouns, verbs, adjectives, adverbs) from the sentence and the entire text. This algorithm is referred to as *WB1-TT* in Table 12.1, which stands for *word-based one, with total text*. The content words were identified using algorithms from Coh-Metrix, an automated tool that yields various measures of cohesion, readability, other characteristics of language (Graesser, McNamara, Louwerse, & Cai, 2004; McNamara, Louwerse, & Cai, chap. 19 in this volume; McNamara, Louwerse, & Graesser, 2002). The iSTART system then compares the words in the self-explanation to the content words from current sentence, prior sentences, and subsequent sentences in the target text, and does a word-based match to determine the number of content words in the self-explanation from each source in the text.

Some hand-coding remained in *WB1-TT* because the length criterion for an explanation was calculated based on the average length of explanations of that sentence collected from a separate pool of participants and on the importance of the sentence according to a manual text analysis. Besides being relatively subjective, this process was time consuming because it required an expert in discourse analysis as well as the collection of self-explanation protocols. Thus, the hand-coded length criteria were replaced with automated criteria based solely on the number of words and content words in the target sentence (i.e., *word-based two, with total text, or WB2-TT* in Table 12.1).

While the first version of iSTART was in use, the first version of the LSA-based system was created (*LSA1* in Table 12.1). The original goal of identifying particular strategies in an explanation had been replaced with the lesser ambition of rating the explanation as one of three levels (Millis et al., 2004; Millis et al., chap. 11 in this volume). The highest level of explanation, called "global-focused," integrates the sentence material in a deep understanding of the text. A "local-focused" explanation explores the sentence in the context of its immediate predecessors. Finally, a "sentence-focused" explanation goes little beyond paraphrasing. To assess the level of an explanation, it is compared to four benchmarks or bags of words. The rating is based on a weighted sum of the four LSA cosines between the explanation and the four benchmarks.

The four benchmarks include the words in the title of the passage, the words in the sentence, prior words or sentences in the text that are causally related to the sentence, and related words from verbal protocols that did not appear in the text. Two of the four benchmarks are created automatically: the words in the title and the words in the current sentence. However, two of the benchmarks require more effort to generate. The prior-text benchmark depends on a causal analysis of the conceptual structure of the text, relating each sentence to previous sentences. This analysis requires both time and expertise. The world knowledge benchmark consists of words that appeared more than once in the previously collected explanations and did not appear in the other benchmarks.

In sum, *LSA1* required a good deal of manual coding to adapt the algorithm to a particular text. Thus, it too was not suitable for an iSTART program that would be readily adaptable to multiple practice texts. Therefore, we experimented with formulae that would simplify the data gathering requirements. Instead of the four benchmarks mentioned previously, we discarded the world knowledge benchmark entirely and replaced the benchmark based on causal-analysis of prior text with one that consisted of the previous two sentences (*LSA2* in Table 12.1). We could do this because the texts being considered were from science textbooks. Specifically, we took advantage of the highly linear argumentation in science texts and used the two immediately prior sentences as stand-ins for the set of causally related sentences. It should be noted that this approach may not succeed so well with other genres, such as fictional texts.

Finally, we developed two systems that were combinations of the word-based and LSA approaches (*LSA1/WB2-TT* and *LSA2/WB2-TT* in Table 12.1). In these combinatory systems, we combine a weighted sum of the factors used in the fully automated word-based systems and those in LSA1 and LSA2. These combinations allowed us to examine the benefits of using the world knowledge benchmark (in LSA1) when LSA was combined with a fully automated word-based system.

iSTART: EVALUATION OF FEEDBACK SYSTEMS

We describe two experiments conducted to evaluate the performance of the systems. In Experiment 1, we compare the seven systems that vary as a function of approach (word-based, LSA, combination) and coding (man-

TABLE 12.1
Descriptions of Evaluation Systems in Terms of Whether Word-Based or
LSA-Based Factors Are Included and the Amount of Hand-Coding Used

		Word-Based		
		-no Word-Based Factors -	Hand-Coded Important Words, Association List, Length Criteria	Automated Selection of Content Words, Total Text Replaces Association List	
				Hand-Coded Length Criteria	Automated Length Criteria
	- no LSA-based factors -	-	WB1-Assoc	WB1-TT	WB2-TT
LSA-Based	Hand-Coded Benchmarks	LSA1	-	-	LSA1/ WB2-TT
	No Hand-Coded Benchmarks	LSA2	-	-	LSA2/WB2-TT

ual, automatic) presented in Table 12.1. They are evaluated by being applied to a database of self-explanation protocols by college students that were evaluated by a human expert on a scale of 0–3. In Experiment 2, we compare the word-based, LSA, and combined systems using a database of explanations by middle school students.

Experiment 1

Self-Explanations. The self-explanations were collected from college students who were provided with SERT training and then tested with two texts, Thunderstorm and Coal. Both texts consisted of 20 sentences. The Thunderstorm text was self-explained by 36 students and the Coal text was self-explained by 38 students. The self-explanations were coded by an expert according to the following 4-point scale: 0 = vague or irrelevant, 1 = sentence-focused (restatement or paraphrase of the sentence), 2 = local-focused (includes concepts from immediately previous sentences), 3 = global-focused (using prior knowledge).

The coding system was intended to reveal the extent to which the participant elaborated the current sentence. Sentence-focused explanations do not provide any new information beyond the current sentence. Local-focused explanations might include an elaboration of a concept mentioned in the current or immediately prior sentence, but there is no attempt to link the current sentence to the theme of the text. Self-explanations that linked the sentence to the theme of the text with world knowledge were coded as "global-focused." Global-focused explanations tend to use multiple reading strategies, and indicate the most active level of processing.

Results.   Each of the seven systems produces an evaluation comparable to the human ratings on a 4-point scale. Hence, we calculated the correlations and percent agreement between the human and system evaluations (see Table 12.2). Additionally, d primes (d's) were computed for each strategy type as a measure of how well the system could discriminate among the different strategies. The ds were computed from hit and false alarm rates. A hit would occur if the system assigned the same self-explanation to a category (e.g., global-focused strategy) as the human judges. A false alarm would occur if the system assigned the self-explanation to a category (e.g., global-focused) different from the human judges (i.e., it was not a global-focused strategy). The d's are highest to the extent that hits are high and false alarms are low. In this context, d's refer to the correspondence between the human and system in standard deviation units. A d' of 0 indicates chance performance, whereas greater d's indicate greater correspondence.

TABLE 12.2
Measures of Agreement for the Thunderstorm and Coal Texts Between the Seven System Evaluations and the Human Ratings of the Self-Explanations

Thunderstorm Text	*WB1-Assoc*	*WB1-TT*	*WB2-TT*	*LSA1*	*LSA2*	*LSA1/WB2-TT*	*LSA2/WB2-TT*
Correlation	.47	.52	.43	.60	.61	.65	.64
% Agreement	48%	50%	27%	55%	57%	60%	62%
d' of 0s	2.21	2.26	.97	2.13	2.19	2.00	2.21
d' of 1s	.84	.79	.66	1.32	1.44	1.53	1.45
d' of 2s	.23	.36	−.43	.47	.59	.76	.85
d' of 3s	1.38	1.52	1.41	1.46	1.48	1.53	1.65
Avg d'	1.17	1.23	.65	1.34	1.43	1.46	1.54

Coal Text	*WB1-Assoc*	*WB1-TT*	*WB2-TT*	*LSA1*	*LSA2*	*LSA1/WB2-TT*	*LSA2/WB2-TT*
Correlation	.51	.47	.41	.66	.67	.70	.71
% Agreement	41%	41%	29%	56%	57%	61%	64%
d' of 0s	4.67	4.73	1.65	2.52	2.99	2.52	2.93
d' of 1s	1.06	.89	.96	1.21	1.29	1.55	1.50
d' of 2s	.09	.13	−.37	.45	.49	.83	.94
d' of 3s	−.16	1.15	1.28	1.59	1.59	1.73	1.79
Avg d'	1.42	1.73	.88	1.44	1.59	1.66	1.79

One thing to note is that there is general improvement according to all of the measures going from left to right. As might be expected, the systems with LSA faired far better than those without LSA, and the combined systems were the most successful. The word-based systems tended to perform worse as the criteria increased (from 0 to 3), but performed relatively well at identifying poor self-explanations and paraphrases. All of the systems, however, identified less successfully the sentence-focused (i.e., 2s) explanations. However, the d's for the sentence focused explanations approach 1.0 as LSA is incorporated, particularly when LSA is combined with the word-based algorithms.

Apart from better performance with LSA than without, the performance is also more stable with LSA. Whereas the word-based systems did not perform equally well on the Thunderstorm and Coal texts, there is a high level of agreement for the LSA-based formulas (i.e., the numbers are virtually identical in the two tables). This indicates that if we were to apply the word-based formulas to yet another text, we have less assurance of finding the same performance, whereas the LSA-based formulas are more likely to replicate across texts.

Figure 12.1 provides a closer look at the data for the combined, automated system, LSA2/WB2-TT. As the d's indicated, the system's perfor-

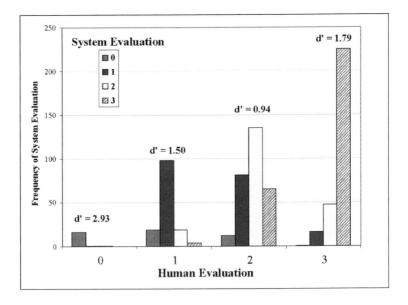

Figure 12.1. Correspondence between human evaluations of the self-explanations and the combined (LSA and word-based), automated system (i.e., LSA2/WB2-TT). Explanations were evaluated by humans as vague or irrelevant (0), sentence-focused (1), local-focused (2), or global (3).

mance is quite good for explanations that were given human ratings of 0, 1, or 3. Thus, the system successfully identifies poor explanations, paraphrases, and very good explanations. It is less successful for identifying explanations that consist of paraphrases in addition to some information from the previous sentence or from world knowledge. As one might expect, some are classified as paraphrases and some as global by the system. Although not perfect, we consider this result a success because so few were misclassified as poor explanations.

Experiment 2

Self-Explanations. The self-explanations were collected from 45 middle school students (entering eighth and ninth grades) who were provided with iSTART training and then tested with two texts, Thunderstorm and Coal. The texts were shortened versions of the texts used in Experiment 1, consisting of 13 and 12 sentences, respectively. This chapter presents only the data from the Thunderstorm text.

The self-explanations from this text were categorized as paraphrases, irrelevant elaborations, text-based elaborations, or knowledge-based elaborations. Paraphrases did not go beyond the meaning of the target sentence. Irrelevant elaborations may have been related to the sentence superficially or tangentially, but were not related to the overall meaning of the text and did not add to the meaning of the text. For example, indicating having seen a thunderstorm would be categorized as an irrelevant elaboration if the visual aspects of thunderstorms were not pertinent to understanding the sentence. Text-based elaborations included bridging inferences that made links to information presented in the text prior to the sentence. Knowledge-based elaborations included the use of prior knowledge to add meaning to the sentence. This latter category is analogous to, but not the same as, the global-focused category in Experiment 1.

Results. In contrast to the human coding system used in Experiment 1, the coding system applied to this data was not intended to map directly onto the iSTART evaluation systems. In this case, the codes are categorical and do not necessarily translate to a 0–3 quality range. However, our interest here was to examine which systems best distinguished between the four types of strategies. One important goal, for example, is to be able to distinguish between paraphrases and elaborations (see also, Millis et al., chap. 11 in this volume). If a system makes such a distinction, then the evaluation scores should yield a significant difference between the categories.

We focus our analyses on three systems (WB1-TT, LSA2, and LSA2/WB2-TT), which are essentially the best representatives of the word-based, LSA, and combined systems. A 3×4 GLM mixed ANOVA was conducted on the scores for each explanation, including the within-items factor of system (word-based, LSA, combined) and the between-items factor of strategy (paraphrase, irrelevant elaboration, text-based elaboration, knowledge-based elaboration). There was a main effect of system, $F(2,1072) = 5.3$, MSE = .301, $p < .01$ ($M_{WB} = 2.06$, $SE_{WB} = .05$; $M_{LSA} = 2.21$, $SE_{LSA} = .04$; $M_{CO} = 2.08$, $SE_{CO} = .05$), showing significantly higher scores using the LSA system than the word-based or combined systems. A main effect of strategy, $F(1, 536)=70.1$, MSE = .285, $p < .001$, indicated significant differences in scores as a function of the four categories ($M_P = 1.62$, $SE_P = .03$; $M_{IE} = 2.04$, $SE_{IE} = .08$; $M_{TE} = 2.29$, $SE_{TE} = .04$; $M_{KE} = 2.52$, $SE_{KE} = .11$). Post-hoc Tukey HSD tests indicated significant differences between all categories except text-based and knowledge-based elaborations.

As shown in Figure 12.2, there was a reliable interaction of system and strategy, $F(6,1072) = 6.9$, MSE = .301, $p < .001$. Of most interest is observing which system best distinguishes between the four strategies. It is visually apparent that the combined system best accomplishes that goal because it led to the largest difference. To quantify that observation, we calculated the effect sizes (i.e., using Cohen's d) of the differences between each strategy for each of the systems, which takes into account both the size of the difference and the amount of variance. The average effect sizes comparing each consecutive category (i.e., the smallest differences) were .31 ($SD = .10$) for the word-based system, .45 ($SD = .39$) for LSA, and .48 ($SD = .04$) for the

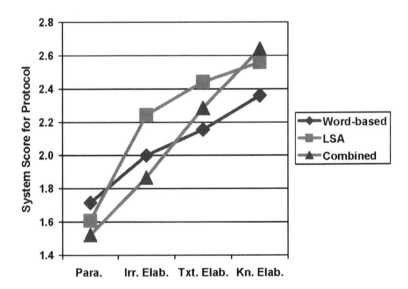

Figure 12.2. Comparison of the scores generated by three systems (word-based, LSA, and combined) as a function of experts' classification of the self-explanation.

combined system. Although, LSA showed comparable average effect sizes, there was greater variation in differences than observed for the combined system. The average effect sizes comparing paraphrases to text-based elaborations and irrelevant elaborations to knowledge-based elaborations were .60 (SD = .06) for the word-based system, .87 (SD = .60) for LSA, and .99 (SD = .01) for the combined system. Finally, comparing the difference between paraphrases and knowledge-based elaborations, the effect size was 1.16 for the word-based system, 1.47 for LSA, and 1.50 for the combined system. Thus, both LSA and the combined system show very good discrimination, but the combined system most consistently discriminated between the strategies. Better discrimination between strategies improves the system's ability to appropriately respond to the student.

DISCUSSION

Our results indicate that the systems that incorporated LSA more accurately classified self-explanations than did the word-based systems, and the combined systems were most successful. Of these latter two systems, the fully automated system (i.e., LSA2/WB2-TT) performed best. In this system, manual coding, such as choosing associated words or benchmarks, is replaced by computational algorithms. This is indeed fortunate for iSTART because it indicates that a large variety of texts can be adapted to its practice module. Thus, one practical implication is that teachers may more readily specify texts for their students to use when learning how to self-explain and when practicing self-explanation.

One valuable contribution of the current study is that it systematically compared the utility of traditional word-based methods to LSA. Because the combined systems did better than either alone, it appears that both approaches have unique merits. One feature of the word-based system is that it looks for specific words in the self-explanation. If a key word is present, then the system knows that the student had used that word, regardless of the other words present in the self-explanation. On the other hand, an LSA-generated cosine between two texts, or a benchmark and a self-explanation, will depend on the presence of other words in either one. For example, the cosine between the benchmark "rain" and the word "rain" is 1.00, but the cosine between "rain" and "When the rain is heavy, it falls" is slightly lower at .94. This suggests that if the evaluation of a self-explanation depends on the use of a particular word, as it might be at specific text locations, then a word-based approach might be more desirable. Of course, one of LSA's strength is that it recognizes the latent structure of word meanings. For example, a word-based system looking for the word "rain" would not give any credit to the explanation "when it is heavy, it falls" because the word is absent from the utterance. However, the LSA-generated cosine between "rain" and "when it is heavy, it falls" is .61. Although this cosine is lower than when "rain" is present in the explanation, it is well above 0, indicating some confidence that the explanation is addressing the concept of "rain." Therefore, if an evaluation depends on a cluster of concepts or ideas rather than particular words, then an LSA approach should fare better than a word-based approach.

In summary, both LSA and more traditional word-based algorithms have played important roles to the development of iSTART. For iSTART to effectively teach reading strategies, it must be able to deliver valid feedback on the quality of the self-explanations that a student types during practice. In order to deliver feedback, the system must understand, at least to some extent, what students are saying in their self-explanation. Of course, automating natural language understanding has been extremely challenging, especially for nonrestrictive content domains like self-explaining a text in which a student might say one of any number of things. This study, in addition to others in the volume (Graesser et al., chap. 13 in this volume; E. Kintsch et al., chap. 14 in this volume; Millis et al., chap. 11 in this volume; Streeter et al., chap. 15 in this volume), fortify the assumption that LSA can be used to solve problems encountered in natural language understanding, and point to adaptive techniques that improve the meaning-seeking process.

ACKNOWLEDGMENTS

This project was supported by the NSF (IERI Award No. 0241144). Any opinions, findings, and conclusions or recommendations expressed in this material are those of the authors and do not necessarily reflect the views of NSF.

REFERENCES

Bransford, J., Brown, A., & Cocking, R.(Eds.). (2000). *How people learn: Brain, mind, experience, and school.* Washington, DC: National Academy Press.
Chi, M. T. H., Bassok, M., Lewis, M. W., Reimann, R., & Glaser, R. (1989). Self-explanation: How students study and use examples in learning to solve problems. *Cognitive Science, 13,* 145–182.
Chi, M. T. H., De Leeuw, N., Chiu, M., & LaVancher, C. (1994). Eliciting self-explanations improves understanding. *Cognitive Science, 18,* 439–477.
Graesser, A. C., Hu, X., & McNamara, D. S. (2005). Computerized learning environments that incorporate research in discourse psychology, cognitive science, and computational linguistics. In A. F. Healy (Ed.), *Experimental cognitive psychology and its applications: Festschrift in Honor of Lyle Bourne, Walter Kintsch, and Thomas Landauer* (pp. 183–194). Washington, DC: American Psychological Association.

Graesser, A. C., Hu, X., & Person, N. (2001). Teaching with the help of talking heads. In T. Okamoto, R. Hartley, Kinshuk, & J. P. Klus (Eds.), *Proceedings IEEE International Conference on Advanced Learning Technology: Issues, achievements and challenges* (pp. 460–461). Los Alamos, CA: IEEE Computer Society.

Graesser, A. C., McNamara, D. S., Louwerse, M. M., & Cai, Z. (2004). Coh-Metrix: Analysis of text on cohesion and language. *Behavior Research Methods, Instruments, and Computers, 36*, 193–202.

Louwerse, M. M., Graesser, A. C., Olney, A., & the Tutoring Research Group. (2002). Good computational manners: Mixed-initiative dialog in conversational agents. In C. Miller (Ed.), *Etiquette for human–computer work, papers from the 2002 fall symposium* (Tech. Rep. No. FS-02-02, pp. 71–76). Menlo Park, CA: AAAI Press.

Magliano, J. P., Todaro, S., Millis, K. K., Wiemer-Hastings, K., Kim, H. J., & McNamara, D. S. (2005). Changes in reading strategies as a function of reading training: A comparison of live and computerized training. *Journal of Educational Computing Research, 32*(2), 185–208.

McNamara, D. S. (2004). SERT: Self-explanation reading training. *Discourse Processes, 38*, 1–30.

McNamara, D. S., Levinstein, I. B., & Boonthum, C. (2004). iSTART: Interactive strategy training for active reading and thinking. *Behavior Research Methods, Instruments, and Computers, 36*, 222–233.

McNamara, D. S., Louwerse, M. M., & Graesser, A. C. (2002). *Coh-Metrix: Automated cohesion and coherence scores to predict text readability and facilitate comprehension.* Technical report, Institute for Intelligent Systems, University of Memphis, Memphis, TN.

McNamara, D. S., & Scott, J. L. (1999). Training reading strategies. In M. Hahn & S. C. Stoness (Eds.), *Proceedings of the 21st Annual Meeting of the Cognitive Science Society* (pp. 387–392). Hillsdale, NJ: Lawrence Erlbaum Associates.

Millis, K. K., Kim, H. J., Todaro, S. Magliano, J. P., Wiemer-Hastings, K., & McNamara, D. S. (2004). Identifying reading strategies using latent semantic analysis: Comparing semantic benchmarks. *Behavior Research Methods, Instruments, and Computers, 36*, 213–221.

O'Reilly, T., Best, R., & McNamara, D. S. (2004). Self-explanation reading training: Effects for low-knowledge readers. In K. Forbus, D. Gentner, & T. Regier (Eds.), *Proceedings of the 26th Annual Meeting of the Cognitive Science Society* (pp. 1053–1058). Mahwah, NJ: Lawrence Erlbaum Associates.

O'Reilly, T., Sinclair, G. P., & McNamara, D. S. (2004). Reading strategy training: Automated verses live. In K. Forbus, D. Gentner, & T. Regier (Eds.), *Proceedings of the 26th Annual Meeting of the Cognitive Science Society* (pp. 1059–1064). Mahwah, NJ: Lawrence Erlbaum Associates.

13

Using LSA in AutoTutor: Learning Through Mixed-Initiative Dialogue in Natural Language

Art Graesser, Phanni Penumatsa, Matthew Ventura,
Zhiqiang Cai, and Xiangen Hu
University of Memphis

AutoTutor is a computer tutor that holds conversations with students in natural language (Graesser, Hu, & McNamara, 2005; Graesser, Lu, et al., 2004; Graesser, Person, Harter, & the Tutoring Research Group, 2001; Graesser, VanLehn, Rose, Jordan, & Harter, 2001; Graesser, K. Wiemer-Hastings, P. Wiemer-Hastings, Kreuz, & Harter, 1999). AutoTutor simulates the discourse patterns of human tutors and a number of ideal tutoring strategies. It presents a series of challenging problems (or questions) from a curriculum script and engages in collaborative, mixed initiative dialog while constructing answers. AutoTutor speaks the content of its turns through an animated conversational agent with a speech engine; it was designed to be a good conversational partner that comprehends, speaks, points, and displays emotions, all in a coordinated fashion. For some topics, there are graphical displays, animations of causal mechanisms, or interactive simulation environments (Graesser, Chipman, Haynes, & Olney, 2005). So far, AutoTutor has been developed and tested for topics in Newtonian physics (VanLehn et al., in press) and computer literacy (Graesser, Lu, et al., 2004), showing impressive learning gains compared to pretest measures and suitable control conditions. One notable characteristic of AutoTutor, from the standpoint of the present edited volume, is that latent semantic analysis (LSA) was adopted as its primary representation of world knowledge.

This chapter begins by briefly describing AutoTutor and how LSA is used to track the learner's coverage of the subject matter. We subsequently report a serious of analyses that assess how well LSA performs in determining whether paragraph-length or sentence-length information packages are covered by the learner. These evaluations have been performed on student essays and on the dynamic conversations that emerge over multiple turns in tutorial dialogue.

A QUICK SKETCH OF AUTOTUTOR

Figure 13.1 shows a screen shot of AutoTutor on the topic of computer literacy. At the top window is the main question that requires deep reasoning to

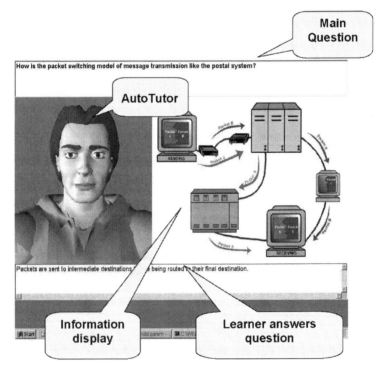

Figure 13.1.   A computer screen of AutoTutor for the subject matter of introductory computer literacy.

answer: *How is the packet switching model of message transmission like the postal system?* An answer to this question involves analogical reasoning, which requires a comparatively deep level of comprehension and application of knowledge (Bloom, 1956; Graesser & Person, 1994). An ideal answer to the question would require approximately seven sentences of information, the size of a typical paragraph. It typically takes 50–200 conversational turns between the tutor and student to answer this main question. This is approximately the same number of turns it takes between human tutors and students who collaboratively answer similar problems that involve deep reasoning. The student types in the answer content in the window at the bottom of the screen. The conversational agent at the left speaks the content of AutoTutor, with appropriate facial expressions and occasional gestures. This question has an associated diagram for the learner to view.

When students are asked questions that require paragraph-length answers and deep reasoning, initial answers to these questions are typically only one or two sentences in length. However, one or two sentences is hardly enough information to adequately answer the question. This is where tutorial dialog is particularly helpful. AutoTutor engages the student in a mixed initiative dialog that assists in the evolution of an improved answer and draws out more of what the student knows. AutoTutor provides *feedback* to the student on what the student types in (positive, neutral, vs. negative feedback), *pumps* the student for more information ("What else?"), *prompts* the student to fill in missing words, gives the student *hints*, fills in missing information with *assertions*, identifies and *corrects* erroneous ideas and misconceptions, *answers* the student's questions, and *summarizes* answers. These acts of feedback, pumps, prompts, hints, assertions, corrections, answers, and summaries are important *dialogue moves* of AutoTutor. A full answer to the question is eventually constructed during this dialog. For readers who desire a more concrete impression of the tutorial dialogue, appendix A has example excerpts from a AutoTutor–student dialogue on conceptual physics.

The tutorial dialog patterns of AutoTutor were motivated by research in discourse processing, cognition, and education. AutoTutor's design was inspired by constructivist theories of learning that emphasize the importance of explanations (Aleven & Koedinger, 2002; Chi, de Leeuw, Chiu, & LaVancher, 1994; McNamara, 2004; McNamara et al., chap. 12 in this volume), by cognitive tutors that adaptively respond to student knowledge (Anderson Corbett, Koedinger, & Pelletier, 1995; VanLehn et al., 2002), and by previous empirical research that has documented the collaborative constructive activities that routinely occur during human tutoring (Chi, Siler, Jeong, Yamauchi, & Hausmann, 2001; Fox, 1993; Graesser, Person, & Magliano, 1995). The process of actively constructing explanations and elaborations of the learning material allegedly produces better learning than merely presenting information to students.

Rather surprisingly, the dialog moves of most human tutors are not particularly sophisticated from the standpoint of today's pedagogical theories and intelligent tutoring systems. Human tutors normally coach the student by filling in missing pieces of information in an expected answer and they fix bugs and misconceptions that are manifested by the student during the tutorial dialog. We refer to this tutoring mechanism as *Expectation and Misconception Tailored Dialog*. Human tutors rarely implement bona fide Socratic tutoring strategies, modeling-scaffolding-fading, reciprocal training, building on prerequisites, and other sophisticated pedagogical techniques. AutoTutor simulates the dialog moves of human tutors who coach students in constructing explanations and answers to open-ended questions.

EXPECTATIONS AND MISCONCEPTIONS ASSOCIATED WITH QUESTIONS IN CURRICULUM SCRIPTS

AutoTutor's curriculum script contains a set of questions (or problems) about a subject matter that requires deep reasoning. Various forms of content are affiliated with each main question, but the following components are relevant to the present chapter.

MAIN QUESTION:

If a lightweight car and a massive truck have a head-on collision, upon which vehicle is the impact force greater? Which vehicle undergoes the greater change in its motion? Explain why.

IDEAL ANSWER:

The force of impact on each of the colliding bodies is due to interaction between them. The forces experienced by these bodies are thus an action–reaction pair. In terms of Newton's third law of motion, these forces will be equal in magnitude and opposite in direction. The magnitude of the acceleration produced by a force on different objects is inversely proportional to their masses. Hence, the magnitude of the car's acceleration due to the force of impact will be much larger than that of the more massive truck. A larger magnitude of acceleration implies a larger rate of change of velocity, which may be interpreted as greater change in motion. Therefore, the car undergoes greater change in its motion.

EXPECTATIONS:

(E1) The magnitudes of the forces exerted by the two objects on each other are equal.

(E2) If one object exerts a force on a second object, then the second object exerts a force on the first object in the opposite direction.
(E3) The same force will produce a larger acceleration in a less massive object than a more massive object.

MISCONCEPTIONS:

(M1) A lighter/smaller object exerts no force on a heavier/larger object.
(M2) A lighter/smaller object exerts less force on other objects than a heavier/larger object.
(M3) The force acting on a body is dependent on the mass of the body.
(M4) Heavier objects accelerate faster for the same force than lighter objects.
(M5) Action and reaction forces do not have the same magnitude.

FUNCTIONALLY EQUIVALENT CONCEPTS:

car, vehicle, object
truck, vehicle, object

The learner would ideally articulate the ideal answer to this question, but that far exceeds what would be anticipated by AutoTutor's mechanisms. Natural language is much too imprecise, fragmentary, vague, ungrammatical, and elliptical to require such semantically well-formed and complete responses. LSA is used to evaluate the extent to which the information within the student turns (i.e., an individual turn, a combination of turns, or collective sequence of turns) matches the ideal answer. AutoTutor requires that the learner articulate each of the expectations before it considers the question answered. The system periodically identifies a missing expectation during the course of the dialogue and posts the goal of covering the expectation. When expectation E is missed and therefore posted, AutoTutor attempts to get the student to articulate it by generating hints and prompts to encourage the learner's filling in missing words and propositions. Expectation E is considered covered if the content of the learner's cumulative set of turns meets or exceeds a threshold T in its LSA cosine value. That is, E is covered if the cosine match between E and the student input I (turns 1 though N) is high enough: cosine (E, I) $\geq$ T. The threshold has varied between .40 and .75 in previous instantiations of AutoTutor. Each expectation E has a family of prompts and hints to get the student to fill in most or all of the content words and propositions in E. Prompts and hints are selected to maximize an increase in the LSA cosine match score (hereafter called the *match score*) when answered successfully. Sometimes the student expresses misconceptions during the dialogue. This happens when the student input I matches a misconception M with a sufficiently high match score. At that point AutoTutor corrects the misconception and goes on.

AutoTutor systematically manages its dialogue when it attempts to get the learner to articulate expectation E. AutoTutor stays on topic by completing the subdialog that covers expectation E before starting a subdialog on another expectation. Learners often leave out a content word, phrase, or entire clause within E. In order to fill in the missing information, and achieve pattern completion, AutoTutor selects particular prompts and hints that elicit answers that would fill in the missing information and thereby boosts the match score above threshold. For example, suppose that expectation E1 needs to be articulated in the answer. The following family of candidate prompts is available for selection by AutoTutor to encourage the student to articulate particular content words in expectation E1 (*The magnitudes of the forces exerted by two objects on each other are equal*):

1. The magnitudes of the forces exerted by two objects on each other are ____.

2. The magnitudes of forces are equal for the two _____.
3. The two vehicles exert on each other an equal magnitude of _____.
4. The force of the two vehicles on each other are equal in _____.

If the student has failed to articulate one of the four content words (*equal, objects, force, magnitude*), then AutoTutor selects the corresponding prompt (1, 2, 3, and 4, respectively).

LSA plays a prominent role in AutoTutor in several ways. LSA is the primary method of representing world knowledge. It serves as a conceptual pattern matcher as it constantly is comparing student input to expectations and misconceptions. It provides a quantitative metric for evaluating the extent to which any two bags of words meet or exceed a threshold criterion. LSA provides a statistical metric for performing pattern recognition, pattern matching, and pattern completion operations instead of relying on brittle symbolic systems (Kintsch, 1998, 2001; Landauer, chap. 1 in this volume; Landauer & Dumais, 1997; Landauer, Laham, & Foltz, 2003).

METRICS THAT ASSESS COVERAGE OF EXPECTATIONS AND MISCONCEPTIONS

There is a large family of metrics that could potentially be used to assess the coverage of expectations and misconceptions. This section reports some of the analyses that we have conducted in our evaluations of the extent to which LSA accurately assesses coverage. We have considered different units of analysis, spans of text, and algorithms in these assessments. These assessments of LSA have been applied to computer science (Graesser et al., 2000; P. Wiemer-Hastings, K. Wiemer-Hastings, & Graesser, 1999), Newtonian physics (Olde, Franceschetti, Karnavat, Graesser, & the Tutoring Research Group, 2002), and research ethics (Graesser, Hu, Person, Jackson, & Toth, 2004).

A few words should be said about the corpora we used when we created the LSA spaces for AutoTutor. The version of AutoTutor for computer literacy covered the topics of hardware, operating systems, and the Internet. The corpus consisted of a textbook on computer literacy, the curriculum script, and 30 articles, namely 10 for each of the three topics (approximately 1 million words). The version of AutoTutor for physics consisted of the curriculum script, 8 relevant chapters in a textbook written by Hewitt (1998), 6 volumes of a comprehensive text aimed at college student majors in technical or life sciences, 2 advanced texts in electromagnetism, and 2 physics texts electronically available (approximately 1 million words). There were 6,536 unique terms in the physics corpus (see Olde et al., 2002). We used 300 dimensions in the LSA space for all of these tutors. We discovered that 300 dimensions yielded the best performance (i.e., correlations between LSA metrics and expert ratings of student essay quality) when varying the number of dimensions (100, 200, 300, 400, vs. 500) and various threshold parameters on coverage of expectations (Olde et al., 2002; P. Wiemer-Hastings et al., 1999). The performance of LSA did not improve much when we attempted to sanitize the corpus by including only relevant documents and content (Olde et al., 2002). However, we are convinced that the performance would substantially improve by increasing the size of corpus (ideally by an order of magnitude, from 1 to 10 million words). As a consequence, the data reported in this chapter probably underestimates how well LSA would perform if we had invested more time and effort in creating a larger corpus.

Evaluating Answer Essays

One of the performance assessments of AutoTutor is an essay test given before and after AutoTutor training. The essays consist of students answering qualitative physics questions on their own, without any assistance. A different sample of questions is given at pretest and posttest, in a fully counterbalanced design. The major research question is how well LSA fares in grading these essays. Automated essay graders have frequently adopted LSA metrics (Foltz, Gilliam, & Kendall, 2000; Landauer et al., 2003), so we pursued a similar assessment for AutoTutor. The standard approach is to compare LSA-based grades of essays with essay quality ratings of subject matter experts.

We have we asked experts in physics or computer literacy to make judgments about the quality of the student essays, which averaged approximately 100 words in length. An expert's *quality rating* was operationally defined as the proportion of expectations in an essay that judges believed were covered, using either stringent or lenient criteria. Similarly, LSA was used to compute the proportion of expectations covered, using varying thresholds of match scores on whether information in the student essay covered each expectation. In our studies on computer literacy, 192 answer essays were graded by 4 experts in computer science; there were 24 questions and 8 answers per question. In our studies on physics, approximately 1,000 essays were graded by 5 physics experts; there were 53 questions and approximately 20 essays per question. Correlations between the LSA scores and the judges' quality ratings (i.e., the mean rating across judges) were approximately .50 for both conceptual physics (Olde et al., TRG, 2002) and computer literacy (Graesser et al., 2000; P. Wiemer-Hastings et al., 1999). Correlations have generally increased as the length of the text increases, yielding correlations of .73 or higher in other laboratories (Foltz et al., 2000; Landauer et al., 2003). We believe that our LSA-based assessments would exceed the .50 correlation if the answers had more words and the corpus was much larger. It is informative to note that the correlations between a pair of experts in our studies was approximately .65, so LSA agrees with experts approximately as well as two experts agree with each other.

We performed some follow-up analyses that considered alternative units of analysis and some different structural decompositions of the verbal content. In each of these analyses, the quality ratings of the experts were the same, but we varied the LSA-based algorithms for computing essay coverage scores. In our analysis of conceptual physics, the complete good answer was defined as the set of expectations (e.g., E1, E2, and E3 in our example) and a student's essay was defined as the total set of sentences in the essay (e.g., sentence S1, S2, ... Sn). If the unit of analysis is a whole paragraph, then we would compute one LSA cosine between the complete good answer (E1 + E2 + E3) and the entire student essay (S1 + S2 + ... Sn). For this metric that considered the entire paragraph as the unit of analysis, the overall correlation with the experts' quality ratings was $r = .35$. If the unit of analysis is the sentence, then we would compute a maximum cosine score for each expectation separately when comparing an expectation E with each student sentence and all combinations of student sentences. In essence, such a measure captures how well each individual expectation resonates with any of the content in the student essay. The mean of these maximum cosine scores is computed across the set of expectations in the good complete answer. For this metric that considers the sentence as the unit of analysis, the correlation with the experts' quality ratings was a bit higher, namely, $r = .44$. Next, we considered whether it would be worthwhile to break each expectation and student sentence into subject-predicate syntactic constituents and compare the constituents of the good answers and student essays. After considering a variety of analyses and metrics using syntactic decomposition, the highest correlation with the experts' quality ratings was actually lower, $r = .26$. A similar curvilinear pattern occurred for computer literacy and research methods. Therefore, it appears to be worthwhile to decompose paragraphs into sentences, but not to worry about breaking sentences into syntactic constituents.

User Modeling

LSA is used to perform user modeling during the course of training with AutoTutor. As students contribute information, turn by turn, their content is compared with the expectations and misconceptions in the curriculum script. How well does LSA perform this user modeling? We have performed some analyses on the LSA cosine scores in AutoTutor's log files in order to answer this question.

In one analysis of conceptual physics, we used pretest scores on a multiple-choice test as the gold standard of the students' pre-experimental knowledge of physics before they started the AutoTutor training. The multiple-choice test was similar to a frequently used test developed by Hestenes, Wells, and Swackhamer (1992), called the force concept inventory. If AutoTutor is performing effective user modeling, then the dialogue moves selected by AutoTutor should be systematically affected by the students' prior knowledge of physics. This indeed appeared to be the case when we analyzed the dialogue moves of AutoTutor in response to students of varying ability (see Jackson, Person, & Graesser, 2004, for one study). Consider first, the short feedback that AutoTutor gives to the student after most of the student's turns. The short feedback is either positive, neutral, or negative. The students' physics knowledge had a significant positive correlation with proportion of short feedbacks that were positive ($r = .38$) and a negative correlation with negative feedback ($r = -.37$). These correlations are based on 30 or more students in an analysis and are therefore statistically significant. Next consider the corrections that AutoTutor made when identifying student errors and misconceptions. The correlation was negative ($r = -.24$), and marginally significant, with the frequency of corrections by AutoTutor. Consider, finally, the four dialogue move categories that attempt to cover the content of the expectations in the curriculum script: pumps, hints, prompts, and assertions. The proportion of dialogue moves in these categories should be sensitive to student knowledge of physics. There is a continuum from the student supplying information to the tutor supplying information as we move from pumps, to hints, to prompts, to assertions. The correlations with student knowledge reflected this continuum perfectly, with correlations of .49, .24, −.19, and −.40. For students with more knowledge of physics, all AutoTutor needs to do is primarily pump and hint, thereby encouraging or nudging the student to supply the answer to the question and articulate the expectations. For students with less knowledge of physics, AutoTutor needs to generate prompts for specific words or to assert the correct information, thereby extracting knowledge piecemeal or telling the student the correct information. These results support the claim that AutoTutor performs user modeling with some modicum of accuracy and adaptively responds to the learner's level of knowledge.

A different approach to assessing user modeling is analyzing the evolution of answers to the main questions. As the student contributes information, turn by turn, the LSA coverage scores should increase. *Coverage characteristics curves* (CC-curves) were prepared in order to assess whether this is case. A CC-curve is the LSA score for an expectation E plotted as a function of conversational turns or as a function of particular states in the evolution of the answer. For example, Graesser et al. (2000) reported CC-curves for computer literacy by plotting mean cumulative LSA cosine scores for each expectation as a function of conversational turns. The scores were cumulative in the sense that the student's content in turn $N + 1$ includes all of the content articulated by the student in turns 1 through N. The mean LSA scores increased significantly, with means of .27, .39, .45, .62, .66, and .76 for turns 1, 2, 3, 4, 5, and 6, respectively. These data support the claim that LSA adequately tracks the evolving evolution of a correct answer over conversational turns. It should be noted that these scores are considerably above what would be expected by chance if words in a student's turn were randomly sampled from the corpus of texts.

There are different metrics for tracking the coverage of expectations during the evolution of a conversational dialogue. One is simply the mean cumulative LSA value, as reported earlier in the Graesser et al. (2000) study. One potential problem with this method is that there can be decreases or distortions in LSA scores to the extent that vague or extraneous information is mixed in with the correct information. An *all subsets method* was subsequently used to mitigate this problem as a second content coverage algorithm. This method converges on and considers information that has a high resonance to the expectation, and minimizes the influence of extraneous and vague information. At student turn $N + 1$ for a particular main question, the student has articulated a set of speech acts 1 through M. An LSA cosine score is computed between (a) an expectation E and (b) each individual speech act and all combinations (subsets) of speech acts. The maximum cosine score from this subset comparison algorithm is declared as the coverage score for expectation E at student turn $N + 1$. This method guarantees a monotonic increase in LSA coverage scores over the evolution of the conversation. Unfortunately, a serious downside to this algorithm is that there is a combinatorial explosion problem as the value of M gets large. If the student were to express 25 speech acts, for example, there would be $(2^{25}-1)$ cosines to compute, nearly 34 million. Although these cosines would be somewhat distributed over turns, it ended up being impractical. As a consequence, a *span* method was used as an alternative algorithm that was not computationally expensive and accomplished similar goals. It is beyond the scope of this chapter to discuss the span method (Hu et al., 2003; Hu et al., chap. 20 in this volume) other than to say that it segregates the student's contribution at turn $N + 1$ into old versus new content with respect to expectation E and that it is incorporated in the most recent versions of AutoTutor.

We prepared some CC-curves for one of our recent experiments on physics. We identified the total set of dialogue sequences in which the student had trouble articulating a particular expectation E. The LSA coverage score for E was recorded at 5 points: (a) after the question was first asked and AutoTutor pumped the student for information for one turn, (b) a first hint was given, (c) a first prompt was given (always after a first hint), (d) a second hint was given, and (e) a second prompt was given (always after the second hint). Figure 13.2 plots the mean LSA scores as a function of these five states in the dialogue history for an expectation E. As can be seen in Figure 13.2, there was a monotonic increase in LSA values over turns. The values were also significantly higher for students with high than low pre-experimental knowledge about physics. Therefore, AutoTutor's LSA

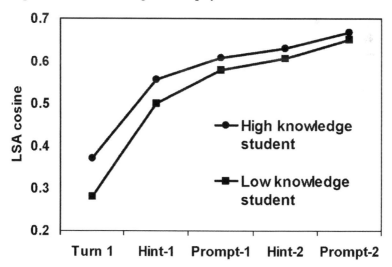

Figure 13.2. Relationship between LSA cosine and number of student contributions in AutoTutor's physics tutor.

component does a decent job performing student modeling and tracking the coverage of an expectation over the tutorial dialogue.

There is a very important word of caution, however, in the current span method of tracking content coverage for expectations. Base rate LSA scores significantly increase as a function of the number of words in the expectations and student answers (Penumatsa, Ventura, Olde, Franceschetti, & Graesser, 2004). Figure 13.3 shows base rate scores that were generated by randomly sampling words from a physics textbook. That is, how high would LSA scores be if the words in expectations and the words in the students' contributions were simply randomly sampled from the corpus of physics texts? We compared 8 versus 16 words, roughly the range in word length of an expectation. We compared sizes of words that reflect the student contributions, from 2 to 256 words. The base rate is noticeably high (about .4) for an expectation of 16 words and a student's contribution of 256 words, even though the bags of words were randomly sampled from a physics textbook. It is important to acknowledge that these base rate scores are appreciably lower than the CC-curves in Figures 13.2 and 13.3, so AutoTutor's tracking of the students' knowledge is quite a bit better than chance. In the future, we will need to somehow adjust for the baserate LSA scores when we conduct student modeling (Hu et al., chap. 20 in this volume).

ANALYSIS OF SENTENTIAL UNITS WITH LSA

Previous LSA research has adequately demonstrated that LSA is successful in reliably handling texts of several paragraphs. However, the status of LSA

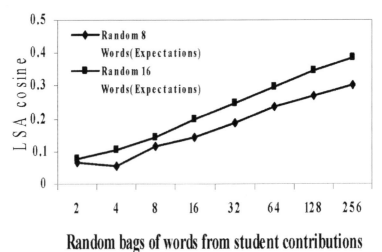

Figure 13.3.   The sensitivity of LSA scores to text size.

in handling sentential units is either disappointing or uncertain. The primary worry is that most sentences do not contain enough words to afford a reliable LSA score. The more optimistic possibility is that a modest LSA coverage score provides sufficient information to be useful. The importance of sentential units is inherent to AutoTutor because expectations are sentential units. It is also the case that the vast majority of the student turns are two or fewer sentences, so any evaluation of a single student turn will potentially be limited; instead, the accumulation of contributions from turns 1 through N might provide the only trustworthy analysis of student modeling. Therefore, this section reports some LSA analyses of sentential units.

Presence of Expectations and Misconceptions in Essays

Essay answers were analyzed to see whether any subset of information within an essay matches particular sentential expectations and misconceptions. Five physics experts made judgments of whether each particular expectation E was covered anywhere in the student's essay. There were three values in these judgments: (1) explicitly present, (2) implicitly present, versus (3) absent. A stringent criterion was a rating of 1, whereas a lenient criterion was a rating of 1 or 2. Similarly, misconceptions were judged on a 3-point scale. When considering all judges, an expectation or misconception was considered covered if the majority of experts scored it as covered (given the operative criterion).

Figure 13.4 plots recall and precision scores as a function of the LSA cosine threshold that determines whether an expectation is covered. The recall score is the probability that LSA scores the expectation as covered, given that human judges consider it covered. This score is expected to decrease with higher LSA thresholds because more information is required in the student essay before the LSA criterion is met. The fact that the slope of the line is so steep indicates that small changes in the threshold setting can have rather dramatic effects on the LSA-based detection of expectations. AutoTutor researchers will therefore need to spend time carefully setting the threshold parameter. As it is set higher, the learner is expected to be more precise in the articulation of the answer. In contrast, the precision score is virtually flat. The precision score is the probability that the humans judge the expectation as covered, given that LSA scores it as covered. What this means is that humans would likely consider an expectation covered if it was detected by LSA. These two curves together suggest that it would be wise to set the threshold score lower rather than higher. However, the threshold cannot be too low because it would run the risk of being indistinguishable from base rate levels (Fig. 13.3).

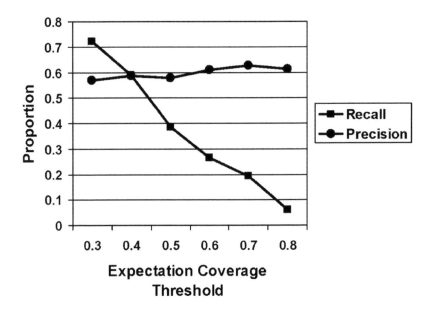

Figure 13.4.   Recall and precision scores as a function of LSA coverage thresholds.

Which Expectations Are LSA-Worthy?

It is conceivable that some expectations would be more amenable to LSA computations than would others. For example, expectations that have high-frequency words should have poorer performance because there would not be enough distinctive content. Ideally, AutoTutor would have a principled way of determining whether or not an expectation is *LSA-worthy*. An expectation is defined as LSA-worthy if there is a high correlation between LSA and human experts in its being covered in the essays. If AutoTutor could predict the LSA worthiness of an expectation in a principled way, then that could guide whether it trusted the LSA metrics. LSA metrics would be used for expectations that are LSA-worthy, but other algorithms would be used for expectations that are not LSA-worthy.

We computed LSA-worthiness scores for approximately 40 expectations associated with the physics problems that were used in the pretest and posttest essays (with 30 or more student scores per expectation). The LSA worthiness score for expectation E is simply a correlation between the LSA coverage scores for E on a sample of 30 or more essays and the mean expectation coverage rating among the 5 expert judges. This score should approach 1.0 to the extent an expectation is LSA-worthy. Some examples of these scores are listed for 4 of the expectations:

1. After the release, the only force on the balls is the force of the moon's gravity ($r = .71$).
2. A larger object will experience a smaller acceleration for the same force ($r = .12$).
3. Force equals mass times acceleration ($r = .67$).
4. The boxes are in free fall ($r = .21$).

The first and third of these expectations would be considered LSA-worthy, but not the second and fourth. It is fortunate that the third expectation is LSA-worthy because it captures Newton's second law.

We performed some analyses that assessed whether there were linguistic or conceptual properties of the expectations that would correlate with the LSA-worthiness scores. If there were, we would have a principled way for AutoTutor to gauge whether the LSA assessments can be trusted. We have examined dozens of linguistic and conceptual properties of the 40 expectations, but only 2 of them significantly correlated with LSA-worthiness: Number of infrequent words ($r = .23$) and negations ($r = -.29$). Among the other properties that had near-zero correlations were number of words, content words, glossary terms, relative terms (e.g., *small, fast*), quantifiers (e.g., *some, all, one, two*), deictic expressions (e.g., *this, that*), and vector length. These modest correlations suggest it may be difficult to predict a priori which of the expectations will end up being LSA-worthy.

Matching Sentential Expectations to Learners' Sentential Contributions

One expert physicist rated the degree to which particular speech acts expressed during AutoTutor training matched particular expectations. These judgments were made on a sample of 25 physics expectations and 5 randomly sampled student answers per expectation, yielding a total of 125 pairs of expressions. The learner answers were always responses to the first hint for that expectation. The question is how well the expert ratings correlate with LSA coverage scores. It should be noted that this analysis involves comparisons between sentential expectations and single student speech acts during training; this is not the same as previous analyses in which an expectation is compared with content of an entire student essay.

The correlation between an expert judge's rating and the LSA cosine was modest—only $r = .29$—but significant in accounting for the 125 items. We scaled the 125 items on two other scales to see how they would compare with LSA. First, we computed overlap scores between the words in the two sentential units (minus *a, an, the*). If an expectation has A content words, a student speech act has B content words, and there are C common words between the two sentential units, then the overlap score is computed as $[2C/(A$

+ *B*)]. The correlation between expert ratings and word overlap scores was .39. So a simple word overlap metric does a somewhat better job than LSA per se when sentential units are compared (see also McNamara et al., chap. 12 in this volume). Second, we scaled whether the serial order of common content words was similar between the two sentential units by computing Kendall's Tau scores (see Dennis, chap. 22 in this volume). This word order similarity metric had a .25 correlation with the expert ratings. We performed a multiple regression analysis that assessed whether the expert ratings could be predicted by LSA, word overlap, and Kendall's Tau together. The three predictors accounted for a significant $r = .42$. Therefore, we believe that analyses of sentences would benefit from a hybrid computational algorithm that considers both LSA and alternative algorithms. Alternative algorithms would consider: (a) associates of the content words computed as nearest neighbors in the LSA space (Kintsch, 2001), (b) word combinations in the actual corpus (Ventura et al., 2004), (c) content word overlap (Graesser, Hu et al., 2004; Millis et al., 2004), and (d) word sequences in the actual corpus (Dennis, chap. 22 in this volume). Of course, we could also consider symbolic models of syntax and meaning in a hybrid model.

CONCLUSIONS

We are convinced that LSA has been moderately successful as a foundational representational system for AutoTutor. It was capable of grading essays in physics and computer literacy ($r = .5$) almost as well as experts. It could significantly perform user modeling and track the coverage of expectations during the evolution of collaborative dialogue. We found some added value in breaking up paragraphs into sentences in our LSA analyses, but no incremental value in decomposing sentences syntactically. Sentence unit matches with LSA were limited ($r = .3$), however, so it is important to consider explicit word overlap and ordering of words when sentential units are compared. We know that some expectations can be reliably computed with LSA, but others cannot be and will require more hybrid architectures for conceptual pattern matching. We will explore some theoretically principled hybrid models in our quest for an adequate sentential pattern matcher.

ACKNOWLEDGMENTS

The Tutoring Research Group (TRG) is an interdisciplinary research team comprised of approximately 35 researchers from psychology, computer science, physics, and education (visit http://www.autotutor.org). The research on AutoTutor was supported by the National Science Foundation (SBR 9720314, REC 0106965, REC 0126265, ITR 0325428) and the Department of Defense Multidisciplinary University Research Initiative administered by the Office of Naval Research under grant N00014-00-1-0600. Any opinions, findings, and conclusions or recommendations expressed in this material are those of the authors and do not necessarily reflect the views of the DoD, ONR, or NSF.

REFERENCES

Aleven, V., & Koedinger, K. R. (2002). An effective metacognitive strategy: Learning by doing and explaining with a computer-based cognitive tutor. *Cognitive Science, 26,* 147–179.

Anderson, J. R., Corbett, A. T., Koedinger, K. R., & Pelletier, R. (1995). Cognitive tutors: Lessons learned. *Journal of the Learning Sciences, 4,* 167–207.

Bloom, B. S. (1956). *Taxonomy of educational objectives: The classification of educational goals. Handbook I: Cognitive domain.* New York: McKay.

Chi, M. T. H., de Leeuw, N., Chiu, M., & LaVancher, C. (1994) Eliciting self-explanation improves understanding. *Cognitive Science, 18,* 439–477.

Chi, M. T. H., Siler, S., Jeong, H., Yamauchi, T., & Hausmann, R. G. (2001). Learning from human tutoring. *Cognitive Science, 25,* 471–533.

Foltz, P. W., Gilliam, S., & Kendall, S. (2000). Supporting content-based feedback in on-line writing evaluation with LSA. *Interactive Learning Environments, 8,* 111–127.

Fox, B. (1993). *The human tutorial dialog project.* Hillsdale, NJ: Lawrence Erlbaum Associates.

Graesser, A. C., Chipman, P., Haynes, B. C., & Olney, A. (2005). AutoTutor: An intelligent tutoring system with mixed-initiative dialogue. *IEEE Transactions in Education, 48,* 612–618 .

Graesser, A. C., Hu, X., & McNamara, D. S. (2005). Computerized learning environments that incorporate research in discourse psychology, cognitive science, and computational linguistics. In A. F. Healy (Ed.), *Experimental cognitive psychology and its applications: Fetschrift in honor of Lyle Bourne, Walter Kintsch, and Thomas Landauer* (pp. 183–194). Washington, DC: American Psychological Association.

Graesser, A. C., Hu, X., Person, P., Jackson, T., & Toth, J. (2004). Modules and information retrieval facilities of the human use regulatory affairs advisor (HURAA). *International Journal on eLearning, 3,* 29–39.

Graesser, A. C., Lu, S., Jackson, G. T., Mitchell, H., Ventura, M., Olney, A., & Louwerse, M. M. (2004). AutoTutor: A tutor with dialogue in natural language. *Behavioral Research Methods, Instruments, and Computers, 36,* 180–193.

Graesser, A. C., & Person, N. K. (1994). Question asking during tutoring. *American Educational Research Journal, 31,* 104–137.

Graesser, A. C., Person, N., Harter, D., & the Tutoring Research Group (2001). Teaching tactics and dialog in AutoTutor. *International Journal of Artificial Intelligence in Education, 12,* 257–279.

Graesser, A. C., Person, N. K., & Magliano, J. P. (1995). Collaborative dialogue patterns in naturalistic one-to-one tutoring. *Applied Cognitive Psychology, 9,* 1–28.

Graesser, A. C., VanLehn, K., Rose, C., Jordan, P., & Harter, D. (2001). Intelligent tutoring systems with conversational dialogue. *AI Magazine, 22,* 39–51.

Graesser, A. C., Wiemer-Hastings, K., Wiemer-Hastings, P., Kreuz, R., & the Tutoring Research Group (1999). Auto Tutor: A simulation of a human tutor. *Journal of Cognitive Systems Research, 1*, 35–51.

Graesser, A. C., Wiemer-Hastings, P., Wiemer-Hastings, K., Harter, D., Person, N., & the Tutoring Research Group (2000). Using latent semantic analysis to evaluate the contributions of students in AutoTutor. *Interactive Learning Environments, 8*, 129–148.

Hestenes, D., Wells, M., & Swackhamer, G. (1992). Force concept inventory. *The Physics Teacher, 30*, 141–158.

Hewitt, P. G. (1998). *Conceptual physics* (8th ed.). Menlo Park, CA: Addison-Wesley.

Hu, X., Cai, Z., Graesser, A. C., Louwerse, M. M., Penumatsa, P., Olney, A., & the Tutoring Research Group (2003). An improved LSA algorithm to evaluate student contributions in tutoring dialogue. In G. Gottlob & T. Walsh (Eds.), *Proceedings of 18th International Joint Conference in Artificial Intelligence* (pp. 1489–4491). San Francisco: Morgan Kaufmann.

Jackson, G. T., Person, N. K., & Graesser, A. C. (2004). Adaptive tutorial dialogue in AutoTutor. *Proceedings of the Workshop on Dialog-Based Intelligent Tutoring Systems at the Seventh International Conference on Intelligent Tutoring Systems* (pp. 368–372). Universidade Federal de Alagoas, Brazil.

Kintsch, W. (1998). *Comprehension: A paradigm for cognition*. Cambridge, MA: Cambridge University Press.

Kintsch, W. (2001). Predication. *Cognitive Science, 25*, 173–202.

Landauer, T. K., & Dumais, S. T. (1997). A solution to Plato's problem: The latent semantic analysis theory of the acquisition, induction, and representation of knowledge. *Psychological Review, 104*, 211–240.

Landauer, T. K., Laham, D., & Foltz, P. W. (2003). Automatic scoring and automation of essays with the Intelligent Essay Assessor. In M. D. Shermis & J. Burstein (Eds.), *Automated essay scoring: A cross-disciplinary perspective* (pp. 87–112). Mahwah, NJ: Lawrence Erlbaum Associates.

McNamara, D. S. (2004). SERT: Self-explanation reading training. *Discourse Processes, 38*, 1–30.

Millis, K. K., Kim, H. J., Todaro, S., Magliano, J. P., Wiemer-Hastings, K., & McNamara, D. S. (2004). Identifying reading strategies using latent semantic analysis: Comparing semantic benchmarks. *Behavior Research Methods, Instruments, and Computers, 36*, 213–221.

Olde, B. A., Franceschetti, D. R., Karnavat, Graesser, A. C., & the Tutoring Research Group (2002). The right stuff: Do you need to sanitize your corpus when using latent semantic analysis? In W. Gray & C. D. Schunn (Eds.), *Proceedings of the 24th Annual Conference of the Cognitive Science Society* (pp. 708–713). Mahwah, NJ: Lawrence Erlbaum Associates.

Penumatsa, P., Ventura, M., Graesser, A. C., Franceschetti, D. R., Louwerse, M., Hu, X., Cai, Z., & the Tutoring Research Group (2004). The right threshold value: What is the right threshold of cosine measure when using latent semantic analysis for evaluating student answers? *International Journal of Artificial Intelligence Tools, 12*, 257–279.

VanLehn, K., Graesser, A. C., Jackson, G. T., Jordan, P., Olney, A., & Rosé, C. P. (in press). When are tutorial dialogues more effective than reading? *Cognitive Science*.

VanLehn, K., Jordan, P., Rosé, C. P., Bhembe, D., Bottner, M., Gaydos, A., et al. (2002). The architecture of Why2-Atlas: A coach for qualitative physics essay writing. In S. A. Cerri, G. Gouarderes, & F. Paraguacu (Eds.), *Proceedings of the Sixth International Conference on Intelligent Tutoring* (pp.158–167). Berlin: Springer–Verlag.

Ventura, M., Hu, X., Graesser, A. C., Louwerse, M. M., & Olney, A. (2004). The context dependent sentence abstraction model. In K. D. Forbus, D. Gentner, & T. Regier (Eds.), *Proceedings of the 26th Annual Meeting of the Cognitive Science Society* (pp. 1387–1392). Mahwah, NJ: Lawrence Erlbaum Associates.

Wiemer-Hastings, P., Wiemer-Hastings, K., & Graesser, A. (1999). Improving an intelligent tutor's comprehension of students with latent semantic analysis. In S. P. Lajoie & M. Vivet (Eds.), *Artificial intelligence in education* (pp. 535–542). Amsterdam: IOS Press.

APPENDIX

Example AutoTutor–student dialogue with classified dialogue moves of AutoTutor, classified speech acts of the student, and comments.

AutoTutor: *When a car without headrests on the seats is struck from behind, the passengers often suffer neck injuries? Explain why.* (MAIN QUESTION: This is a main question selected from AutoTutor's curriculum script, which will take approximately 50–200 conversation turns to collaborately answer.)

Student: *I don't know.* (This expression by the student is classified as a metacognitive speech act because it conveys what the student knows about his/her own knowledge.)

AutoTutor: *Could you at least try to give me an answer? That way, we'll have something as a starting place to work from.* (PUMP: This dialogue move encourages the student to say more, but does not direct the student to express particular information.)

[Later]

AutoTutor: *Uh Huh* (SHORT NEUTRAL FEADBACK) *Let's try this together.* (DISCOURSE MARKER: This is a discourse marker that connects different dialogue moves within a turn. Another good discourse marker is "Okay.") *When the neck provides a large force to accelerate the head, what could happen to the neck?* (HINT: This dialogue move leads the student to articulate a particular sentence, clauses, or proposition.)

Student: *What is a force?* (The student can ask questions during an AutoTutor session.)

AutoTutor: *I'll take a crack at answering your question.* (DISCOURSE MARKER) *Force is any influence that tends to accelerate an object; a push or pull; measured in newtons. Force is a vector quantity.* (ANSWER: AutoTutor answers the student's direct question by searching and fetching information from a glossary or a textbook.) *Was that what you were looking for?* (QUESTION SOLICITATION: AutoTutor allows the student the opportunity to rephrase his question.)

[Later]

AutoTutor: *See if you know the answer to this.* (DISCOURSE MARKER: AutoTutor prepares the student for a direct question.) *When the head and body are moving at the same acceleration, they are moving at the same _____?* (PROMPT: This dialogue move encourages the student to fill in a particular word or phrase of information, in this case the word "rate." Prompts are needed for students who are low verbal and to elicit a particular noun, verb, or adjective.)

Student: *distance*

AutoTutor: *Moving at the same rate.* (PROMPT COMPLETION: AutoTutor splices in the correct information if the student provides an incorrect answer to its prompt.)

[Later]

AutoTutor: *Okay, now, let's recap.* (DISCOURSE MARKER) *In the collision notice the person's body and head move along together. In order for this to occur the body and head must have the same acceleration. This concept applies to all situations where two bodies are moving together through space.* (SUMMARY: AutoTutor recaps what the student has learned.)

14

Summary Street®: Computer-Guided Summary Writing

Eileen Kintsch, Donna Caccamise, Marita Franzke,
and Nina Johnson
University of Colorado, Boulder

Scott Dooley
Pearson Knowledge Technologies

There is a need for a tutor that coaches students through the process of composing a written summary. Summarizing is increasingly valued by teachers, as well as by school accountability experts, not only as an important skill in its own right, but as a means of promoting deeper levels of comprehension and learning. *How* to teach kids to summarize is the problem. Conveying the underlying strategies is the easy part, but like most skills, one learns by doing, and in this case it takes a lot of practice. Few schools have the resources to guide individual students through multiple drafts and revisions of their summaries or essays. Summary Street® was designed to address this problem by giving students lots of opportunity to summarize informational text guided by individualized feedback. As a true offspring of LSA, feedback from Summary Street® is directed at the content of the writing. It tells the writer whether the summary conveys enough information about each of the main topics of a text; whether the summary is of the appropriate length; and whether it contains repeated information or information that is not highly relevant to the overall topic. It also warns the writer if too much of the material has been lifted directly from the source text and, of course, it provides a spell check. However, Summary Street® does not provide feedback on other problems with the mechanics of writing, such as sentence structure and punctuation, nor does it assess style, organization, and the truth value of the content.

The evolution of Summary Street® into a robust, engaging, and practical educational tool that is increasingly used in Colorado school classes was the product of many minds and a long development process. The process from theoretical insights to something that functions in the messy real world of the classroom was hardly straightforward, and LSA researchers owe a debt of gratitude to David Wade-Stein, who programmed the first workable version of Summary Street®, and to two talented teachers—Cindy Matthews and Ronald Lamb, of Platt Middle School in Boulder—who helped translate the researchers' vision into a classroom success. Indeed, collaborative design among researchers, teachers, and their students continues to guide our efforts to improve and refine the software.

In a sense, providing feedback on written summaries is a natural application of the LSA technology: To do so, Summary Street® simply matches the student summary with the source text. (Alternatively, the summary could be matched with a teacher's "golden summary" or with a large database of human scored summaries—the method used by the Intelligent Essay Assessor, IEA, to score essays. However, these approaches involve considerable effort and are less practical for assessing summaries of a large number of different texts.)

HOW SUMMARY STREET® WORKS

Summary Street® is accessible over a set of specifically assigned Internet pages (see http://www.colit.org or http://www.knowledge-technologies.com to try a demonstration). Students compose their summaries in an editing field, or textbox, or they may copy and paste in a prepared summary. Clicking on the feedback button sends the summary via the Internet to Pearson Knowledge Technologies for analysis by LSA, which compares the content of the summary with the content of the text on which it was based. For the most part, LSA uses the General Reading Space to perform the analyses of middle and high school summaries. However, for a few specialized topics (e.g., the circulatory system), the feedback is more reliable when a specific space (e.g., biology) is used. Feedback is returned almost instantaneously in the graphic form shown in Figure 14.1. Most texts that students summarize consist of several sections corresponding to the main topics covered (e.g., the text on Kenya has five sections: Introduction, Life in Urban and Rural Africa, Tribal Ties, and The Future). The Summary Street® feedback screen shows a stack of horizontal bars, each one corresponding to a main section heading of the text. The bars turn from orange to green and extend past a vertical black line (representing the cosine threshold for that section) when the content for that section is adequately covered. Although the content threshold is represented by a single, black vertical line, in fact the threshold cosines differ for each section of the text.[1] Thus, students can see at a glance what sections contain enough information about a particular topic and which need more work.

A vertical bar at the right with min–max indicators shows whether the summary falls within the word length proscribed by the teacher. Buttons at the bottom of the feedback page allow access to the additional tools noted earlier: a spell check, redundant, irrelevant, and plagiarized sentence checks. Guided by these kinds of feedback on the content of their writing, students

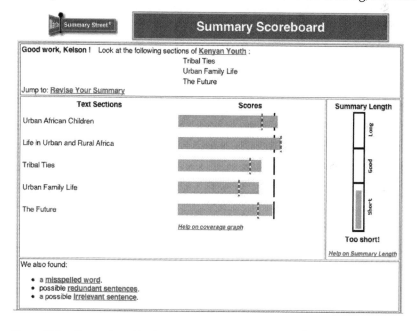

Figure 14.1.   Screenshot of feedback window in Summary Street®. Horizontal bars representing topic sections of the text change from orange to green when the content coverage is sufficient. Dotted lines that bisect the feedback bars indicate progress from last request for feedback. The summary length bar is orange when the summary is too brief or too long and green when it is within the specified range.

---

[1]The threshold cosines are derived using a mathematical algorithm that takes into account both content similarity and word length. The method is described in detail in Wade-Stein and E. Kintsch (2004).

thus engage in successive cycles of revision and feedback requests. In order to encourage more thoughtful revisions, the current version of Summary Street® limits the number of times students may request feedback for a particular summary to 10 tries. It is important to note that the feedback does not provide correct answers, but rather gives students enough support to allow them to debug their own writing problems. Students' interactions with Summary Street® have a gamelike character. Even students who do not like writing tasks get involved in how to get the bars to pass the thresholds and turn green. And, in so doing, they write better summaries. An additional function that Summary Street® now offers is authoring tools. This interface makes it possible for teachers to see at a glance how their students are doing, either by zooming in on a working session (The Class Snapshot tool, shown in Fig. 14.2) or by requesting overview data at a later time. The authoring tools also provide a forum in which teachers and researchers can add and edit students' names, classes, and texts.

More complete descriptions of how Summary Street® works are available in Franzke, E. Kintsch, Caccamise, Johnson, and Dooley (2005), E. Kintsch et al. (2000), and in Wade-Stein and E. Kintsch (2004). This chapter provides a brief overview of how Summary Street® is being implemented in schools and summarizes the results of several classroom trials documenting its efficacy. We conclude with an outline of future research endeavors that we are planning.

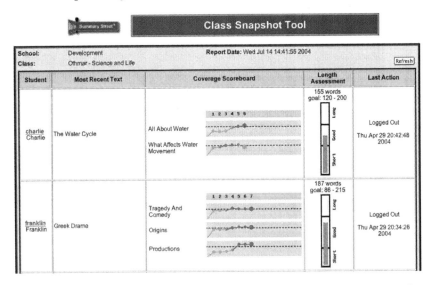

Figure 14.2. Screenshot showing Class Snapshot, one of the Summary Street® authoring tools. The bar graph shows the student's progress across multiple feedback requests for each text section. Section numbers appear at the top of the graph, and horizontal dotted lines indicate the cosine thresholds for each section.

OUTREACH EFFORTS

Use of Summary Street®

Summary Street® is currently being used by some 2,500 students in 65 5th-through 12th-grade classrooms in Colorado. The schools are located in seven urban, rural, and suburban districts. The number of students using the tool has greatly expanded in the last 2 years via word-of-mouth interactions as well as teacher training workshops. During the workshops, teachers in a specific district or school learn what Summary Street® does, how to navigate the user interface and editing tools, and how it can be implemented in their classrooms. Most importantly, teachers get firsthand experience by writing a summary on the program, which helps them imagine how it could be used in their own classes, and to realize how students would benefit from it. Interest in Summary Street® has been generated both from the top down (by contacting school principals and district superintendents to organize training sessions) and bottom up, as teachers observe their peers using Summary Street® and request to use it too.

Integrating Summary Street® Into Instruction

The Summary Street® library of now includes some 140 texts, covering a broad range of topics in biography, history, science (e.g., environmental science, life science, physical science), and social issues. Textbooks are not included due to copyright restrictions, but also because the unelaborated listlike presentation of science information in many textbooks makes them unsuitable for summarizing. Instead, teachers use the texts in the Summary Street® library to enrich the instructional materials and to emphasize key concepts.

Teachers' goals in using Summary Street® differ depending on the subject matter they teach. Language arts teachers are typically interested in strengthening their students' summary writing skills. Hence, their students work through multiple drafts of their writing, using the system's tools to deal with problems in content coverage, redundancy, relevance, and length in their revisions. One teacher finds it especially helpful as a context for discussing how to go about making a summary more concise, using strategies such as focusing on important words, combining ideas in a single sentence, and generalizing across details. Among social studies or science teachers, on the other hand, the focus is more on understanding a particular content, rather than resolving writing problems. In these classes, Summary Street® serves both to direct students' attention to the main ideas and to deepen their learning by having them express the meaning in their own words.

Students' age and skill level also influence how Summary Street® is used. For fifth graders, it provides an initial starting point for learning about summary writing with many opportunities for guided practice with different texts. Summary Street® feedback, geared to a text's main topic sections, is especially helpful for the younger students, who have difficulty locating the important information in a text. High school students should (although often don't) know how to compose a summary, but now need to apply the skill to gathering information for a written report. Relevance of the information to their topic and conciseness are paramount concerns. Summary Street® can accommodate these goals by greatly restricting the allowable word length.

Many special education teachers have expressed interest in using Summary Street® with their students. The tutor can be readily adapted to their needs by choosing texts appropriate to their reading skill level, by lowering the section thresholds and adjusting length constraints, and by providing extra support at the outset. Thus, lower achieving students may need more instruction in how to summarize, as well as help with particular problems they encounter composing and revising. Once they catch on, we find that Summary Street® becomes a highly motivating context in which they can also experience success. Furthermore, we find that it works especially well with pairs of students working collaboratively.

Just as teachers' goals differ with content area, grade, and ability level, logistics—such as the availability of computer lab time—to some extent also dictate how Summary Street® is used and how often. Depending on how well summary writing sessions fit specific curricular plans, the tool may be used as often as two or three times a month, or as little as two to three times a year. Unfortunately, in many schools, computer availability is still very limited. Teachers compensate by assigning Summary Street® sessions as homework, by having students work as pairs or teams at a single computer, and by having students write their summaries in advance, using the tool to revise them in the lab. All of these methods work, as Summary Street® is remarkably flexible and has minimal technology requirements: A reliable Internet connection with a fairly recent web browser, such as Internet Explorer 5.1 or Netscape 7.0 or higher, is all that is required.

EMPIRICAL FINDINGS FROM CLASSROOM STUDIES

Several studies (Franzke et al., 2005; E. Kintsch et al., 2000; Wade-Stein & E. Kintsch, 2004) have been conducted on classroom use of Summary Street®, both to assess usability issues and guide its further development, and to evaluate its effectiveness as a learning tool. The educational issues concern first, whether the content feedback does help students write better summaries, as we predicted. And if so, what aspects of their writing are improved? Further, does guided practice in writing summaries over a longer period of use transfer to reading strategies, that is, does it promote more active, attentive reading, as reflected by scores on an independent test of comprehension? What other aspects of students' behavior are affected, for example, the amount of time spent on summary writing and their awareness of summarization strategies. Does Summary Street® use affect students' summaries in a negative manner by encouraging too many low-level revisions or the tendency to lift sentences directly from the source text? In these studies, we also looked at individual differences among students, asking for whom Summary Street® is most useful and under what conditions?

Altogether, some 300 6th- and 8th-grade students from public schools in Boulder and Thornton, Colorado, participated in this research. Their use of the tool ranged from two texts across two long sessions to multiple uses during class for a 4-week period. One classroom trial with 52 sixth-grade participants (Wade-Stein & E. Kintsch, 2004) employed a within-subjects design; the other (Franzke et al., 2005) involved a between-subjects, experimental versus control group comparison with 121 8th-grade participants.

Effects on Summary Quality

The summaries collected from the students in both studies were blind scored either by their classroom teachers or by hired scorers (former teachers) for their overall quality and specific content coverage of each section of a given text. Specifically, the section content was scored on a scale of 0 to 2 points (0 = no information on this section, 1 = some, but not enough, 2 = adequate coverage). For some of the summaries, they also provided separate scores to rate style, organization, conciseness, and mechanics. Summarizing the results across all these trials we found the following effects on summaries written with the guidance of LSA-based feedback (content coverage, length, relevance, and redundancy checks).

Summaries by students using Summary Street® were rated consistently better in overall quality and in content coverage. As seen in Figure 14.3, when students were using Summary Street® their summaries contained information from all four to six sections of the longer texts, whereas summaries written without support typically covered only the first two or three sections. Moreover, Summary Street® feedback was especially helpful when students worked with more difficult texts that they found challeng-

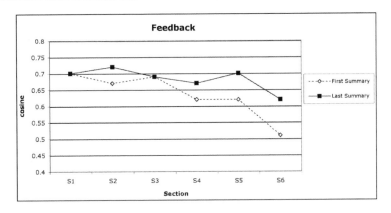

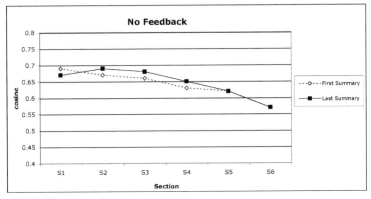

Figure 14.3. Comparison of first and last summaries by feedback condition. From "Summary Street: Interactive Computer Support for Writing," by D. Wade-Stein and E. Kintsch, 2004, *Cognition and Instruction, 22*(3), p. 353. Copyright © 2004 by Lawrence Erlbaum Associates. Reprinted with permission.

ing to understand and to summarize. Figure 14.4 compares summaries of students using Summary Street® and control group students, who used a word processor as they worked through a series of texts of increasing difficulty, both in terms of length (from one to four sections) and in terms of conceptual complexity. Despite the increasing difficulty of the texts, Summary Street® users maintained consistently high scores, whereas the scores of control group students declined as the texts got harder.

When guided by the feedback, students spent much longer working on their summaries—more than twice as long as when they wrote without the support (70 min. vs. 30 min., respectively), which probably also contributed to the quality of the product.

There is evidence (Wade-Stein & E. Kintsch, 2004) suggesting that the effects of guided practice with Summary Street® may persist over time: Students whose first summaries were composed with Summary Street® wrote equally good summaries of a different text 2 weeks later when they received no feedback on their content coverage.

The study by Franzke et al. (2005) looked in more detail at the particular characteristics of the eighth-grade summaries that were influenced by using Summary Street® over a longer period of use (4 weeks). Thus, in addition to overall quality and content coverage scores, a subset of the summaries was graded for characteristics that are traditionally considered by teachers in their evaluations of student writing: namely, organization, writing style, the amount of unnecessary detail in the summaries, writing mechanics (spelling, punctuation, sentence structure), and plagiarism. In blind scoring (using a 1- to 5-point scale) Summary Street® summaries were rated significantly better in terms of their organization, style, and conciseness (exclusion of details) than the control group summaries, which are not directly targeted by the feedback that Summary Street® gives. It appears, then, that several other aspects of writing fall into place when one has expressed the right content (cf. Foltz, Laham, & Landauer, 1999). However, we found no effects on punctuation, spelling, and grammar by Summary Street® use, nor is there any reason to expect such effects, because writing mechanics are not specifically addressed by the tool. We had some concern that Summary Street® might encourage students to lift material directly from the source text. On the contrary, experimental and control group summaries were equivalent in the amount of plagiarized material they contained, which was gratifyingly low in both groups. Students apparently

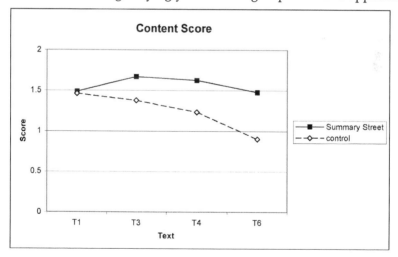

Figure 14.4.   Content scores by text (T1, T3, T4, & T6) and condition. From *Summary Street®: Computer support for comprehension and writing* (p. 70), by M. Franzke, E. Kintsch, D. Caccamise, N. Johnson, and S. Dooley, 2005, Amityville, NY: Baywood Publishing Co., Inc. Copyright © 2005 by Baywood Publishing Co., Inc. Reprinted with permission.
Note: T1 has a single section, T3 has two sections, T4 and T6 each have four sections.

realized that using their own words was the only way to cover the information within the rather tight length constraints.

One should be cautious about overgeneralizing these results, of course, because different age groups and students of different ability levels probably respond somewhat differently to the kind of guidance that Summary Street® offers. For example, our research shows that although all users wrote better summaries when using the tool, those of low and moderate ability levels (those with scores in the lower and middle thirds on the Colorado standards test) benefited more than higher ability students (who scored in the upper third). Presumably, the latter group was able to summarize the texts fairly well without the support; Summary Street®, however, did help students who were especially challenged by the task, allowing them to perform at the same level as their higher achieving peers (see Fig. 14.5). We are encouraged by these results because they suggest that the tool may be helpful to a broad range of student age and ability levels, providing of course that they have the keyboard and writing skills to perform an extended writing task. Currently, fifth-graders are the youngest students using the system.

Evidence of Transfer Effects

In addition to analyses of summary quality, the study by Franzke et al. (2005) explored whether use of Summary Street® over an extended period of practice—twice weekly over 4 weeks—would influence how students read and comprehend informational text in a generalized manner. An inde-

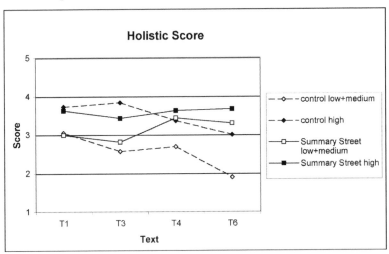

Figure 14.5. Holistic quality scores as a function of text difficulty and ability level. *Summary Street®: Computer support for comprehension and writing* (p. 75), by M. Franzke, E. Kintsch, D. Caccamise, N. Johnson, and S. Dooley, 2005, Amityville, NY: Baywood Publishing Co., Inc. Copyright © 2005 by Baywood Publishing Co., Inc. Reprinted with permission.

pendent test of comprehension composed of retired test items from the Colorado standards test (called the CSAP) was used to test this in a pre–post intervention design.

We found that 4 weeks of guided summary practice did not result in overall gains from pre- to posttest performance for either the experimental or the control students. This amount of practice was probably not sufficient to affect comprehension in a global fashion. However, the composite scores provided by standards tests are based on several different kinds of questions, some of which could be expected to benefit from the kind of processes that Summary Street® supports, and others not. Thus, in order to gain a more sensitive gauge of the effects of the intervention, we examined the scores for individual test item types: summary questions, inference questions, and "other" questions (the latter category included fact finding, vocabulary, literary analysis questions, and a few hard-to-classify types). In order to compare performance across item categories, the analyses examined percent improvement per item type.

The results revealed significant improvement for all students on one type of test item, namely, those that involved inferential reasoning. Because writing summaries requires deep engagement with the meaning, practicing this skill may have caused students to read the test items with more attention and better comprehension than usual, which resulted in improved performance on the inference items. In contrast, the performance of the experimental and control groups did diverge on another type of test item, namely, the summary questions: Summary Street® users scored significantly higher on these items than students who practiced summary writing using a word processor. We attribute this to the focus on the macrostructure, or gist level comprehension, fostered by Summary Street®. After a longer period of practice, students got into the habit of identifying and paying attention to all the main topics in a text, which subsequently influenced their reading behavior. Students who practiced summary writing without this support did not improve their scores on the summary questions; indeed, their scores actually declined somewhat. The role of feedback thus appears to be crucial in directing the eighth-grade students to the important information. Simply practicing summary writing without this feedback does not appear to benefit their comprehension; indeed, it may reinforce bad habits. The other types of questions (fact finding, literary interpretation, and vocabulary items) showed no effect of the intervention, nor was any expected for these test items.

Finally, postintervention interviews with a small subgroup of students who participated in this study revealed some interesting differences in students' awareness of the task demands of summary writing. The responses of 10 Summary Street® users to an open-ended question about what one has to do to write a summary indicated a better sense of the strategic processes involved than those of the 8 control group individuals. The former group often mentioned specific strategies and several different ones (e.g., "cover each paragraph" and "keep it short"), whereas the latter group's responses tended to be rather vague and general (e.g., "make it interesting to the reader"). Whereas 8 of the 10 Summary Street® users mentioned "cover the main points" as an important strategy, only half of the students in the control group did so. This indication of possible metacognitive benefits of Summary Street® on students' awareness of summarization strategies is currently being investigated in a study using verbal reports while writing and revising summaries.

In sum, our results on transfer effects, although preliminary, support the claim that practicing writing summaries is a worthwhile educational activity: One cannot, after all, write a good summary without really comprehending the source text, that is, without constructing a coherent and comprehensive macrostructure. The fact that the eighth-grade students who used Summary Street® in the study by Franzke et al. (2005) benefited more, in terms of both the quality of their summaries and their performance on summary items of the comprehension posttest, supports our claim that *guided* practice from a tutor like Summary Street® is more effective than unsupported practice, because it helps students build a good macrostructure as a foundation for their learning. Finding and then expressing in their own words all the main ideas in a text is especially difficult for younger students. However, the support may also benefit more experienced readers and writers when they must deal with instructional texts that are structurally and conceptually more complex. Thus, in our future research, we plan to explore whether Summary Street® is as effective as a comprehension and learning tutor as it is a writing tutor. The following section provides a brief overview of these plans.

FUTURE DIRECTIONS AND OPEN QUESTIONS

Our future research will continue to look for beneficial fall-out from Summary Street® use. Evaluation in the coming 2 years is using a two-tiered approach: (a) comparisons of standardized test scores will track effects over longer periods of use; and (b) individual studies, both in the classroom and in a controlled laboratory setting, will focus on particular issues of pedagogical and methodological interest. In addition, teachers' and students' responses to questionnaires will provide qualitative data about implementing Summary Street®, about the users themselves and their reactions.

Broad-Scale, Long-Term Evaluation

In addition to districtwide test scores, this evaluation is using pre- and postintervention summaries written without support of Summary Street®

together with short answer quizzes to compare classes who are using the system and control group classes who receive traditional instruction. The standardized tests are, of course, a very distant test of transfer, and the scores may be too global to detect reliable differences. The pre- and postsummaries, however, should provide evidence of transfer from long-term practice in summary writing with Summary Street® to writing without that support. Adequacy of content coverage will be the primary variable of interest for evaluating the summaries, and quiz scores may show some effects on content learning.

Focused Studies

Our previous research has demonstrated that middle school students compose better summaries when guided by feedback from Summary Street® than when using a word processor. There is, furthermore, some preliminary evidence that the tool may encourage better attention to main ideas while reading and better awareness of summarization strategies. What happens, then, following a longer period of practice in summary writing? Namely, if this kind of intervention does prompt students to read in a more active, engaged manner, we would expect this to show up in a better grasp of the content. Hence, several classroom and laboratory studies are planned in order to explore possible transfer effects of summarization, with and without guidance, on reading comprehension processes, on awareness of comprehension strategies, and on content learning. Learning gains will be measured using assessments that target depth of understanding of the topic, both at the level of the textbase and of the situation model. Our goal is to provide evidence that broad and extensive use of Summary Street® can provide an effective means to address the pervasive problem among students at all grade levels of passive, uninvolved reading and the inert, unusable knowledge that results (cf. W. Kintsch & E. Kintsch, 2005). Better learning depends on deep-level comprehension processes and the ability to detect and remedy gaps in understanding. Thus, we would expect to find evidence that longtime Summary Street® users also exhibit a greater awareness of appropriate comprehension and revising strategies. How do students of differing learning abilities respond to the feedback that Summary Street® provides? Possible interactions between ability level and text difficulty are the issue here. Our findings on measures of summary quality suggest that low-to-moderate ability students benefit more than higher ability students. This was the case when all students read and summarized the same texts. However, adjusting the difficulty level of the text to individual students' capabilities may show whether the tool is helpful to a range of students as long as text and task pose a significant but not insurmountable challenge. In some cases, the summarization task itself may prove overwhelming, especially for students with deficient language skills. Summary Street® could be modified by adding support (e.g., in the form of question prompts) to help such students build a summary. Studies of individual differences will provide a better understanding of appropriate text and task choices for different groups of students.

We have received a number of inquiries about Summary Street® from educators and researchers in foreign countries. Although Summary Street® itself could easily be adapted to use in languages other than English, the LSA conversion is not simple. Each language requires its own semantic space, and the time and effort required to construct a new space can pose a major obstacle. Several semantic spaces exist for French, which were constructed by Denhière and are described in chapter 8 of the present volume. Limited semantic spaces have also been constructed in Arabic, Chinese, German, Hindi, Swahili, and Spanish. So far, the foreign language spaces have only been used for research or special projects and not in educational applications.

CONCLUSIONS

Summary Street® has come a long way since its inception some 6 years ago. Although not quite as sensitive as a good human tutor, it does a remarkable job of providing useful and individualized feedback that helps to guide students through a complex writing task. It does not seek to replace teachers, but to enhance their effectiveness by giving students tools they can use to correct many writing problems on their own. A teacher's final evaluation of their summaries remains as important as always. Students sometimes complain that Summary Street® makes them work so hard, but they are invariably proud when their summary passes all the thresholds and all the bars turn green. Teachers like the fact that Summary Street® really makes students think, which, after all, should be the goal of academic training.

ACKNOWLEDGMENTS

This research was supported by Grant No. 96–36 from the James S. McDonnell Foundation and Grant No. 030.05.0431B from the Interagency Educational Research Initiative of the National Science Foundation.

REFERENCES

Foltz, P. W., Laham, D., & Landauer, T. K. (1999). The Intelligent Essay Assessor: Applications to educational technology. *Interactive Multimedia Electronic Journal of Computer-Enhanced Learning, 1*. Retrieved June 29, 2004, from http://www.knowledge-technologies.com

Franzke, M., Kintsch, E., Caccamise, D., Johnson, N., & Dooley, S. (2005). Summary Street®: Computer support for comprehension and writing. *Journal of Educational Computing Research, 33*(1), 53–80.

Kintsch, W., & Kintsch, E. (2005). Comprehension. In S. G. Paris & S. A. Stahl (Eds.), *Current issues in reading comprehension and assessment* (pp. 71–92). Mahwah, NJ: Lawrence Erlbaum Associates.

Kintsch, E., Steinhart, D., Stahl, G., LSA Research Group, Matthews, C., & Lamb, R. (2000). Developing summarization skills through the use of LSA-based feedback. *Interactive Learning Environments, 8,* 87–109.

Wade-Stein, D., & Kintsch, E. (2004). Summary Street: Interactive computer support for writing. *Cognition and Instruction, 22,* 333–362.

15

Automated Tools for Collaborative Learning Environments

Lynn A. Streeter, Karen E. Lochbaum,
and Noelle LaVoie
Pearson Knowledge Technologies

Joseph E. Psotka
*U.S. Army Research Institute for the Behavioral
and Social Sciences*

Our applications of LSA over the last two decades have focused on software that augments problem solving in organizational settings. In the late 1980s, we (Streeter & Lochbaum, 1988; Lochbaum & Streeter, 1989) built an expert-expert locator that was used for many years at Bellcore (now Telcordia) by the staff in a 5,000-person company. Bellcore, a telecommunications R&D company was quite diverse, covering research on rare earth metals to software development for large billing systems. The *Bellcore Advisor* processed a user query, such as "expert systems based on natural language processing" and using LSA compared it against work plans of about 500 department and supervisory groups, returning the three most similar groups along with the managers' contact information. Its usefulness derived from the fact that its knowledge of the company was based on materials that were required of organizations in the normal course of doing business. It entailed no extra work on the part of staff members, such as filling out expertise questionnaires and updating them at regular intervals. The Advisor thus avoided the Problem of the Commons, the downfall of most such well-intentioned systems.

As computing advances have made possible greater person-to-person interactivity, the focus of our applications shifted. Current work has expanded LSA from passive information retrieval to active monitoring and assessment of individuals and groups involved in online discussions. For example, we have developed software agents that can detect whether a group has reached a consensus solution, as well as when a discussion has lost its thread. Applications such as these and their technological underpinnings form the core of this chapter.

DISTANCE LEARNING

Economic factors, including decreased travel and more efficient use of time, have fueled the demand for distance learning. In 2002, an estimated 11 million students in the United States participated in at least one distance learning course (Allen & Seaman, 2003). In the last several years, the delivery environment for such courses has improved. There is mounting evidence that properly constructed and administered online learning courses are as least as effective as traditional classroom courses. In a meta-analysis of 19 independent case and controlled studies, Hiltz, Zhang, and Turoff (2002) found that when asynchronous learning networks are instructor moderated, and engage both students and instructors, learning effectiveness is as high as face-to-face instruction and in some instances higher. Asynchronous learning networks emphasize interaction between students and instructors, unlike distance learning courses, which may simply post material on the Web, use e-mail, or rely on video conferencing. Learning outcomes were measured differently in different studies, but include objective measures such as exam and course grades, quality of work, and participation rates, as well as more subjective measures, such as the overall amount of student learning, level of motivation, and frequency of access to instructors.

Although instructor-led and moderated distance learning courses contribute to success, they also take more instructors' time than most are able to give. Instructors report that constructing online courses takes more time than traditional courses and moderating asynchronously held discussion groups is time consuming. For students, information management and summarization quickly become a problem with an active discussion group, especially figuring out which postings are relevant to the current topic, and which postings to read and respond to. An additional complexity with threaded discussion groups is determining whether individuals and groups have mastered the subject matter. To do these things automatically would be a boon to distance learning technology.

Over the last several years, we have built software tools to aid students and instructors in online discussion groups. The system, called *Knowledge Post®*, adds significant power to the standard threaded discussion group (LaVoie, Psotka, Lochbaum, & Krupnick, 2004; Lochbaum, Streeter, & Psotka, 2002). In addition to supporting synchronous or asynchronous team problem-solving discussions, *Knowledge Post®* uses LSA to monitor and enhance the discussion in novel ways. For example, *Knowledge Post®* connects relevant comments to each other; finds relevant information in a large electronic library; generates automatic summaries of contributions; and interactively monitors, assesses, and mentors the strategic thinking of individual participants and the group as a whole, based on the content of free-form verbal contributions. We have conducted experiments that demonstrate the effectiveness of *Knowledge Post®* for improving the quality of individual contributions as compared to face-to-face discussions, and the ability to monitor and assess group and individual performance.

Knowledge Post® started with a commercial off-the-shelf threaded discussion group to which substantial enhancements were then added. Today the system has the following features (those added by Pearson Knowledge Technologies are indicated by a star):

- Users read assignments or scenarios stored as notes within the discussion forum.
- Users write notes in response to those assignments.
- Users read and respond to the notes of other users.
- ❖ Users can search for notes that are semantically similar to others in the current discussion area or the special library.
- ❖ Users can "mouse over" a note and see an automatically generated summary of its content.
- ❖ Users can have their responses evaluated by the Intelligent Essay Assessor.
- ❖ Instructors can monitor the students' progress both individually and collectively through reports generated by the system.
- ❖ The system can perform automated embedded assessment of whole discussion groups as well as the participants.
- ❖ The system can automatically track discussion groups to distinguish planning and coordination comments from high content, on-topic comments to alert instructors to groups requiring special attention.
- ❖ The system can select the next best posting for the students to read, which is usually of higher quality than their contribution.

The following screen shots demonstrate some of these unique features as realized in a discussion among a group of U.S. Army Captains at Ft. Riley. The Captains discuss a Think Like a Commander scenario (created by the Army Research Institute at Ft. Leavenworth) called "Trouble in McLouth," which describes a situation in which refugees have fled a refugee camp outside of McLouth, intercepting Army fuel tankers and blocking major roads. Figure 15.1 illustrates the "Find Related Notes" feature. Here the user has asked to see those notes that are semantically most similar to the note entitled "Where's PAO"[1] displayed near the bottom of the screen. By using LSA to locate the notes that have the highest cosine to the "Where's PAO" note, this feature allows users to traverse what could be a very large space of notes by finding those related to a note or topic they have already identified to be of interest. Figure 15.1 also illustrates the summary feature whereby an *automatically* generated summary of a note is displayed when the mouse is rolled over it. This feature gives users more information about the content of the note than just the title and again provides a useful tool for navigating a large space of notes. The summary feature works by finding the most representative sentence in the note—the sentence with the closest cosine to the whole note. Whereas Figure 15.1 shows the result of finding notes related to a given note within the current discussion board, the functionality is also available to find semantically related library reference materials, books, and articles. This functionality works in the same way, using LSA to identify the reference material that has the highest cosine to a given note.

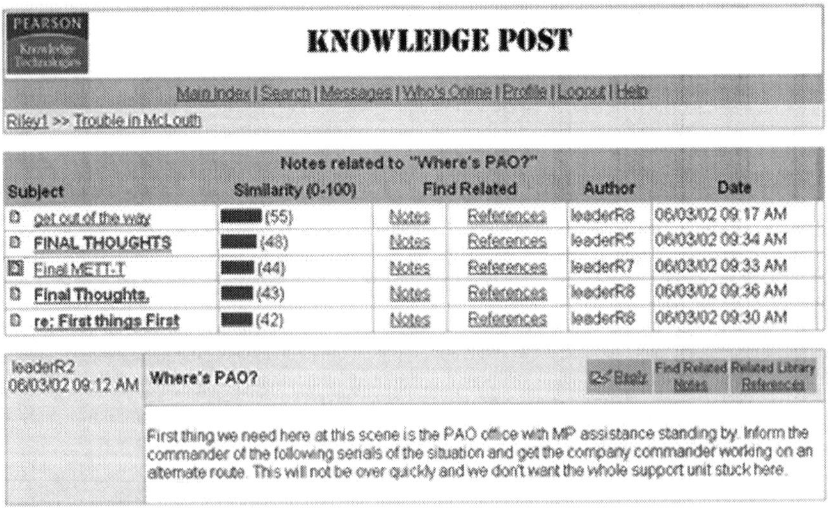

Figure 15.1.   Find related notes feature.

---

[1]PAO refers to the Army's Public Affairs Office.

Figure 15.2 provides an example of automated assessment. Responses to the Trouble in McLouth scenario were collected, scored by military experts, analyzed by the Intelligent Essay Assessor, and then embodied in an automatic grading model. Figure 15.2 shows the feedback that leaderR7 received, in this case at the end of the discussion. The sum total of his contributions has been scored and rated "Excellent" overall. In addition, the system provides feedback about two aspects of the scenario "Alternate Route" and "Mission" that leaderR7 could address more thoroughly. To determine feedback on the components of the scenario, leaderR7's response to the scenario was compared to each of the components of an expert-constructed ideal answer. Those components with the lowest cosines, indicating least similarity, were returned to the user as areas for further elaboration.

Several hundred Army officers, including Lieutenants, Captains, Majors, and Lieutenant Colonels have discussed military scenarios of this sort either face-to-face or using *Knowledge Post*®. Across a broad range of managerial and military scenarios, officers learn more using the threaded discussion tool than they do in face-to-face discussions. The scenarios used in these experiments were either "Think Like a Commander" (TLAC) scenarios developed at Ft. Leavenworth or "Tacit Knowledge of Military Leadership" (TKML) scenarios developed jointly by the Army Research Institute and Yale University (Hedlund et al., 1998). The TLAC scenarios were developed to teach tactical and strategic thinking skills. The TKML scenarios are based on a carefully developed set of representative scenarios of challenging interpersonal leadership situations that are commonly encountered by Army officers, along with sets of alternative actions that a leader might take.

Figure 15.2. Assessment results for leaderR7.

Thirty-eight officers discussed the scenarios face-to-face and wrote their responses using pencil and paper, and 28 typed their thoughts and eventual "solutions" into the online discussion environment. The electronic discussion group entered an initial response and then a final response after an online synchronous discussion. All responses were randomly sorted and the rank of the officers removed before they were then "blind" graded by two military leadership experts. The grading was based on their expert assessment of the quality of the proposed actions and comments. The results are shown in Figure 15.3 for all of the TLAC scenarios for one rater. (The same pattern of results has been found for the TKML scenarios and the other raters.) The rated quality of responses, on a 10-point scale, is plotted for each of the four officer categories as a function of whether they were in a face-to-face discussion group and summarized their views using pencil and paper or whether they were in the electronic discussion group. Whether the discussion took place face-to-face or electronically made a large difference—those who used the electronic discussion group contributed much higher quality initial responses (shown as First *Knowledge Post*[®] in the figure) than those in the paper-and-pencil group. In addition, the lower ranking officers (Lieutenants and Captains) learned more using the electronic discussion group than did the same ranks of face-to-face participants.

Although senior officers (Majors and Lieutenant Colonels) had a slight superiority in the paper-based version, all officer groups improved through the *Knowledge Post*[®] discussion. Even the first response in the online format was superior to the final responses in the face-to-face discussion; this may have been facilitated by the fact that officers knew their first response in the *Knowledge Post*[®] environment would be seen by a peer, a fellow officer, and not just a civilian researcher or anonymous General.

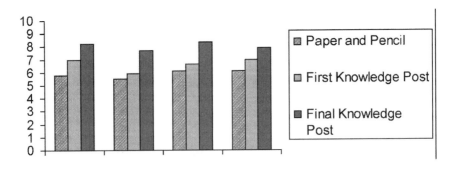

Figure 15.3.   Comparison of paper-and-pencil response to first and final Knowledge Post[®] response by officer rank for all TLAC scenarios.

Several factors may contribute to the better discussion and learning in the electronic medium. One is the natural desire of humans to communicate with each other. Another is the parallel nature of the discussion—members of an electronic discussion can contribute simultaneously, thereby making more effective use of the time available. This is not possible in face-to-face discussions. An additional factor is the anonymity that contributing to an online discussion provides. The simultaneity of input, coupled with greater equality of participation and anonymity, results in a richer set of ideas generated by a greater number of people.

MODELING CONSENSUS

We have looked at the distribution of officers' responses in the LSA space and found that the distribution of responses is highly asymmetric—lower quality responses are quite spread apart, whereas good responses cluster around the centroid of the distribution. We conjectured that answers near the centroid are best because they capture most of the consensual components of experts. With Army officers, the centroid represents aspects of the solution that have been agreed on by different people, omitting those components that are not generally agreed on. In this respect, it is better than the average contribution. To empirically test this, we used four tacit knowledge scenarios that had 9-point rating alternatives that had been normed by hundreds of officers (see Hedlund, Sternberg, & Psotka, 2000, for a description of the scenario development). Some alternatives are rated as decidedly better than others by high-level officers. Examples of good and bad alternatives are shown here. In this scenario, the new platoon leader failed Ranger School and has been put in command of soldiers who have just returned from combat:

- Ask the members of the platoon to share their combat experience: Ask what they learned and how it can help the platoon."
  (median 9 "extremely good" on a 9-point scale $N = 358$)
- Announce right up front that you are in charge and the soldiers must accept this fact and treat you with appropriate respect."
  (median = 3 "somewhat bad" on a 9-point scale, $N = 358$)

To examine whether the centroid contribution had more elements of good responses, we compared a note constructed of all good alternatives (median rating of at least 8), selected from the forced choice text versions of the tacit knowledge scenarios, with the centroid as well as with the best and worst one-sixth contributions for each of the platoon scenarios. Low-quality discussion contributions have significantly less similarity to the centroid, $M = .60$, than do high- quality contributions, $M = .74$, $t(62) = 6.84$, $p < .01$. The contributions that were combined from the text of good alternatives to the scenarios are closer to the high-quality contributions, $M = .30$, than the low, $M = .19$, $t(62) = 4.38$, $p < .01$. However, the magnitude of these cosines is significantly less, $p < .001$, than the real contributions. Evidently, the actual discussion contributions are more detailed than the distilled response alternatives in the scenarios.

That LSA models consensus in this way has important implications for tutoring. Namely, it provides a mechanism for automatically selecting the next best piece of text for a student to read—by selecting the nearest semantically similar note to the students' note, that is the note with the highest cosine with the students' note. This will, for the most part, be a note just slightly higher in quality, not too easy or too hard, but just right to best facilitate learning. Additional research on the utility of LSA consensus for tutoring will require skilled human raters to judge the quality of notes and the appropriateness of the notes for increasing student learning.

AUTOMATED TRACKING OF GROUP DISCUSSIONS

Discussion groups that are floundering may have a characteristic signature aside from low participation rate. We reasoned that one indication of a group's being in trouble was spending too much time coordinating and planning the task—figuring out who was going to do what—as opposed to discussing the content of the assignment. We thus put LSA to work to differentiate content comments from coordination and planning comments automatically.

We obtained an electronic copy of an asynchronous distance learning course given at the U.S. Army War College to several hundred senior officers in 2003. Officers were divided into 20 discussion groups with from 12 to 15 participants per group. The course dealt with U.S. foreign and security policy and the future of NATO. All comments ($N = 1,605$) dealing with the future of NATO were rated by one of the researchers as either a planning and coordination comment (0) or a content comment (1). Four graders scored a subset of the content comments, and the Intelligent Essay Assessor (IEA) was used to model these scores. The resulting IEA model was then used to score all comments. The matrix of LSA cosines for all comments was transformed, and together with the IEA scores, submitted to a discriminant function analysis, $\chi^2(2) = 2012.06$, $p < .001$. The resulting classification of comments is shown in Table 15.1.

The following are examples of the comment types:

• Coordination: I just want to say "Thank You" to each of you in our group. It's been great teamwork. Look forward to meeting you all in June. God bless. Jim
• Content: The EU military capability needs to be more than a collective security (defensive) organization, it also needs to have a power pro-

TABLE 15.1
Classification of Comments by Type

	Classified Coordination	Classified Content	Total
Coordination	394	55	449
Content	24	1132	1156

jection capability to react to global contingencies that affect Europe. If the concerns can be overcome with effective cooperation and coordination between NATO and the EU, then the U.S. should support the EU's ESDP.

• Content Misclassified as Coordination: Mark and Al: Greetings from San Antonio The paper here says that the Germans and the French do not like our President's straight forward, Texas way. Well I guess they probably did not like LBJ in the 60's. Mark: I read your paper and then I read the Kennedy's comments. Pretty good stuff. I agree with Gary that the State may water down what comes out of the PCC in order not to offend. This is what Steve L. pointed out during his AAR. I am a little bit unsure on what happens next. Do we sell Kennedy on trying to revise his language to be more direct and if so who does? I am reaching here. For now though I will look and see what the IPS Gazette has to say for today.

Figure 15.4 shows the same data as a scatter plot using two LSA dimensions as an example. The content comments are shown in red and the coordination comments in yellow. This sort of a display can be rotated in three dimensions to achieve the best separation. With this data set, because the differences are so clear, the separation is evident in every rotation. Notice that the yellow coordination comments form a distinct cluster that goes from highly laudatory and cohesive comments at the apex where both students and instructors make brief, positive, "thank you" kind of comments to the other end where they are coordinating the NATO work and so verging on red content comments. This ability of LSA to monitor aspects of the discussion (e.g., the cohesive components of comments) can be implemented systematically and automatically to look for explicit events and provide instantaneous feedback to instructors about which groups have a large percentage of coordination comments are may need help.

EVALUATING THE CONTRIBUTION OF INDIVIDUALS

One problem instructors have with online discussion groups, or any group project for that matter, is evaluating the relative contribution of individuals apart from the performance of the group. The technique used previously could be used to generate content scores for each comment. These scores

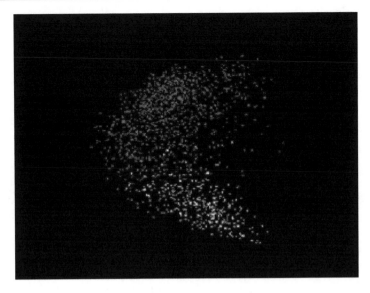

Figure 15.4.   Visualization of coordination (yellow) and content (red) comments.

could be averaged to get one measure of an individual's contribution. Other measures are certainly relevant, such as the percentage of content comments, participation rate, consistency of participation rate throughout the course, grades on assignments, and so on. However, this automatic method for assigning content grades appears to have wide applicability in the online environment.

FUTURE DIRECTIONS

The functionality of software agents for moderating and evaluating on-line discussion groups could be greatly expanded with more research and design. The visualizations that LSA makes possible have applicability to tracking, in real time, finer grained aspects of the discussion. For instance, discussions have juncture points where they shift from one topic to another. Often this can be traced to a seminal comment made by one individual who proves to be more influential than the others. LSA content scores and visualizations may make it possible to find when the discussion has shifted and at what point in the discussion the shift occurred. Other uses of the content scores include when to suggest instructor intervention for individuals as well as groups. Instructors can be alerted on a periodic basis about the progress of individuals and groups. Perhaps one group is having trouble focusing on the task at hand, which is evidenced by a large number of planning and coordination comments. Perhaps particular individuals are not contributing comments that are in line with their fellow group participants' ideas. Alerting could also be used to draw the attention of participants to particularly astute comments in other groups.

The LSA technology makes it feasible now to tie online resources, such as electronic libraries and the Internet, to discussions, even for very large reference collections. In our work thus far, we have been disappointed in students' use of the library facilities that were available to them—they rarely use them. We have conjectured that discussing and searching are seen as separate activities for learners. Perhaps finding material is a solitary activity. One reads an assignment and then discusses it using the information already in one's head. Alternatively, the resources that we have supplied may have been inadequate. But, as tasks become more complex and beyond the grasp of the participants, the need to pull in outside information, whether from text resources or people outside the group, will become more pressing. LSA or its descendants can be there to help.

ACKNOWLEDGMENTS

The research reported in this chapter was supported by the U.S. Army Research Institute and the Army War College, but the views expressed do not represent official Army policy.

REFERENCES

Allen, I. E., & Seaman, J. (2003). *Sizing the opportunity: The quality and extent of online education in the United States, 2002 and 2003*. Needham, MA: The Sloan Consortium.

Hedlund, J., Horvath, J. A., Forsythe, G. B., Snook, S., Bullis, R. C., Williams, W. M., et al. (1998). *Tacit knowledge in military leadership: Evidence of construct validity* (Tech. Rep. No. 1018). Alexandria, VA: U.S. Army Research Institute for the Behavioral and Social Sciences.

Hedlund, J., Sternberg, R. J., & Psotka, J. (2000). *Tacit knowledge for military leadership: Seeking insight into the acquisition and use of practical knowledge* (Tech. Rep. No. ARI TR 1105). Alexandria, VA: U. S. Army Research Institute.

Hiltz, S. R., Zhang, Y., & Turoff, M. (2002). Studies of effectiveness of learning networks. In J. Bourne & J. C. Moore (Eds.), *Elements of quality online education* (pp. 15–41). Needham, MA: The Sloan Consortium.

LaVoie, N., Psotka, J., Lochbaum, K., & Krupnick, C. (2004, February). *Automated tools for distance learning*. Paper present at the New Learning Technologies Conference, Orlando, FL.

Lochbaum, K. E., & Streeter, L. A. (1989). Comparing and combining the effectiveness of latent semantic indexing and the ordinary vector space model for information retrieval. *Information Processing and Management, 25*(6), 665–676.

Lochbaum, K., Streeter, L. A., & Psotka, J. (2002, December). *Exploiting technology to harness the power of peers.* Paper presented at the Interservice/Industry Training, Simulation and Education Conference, Orlando, FL.

Streeter, L. A., & Lochbaum, K. E. (1988). Who knows: A system based on automatic representation of semantic structure. *RIAO 88: User-Oriented Content-Based Text and Image Handling,* 379–388.

IV

Information Retrieval and HCI Applications of LSA

16

LSA and Information Retrieval: Getting Back to Basics

Susan T. Dumais
Microsoft Research

Latent semantic analysis (LSA) was first introduced in Dumais, Furnas, Landauer, Deerwester, and Harshman (1988) and Deerwester, Dumais, Furnas, Landauer, and Harshman (1990) as a technique for improving information retrieval. Most web, enterprise, and desktop search engines work by matching words in a user's query with words in documents. Information retrieval systems that depend on lexical matching suffer from two problems. First, because the same literal word can have many different meanings, irrelevant information is retrieved when searching. Second, because there are different ways to describe the same object or concept, relevant information can be missed. LSA was designed to address these fundamental retrieval problems. The key idea in LSA was to use dimension reduction techniques to map documents and terms into a lower dimensional semantic space.

Latent semantic indexing (LSI) was the phrase used in this early work to refer to the use of dimension reduction techniques to improve *indexing* of textual content. As outlined in other chapters in this volume, the same ideas have subsequently been applied to a wider range of problems, including modeling various aspects of human memory, where the approach is usually referred to as LSA. We use the more general terminology, LSA, in this chapter for consistency. This chapter provides an overview of the development of LSA for information retrieval. We first describe the basic analytical framework, examine the performance of LSA on information retrieval problems, and consider extensions to several related areas including text classification, text clustering, and link analysis.

Fundamental characteristics of human word usage underlie the failures of word matching systems. People use a wide variety of words to describe the same object or concept (*synonymy*). Furnas, Landauer, Gomez, and Dumais (1987) showed that people generate the same keyword to describe well-known objects only 20% of the time. Poor agreement was also observed in studies of inter-indexer consistency (e.g., Chan, 1989; Tarr & Borko, 1974) and in the generation of search terms (e.g., Bates, 1986; Fidel, 1985). Because searchers often use different words than authors, relevant materials are missed. Someone looking for documents on "LSA" will not find articles that use only the word "LSI" or the phrase "latent semantic indexing." The reduced dimensional representation that LSA uses helps alleviate this problem. People also use the same word to refer to different things (*polysemy*). Words like "jaguar," "chip," or even "LSI" have several different meanings. Thus, a short query like "LSI" returns many irrelevant documents having to do with "large scale integration," "language studies international," or "legal secretaries incorporated."

Several approaches have been used in information retrieval to address the problems caused by the variability in word usage. *Stemming* is a popular technique used to normalize some kinds of surface-level variability by converting words to their morphological root. For example, the words "retrieve," "retrieval," "retrieved," and "retrieving" would all be converted to their root form, "retrieve." The root form is used for both document and query processing. Stemming helps retrieval accuracy sometimes, although not by much (Harman, 1991; Hull, 1996). And, it does not address cases where related words are not morphologically related (e.g., physician and doctor). *Controlled vocabularies* have also been used to limit variability by requiring that query and index terms belong to a predefined set of indexing terms. Library of Congress Subject Headings, Medical Subject Headings, ACM keywords, and Yellow Page headings are examples of controlled vocabularies. If searchers can find the right controlled vocabulary term, then they do not have to think of all the morphological related or synonymous terms that authors might have used. However, assigning controlled vocabulary terms in a consistent and thorough manner is a time consuming process, and untrained users cannot be expected to know what terms to use, exacerbating the synonymy problem. The combination of both full text and controlled vocabularies is often better than either alone, although the size of the advantage is variable (Bates, 1998; Lancaster, 1986). *Thesauri* have also been used to provide synonyms, generalizations, and specializations of users' search terms. As with controlled vocabularies, thesauri are expensive to construct and have variable effects on retrieval accuracy (see Srinivasan, 1992, for a review). *Adaptive indexing* techniques in which the words associated with each document are augmented through interaction with searchers have also been explored with some success (Furnas, 1985; Reisner, 1966). Adaptation is quite successful when one can close-the-loop and get users to provide additional terms for documents. An interesting variant of adaptive indexing occurs on the Web. Anchor texts are short humanly generated links to pages that are used in addition to web page content for retrieval. Anchor texts bear a close resemblance to user queries (Eiron & McCurley, 2003) and substantially improve retrieval accuracy for some tasks (Craswell, Hawking, & Robertson, 2001; Westerveld, Kraaij, & Hiemstra, 2002).

With the advent of large-scale collections of full text, *statistical approaches* are being used more and more to analyze the relationships among terms and documents. LSA takes this approach. LSA induces knowledge about the relationships among documents and words by analyzing large collections of texts. The approach simultaneously models the relationships among documents based on their constituent words, and the relationships between words based on their occurrence in documents. By using fewer dimensions for representation than there are unique words, LSA induces similarities among terms including ones that have never occurred together.

LSA AND INFORMATION RETRIEVAL

Mathematical Framework

More complete mathematical details of the LSA approach to information retrieval are presented in Deerwester et al. (1990), Berry, Dumais, and O'Brien (1995), and Martin and Berry (chap. 2 in this volume). Here we highlight the main steps involved in applying LSA to the problem of information retrieval.

LSA is a variant of the popular *vector space* model of information retrieval pioneered by Salton and his colleagues (Salton, 1968; Salton & McGill, 1983). In the vector space model, terms form the dimensions of an indexing space. Documents and queries are represented by vectors in this space. Queries are compared to documents using a measure of similarity such as the inner product or the cosine. LSA is similar to the vector space model, except that derived indexing dimensions (not terms) form the dimensions of the indexing space. The LSA analysis consists of four main steps. The first two steps are also used in more traditional retrieval models such as vector space or probabilistic models. The third step (dimension reduction) is the key difference in LSA.

Term-Document Matrix.   A large collection of text is represented as a term by document matrix. Rows are words and columns are documents or smaller units such as passages or sentence, as appropriate for each application. Individual cell entries represent the frequency with which a term occurs in a document. Note that the order of words in the document is unimportant in this matrix representation, thus the name "bag of words" representation is often used, although the "bags" in LSA contain only sets of words that together express a coherent meaning.

Transformed Term-Document Matrix.   Instead of working with raw term frequencies, the entries in the term-document matrix are often transformed. The best retrieval performance is observed when frequencies are cumulated in a sublinear fashion—typically, $log(freq_{ij}+1)$—and inversely with the overall occurrence of the term in the collection—typically, an inverse document frequency or entropy-based score.

Dimension Reduction.   A reduced-rank singular value decomposition (SVD) is performed on the matrix, in which the k largest singular values are retained and the remainder set to 0. The resulting reduced-dimension SVD representation is the best k-dimensional approximation to the original matrix, in the least-squares sense. Each document and term is now represented as a k-dimensional vector in the space derived by the SVD. The SVD technique is closely related to eigenvector analysis, factor analysis, principal components analysis, and linear neural networks.

Retrieval in Reduced Space.   Similarities are computed among entities in the reduced-dimensional space, rather than in the original term-document matrix. The cosine or angular distance between vectors is used as the measure of their similarity because it has been shown to be effective for many information retrieval applications. Because both documents and terms are represented as vectors in the space, document-document, term-term, and term-document similarities are all straightforward to compute. In addition, terms and/or documents can be combined to create new vectors in space, which can be compared in the same way. This is how queries are handled. A new query vector is formed at the *centroid*, or weighted average, of its constituent term vectors and then compared to document vectors to find the most similar documents.

Mathematically, information retrieval problems begin with a rectangular **t** × **d** matrix of terms and documents, **X**. Any rectangular matrix can be decomposed into the product of three other matrices using the SVD (Golub & van Loan, 1989). Thus,

$$X = T^*S^* D^T,$$ 16.1

is the SVD of a matrix **X**, where **T** is a t × r matrix with orthonormal columns, **D** is a d × r matrix with orthonormal columns, and **S** is an r × r diagonal matrix with the entries sorted in decreasing order. The entries of the **S** matrix are the singular values, and the **T** and **D** matrices are the left and right singular vectors, corresponding to term and document vectors for information retrieval problems. This is simply a re-representation of the **X** matrix using orthogonal indexing dimensions. LSA uses a truncated SVD, keeping only the k largest singular values and their associated vectors, so

$$X \approx T_k^*S_k^* D_k^T.$$ 16.2

is the reduced-dimension SVD, as used in LSA. This is the best least squares approximation to **X** with k parameters, and is what LSA uses for its semantic space. The rows in T_k are the term vectors in LSA space and the rows in D_k are the document vectors in LSA space. Document-document, term-term, and term-document similarities are computed in the reduced dimensional approximation to **X**.

A geometric analogy highlights the differences between traditional vector retrieval systems and the reduced-dimension LSA approach. The vector retrieval model has a natural geometric interpretation, as shown in the left panel of Figure 16.1. Terms form the dimensions or axes of the space. Documents are represented as vectors in this term space, with the entries in the term-document matrix determining the length and direction of the vectors. Note that in this representation, terms are orthogonal because they form the

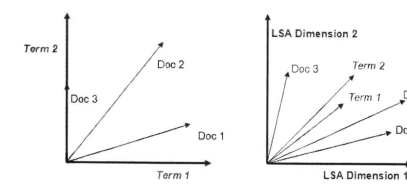

Figure 16.1.   Comparison of vector space (left) and LSA (right) representations. The dimensionality of the vector space is the number of unique terms in the collection. The dimensionality of LSA is k, which is much less than the number of terms in the collection.

axes of the space. An important consequence of this is that if a document does not contain a term, it has similarity 0 with a query consisting of just that term. If you ask a query about *cars*, then you will not retrieve any documents containing *automobile* (and not car). In Figure 16.1, for example, Doc 3 cannot be retrieved by Term 1.

The geometric representation of LSA is shown in the right panel of Figure 16.1. The axes are those derived from the SVD; they are linear combinations of terms. Both terms and documents are represented as vectors in this *k*-dimensional LSA space. In this representation, the derived indexing dimensions are orthogonal, but terms are not. The location of term vectors reflects the correlations in their usage across documents. An important consequence of the dimension reduction is that terms are no longer independent. Because of this, a query can match documents even though the documents do not contain the query terms. For example, Doc 3 can now be retrieved by Term 1 (which does not occur in Doc 3).

In the information retrieval literature, the idea of aiding information retrieval by discovering latent proximity structure predates the work on LSA. Term and document clustering was used by several researchers, primarily to improve retrieval efficiency (Jardin & van Rijsbergen, 1971; Salton, 1968; Sparck Jones, 1971). Latent class analysis (Baker, 1962) and factor analysis (Borko & Bernick, 1963; Ossorio, 1966), techniques closely related to LSA, were explored for automatic document indexing and retrieval. These earlier approaches typically focused on representing either terms or documents, but not both in the same space. One exception to this was a proposal by Koll (1979) to represent both terms and documents in the same concept space. Although Koll's approach is similar in spirit to LSA, the concept space he used was of very low dimensionality, and the dimensions were hand-chosen and not truly orthogonal as with the SVD. In addition, all of these early attempts were limited by lack of computer processing power and the availability of large collections of text in machine readable form. These problems are now largely solved, so progress in the field has been rapid.

Information Retrieval

Dumais et al. (1988) and Deerwester et al. (1990) described the application of LSA to information retrieval and evaluated it using several information retrieval test collections. They compared LSA retrieval to traditional vector retrieval. For both LSA and vector retrieval, the same matrix (obtained after the second step outlined in the previous section) is used. For vector retrieval, the similarity between queries and documents is computed using the full dimensional term-document matrix. For LSA retrieval, dimension reduction is also performed and the similarity is computed using the reduced dimension representation. The term *word matching* is used synonymously with *vector matching* in this chapter. It is used to highlight the fact that vector matching depends on literal word overlap, whereas LSA can retrieve documents even when they do not contain query terms.

Information retrieval test collections typically consist of a corpus of documents, user queries, and relevance judgments describing which documents are relevant to each query. For each query, the documents in the collection are ranked by their similarity to the query (using either the LSA or vector representation). The performance of information retrieval system is usually summarized using two measures, precision and recall. *Recall* is the proportion of relevant documents in the collection that are retrieved by the system. *Precision* is the proportion of relevant documents in the set returned to the user. Precision is calculated at several levels of recall to generate a curve showing the trade-off between precision and recall. Other summary measures, such as the precision at fixed numbers of documents (e.g., precision in the first 10 documents), are often used when the collection is large and exhaustive relevance judgments are not available, but we use precision-recall measures when possible.

Figure 16.2 shows the results for the MED test collection (Salton, 1969). This test collection consists of 1,033 medical abstracts (documents) and 5,831 unique terms. Precision is plotted as a function of recall, averaged over the 30 queries available for this collection. As is typical in retrieval applications, precision drops as recall increases. This reflects the fact that it is easy to find a few relevant documents, but finding all of the relevant documents requires examining many irrelevant documents. As can be seen, LSA performance is substantially better than the standard word matching con-

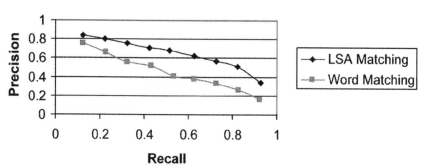

Figure 16.2.   Precision-recall curve for the MED test collection.

trol for the entire range of recall values, with an average advantage of about 30%. The advantages for LSA are somewhat larger at higher levels of recall, as expected. At 50% recall, for example, 68% of the documents returned by LSA are relevant, as compared with 40% of the documents returned by simple word matching.

A similar pattern of retrieval advantages for LSA compared with word matching has been shown for several other test collections (e.g., Deerwester et al., 1990; Dumais, 1995; Jiang & Littman, 2000) and applications (e.g., Lochbaum & Streeter, 1989). Sometimes, however, performance with LSA is no better than word matching (e.g., the CISI collection in Deerwester et al., 1990; the TREC-6 collection in Husbands, Simon, & Ding, 2000, and the TREC-AP-1990 collection in Jiang & Littman, 2000). The reasons for the inconsistent advantages of LSA compared to word matching baselines are not well understood and require further research. The diversity and size of the collection, and the number of singular values that are extracted, have been mentioned as possible factors. In the case of TREC, an additional factor is that the queries (topics) are quite long. In TREC-3, queries contained an average of 35 content words. With long queries, there are less likely to be relevant documents that do not share *any* terms with the query. Indeed, others have reported that query expansion techniques do not work very well on already long queries (Jing & Croft, 1994; Voorhees, 1994). Performance advantages of between 5% and 30% have been for information retrieval tasks, with the largest advantages occurring when queries and/or documents are short (thus subject to retrieval misses) and when high recall is needed.

There are some algorithmic improvements, based on analysis of the singular values (S_k), which can improve the performance of LSA, even for large heterogeneous collections such as TREC. Jiang and Littman (2000) proposed a technique called approximate dimension equalization (ADE), which combines LSA and a generalized vector space model (GVSM) that captures direct term associations. The approach works well on monolingual collections in reducing the gap between LSA and vector retrieval, and especially well in cross-lingual retrieval (which we discuss later). Husbands et al. (2000) developed a technique called normalized LSI (NLSI). Their initial experiments found retrieval advantages for LSA with the MED collection, no differences for the NPL collection, and an advantage for vector retrieval for the much larger and more diverse TREC-6 collection. They developed a technique to normalize the length of the projected reduced-dimension term vectors ($\mathbf{T}_k{}^*\mathbf{S}_k$), and found improved performance, compared with vector retrieval, for the TREC-6 collection and all others they tested.

LSA retrieval also involves the parameter k, the number of dimensions used in the reduced space. In Figure 16.2, 90 dimensions were used in the LSA analysis. For the vector analysis, 5,831 dimensions (one for each term) were used. Figure 16.3 shows LSA performance as a function of number of

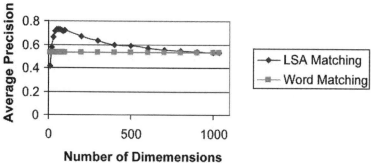

Figure 16.3.   Precision as a function of number of dimensions for the MED test collection.

dimensions for the medical collection described earlier. The measure of performance shown in this figure is average precision; that is, the precision averaged over the 9 levels of recall shown in Figure 16.2. For $k = 90$, the average precision is .71. Similar values are computed for other values of k. Word matching performance, which is constant across dimensions, is also shown for comparison.

LSA performance is poor with too few dimensions, and performance is the same as word matching with too many dimensions. In between these two, there is a substantial range over which LSA performance is better than word matching. For the medical collection, performance peaks at about 90 dimensions. This pattern of initial poor LSA performance with very few dimensions, an increase in performance over a substantial range, and then a decrease to word matching level is observed for other collections as well (see Landauer & Dumais, 1997, Fig.). Choosing the right dimensionality is required for successful application of the LSA approach to information retrieval. Choosing the appropriate value of k can be difficult when relevance judgments are not available ahead of time, but this is the subject of active research. However, there is a fairly large range of values of k for which LSA performance is substantially better than the standard word matching approach.

Several techniques have been used to improve the precision and recall of information retrieval systems. One of the most important and robust techniques involves *term weighting*, the transformations described in the second step discussed earlier (e.g., Sparck Jones, 1972). LSA performance can also be improved by using transformations of the term-document such as the popular $tf*idf$ approaches. Dumais (1991) reports that the best performance is observed when frequencies are cumulated in a sublinear fashion, $log(freq_{ij} + 1)$, and inversely with the overall occurrence of the term in the collection (idf or $entropy$ scores). Another approach to improving information retrieval uses *relevance feedback*, which involves iterative retrieval based on user interaction (e.g., Salton & Buckley, 1990). Relevance feedback techniques can also be used to improve LSA performance (Dumais, 1991).

Many information tasks involve matching a user's query with documents in a collection. However, LSA dimension reduction ideas can be applied to a variety of other retrieval problems, in which either terms, documents, or queries are interpreted more abstractly. In one interesting example, Streeter and Lochbaum (1987) used LSA to retrieve corporate organizations using a combination of word and phrase features. The application was one in which organizations with likely experts were to be retrieved in response to queries. They represented organizations using abstracts of work descriptions produced by the organizations. They used both individual words and nominal compounds as indexing entries. The matrix to which LSA was applied consisted of 7,100 terms + compounds by 728 organizational work descriptions. Queries were abstracts of new work projects, and the goal was to retrieve the organization that actually wrote the work description. A total of 236 queries were used in the evaluation. Because there was only one relevant item for each query, the measure of performance was the rank at which the target organization was retrieved. LSA performed better than vector matching (median rank of 3 vs. 4), and a combination of the two approaches was better than either alone (median rank 1). In another example, Dumais and Nielsen (1992) used LSA to automatically assign reviewers to technical papers for a hypertext conference. LSA spaces were built using several different collections of materials from the hypertext domain (abstracts submitted to the conference, three hypertext text books, ACM hypertext compendium, human–computer interaction bibliography). Reviewers were represented as a vector in the LSA space, located at the centroid of the abstracts of papers they had written. Conference submissions were also added to the LSA space in the same manner, and the nearest reviewers identified. LSA assignments of papers to reviewers were compared to assignments by three human experts. The best LSA space was that based on all the sources combined. The relevance of automatically assigned papers was as high as those assigned by one human expert and somewhat worse than those from the two other human experts. Heinrich et al. (2003) used LSA for a related problem of organizing a conference into sessions. The term by conference paper matrix is analyzed in the usual way. The queries were the topics associated with each session. The best matching documents were returned and edited by the conference organizers to form sessions.

The success of LSA in information retrieval applications is attributable to the dimension reduction step. By adding the constraint that the observed term-document relationships must be modeled by many fewer parameters than there are unique words, LSA requires that relationships among words be represented. This reduced space is what is referred to as the "semantic" space, because key relationships among words (and documents) are captured. One important consequence of this in the context of information retrieval is that a query can be very similar to a document even though the two do not share any words. In an encyclopedia collection, for example, the words "physician" and "doctor" never co-occur in a single article, but they are quite similar in the reduced LSA space (Landauer & Dumais, 1997). This is because they occur in many of the same contexts (e.g., with words like patient, hospital, sick, recovery, surgery, nurse, etc.) and when dimension constraints are imposed, the vectors for doctor and physician are near each other in the reduced LSA space. This inferred similarity among words can also be thought of as a kind of query expansion (Xu & Croft, 1996). Not only does a query word match documents that contain it, but it matches documents that contain similar words as well. Query expansion is typically done on-the-fly, but with LSA there is no need to explicitly augment a query; that process happens implicitly during the dimension reduction step.

Cross-Language Information Retrieval

LSA was designed to overcome the vocabulary mismatch problem between searchers and document creators. An extreme example of mismatch occurs when queries and documents are in different languages. In cross-language retrieval, queries in one language are used to retrieve documents in other languages as well as the original language. Cross-language LSA (CL-LSA) has been applied to this problem with good results. The techniques of LSA applies directly to this problem by using a slightly different notion of the "document" (Landauer & Littman, 1990).

In many cross-language applications, parallel corpora are available (i.e., the same documents are available in two or more languages) and can be used to train a multilingual semantic space. For ease of exposition, we talk about French and English documents, but the approach works for any set of languages. When a parallel corpus is available, a dual-language document is created by concatenating the French and English versions of the document. For each dual-language document, some of the rows in the term by dual-language document matrix are French words and others are English words. The SVD is computed on the term by a dual-language document matrix. The resulting LSA space contains both French and English terms, with those sharing many contexts being near each other. The dual-language LSA space is a kind of learned interlingua in which cross-language retrieval is performed. The multilingual LSA space also contains the dual-language documents, but these are not of interest for retrieval. Mono-lingual French and English documents are added into to the LSA space as vectors located at the centroid of their constituent words (a process called *folding in*). The LSA space now consists of French and English documents and words. Queries in English (French) can retrieve the most similar docu-ments regardless of the language in which they are written. Unlike many approaches to cross-language retrieval, CL-LSA does not require any dic-tionaries, lexical resources, or translation of either documents or terms. The relationships among words are inferred using the parallel corpus. The dual-language LSA space reflects these relationships and is used for cross-language retrieval. Sheridan and Ballerini's (1996) similarity thesaurus approach to cross-language retrieval is related to CL-LSA.

Early work with CL-LSA used a mate-retrieval task for evaluation (Dumais, Littman, & Landauer, 1998; Landauer & Littman, 1990). In the mate-retrieval task, an English (French) document is used as a query, and is compared with each French (English) document. The mate-retrieval task represents the extent to which the LSA representation places the same doc-uments near each other and is independent of specific user queries. The rank at which the mate is found is used to summarize performance. Landauer and Littman used parallel documents from the Hansard collec-tion of Canadian Parliment texts. They worked with 2,482 paragraphs con-taining at least 5 sentences. They randomly selected 900 dual-language documents to build the dual-language LSA space, and used the remaining 1,582 documents for testing. The test documents were first folded-in to the LSA space. For the retrieval test, each French (English) document was is-sued as a query and the closest English (French) documents returned. For CL-LSA approach, a document in one language returned its mate in the other language as the most similar document 98.4% of the time. When the same test was performed using standard word matching without dimen-sion reduction, the mate was returned first only 48.6% of the time. Dumais et al. (1998) explored extensions of the CL-LSA approach to situations in which machine translation was used to generate a parallel corpus, and to situations in which short queries rather than full documents (typically used in mate-retrieval tasks) were used as queries.

More traditional cross-language information retrieval experiments us-ing short queries and explicit relevance judgments have subsequently been conducted (Carbonell et al., 1997; Rehder, Littman, Dumais, & Landauer, 1997). Carbonell et al. (1997) compared LSA to the generalized vector space model (GVSM). In GVSM, documents form the axes of the retrieval space, and terms are located based on their usage in documents. Performance was evaluated using 30 queries they developed for the UNICEF English–Spanish Corpus. Average precision was approximately the same for GVSM and LSA (.39 vs. .38). Littman and Jiang (1998) replicated these experiments using the same collection but correcting an error in the LSA implementation. They found that LSA outperformed GVSM over a number of different values of k (e.g., .44 at 800 dimensions vs. .36). Jiang and Littman also examined CL-LSA performance for the much larger TREC French and TREC German collections. CL-LSA outperformed GVSM in both French to German and German to French cross-lingual retrieval (.02 vs. .11 for German to French, and .02 vs. .15 for French to German). The approximate dimension equalization variant of CL-LSA described earlier showed even higher average precision (.17 and .22 for the two tasks, respectively).

The CL-LSA method has been applied to many other languages, including English-French (Dumais et al., 1998; Landauer & Littman, 1990), English-Spanish (Carbonell et al., 1997; Evans et al., 1998; Oard & Dorr, 1998), English-Greek (Berry & Young, 1995), Portuguese-English (Orengo & Huyck, 2002), and English-Japanese (Jiang & Littman, 2001; Mori, Kokubu & Tanaka, 2001). It has also been applied to language triples such as English-French-Spanish and English-French-German, where three-way document-aligned corpora were available (Littman, Jiang & Keim, 1998; Rehder et al., 1997).

Littman et al. (1998) developed an important extension to CL-LSA that allows LSA analyses to be performed when fully aligned corpora are not available. The technique is based on Procrustes analysis, which identifies the rotation matrix that gives the best possible mapping of vectors from one vector space to another (Golub & Van Loan, 1989). Littman et al. (1998) applied the technique to retrieval from three languages when only partial alignments were available. They showed how Procrustes analysis could be used for English-Spanish retrieval, even when only French-English and French-Spanish corpora were available. In one analysis, separate CL-LSA spaces were developed for French-Engligh and French-Spanish. French terms that are common to the two spaces can be used for alignment. In another analysis, French documents from both collections are used to derive a more stable French-only LSA space. French terms or documents can now be used to transform vectors in the CL-LSA space. The most successful technique in this application was to align the spaces using the documents from the French-only space, resulting in a median rank of 1 (and mean rank of 14) for a mate retrieval evaluation. The approach can also be applied in cases where two monolingual spaces are available, as long as there are some common term or document vectors that can be used for alignment. Landauer and colleagues (personal communication) have recently used a variant of the method to create a Hindi, Arabic, Swahili, English multilingual representation.

Evans et al. (1998) explored the use of LSA and CL-LSA to associate terms to specialized indexing concepts. Experiments associating English terms with Spanish medical concepts appear to be promising, but no comparisons to monolingual approaches were reported. Vinokourov, Shawe-Taylor, and Cristianini (2002) applied a variant of LSA that uses canonical correlation analysis rather than SVD for cross-language retrieval (CL-KCCA). Using the Hansard corpus, they find that KCCA outperforms LSA (e.g., .99 vs. .95 for mate retrieval using $k = 400$). This technique appears promising, but is more computationally expensive than LSA.

LSA AND OTHER RETRIEVAL-RELATED PROBLEMS

LSA has also been used for a variety of text applications, including information filtering, document clustering, and link analysis. We briefly summarize a few here, and more details are available in Dumais (2004) and in the individual chapters.

Information Filtering/Classification

In *information retrieval*, the document collection is relatively stable, and new queries are issued constantly. In *information filtering* (also known as classification or routing), the queries are fixed, and new documents are added to the collection constantly. The task is to match new documents against these standing queries or profiles of interest that reflect persistent information needs. The user profile is specified by means of words and/or known relevant documents describing the user's interest. The nature of the user profile and the number of known relevant documents can vary depending on the application. In routing, many relevant documents are known ahead of time and the task is to rank a set of new documents (e.g., a daily or weekly alerting service). In filtering, at most, a few relevant documents are known and the task is to mark new documents as relevant or not as they come along (e.g., a real-time alerting service). For filtering, a binary decision must be made about every document as it arrives. Robertson and Soboroff (2001) provide a more detailed description of filtering tasks and performance measures.

Applying LSA to information filtering is straightforward. Any LSA space can be used as a starting point. A user profile is added to the space to reflect a user's interests (e.g., the vector is often located at the centroid of words and/or documents in which the user is interested). As new documents arrive, they are added into the LSA space and are compared with existing profiles. If the new document vector is similar enough to the user profile vector, then it is returned to the user. The user profile can be adjusted if relevance judgments about the returned documents become available during the process.

Foltz and Dumais (1992) conducted an early evaluation of LSA for use in a filtering application. They compared several methods for predicting which technical memoranda people would like to receive. They varied the matching algorithm (LSA vs. vector retrieval) and the method in which the profile was created (free-form interest statement vs. example relevant documents). Their "LSA match-document profile" approach, which combined LSA with some knowledge of previously relevant technical memoranda, was the most successful technique for all performance measures examined.

Wiener, Pedersen, and Weigend (1995) evaluated LSA for text filtering using the popular Reuters-22173 collection. The Reuters collection consists of 22,173 news articles organized into 92 categories. The collection is split into a training set, used for creating a LSA space, and a testing set, used for evaluating the quality of the LSA space by finding the most similar categories for each test article. In addition to performing a global LSA on all of the training documents, Wiener et al. explored what they called local LSA analyses. For the local representations, separate LSA analyses were computed for each category or groups of similar categories. LSA showed small 5% advantages compared to term matching, and larger advantages (22% compared to LSA) were observed when a separate local LSA analysis was performed for each category.

Dumais (1995) evaluated the LSA approach to filtering (called routing in TREC) on the larger standard TREC-3 collection. For this evaluation, 50 profiles were compared to a stream of 336k new documents. The LSA space was created by analyzing 38k training documents related to one or more of the topics. User profiles were represented using a free-form interest statement (called topics in TREC) or known relevant documents. Dumais also found that creating a user profile using known relevant documents (the "lsir2" run) was more effective than using the topic description. Precision over the first 10 documents was .62 for the topic profile and .69 for the document profile, and overall 10% more relevant documents were retrieved. Dumais also explored combinations of the topic and document profiles by taking linear combinations of the two vectors, and observed small advantages in precision. Compared with other systems that completed the TREC routing task, the LSA relevant topic profile did quite well. LSA was better than the median on 41 of the 50 routing topics and the best system for 9 of them.

Hull (1994), Schütze, Hull, and Pedersen (1995), and Hull, Pedersen, and Schütze (1996) also looked at LSA for information filtering. They found a small but consistent advantage for LSA compared to no dimension reduction, using the TREC-2 and TREC-3 routing topics. Schütze et al. (1995) compared different techniques for representing documents (LSA, important terms, LSA and important terms) and for learning the profiles (centroid, logistic regression, neural network, linear discriminant analysis). They used a local LSA analysis in which a separate LSA space was computed for every topic using the 2,000 best matching documents for the topic description. This is an interesting variant of the approach described earlier, where all topics were represented in the same global LSA space. The best average precision scores were obtained when the LSA representation was combined with a discriminative classification approach (discriminative analysis or neural nets). Discriminative approaches use information about both positive and negative instances to learn a topic model. Nondiscriminative approaches, like the centroid method, use just the relevant items. In many experiments, advanced discriminative methods from machine learning, such as support vector machines or random forests, are more accurate at classifying new test instances.

Zelikovitz and Hirsh (2001) use another technique from machine learning to improve information filtering using LSA. They worked with four text classification collections (technical papers, web page titles, WebKB, and 20 Newsgroups). Each data set has documents that are relevant to different classes or profiles from which LSA spaces can be derived. They augmented this training data with additional documents that they call background documents. Although these additional documents do not have explicit labels vis-à-vis the filtering task, they do contain many words and contexts, which should help in establishing a useful LSA space. They compared LSA analyses with and without additional background documents. They found consistently lower error rates when the background knowledge was used, and the advantages were larger when there was less labeled training data. This approach should have wide applicability because it is often difficult to obtain labeled data but easy to obtain many background documents, although many details regarding the number and similarity of labeled and unlabeled documents need to be explored more thoroughly.

A simple kind of information filtering or classification problem is a two-class problem in which items are either in a class or not. Spam is an example of this—an e-mail message is either spam or it is not spam, although the classification of a message may depend on the user. A large collection of e-mail could be analyzed using LSA, and a spam profile vector created at the centroid of known spam messages. If a new e-mail is near enough the spam vector, then it would be labeled as spam. The spam vector can be personalized to individual users if they provide individual feedback. There have been reports that the spam filter in Apple's OS X uses an adaptive LSA-based dimension reduction approach for its spam filter, although few technical details have been released (de Kermadec, 2004).

Clustering

Document clustering seeks to discover relationships among documents. This requires that the similarity between all document-document pairs be computed. This can be very inefficient when each document is represented by thousands of features. Schütze and Silverstein (1996) explored two methods for reducing the dimensionality of the problem—one used LSA and the other used a word selection algorithm based on global term frequencies. Accurate performance could be achieved using only a small number of dimensions (20–100). With this amount of dimension reduction, LSA and projection were two orders of magnitude more efficient than initial computations. Retrieval performance for 49 queries was also explored. LSA with $k = 20$ achieved the highest average precision and average rank.

Literature-Based Discovery

Gordon and Dumais (1998) applied LSA to literature-based discovery problems pioneered by Swanson (1989). They applied LSA to 560 documents published during the years 1983–1985 containing the term *Raynaud's*. The nearest words to term *Raynaud's* in the LSA space were identified. These words were compared to the top 40 terms and phrases obtained from several statistical techniques proposed by Gordon and Lindsay (1996). A high percentage of terms LSA found as similar to Raynaud's had been identified by Gordon and Lindsay's methods (e.g., 9 of the top 10 terms; 15 of the top 20). A rank correlation of the top 40 phrases by both methods showed that the position on one list predicts position on the other ($r = .57$). LSA closely reproduces the set of terms that Gordon and Lindsay (1996) showed were a useful starting poring for literature-based discovery.

Noisy Content

Because LSA does not depend on the literal matching of query words to document words, it is useful in applications where the query or document words are noisy, as occurs with optical character recognition, handwriting recognition, or speech input. When there are document scanning errors, for example, the word *Dumais* can be misrecognized as *Duniais*. If the variants of a word occur in the same contexts (e.g., with words like information retrieval, LSA, human–computer interaction, Landauer) then they will wind up near each other in the reduced dimension LSA space and queries about Dumais can retrieve documents containing only Duniais. Nielsen, Philips, and Dumais (1992) used LSA to index a small collection of abstracts input by a commercially available pen machine in its standard recognizer mode. Even though word error rates were almost 9%, information retrieval using the LSA representation was not disrupted compared to matching on the uncorrupted texts. Kurimo (2000) and Wolf and Raj (2002) used an SVD-based representation for spoken documents to overcome the noisy input that happens when queries are spoken rather than typed.

Citation and Link Analysis

Garfield (1972) pioneered the use of citation data to model the importance of technical journals. Under his initial definition, the impact factor of a journal in a year was the average number citations received by papers published in the previous 2 years. Pinski and Narin (1976) suggested an important modification based on the observation that not all citations are equally important. They proposed a recursive definition in which a journal is influential if it is heavily cited by other influential journals. In the citation application an $N \times N$ matrix, A, is generated in which both rows and columns represent journals. The (i, j) entry represents the proportion of times that journal i is cited by journal j. The solution to the recursive problem of finding influence weights for each journal ($w = A^T w$) corresponds to finding the first eigenvector of the matrix A^T. The citation influence application uses only the first eigenvector of a link by link matrix, whereas LSA uses many more singular values of a term by document matrix.

Brin and Page (1998) proposed a similar idea using the link structure of the web. An $N \times N$ matrix, A, is generated in which both rows and columns represent web pages. A cell entry (i,j) is non-zero if there is a link from page i to page j and 0 otherwise. The link matrix is normalized and a random jump probability is introduced to reflect the fact that a surfer can go from one page to another without following links between the two. An iterative algorithm is used to compute the principal eigenvector of the normalized link matrix A, and this is called the PageRank for each page.

Kleinberg's (1998) work on hyperlink induced topic search (HITS) also uses web links to model the quality of web pages. Instead of propagating importance directly from one page to another, he uses the intermediate notion of hub and authority pages. Authority pages are those pointed to by many others. Hubs pages are those that are linked to many authorities. An iterative algorithm is used to compute these scores until convergence. Instead of computing a global importance score for every page, a query is first issued, and importance scores are computed for only a small subgraph seeded with the search results. Bharat and Henzinger (1998) used HITS techniques to rank search results. They prune the HITS node expansion using the content-based similarity of nodes and showed retrieval improvements. Cohn and Hofmann (2001) used a probabilistic version of LSA and HITS for combining context and link information. They used a mixture model to perform a simultaneous decomposition of the matrices associated with word occurrences (content) and link (connectivity) patterns. They applied the model to two text classification problems with promising results.

Summarization

Gong and Liu (2001) used LSA to select important sentences in documents for creating generic text summaries. Summaries generated by LSA and summaries generated by vector space models were compared to summaries generated by humans. LSA-based summaries showed somewhat better correspondence (5% improvement) for a range of different compression ratios and term weighting schemes. Shen et al. (2004) extended these ideas to using summaries generated by LSA as input to text classification algorithms. LSA summarization improved text classification accuracy by roughly 7% compared to a baseline with no summarization. Further improvements were observed by combining different summarization techniques.

RELATED DIMENSION REDUCTION TECHNIQUES

LSA was designed to overcome the variability in vocabulary used by authors and searchers. The observed term-document matrix is approximated using fewer parameters (dimensions) than the original matrix using techniques from matrix algebra. The early work on LSA led to several information retrieval experiments and applications, as summarized earlier. It also stimulated new theoretical work on alternative dimension reduction techniques and generalizations. We mention only a few of the more influential in the information retrieval community here; additional details can be found in Dumais (2004) and Martin and Berry's chapter (chap. 2 in this volume). There is a close similarity between linear neural networks and LSA, as described in Caid, Dumais, and Gallant (1995). Bartell, Cottrell, and Belew (1992) described the similarities between LSA and multidimensional scaling (MDS). MDS allows generalization of the analysis beyond term-document relationships to other sources of document-document similarity information. There are many other possible sources of such information, including bibliometric relationships or relevance feedback.

Hofmann (1999) developed a generative probabilistic model, which he calls probabilistic LSA (or PLSA). In this model, documents are represented as a multinomial probability distribution over topics (z), which are assumed but not directly observed. The joint probability of a document and word is: $P(d, w) = P(d) * P(w \mid d)$, where $P(w \mid d) = \Sigma P(w \mid d) * P(z \mid d)$. Expectation maximization, a standard machine learning technique for maximum likelihood estimation in latent variable models, is used to estimate the model parameters. The approach is very similar in spirit to LSA, with the main difference being how model parameters are estimated. In LSA, the sum of squared distances (the L_2 norm) between the full- and reduced-dimension vectors is minimized. PLSA uses the likelihood function of multinomial sampling and maximizes the predictive power of the model. Hofmann compared performance of the standard vector space model with LSA and PLSA for four small text retrieval collections (MED, CRAN, CACM, and CISI). The LSA and PLSA results reported used a linear combination of cosine similarities from the vector space and cosines from the LSA or PLSA model. Both LSA and PLSA showed improvements compared with the vector space model, ranging from 8%–32% for LSA and 15%–47% for PLSA. PLSA has also been applied to text clustering, collaborative filtering, and to combinations of link and content retrieval and collaborative and content filtering. Griffiths and Steyvers (2002) developed a variant of PLSA that assumes the mixture proportions $(P(z))$ are distributed as a latent Dirichelet random variable. Their approach has been used to model characteristics of semantic word associations. Although the technique has not been applied to standard information retrieval problems, it has been used to support data exploration of topics, authors and the relations between them (Steyvers, Smyth, & Griffiths, 2004). Ding (1999) and Girolami (2000) also explored probabilistic variants of LSA for information retrieval applications.

Ando and Lee (2001) described a generalization of LSA using a subspace-based framework, which they call iterative residual rescaling (IRR). The basic idea is to repeatedly rescale the vectors to amplify the presence of documents that are poorly represented in earlier iterations. This results in 8%–10% improvements over LSA in retrieval and clustering applications. Isbell and Viola (1998) described an analysis in which sets of highly related words form the basis of the representation. Documents and queries are represented by their distance to these sets. As applied to information filtering, documents related to a topic are used to identify sets of words that discriminate that topic from others. This technique is efficient to compute and related theoretically to the independent components analysis. Karypis and Han (2000) describe a "concept indexing" technique, which first uses a fast clustering technique to find the axes of the reduced dimensional space. They report that this technique is roughly an order of magnitude faster than LSA for several retrieval problems and about as accurate. Cristianini, Shawe-Taylor, and Lodhi (2001) described an approach that combines aspects of LSA and support vector machines, a popular discriminative learning technique, for a text classification problem. Instead of taking the usual dot product as a measure of similarity between two documents, they develop a latent semantic kernel that incorporates term co-occurrence information in the similarity measure. These techniques all extend LSA by examining new modeling formalisms, but they all share a common focus on dimension reduction.

COMPUTATIONAL CONSIDERATIONS

Martin and Berry (chap. 2 in this volume) describes computational issues with LSA in greater detail. We highlight here only a few that are important for information retrieval applications—initial SVD decomposition, updating with new terms and documents, estimating the appropriate value of k, and query processing.

Initial Decomposition

There has been some significant work in improving the speed with which the SVD can be computed as well as in minimizing memory requirements. In general, the approaches reduce the number of terms or documents analyzed by sampling or transform the cell entries to binary values so that the arithmetic operations can be performed more quickly.

Papadimitriou, Raghaven, Tamaki, and Vempala (1995) proposed a technique of "random projections" to speed up the SVD computations. By randomly projecting the term-document matrix onto a lower dimensional subspace, the SVD computations can be speeded up while at the same time preserving accuracy within provable bounds. Frieze, Kannan, and Vempala (1998) showed that by taking a weighted sample of the documents with a probability proportional to the length of the document, they could analyze a matrix that depended on k rather than the number of terms or documents. Aclioptas and McSherry (2001) also sample matrix entries to achieve more efficient decomposition. They further reduce computation costs by converting the matrix entries to $1/0$, using nonuniform sampling when the magnitudes of the entries vary significantly. In some image analysis problems, more than 90% of the data can be removed without introducing noticeable error in the SVD. The amount of reduction possible in information retrieval problems has not yet been investigated empirically. Jiang, Kannan, Littman, and Vempala (1999) developed a weighted sampling technique that is based on the vector length of documents. The term-document matrices generated by this process are somewhat less sparse than those generated by uniform sampling (.16% vs. .13% for a TREC collection), but show lower approximation error and somewhat better retrieval performance. Kolda and O'Leary (1998) use a semi-discrete matrix decomposition in which vector components are constrained to have discrete values –1, 0, or 1, thus reducing storage costs for the reduced model and faster query processing speed. The disadvantage is longer decomposition time and somewhat poorer retrieval performance.

Updating

When new documents are added to a collection, the relationships among terms can change. Recomputing the SVD of a new matrix can be costly, especially for large collections with rapidly changing content (e.g., the Web). Computationally less expensive approximations such as *folding-in* (Berry et al., 1995; Deerwester et al., 1990) and *SVD-updating* (Berry et al., 1995; Zha & Simon, 1999) have been developed.

Estimating Dimensionality

As described earlier, retrieval performance certainly depends on the number of dimensions, *k*—with too few dimensions performance is poor, and with too many dimensions performance is also poor. Although there is usually a pretty wide region of *k* where performance is above the standard vector approach, methods for estimating an optimal *k* are still helpful. Efron (2002) developed a technique call amended parallel analysis (APA) for estimating *k*. APA is a resampling technique that analyzes the departure of the observed singular values from those expected under the hypothesis. The probabilistic approaches by Ding (1999) and Hofmann (1999) can also be used to predict an optimal region for *k*.

Query Processing

A final computational issue with LSA is the computation of query to document similarities. For standard term-document databases, efficient retrieval structures can be used because only documents containing query terms need to be examined. With LSA, every query is related to every document to some extent, so all documents must be examined. Chen et al. (2001) describe a technique for reducing the precision with which singular vectors are stored to improve the time for core arithmetic operations. Gao and Zheng (2003) and Kontostathis, Pottenger, and Davison (2004) explored techniques for selectively setting some of the entries in the singular vectors to 0. Kontosthathis et al. (2004) found that for most collections they could remove 70% of the values in T_k and $S_k D_k$ without impacting retrieval quality, and on one collection (OHSUMED) sparsification helped retrieval accuracy.

SUMMARY AND CONCLUSIONS

Latent semantic analysis (LSA) was first introduced more than a decade ago as a technique to improve information retrieval. The main idea was to reduce the dimensionality of the information retrieval problem as a means of overcoming the vocabulary mismatch problems observed in standard vector space and probabilistic models. A technique from linear algebra, singular value decomposition, was used to accomplish the dimension reduction. One of the major advantages of LSA in information retrieval and filtering applications is that documents can be retrieved even when they do not match any query words. In many cases, LSA provides retrieval advantages compared to word matching techniques; other times performance is the same. LSA has also been applied to many IR-related problems, including text classification, text clustering, link analysis, and so on. It appears to be especially useful for problems where input is noisy (e.g., speech input) and standard lexical matching techniques fail. Understanding the full range of circumstances under which LSA provides retrieval benefits (e.g., size and breadth of the collections, the distribution of singular values) is an open research area.

In addition to the wide range of applications, there has been a good deal of theoretical work aimed at better understanding why LSA works using a variety of alternative formalisms and extensions. Probabilistic aspect models have received the most attention and development. Computational issues have also been addressed, although they continue to be a challenge for large and rapidly changing collections.

REFERENCES

Aclioptas, D., & McSherry, F. (2001). Fast computation of low rank matrix approximations. *Proceedings of the 33rd Annual ACM Symposium on Theory of Computing*, 611–618.

Ando, R. K., & Lee, L. (2001). Iterative residual rescaling: An analysis and generalization of LSI. *Proceedings of the 24th Annual International ACM SIGIR Conference on Research and Development in Information Retrieval*, 154–162.

Baker, F. B. (1962). Information retrieval based on latent class analysis. *Journal of the ACM, 9*, 512–521.

Bartell, B. T., Cottrell, G. W., & Belew, R. K. (1992). Latent semantic indexing is an optimal special case of multidimensional scaling. *Proceedings of the 15th Annual International ACM SIGIR Conference on Research and Development in Information Retrieval*, 161–167.

Bates, M. (1986). Subject access in online catalogs: A design model. *Journal of the American Society for Information Science, 37*, 357–376.

Bates, M. (1998, November). How to use controlled vocabularies more effectively in online searching. *Online*, 45–56.

Berry, M. W,. & Young, P. G. (1995). Using latent semantic indexing for multilingual information retrieval. *Computers and the Humanities, 29*(6), 413–419.

Berry, M. W., Dumais, S. T., & O'Brien, G. W. (1995). Using linear algebra for intelligent information retrieval. *SIAM: Review, 37*(4), 573–595.

Bharat, K., & Henzinger, M. (1998). Improved algorithms for topic distillation in a hyperlinked environment. *Proceedings of the 21st Annual International ACM SIGIR Conference on Research and Development in Information Retrieval*, 104–111.

Borko, H., & Bernick, M. D. (1963). Automatic document classification. *Journal of the ACM, 10*, 151–162.

Brin, S., & Page, L. (1998). Anatomy of a large-scale hypertextual web search engine. *Proceedings of the 7th International World Wide Web Conference/Computer Networks, 30*(1–7), 107–117.

Caid, W. R., Dumais, S. T., & Gallant, S. I. (1995). Learned vector space models for information retrieval. *Information Processing and Management, 31*(3), 419–429.

Carbonell, J., Yang, Y., Frederking, R., Brown, R. D., Geng, Y., & Lee, D. (1997). Translingual information retrieval: A comparative evaluation. *Proceedings of the 15th International Joint Conference on Artificial Intelligence,* 323–345.

Chan, L. M. (1989). Inter-indexer consistency in subject cataloging. *Information Technology and Libraries, 8*(4), 349–358.

Chen, C-M., Stoffel, N., Post, M., Basu, C., Bassu, D., & Behrens, C. (2001). Telcordia LSI engine: Implementation and scalability issues. *Proceedings of the 11th International Workshop on Research Issues in Data Engineering,* 51–58.

Cristianini, N., Shawe-Taylor, J., & Lodhi, H. (2001). Latent semantic kernels. *Proceedings of ICML-01, 18th International Conference on Machine Learning,* 66–73.

Cohn, D., & Hofmann, T. (2001). The missing link: A probabilistic model of document content and hypertext connectivity. In T. K. Leen, T. G. Dietterich, & V. Tresp (Eds.), *Advances in Neural Information Processing Systems* (pp. 430–436). Cambridge, MA: MIT Press

Craswell, N., Hawking, D., & Robertson, S. E. (2001). Effective site finding using anchor text information. *Proceedings of the 24th Annual International ACM SIGIR Conference on Research and Development in Information Retrieval,* 250–257.

Deerwester, S., Dumais, S. T., Furnas, G. W., Landauer, T. K., & Harshman, R. (1990). Indexing by latent semantic analysis. *Journal of the American Society for Information Science, 41,* 391–407.

de Kermadec, F. J. (2004). *The fight against spam, part 2. O'Reilly Mac Developer.* Retrieved August 25, 2006, from http://www.macdevcenter.com/pub/a/mac/2004/05/18/spam_pt2.html?page=1 and http://www.aple.com/lae/macosx/jaguar/mail.html

Ding, C. H. Q. (1999). A similarity-based probability model for latent semantic indexing. *Proceedings of 22nd Annual International ACM SIGIR Conference on Research and Development in Information Retrieval,* 59–65.

Dumais, S. T. (1991). Improving the retrieval of information from external sources. *Behavior Research Methods, Instruments and Computers, 23*(2), 229–236.

Dumais, S. T. (1995). Using LSI for information filtering: TREC-3 experiments. In D. Harman (Ed.), *The Third Text REtrieval Conference (TREC-3) National Institute of Standards and Technology* (Special Publication 500–225, pp. 219–230). Washington, DC: U.S. Government Printing Office.

Dumais, S. T. (2004). Latent semantic analysis. *Annual Review of Information Science and Technology (ARIST), 38,* 189–230.

Dumais, S. T., Furnas, G. W., Landauer, T. K., Deerwester, S., & Harshman, R. (1988). Using latent semantic analysis to improve information retrieval. *Proceedings of SIGCHI Conference on Human Factors in Computing Systems,* 281–285.

Dumais, S. T., Littman, M. L., & Landauer, T. K. (1998). Automatic cross-linguistic information retrieval using latent semantic analysis. In G. Grefenstette (Ed.), *Cross language information retrieval* (pp. 51–62). Boston: Kluwer Academix Publishers.

Dumais, S. T., & Nielsen, J. (1992). Automating the assignment of submitted manuscripts to reviewers. *Proceedings of the 15th Annual International ACM SIGIR Conference on Research and Development in Information Retrieval,* 233–244.

Efron, M. (2002). *Amended parallel analysis for optimal dimensionality estimation in latent semantic indexing* (SLIS Tech. Rep. No. TR-2002-03). University of North Carolina, Chapel Hill.

Eiron, N., & McCurley, K. S. (2003). Analysis of anchor texts for web search. *Proceedings of the 26th Annual International ACM SIGIR Conference on Research and Development in Information Retrieval*, 459–460.

Evans, D. A., Handerson, S. K., Monarch, I. A., Pereiro, J., Delon, L., & Hersh, W. R. (1998). Mapping vocabularies using "latent semantics." In G. Grefenstette (Ed.), *Cross language information retrieval* (pp. 63–80). Boston: Kluwer Academic Publishers.

Fidel, R. (1985). Individual variability in online searching behavior. *Proceedings of the American Society for Information Science 48th Annual Meeting*, 69–72.

Foltz, P. W., & Dumais, S. T. (1992). Personalized information delivery: An analysis of information filtering methods. *Communications of the ACM, 35*(12), 51–60.

Frieze, A., Kannan, R., & Vempala, S. (1998). Fast Monte-Carlo algorithms for finding low-rank approximations. *Proceedings of the 39th Annual Symposium on Foundations of Computer Science*, 370–378.

Furnas, G. (1985). Experience with an adaptive indexing scheme. *Proceedings of the SIGCHI Conference on Human Factors in Computing*, 131–135.

Furnas, G. W., Landauer, T. K., Gomez, L. M,. & Dumais, S. T. (1987). The vocabulary problem in human-computer interaction. *Communications of the ACM, 30*(11), 964–971.

Gao, J., & Zhang, J. (2003). *Sparsification strategies in latent semantic indexing.* (Tech. Rep. No. 368–03). University of Kentucky: Department of Computer Science.

Garfield, E. (1972). Citation analysis as a tool in journal evaluation. *Science, 178*, 471–479.

Girolami, M. (2000). Document representations based on generative multivariate Bernoulli latent topic models. *Proceedings of the BCS-Information Retrieval Specialist Group 22nd Annual Colloquium on Information Retrieval Research*, 194–201.

Golub, G. H., & Van Loan, C. F. (1989). *Matrix computations* (2nd ed.). Baltimore: Johns Hopkins University Press.

Gong, Y. H., & Liu, X. (2001). Generic text summarization using relevance measure and latent semantic analysis. *Proceedings of the 24th Annual International ACM SIGIR Conference on Research and Development in Information Retrieval*, 19–25.

Gordon, M. D., & Dumais, S. T. (1998). Using latent semantic indexing for literature based discovery. *Journal of the American Society for Information Science, 49*(8), 674–685.

Gordon, M. D., & Lindsay, R. K. (1996). Toward discovery support systems: A replication, re-examination, and extension of Swanson's work on literature based discovery of a connection between Raynaud's and Fish Oil. *Journal of the American Society for Information Science, 47*(2), 116–128.

Griffiths, T. L., & Steyvers, M. (2002). A probabilistic approach to semantic representation. In W. D. Gray & C. D. Schunn (Eds.), *Proceedings of 24th Annual Cognitive Science Conference*, 381–386.

Harman, D. (1991). How effective is suffixing? *Journal of the American Society for Information Science, 42*(1), 7–15.

Heinrich, K., Berry, M., Dongarra, J. J., & Vadhiyar, S. (2003). The semantic conference organizer. In H. Bozdogan (Ed.), *Statistical data mining and knowledge discovery* (pp. 571–581). Boca Raton, FL: CRC Press.

Hull, D. A. (1996). Stemming algorithms: a case study for detailed evaluation. *Journal of the American Society for Information Science, 47*(1), 70–84.

Hofmann, T. (1999). Probabilistic latent semantic analysis. *Proceedings of 22nd Annual International ACM SIGIR Conference on Research and Development in Information Retrieval,* 50–57.

Hull, D. A. (1994). Improving text retrieval for the routing problem using latent semantic indexing. *Proceedings of the 17th Annual International ACM SIGIR Conference on Research and Development in Information Retrieval,* 282–290.

Hull, D. A., Pedersen, J. O., & Schütze, H. (1996). Method combination for document filtering. *Proceedings of the 19th Annual International ACM SIGIR Conference on Research and Development in Information Retrieval,* 279–288.

Husbands, P., Simon, H., & Ding, C. (2000, October). On the use of singular value decomposition for text retrieval. *Proceedings of the First SIAM Computational Information Retrieval Workshop.* Retrieved August 25, 2006, from http://www-library.lbl.gov/docs/LBNL/471/70/PDF/LBNL-47170.pdf

Isbell, C. L., & Viola, P. (1998). Restructuring sparse high-dimensional data for effective retrieval. *Advances in Neural Information Processing, NIPS11,* 480–486.

Jardin, N., & van Rijsbergen, C. J. (1971). The use of hierarchical clustering in information retrieval. *Information Storage and Retrieval, 7,* 214–240.

Jiang, F., Kannan, R. Littman, M. L., & Vempala, S. (1999, February). *Efficient singular value decomposition via improved document sampling* (Tech. Rep. No. CS-99-5). Duke University, Department of Computer Science, Durham, NC.

Jiang, F., & Littman, M. L. (2000). Approximate dimension equalization in vector-based information retrieval. *Proceedings of the 17th International Conference on Machine Learning,* 423–430.

Jiang, F., & Littman, M. L. (2001). Approximate dimension reduction at NTCIR. *Proceedings of NTCIR Workshop 2: Proceeding of the Second NTCIR Workshop on Research in Chinese and Japenese Text Retrieval and Text Summarization.* Retrieved August 25, 2006, from http://research.nii.ac.jp/ntcir/workshop/OnlineProceedings2/michael.pdf

Jing, Y., & Croft, W. B. (1994). An association thesaurus for information retrieval. *Proceedings of RIAO'94,* 146–160.

Karypis, G., & Han, E-H. (2000). Fast supervised dimensionality reduction algorithm with applications to document categorization and retrieval. *Proceedings of the Ninth Annual International ACM SIGIR International Conference on Information and Knowledge Management,* 12–19.

Kleinberg, J. (1998). Authoritative sources in a hyperlinked environment. *Proceedings of the ACM-SIAM Symposium on Discrete Algorithms,* 668–677.

Kolda, T. G., & O'Leary, D. P. (1998). A semidiscrete matrix decomposition for latent semantic indexing in information retrieval. *ACM Transactions on Information Systems (TOIS), 16*(4), 322–346.

Koll, M. (1979). An approach to concept-based information. *ACM SIGIR Forum, 13,* 32–50.

Kontostathis, A., Pottenger, W. M., & Davison, B. D. (2004). Assessing the impact of sparsification on LSI performance. *Proceedings of the 2004 Grace Hopper Celebra-*

tion of Women in Computing Conference. Retrieved August 25, 2006, from http://webpages.ursins.edu/akontostathis/KontostathisGH.pdf

Kurimo, M. (2000). Fast latent semantic indexing of spoken documents by using self-organizing maps. *Proceedings of the IEEE International Conference on Acoustics, Speech and Signal Processing ICASSP'2000*, 2425–2428.

Lancaster, F. (1986). *Vocabulary control for information retrieval* (2nd ed.). Arlington, VA: Information Resources.

Landauer, T. K., & Dumais, S. T. (1997). A solution to Plato's problem: The latent semantic analysis theory of the acquisition, induction, and representation of knowledge. *Psychological Review, 104*, 211–240.

Landauer, T. K., & Littman, M. L. (1990). Fully automatic cross-language document retrieval using latent semantic indexing. *Proceedings of the Sixth Annual Conference on Electronic Text Research, 31–38.*

Littman, M. L., & Jiang, F. (1998, June). *A comparison of two corpus-based methods for translingual information retrieval* (Tech. Rep. No. CS-1998–11). Department of Computer Science, Duke University.

Littman, M. L., Jiang, F., & Keim, G. A. (1998). Learning a language-independent representation for terms from a partially aligned corpus. *Proceedings of the 15th International Conference on Machine Learning*, 314–322.

Lochbaum, K., & Streeter, L. A. (1989). Comparing and combining the effectiveness of latent semantic indexing and the ordinary vector space model for information retrieval. *Information Processing and Management, 25*(6), 665–676.

Mori, T., Kokubu, T., & Tanaka, T. (2001). Cross-lingual information retrieval based on LSI with multiple word spaces. *Proceedings of NTCIR Workshop 2: Proceeding of the Second NTCIR Workshop on Research in Chinese and Japanese Text Retrieval and Text Summarization.* Retrieved August 25, 2006, from http://research.nii.ac.jp/ntcir/workshop/OnlineProceedings2/mori-ir.pdf

Nielsen, J., Phillips, V. L., & Dumais, S. T. (1992, August). Retrieving imperfectly recognized handwritten notes. *Bellcore Technical Memorandum, TM-ARH-021781.*

Oard, D. W., & Dorr, B. J. (1998). Evaluating cross-language text filtering effectiveness. In G. Grefenstette (Ed.), *Cross language information retrieval* (pp. 151–161).

Orengo, V. M., & Huyck, C. (2002, September). Portuguese-English experiments using latent semantic indexing. *Proceedings of the Third Workshop of the Cross-Language Evaluation Forum, CLEF 2002*, 147–154.

Ossorio, P. G. (1966). Classification space: A multivariate procedure for automatic document indexing and retrieval. *Multivariate Behavior Research*, 479–524.

Page, E. B. (1994). Computer grading of student prose using modern concepts and software. *Journal of Experimental Education, 62*, 127–142.

Papadimitriou, C. H., Raghavan, P., Tamaki, H., & Vempala, S. (1995). Latent semantic indexing: A probabilistic analysis. *Proceedings of the 17th Annual Symposium on Principles of Database Systems*, 159–169.

Pinski, G., & Narin, F. (1976). Citation influence for journal aggregates of scientific publications: Theory with application to the literature of physics. *Information Processing and Management, 12*(5), 297–312.

Reisner, P. (1966, August). *Evaluation of a growing thesaurus* (IBM Research Paper No. RC–1662). Yorktown Heights, NY: IBM Watson Research Center.

Rehder, B., Littman, M. L., Dumais, S. T., & Landauer, T. K. (1997). Automatic 3-language cross-language information retrieval with latent semantic indexing. *NIST Special Publication 500–240: The Sixth Text Retrieval Conference (TREC-6)*, 233–240.

Robertson, S. E., & Soboroff, I. (2001). The TREC 2001 filtering track report. In E. Voorhees (Ed.), *NIST Special Publication 500–250: The Tenth Text REtrieval Conference*, 26–37.

Salton, G. (1968). *Automatic information organization and retrieval.* New York: McGraw-Hill.

Salton, G. (1969). A comparison between manual and automatic indexing methods. *American Documentation, 20*(1), 61–71.

Salton, G., & Buckley, C. (1990). Improving retrieval by relevance feedback. *Journal of the American Society for Information Science, 41*(4), 288–297.

Salton, G. & McGill, M. (1983). *Introduction to modern information retrieval.* McGraw-Hill.

Schütze, H., Hull, D. A., & Pedersen, J. (1995). A comparison of classifiers and document representation for the routing problem. *Proceedings of the 18th Annual International ACM SIGIR Conference on Research and Development in Information Retrieval*, 229–237.

Schütze, H., & Silverstein, C. (1997). A comparison of projections for efficient document clustering. *Proceedings of the 20th Annual International ACM SIGIR Conference on Research and Development in Information Retrieval*, 74–81.

Shen, D., Chen, Z., Yang, Q., Zeng, H-J., Zhang, B., Lu, Y., & Ma, W-Y. (2004). Text classification through summarization. *Proceedings of the 27th Annual International ACM SIGIR Conference on Research and Development in Information Retrieval*, 242–249.

Sheridan, P., & Ballerini, J. P. (1996). Experiments in multilingual information retrieval using the SPIDER system. *Proceedings of the 19th Annual International ACM SIGIR Conference on Research and Development in Information Retrieval*, 58–65.

Sparck Jones, K. (1971). *Automatic keyword classification in information retrieval.* London: Buttersworth.

Sparck Jones, K. (1972). A statistical interpretation of term specificity and its application in retrieval. *Journal of Documentation, 28*, 11–21.

Srinivasan, P. (1992). Thesaurus construction. In W. B. Frakes & R. Baeza-Yates (Eds.), *Information retrieval: Data structures and algorithms* (pp. 161–218). Englewood Cliffs, NJ: Prentice-Hall.

Streeter, L. A., & Lochbaum, K. E. (1987). An expert/expert-locating system based on automatic representation of semantic structure. *Proceedings of the Fourth Conference on Artificial Intelligence Applications*, 345–350.

Steyvers, M., Smyth, P., & Griffiths, T. (2004). Probabilistic author-topic models for information discovery. *Proceedings of the 10th ACM SIGKDD International Conference on Knowledge Discovery and Data Mining*, 306–315.

Swanson, D. R. (1989). Online search for logically-related noninteractive medical literatures: A systematic trial-and-error strategy. *Journal of the American Society for Information Science, 40*(5), 356–358.

Tarr, D., & Borko, H. (1974). Factors influencing inter-indexer consistency. *Proceedings of the American Society for Information Science 37th Annual Meeting, 11,* 50–55.

Vinokourov, A., Shawe-Taylor, J., & Cristianini, N. (2002). Inferring a semantic representation of text via cross-language correlation analysis. *Advances in Neural Information Processing Systems,* 1473–1480.

Voorhees, E. (1994). Query expansion using lexical-semantic relations. *Proceedings of the 17th Annual International ACM SIGIR Conference on Research and Development in Information Retrieval,* 61–70.

Wiener, E., Pedersen, J. O., & Weigend, A. S. (1995). A neural network approach to topic spotting. *Proceedings of SDAIR-95, Fourth Annual Symposium on Document Analysis and Information Retrieval,* 317–332.

Westerveld, T., Kraaij, W., & Hiemstra, D. (2002). Retrieving web pages using content, links, URLs and anchors. *Proceedings of the Tenth Text REtrieval Conference (TREC-10),* 663–672.

Wolf, P., & Raj, B. (2002). The MERL spoken query information retrieval system: A system for retrieving pertinent documents from a spoken query. *IEEE International Conference on Multimedia and Expo (ICME'2002),* 317–320.

Xu, J., & Croft, W.B. (1996). Query expansion using local and global document analysis. *Proceedings of the 19th Annual International ACM SIGIR Conference on Research and Development in Information Retrieval,* 4–11.

Zelikovitz, S., & Hirsh, H. (2001). Using LSI for text classification in the presence of background text. *Proceedings of the 2005 ACM CIKM International Conference on Information and Knowledge Management,* 113–118.

Zha, H., & Simon, H. (1999). On updating problems in latent semantic indexing. *SIAM Journal on Scientific Computing, 21*(2), 782–791.

17

Helping People Find and Learn From Documents: Exploiting Synergies Between Human and Computer Retrieval With SuperManual®

Peter W. Foltz
Pearson Knowledge Technologies and New Mexico State University

Thomas K Landauer
Pearson Knowledge Technologies and University of Colorado, Boulder

As increasingly complex technological systems are developed, there is a concomitant increase in the complexity and amount of information needed to maintain them. This presents a critical and difficult challenge for defense, government, and private sector organizations whose personnel keep the systems running. Increasingly, personnel trained or experienced on one system must quickly switch to working on another. Traditional print media and current online systems assume greater familiarity with specialized parts, procedures, concepts, and vocabulary than can be expected from maintenance personnel. Thus, even current approaches to online manuals are not adequate. This chapter provides an overview of the SuperManual® project, whose object is to identify, develop, and test better ways to organize and present information that adapt to individual maintainers' background knowledge and levels of expertise. The long-term goal is a next-generation system that can permit users to have order-of-magnitude more efficient finding and improved comprehension of needed information under the operational maintenance conditions of the future.

There are a variety of issues involved in the design of online manuals, ranging from physical device form, to screen resolution, computational power, font and graphics design, color, word choice, sentential syntax, and accuracy of content—to mention only a few. Although many such matters can be of considerable importance in the success or failure of such systems, the research in this project is primarily concerned with following problems. Given that a maintenance manual has been written with adequate content in an acceptable manner at the level of description and comprehensibility of individual system components and procedures, how can computational techniques be used to improve the user's ability to find and understand how to accomplish maintenance tasks? Thus, our concern is with matters of organization, navigation, and presentation of information at the conceptual level. Whereas it is likely that new system designs and design principles arising from this research will include ways to assess and improve the quality and utility of written and graphic components as such, this will not be the main concern. The main concern will be how to get an individual user to all the necessary information most efficiently and effectively.

The goal is being pursued by using the capabilities of the latent semantic analysis (LSA) to help improve the finding of material along with determining the optimum sequence of texts to provide just the right material to support a given task for a given individual. This is combined with the proven functionality and features of the SuperBook hypertext browser, and with other newer techniques for presentation of text and graphics. This chapter provides an overview of the relevant technologies and issues in developing interactive electronic technical manuals (IETMs) and describes how LSA-based, as well as other technologies, are implemented in a SuperManual®.

OVERVIEW OF THE SUPERBOOK BROWSER

In order to see how these features are implemented, it is important to review the functionality of the original SuperBook browser. Developed at Bellcore in the early 1990s, SuperBook is a system that automatically constructs efficiently navigable electronic versions of existing textbooks and manuals. Order-of-magnitude increases in the speed and accuracy with which users could perform information-dependent tasks were demonstrated empirically, and the system was used in maintenance-related jobs by over 40,000 telecommunication workers (most using small, low-resolution terminals) with major measured efficiency gains (Egan et al., 1991).

One of the key characteristics in the development of SuperBook was the formative design-evaluation approach used by Egan, Landauer, and colleagues. Background research, iterative user-centered design, and field evaluation for the SuperBook system was done at Bellcore (Egan et al., 1989; Landauer et al., 1993). In SuperBook, text in electronic form is automatically converted into a form of hypertext. A dynamic "fisheye" table of contents is created from the heading structure of the text itself. The dynamic table of contents is displayed in one window, with the major headings appearing first, and successively lower level subheadings being opened by mouse clicks. The value of this is that the meaning of deep sub-sub-sections (e.g., "7.2.3.1 YB-4A6") are made clear by the context of the larger table of contents in which they are viewed. This can be highly useful, even on a small screen device. Clicking on any heading or subheading displays the first page in that section in another window, along with its three nested superordinate headings. Scrolling and "jumping" in both text and table of contents is provided. As observed in empirical studies, with these facilities alone, users much more easily find their way to sections containing information for which they are specifically looking. The dynamic fisheye view largely prevented users from following unintended paths.

The second characteristic of SuperBook that was demonstrably successful was its specialized search facilities, which produced another large increment in the user's ability to navigate large texts effectively. When a user entered any word or set of words into a query box, the system found all of the sections in which one or more of the words appear. This "keyword-based search" is, of course, now a common feature of hypertext search engines and "find" features. However, the effective functionality that SuperBook added, and that is not always implemented, is that when a search is initiated, before taking the user to a target page, all occurrences of the search terms are first posted against the dynamic table of contents. Thus, the user can see every place that the query word appeared and how often it appeared in various sections. The result was that users usually went only to those places where the term appeared in the right context, rather than marching one at a time back and forth through irrelevant occurrences, which was a frequent strategy in control comparisons systems lacking this feature. When the user selects a section from the table of contents, the document is opened to that place, occurrences of the query word(s) are highlighted and the first paragraph in the section containing a search term is brought to the top of the page. This prevented users from missing information buried low on a page, a frequent occurrence in comparison systems that were only indexed to static pages.

Graphics were handled in SuperBook by showing a miniature icon of the graphic as a clickable link in the margin and allowing the user to open graphics only as needed, rather than displaying them and using up screen space unnecessarily. This feature was not uniformly successful; in tests, users often failed to open graphics that were needed for learning or performance. On the other hand, always presenting graphics made users less efficient. Ways to overcome this dilemma are still needed.

The most important aspect of the SuperBook development was clearly the iterative test, design, test, design, and test methodology by which its effectiveness for finding focused information was eventually increased more than seven-fold (Landauer et al., 1993). Significantly, as much was gained by deleting or replacing features found ineffective as by adding attractive new ones. For example, inclusion of Boolean word combination searches had deleterious effects, as did allowing users to move through the text to successive occurrences of a search term by merely clicking a button.

Since its development, many of SuperBook's features and principles have been incorporated into widely used text presentation systems (e.g., fisheye views), usually with more powerful hardware and software, but never with the same iterative empirical evaluation of resulting usefulness and usability that was at the heart of SuperBook's success. However, not all features of SuperBook have been incorporated into existing commercial text presentation systems. In fact, some of the superior functionalities identified in SuperBook's formative evaluations have been abandoned in favor of those shown by the research to be significantly inferior, and many simplifications that were embodied in SuperBook to demonstrated advantage—getting rid of commonly used techniques that were found to be difficult or inefficient for ordinary users (e.g., Boolean queries), and getting rid of too many different features that served mostly to confuse and slow down users—have unfortunately been reintroduced into many systems.

REVIEW OF THE STATE OF THE ART IN ONLINE MANUALS

Based on a review of empirical studies of online manuals and hypertexts, Foltz, Landauer, and Parker, (2001) concluded that since Landauer (1994), Landauer et al. (1993), and Egan et al. (1991), there had been disappointing little empirical study of the relative merits of different functionality, features, and measured utility of document systems for helping individuals perform jobs. There have been only few and scattered evaluations of feature comparisons and proposed new features and a few reports of inadequately designed trials of new integrated systems. None of the other reported hypertext system evaluations of which we are aware were based on extended formative evaluation and redesign research comparable to that carried out for SuperBook. Indeed, most reports are either a single comparison of two systems, or with two versions of the same system with variations in one or more component functions or features. In the latter case, the main difference from the studies reviewed on feature evaluations is that the features are embedded in full functioning systems. On the other hand, some more recent research has provided additional confirmation of the potential advantages of LSA-based interactive organization and search methods.

The state of the art in IETM technology as represented in existing systems and proposed standards and purchasing specifications and guidelines has advanced from that in 1994 by adding some features and functionalities made possible by web-based technologies, such as HTML hyperlinks. In addition, some of the provably effective features of SuperBook, in particular, dynamic tables of contents with selectable direct access to document sections and query based search, have become common, but not universal, in IETMs and IETM-like systems. On the other hand, some features, such as the requirement to use formal Boolean queries, that were shown to be detrimental have continued to be included and other demonstrably advantageous functionalities, such as adaptive indexing, have not found their way into use. There is no direct evidence that hypertext manuals or their component features have become significantly better than paper manuals. Nor is their good empirical reason to believe that the designs of the current crop of IETMs will significantly alleviate the problems of finding and understanding needed technical information.

Thus, in order to improve online manuals, we must take advantage of new technology and research in information finding to provide a robust environment for finding and using maintenance materials. The goal of the SuperManual® project is to use the capabilities of SuperBook while integrating additional features that can improve users' performance in finding and using electronic manuals.

OVERVIEW OF SUPERMANUAL® INNOVATIONS

One of the principal problems in information finding is vocabulary. In order to find information either by indexes in paper books or by search in electronic ones, users need to know the words used to label or describe what they need within the document. This problem is especially severe in the case of using maintenance manuals when personnel must switch from one system to another, where names for equivalent parts or functions are different, work on a given system or problem is infrequent, or the maintainer has had limited training or experience on the relevant task.

The Bellcore research showed that the vocabulary problem, also known as the synonymy problem (multiple ways of referring to the same thing), was a major cause of slow and inefficient use of manuals (see Dumais, chap. 16 in this volume) To overcome this hurdle, several then-novel features were developed and usability tested, and an optimal selection and combination thereof was implemented. The most powerful improvements were dynamic fisheye tables of content with search result posting, adaptive indexing (both described later) and, importantly, simplification of functionality to remove certain common search techniques that slow and confuse most users, an example being complex Boolean search.

However, the most important innovations being developed and used in SuperManual® are those based on latent semantic analysis (LSA). LSA makes it possible to connect queries to paragraphs or sections of a text, and from one paragraph or section to another, by their meaning, independent of the particular words used in either query or target text. This capability is exploited to augment the utility of the dynamic table of contents, to improve search effectiveness, particularly for users lacking thorough knowledge of a system and its nomenclature, and to support a novel feature that will guide users through a manual so as to acquire needed knowledge for a given maintenance task in the most efficient manner.

DEVELOPMENT OF A SUPERMANUAL®

The SuperManual® prototype has been implemented as a client-server web-based system running a Java applet. The Java applet provides the user interface and communicates with the server, which maintains the information and performs the majority of the required computing to display the appropriate information. This approach provides flexibility so that information can be delivered by Internet or used as a stand-alone application on one computer. It also permits the system to be used on any range of computers including laptops, tablets, hand-held, and wearable devices.

The developed SuperManual® has been primarily tested on a Naval Manual used for maintenance of the Navy's SLQ-32 system. The SLQ-32 is a system for providing early warning of incoming threats, such anti-ship missiles. Ships currently use paper documentation, divided up into different volumes, which take up several feet of bookshelf space. Maintainers of the SLQ-32 must have special training on the SLQ-32 in order to have specific knowledge of the circuitry and functionality. The maintainers also need to have had background training in electronics. Nevertheless, maintainers are often put on ships with limited experience using and maintaining the system, and therefore must rely on other more experienced maintainers for help.

On the ship, the SLQ-32 components are spread across multiple locations (the user interface for some of the equipment is in the Command Information Center, the main processors are in a machine room, and the radars are on the exterior superstructure). Thus, maintainers need to carry the required manuals to different areas of the ship. Due to the limited space onboard, there is seldom room to lay out the necessary volumes to perform maintenance. Thus, a computer-based solution would need to allow maintainers to efficiently locate and use information across the different volumes using a single monitor for viewing the manuals.

The current SLQ-32 manual consists of over 1.4 million running words printed on 4,230 paper pages, divided up into 5,930 sections along with 2,224 images. A semantic space was developed for the SLQ-32 manuals comprising a number of Naval Ships Technical Manuals and over 17,000 training documents from the Surface Warfare Officer School. Additional SuperManuals® have been built for other manuals. Although a majority of the examples shown in this chapter are taken from the SLQ-32 manual, some examples are used from other manuals.

Next, we outline a series of features that have been implemented in SuperManuals®. We then describe the applicability of the SuperManual® functionality to other tasks that require finding information in large repositories. The SuperManual® project is implementing the features described previously into a prototype system running existing military maintenance manuals. This is an ongoing project, and thus we have not fully reported in this chapter on usability and performance assessment with SuperManual®. Many of the features have been incorporated and are being tested. The remaining features have been tested individually and are being incorporated in successive iterative design and testing cycles.

Primary Windows in a SuperManual®

The primary windows in SuperManual® are shown in Figure 17.1. They will be introduced here and details will be provided later. On the right is the primary text window that displays text and inline graphics. Above it, a display shows the superordinate sections of the manual so that users are continually aware of where they are in a manual. On the left is a dynamic table of contents, which displays a fisheye view of the document, as well as graphically displaying the location of search results. Below it is a window permitting users to perform searches.

Fisheye View

Fisheye views were introduced by Furnas (1986) with both formal theoretical justification and empirical demonstration of effectiveness. A dynamic "fisheye" table of contents is created from the heading structure of the text itself. The dynamic table of contents is displayed in one window, with the

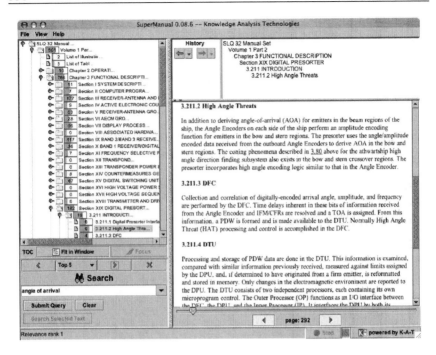

Figure 17.1.   SuperManual® for the SLQ-32 manual.

major headings appearing first, and successively lower level subheadings being opened by mouse clicks. The value of a fisheye view is that the contextual meaning of deep sub-sub-sections (e.g., "320–1.3.3.2") are made clear by the context of the larger table of contents in which they are viewed. (see Figure 17.2 for a fisheye view of a *Naval Ships Technical Manual on Electric Power Distribution Systems* displayed in SuperManual®). This approach can be especially useful on a small screen device.

Clicking on any heading or subheading displays the first page in that section in another window, along with its nested superordinate headings. Scrolling and "jumping" in both text and table of contents is provided.

As observed in empirical studies, with these facilities alone users much more easily find their way to sections containing information that they are specifically looking for. The dynamic fisheye view largely prevents users from following unintended paths (see Landauer, 1994; Landauer et al., 1993).

Search

When a user enters any word or set of words into a query box, the system finds all of the sections in which one or more of the words appear. In SuperManual®, this capability is for the first time supplemented with meaning-based search based on Pearson Knowledge Technologies' version of LSA.

SuperManual® incorporates two primary types of searches based on user entry of queries. The first, simple keyword search means only the entry of single or implicitly "or" combined words that find all passages of task-appropriate length (e.g., procedure descriptions) containing one or more of the query words. The second type of search uses LSA-based natural language, meaning-based search. In addition to keyword search, users can enter natural language queries of any length and be shown the relative relevance of all TOC-titled sections. With LSA, a natural language query formed either as an ad-hoc keyword list, phrase, or sentence composed by the user, user selected set of words or section of the current text, or a cut-and-paste from another source. (Whole passages expressing ideas are especially good queries for LSA-based search.)

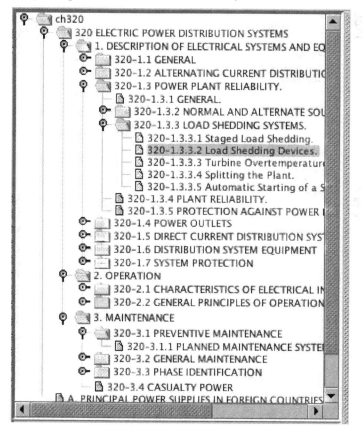

Figure 17.2.   Fisheye view of the table of contents of *Naval Ships Technical Manual on Electric Power Distribution Systems*.

Dual Posting of Search Results

The results of all searches are posted against the fisheye table of contents (TOC; see Fig. 17.3). The results of simple keyword searches are displayed as numbers to the left of each section indicating how many words matched in that section. The results of the meaning-based natural language search are displayed as bars to the left of the text sections. All words in search strings that appear as literals in found or TOC-selected text are highlighted in both the TOC and the

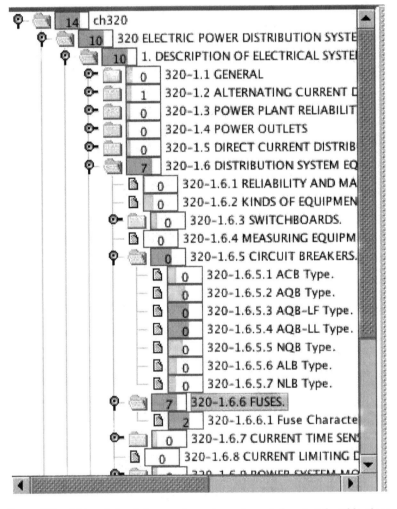

Figure 17.3.   LSA and simple keyword search results posted against the table of contents for the query "fuse." Note that LSA finds relevant sections under "Circuit breakers" even though the word "fuse" does not occur in the sections.

text itself. Because the meaning-based LSA search is matching at a conceptual level, it can identify relevant text sections that do not contain any of the keywords in the query. For example, in Figure 17.3, the meaning-based search identifies the sections on "circuit breakers" as relevant to the query "fuse," even though the word "fuse" does not occur in those sections.

Find Like-Paragraphs in Manuals or Libraries

Facilities to find related paragraphs or sections to the one currently being read are also provided in SuperManual®. With this capability, a user can create a query from a selected paragraph from any text that describes the maintenance task that the individual currently needs to perform. The most similar paragraphs in the whole set of relevant documentation will then be identified. Alternatively, the query paragraph could be one that represents the special knowledge a particular trainee or mission team needs but lacks. It would be selected by individuals themselves, by easily navigating in the browser. In the SuperManual® interface, users can click on the text of any section and instantly see the 10 most similar sections in the manual, along with the ability to choose and jump to those sections. For example, in Figure 17.4, a user has clicked on a text section called "Angle Determination" and is provided a selectable list of the 10 most similar sections.

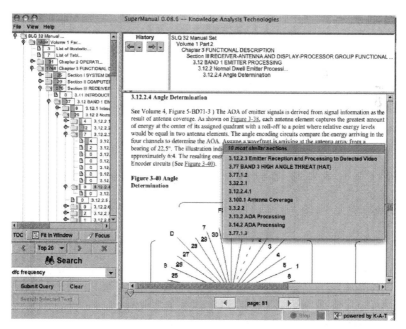

Figure 17.4. Example of finding the 10 most similar sections to a section on "Angle Determination."

SuperManual® can further enable searches from within the IETM to materials contained in any part of a virtually unlimited library of relevant text. By clicking on a library search icon for a paragraph, a user can have returned the reference to, a summary of, and, with another click, the texts of the most similar paragraphs anywhere in a whole library. These can include instructional, manual sections regarding other uses or common problems with the same or related systems or parts, access to diagrams not in the current manual, instructional curriculum and logs of comments by other maintainers. Any section or paragraph so-found can itself become a query to find, for example, the two most similar to it in the repository. These features can be useful in IETMs by allowing users to find related procedures that may help clarify the tasks needed to be done in a current procedure. For example, if a user is unable to understand the current section being read, other sections that discuss related material can be easily located.

Autosummarization

Often heading and subheading titles are insufficiently informative, even in fisheye view hierarchical context, to tell the user whether the text contains the desired content. Even the beginning portion of the text itself, especially if displayed in a window on a small screen, is sometimes not enough to judge its relevance. To reduce the time and difficulty of determining relevance, we have developed two new automatic summarization techniques that give additional information about the contents of any selected portion of a text. These differ from current ones available in systems like Microsoft Word by being based on semantics rather than surface level formatting, syntactic, markup, or trigger-word clues. One of them produces a four- or five-word keyword summary, the other selects the one contained sentence that best covers the content of the entire selected text.

The keyword summary method uses LSA to choose keywords that are most semantically similar to the section and describe the greatest amount of information about the section. The keywords do not have to have occurred within the section to be chosen. As an example of the keyword summary, if the original text were:

Security Clearances. Introduction. Qualifications. Investigation. Self Check. Sailors in many Navy ratings may require access to classified information. The Commanding Officer (CO) determines your need for a security clearance based on your assignment at their command or potential assignment on transfer. To apply for a security clearance, you must be a US citizen. Each Sailor needing a clearance will require an investigation. This investigation determines the Sailor's potential to protect information during the course of their duties. Once issued, a security clearance remains valid provided the Sailor continues compliance with personnel security standards and has no subsequent break in service exceeding 24 months.

The best 20 keywords chosen were:

security_clearance, national_agency_check, background_investigation, ENTNAC, SSO, clearance, eligibility, security, security_officer, CAF, person-nel_screening, DON_CAF, Clearances, NAC, eligible , disclosure, grant, in-vestigative, classified, suitability

In the example, none of the underlined keywords occur in the actual doc-ument, yet are all highly relevant to the section. It should be noted that not all text sections provide such perfect results and a full evaluation of the per-formance of the summarization algorithm has not as yet been performed.

Because LSA can work on any size unit of text, summaries can be pro-vided at any level. For sentence summaries, an algorithm chooses the sen-tences that best describe the whole text section. For selecting the sentences, instead of assuming that selected text always begins with a good summa-rizing sentence or the like, the LSA-based technique compares the meaning of each sentence with each other and finds the one whose average similarity to all others is greatest. This produces one or more summary sentences which best cover the overall meaning of the section.

Learning Paths

It is becoming impossible to train personnel for all maintenance tasks that they may encounter. Therefore, maintenance manual readers may read sec-tions in a manual in which they are unfamiliar with the procedures or ter-minology. What is needed is a tool to permit them to quickly learn the additional relevant pieces of information that would make their current task understandable. *Learning Path*© is a technique that helps users find an optimal path through the manual to provide the additional background in-formation they need to complete a task. Like the "find-like paragraphs" functionality described earlier, the Learning Path dynamically finds re-lated sections, however, it finds sections within the manual and orders them in a way that helps the user understand the current section that is being read.

To use a learning path, the user selects a "knowledge target" from the text, or a set of focused paragraphs is selected by a trainer or leader to repre-sent the needed knowledge for a particular, system, job, or mission. The LSA-system then suggests a minimum sequence of text sections, or steps, for the individual or team members to read in order to be able to under-stand the "knowledge target" (see Fig. 17.5). To generate a learning path, the system uses LSA-based technology to find relevant material (i.e., that is semantically similar), as well as to order the information in a coherent man-ner (see Foltz, Kintsch, & Landauer, 1998; Rehder et al., 1998). This coherent ordering is done so that each step builds on the information in the previous

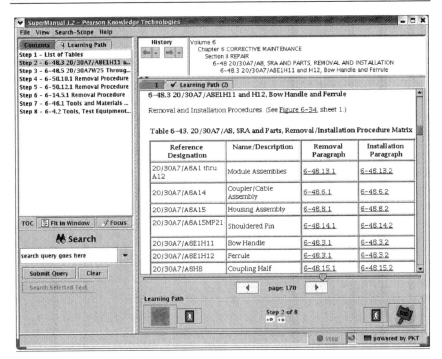

Figure 17.5.   Illustration of a learning path generated by a user reading section 6–4.2.

steps. Figure 17.5 shows a Learning Path computed from a section on tools and test equipment required for a particular procedure. The system suggests steps that should be read in order to best understand the tools and test equipment section. These steps are displayed in a separate table of contents, which allows users to easily click through each step. Because the "dynamic path to knowledge" is entirely automatic, it can be generated on the fly for any task a user might encounter. Although the technology has been developed and integrated into SuperManual, additional work will be performed to evaluate the performance and potential learning gains of users of the learning paths.

Just in Time Glossary: Word Equivalence With Contextual Reference

Users of complex manuals often are unable to acquire the vocabulary knowledge for all potential parts of the manual. Thus, they may encounter novel concepts or part descriptors that are unfamiliar. SuperManual® seeks to alleviate this problem by providing an automatically derived glossary. Users can select a word to bring up a glossary definition. In addition, by

LSA search, one or more additional paragraphs containing the word used in the same sense is also returned. Therefore, the user is able to both learn the definition of the word and see its use in conceptually related contexts. By training the system on technical documents from multiple systems, for example, earlier or later versions, LSA can automatically associate alternative technical terms with the same or highly similar meaning, including corresponding part numbers. Similarly, in more academic educational domains, by training the system on multiple textbooks, a user can see how multiple authors have explained similar concepts.

Adaptive Indexing

Adaptive indexing is a highly useful aid that exploits information gained in actual use by an individual or group. This system learns from users what search terms they spontaneously think of when faced with a particular problem or looking for a particular kind of information. The system keeps track of the words that users try which do not succeed. If and when the user finally finds a sought item, then the system asks whether some of the users' words that did not find the desired content but ought to have been added to the list of index terms for that item. If the user concurs, then the new key words are promoted to definitive pointers that remain available for that and other users in the future. When the same or another user enters one of these keys in an ad-hoc query, the top k texts or graphics that previously satisfied any user in response to the same term would be marked in the table of contents along with an indication of how many times the particular target had previously been endorsed as a proper response to the query word(s). With a moderate amount of use, this technique largely overcomes the synonymy and ambiguity problems in search (Furnas, Landauer, Gomez, & Dumais, 1987); in trials it quickly increased success rates in finding needed information by 50% (Furnas, 1985). (Note that adaptive indexing does not produce a retrieval explosion the way ordinary term expansion often does, because the pointers are specific only to a limited number of targets for which they have been endorsed, not treated as universal synonyms.)

Integration of Graphics and Interactive Content

Small, low resolution screens prohibit the display of large, detailed diagrams, pictures, and animations. Merely displaying graphics can sometimes be counterproductive because they displace large amounts of valuable text and use up valuable time downloading, sometimes to little or no actual advantage. Research literature on graphics for learning, and even for understanding data, shows that their value is often overestimated.

However, graphics are frequently used to good effect: Part and wiring diagrams are often critical tools and animations of procedures can be valuable. Thus, it is important both to display graphics and to find ways to use graphics selectively and effectively.

SuperManual® is designed to deal with a range of means of presenting graphics as well as other web-based content. The graphics may be presented inline with the text or as separate windows that can be zoomed or scrolled. Figure 17.6 shows an example of graphics and videos incorporated into a SuperManual® based on a biology textbook. In order to improve readability of the text, thumbnail icons of the graphics can be provided next to the text, which can be expanded into the complete graphic. In addition, because graphics often contain useful information that may need to be located by users, SuperManual® provides search on captions and text items in graphics.

An important research objective still underway will be to determine by empirical usability testing the extent to which large graphical displays on small screens will be satisfactory, and under what circumstances they should be augmented by other display technologies such as Just In Time printed paper.

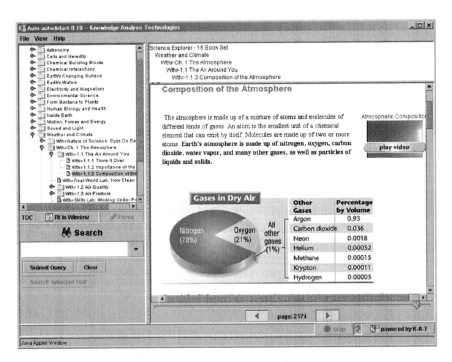

Figure 17.6. Example of graphics within a SuperManual® for a biology textbook.

Applications of SuperManual® Technology in Other Types of Information

Whereas the examples in this chapter have focused primarily on applying the technology to Naval maintenance, it should be noted that the SuperManual® technology is not limited to online manuals. Indeed, it can be applied to any domain in which there is a large amount of hierarchically structured information that must be navigated in an efficient manner. As an example of a highly different domain, we have developed an application called StandardSeeker for matching state standards to educational material.

Virtually all states, as well as several national organizations, have created sets of standards or learning objectives for each grade school educational level. Each standard for each level and topic can have hundreds to thousands of individual concepts that a student is expected to master in that grade level. As schools move toward greater standards-based education, they must know how well any piece of educational material in the curriculum (e.g., textbook sections, individual questions, lesson plans, classroom exercises) aligns with the state standards. Thus, a challenge for creators of educational material is to align all this material to each of the state standards. Currently, all of this work is done manually by "standards correlators," who read the material and then create indices of the relationship between the material and each standard.

StandardSeeker was developed as a semi-automatic system to match any text-based curriculum material to any state standards. It can be used to match textbooks, skill lists, standards, objectives, problem metadata statements, or lesson plans to any set of state standards or skills lists. The philosophy behind its "human–computer symbiotic" approach is that all information retrieval systems are far from perfect. Even with LSA enhanced retrieval, the system will suggest some standards that are not appropriate matches. Using a SuperManual®-based interface, the system automatically displays the best matches between the educational material and a standard. By displaying the hits against the standards within the hierarchical context of the fisheye view, the user interface aids the users in judging the quality of the computer matches, navigating and choosing those that look most appropriate for the context. The search engine insures wider coverage of potential matches than would typically be retrieved by a manual correlation alone.

An example of the StandardSeeker interface is shown in Figure 17.7. In this case, a user has entered a problem statement from a math problem "Find the volume of a sphere." The system has matched this problem statement against the Florida Grade 8 math standards. The best match in this case (with a cosine of .57) is the standard involving "finding the volume of

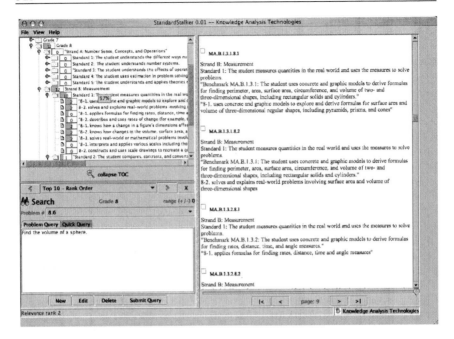

Figure 17.7. StandardSeeker interface displaying Florida math standards.

two and three dimensional shapes." It should be noted, that the word "sphere" was not used in the standard, yet the best match is to a standard that includes other "three dimensional regular shapes, including pyramids, prisms and cones."

Using StandardSeeker as an aid to correlating educational material, a user can quickly determine what learning objectives have been covered by the material. Output from the system can include a list of objectives covered by pages, sections, or paragraphs in the learning material. This can be easily used to identify coverage gaps within the material (e.g., when an author has not covered particular learning objectives).

One evaluation has been performed on using LSA for standards matching. One hundred and twelve math problem statements were matched against the Florida math standards by two human correlators. Across the problem statements, the overlap of chosen standards between the two humans was 46%. This result appears to be quite typical for this task, in which there are many possible matches and many ambiguous standards and problem statements. Correlators typically chose just one standard as a match, even though several may be relevant. LSA was used to pick the five best standards matching each problem statement. Of the top five chosen, LSA agreed with at least one of the human correlator's chosen standards

76% of the time. In addition, 59% of the time all of the standards chosen by the correlators were in the top five of those chosen by LSA. These results suggest that LSA provides fairly robust matching performance. By displaying these hits within the SuperManual interface, a correlator can then quickly identify which of those top hits are relevant.

CONCLUSIONS

The purpose of this chapter is to provide an overview of techniques and technologies that may be applied to electronic technical manuals and other types of online information in order to enhance users' performance in tasks requiring dynamic human use of stored information. SuperManual® provides a test bed for iterative research, development, and testing of tools for a personally adaptive electronic maintenance manual that can permit personnel to rapidly locate and apply information. SuperManual® synergistically combines the functionalities of two technologies. One is the powerful capabilities of LSA; the other major technological basis is the usability tested and application-proven functionality and features of the SuperBook hypertext browser. SuperManual® derives great benefit from LSA-based technology for a number of its features. These features include improved search for sections and figures, providing instant linking between relevant sections, automated summarization of material, ordering of the material within the manual so that it can provide efficient learning, and contextual examples of word usage to help improve learning of new vocabulary.

Search within large documents and linked texts often results in users being "lost in hyperspace." Users can be lost both in terms of not knowing where they are in the manual and not being able to comprehend the current information being displayed. In domains such as complex system maintenance, users must be able to locate, comprehend, and perform actions based on what they have learned from the manual. The approach described provides a system that allows users to navigate large documents while supporting the users' comprehension of the text. This permits the use of a SuperManual® by users at varying levels of expertise.

Because SuperManuals® are produced virtually automatically from existing instructional and operations-support texts, they can be constructed much more quickly for new systems, and at much lower costs than current electronic manuals. In addition, because maintenance manuals must be used in a range of environments and situations and for varied tasks, the SuperManual® architecture is designed to be extensible to a number of hardware platforms. It can run on existing PC-based web-browsers and can be used on desktop PCs, laptops, tablets, and wearables. It can further incorporate hyper-links to other training or technical material in other computer-based formats.

A critically important part of this effort is iterative usefulness and usability testing. Prior research (Landauer, 1994) has shown that user–system interaction functions and interface designs typically have around 40 flaws on first trial—flaws that, in the case of online manuals, often make them significantly harder to use than the paper manuals they are intended to replace. Fortunately, it has also been found that most of such flaws can be detected by observing trials of the system by two to four people, and most of these are easily corrected. Such iterative empirical user-centered design (Landauer, 1994) also allows for discovery of innovative design solutions that can have favorable effects. The SuperManual® research and development program is exploiting this methodology.

As noted earlier, SuperManuals® are not limited to just maintenance manuals. The components developed in the SuperManual® project have been integrated into a range of products, such as online textbooks and standards matching systems. Indeed, different components may be more appropriate for different contexts, tasks, and users. For example, learning paths may be more appropriate in training material, whereas material for more expert users may benefit more from section-to-section search.

Present systems have not taken sufficient advantage of what is known about optimal design for efficient information use, and they have not incorporated certain promising new technologies for dynamic adaptation to user knowledge and vocabulary differences. The tools and techniques developed through the SuperManual® project are based on applied research in information finding and on the results of iterative testing. The results can be used to inform the design of future online information repositories of many kinds. They promise to provide faster and more accurate learning and task performance through the ability to locate and understand relevant information better and more quickly when needed.

ACKNOWLEDGMENTS

This chapter is based on research funded by contracts from the Office of Naval Research, Susan Chipman (COR) and Naval Air Warfare Center Training Systems Division, Katie Ricci (COR). The work has also benefited from contributions from Brent Halsey, Kyle Habermehl, Marcia Derr, Noelle LaVoie, Terry Drissell, and James Parker.

REFERENCES

Egan, D. E., Lesk, M. E., Ketchum, R. D., Lochbaum, C. C., Littman, M. L., & Landauer, T. K. (1991). Hypertext for the electronic library? CORE sample results. *Proceedings of the Third Annual ACM Conference on Hypertext*, 299–312.

Egan, D. E., Remde, J. R., Gomez, L. M., Landauer, T. K., Eberhardt, J., & Lochbaum, C. C. (1989). Formative design evaluation of SuperBook. *ACM Transactions on Information Systems, 7*(1), 30–57.

Foltz, P. W., Kintsch, W., & Landauer, T. K (1998). The measurement of textual coherence with latent semantic analysis. *Discourse Processes, 25*(2&3), 285–307.

Foltz, P. W., Landauer, T. K., & Parker, J. (2001). *Design principles for organization and navigation in interactive electronic technical manuals: A review of relevant science and technology.* Knowledge Analysis Technologies Technical Report submitted to the Office of Naval Research.

Furnas, G. W. (1985). Experience with an adaptive indexing scheme. *Proceedings of the SIGCHI Conference on Human Factors in Computing Systems,* 131–135.

Furnas, G. W. (1986, April). Generalized fisheye views. *Proceedings of the SIGCHI Conference on Human Factors in Computing Systems,* 16–23.

Furnas, G. W., Landauer, T. K., Gomez, L. M., & Dumais, S. T. (1987). The vocabulary problem in human system communication. *Communications of the ACM, 30*(11), 946–971.

Landauer, T. K. (1994). *The trouble with computers: Usefulness, usability, and productivity.* Cambridge, MA: MIT Press.

Landauer, T. K., Egan, D. E., Remde, J. R., Lesk, M. E., Lochbaum, C. C., & Ketchum, R. D. (1993). Enhancing the usability of text through computer delivery and formative design evaluation. In A. Dillon, C. McNight, & J. Richardson (Eds.), *Hypertext: A psychological perspective* (pp. 71–136). New York: Ellis Horwood.

Rehder, B., Schreiner, M. E., Wolfe, M. B. W., Laham, D., Landauer, T. K., & Kintsch, W. (1998). Using latent semantic analysis to assess knowledge: Some technical considerations. *Discourse Processes, 25*(2&3), 337–354.

18

Automating Usability Evaluation: Cognitive Walkthrough for the Web Puts LSA to Work on Real-World HCI Design Problems

Marilyn Hughes Blackmon
Dipti R. Mandalia
Peter G. Polson
University of Colorado, Boulder

Muneo Kitajima
*National Institute of Advanced Industrial Science and
Technology (AIST), Japan*

When people navigate a relevant Web site for information needed to solve a problem, they encounter two subproblems. The first is navigating within the Web site to find a relevant web page(s) or a relevant document downloadable from the Web site. The second subproblem is comprehending the retrieved information.

345

For the past 5 years, we have addressed the first subproblem by developing a usability evaluation method (UEM) called the Cognitive Walkthrough for the Web (CWW). This chapter focuses primarily on how CWW employs LSA to identify and repair usability problems that impair navigation of large, complex Web sites. By now we have collected a large amount of evidence demonstrating that CWW reliably and validly predicts the usability problems that impede navigation of a Web site to retrieve information (Blackmon et al., 2002, 2003, 2005).

The special genius of LSA is its versatility to switch among a variety of different semantic spaces. Each LSA semantic space used by CWW is constructed from a scientifically sampled corpus of documents, emulating Zeno, Ivens, Millard, and Duvvuri (1995).[1] Scientifically sampled corpora ensure that the semantic space faithfully represents the background knowledge and general reading ability of a particular population, such as 3rd-, 6th-, 9th-, or 12th-grade general reading knowledge of American English. This versatility of LSA enables us to apply CWW to evaluate the usability of a given Web site for a diverse array of user populations. For example, CWW might simulate navigating a one-size-fits-all online encyclopedia to answer a range of information needs, predicting that users with college-level general reading knowledge would be successful, but that users with 3rd- or 6th-grade reading knowledge would experience frustration and probably fail to find the information they needed in the same online encyclopedia.

Recently, one of us (Mandalia, 2004) extended the research program in a new direction by addressing the second subproblem users face: whether users can comprehend the content that they find. Mandalia created a new LSA-based tool that integrates with the workflow of content writers. A section near the end of this chapter describes how this tool supports content writers in improving the comprehensibility of content material made available on the Web site, and targeting one or more particular user groups whose level of background knowledge differs markedly from the writers' own level of background knowledge.

THEORETICAL ROOTS UNDERLYING CWW

Theories of How People Navigate Complex Informational Web Sites

There is widespread agreement that a common problem-solving process underlies both navigating a Web site to find specific information (or to find

---

[1]The five tasa semantic spaces were built from the scientifically sampled corpora that Zeno et al. (1995) collected to create their definitive guide to word frequency for American educators. The five corpora are divided by applying the degrees of reading power (DRP) measure of readability found at http://www.tasaliteracy.com/

a product), and performing a novel task using a complex Macintosh or Windows application. This common problem-solving process is the process of learning or performing by exploration (Chi, Pirolli, Chen, & Pitkow, 2001; Kitajima, Blackmon, & Polson, 2000, 2005; Kitajima & Polson, 1997; Pirolli, 2005; Pirolli & Card, 1999; Pirolli & Fu, 2003; Pirolli, Fu, Chi, & Farahat, 2005; Rieman, Young, & Howes, 1996; Soto, 1999). Simulation models of performing by exploration have been derived from different theoretical foundations, but all share the underlying assumption that exploratory behavior is guided by perceptions of semantic similarity. The most common heuristic for directing exploratory behavior is to act on an object in a display (e.g., release on a menu item, click on a link) whose description is perceived by a user to be semantically similar to the user's current goal.

When reporting how users perform Web site navigation tasks by exploration, there is consensus among researchers that users follow a trail of *scent*, or *information scent*, that involves users' perceptions of semantic similarity between their current goal and each of the links they might click on any web page they visit in a particular Web site (Blackmon et al., 2002, 2003, 2005; Chi et al., 2001, 2003; Furnas, 1997; Pirolli, 2005; Pirolli & Card, 1999; Pirolli & Fu, 2003; Pirolli et al., 2005). Although CWW researchers follow the consensus and employ the term *information scent*, CWW researchers diverge from the consensus both by measuring information scent within a particular LSA semantic space and by distinguishing two dimensions of information scent: semantic similarity between the user's goal and web page texts and familiarity of the terms in the web page texts.

CWW is designed to identify and repair design flaws in a Web site that would cause navigating by scent-following to fail, and the heuristic of guiding navigation by following a scent trail can fail in any of three different scenarios. In the first scenario, scent can be weak or nonexistent for the correct heading or link, failing to provide users with any guidance on what link to click. In the second scenario, the heading or link text may be unfamiliar and, thus, relatively meaningless to users (e.g., a correct link that uses a low-frequency scientific or medical term). In the third scenario, following a strong scent actively misdirects users, causing them to detour away from solution paths that would lead to achieving their goals.

Designers of Web sites, therefore, need to accurately predict users' perceptions of similarity and familiarity, but designers and users frequently do not share common understandings and therefore have very different perceptions of similarity and familiarity. Even when compared to a typical college-educated user, the typical Web site designer has a great deal more knowledge than the typical user has, including exceptional knowledge of the content domain, specialized terms used in heading and link descriptions, and web page layout conventions. Thus, designers' subjective judgments of similarity and familiarity, unaided by CWW, can be very different from perceptions of similarity and familiarity of target user populations. Thus, the validity of the CWW design evaluation and repair processes described in this chapter depends on designers being able to set CWW to a particular LSA semantic space to accurately simulate users' judgments of similarity and familiarity.

CoLiDeS Cognitive Model and the
Construction-Integration Cognitive Architecture

Our CWW research began by adapting the Cognitive Walkthrough (CW), a widely used UEM originally developed to support the design and evaluation of application interfaces (Blackmon, 2004; Wharton, Rieman, Lewis, & Polson, 1994). CW has been applied to evaluating how well users could execute tasks on a walk-up-and-use interface (e.g., an ATM) or perform novel or infrequent tasks in a complex suite of applications, such as Microsoft Office. CWW retains a major advantage of CW: Designers can apply it early in the process of designing and building an application or Web site, avoiding the necessity of making expensive major changes to fix usability problems after the application or Web site has already been designed and built.

Kitajima and Polson (1997; Kitajima, Blackmon, & Polson, 2000, 2005) exploited the fact that their earlier theoretical models of learning and performing by exploration could be extended to analyze how to design Web sites to facilitate successful forward search (relying on hill-climbing, a general problem-solving method) and to prevent Web site design flaws that hinder successful navigation. The resulting model for Web site navigation is CoLiDeS, an acronym for *C*omprehension-based *Li*nked model of *De*liberate *S*earch (Kitajima, Blackmon, & Polson, 2000, 2005). The action-planning processes of learning by exploration are comprehension based, and CoLiDeS is based on Kintsch's (1998) construction-integration (CI) theory of text comprehension and action planning. Information scent is generated by processes closely related to text comprehension, and scent, like text comprehension, depends on background knowledge.

A CI model of web navigation requires a robust, realistic model of attention processes, because clicking a link confronts the user with a new page containing many targets for action. Accordingly, CoLiDeS incorporates a model of attention management and a two-phase model of action planning. Each phase uses a pair of CI cycles. In the first phase of action planning, the user parses the web page into subregions and generates text descriptions of each region, perhaps describing one region as a "hierarchically organized side navigation menu" and another region as a "collection of links to physics, chemistry, and other physical sciences." Contingent on the user's own particular background knowledge, the user derives descriptions of subregions from (a) comprehension of heading texts, if any headings are used on the web page, and (b) knowledge of the functions of various subregions of a particular Web site (if the user has enough prior experience with that Web site) or default conventions for a typical Web site (if the user has prior experience with Web sites and can recognize, and know the conventional functions of, the side navigation bar, top navigation bar, content area, site logo, etc.). At the end of the first phase of action planning, a user focuses attention on a subregion of the web page whose description is familiar to the user and semantically similar to the user's goal. In sum, during the first phase of action planning, a pair of CI cycles parses the web page into subregions and ends by focusing attention on a subregion of a web page most similar to the user's goal (an attention action).

In the second phase of action planning, the first CI cycle identifies each possible target for action within the focused-on subregion (e.g., links, buttons, graphics), comprehends link label texts in that subregion, and generates a description for each target for action. Background knowledge is critical for understanding the consequences of clicking the various specific links, such as what to expect after clicking a link labeled "Music." At the end of the second phase of action planning, the second CI cycle selects a specific action on an object from the attended-to subregion, for example, clicking the link labeled "Music." CoLiDeS assumes the target for action is familiar to the user and semantically similar to the user's goal.[2]

CoLiDeS uses LSA to model users' perceptions of similarity and familiarity and combines them with prior experience with Web site widgets into a complex measure of information scent. In a full running simulation of CoLiDeS, the complex measure of information scent would be integrated into a single activation value, that is, a measure of the probability that the user will select a particular link or other screen object (Kitajima, Blackmon, & Polson, 2005).

When CoLiDeS simulates a human user successfully navigating a Web site by pure forward search, the heading and link that are semantically most similar to the user's goal must also be *correct* and use *familiar* text labels. Throughout this chapter, the term *correct* consistently means that clicking the *correct* link nested under the *correct* heading in the *correct* subregion of the web page actually leads the user expeditiously to the target web page and, thus, to accomplishment of the user's goal in the minimum number of clicks. The term *familiar* consistently means that the user can comprehend the term or terms used to label the heading and link and has sufficient background knowledge to select the correct heading and link. In contrast, if the correct heading and link are unfamiliar or not semantically similar to the user's goal, CoLiDeS, simulating the human user, will flounder and be forced to backtrack or detour. If the problems are severe, then a human

---

[2]A demonstration of CoLiDeS can be found at http://www.staff.aist.go.jp/kitajima.muneo/CoLiDeS_Demo.html

user—or CoLiDeS simulating a human user—is likely to experience task failure (i.e., fail to accomplish the goal and give up navigating the Web site).

USABILITY PROBLEMS IDENTIFIED BY CWW

In order to identify usability problems with the navigation system of a web page, the CWW analyst must determine which link(s), heading(s), and sub-region(s) are *correct* for accomplishing that goal on the web page. In contrast, CoLiDeS simulates human users and, like users, has no way of distinguishing whether a particular link, heading, or subregion is correct or incorrect. Thus, CoLiDeS, like human users, struggles when it encounters the following four types of CWW-identified usability problems while navigating Web sites to accomplish particular tasks. The first three of the following four types of usability problems have been verified by experiments reported in the earliest publications (Blackmon et al., 2002, 2003). The fourth has emerged more recently and, as CWW has evolved, we have made slight changes in the parameters for problem identification (Blackmon, Kitajima, & Polson, 2005). Appendix A lists the exact, automatable rules and LSA parameters that CWW now uses to identify these four usability problems.

An *unfamiliar correct link* problem can potentially occur whenever target users of the Web site lack sufficient background knowledge to comprehend a link text and accurately estimate its similarity to their current goals. A short LSA term vector length has empirically proved to be the most useful CWW index of insufficient background knowledge. Low word frequency in the selected LSA semantic space is, however, another important marker, because typical users cannot recognize or comprehend low-frequency technical terms and other low-frequency words. In some cases, such as *paleontology*, a link label is both a low-frequency word and a term that has a short-term vector length. In other cases, such as *anthropology* in the college-level semantic space, a link is not a low-frequency word but nevertheless has a short-term vector length. Thus, although college-level users recognize the word, they tend, even so, to have only sparse, vague knowledge of the full range of information that falls within the scope of anthropology. Both users and CoLiDeS tend to ignore links they fail to understand clearly, and ignoring an *unfamiliar correct link* causes serious problems because users must click that link to reach the target web page that accomplishes their goal. A preventive repair strategy is best to avoid *unfamiliar correct link* problems. Designers would ideally identify and repair all unfamiliar link texts on each web page before posting the web page on the Internet.

A *competing heading* problem arises when any heading and its associated subregion is semantically very similar to the user goal but does not contain a correct link that leads to accomplishing the user goal. Like users, CoLiDeS follows the information scent trail and has no way of knowing if a given subregion contains a correct link(s). Competing headings problems are liable to be serious problems, because they divert the user's attention away from the "correct" subregion. Users often click several links under a focused-on subregion before switching their attention from that subregion to another semantically similar subregion. Indeed, Blackmon et al. (2005) found that the best measure of competing heading problems is the number of attractive links within all competing subregions, called *competing links nested under competing headings*. Many high-scent links increase the user's perception that the correct link is somewhere within a high-scent competing subregion, so a user will probably click many links in that competing subregion, even exhaustively clicking relatively unlikely links, before leaving that subregion. Designers can prevent some competing heading problems by using high-quality link and heading labels (Blackmon et al., 2003; Miller & Remington, 2004), but some goals inevitably require cross-classification under two or more subregions (e.g., users search for information about music therapy under music, psychotherapy, and medicine links that necessarily belong in three different subregions).

A *competing link* problem occurs when a correct or competing subregion contains one or more links that are semantically similar to the user goal but not on the solution path. In recent work (Blackmon et al., 2005), we have begun using the more precise term *competing links nested under a correct heading*. Competing links located within a correct subregion may distract the user momentarily, but the user usually persists and eventually clicks the "correct" link before abandoning the "correct" subregion. *Competing links nested under competing headings* are more serious, as already indicated. A designer can prevent many competing links problems by changing link label text to reduce similarity among link labels within each subregion (Blackmon et al., 2003).

A *weak-scent correct link* problem refers to the situation when a correct link is semantically unrelated to the user goal (near-zero LSA cosine), and when there are no other correct links that have moderate or strong scent. CoLiDeS and human users generally ignore links that they perceive as semantically unrelated to the current user goal and have no way of knowing which link is correct. Therefore, a weak-scent correct link causes serious problems. Designers can prevent weak-scent correct links by devising high-quality link labels and testing the scent of each link label for a large set of typical user goals that will require users to click that link.

CONCRETE EXAMPLE OF AN EXPERIMENTAL TASK

A concrete example offers the simplest way to grasp how the CoLiDeS model guides experimental design, how CWW can be used to predict the difficulty of doing a specific task on a particular web page, and how we test the psychological validity of CWW predictions using controlled laboratory experiments. We have deliberately selected a task that CWW predicts will be very difficult for users (or for CoLiDeS simulations of human users), because users will encounter all four of the usability problems described previously while doing this task.

The particular task—Find Hmong—involves finding an article about the Hmong people by navigating an online encyclopedia. The main web page for the Find Hmong task in our controlled laboratory experiments is shown in Figure 18.1, a web page that closely simulates a popular online encyclopedia Web site and has 93 topic links nested under nine category headings. "Anthropology" is the only link that leads to the article on Hmong in the actual online encyclopedia Web site simulated in our experiment. Therefore, to complete the Find Hmong task on the experimental Web site, experimental participants had to click the correct link "Anthropology" nested under the correct heading "Social Science."

Experimental participants who did this task could see and read the Find Hmong user goal in the box at the top of the web page shown in Figure 18.1. The Find Hmong goal is a 205-word summary of the full encyclopedia article on Hmong, and accurately represents the actual article because it has an LSA cosine of .82 with the full article. (If the summary had contained ex-

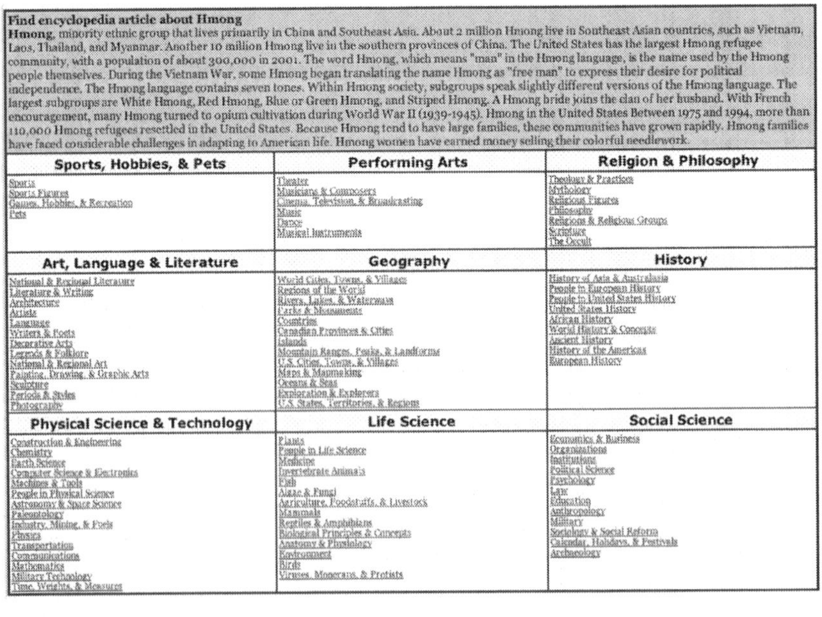

Figure 18.1.   Web page for Find Hmong Task.

actly the same text as the article the cosine would be 1.00, and if the summary had essentially no semantic similarity to the article, then the cosine would be approximately zero. Therefore, a cosine of .82 shows a high degree of semantic similarity.)

The 76 experimental participants who did the Find Hmong task were all undergraduates, so we selected the LSA semantic space for first-year college general reading knowledge. To determine which headings and links have the highest information scent for the Find Hmong goal, we performed a One-to-Many LSA analysis comparing the Find Hmong goal with each of the nine headings and 93 links shown in Figure 18.1. Then we sorted both the goal-heading cosines and the goal-link cosines by decreasing cosine value. To simulate the way that human beings elaborate text during comprehension, we had previously elaborated the link and heading texts with additional words that are both highly similar and highly familiar (see Appendix B for details about elaboration of link and heading texts).

Following the CoLiDeS model, CWW assumes experimental participants will first parse the web page into subregions and focus on the subregion and heading most similar to the goal. History and Geography are the subregions with the highest scent for the Find Hmong goal (goal-heading cosines of .30 and .19, respectively), and both have stronger information scent than does the correct heading, Social Science (goal-heading cosine of only .08). Thus, CWW expects that users' attention will be actively misdirected from the correct heading to History and Geography and identifies *competing headings* problems for these two subregions. Nested under these two competing headings, History and Geography, are five high-scent links that CWW identifies as *competing links nested under competing headings* (goal-link cosines ranging from .37 down to .22), and CWW predicts that people will click many or all of these attractive links before switching attention to the correct subregion, "Social Science."

If and when the experimental participant finally gets to the correct Social Science subregion, there is still a fairly low probability of clicking the correct link. Examination of the goal-link cosines indicates that the correct link "Anthropology" has weak-scent (.08) for the Find Hmong goal—CWW calls this a *weak-scent correct link* problem—and that there is a higher scent competing link nested in the same subregion—called a *competing link nested under a correct heading*. In addition, the link "Anthropology" is an *unfamiliar correct link*, because the short-term vector for "anthropology" suggests that even college-educated users generally have inadequate background knowledge of anthropology to realize that anthropologists study the cultures and social organization of peoples like the Hmong.

In short, CWW predicts that users will encounter great difficulty finding the correct link to complete the Find Hmong task. Having identified the highest scent headings and links, however, it is now possible to design a repaired web page that would make it possible for people to do the Find Hmong task using pure forward search. The repaired web page built for the experiment makes it possible to find the encyclopedia article exactly where CWW predicts users are most apt to look for it, not just where an encyclopedia expert thinks the item is properly classified. More specifically, the repaired web page for Find Hmong makes it possible to find the Hmong article by clicking the highest scent links under History or Geography, as well as by clicking the "Anthropology" link designated correct by the designers. On the repaired web page, CWW predicts experimental participants will quickly click one of the links that actually leads to the Find Hmong article.

The performance of experimental participants closely matches CWW predictions, with 45% of the first-clicks falling on a link nested under History, 21% of the first-clicks falling on a link nested under Geography, and a mere 5% of the first-clicks falling on a link nested under Social Science. Table 18.1 shows the observed mean total clicks for the Find Hmong task for the 76 college students who did the task in our laboratory study, including 38 participants in the unrepaired web page condition and 38 participants in the repaired web page condition. For the unrepaired condition, the Find Hmong task took 9.026 mean total clicks compared with 2.135 mean total clicks in the repaired condition. The difference (measured in mean total clicks) between the two conditions of the Find Hmong task is significant, $F(1, 73) = 98.9$, $p < .0001$.

Only 26% of the students in the unrepaired web page condition ever found the Hmong article within the time limit of 130 seconds. In contrast, 100% of the students in the repaired web page condition were successful in finding the Hmong article and did it in a mean time of 41 seconds. Armed with an accurate way of predicting which links people are most apt to click, therefore, it is possible to build web pages where people accomplish their goals with pure forward search, the ideal situation according to the CoLiDeS model.

TABLE 18.1
Find Hmong Task: Repaired Versus Unrepaired Condition

Performance Measure	Find Hmong Web Page Condition	
	Unrepaired	Repaired
First-click success rate	3%	43%
Actual mean total clicks	9.0	2.1
Success rate	26%	100%
Mean solution time	124 s	41 s
Experimental participants in each condition (76 total)	38	38

HOW THE RELIABILITY OF CWW DEPENDS ON LSA

Hertzum and Jacobsen (2003) have demonstrated that there is a disturbingly high "evaluator effect" for usability evaluation methods (UEMs) that rely on the human judgments of usability experts and developers. Similarity and familiarity judgments of human evaluators are subjective judgments anchored in the experience of individuals and can be far different from the perceptions of actual users. Hertzum and Jacobsen (2003) reviewed the available evidence for various UEM methods and demonstrated that agreement is unreliably low between the judgments of any pair of individual analysts. Increasing the number of analysts making a given set of judgments may improve the reliability of the judgments but drives up the cost of the usability evaluation.

CWW solves the UEM interrater reliability problem by substituting LSA measures of semantic similarity and familiarity in place of developers' judgments of similarity and familiarity. CWW uses LSA measures of similarity (i.e., cosines) because LSA cosines are objective measures of semantic similarity that can be precisely replicated by any analyst using the same procedure and selecting the same semantic space. Similarly, LSA provides objective, replicable measures of familiarity (term vector length and term frequency).

A notable advantage of relying on LSA measures of similarity and familiarity is the capacity of LSA to make accurate, objective similarity and familiarity judgments for users very different from the analyst. LSA measures of similarity and familiarity are invaluable for designing heading and link labels that are usable by target audiences that have less advanced knowledge. It is particularly crucial to rely on objective LSA judgments of familiarity. People who design Web sites typically have fluent college-level general reading knowledge and high domain-specific background knowledge for the domain of the Web site. Unaided by LSA measures of familiarity, it is virtually impossible for a designer with advanced knowledge to accurately detect and flag all the terms that would be unfamiliar to users with third- or sixth-grade general reading knowledge, or unfamiliar to bicultural users whose native language and cultural background differ from the designer's own native language and culture.

HOW THE PSYCHOLOGICAL VALIDITY OF CWW DEPENDS ON LSA

Blackmon et al. (2002, 2003) identified three types of usability problems with navigation systems—unfamiliar correct link problems, competing headings, and competing links problems—and reported a series of experiments that verified the psychological validity of CWW problem identifications and the success of CWW repairs. More recently, CWW added a new category of usability problems—called weak-scent correct link problems—and eliminated a confound in earlier data by distinguishing competing links nested under competing headings from competing links nested under a correct heading (Blackmon, Kitajima, & Polson, 2005). To identify and repair CWW problems, CWW harnesses the complete array of LSA analyses and measures and uses particular parameters in order to provide completely objective, fully automated measures of similarity and familiarity. For readers who wish to know all the details, the current procedures for CWW problem identification are precisely described in Appendix A and Appendix B.

After running many experiments (Blackmon et al., 2002, 2003, 2005), we had accumulated enough evidence to rise to the higher standard of proof for UEMs advocated by Gray and Salzman (1998a, 1998b). To meet the higher standard, we had to accomplish four subgoals, described in the following subsections. First, we started by building a multiple regression model and extracting a prediction formula from the model. Second, we cross-validated the regression model using an independent dataset, ensuring that our new CWW prediction formula was an accurate measure of problem severity. Third, to further test the prediction formula, we examined rates of hits versus false alarms and correct rejections versus misses. Finally, we tested the success rate for CWW-guided repairs of usability problems.

Multiple Regression Model for a Large Dataset

To create a multiple regression model and associated formula for predicting problem severity, the first step, as reported previously (Blackmon et al, 2005), was to compile results from completed CWW experiments that used pairs of tasks and met the following four specific criteria for inclusion. These four criteria for inclusion were met by 82 pairs of tasks, 164 tasks altogether, drawn from four different CWW experiments (reported in Blackmon et al., 2002, 2003, 2005), and no tasks done by these experimental groups were excluded from the dataset for reanalysis:

1. For each pair of tasks, the first criterion specified that the goal was identical for two well-matched experimental groups, but one experimental group tried to accomplish the goal on an unrepaired web page and a second group tried to accomplish the same goal on a repaired web page.
2. We set a minimum .76 cosine between the actual web page content article and the short, 100- to 200-word summary of the article that experimental participants saw on the web page (e.g., the description of the

Hmong goal in Fig. 18.1). This criterion ensured that experimental participants had a fair, accurate representation of the complete target article they were trying to find in the Web site.

3. For the sample of tasks done in the unrepaired web page condition, the tasks manifested diverse combinations of unfamiliar links, and weak-scent links, competing headings, and competing links nested under both competing and correct headings.

4. Problem-solving data typically have high between-subject variance, so to ensure stable mean total click data for all 164 tasks, we required all tasks to be based on data from a minimum of 20 participants. In fact, the means for 144 of the 164 tasks were based on data from 38 or more experimental participants, and means for the remaining 20 tasks were based on data from 23 or more experimental participants.

The second step toward completing the multiple regression analysis was to develop a uniform, completely objective procedure for reanalyzing all 164 tasks in the dataset. This goal required iteratively rescoring the set of 164 tasks until we had created a set of automatable rules for identifying unfamiliar links, weak-scent links, competing headings, competing links nested under competing headings, and competing links nested under correct headings. Appendix A displays the automatable rules, and appendix B describes, step-by-step, the complex CWW procedure with the current edition of its parameters.[3]

The seven automatable rules in appendix A are all written as if–then production rules, so that a computer programmer can easily convert the rules to code. For example, two different automatable rules specify precisely defined conditions that can independently prompt classification of the heading as a competing heading. The first of the two rules specifies four conditions that must all be simultaneously met in order to trigger firing of this rule and consequent identification of a competing heading: (a) the particular heading is not a correct heading, (b) the goal-heading cosine of the heading must be greater than or equal to .8 times the goal-heading cosine of any correct heading, (c) the goal-heading cosine must be greater than or equal to .10 (i.e., not weak-scent), and (d) the highest goal-link cosine for the links nested under the heading must be greater than or equal to .20.

The seven automatable rules in appendix A paved the way for more complete automation of CWW by eliminating the subjective, time-consuming hand editing of LSA analyses[4] that we originally thought necessary

---

[3]For further details and concrete examples, download the file AutoCWWTutorialA.pdf at http://www.autocww.colorado.edu/~blackmon

[4]Hand editing uses human judgment to weed out likely false alarms, that is, headings and links that real people would be unlikely to focus on or select despite relatively high goal-heading or goal-link cosines.

(Blackmon et al., 2002). Brown (2005) built a new web-based interface for doing CWW, called ACWW (http://www.autocww.colo-rado.edu/~brownr/ACWW.php), which implements all the automatable rules in appendix A and follows the procedures defined in appendix B. ACWW automatically identifies usability problems and predicts task difficulty for any set of one or more goals performed on one or more web pages.[5]

The third step was to develop the multiple regression model of task difficulty. For our initial laboratory studies (Blackmon et al., 2002, 2003), we had deliberately selected tasks that each epitomized one class of usability problems, but in actual fact few tasks are pure examples of just one type of usability problem. Most tasks are afflicted by two or more types of usability problems, and some tasks (e.g., Find Hmong) are simultaneously afflicted by all of the CWW-identified usability problems.

By doing a multiple regression analysis of the 164-task dataset we tried to account for the variance in task difficulty, indexed by mean total clicks. For the full 164-item dataset, the mean total clicks ranges from 1.0 click to 10.3 clicks with a mean of 3.7 clicks. The multiple regression tested whether four hypothesized factors—number of competing links nested under competing headings, number of competing links nested under correct headings, unfamiliar correct links, and weak-scent correct links—were all statistically significant independent variables and how much each contributed to the overall difficulty level. For example, Find Hmong is a very difficult task (9.0 mean total clicks in the unrepaired condition), a task so difficult that it was completed by only 26% of the people who attempted to do it in the unrepaired condition. Could we have predicted that the Find Hmong task would be that difficult from knowing that it had five competing links nested under two competing headings, one competing link nested under the correct heading, an unfamiliar correct link, and a weak-scent correct link?

The multiple regression analysis explains 57% of the variance in observed mean total clicks as a function of three of the four hypothesized independent variables, $F (4, 160) = 74.22$, $p < .0001$, adjusted $R^2 = .574$. The fourth hypothesized independent variable, number of competing links nested under correct headings, was not significant. All three independent variables are statistically significant—number of competing headings, whether or not the only correct link was unfamiliar, and whether or not the only correct link as a weak-scent link—and the intercept is also significant. We were also able to show, with a secondary analysis, that the number of competing links nested under competing headings explained a higher per-

---

[5]The final step in the ACWW interface enables the analyst to choose to run multiple analyses on the selected goals and web pages, including running analyses to be run in two or more different semantic spaces, and specifying a unique set of parameters for elaborating the headings and links for different analysis run on a particular semantic space.

centage of the variance than the alternate variable, number of competing headings.

The minimum solution path for all 164 tasks was a single click, but the statistically significant intercept of 2.199 reveals that even the non-problem tasks took an average of over two clicks to complete. The intercept and un-weighted regression coefficients give us a working formula for predicting the mean total clicks:

Mean total clicks = 2.199
+ 1.656 if the correct link is unfamiliar
+ 1.464 if the correct link has weak-scent
+ 0.754 times the number of competing links nested under competing headings.

The next step after completing the multiple regression analysis was to apply the multiple regression formula to predict the mean total clicks for each of the 164 tasks in the dataset. Applying this formula to the Find Hmong task, for example, we predict 9.089 clicks for the unrepaired condition and 2.199 for the repaired condition, very close to the observed results of 9.0 for the unrepaired and 2.1 for the repaired condition. Figure 18.2 displays the accuracy of the predictions by comparing predicted and observed mean total clicks for all 164 tasks. The right half of Figure 18.2 displays nearly identical values of predicted and observed mean total clicks for the 82 unrepaired tasks in the 164-task dataset and for the 82 repaired tasks. To

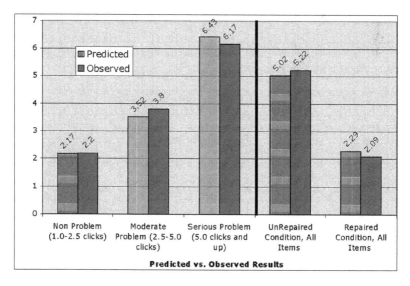

Figure 18.2.   Comparison of observed and predicated scores for 164-item dataset.

test for consistency of the formula across increasing levels of task difficulty, the left half of Figure 18.2 first pooled the unrepaired and repaired tasks into a single set and then regrouped the 164 items into three groups: (a) one group of 83 *non-problem* tasks, mostly repaired tasks, that the CWW formula predicted people could do in fewer than 2.5 mean total clicks; (b) a second group of 35 *moderate problem* tasks, mostly unrepaired tasks, that the CWW formula predicted people would do in between 2.5 and 5.0 clicks; and (c) a third group of 46 *serious problem* tasks, all unrepaired tasks, that CWW predicted would take people 5.0 or more clicks. For all three groups, the predicted and observed mean total clicks are very close in value.

To test whether these thresholds—2.5 clicks and 5.0 clicks—were reasonable for distinguishing non-problems from moderate problems and moderate problems from serious problems, we found 100 tasks from the 164-item dataset for which we have recorded the percentages of experimental participants who could not complete the task within the allotted time (usually 130 seconds). A simple regression of the percentages of task failure per task on observed mean total clicks for the same task yields a correlation of .93, F $(1, 98) = 651.78, p < .0001$, adjusted $R^2 = .87$. Using the regression formula derived from the analysis—percent task failure = (.082 times observed mean total clicks – .154)* 100—we estimated a task failure rate of 5% at 2.5 mean total clicks (operationally defined as the threshold between non-problem and problem items), 26% at 5.0 mean total clicks (operationally defined as the threshold between moderate and severe problems), 51% at 8.0 mean total clicks, and 76% at 11.0 mean total clicks. It is a matter of judgment whether it is a "serious" problem when the task failure rate exceeds 25%, but in our judgment 25% task failure is an unacceptable failure rate, particularly considering that this is the failure rate for college-educated users, and we can assume that task failure rates will be higher for people with more modest levels of general reading knowledge.

Cross-Validation of Multiple Regression Model

It is crucial to replicate a multiple regression model on a completely new set of tasks, so we gathered new data that addressed the same four criteria (see earlier) but with two significant changes. Instead of comparing the same tasks on repaired and unrepaired web pages, as specified by the first criterion, we selected 28 tasks that CWW predicted to have usability problems and 36 tasks predicted to cause no problems. The 64 tasks were all done on a simulation of the online encyclopedia Web site with 93 links nested under nine categories, and for each task only one of the 93 links was correct. Thus, the comparison between problems and non-problems controlled for number of correct links, a variable that was not controlled in the 164-task dataset, where problem tasks generally had just one correct link but repaired tasks usually had two or more correct links.

Although the dataset is smaller (64 tasks instead of 164 tasks), the multiple regression analysis fully replicated the results of the original multiple regression analysis (as reported in Blackmon et al., 2005). The same three independent variables and intercept were all highly significant, the competing links under competing headings was still superior to the competing headings variable, and the competing links under correct heading variable was still nonsignificant. For the 64-task dataset, the multiple regression model explained 50% of the variance, F (3, 60) = 22.042, $p < .0001$, adjusted $R^2 = .50$. Table 18.2 compares the coefficients from the two multiple regression analyses, the original and cross-validation studies, putting the cross-validation study values in parentheses.

Hits Versus False Alarms

Table 18.2 shows a close alignment between the original and cross-validation study, and Figure 18.2 shows little discrepancy between predicted and observed mean total clicks. Nevertheless, to meet the standards advocated by Gray and Salzman (1998a, 1998b), we must also report the rates of hits versus false alarms for tasks that CWW predicts to have usability problems.

At the time the experiments were performed, all 82 unrepaired tasks from the 164-task dataset had been classified as usability problems by then-defined criteria, but by current refined CWW procedures, only 75 of the 82 tasks in the 164-task dataset are predicted to have usability problems (i.e., predicted to take 2.5 or more clicks to complete). The overall hit rate for these 75 tasks in the unrepaired condition is 69/75 (92%), and the false alarm rate was 6/75 (8%). In other words, 92% of the tasks predicted to require 2.5 mean total clicks or more actually did require 2.5 clicks or more,

TABLE 18.2
Multiple Regression of Actual Mean Total Clicks on Three Independent
Variables for Two Datasets: 164-Task Original Dataset Versus 64-Task
Cross-Validation Dataset Shown in Parentheses

Independent Variable	Unweighted Coefficient	Standard Error	Standard Coefficient	t-Value	p-Value
Intercept	2.199	.157	2.199	14.010	< .0001
	(2.481)	(.257)	(2.481)	(9.656)	(< .0001)
Number of competing links under competing headings	.754	.070	.578	10.774	< .0001
	(0.551)	(.123)	(.423)	(4.492)	(< .0001)
Unfamiliar correct link	1.656	.324	.264	5.104	< .0001
	(2.040)	(.571)	(.330)	(3.573)	(.0007)
Weak scent correct link	1.464	.306	.254	4.785	< .0001
	(1.484)	(.491)	(.280)	(3.021)	(.0037)

and the remaining 8% actually required fewer than 2.5 clicks. Because usability experts prioritize identifying and repairing the most serious usability problems, we narrowed our focus to the subset of 46 tasks predicted to pose serious problems (i.e., those problems that CWW predicted would take 5.0 or more mean total clicks), finding a hit rate of 46/46 (100%) for serious problems (meaning that experimental participants took at least 2.5 clicks to complete all of these tasks).

For the cross-validation study (64-task dataset), the hit rate was 26/29 (90%), and the false alarm rate was 3/29 (10%). For the subset of 17 serious problems (predicted mean clicks 5.0 or higher), the hit rate was 15/17 (88%).

Correct Rejections Versus Misses

The rates for correct rejections versus misses come only from cross-validation study data, because the cross-validation study was the only CWW experiment done to date that tested tasks predicted to be non-problems. For the 35 tasks predicted to be non-problem items, the correct rejection rate was 24/35 (69%), and the rate of misses (observed mean clicks equal to or higher than 2.5) was 11/35 (31%). Nevertheless, most of the misses posed only minor problems, and the remaining 4/35 (11%) of the predicted non-problems had observed mean clicks greater than 3.5 but fewer than 5.0. Thus, none of the misses were observed to pose serious problems.

Success Rates for Repairs

Another important question concerns the success rate for CWW-guided repairs of the usability problems that CWW identifies (Blackmon et al., 2003, 2005), a question that can only be answered by data from the original 164-task dataset that compared tasks done on repaired and unrepaired web page conditions.

A rigorous standard for defining a "successful repair" for a given task is to require statistically significant superiority in performance for the task done on a repaired web page compared to the same task done on an unrepaired web page. We can then tally the number of tasks that meet this rigorous standard and divide it by the total number of tasks. Out of the 82 unrepaired tasks in the original dataset, 75 are still predicted to be problems by current CWW criteria, and the overall success rate for repairs for these 75 problems is 83% (62/75). Because usability experts are often under time constraints that force them to prioritize identifying and repairing the most serious problems, it is important to narrow our attention to the 46 problems predicted to be serious problems. As already mentioned, there was a 100% hit rate for these 46 tasks, and the success rate for repairing the usability problems for these tasks was 93% (43/46).

CWW-Guided Methods of Repair

We completed one study comparing the performance of rigorous but time-consuming methods of repairing usability problems with the performance of a discount repair method, finding that the discount method delivers most of the performance gains with less investment of time (Blackmon et al., 2003). That study looked only at performance gains on the repaired web page, ignoring consequences for the Web site. For each user goal that encounters usability problems on a given web page, the discount method of repair Web site generally activates two or more links and the web developer must consequently continue these paths down through the hierarchy until they reach the target web page. Thus, the discount method quickly solves the usability problem on one web page, but there is a trade-off for the Web site as a whole: Each subordinate page must then be repaired to ensure that users can ultimately get to the target web page. The repairs to subordinate web pages are particularly costly if the Web site has a deep hierarchy. If multiple links are activated on these subordinate pages, then the effects branch out to require repairs on many web pages at many levels of the Web site.

In contrast, the more rigorous method of repair changes minimizes the need for activating multiple links by first improving the quality of the link and heading labels. Recently, Miller and Remington (2004) showed that improving "link quality" can make a deeply hierarchical site architecture function well. To improve "link quality," the rigorous CWW repair method uses LSA similarity and familiarity measures. One goal is to improve the coherence within each spatially distinct group of links, aiming for (a) high similarity between each pair of links within a group, (b) high similarity between the heading for the group and each link in the group, and (c) sufficient semantic distance between each pair of groups to minimize competing headings problems.

The rigorous CWW repair method also repairs unfamiliar problems by inserting or substituting familiar words. For example, the link label "Paleontology" has low word frequency and a short-term vector length, and it can be repaired by changing the link label to "Paleontology and Fossils" or "Fossils of Extinct Species," or "Fossils and Prehistoric Species." In the empirical study of repairs (Blackmon et al., 2003), changing the link label produced performance gains in some cases, but there is no quick and easy way to compensate for users' low background knowledge of a particular topic.

HOW LSA ENABLES CWW TO SCALE UP TO EVALUATING LARGE WEB SITES

Earlier UEMs had a serious problem of scale. Because it is very time consuming to perform these UEMs, they do not scale to the evaluation of large applications or Web sites. In contrast, the LSA component of CWW makes it feasible for CWW to scale up to the evaluation of large Web sites. Kitajima, Kariya, Takagi, and Zhang (2005) tested this by writing computer programs to perform CWW for finding all the encyclopedia articles in a particular on-line encyclopedia, an encyclopedia with over 40,000 content pages. Blackmon (2003) subsequently built an experimental Web site to test 20 tasks that the automated usability analysis had predicted to be serious competing headings problems and 20 tasks predicted to be unfamiliar problems. All 40 unrepaired tasks proved to be serious or moderate usability problems when tested in the lab, producing a 100% hit rate for the sample of 40 tasks produced by the CWW of the large-scale Web site.

LSA is essential for automated CWW analyses of large Web sites. Our development of automatable rules for identifying usability problems, the multiple regression analysis of the 164-item dataset, and its cross-validation with an independent 64-task dataset, took a giant leap toward full automation of CWW. ACWW, the new, more automated web-based interface for doing CWW (http://www.autocww.colorado.edu/~brownr/ACWW.php) built by Brown (2005) currently requires the analyst to manually input a set of one or more user goals and a set of one or more web pages. ACWW then automatically identifies CWW usability problems (unfamiliar correct link, weak-scent correct link, and number of competing links nested under competing headings) for each goal on each web page. Then ACWW computes predicted mean total clicks for each goal on each web page, enabling the analyst to identify web pages that must be repaired for particular user goals/tasks. The modular design of ACWW makes it easy to more fully automate or refine each individual module independently. Thus, it would be possible to replace the current manual input of web pages with a more automated module that takes a web page(s) as input or even a set of URLs. It would also be possible to more fully automate the output, so that the analyst receives summary statistics for a web page or a Web site.

WRITERS' TOOL FOR IMPROVING WEB PAGE READABILITY

In order to design usable Web sites, designers must create content articles well matched to users' background knowledge and level of reading comprehension, and design Web sites that enable users to navigate by pure forward search and find the content easily. One of us (Mandalia, 2004) has developed a readability evaluation tool for developing content, and it can actually support both of the aforementioned design goals.

The readability evaluation tool affords a theory-based approach to content development by assisting the writer in monitoring and controlling three characteristics of expository text that have proven effects on comprehension and learning: percentage of low-frequency words, text coherence, and elaboration of key concepts. When using the tool to design content for optimal learning, published research on text comprehension and learning from text indicated that it would be best for writers to target about 5% low-frequency words, maintain high sentence-to-sentence coherence, and select familiar words and ideas to elaborate the key concept in a paragraph or section of text (the key concept is the concept, principle, process, or main idea that a writer is attempting to communicate in a passage).

When applying the tool to design or repair the navigation system—meaning the link and heading texts and groupings of links—the tool makes it easy for the designer to eliminate low-frequency words in link and heading texts, monitor coherence between pairs of links grouped together under a heading, and evaluate the heading text to make sure that it effectively expresses the key concept or relationship that unites a group of links.

Following user-centered design practices, Mandalia (2004) interviewed science and medical writers who have advanced degrees and who write science or medical articles intended for younger or less knowledgeable audiences (elementary, middle, and high school readers). Mandalia discovered that it was necessary to design the tool as an add-in to Microsoft Word to ensure seamless integration with the writers' workflow while revising texts for readability.

The multifunctional readability evaluation tool, like CWW, employs LSA measures of similarity and familiarity and represents the target user by a particular LSA semantic space. The first step in using the tool is to select the particular LSA semantic space that best represents the background knowledge of the target audience: 3rd-, 6th-, 9th-, 12th-grade, or first-year-college general reading knowledge. One function of the tool is to identify and highlight (in red font) all the low-frequency words in a text for a particular reading level and then to support the writer in attaining the target percentage of low-frequency words in the text. A second function supports monitoring and revision of the text to improve coherence, and a third function supports revision that optimally elaborates the key concepts the writer intends to communicate.

The readability evaluation tool was evaluated by doing user testing with the same science writers interviewed prior to building the tool. The user testing revealed that, apart from minor usability issues, the writers liked the overall organization and functionality of the tool. The psychological validity of the tool was empirically verified by a large experiment ($n = 168$) that found significantly higher learning gains for texts that the science writers had revised with the tool compared to texts revised without the tool. The empirical evaluation also provided evidence that the percentage of low-frequency words, text coherence, and key concepts elaboration do, indeed, influence text comprehension and learning gains, and the tool assists writers in better achieving these characteristics when producing content articles.

To verify these initial findings, it is necessary to run more experiments and replicate the results of the first experiment with more texts and with a broader sample of writers, and it is also necessary to test the tool with designers of navigation systems. The current version of the readability evaluation tool, the manual for using the tool, and papers about the user-centered design and the experiment are available for download on our research Web site.[6]

CONCLUSIONS

LSA has proved invaluable for CWW and for the readability evaluation tool, as it has for the practical applications and research reported in other chapters in this volume. LSA has enabled CWW to overcome all three of the crucial limitations of other UEMs. First, LSA provides reliable, objective ratings of similarity and familiarity that CWW substitutes for unreliable, subjective human judgments of similarity and familiarity. Second, CWW predictions, guided by the CoLiDeS cognitive model, have used LSA functionality to produce predictions of human navigation with high psychological validity. Finally, LSA enables us to solve the problem of scale, making it possible to build an automated version of CWW that can be applied to very large Web sites with 40,000 pages or more.

In addition to overcoming the limitations of other UEMs, each distinct LSA semantic space offers the means for simulating the influence of background knowledge on reading comprehension for a particular population of users. The versatility of LSA is its ability to simulate a multitude of user groups with high psychological validity by constructing a semantic space for each and every possible user group. Accordingly, an important goal for the immediate future is to extend the CWW research to other user groups and semantic spaces. Empirical evidence to date (Blackmon et al., 2002, 2003, 2005) has tested CWW predictions of heading and link selection only for college-educated users, using the college-level LSA semantic space. A driving motivation for the CWW research has been our hypothesis that we can successfully extend the CWW to evaluating Web sites for user groups who speak any language at any level of general reading knowledge. The first step toward verifying that hypothesis will be to make predictions from the third-grade semantic space with groups of experimental participants who have third-grade general reading knowledge.

---

[6]Download the readability evaluation tool, manual, and papers on the work at http://www.autocww.colorado.edu/~blackmon/Readability/ReadabilityTool.html

REFERENCES

Blackmon, M. H. (2003). [Test of 40 CWW predictions from automated CWW analysis over 40,000 webpages of the complete Encarta.msn.com website: Web-based experiment available at http://autocww.coloado.edu/~blackmon/Expt030303Home.html]. Unpublished raw data.

Blackmon, M. H. (2004). Cognitive Walkthrough. In W. S. Bainbridge (Ed.), *Encyclopedia of human-computer interaction* (2 vols.). Great Barrington, MA: Berkshire Publishing.

Blackmon, M. H., Kitajima, M., & Polson, P. G. (2003). Repairing usability problems identified by the Cognitive Walkthrough for the Web. *CHI Letters, 5: Proceedings of CHI 2003*, 497–504.

Blackmon, M.H., Kitajima, M., & Polson, P. G. (2005). Tool for accurately predicting website navigation problems, non-problems, problem severity, and effectiveness of repairs. *CHI Letters, 7: Proceedings of CHI 2005*, 31–41.

Blackmon, M. H., Polson, P. G., Kitajima, M., & Lewis, C. (2002). Cognitive Walkthrough for the Web. *CHI Letters, 4: Proceedings of CHI 2002*, 463–470.

Brown, R. (2005). *ACWW: Adding automation to the Cognitive Walkthrough for the Web (CWW)*. Unpublished Master's thesis, University of North Florida.

Chi, E. H., Pirolli, P., Chen, K., & Pitkow, J. (2001). Using information scent to model user information needs and actions and the Web. *CHI Letters, 3: Proceedings of CHI 2001*, 490–497.

Chi, E. H., Rosien, A., Supattanasiri, G., Williams, A., Royer, C., Chow, C., Robles, E., Dalal, B., Chen, J., & Cousins, S. (2003). The Bloodhound Project: Automating discovery of web usability issues using the InfoScent™ Simulator. *CHI Letters, 5: Proceedings of CHI 2003*, 505–512.

Furnas, G. W. (1997). Effective view navigation. *Proceedings of the SIGCHI Conference on Human Factors in Computing Systems*, 367–374.

Gray, W. D., & Salzman, M. C. (1998a). Damaged merchandise? A review of experiments that compare usability evaluation methods. *Human–Computer Interaction, 13*, 203–261.

Gray, W. D., & Salzman, M. C. (1998b). Repairing damaged merchandise: A rejoinder. *Human–Computer Interaction, 13*, 325–335.

Hertzum, M., & Jacobsen, N. E. (2003). The evaluator effect: A chilling fact about usability evaluation methods. *International Journal of Human–Computer Interaction, 15*(1), 183–204.

Kintsch, W. (1998). *Comprehension: A paradigm for cognition*. Cambridge, England: Cambridge University Press.

Kitajima, M., Blackmon, M. H., & Polson, P. G. (2000). A comprehension-based model of Web navigation and its application to Web usability analysis. In S. McDonald, Y. Waern, & G. Cockton (Eds.), *People and computers XIV—usability or else!* (pp. 357–373). New York: Springer.

Kitajima, M., Blackmon, M. H., & Polson, P. G. (2005). Cognitive architecture for website design and usability evaluation: Comprehension and information scent in performing by exploration. Invited session on Cognitive Architectures in HCI. *HCI-International 2005 Conference Proceedings* [CD-ROM].

Kitajima, M., Kariya, N., Takagi, H., & Zhang, Y. (2005). Evaluation of website usability using Markov chains and latent semantic analysis. *IEICE Transactions Online, Vol. E88-B*, 1467–1475.

Kitajima, M. & Polson, P. G. (1997). A comprehension-based model of exploration. *Human–Computer Interaction, 12*, 345–389.

Mandalia, D. R. (2004). *User-centered design of a content analysis tool for domain experts.* Unpublished master's thesis, University of Colorado, Boulder.

Miller, C. S., & Remington, R. W. (2004). Modeling information navigation: Implications for information architecture. *Human–Computer Interaction, 19*, 225–271.

Pirolli, P. (2005). Rational analyses of information foraging on the Web. *Cognitive Science, 29*, 343–373.

Pirolli, P., & Card, S. K. (1999). Information foraging. *Psychological Review, 106*(4), 643–675.

Pirolli, P. L., & Fu, W. (2003). SNIF-ACT: A model of information foraging on the World Wide Web (9th International Conference on User Modeling, June 22–26, 2003, Johnstown, PA). *Lecture Notes in Artificial Intelligence, 2702*, 45–54.

Pirolli, P. (2005). Rational analyses of information foraging on the Web. *Cognitive Science, 29*, 343–373.

Pirolli, P., Fu, W-T, Chi, E., & Farahat, A. (2005). Information scent and web navigation: Theory, models and automated usability evaluation. Invited session on Cognitive Architectures in HCI. *HCI-International 2005 Conference Proceedings* [CD-ROM].

Rieman, J., Young, R. M., & Howes, A. (1996). A dual space model of iteratively deepening exploratory learning. *International Journal of Human–Computer Studies, 44*, 743–775.

Soto, R. (1999). Learning and performing by exploration: Label quality measured by latent semantic analysis. *CHI Letters, 1: Proceedings of CHI 1999*, 418–425.

Wharton, C., Rieman, J., Lewis, C., & Polson, P. (1994). The Cognitive Walkthrough method: A practitioner's guide. In J. Nielsen & R. L. Mack (Eds.), *Usability inspection methods* (pp. 105–140). New York: Wiley.

Zeno, S. M., Ivens, S. H., Millard, R. T., & Duvvuri, R. (1995). *The educator's word frequency guide.* Brewster, NY: Touchstone Applied Science Associates.

APPENDIX A

Classify It as a Competing Heading

Rule 1

If the heading is not a correct heading
And if the heading has a goal-heading cosine ≥ .8 times the goal-heading cosine of the correct heading or the goal-heading cosine of the correct heading that has the highest goal-heading cosine if there are two or more correct headings
And if the goal-heading cosine of the heading ≥ .10 (i.e., NOT weak-scent)
And if the highest goal-link cosine of links nested under the heading ≥ .20

Then classify it as a competing heading.

Rationale. Users' attention is pulled to headings that are stronger than the correct heading, but it is meaningless to speak of "stronger than" when the higher goal-heading cosine is a weak-scent heading "in the noise." Requiring the competing heading to have a goal-heading cosine ≥ .8 times the goal-heading cosine of the correct heading is consistent with the way we compute competing links (i.e., as links with goal-link cosines ≥ .8 times the goal-link cosine of the correct heading).

Rule 2

If the heading is not a correct heading
And if the highest goal-link cosine for any link nested under that heading ≥ .30 (i.e., strong-scent link)
Then classify it as a competing heading.

Rationale. Sometimes users are drawn to a particular heading by a strong information scent for a specific link(s) nested under the heading. Even if the strong-scent link does not work, the user will then search for other links similar to the strong-scent link under the same heading. For example, a person might first think "Chemistry" and then look for the heading where they would find the "Chemistry" link, that is, "Physical Science & Technology." Even if "Chemistry" turns out to not work, the user will think, "I must be close" and continue to search for other links with sufficient scent under the same goal.

Classify It as a Competing Heading Competing Link

Rule 1

If the link is nested under a competing heading
And if the goal-link cosine of the link ≥ .8 times the highest goal-link cosine of all the links nested under the competing heading
And if the goal-link cosine of the link ≥ .10
And if the goal-link cosine of the link is ranked no lower than fourth place when the goal-link cosines of links under the same heading are ranked in descending order, *or if* the goal-link cosine ≥ .30 (i.e., a strong-scent link)
Then classify it as a competing heading competing link.

Rationale. If the user's attention has been drawn to a competing heading, the user is apt to click links under that heading in order of decreasing information scent and then give up after clicking several high scent links under that heading, or even all links that are not weak-scent.

Rule 2

If the link is nested under a competing heading
And if the goal-link cosine of the link $\geq$ .20
And if there is no more than one link under the same heading with a higher goal-link cosine
Then classify it as a competing heading competing link.

Rationale. There are subregions where the highest-ranking link has such strong information scent that no other links under the same heading are $\geq$ .8 times the highest-ranking link. Nevertheless, users who focus on a heading and click the link with the highest goal-link cosine in that subregion, are likely to click at least one more link in that same subregion if they see one with fairly strong information scent (operationally defined as a goal-link cosine $\geq$ .20).

Classify It as a Correct Heading Competing Link

If the link is nested under a correct heading
And if the goal-link cosine of the link $\geq$ .8 times the goal-link cosine of the correct link
And if the goal-link cosine of the link $\geq$ .10
And if the goal-link cosine of the link is ranked no lower than fourth place when the goal-link cosines of links under the same heading are ranked in descending order, *or if* the goal-link cosine $\geq$ .30 (i.e., a strong-scent link)
Then classify it as a correct heading competing link.

Rationale. If the user's attention has been drawn to the correct heading, the user is apt to click links under that heading in order of decreasing information scent and then give up after clicking several high scent links under that heading, or even all links that are not weak-scent.

Classify It as a Weak-Scent Correct Link

If the link has a goal-link cosine < .10
And if the link is a correct link
And if there are no correct links with a goal-link cosine $\geq$ .10
Then classify it as a weak-scent correct link.

Rationale. A weak-scent link refers to the situation when a correct link is not semantically similar to the user goal and there are no other correct links that have moderate or strong scent. Weak-scent on the correct link makes the link an unlikely target of action, whether or not there is competition from other, higher scent links.

Classify It as an Unfamiliar Correct Link

If the text of a correct link is unfamiliar (i.e., *if* it has only one word and the word has a term vector length ≤ .55 *or if* the text of a correct link contains two or more words with a term vector length < .80)
And if there are no correct links that are not unfamiliar
Then classify it as an unfamiliar correct link

Rationale. Empirical evidence indicates that the term vector length is an approximate index of the amount of background knowledge that typical users have about a topic, and that unfamiliar problems happen when the term vector is low and typical users know little about the topic. The unfamiliarity partially or completely reduces the information scent, even in cases where the goal-link cosine is high. When some or all of the words in the link labels are low-frequency words, users may not even comprehend the meaning of the link, but these cases seem to be captured by short-term vector length without complicating the situation by examining word frequency.

APPENDIX B

Step 1: Select or Build and Select a Semantic Space

The first step in the CWW method is to select the most appropriate semantic space to represent a particular user group. Because the laboratory studies we have done to date all use college-educated experimental participants, we have consistently selected the semantic space for college-level general reading knowledge of American English. For a sixth-grade class in an American public school we would use the sixth-grade semantic space if about 50% of the students were proficient or above on the state achievement test for reading. Among both college-educated and sixth-grade groups, there are marked individual differences in reading ability and background knowledge, but in laboratory studies it is adequate to ignore these individual differences and use a single semantic space for the entire group.

If an appropriate semantic space does not exist already, it is possible to collect a scientifically sampled corpus of the documents (emulating Zeno et al., 1995) that are likely to have been read by a given user population. Using that corpus, the analyst can build a psychologically valid representation of the population. LSA semantic spaces can thus be built to provide a psychologically valid representation of virtually any user population with any level of background knowledge in any language or bilingual competence in two languages.

Step 2: Collect Set of User Goals

The next step is to collect a set of user goals to represent what that user group is likely to want to accomplish on the Web site under analysis. Ideally, user goals would be elicited by interviewing large samples of target users, and each user goal text would be a 100- to 200-word narrative description of what a particular user is looking for in a Web site.

As experimenters, we have not had the resources to collect user goals directly from users. In addition, it is useful to get data from 20 or more different persons completing the same assigned task. To perform a controlled laboratory test of the usability of the navigation system on an informational Web site, such as an online encyclopedia, we make the realistic assumption that the content articles presented on the Web site are valuable to users, and that users will invest considerable effort to surmount usability problems in a Web site if the Web site presents content that they find valuable. That assumption allows us to create user goal statements by using a summary of the target web page that we ask experimental participants to find in the Web site (e.g., the content article in an online encyclopedia).

The summary must be short (100 to 200 words), because experimental participants have been given only 130 seconds to complete the task. The summary also must be extremely similar to the actual article so that experimental participants have an accurate representation of the actual content they are trying to find in the Web site. We currently use the Summary tool of Microsoft Word to produce a summary of the complete online encyclopedia article we ask experimental participants to find. Then we use the LSA One-to-Many Comparison to compute the cosine between the text of the summary and the text of the complete article in the actual online encyclopedia. To ensure that the summary is an accurate representation of the content article, we aim for very high semantic similarity (operationally defined as a minimum cosine greater than .76). For the sample of 82 goal statements used in the first multiple regression analysis reported in this chapter, the mean summary-article cosine was .91, ranging from .76 to 1.00.

Step 3: Parse the Web Page and Identify Link and Heading Texts

Step three simulates how the user will parse the web page and identifies all the individual subregions of the web page. For example, CWW identifies nine subregions for the simple matrix web page layout in Figure 18.1, one subregion for each of the nine heading texts and cluster of links nested under the heading (e.g., the "Sports, Hobbies, & Pets" has a cluster of four links). The texts submitted to LSA include the link texts, meaning the texts that label each and every link on the web page. Heading texts will also be included in the LSA analysis if the web page designer decided to group related links together in the content area, or in one or more navigation bars. In some cases, the grouping of links has no heading text, but in that case the analyst can add together the texts of all the links in the group to create a pseudo-heading text, ensuring that LSA creates a single document vector for the link grouping. In other cases the designer uses an actual heading text to label the group. For example, Figure 18.1 shows a content area subdivided into nine groupings of links, and each grouping is labeled with a heading text that enables the user to scan the web page looking for the correct heading.

Step 4: Identify the Unfamiliar Heading and Link Texts

Familiarity measures include (a) term vector length for web page link texts and heading texts as an estimate of users' background knowledge of a given topic, and (b) word frequency within the selected semantic space. Current parameters identify a link or heading as an unfamiliar topic if the term vector length is .55 or less for a single-word text or less than .80 for a link/heading label with two or more words. Low-frequency words are defined as having a frequency of 15 or fewer in the corpus for the selected semantic space. CWW-guided repairs include substitution of familiar words for low-frequency words, but at present only the term vector length is used to identify unfamiliar heading and link texts.

Step 5: Elaborate the Heading and Link Texts

CoLiDeS and CWW also set simultaneous constraints on similarity and familiarity by using the near neighbors LSA analysis to simulate the process of elaboration that occurs during comprehension of short heading and link texts on a web page. The underlying CoLiDeS assumption is that the terms most likely to be activated by reading a web page text are those that are highly similar to the text and are also high frequency, familiar terms, so current parameters for elaborating texts with near neighbors specify a minimum document-to-document cosine of .50 and a minimum word frequency of 50. Elaborating link texts adds the near neighbors to the original, unelaborated link text that appears on the web page. The Elaborate Links function at http://www.autocww.colorado.edu can apply near neighbors analysis for up to about 50 link/heading texts input in a single batch with blank lines separating them.

Elaborating heading texts is more complicated than elaborating links. For example, under the heading "Life Science," the heading text expands to the string of words "Life Science science sciences biology scientific geology physics life biologist physicists," the link label "Birds" expands to the elaborated link label "Birds, birds bird feathers beak wings eagle nest nests fly wing geese hawk flew pigeons feather eagles owls fluttered flying," and the link label "Medicine" expands to "Medicine, medicine medicines doctor doctors prescription sick medical clinic." To create the full elaboration for the heading text for "Life Science" CWW combines the elaboration of the words "life science" with the elaborated link texts for all 14 links nested under Life Science, resulting in a 268-word text to represent the semantic meaning of "Life Science" for college-level users confronting the web page shown in Figure 18.1.

Step 6: Use LSA to Compute Goal-Link and Goal-Heading Cosines

The next step applies the LSA one-to-many analysis to compare the goal statement with the elaborated headings and links, set to produce document-to-document cosines. Thus, cosines are based on comparing a 100- to 200-word goal statement with the elaborated versions of each link and heading text, not just the link and heading texts printed on the web page.

We then separate the results into a group of heading-goal cosines and a group of link-goal cosines, sorting each group by decreasing cosine value. Next, we examine the sorted results and identify and mark the correct heading(s) and link(s), the ones that actually lead to accomplishing the goal in the actual online Web site being simulated.

Step 7: Apply Automatable Rules to Identify Usability Problems

The sixth step is to apply an automatable set of rules (see appendix A) for distinguishing unfamiliar correct links, weak-scent correct links, competing links nested under competing headings, and competing links nested under correct headings.

Step 8: Follow CWW Guidelines for Repairing Problems

Next we examine the results and see how to repair the problems. When fully repaired, the CoLiDeS model leads us to expect users to be able to accomplish the goal on the repaired page with pure forward search, following the high information scent on any of the competing heading and competing links. CWW does not yet have a set of automatable rules for repairing usability problems, but the general processes of repair are covered in Blackmon, Kitajima, and Polson (2003) and in the text of this chapter.

Step 9: Use CWW Formula to Predict Mean Total Clicks

At the final step, we apply a newly developed CWW formula for predicting the mean total clicks under both the repaired and unrepaired condition. The current formula is derived from a compilation of 228 tasks, pooling both the 164-task dataset and 64-task cross-validation study:

> Predicted mean total clicks required to find the item on a Web site = 2.292
> + 1.757 if there is an unfamiliar correct link
> + 1.516 if there is a weak-scent correct link
> + 0.655 times the number of competing links nested under competing headings

V

Extensions to LSA

19

Optimizing LSA Measures of Cohesion

Danielle S. McNamara
Zhiqiang Cai
Max M. Louwerse
University of Memphis

One important application of LSA has been to measure cohesion in text and to predict the effects of cohesion on comprehension (see Foltz, chap. 9 in this volume; Foltz, W. Kintsch, & Landauer, 1998; Louwerse, 2004; Shapiro & McNamara, 2000). We use the term *cohesion* to refer to the elements or cues in the text, and *coherence* to refer to how these cues are used in the construction of a mental representation (Graesser, McNamara, & Louwerse, 2003; Louwerse, 2002; Louwerse & Graesser, 2005). Many studies have shown how cohesive cues facilitate the coherence of readers' comprehension, as evidenced by measures such as summarization, recall, question answering, and keyword sorting (Britton & Gulgoz, 1991; Gernsbacher, 1990; Zwaan & Radvansky, 1998). For example, referential cohesion, or argument overlap, between two sentences can help the reader to make links between the sentences and better understand the relationship between them. Cohesion can arise from a variety of sources, including explicit argument overlap and causal relationships, and can operate between sentences, groups of sentences, paragraphs, and chapters. Cohesion between sentences is generally identified as local cohesion, whereas cohesion between larger chunks of texts is generally identified as global cohesion (Givón, 1995; W. Kintsch, 1995; Louwerse, 2005). A cohesion gap in a text forces the reader to make inferences to fill in the gaps, which if successful can improve comprehension (McNamara, 2001; McNamara & W. Kintsch, 1996; McNamara, E. Kintsch, Songer, & W. Kintsch, 1996). However, the reader often lacks either the knowledge or skill to generate the inferences, resulting in poor comprehension of the text. Thus, for the most part, cohesion facilitates comprehension and coherence.

Advances in computational linguistics allow us to measure cohesion automatically. There are a number of reasons why this is beneficial. First, such computational methods, when compared to psychological data, may shed light on some of the components involved in discourse processing. Second, such computational methods are useful in a variety of computational linguistic applications, including intelligent systems, summarization techniques, text generation, speech recognition, and question answering systems. Recently, the notion of cohesion facilitating coherence has led to the development of a computational tool, called Coh-Metrix. This tool is intended to augment conventional readability formulas with computational measures of text difficulty. Coh-Metrix analyzes texts on over 200 types of cohesion relations and measures of language, text, and readability (Graesser, McNamara, Louwerse, & Cai, 2004; Louwerse, McCarthy, McNamara, & Graesser, 2004; McNamara, Louwerse, & Graesser, 2002). The modules of Coh-Metrix use lexicons, part-of-speech classifiers, syntactic parsers, templates, corpora, latent semantic analysis (LSA), and other components that are widely used in computational linguistics. For example, the MRC database (Coltheart, 1981) is used for psycholinguistic information; WordNet (G. A. Miller, Beckwith, Fellbaum, Gross, & K. Miller, 1990) for hypernymy and hyponymy relations; LSA (Landauer & Dumais, 1997) for the semantic similarities between words, sentences, and paragraphs; and the ApplePie parser (Sekine & Grishman, 1995) and the Brill (1995) part-of-speech tagger for a variety of syntactic categories. Graesser et al. (2004) provide an extensive overview of the various indices. One of the goals in the Coh-Metrix project is to compare a variety of indices and determine which ones best account for cohesion and coherence.

One measure of cohesion used in Coh-Metrix is LSA. Although LSA has generally been successful in measuring cohesion (Foltz, chap. 9 in this volume; Foltz, W. Kintsch, & Landauer, 1998; Shapiro & McNamara, 2000), the question can be posed as to whether modifications of existing LSA algorithms could enhance the performance of LSA and thereby of Coh-Metrix. This question becomes particularly important when we consider that LSA may be more appropriate for comparing larger chunks of text or global levels of discourse than for smaller amounts of text or local levels of cohesion (Landauer & Dumais, 1997).

This chapter examines the effects of varying two factors in LSA. The first factor is term weighting. LSA provides a vector representation for each word (or *term*) in a space and provides a similarity measure between any two words in the space using the cosine between the vectors. Linear combinations of word vectors are used to form vector representations of texts. The coefficients in the linear combination can be selected to reflect certain biases to some words that dominate the meaning of the text. For example, coefficients can be used to either emphasize or de-emphasize the effects of frequent words on the vectors. In this chapter, we manipulate those coefficients to vary the degree to which frequent or rare words are emphasized within the linear combination of vector representations.

The second factor is the level of strictness for similarity between words. When two text chunks are compared, the cosine between two text chunk vectors can be expressed by the number of occurrences of words in each text chunk, the weights in the linear combination, and the word similarities. Usually, LSA takes into account all word similarities, remote or close, weak or strong. In that case, the definition of similarity is relatively loose. However, we can set a threshold for the cosine values such that small values, or weak similarities, are eliminated. As such, the definition of similarity is more "strict." This chapter considers three thresholds for word similarity that result in loose, medium, or strict similarities.

We investigate the effects of term weighting and similarity strictness selection on how well different cohesion manipulations are detected. In Experiment 1, cohesion, or relatedness, is varied between sentences in narrative text by pairing each of 16 sentences with a paraphrase of the sentence, other sentences from within the same text, and sentences from a different text. In Experiment 2, we use the expository texts from McNamara et al.(1996), in which cohesion was manipulated at both local and global levels to produce four levels of text cohesion. The next section describes in greater detail the modifications made to the LSA algorithm.

LSA MODIFICATIONS: TERM WEIGHTING AND SIMILARITY STRICTNESS

An LSA space is a set of vector representations for terms and documents contained in a given corpus. An LSA space is determined by the corpus and several other parameters, such as the number of dimensions, the local and global weighting, and the minimum occurrence of a term. The LSA space we use in this study is generated from the corpus provided by the Touchstone Applied Science Association (TASA). The term-document matrix was weighted by "log-entropy" before singular value decomposition (SVD) was applied (with 326 dimensions). For any two text chunks, T_1 and T_2, the similarity is computed as the cosine of the vector representations of the chunks, following Equation 19.1:

$$sim(T_1, T_2) = \frac{(\sum_{i=1}^{n} a_i v_i)(\sum_{i=1}^{n} b_i v_i)^T}{\left\| \sum_{i=1}^{n} a_i v_i \right\| \left\| \sum_{i=1}^{n} b_i v_i \right\|} \qquad \textbf{19.1}$$

where n is the number of terms in the space; v_i is the vector representation of term i; a_i is the number of times term i appeared in the text chunk T_1; and b_i is the number of times term i appeared in the text chunk T_2. Equation 19.1 will be referred to in this study as "LSA similarity."

A text chunk (sentence, paragraph, etc.) is represented by a linear combination of the vectors corresponding to the words appearing in the text chunk. In Equation 19.1, the text chunk representation is a simple summation of the word vectors, that is, the coefficients are all set to 1 in the linear combination. For convenience of further discussion, consider a sentence from the famous Czar story that will be used in Experiment 1: "As they were being dragged off, they cried for help." There are 10 words in this sentence. Denote the vector for each word by $v_i (i = 1, 2, \ldots, 10)$. In Equation 19.2, the sentence vector $\mathbf{v}$ is the summation of the 10 vectors:

$$\mathbf{v} = \mathbf{v}_1 + \mathbf{v}_2 + \ldots + \mathbf{v}_{10}. \qquad \textbf{19.2}$$

The question can be raised concerning whether each word equally contributes to the overall meaning of this sentence. In other words, are these 10 words equally important in this vector representation when the vector is used to compare the meaning with other sentences?

To answer this question, we need to begin by measuring the contribution of each word in the vector construction. Vector length is a good measure for such a contribution. It would seem that the words with larger vector lengths would have more influence on the similarity score when the sentence vector is used in comparison. The LSA vectors are very different in length, ranging from 0 to 1. In our example sentence, the word "dragged" has a very small vector length, .04, whereas the word "help" has a large length, .56 (see Table 19.1). To see the effect of the vector length in meaning construction, we can remove one word, say "dragged" from the sentence, and then compare this reduced sentence to the original sentence. Because the vector length of "dragged" is so small, the difference that this one word makes on the overall meaning is expected to be small. A simple test confirms this expectation: The LSA cosine of the original sentence to the modified sentence with all words except "dragged" was .999. However, when the word "help" was removed, the change was much larger, with the LSA value dropping to .872. We computed such changes for every word in this sentence and found that the overall correlation of the LSA values to the vector lengths was −.94 ($n = 9$), $p < .01$.

This simple test shows that the meaning of a text chunk is dominated by the words with larger vector length. The question now needs to be raised concerning which words have larger vector lengths. Recall that we applied log-entropy weights to the terms in the term-document matrix before SVD was applied. The prediction can therefore be made that words with larger entropy weights have larger vector lengths. This, however, is not true: For the words in the previous example sentence, the correlation between the vector lengths and the entropy weights (α_i) is −.19. This shows that the words that were emphasized in the term-document matrix are not necessarily emphasized in the text chunk vector construction.

Here we examine the impact of three term weighting schemes for the text chunk meaning construction: normalized scheme, rare words dominated (RWD) scheme, and frequent words dominated (FWD) scheme. In the normalized scheme, each vector is normalized to unit length, thereby placing equal bias to all words in a sentence. RWD scheme can be formed by applying entropy weights to the normalized vectors. Therefore, small weights are assigned to familiar words and large weights are assigned to rare words. Conversely, in the FWD scheme, a term i in the space is assigned a weight ($1 - \alpha_i$) to emphasize frequent words. The similarity between two text chunks with different schemes is computed by Equation 19.3.

TABLE 19.1
LSA Cosines Between Original and Word-Reduced Sentence, the Length of the Word Vectors, and the Entropy α_i Weights(α_i) for the Sentence "As They Were Being Dragged Off, They Cried For Help"

	LSA	*Length*	α_i
as	.996	.10	.04
they	.969	.32	.07
were	.958	.34	.09
being	.962	.31	.20
dragged	.999	.04	.51
off	.953	.35	.19
cried	.987	.19	.35
for	.998	.08	.03
help	.872	.56	.20

$$sim(T_1, T_2) = \frac{(\sum_{i=1}^{n} a_i w_i \frac{v}{\|v_i\|})(\sum_{i=1}^{n} b_i w_i \frac{v}{\|v_i\|})^T}{\left\|\sum_{i=1}^{n} a_i w_i \frac{v}{\|v_i\|}\right\| \left\|\sum_{i=1}^{n} b_i w_i \frac{v}{\|v_i\|}\right\|} \qquad 19.3$$

where the weights w_i are chosen as follows,

$$w_i = \begin{cases} 1, normalized \\ \alpha_{i,} \ RWD \\ 1-\alpha_{1,} \ FWD \end{cases}$$

In addition to using varying weighting schemes, we can also modify the LSA measure by applying adjustments that vary levels of similarity strictness. To do so, Equation 19.3 is revised as follows:

$$sim(T_1, T_2) = \frac{\sum_{i,j=1}^{n} a_i b_j w_i w_j \frac{v_i v_j^T}{\|v_i\| \|v_j\|}}{\sqrt{\sum_{i,j=1}^{n} a_i a_j w_i w_j \frac{v_i v_j^T}{\|v_i\| \|v_j\|}} \sqrt{\sum_{i,j=1}^{n} b_i b_j w_i w_j \frac{v_i v_j^T}{\|v_i\| \|v_j\|}}} \qquad 19.4$$

Notice that in Equation 19.4, $\frac{v_i v_j^T}{\|v_i\| \|v_j\|}$ is actually the similarity between the terms with indices i and j in the space. This similarity is the same for LSA and its variations with the three weighting schemes, because the computation is between two single terms. Denoting this similarity by s_{ij}, we have

$$sim(T_1, T_2) = \frac{\sum_{i,j=1}^{n} a_i b_j w_i w_j s_{ij}}{\sqrt{\sum_{i,j=1}^{n} a_i a_j w_i w_j s_{ij}} \sqrt{\sum_{i,j=1}^{n} b_i b_j w_i w_j s_{ij}}} \qquad 19.5$$

The matrix formed by (s_{ij}) is a word-to-word similarity matrix. One would hope that this word-to-word similarity matrix reflects the semantic similarity we desire for all word pairs. Unfortunately, this matrix looks quite noisy. Suppose we want to compare two sentences: "The boy took mathematics" and "The girl chose physics." Let us assume that we want to count the similarities in the following pairs: boy-girl, took-chose, mathematics-physics. Table 19.2 shows that the cosine values representing the similarity of these pairs are .50, .16, and .58, respectively. However, other word pairs also have nonzero values that may reflect noise. To remove this noise, we set up a cut off threshold H and set those s_{ij} that are less than H to be 0. Thus Equation 19.5 is modified to

$$sim(T_1, T_2) = \frac{\sum\limits_{i,j=1, s_{ij}>H}^{n} a_i b_j w_i w_j s_{ij}}{\sqrt{\sum\limits_{i,j=1, s_{ij}>H}^{n} a_i a_j w_i w_j s_{ij}} \sqrt{\sum\limits_{i,j=1, s_{ij}>H}^{n} b_i b_j w_i w_j s_{ij}}} \qquad 19.6$$

In this chapter, we consider three threshold values for H: -1, 0, and 1. When the threshold is -1, no s_{ij} is set to zero and we consider a "loose similarity." Thus, all of the values in Table 19.2 would be included, as they would in an unaltered LSA measure. When the threshold is 0, all negative s_{ij} are set to zero, which we consider a "medium similarity." When the threshold is 1, all off-diagonal values in Table 19.2 would be set to 0, and Equation 19.6 becomes a word matching algorithm, which we consider "strict similarity."

EXPERIMENTS

Two experiments were conducted to examine the ability of the modified algorithms to predict cohesion. A total of 10 algorithms were examined. The first is an unmodified version of LSA. The remaining 9 vary as a function of term weighting scheme (normalized, RWD, FWD) and similarity strictness (loose, medium, strict). In Experiment 1, we tested whether the algorithms

TABLE 19.2
Cosine Values Between Words in the Two Sentences: "The Boy Took Mathematics" and "The Girl Chose Physics"

	The	Boy	Took	Mathematics	Girl	Chose	Physics
The	1.00	.01	.05	−.08	.02	.02	−.04
Boy	.01	1.00	.09	−.05	.50	.01	.02
Took	.05	.09	1.00	.07	−.01	.16	.02
Mathematics	−.08	−.05	.07	1.00	−.06	−.04	.58
Girl	.02	.50	−.01	−.06	1.00	−.03	.02
Chose	.02	.01	.16	−.04	−.03	1.00	−.03
Physics	−.04	.02	.02	.58	.02	−.03	1.00

would detect degrees of relatedness between sentences in four narrative passages and which algorithms would be most successful. To this end, we manipulated semantic cohesion by pairing sentences with other sentences that were more or less related to the target sentences. In Experiment 2, we tested how well the algorithms would detect degrees of relatedness between sentences in expository text passages from McNamara et al. (1996) about types of and treatments for heart disease.

LSA is presumed to not work optimally for sentence comparisons (e.g., Landauer & Dumais, 1997; Graesser et al., 2000). It assumedly requires a context that is sufficiently large to determine higher order relationships between neighbors, usually the size of paragraphs. Here we examine whether different emphases on word frequency using term weighting and varying level of similarity strictness improve the ability of LSA to detect variations in cohesion. In addition, the success or failure of the modified algorithms was expected to provide insight into how these variables affect sentence level comparisons using LSA.

Experiment 1

The purpose of Experiment 1 was to examine the ability of the algorithms to predict relatedness in narrative texts. Four passages were obtained from Graesser, Robertson, and Anderson (1981), including the narratives: *The Czar and His Daughters*, *The Boy and His Dog*, *John at Leone's*, and *The Ant and the Dove*. We examined the ability of the algorithms to discriminate between three types of sentences and to predict human judgments of the relatedness between sentence pairs. Relatedness was varied by pairing a given sentence with either a paraphrase of that sentence, a sentence within the same passage, or a sentence from a different passage. Thus, three classes of sentences were compared to the target sentences: paraphrases, within-text sentences, and cross-text sentences. The reasoning was that the paraphrase should be most related and thus most cohesive with the target sentence, and the sentence from a different text should be least cohesive with the target sentence.

The four passages each contained between 9 and 12 sentences. The first, third, fifth, and seventh sentences of each passage were used as target sentences. The other sentences were used to form within-text and cross-text pairs with the target sentences. We used the 10 algorithms described earlier to computationally determine the relatedness between these three types of pairs.

First, we examined whether the algorithms showed differences in relatedness rating as a function of sentence pair type. Second, we examined whether the relatedness estimates correlated with human estimates of relatedness.

Sentence-Pairs

Paraphrase (16 Pairs).   For each of the 16 target sentences, a paraphrase was created by the authors using the rules that at least 30% of the content words in each of the target sentences be replaced by new words and the meaning of the sentence remain the same. For example, the paraphrase for "As they were being dragged off, they cried for help" was "They screamed to be rescued as they were being taken away."

Within-Text Sentences (32 Pairs).   For each of the target sentences, two sentences in the same passage of the target sentence were selected to form two within-text pairs with the target sentence (n). One was the sentence that immediately followed the target sentence in the passage (i.e., $n + 1$) and the other one was the third sentence after the target sentence (i.e., $n + 3$). For example, if the target sentence was the first sentence in a passage, then the second and the fourth sentences were selected to form the pairs with the first sentence.

Cross-Text Sentences (48 Pairs).   For each of the target sentences, three sentences that were not target sentences or within-text pairs were selected from the other three passages.

Relatedness Estimates

The algorithms' estimates of relatedness between the three pair types (paraphrase, within-text, cross-text) are presented in Table 19.3. The results for all of the algorithms reflect the probability of semantic relatedness as highest for the 16 paraphrase pairs and lowest for the 48 cross-text pairs, with the 32 within-text pairs somewhere in between. To examine whether the algorithms significantly detected that the relatedness between the three types of sentence pairs were different, separate analyses of variance (ANOVA) were conducted on the similarity ratings with pair type as the between-items variable. As shown in Table 19.3, all algorithms showed a significant effect of pair type in the expected direction (paraphrase > within-text > cross-text), and the differences were reliable between all of the pair types.

The LSA algorithm that emphasized rare words (RWD) shows the largest differences between pair types and that the LSA algorithm emphasizing more frequent words (FWD) shows the smallest differences. This indicates that the differences between the pair types are dominated by the relationships between relatively rare words. However, the strict similarity (i.e., word matching) algorithm yielded much lower differences between pair types in the RWD scheme. This indicates that LSA word similarity contributes positively to the discrimination between pair types.

TABLE 19.3
Cosine Means and Standard Deviations Reflecting the Relationships Between
the Target Sentences and Their Paraphrases, Within-Text Sentences, and
Cross-Text Sentences, and the F Values, and Cohen's d Effect Sizes Reflecting
the Differences Between the Three Mean, as a Function of the Type of
Modification to the LSA Algorithm

		Paraphrase		Within-Text		Cross-Text			Cohen's d Effect Sizes		
		Mean	STD	Mean	STD	Mean	STD	F (2, 93)	P-W	W-C	P-C
Unmodified LSA		.64	.26	.38	.32	.05	.12	46.4**	.89	1.37	2.91
Frequent	Loose	.81	.16	.58	.18	.40	.27	2.8**	1.35	.78	1.85
word	Medium	.82	.14	.62	.15	.47	.22	22.6**	1.38	.80	1.90
dominated	Strict	.70	.15	.39	.22	.27	.23	24.3**	1.65	.53	2.21
	Loose	.74	.15	.51	.17	.31	.21	35.3**	1.43	1.05	2.36
Normalized	Medium	.77	.13	.56	.14	.39	.17	39.1**	1.55	1.09	2.51
	Strict	.59	.13	.32	.19	.19	.16	33.9**	1.66	.74	2.74
Rare	Loose	.55	.19	.31	.22	.04	.08	72.5**	1.17	1.63	3.50
word	Medium	.58	.18	.35	.20	.11	.06	73.0**	1.21	1.63	3.50
dominated	Strict	.35	.23	.16	.18	.00	.01	39.5**	.92	1.26	2.15

Note. P-W is the effect size of the difference between paraphrase and within-text
comparisons; W-C corresponds to that difference for the within-text and cross-text
comparisons; P-C refers to the paraphrase and cross-text difference.
**$p < .01$.

These results confirm that the cohesion (or relatedness) between the target
sentence and the sentence pair decreases going from paraphrases to
within-text pairs to cross-text pairs. The ability of an algorithm to distinguish
between these cohesion ratings from category to category is indicative of its
success in measuring cohesion. That is, if an algorithm successfully measures
cohesion, then its estimate of relatedness for a highly related pair such as a target sentence with its paraphrase should be significantly different from a less
related pair, such as a target sentence paired with a sentence from a different
text. These results indicate that all of the algorithms successfully discriminated
degrees of relatedness between the different pairs. The most successful was
the RWD scheme with either loose or medium similarity strictness. Thus, LSA
performance was optimized by emphasizing rare words in the vectors, and
benefited from going beyond simple word matching.

Human Ratings

The question addressed in the previous section regards the degree to
which the algorithms detect differences between sentence pairs with ma-

nipulated differences in relatedness. A second question is whether the performance of the algorithms mimics human performance. To address this question, we asked 16 experts in discourse psychology (faculty and student members of the Institute for Intelligent Systems) to rate the relatedness of the pairs on a 6-point Likert scale, and compared their ratings to the LSA cosines.

The participants were asked to rate each pair of sentences according to how similar they seemed. They were asked to take the sentences at face value without additional context and to consider only relationships between sentences that would be evoked for most people, rather than relationships that would only be evoked for the raters. Examples were given for high similarity sentences (*She smelled the flower* and *The girl smelled the rose*), moderate similarity sentences (*She smelled the flower* and *She walked in the garden*) and low similarity sentences (*She smelled the flower* and *The boy rode on the train*).

Differences in Ratings Between Pair Types.   To verify that the three types of sentence pairs were perceived as significantly different by the participants, an ANOVA was conducted including pair type as a within-subjects variable on the similarity ratings. As expected, there was a significant difference between paraphrases ($M = 5.38$, $SD = .51$), within-text pairs ($M = 2.42$, $SD = .87$), and cross-text pairs ($M = 1.14$, $SD = .19$), $F(2, 30) = 296.78$, $p < .001$. Thus, the participants were sensitive to the differences in cohesion.

Correlations.   Pearson correlations between the average human ratings and the computational ratings were calculated to examine which algorithms best predicted the human ratings. For the purpose of comparison, we also computed the correlations between each rater's ratings and the average human ratings. The average and standard deviation of these correlations are presented in the bottom row of Table 19.4.

The results shown in Table 19.4 indicate that differences in relatedness between paraphrases were reliably detected only by the FWD scheme with loose or medium similarity strictness and the normalized scheme with medium similarity strictness. Indeed, these algorithm-to-human correlations exceed the average human-to-human correlations (i.e., $r = .44$). Thus, human estimates of close pairs are best captured by frequent words in the vector representations.

Differences in relatedness for the within-text sentence pairs was reliably detected by 8 of the 10 algorithms, but best detected by RWD, regardless of similarity strictness. The RWD scheme was also the only algorithm to correlate with human judgments of cross-text pairs, but only with medium or loose similarity strictness. Word-to-word matching captured by the strict algorithm did not correlate with human's estimates of cross-text differences in relatedness.

TABLE 19.4
Correlations Between Human and Computational Ratings of Relatedness
for the Three Types of Sentence Pairs

		Paraphrase	Within-Text	Cross-Text
Unmodified LSA		.20	.16	.04
Frequent	*Loose*	.54*	.41*	.16
word	*Medium*	.55*	.37*	.17
dominated	*Strict*	.43	.28	.06
	Loose	.48	.49**	.20
Normalized	*Medium*	.50*	.46**	.24
	Strict	.37	.37*	.07
Rare	*Loose*	.03	.53**	.30*
word	*Medium*	.08	.55**	.46**
dominated	*Strict*	.04	.54**	−.06
Human to Human		.44 (.22)	.69**(.11)	.39*(.24)

Note. Human to Human correlation standard deviations are in parentheses.

*p < .05, **p < .01

Most notable in these comparisons is that the conventional LSA algorithm did not significantly correlate with the human ratings. Thus, the variations in the LSA algorithm significantly improved its performance in detecting differences in cohesion. Furthermore, the success of the algorithms depended on the level of comparison. The variations in relatedness between the paraphrases (to their target sentences) were best captured by emphasizing frequent words in LSA vector. In contrast, cross-text comparisons benefited from emphasizing rare words.

Experiment 2

The goal of Experiment 2 was to examine the ability of the algorithms to capture manipulated cohesion in expository texts. This experiment was modeled after the work by Foltz et al. (1998) to predict the cohesion manipulations of McNamara et al. (1996). McNamara et al. used four versions of a text about heart disease, including an original, low-cohesion text that had both low local and low global cohesion (cm), a high-cohesion text (CM), and two texts that were high in either local (C) or global (M) cohesion (i.e., Cm and cM). We adopt the acronyms used by McNamara et al., where C represents local *cohesion*, and M represents global (or *macro*level) cohesion. Local cohesion was primarily increased by adding causal connections and referential overlap. Global cohesion was increased by adding headers and topic sentences to the paragraphs.

The participants were 56 middle school students who read one of the text versions, recalled the text, and answered open-ended questions to assess comprehension. There were four types of questions: text-based, bridging inference, elaborative inference, and problem solving. The comprehension measures were designed to assess different levels of readers' comprehension. Recall and text-based questions were designed to assess readers' text-based level of understanding, or their memory for the individual concepts conveyed in the text. Recall is considered primarily text-based because readers generally make few and various inferences while recalling information from a text. That is, the inferences are scarce and not likely to be the same across participants. The scarcity and wide variety of inferences result in a recall score that taps mainly the text. Text-based questions are those that require only one sentence, or few propositions from the text, and do not require making cross-sentential inferences to answer. The bridging inference and problem-solving questions were designed to assess readers' situation model level of understanding, that is, their deeper level understanding of the relationships between ideas in the text. Bridging inference questions require several sentences from the text to answer, and thus require that the reader had made inferences concerning the relationships between ideas in the text. Elaborative inference questions are those that require information from the text and outside the text, with the notion that answering the question requires making inferences that link the text to prior knowledge. Problem-solving questions require the reader to apply some information from the text to a novel situation; in the case of McNamara et al. (1996), the reader applied the information to physical problems exhibited by individuals. Participants' prior knowledge was measured by a pretest about the heart and its functions. Based on this measure, students were categorized using a median split on the test as high or low in prior knowledge of the heart's structure and function.

The results of the McNamara et al. (1996) study indicated that low-knowledge participants benefited from the high-cohesion text in comparison to the low-cohesion text. They performed better on all of the measures if they had read a text with added cohesion rather than the low-cohesion version of the text. It was assumed that low-knowledge readers need the added cohesion because they do not possess enough knowledge to bridge the conceptual gaps in the texts. So, when cohesion gaps are encountered in low-cohesion texts, low-knowledge readers do not possess enough knowledge to understand difficult concepts and make inferences to understand relationships between concepts. Thus, added cohesion benefits both memory and learning for low-knowledge readers.

In contrast, the high-knowledge participants showed better deep comprehension, in terms of the bridging-inference and problem-solving questions, if they had read the low-cohesion text rather than one of the three texts with added cohesion. An explanation for this phenomenon proposed by McNamara and colleagues (1996) relates to the importance of active processing while learning (e.g., McNamara & Healy, 2000). That is, learning improves when readers are forced to make more inferences and link new information with prior knowledge. Because high-knowledge readers are more likely to possess the knowledge necessary to generate successful inferences while reading, those inferences should benefit learning by ensuring that prior knowledge is activated and used to understand the text. Whereas low-knowledge readers need the added cohesion because they do not possess enough knowledge to fill in the gaps in the texts, the high-knowledge readers benefit from being forced to generate the gap-filling inferences (see also, McNamara, 2001; McNamara & W. Kintsch, 1996). Thus, increased cohesion is beneficial to low-knowledge readers, but can be detrimental to readers who possess the knowledge to generate the necessary inferences in a lower cohesion text.

The goal of the computations is to examine the correspondence between the estimates of cohesion by each of the algorithms and the comprehension performance by low-knowledge and high-knowledge participants. We should expect positive correlations between cohesion estimates and comprehension performance for the low-knowledge readers. In contrast, negative correlations are expected between cohesion estimates and comprehension performance for the high-knowledge readers—particularly on the situation model measures of comprehension. That is, when cohesion is low, we expect better comprehension for the high-knowledge readers.

Cohesion Estimates

The estimates of relatedness in the four text versions for standard LSA and the nine experimental algorithms are presented in Table 19.5. All of the algorithms showed semilinear trends such that the low-cohesion text (cm) was estimated to have the lowest cohesion and the high-cohesion text (CM) was estimated to have the highest cohesion. As shown in Table 19.5, six of the nine modified algorithms showed significant differences between the highly cohesive (CM) and least cohesive (cm) texts. The modified algorithms with medium similarity strictness showed the largest cohesion differences, whereas the strict similarity algorithm, or word overlap, did not show reliable differences. LSA yielded a marginal difference.

The design of the McNamara et al. (1996) experiment allows us to examine whether the algorithms detect local or global cohesion. Table 19.6 shows the F values and Cohen's d effect sizes for text comparisons that reveal either local or global manipulations. None of the algorithms detected global

Average Cosine Values for the Four Text Versions and the F Values Indicating
Differences Between the High and Low Cohesion Versions of the Text

		CM		Cm		cM		cm		CM-cm	
		Mean	STD	Mean	STD	Mean	STD	Mean	STD	F (1,123)	p
Unmodified LSA		.37	.2	.34	.19	.32	.22	.30	.23	3.56	.061
Frequent	Loose	.51	.16	.52	.17	.43	.2	.43	.22	5.19	.024
word	Medium	.57	.14	.57	.15	.50	.17	.50	.20	5.96	.016
dominated	Strict	.25	.15	.25	.16	.21	.16	.22	.18	.52	.473
	Loose	.48	.16	.47	.17	.40	.18	.39	.20	6.95	.009
Normalized	Medium	.54	.14	.54	.14	.47	.16	.46	.18	8.08	.005
	Strict	.21	.13	.21	.13	.17	.12	.18	.14	1.86	.175
Rare	Loose	.38	.24	.35	.24	.33	.23	.29	.23	4.23	.042
word	Medium	.43	.21	.41	.21	.38	.21	.34	.21	5.20	.024
dominated	Strict	.14	.17	.11	.15	.11	.17	.09	.16	2.49	.117

Note. cm indicates low local and global cohesion, cM indicates low local and high global cohesion, Cm indicates high local and low global cohesion, and CM indicates high local and global cohesion.

manipulations of cohesion. That is, they did not detect the addition of topic sentences and headers. Local cohesion was picked up best by FWD and normalized schemes, with loose or medium similarity strictness.

Correlations

Following the methodology used by Foltz et al. (1998), we correlated the average cohesion scores from the algorithms with the comprehension scores. In contrast to Foltz et al. (1998), who only focused on scores for low-knowledge participants, we present the correlations for both high-knowledge and low-knowledge participants. The correlations between the algorithms' cohesion estimates and the comprehension scores for high-knowledge and low-knowledge participants are presented in Table 19.7. First, note a general pattern; the correlations are positive for low-knowledge participants, as well as for high-knowledge participants' recall and text-based question performance. In contrast, the correlations are negative for high-knowledge participants' performance on inference questions. This pattern reflects the finding that high-knowledge participants' showed a reverse cohesion effect (advantage for low-cohesion text) on inference level questions in the McNamara et al. (1996) study.

TABLE 19.6
F Values and Cohen's *d* Effect Sizes for Differences Between Text Versions
Indicating Which Algorithms Best Detected Local and Global
Cohesion Manipulations

		Global				Local			
		CM-Cm		cM-cm		CM-cM		Cm-cm	
		F (1,123)	Cohen's d	F (1,123)	Cohen's d	F (1,123)	Cohen's d	F (1,123)	Cohen's d
LSA		.46	.15	.30	.13	1.88	.24	1.62	.24
Frequent	*Loose*	.04	-.06	.01	.00	6.80*	.44	5.28*	.46
word	*Medium*	.02	.00	.01	.00	7.03**	.45	5.86*	.40
dominated	*Strict*	.02	.00	.23	-.06	1.84	.26	.63	.03
	Loose	.01	.06	.05	.05	6.69*	.47	5.88*	.43
Normalized	*Medium*	.02	.00	.11	.06	7.15**	.47	6.64*	.51
	Strict	.05	.00	.03	-.08	2.85	.32	1.25	.22
Rare	*Loose*	.34	.13	.62	.17	1.75	.21	2.08	.26
word	*Medium*	.45	.10	.72	.19	2.16	.24	2.53	.33
dominated	*Strict*	.82	.19	.49	.12	.77	.18	.57	.13

Note. cm indicates low local and global cohesion, cM indicates low local and high global cohesion, Cm indicates high local and low global cohesion, and CM indicates high local and global cohesion.

*$p < .05$, **$p < .01$

In general, low-knowledge participants' performance was best captured by the RWD scheme. Thus, their performance was most driven by overlap between relatively rare words. Overlap between more common words probably had less of an effect on their comprehension. This result can be expected because the less common words are the ones that require more prior knowledge to understand, which low-knowledge readers lack. On text-based questions, only RWD with strict similarity showed a reliable correlation—this indicates that their textbase comprehension is mainly affected by explicit word overlap within the text, and this occurs mainly as a function of the less common words. In contrast, elaborative inference question performance significantly correlated with RWD and LSA. These results indicate that performance on these inference questions relied more on overlap between less common words, but that the necessary overlap was conceptual as well as word based.

TABLE 19.7

Correlations Between Cohesion Scores and Comprehension Scores for Low-Knowledge and High-Knowledge Participants

	LSA	Frequent Word Dominated			Normalized			Rare Word Dominated		
		Loose	Med	Strict	Loose	Med	Strict	Loose	Med	Strict
Low Knowledge										
Recall	.45	.26	.29	-.04	.33	.36	.17	.53	.52	.51
Text-based Q	.83	.48	.51	.26	.57	.60	.53	.84	.84	.97*
Bridging-inference Q	.53	.19	.23	-.12	.30	.33	.15	.59	.59	.69
Elaborative-inference Q	.93*	.67	.70	.44	.75	.78	.68	.95*	.96*	.99*
Problem-solving Q	.84	.64	.67	.38	.72	.75	.60	.88	.88	.86
High Knowledge										
Recall	.82	.89	.88	.93*	.88	.87	.94*	.77	.77	.67
Text-based Q	.32	.03	.05	.06	.08	.10	.18	.28	.28	.50
Bridging-inference Q	-.57	-.37	-.40	-.08	-.45	-.48	-.29	-.63	-.63	-.61
Elaborative-inference Q	-.01	.06	.04	.30	.02	-.00	.19	-.10	-.09	-.04
Problem-solving Q	-.31	-.15	-.17	.14	-.21	-.24	-.04	-.39	-.38	-.37

*p < .05, **p < .01.

GENERAL DISCUSSION

LSA essentially opened up the field to examine semantic relatedness (see Dumais, chap. 16 in this volume; Landauer, chap. 1 in this volume). It was used in the early 1990s as a method for information retrieval (Deerwester et al., 1990). We now know that it can also be used successfully for essay grading (Landauer, Laham, & Foltz, 2003) and measuring cohesion (Foltz et al., 1998). In most of these experiments, the units that are analyzed are at the (global) text level rather than the (local) sentence level. Although there are cases where LSA has also successfully been used to compare single student contributions to ideal answers (AutoTutor: Graesser et al., 2000), many have found that LSA is less successful with smaller chunks of text, such as words or sentences (Landauer & Dumais, 1997). We evaluated variations of the LSA algorithm to examine whether the performance of LSA could be improved by varying two factors: emphasis on high- or low-frequency words, and similarity strictness.

We examined cohesion in two experiments. In Experiment 1, we compared the ability of the algorithms to discriminate between paraphrases, within-passage sentences, and cross-passage sentences from four short narrative passages (from Graesser et al., 1981). We created paraphrases of the passages and calculated the predicted cohesion between the passage sentences, the paraphrases, other passage sentences, and sentences outside the passage. Our goal was to examine the ability of the algorithms to discriminate between paraphrases, within-text sentences, and cross-text sentences.

The results indicated that all of the algorithms successfully captured the differences in relatedness between the three types of sentence pairs. However, RWD showed the largest differences, indicating that emphasizing rare words in the vector representations improved LSA performance. RWD also correlated well with human ratings of the relationship between the target sentence and sentences within the same text and sentences from different texts. In contrast, correlations with human ratings of the paraphrases were highest when more frequent words were emphasized within the FWD algorithm. Thus, human discriminations between close distinctions, such as comparisons of a sentence and its paraphrase, seem more driven by overlap in frequent words than less frequent words. Overall, the results indicate that an emphasis on particular word types can improve LSA performance, and the type of word to be emphasized may depend on the task at hand.

In Experiment 2, we examined the ability of the algorithms to discriminate between expository texts with cohesion manipulations (McNamara et al., 1996). The algorithms did not show differences as a function of global cohesion manipulations. This result is not surprising in that the cohesion scores (between adjacent sentences) are primarily aimed at local cohesion differences. As in Experiment 1, the modified LSA formulas outperformed LSA in discriminating between the maximally high- and low-cohesion texts (CM-cm), and the medium similarity algorithms that had some noise reduction by removing negative cosines in the word vectors showed the largest differences. However, whereas the emphasis on word frequency had the largest effects on LSA performance in Experiment 1, the normalized scheme (with the effect of vector length removed) showed the largest differences in cohesion in Experiment 2. Nonetheless, when the average cosines were correlated with average comprehension performance, RWD showed the highest correlations overall. Thus, the emphasis on rare words in RWD improves the ability of LSA to predict comprehension performance.

We also examined the correlations between predicted cohesion and the comprehension results for high- and low-knowledge readers. Low-knowledge readers' comprehension was best predicted by RWD and LSA. High-knowledge readers' recall was correlated with all of the algorithms. Their performance on situation model measures was negatively correlated with the algorithms' predictions (see also, Shapiro & McNamara, 2000). This result nicely reflects the empirical result that high-knowledge readers' performance on the bridging inference questions was negatively related to cohesion, with better comprehension emerging from the low-cohesion text than the high-cohesion text.

The results of Experiments 1 and 2 collectively indicate that weighting LSA to emphasize rare words and remove noise from negative cosines more accurately predicts effects of cohesion between sentences in text. This result emerged for both narrative and expository texts. This suggests that one may want to use different models, depending on the type of cohesion, texts, or level of comprehension to be analyzed in a study. Establishing the appropriateness of different computational linguistic techniques for measuring various aspects of cohesion will enhance tools that automatically measure readability and cohesion of texts, including Coh-Metrix.

This study shows that various parameters in LSA can be manipulated depending on the level of language that is of interest. However, there are larger implications of this study. Although we have centered on one aspect of language, cohesion, there are innumerable facets of language and cognition that could be explored capitalizing on these types of parameter adjustments to LSA. One potential application would be to explore what aspects of language most influence human judgments and decision making. Here, for example, we found that human ratings of paraphrases were most influenced by the proportion of frequent words shared by two sentences, whereas comparisons of within-text and cross-text sentences were influenced by the relationship between less frequent words. Further research might be directed both at better understanding the cognitive processes behind these results and also exploring these types of phenomenon with other types of judgment tasks. In sum, this work not only points toward ways to improve LSA scoring, but also opens doors to new kinds of questions that can be asked and computationally tested.

ACKNOWLEDGMENTS

The research was supported by grants from the Institute of Education Sciences (IES R3056020018-02), the National Science Foundation (IIS-0416128, ITR0325428, REC0106965, SBR 9720314), and the Office of Naval Research (N00014-02-M-0248). Any opinions, findings, and conclusions or recommendations expressed in this material are those of the authors and do not necessarily reflect the views of the IES, ONR, or NSF. We thank Courtney Bell and Christian Hempelman for comments on an earlier version of this chapter. The TASA corpus used was generously provided by Touchstone Applied Science Associates, Newburg, NY, who developed it for data on which to base their Educators Word Frequency Guide.

REFERENCES

Brill, E. (1995). Transformation-based error-driven learning and natural language processing: A case study in part-of-speech tagging. *Computational Linguistics, 21*, 543–566.

Britton, B. K., & Gulgoz, S. (1991). Using Kintsch's computational model to improve instructional text: Effects of repairing inference calls on recall and cognitive structures. *Journal of Educational Psychology, 83*, 329–345.

Coltheart, M. (1981). The MRC psycholinguistic database. *Quarterly Journal of Experimental Psychology, 33*, 497–505.

Deerwester, S., Dumais, S. T., Furnas, G. W., Landauer, T. K., & Harshman, R. (1990). Indexing by latent semantic analysis. *Journal of the American Society for Information Science, 41*, 391–407.

Foltz, P. W., Kintsch, W., & Landauer, T. K. (1998). The measurement of textual coherence with latent semantic analysis. *Discourse Processes, 25*, 285–307.

Gernsbacher, M. A. (1990). *Language comprehension as structure building*. Hillsdale, NJ: Lawrence Erlbaum Associates.

Givón, T. (1995). Coherence in the text and coherence in the mind. In M. A. Gernsbacher & T. Givón (Eds.), *Coherence in spontaneous text* (pp. 59–115). Amsterdam: Benjamins.

Graesser, A. C., McNamara, D. S., & Louwerse, M. M. (2003). What do readers need to learn in order to process coherence relations in narrative and expository text. In A. P. Sweet & C. E. Snow (Eds.), *Rethinking reading comprehension* (pp. 82–98). New York: Guilford.

Graesser, A. C., McNamara, D. S., Louwerse, M. M., & Cai, Z. (2004). Coh-Metrix: Analysis of text on cohesion and language. *Behavior Research Methods, Instruments, and Computers, 36*, 193–202.

Graesser, A. C., Robertson, S. E., & Anderson, P. A. (1981). Incorporating inferences in narrative representations: A study of how and why. *Cognitive Psychology, 13,* 1–26.

Graesser, A., Wiemer-Hastings, P., Wiemer-Hastings, K., Harter, D., Person, N., & the Tutoring Research Group. (2000). Using latent semantic analysis to evaluate the contributions of students in AutoTutor. *Interactive Learning Environments, 8,* 149–169.

Kintsch, W. (1995). How readers construct situation models for stories: The role of syntactic cues and causal inferences. In M. A. Gernsbacher & T. Givón, *Coherence in spontaneous text* (pp.139–160). Amsterdam: Benjamins.

Landauer, T. K., & Dumais, S. T. (1997). A solution to Plato's problem: The latent semantic analysis theory of acquisition, induction, and representation of knowledge. *Psychological Review, 104,* 211–240.

Landauer, T. K., Laham, D., & Foltz, P. W. (2003). Automated essay scoring and annotation of essays with the intelligent essay assessor. In M. D. Shermis & J. C. Burstein (Eds.), *Automated Essay Scoring: A Cross Disciplinary Perspective* (pp. 87–112). Mahwah, NJ: Lawrence Erlbaum Associates.

Louwerse, M. M. (2002). Computational retrieval of themes. In M. M. Louwerse & W. van Peer (Eds.), *Thematics: Interdisciplinary studies* (pp. 189–212). Amsterdam: Benjamins.

Louwerse, M. M. (2004). Semantic variation in idiolect and sociolect: Corpus linguistic evidence from literary texts. *Computers and the Humanities, 38,* 207–221.

Louwerse, M. M. (2005). Un modelo conciso de cohesion en el texto y coherencia en la comprehension [A concise model of cohesion in text and coherence in comprehension]. *Revista Signos, 37,* 41–58.

Louwerse, M. M., & Graesser, A. C. (2005). Coherence in discourse. In P. Strazny (Ed.), *Encyclopedia of linguistics* (pp. 216–218). Chicago: Fitzroy Dearborn.

Louwerse, M. M., McCarthy, P. M., McNamara, D. S., & Graesser, A. C. (2004). Variation in language and cohesion across written and spoken registers. In K. D. Forbus, D. Gentner, & T. Regier (Eds.), *Proceedings of the 26th Annual Conference of the Cognitive Science Society* (pp. 843–848). Mahwah, NJ: Lawrence Erlbaum Associates.

McNamara, D. S. (2001). Reading both high and low coherence texts: Effects of text sequence and prior knowledge. *Canadian Journal of Experimental Psychology, 55,* 51–62.

McNamara, D. S., & Healy, A. F. (2000). A procedural explanation of the generation effect for simple and difficult multiplication problems and answers. *Journal of Memory and Language, 43,* 652–679.

McNamara, D. S., Kintsch, E., Songer, N. B., & Kintsch, W. (1996). Are good texts always better? Text coherence, background knowledge, and levels of understanding in learning from text. *Cognition and Instruction, 14,* 1–43.

McNamara, D. S., & Kintsch, W. (1996). Learning from text: Effects of prior knowledge and text coherence. *Discourse Processes, 22,* 247–287.

McNamara, D. S., Louwerse, M. M., & Graesser, A. C. (2002). *Coh-Metrix: Automated cohesion and coherence scores to predict text readability and facilitate comprehension.* Technical report, Institute for Intelligent Systems, University of Memphis, Memphis, TN.

Miller, G. A., Beckwith, R., Fellbaum, C., Gross, D., & Miller, K. (1990). Introduction to WordNet: An on-line lexical database. *Journal of Lexicography, 3,* 234–244.

Sekine, S., & Grishman, R. (1995). A corpus-based probabilistic grammar with only two nonterminals. *Proceedings of the Fourth International Workshop on Parsing Technology,* 216–223.

Shapiro, A. M., & McNamara, D. S. (2000). The use of latent semantic analysis as a tool for the quantitative assessment of understanding and knowledge. *Journal of Educational Computing Research, 22,* 1–36.

Van Dijk, T. A., & Kintsch, W. (1983). *Strategies of discourse comprehension.* New York: Academic Press.

Zwaan, R. A., & Radvansky, G. A. (1998). Situation models in language comprehension and memory. *Psychological Bulletin, 123,* 162–185.

20

Strengths, Limitations, and Extensions of LSA

Xiangen Hu
Zhiqiang Cai
Peter Wiemer-Hastings
Art C. Graesser
Danielle S. McNamara
University of Memphis

As the title indicates, this chapter addresses three goals. The first goal is to identify some important strengths of LSA, whereas the second is to identify some weaknesses. The third goal is to propose a few alternative quantitative models of representation with high-dimensional semantic spaces. As amply demonstrated by the range of applications described in other chapters of this book, there is no need to address the practical strength of LSA. Instead, we approach the first goal by presenting some basic facts about LSA in terms of simple algebra and demonstrate how powerfully this "data-mining" method captures human intuition. Limitations of LSA are observed from two perspectives: empirical evaluations of LSA in applications and formal analysis of LSA algorithms and procedures. Regarding the third goal, we position LSA in a more general framework and then examine possible extensions. These extensions include three methods that adapt to learner perspective, context, and conversational history.

COMPARING TEXT SIMILARITY

The primary task that LSA performs in most applications is to compute the semantic similarity of any two texts. To approach LSA from a different angle, we consider two other text similarity metrics: word-based and context-based measures of text similarity. The discussion of these relatively simple measures will facilitate the introduction of a denotation that allows the consideration of LSA in a new framework.

Word-Based Similarity

Keyword matching is the most frequently used method to measure similarity between two texts. There are many different techniques for keyword matching. We list a few in the order of simplicity.

Word Matching.   The simplest technique is word matching. In this case, all words are of equal importance and the calculation is based on how many words the two texts share. This method does not depend on context or domain knowledge. The similarity measure is a function of the total words and the shared words, which can readily be depicted in a Venn diagram (http://www.groups.dcs.st-and.ac.uk/~history/Mathematicians/Venn.html). The most often-used formula for the computation is the ratio of the shared words to the total words, which restricts the similarity measure between 0 (completely different) and 1 (completely identical). The advantages of word matching are its intuitiveness and computational simplicity. One disadvantage of this method is the lack of emphasis on important words. The next method improves the word matching method by considering which words contribute most to the distinct meaning of the text.

Keyword Matching.   In this case, only keywords are considered. Common words or function words like *it*, *is*, or *the* are ignored (Graesser, Hu, Person, Jackson, & Toth, 2004). This is the most widely used method in document retrieval. The advantage of this method is that it considers the importance of the words' semantic contributions. Some additional requirements need to be satisfied in order to have this method work well, especially in narrowly defined domains. For example, which words are identified as keywords largely depends on the domain. In most cases, the list of keywords is simply the list of glossary items and therefore is domain dependent. One weakness of this method is that it does not consider differential importance as to how much information a particular word may carry. The following method addresses this problem by differentially weighting the keywords.

Weighted Keyword Matching. The advantage of weighting keywords is to emphasize the degree to which a particular word is important to a particular domain. The challenge lies in how to assign the weights, which is often domain dependent. For example, weights can reflect how often a word is used in ordinary written language or spoken language (Graesser, Hu, et al., 2004). Such data can be obtained either by computing the relative frequency from a given corpus (with a one-time computation cost), or by using an established lexical database such as WordNet (Miller, 1985) or the MRC Psycholinguistic Database (Coltheart, 1981). As an alternative, weights can be assigned by an algorithm that computes the importance of the word in context. However, such an algorithm would need to be formulated in a principled fashion and might again depend heavily on domain expertise.

Weighted keyword matching is a powerful abstraction that subsumes word matching and keyword matching. It is also flexible due to the unlimited methods of assigning weights. However, it is limited in that it relies on exact matches between words. The extended weighted keyword matching methods allows consideration of synonyms as well.

Extended Weighted Keyword Matching. This method simply considers each word together with a set of words that are similar in some fashion. For example, each word can be associated with a set of synonyms. This method can provide a similarity rating even when the compared texts do not have any exact words in common. In such cases, the use of synonyms can also be a liability. Synonyms never capture exactly the same meaning as the original word, especially when one considers a range of contexts of use. Thus, the inclusion of synonyms has the potential to significantly distort the meanings of the texts.

Each of the methods mentioned earlier operates by finding exact matches between words. The information affiliated with a word (i.e., its weight and synonyms) can either be calculated by some method from a corpus, or taken from an external resource. As such, the performance of the techniques can depend heavily on the resources used. Databases such as MRC (Coltheart, 1981) and CELEX (http://www.ru.nl/celex/) can provide word frequency information. Corpora such as TASA (Touchstone Applied Science Associates, Inc.), Penn Treebank (http://www.cis.upenn.edu/~treebank/home.html), and the British National Corpus (BNC, http://www.natcorp.ox.ac.uk/) provide samples of actual texts from which word information can be derived. A lexicon like WordNet (http://wordnet.princeton.edu/) can provide synonyms. The information derived from different lexical databases or corpora may be appropriate

for the domain of interest, but it may also be misleading if there is a misalign-
ment between the corpus and the application. The quality of this information
can have a large effect on the overall success of the technique.

Formal Definition of Similarity Between Texts

The various types of word matching methods can be represented within a
unified mathematical formalism. First, consider that the collection of all
possible terms in a given language is a set with m items. One can index all
the terms from 1 to m. Each term t_i (where $i = 1, \ldots m$) can be represented by
an m-dimensional row vector with only one nonzero element. Denoting the
ith row vector by t_i and the jth entry of the ith row by u_{ij}, we have

$$t_i = (u_{ij})^m_{j=1}, \qquad\qquad 20.1$$

where

$$u_{ij} = \begin{Bmatrix} 1 & j = i \\ 0 & otherwise \end{Bmatrix} \qquad\qquad 20.2$$

In other words, t_i is a vector that is 0 everywhere except for the ith element,
which is 1. With this notation, for any text T with K words (not necessarily
distinct), there is an m-dimensional vector representation T, as expressed in
Equation 20.3 in which there are K term vectors in the summation:

$$T = \sum_i n_i t_i \qquad\qquad 20.3$$

where n_i is the number of occurrences of the ith word in the text T.
   The word match similarity between two texts, T_1 and T_2, is computed as
the cosine between the two document vectors:

$$\cos(T_1, T_2) = \frac{T_1 T_2^T}{\sqrt{T_1 T_1^T} \sqrt{T_2 T_2^T}} \qquad\qquad 20.4$$

Notice that T_1 and T_2 are row vectors, so there is a transpose needed for T_2 in
Equation 20.4.
   Assembling all the term vectors together, a diagonal matrix U can be ob-
tained, as expressed in Equation 20.5.

$$U = \begin{pmatrix} n_1 t_1 \\ \vdots \\ n_m t_m \end{pmatrix} = (n_i u_{ij})_{m \times m} \qquad\qquad 20.5$$

With this definition of **U**, we are able to have similar formulas for different types of similarity measures.

Keyword Matching and Weighted Keyword Matching. Consider an $m \times m$ diagonal matrix, $\mathbf{W} = diag\{w_i\}$, where all diagonal elements are non-negative. In this case, the similarity measure based on both keyword matching and weighted keyword matching can be computed with Equation 20.4, where the term vector $\mathbf{t}_i$ is multiplied by the number of occurrence to form the ith row of **WU**. In other words, the matrix **WU** contains term vectors $\mathbf{t}_i$ multiplied by the occurrences and then weighted by w_i ($i = 1, \ldots m$). Note that keyword matching corresponds to the case where elements of **W** only have the value of 0 or 1. A weight of 0 for a common word essentially removes it from consideration.

Extended Weighted Keyword Matching. The similarity measure corresponds to extended weighted keyword matching can be computed as the same as Equation 20.4, where $\mathbf{T} = \mathbf{WUE}$ and $\mathbf{E} = (e_{ij})_{m \times m}$ is a matrix with all elements either 0 or 1. When $e_{ij} = 1$, terms indexed as i and j are synonyms of each other.

We find the previous notations very useful. We can extend the similarity measures from word matching to context matching.

Context-Based Similarity. In the word-based methods, the only way that one could obtain a nonzero similarity measure between two distinct terms is when they are somehow related. This occurs, for example, when there is extended weighted keyword matching and the two terms are synonyms. A similarity measure based on context is different from the keyword-based similarity measure. Consider a corpus, with all of the documents indexed from $1, 2, \ldots, n$. Term $t_i, i = 1, \ldots m$, in the corpus is represented as the n-dimensional vector expressed in Equation 20.6,

$$\mathbf{t}_i = (f_{ij})^n_{j=1} , \qquad \qquad 20.6$$

where f_{ij} is the number of times term t_i appears in document j. Denote $\mathbf{F} = (f_{ij})_{m \times n}$. The similarity measure of any two texts based on context can again be computed with Equation 20.4, where $\mathbf{t}_i$ is the ith row of **F**. As with the word-based measures, we can also apply weighting to terms and documents. In this case, term weights form a diagonal matrix $\mathbf{W}_{m \times m}$ and document weights form a diagonal matrix $\Lambda_{n \times n}$. The similarity measures between two texts is the same as Equation 20.4, except that the term vector $\mathbf{t}_i$ is obtained as the ith row of **WFΛ**. This method of denotation allows us to consider LSA in a new framework, as discussed in the next section.

LSA

The two similarity measures introduced previously have one important common characteristic: The terms are represented as multidimensional vectors. The computational formulas are the same, namely, Equation 20.4. However, the vector representations of the terms differ between the approaches. As we have observed, for all the methods introduced, we always assume the existence of a high-dimensional vector representation. This assumption will bring some difficulty when they are implemented in real applications due to the computational complexity.

Representing terms as vectors and comparing similarity between texts using vector algebra has been a common methodology in several applications. For example, Hyperspace Analog to Language (HAL) uses co-occurrence of word pairs in a corpus to build word vector representations (Burgess, 1998). Non-latent similarity (NLS) uses similarities between explicit word pairs to build word vector representations (Cai et al., 2004). Latent semantic analysis (LSA) is the most well-known example of such methods that use vectors to represent terms. Instead of using high-dimensional vectors (usually, the number of words is in the neighborhood of 10^5 and the number of documents is about the same scale), LSA represents each term as a real vector (of up to 500 dimensions), and the similarity between any two texts is computed using the formula in Equation 20.4.

Basic Steps in LSA

The difference between LSA and other methods that we have introduced previously (Martin and Berry, chap. 2 in this volume) is the mechanism by which the term vectors are obtained. We briefly summarize the LSA procedures for obtaining term vectors: data acquisition, singular value decomposition, and dimension reduction.

Data Acquisition.   The process starts by collecting a massive amount of text data in electronic form. With such data, we prepare the $m \times n$ matrix in Equation 20.7,

$$\mathbf{A} = (f_{ij} \times G(i) \times L(i,j))_{m \times n} \qquad \textbf{20.7}$$

where m is the number of terms and n is the number of documents (usually m and n are very large, and for now, assume $n \geq m$), the value of f_{ij} is a function of the number of times term i appears in document j, $L(i, j)$ is a local weighting of term i in document j, and $G(i)$ is the global weighting for term i. Such a weighting function is used to differentially treat terms and documents to reflect knowledge that is beyond the collection of the documents (see Martin and Berry, chap. 2 in this volume, for detail). Notice the fact that if $L(i, j)$ is multiplicative, namely $L(i, j)$ can be written as,

$$L(i, j) = k(i)l(j), \qquad \text{20.8}$$

where $k(i)$ is a weight for the ith term and $l(j)$ is a weight for the jth document, then Equation 20.7 is a matrix (f_{ij}) multiplied by a diagonal matrix $diag\{k(i)G(i)\}$ on the left and another diagonal matrix $diag\{l(j)\}$ on the right, the same form as $\mathbf{WF\Lambda}$ in the context-based similarity measure.

Singular Value Decomposition (SVD). Singular value decomposition (SVD) decomposes the matrix $\mathbf{A}$ into three matrices

$$\mathbf{A} = \mathbf{U\Sigma V}^T \qquad \text{20.9}$$

where $\mathbf{U}$ is $m \times m$ and $\mathbf{V}$ is $n \times n$ square matrices, such that $\mathbf{UU}^T = \mathbf{I}$; $\mathbf{VV}^T = \mathbf{I}$ (orthonormal matrices), and $\mathbf{\Sigma}$ is an $m \times n$ diagonal matrix with singular values on the diagonal. In addition, the singular values are non-negative and are ordered from largest to smallest in the diagonal of $\mathbf{\Sigma}$ (see Martin and Berry, chap. 2 in this volume for detail of SVD).

Dimension Reduction. By removing dimensions corresponding to small singular values and keeping the dimensions corresponding to larger singular values, the representation of each term is reduced to a smaller vector with only k dimensions. The original SVD Equation 20.9 becomes Equation 20.10.

$$\mathbf{A}_k = \mathbf{U}_k \mathbf{\Sigma}_{k \times k} \mathbf{V}^T_k . \qquad \text{20.10}$$

The new term vectors (rows in the reduced $\mathbf{U}$ matrix, $\mathbf{U}_k$) are no longer orthogonal, but the advantage of this is that only the most important dimensions that correspond to larger singular values are kept. This operation is believed to remove redundant information in the matrix $\mathbf{A}$ and reduce noise from semantic information. In the LSA procedure already described, the Data Acquisition and the Dimension Reduction parts are the most intuitive. The most mysterious part is the SVD. Why and how it works is a very deep mathematical/philosophical question and is beyond the scope of this chapter. For more details, see Martin and Berry (chap. 2 in this volume).

Basic Facts About LSA

After $\mathbf{U}_k$ is obtained, each term has a unique k-dimensional vector representation. Furthermore, any text containing one or more terms will also have a corresponding vector with the same number of dimensions. The vector for a text can be computed as a function of the term vectors. Text vectors are computed differently for different applications. The formula for the text vector is in the same form as Equation 20.3, except that $\mathbf{t}_i$ is the ith row of $\mathbf{W}\mathbf{U}_k\Lambda$ where $\mathbf{W} = \mathrm{diag}\{w_i\}$ is a diagonal matrix and w_i is the weight for term i, $\Lambda = diag\{\lambda_j\}$ is a diagonal matrix where λ_j is the weight of dimension j. The similarity between any two texts is calculated by the formula in Equation 20.4.

The procedure outlined previously is relatively simple. There are several advantages to using LSA, but two of them are primary:

1. It picks up the word importance score from the information provided by the corpus.
2. It sets up semantic similarity between words. This widely extends the synonym relation between words.

In addition to the advantages, there are several key elements in LSA that are not directly obvious:

1. The computation of weights $G(i)$ and $L(i, j)$ in Equation 20.7 is nontrivial. $G(i)$ is a measure of how important a term is in the entire collection of texts. In order to obtain $G(i)$ and $L(i,j)$, one needs to process the entire corpus first to get some kind of importance measure such as frequency of appearance. A direct consequence of this is that the entire matrix $\mathbf{A}$ needs to be recalculated whenever some more documents are put into the corpus, because word frequencies are changed. It presumably encodes the weighting of term i in document j and the importance of document j. Such parameters are needed during the data acquisition/encoding phase. It is very important to note that the influence of the parameters can only be evaluated after the three steps and it is very hard to set the parameters because of the massive amount of computation needed to reach the last step.

2. Selection of the number of dimensions (k) is a challenging task. One needs to specify k before the computation. There is no intuitive way to determine the best k, other than by repeated empirical evaluations (Zha & Zhang, 1999).

3. The computation of Equation 20.4 is task dependent. For example, if one only wants to compare the similarity between two texts, then Λ is an identity matrix ($\lambda_j = 1, j = 1, \ldots, k$). If one wants to retrieve a document from the original corpus and obtain the closest vector in $\mathbf{V}$ then Λ is the inverse of the singular values from the SVD (Berry, 1992). The former similarity computation is called the term method, wherein the later computation is called the document method (see http://www.lsa.colorado.edu/).

4. The first dimension is problematic. Because all entries of the original matrix **A** are non-negative, the first dimension of $\mathbf{U}_k$ always has the same sign (Hu, Cai, Franceschetti, et al., 2003) and the mean of the first dimension values is much larger than that of other dimensions. This trend is illustrated in Figure 20.1. As a result of this, the cosine value between any two documents, if one uses the term method, is monotonically related to number of words contained in the documents. This fact was observed by Buckley, Singhal, Mitra, and Salton (1996). Such trend is illustrated in Figure 20.2.

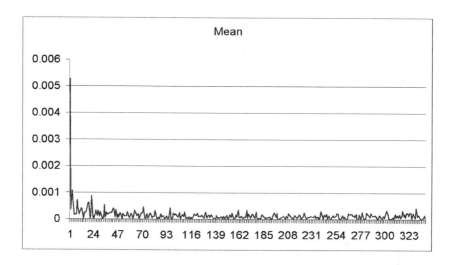

Figure 20.1.   First dimension always has the same sign and its mean is larger than all other dimensions.

Doc B	Document A									
	1	2	4	8	16	32	64	128	256	512
1	0.05	0.02	0.04	0.04	0.05	0.08	0.10	0.11	0.13	0.15
2	0.04	0.02	0.02	0.03	0.05	0.08	0.08	0.10	0.13	0.14
4	0.03	0.02	0.03	0.04	0.05	0.07	0.09	0.11	0.13	0.15
8	0.05	0.03	0.03	0.04	0.05	0.08	0.11	0.13	0.16	0.17
16	0.05	0.05	0.05	0.06	0.09	0.11	0.15	0.18	0.21	0.25
32	0.08	0.06	0.06	0.06	0.11	0.15	0.19	0.24	0.28	0.31
64	0.10	0.07	0.08	0.09	0.13	0.18	0.24	0.28	0.35	0.39
128	0.11	0.08	0.09	0.11	0.15	0.21	0.29	0.34	0.41	0.45
256	0.13	0.10	0.11	0.12	0.17	0.23	0.32	0.38	0.46	0.51

Figure 20.2.   Cosine matches of two documents (i.e., Doc A and B) is a monotonic function of the document size (number of words in each of the two documents).

5. The vector representations for the terms are not fully used. Up to now, their contribution is essentially in the computation of similarities between terms. In other words, in the computation of text similarity, LSA only provides the information about "term similarity." A little mathematics can help to make this clear. Denote the term vectors by t_i ($i = 1, \ldots, n$), the number of occurrences of term i in text 1 by a_i and in text 2 by b_i, then text 1 and text 2 are represented by vectors T_1 and T_2, respectively, where

$$T_1 = (a_1 t_1, a_2 t_2, \ldots, a_n t_n),$$

$$T_2 = (b_1 t_1, b_2 t_2, \ldots, b_n t_n).$$

The similarity between T_1 and T_2 is computed by the cosine of the angle between T_1 and T_2

$$\cos(T_1, T_2) = \frac{T_1 T_2^T}{\sqrt{T_1 T_1^T} \sqrt{T_2 T_2^T}} = \frac{\sum_{i=1}^{n} \sum_{j=1}^{n} a_i b_j t_i t_j^T}{\sqrt{\sum_{i=1}^{n} \sum_{j=1}^{n} a_i a_j t_i t_j^T} \sqrt{\sum_{i=1}^{n} \sum_{j=1}^{n} b_i b_j t_i t_j^T}}$$

$$(20.11)$$

where $t_i t_j^T$, are dot products of the term vectors. When the term vectors are normalized to unit length, the products are similarities between terms. In other words, the obtained $n \times n$ matrix, $P = (s_{ij})_{n \times n}$, where $s_{ij} = t_i t_j^T$, $I, j = 1, 2, \ldots, n$ is the similarity (un-normalized) between term i and term j. Equation 20.11 gives a way to compute text similarities based on the term similarity matrix. However, we need an $n \times n$ matrix to save the un-normalized term similarities. The advantage of vector representation of terms here is the saving of storage space (from $n \times n$ to $n \times k$ real numbers). It may be a significant saving, when n is greater than k. One drawback is the loss of flexibility in constructing the term similarity matrix (Cai et al., 2004).

We end this section by proving a theorem that relates LSA and weighted keyword matching (Hu, Cai, Franceschetti, et al., 2003). This theorem will help to develop other sections of the chapter.

Theorem: Assume k equals the number of nonzero singular values, then

1. If $\Lambda = \Sigma_{k \times k}$ and $L(i, j)$ is multiplicative, as in Equation 20.8, then Equation 20.4 is weighted context matching.
2. If $\Lambda = I_{k \times k}$ then Equation 20.4 is weighted keyword matching.

Based on our discussions in this section, we observed that there are some facts about LSA that are not trivial (facts d and e, e.g.). The next section examines the use of LSA in several applications and points out some weaknesses of LSA.

Limitations of LSA

In order to understand the limitations pointed out here, we briefly describe two applications that use LSA. For details about these two applications, the reader may find more in other chapters in this book (see Graesser et al., chap. 13 in this volume; McNamara, Cai, & Louwerse, chap. 19 in this volume).

AutoTutor. AutoTutor is a natural language tutoring system that teaches conceptual physics and computer literacy via the Internet (Graesser et al., 2000). One challenge for this system is to assess the quality of the student's response to the system. LSA cosine match is used to compare the student's response with the expected answers stored in a curriculum script. The values are used to help AutoTutor provide appropriate feedback for the student.

Coh-Metrix. Coh-Metrix is a web tool that analyzes texts and provides up to 250 measures of cohesion and language characteristics (Graesser, McNamara, Louwerse, & Cai, 2004). Some of the cohesion measures consist of density scores for particular types of cohesion links between text constituents, such as paragraphs, sentences, clauses, or even words. LSA is used in this system to assess the conceptual relatedness of constituents (i.e., the more related, the more cohesive) and to assess co-referential cohesion (i.e., the extent to which content words refer to other constituents in the text).

The Statistical Nature of LSA Values

As we have pointed out previously, the first dimension of all the term vectors have the same sign. This indicates that if one uses the term method to compute the similarity, the value computed by Equation 20.4 is directly influenced by the number of words in the texts. A simple simulation shows that the cosine value between two texts monotonically increases as a function of the number of terms in the two documents (see Fig. 20.2). This property of the term method makes it very hard to interpret text similarity measures without considering the sizes of the texts (Hu, Cai, Franceschetti, et al., 2003). In the case of AutoTutor, students' contributions are compared with stored expectations. AutoTutor selects a fixed value between 0 and 1. If the cosine match between students' contribution and the stored expectation exceed such value, AutoTutor assumes the expectation is covered. The fixed value for this purpose is called a threshold. The issue here is how to set the threshold. The threshold should be a function of the number of terms contained in the student's contribution and the individual expectations. This limitation is not relevant in the case where similarity is computed using the document method, where the influence of the first dimension is minimized, nor in the case where the similarity is used for information retrieval, where only the ordinal property of the similarity value is used (Graesser, Hu, et al., 2004).

The Use of Detailed Dimensional Information

The procedure outlined in the previous section has demonstrated that the original U matrix from the SVD and the truncated U_k are substantially influenced by the information contained in the original corpus. We further observed that even with the remaining k dimensions, LSA only has limited use. In fact, all the remaining dimensions are used only to obtain dot products between terms, as it was shown in Equation 20.11. In the next few sections, we demonstrate that the vector representations of terms and documents contain more information. The information contained in the dimensions can be further used to extend the usefulness of LSA.

EXTENDING LSA

Two observed weaknesses of LSA motivated us to propose two extensions of LSA that address the observations. One extension is to use the statistical characteristics to reduce the text size effect in the LSA similarity computation. The other extension is to make more use of the dimensional information contained in the vector representation.

Statistical Characteristics of LSA

LSA was originally used as a tool for information retrieval (IR; Graesser, Hu, et al., 2004), where recall was more emphasized than precision in most of the applications. In IR, the influence of the first dimension is not as strong as in similarity measure. This is because (a) the query vector is computed from $WU_k\Lambda$ where $\Lambda = \Sigma^{-1}$ so the first dimension was weighted inversely by the largest singular value, and (b) the document vector is from V_k where the rows are normalized before they are truncated. Furthermore, only the ordinal nature of the cosine value is used in IR because the main goal is to fetch the most relevant document to the query. As a consequence, consideration of the statistical nature of the cosine values is not necessary. In the case of the similarity measure, however, the query vector is computed from WU_k, so the first dimension is always the most influential. Furthermore, in some applications, such as AutoTutor, the cosine values are compared with a threshold. As indicated in Figure 20.2 and proven by Hu, Cai, Franceschetti, et al. (2003), the cosine values are always a monotonic function of the texts' size. For example, a cosine value of .2 between two terms may indicate a high degree of similarity, but may not indicate any similarity at all between texts with over 200 terms. This analysis suggests that when using LSA cosine values for the measures of similarity between texts, one needs to consider the sizes of the texts (Buckley et al.,1996; Hu, Cai, Franceschetti, et al., 2003).

Given the weighted term matrix $\mathbf{WU}_k$, one can always obtain some basic statistical information such as the average cosine $\mu(n_1, n_2)$ and the standard deviation $\sigma(n_1, n_2)$ of any two texts with n_1 and n_2 terms, respectively. Furthermore, if the distribution of all possible cosine values between two texts is normally distributed, one can obtain the relative cosine values between two texts using the following simple formula

$$S(\mathbf{T}_1, \mathbf{T}_2) = \frac{\cos(\mathbf{T}_1, \mathbf{T}_2) - \mu(n_1, n_2)}{\sigma(n_1, n_2)} \qquad 20.12$$

where n_1 and n_2 are the number of terms in T_1 and $\mathbf{T}_2$, respectively.

Adaptive Methods of LSA

As we have pointed out in the previous section, the vector representation of terms in LSA space has been used only to produce a numerical value (vector dot product) between two terms. We argue that there are several other ways of using the dimensional information contained in the vector representation. We call this approach the "adaptive method" of LSA. For the purpose of later sections, we briefly review a few concepts in linear algebra.

Some Basic Concepts in Linear Algebra

Linear Combination. A vector **b** is a linear combination of the vectors $\mathbf{v}_1, \mathbf{v}_2 \dots, \mathbf{v}_n$, if $\mathbf{b} = c_1\mathbf{v}_1 + c_2\mathbf{v}_2 + \dots + c_n\mathbf{v}_n$, where $c_1, c_2 \dots, c_n$ are scalars.

Span. Suppose $\mathbf{v}_1, \mathbf{v}_2, \dots, \mathbf{v}_n$ are vectors in a vector space **V**. These vectors are said to span **V** if every vector **v** in **V** can be expressed as a linear combination of these vectors.

Linear Dependence. A set of vectors $\mathbf{v}_1, \mathbf{v}_2, \dots, \mathbf{v}_n$ are linearly dependent if it is possible to express one of the vectors as the others; that is, for some k,

$$v_k = \sum_{\substack{1 \le i \le n \\ i \ne k}} a_i v_i$$

Linear Independence. A set of vectors $\mathbf{v}_1, \mathbf{v}_2, \dots, \mathbf{v}_n$ are linearly independent if it is impossible to express any one of the vectors as the others.

Basis.   A set of vectors $\mathbf{v}_1, \mathbf{v}_2, \ldots, \mathbf{v}_n$ in $\mathbf{V}$ is a basis for $\mathbf{V}$ if the vectors are linearly independent and span $\mathbf{V}$.

Standard Basis.   The set of vectors $\mathbf{e}_1, \mathbf{e}_2, \ldots, \mathbf{e}_n$ where

$$
\begin{aligned}
\mathbf{e}_1 &= (1,0,0,\ldots,0) \\
\mathbf{e}_2 &= (0,1,0,\ldots,0) \\
\mathbf{e}_3 &= (0,0,1,\ldots,0) \\
&\vdots \\
\mathbf{e}_n &= (0,0,0,\ldots,1)
\end{aligned}
\qquad\qquad \text{20.13}
$$

is called the standard basis for $\mathbf{R}^n$.

Dimension.   A vector space $\mathbf{V}$ has a dimension n if $\mathbf{V}$ has a basis consisting of n vectors. The dimension of $\mathbf{V}$ is denoted by dim($\mathbf{V}$).

Representation.   Because every vector can be represented uniquely by the base, meaning and interpretation of any vector can only be understood through the meaning and interpretation of the vectors contained in the base. This is the key notion behind the current claims. LSA vector is "latent" only because the dimensions are implicit (latent).

Adapting to Perspective

The typical feature of LSA is that the dimensions are latent. That means there are no explicit interpretations for the dimensions. Even though this is a fact about LSA, researchers frequently try to find some more information from the dimensions and interpret the values. For example, we observed some special properties of the first dimension (Hu, Cai, Franceschetti, et al., 2003). In this section, we explore two questions that are potentially relevant. First, can we make the latent dimensions explicit? Second, can we find explicit relations between words and between documents? From some initial derivations, we provide a mathematical solution. The basic idea is to represent information on some explicit dimensions. To do so, we simply need to find a new base with meaningful dimensions and transform the entire LSA vector space to the new base.

To illustrate, we consider a very simple example where only two dimensions are involved. If a vector $\mathbf{S}$ is in an arbitrary coordinate system $\mathbf{U} \times \mathbf{V}$, then $\mathbf{S}$ [with coordinates (u,v)] cannot be easily interpreted without an explicit interpretation of $\mathbf{U}$ and $\mathbf{V}$. However, if a new system $\mathbf{X} \times \mathbf{Y}$ is introduced where $\mathbf{X}$ is the horizontal axis and $\mathbf{Y}$ is vertical axis, $\mathbf{S}$ can be interpreted easily, due to the obvious interpretation of $\mathbf{X}$ and $\mathbf{Y}$ (see Fig. 20.3).

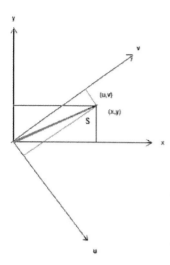

Figure 20.3. Vector **(u, v)** in an arbitrary system cannot be interpreted due to the arbitrariness of the coordinates system **U** and **V**. However, it can be interpreted if a new system (coordinates system **X** and **Y**) is used. The vector **(x, y)** can be obtained from the relations between the two systems, namely, **U-V** coordinates system and **X-Y** coordinates system.

To generalize the previous intuitive example, we derive a general algorithm that can be used in LSA space with k dimensions. Consider the LSA term matrix $\mathbf{H}_{m \times k} = \mathbf{WU}_k \Lambda$ with m term vectors. Furthermore, we may assume $\mathbf{b}_1, \mathbf{b}_2, \ldots, \mathbf{b}_k$ are any set of independent vectors that serve as a base of the space. For example, the base could be k words that represent k distinct categories, or a centroid of some categories that can be interpreted. From linear algebra, for any row in $\mathbf{H}_{m \times k}$, $\mathbf{h}_i = (h_{i1}, h_{i2}, \ldots, h_{ik})$, there is a unique nonzero vector $(e_{i1}, e_{i2} \ldots, e_{ik})$, such that

$$\mathbf{h}_i = \sum_{j=1}^{k} e_{ij} \mathbf{b}_j \qquad 20.14$$

In this case, $\mathbf{e}_i = (e_{i1}, \ldots, e_{ik})$ is the new representation under new base $\mathbf{B} = (\mathbf{b}_1, \mathbf{b}_2, \ldots, \mathbf{b}_k)$. To illustrate, suppose in the original LSA space, two terms are represented by two rows in $\mathbf{H}_{m \times k}$, $\mathbf{h}_s = (h_{s1}, h_{s2}, \ldots, h_{sk})$ and $\mathbf{h}_t = (h_{t1}, h_{t2}, \ldots, h_{tk})$. There exist unique $\mathbf{c}_s = (c_{s1}, c_{s2}, \ldots, c_{sk})$ and $\mathbf{c}_t = (c_{t1}, c_{t2}, \ldots, c_{tk})$, for $\mathbf{h}_s = \mathbf{c}_s \mathbf{B}^\mathsf{T}$ and $\mathbf{h}_t = \mathbf{c}_t \mathbf{B}^\mathsf{T}$, respectively, where $\mathbf{c}_s \mathbf{B}^\mathsf{T}$ and $\mathbf{c}_t \mathbf{B}^\mathsf{T}$ are inner products of vectors. The cosine in the original space is

$$\frac{\mathbf{h}_s \mathbf{h}_t^T}{\|\mathbf{h}_s\| \|\mathbf{h}_t\|} = \frac{(h_{s1}, h_{s2} \ldots, h_{sk})(h_{t1}, h_{t2} \ldots, h_{tk})^T}{\|\mathbf{h}_s\| \|\mathbf{h}_t\|} = \frac{\mathbf{c}_s (\mathbf{B}^T \mathbf{B}) \mathbf{c}_t^T}{\|\mathbf{h}_s\| \|\mathbf{h}_t\|},$$

where $\| \bullet \|$ is the length of a vector. On the other hand, because $\mathbf{c}_s = \mathbf{h}_s (\mathbf{B}^T)^{-1}$ and $\mathbf{c}_t = \mathbf{h}_t (\mathbf{B}^T)^{-1}$, the cosine under the new base can be obtained by

$$
\frac{\mathbf{c}_s \mathbf{c}_t^T}{\|\mathbf{c}_s\| \|\mathbf{c}_t\|} = \frac{(c_{s1}, c_{s2} \ldots, c_{sk})(c_{t1}, c_{t2} \ldots, c_{tk})^T}{\|\mathbf{c}_s\| \|\mathbf{c}_t\|} = \frac{\mathbf{h}_s((\mathbf{B}^T)^{-1}(\mathbf{B})^{-1})\mathbf{h}_t^T}{\|\mathbf{c}_s\| \|\mathbf{c}_t\|},
$$

The interesting question is whether we can find a meaningful base. The answer is yes and the construction of such bases can be very simple. For example, we can choose k key terms that we think are most relevant to our task. If the corresponding term vectors are linearly independent, then these k term vectors form a base. Then, any term in the space can be linearly expressed by these selected k term vectors. By definition, these k term vectors form a base of the k-dimensional space. In the previous description, we have used $(\mathbf{b}_1, \mathbf{b}_2, \ldots, \mathbf{b}_k)$, where k is the rank of $\mathbf{H}_{m \times k} = \mathbf{WU}_k \Lambda$.

In fact, from the previous derivation, we can prove that it is not necessary to specify all k vectors for the base. One could simply specify a few meaningful vectors $(\mathbf{b}_1, \mathbf{b}_2, \ldots, \mathbf{b}_{k0})$ and select $(k - k_0)$ vectors from the old base from Equation 20.13.

Adapting to Context

In AutoTutor, every input from student is compared to several expectations. LSA is used to decide whether each of the expectations is covered. It turned out that some of the expectations have similar LSA vectors. When this occurs, it would be ideal to adjust AutoTutor so that it can detect small differences between the expectations. The process of adjusting LSA to this task is outlined here. We call this the method of "adapting to context."

Before we derive the formal method, consider the following keyword match example to help understand our basic claims. Assume that the two target expectations are A: "The horizontal speed is constant for the moving body" and B: "The vertical speed is zero for the moving body." Assume that the student's input is C: "The moving body will move forward with constant speed." To distinguish A from B, there are some common words (*the, is, for, the, moving, body*) shared by A and B; they will not add much value in discriminating the two alternative expectations. In this case, one can either include common words or exclude common words. When common words are included, the similarity between A and C is .556, whereas the similarity between B and C is .444. When common words are excluded, the similarity between A and C is .258, whereas the similarity between B and C is 0.

As shown from this example, one might prefer the exclusion method so that C is relatively more similar to A than B. In essence, the differences between A and B would be magnified and this would be reflected in the similarity between C and A versus B (see Table 20.1). There needs to be a method to implement this context-sensitive magnification to LSA, where each expectation is represented as an LSA vector. Assume the two target expectations have vectors $\mathbf{A}$ and $\mathbf{B}$, and that the student's input is vector $\mathbf{C}$.

TABLE 20.1
Comparison Between Two Similarity Measures

	Remove Common Words	Keep Common Words
A vs. C	.258	.556
B vs. C	.000	.444

Note. Sentences A: "The horizontal speed is constant for the moving body," B: "The vertical speed is zero for the moving body," and C: "The moving body will move forward with constant speed." Using two methods of keyword matching. The common words in A and B are "the," " speed," " is," "for," " moving," and "body." By removing the common words from A and B, then resulting A, B, and C are three sets of words: A: " horizontal," "constant," B: "vertical," "zero," and C: "will," "move," "forward," "with," "constant."

$$A = (a_1, a_2, \dots, a_k)$$

$$B = (b_1, b_2, \dots, b_k)$$

$$C = (c_1, c_2, \dots, c_k)$$

Further assume that n_A, n_B and n_C are the number of words in A, B, and C, respectively, and that we have identified statistical properties of the LSA space. That is, for each column of $\mathbf{WU}_k \Lambda$ such as column x, there is the mean μ_x and standard deviation σ_x, $x = 1, 2, \dots, k$. Given these statistics and the number of words in A, B, and C, the expected values and variability (standard deviation) of the xth elements of A, B, and C are $(n_A \mu_x, \sqrt{n_A} \sigma_x)$, $(n_B \mu_x, \sqrt{n_B} \sigma_x)$, and $(n_C \mu_x, \sqrt{n_C} \sigma_x)$. With these values computed, we can then decide the difference between $\mathbf{A}$ and $\mathbf{B}$ by comparing quantities computed based on Equation 20.15 for all $x = 1, \dots, k$.

$$\frac{n_A \mu - n_B \mu_x}{\sqrt{n_A \sigma_x^2 + n_B \sigma_x^2}} = z_x \qquad \textbf{20.15}$$

The final comparison between $\mathbf{A}$ and $\mathbf{B}$ versus $\mathbf{B}$ and $\mathbf{C}$ is computed in Equation 20.16,

$$\left\{ \begin{aligned} S'(A,C) &= \frac{\sum_{x=1}^{k} F(z_x) a_x c_x}{\sqrt{\sum_{x=1}^{k} f(z_x) a_x^2} \sqrt{\sum_{x=1}^{k} f(z_x) c_x^2}} \\ S'(B,C) &= \frac{\sum_{x=1}^{k} f(z_x) b_x c_x}{\sqrt{\sum_{x=1}^{k} f(z_x) b_x^2} \sqrt{\sum_{x=1}^{k} f(z_x) c_x^2}} \end{aligned} \right. \qquad \textbf{20.16}$$

where $f(z)$ is a function such that $f(z') \geq f(z'')$ if $z' > z''$ The simplest case for the function $f(z)$ is the function captured in Equation 20.17.

$$f(z) = \begin{cases} 1 & z > \delta \\ 0 & z \leq \delta \end{cases} \qquad\qquad 20.17$$

This function was used in the simulation that we describe next.

Simulation

We explored the previous analysis by a simple simulation (see Fig. 20.4 as an illustration) where **A**, **B**, and **C** are generated random vectors with 300 dimensions. In the simulation, two set of vectors that are "similar" at dimension x if $z_x = 0$. **A** and **B** are similar for 150 of the dimensions, whereas **A** and **C** are similar for those 37 of the 150 dimensions for which **A** and **B** are different. Thus, similarity is based on those dimensions that differentiate **A** and **B**, not all dimensions.

We obtained all simulated values of Equation 20.16, both with and without using the weighting function (Equation 20.17). We observed the difference between S'(**A**, **C**) and S'(**B**, **C**) is larger with Equation 20.17 (upper picture of Fig. 20.5, $d' = 3.05$) than the case in which Equation 20.17 was not used (lower picture of Fig. 20.5, $d' = 2.07$).

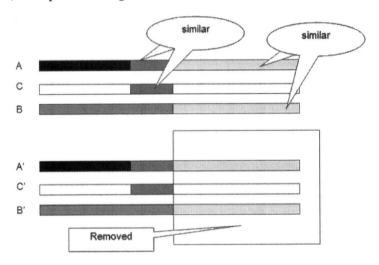

Figure 20.4.   This is an illustration of the simulation. Vectors **A**, **B**, and **C** are generated based on the following rule: **A** and **B** are similar 50% ; **A** and **C** are similar 25% among the dimensions where **A** and **B** are different. In the first simulation, all dimensions are used in the simulation. In the second simulation, the dimensions that **A** and **B** are similar are removed.

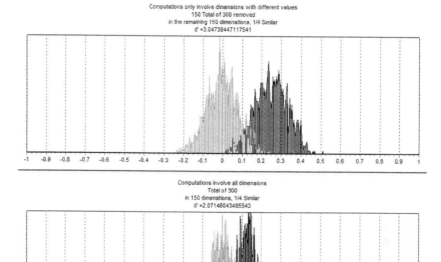

Figure 20.5. Darker distribution is the cosine between **A** and **C**, and lighter distribution is the cosine between **B** and **C**. The difference between the two distribution is $d' =$ 2.07 for the case where all dimensions are used and $d' = 3.047$ when the common dimensions are removed.

From the previous analysis and simulation, we argue that when using LSA similarity to select one option from multiple alternatives (e.g., using *C* to select one of *A* and *B*, as in the example and simulation), considering detailed dimensional information will help the selection. In this method, context constrains and narrows down the alternatives at the level of detailed dimensions. We call this the method of "adapting to context."

Adapting to Dialog History

This is a method especially appropriate in situations where LSA is used to evaluate sequence of contributions (Hu, Cai, Louwerse, et al., 2003). Consider AutoTutor when the tutor's goal is to help the student produce an answer to a question. The student typically gives one piece of information at a time. To furnish a complete answer to a question, the student needs to produce multiple pieces of information. In order for the tutor to be helpful and effective, the tutor needs to evaluate every contribution of the student and to help the student every time a contribution is made. We assume that AutoTutor is suppose to give feedback based on student's contribution toward the answer and that AutoTutor is suppose to give four different context-sensitive feedbacks at every contribution:

Similar to the analysis of the previous method, we first consider what AutoTutor would do if the evaluation method were keyword matching. For an ordered sequence of statements, $S_1, S_2, \ldots, S_N$ and a target statement S_0, for any given i ($2 \le i \le n$), one can decompose S_i into the four different bags of words, as specified here:

1. Words that overlap with words in S_0 (relevant)
   - Appeared in $S_1, S_2, \ldots, S_{i-1}$ (old)
   - Never appeared in $S_1, S_2, \ldots, S_{i-1}$ (new)
2. Words that do not overlap with words in S_0 (irrelevant)
   - Appeared in $S_1, S_2, \ldots, S_{i-1}$ (old)
   - Never appeared in $S_1, S_2, \ldots, S_{i-1}$ (new)

Having established relations between keyword match and LSA in the previous section, the similar decomposition can be achieved in the present case. Denote $\mathbf{s}_i = s_i \mathbf{W} \mathbf{U}_k$, $i = 0, 1, \ldots, n$. For an ordered sequence of statements, $\mathbf{s}_1, \mathbf{s}_2, \ldots, \mathbf{s}_n$ and a target statement $\mathbf{s}_0$ for any given i ($2 \le i \le n$), one can decompose S_i into four different vectors:

1. Vector that is parallel to $\mathbf{s}_0$ (relevant)
   - Parallel to the spanned space of $\mathbf{s}_1, \mathbf{s}_2, \ldots, \mathbf{s}_{i-1}$ (old)
   - Perpendicular to the spanned space of $\mathbf{s}_1, \mathbf{s}_2, \ldots, \mathbf{s}_{i-1}$ (new)
2. Vector that is perpendicular to $\mathbf{s}_0$ (irrelevant)
   - Parallel to the spanned space of $\mathbf{s}_1, \mathbf{s}_2, \ldots, \mathbf{s}_{i-1}$ (old)
   - Perpendicular to the spanned space of $\mathbf{s}_1, \mathbf{s}_2, \ldots, \mathbf{s}_{i-1}$ (new)

TABLE 20.2
Four Types of Feedback the System Provides on the Basis of Relevance and Newness of Student Contribution

	Relevant	*Irrelevant*
New	++	-
Old	+	- -

Note. In the case of keyword matching, treating each sentence as a collection of words, this collection of words can be classified into four different types, based on what is the answer key and all previous contributions.

AutoTutor would ideally provide feedback based on the rate of change on each of the four components. For example, AutoTutor would provide positive feedback if each input from the student contains more new and relevant information (see Table 20.2). Ideally, a student would contribute a sequence of statements toward the answer. In AutoTutor, feedback at step i is based on how much the student has contributed to the coverage of the expected answer until step i. To compute the coverage score, we need to introduce some notations. Let $proj(\mathbf{s}, \mathbf{p})$ denote the projection of vector $\mathbf{s}$ in the subspace $\mathbf{P}$ and $\mathbf{S}_i = \mathrm{span}\{\mathbf{s}_1, \mathbf{s}_2, \ldots, \mathbf{s}_{i-1}\}$. For any given i $(2 \le i \le n)$, the four previous components can be specified in Equation 20.18.

$$
\begin{aligned}
&relevant,\ old\text{: } \mathbf{u}_i = proj(proj(\mathbf{s}_i, span\{\mathbf{s}_0\}), \mathbf{S}_{i'}) \\
&relevant,\ new\text{:} v_i = proj(proj(\mathbf{s}_i, span\{\mathbf{s}_0\}), \mathbf{S}^{\perp}_{i'}) \\
&irrelevant,\ old\text{: } x_i = proj(proj(\mathbf{s}_i, (span\{\mathbf{s}_0\})^{\perp}), \mathbf{S}_{i'}) \\
&irrelevant,\ new\text{: } \mathrm{y}i = proj(proj(\mathbf{s}_i, (span\{\mathbf{s}_0\})^{\perp}), \mathbf{S}^{\perp\perp}_{i'})
\end{aligned}
\qquad 20.18
$$

The accumulation of "relevant, new" information is called coverage. To compute the coverage score, we use an iterative procedure. If c_i is the coverage score for space $\mathbf{S}_i$, then the new coverage score c_{i+1} by the space $\mathbf{S}_{i+1}$ is expressed in Equation 20.19. Figure 20.6 is an illustration of Equation 20.18.

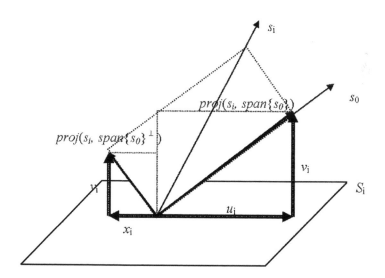

Figure 20.6. A vector $\mathbf{s}_i$ is decomposed into components in the direction of the target vector $\mathbf{s}_0$ and its perpendicular direction. The components are further decomposed in the direction of the ith span $\mathbf{S}_i$ and its perpendicular direction.

$$c_{i+1} = \sqrt{c_i^2 + \frac{\|v_i\|^2}{\|s_o\|^2}}$$
                                                                                                                    20.19

We illustrate the previous arguments by applying to the following example from AutoTutor:

Question: Suppose a runner is running in a straight line at a constant speed and throws a pumpkin straight up. Where will the pumpkin land? Explain why.

Expectation: The pumpkin will land in the runner's hands.

Student's contribution:

1. I think, correct me if I am wrong, it will not land before or behind the guy.
2. The reason is clear; they have the same horizontal speed.
3. The pumpkin will land in the runner's hand.
4. Did I say anything wrong?
5. Come on, I thought I have said that!

We use old LSA (with threshold .8) and adaptive methods to compute coverage of the student's contribution at each step (see Table 20.1). We observed that even when the student produced a perfect answer (e.g., answer 3), the old LSA method failed to detect it (the cosine match was still less than the threshold, due to the fact that contributions 1 and 2 are evaluated with 3 together). Furthermore, the last two of the contributions have very little contribution to the coverage of the expectation, so the old LSA method decreased, as expected. However, when we used the adapting to context method described earlier, we observed the monotonic increase in coverage scores and a perfect match score when the student provided the perfect answer (see Table 20.3).

TABLE 20.3
Example of Student Contibution and Evaluation Based on Two LSA Methods

	Old LSA Cosine Value	New and Relevant	Coverage
1	.431	.431	.431
2	.430	.175	.466
3	.751	.885	1.0
4	.713	.000	1.0
5	.667	.000	1.0

Note. Old LSA Cosine Value is the cosine match between all prior contributions and the answer key (expectation). This is the reason for the observed decreasing cosine values in the second column. New and Relevant is computed by the SPAN method in Equation 20.18. The coverage is computed by Equation 20.19.

The basic idea in this method is to consider the span of the vectors prior to current vector. Hence, the method is called the "span method." As we can see from the previous derivation and example, this method makes use of the dialog history and the dimensional information of the vector representation. One could imagine that Tutor's feedback could be based on other components also. For example, when the student provides old and irrelevant information, AutoTutor may detect that persistent misconceptions are driving the answers. AutoTutor's feedback is largely determined by the values of u_i, v_i, x_i, y_i at any step i. The overall performance is computed as an accumulation score, as in the case of Equation 20.19.

CONCLUSIONS

In this chapter, we have pointed out two limitations of LSA: limited use of statistical information of LSA space and limited use of dimensional information in the vector representation of the terms. Based on these observations, we have proposed a few extensions. These include a modified cosine match, as shown in Equation 20.12, as similarity measures and adaptive methods that intelligently select dimensional information of the vector representations. We have concentrated large portion of the chapter developing the adaptive methods. We have proposed three adaptive methods: adapting to perspective, adapting to context, and adapting to dialog history. All three adaptive methods are developed in the context of the application of AutoTutor with LSA cosine match being used as similarity measure. In this chapter, we primarily concentrated on mathematical derivations and explained the extensions at the conceptual level with simple simulations. The next step is to implement the extensions in real applications.

ACKNOWLEDGMENTS

This research was supported by grants from the Institute for Education Sciences (IES R3056020018-02), the National Science Foundation (SBR 9720314, REC 0106965, REC 0126265, ITR 0325428), and the DoD Multidisciplinary University Research Initiative (MURI) administered by ONR under grant N00014-00-1-0600. The Tutoring Research Group (TRG) is an interdisciplinary research team comprised of approximately 35 researchers from psychology, computer science, physics, and education (visit http://www.autotutor.org). Any opinions, findings, and conclusions or recommendations expressed in this material are those of the authors and do not necessarily reflect the views of the IES, NSF, DoD, or ONR.

REFERENCES

Berry, M. W. (1992). Large scale singular value computations. *International Journal of Supercomputer Applications, 6*(1), 13–49.

Buckley, C., Singhal, A., Mitra, M., & Salton, G. (1996). New retrieval approaches using SMART: TREC 4. *Proceedings of the Fourth Text Retrieval Conference* (NIST Special Publication 500–236), 25–48.

Burgess, C. (1998). From simple associations to the building blocks of language: Modeling meaning in memory with the HAL model. *Behavior Research Methods, Instruments, and Computers, 30,* 188–198

Cai, Z., McNamara, D. S., Louwerse, M. M., Hu, X., Rowe, M. P., & Graesser, A. C. (2004). NLS: A non-latent similarity algorithm. In K. D. Forbus, D. Gentner, & T. Regier (Eds.), *Proceedings of the 26th Annual Conference of the Cognitive Science Society* (pp. 180–185). Mahwah, NJ: Lawrence Erlbaum Associates.

Coltheart, M. (1981). The MRC psycholinguistic database. *Quarterly Journal of Experimental Psychology, 33,* 497–505

Graesser, A. C., McNamara, D.S., Louwerse, M.M., & Cai, Z. (2004). Coh-Metrix: Analysis of text on cohesion and language. *Behavior Research Methods, Instruments, and Computers, 36,* 193–202.

Graesser, A. C., Hu, X., Person, P., Jackson, T., & Toth, J. (2004, October/November). Modules and information retrieval facilities of the Human Use Regulatory Affairs Advisor (HURAA). *International Journal on eLearning,* 29–39.

Graesser, A., Wiemer-Hastings, P., Wiemer-Hastings, K., Harter, D., Person, N., & the Tutoring Research Group. (2000). Using latent semantic analysis to evaluate the contributions of students in AutoTutor. *Interactive Learning Environments, 8,* 149–169.

Hu, X., Cai, Z., Franceschetti, D., Penumatsa, P., Graesser, A. C., Louwerse, M. M., McNamara, D. S., & TRG (2003). LSA: The first dimension and dimensional weighting. In R. Alterman & D. Hirsh (Eds.), *Proceedings of the 25rd Annual Conference of the Cognitive Science Society* (pp. 1–6). Boston: Cognitive Science Society.

Hu, X., Cai, Z., Louwerse, M., Olney, A., Penumatsa, P., Graesser, A. C., & TRG (2003). A revised algorithm for latent semantic analysis. In G. Gottlob & T. Walsh (eds.), *Proceedings of the 2003 International Joint Conference on Artificial Intelligence,* (pp. 1489–1491). San Francisco: Morgan Kaufmann.

McNamara, D. S., Cai, Z., & Louwerse, M. M. (in press). Comparing latent and non-latent measures of cohesion. In T. Landauer, D. S., McNamara, S. Dennis, & W. Kintsch (Eds.), *LSA: A road to meaning.* Mahwah, NJ: Lawrence Erlbaum Associates.

Miller, G. A. (1985).WordNet: A dictionary browser. *Proceedings of the First International Conference on Information in Data*, 25–28.

Zha, H., & Zhang, Z. (1999). Matrices with low-rank-plus-shift structure: Partial SVD and latent semantic indexing. *SIAM Journal on Matrix Analysis and Application*, 21(2), 522–536.

21

Probabilistic Topic Models

Mark Steyvers
University of California, Irvine

Tom Griffiths
University of California, Berkeley

Many chapters in this book illustrate that applying a statistical method such as latent semantic analysis (LSA; Landauer & Dumais, 1997; Landauer, Foltz, & Laham, 1998) to large databases can yield insight into human cognition. The LSA approach makes three claims: that semantic information can be derived from a word-document co-occurrence matrix; that dimensionality reduction is an essential part of this derivation; and that words and documents can be represented as points in Euclidean space. This chapter pursues an approach that is consistent with the first two of these claims, but differs in the third, describing a class of statistical models in which the semantic properties of words and documents are expressed in terms of probabilistic topics.

Topic models (e.g., Blei, Ng, & Jordan, 2003; Griffiths & Steyvers, 2002, 2003, 2004; Hofmann, 1999, 2001) are based on the idea that documents are mixtures of topics, where a topic (Ueda & Saito, 2003) is a probability distribution over words. A topic model is a *generative model* for documents: It specifies a simple probabilistic procedure by which documents can be generated. To make a new document, one chooses a distribution over topics. Then, for each word in that document, one chooses a topic at random according to this distribution, and draws a word from that topic. Standard statistical techniques can be used to invert this process, inferring the set of topics that were responsible for generating a collection of documents. Figure 21.1 shows four example topics that were derived from the TASA corpus, a collection of over 37,000 text passages from educational materials (e.g., language & arts, social studies, health, sciences) collected by Touchstone Applied Science Associates (see Landauer et al., 1998). The figure shows the 16 words that have the highest probability under each topic. The words in these topics relate to drug use, colors, memory and the mind, and doctor visits. Documents with different content can be generated by choosing different distributions over topics. For example, by giving equal probability to the first two topics, one could construct a document about a person that has taken too many drugs, and how that affected color perception. By giving equal probability to the last two topics, one could construct a document about a person who experienced a loss of memory, which required a visit to the doctor.

Representing the content of words and documents with probabilistic topics has one distinct advantage over a purely spatial representation. Each topic is individually interpretable, providing a probability distribution over words that picks out a coherent cluster of correlated terms. Although Figure 21.1 shows only 4 out of 300 topics that were derived, the topics are typically as interpretable as the ones shown here. This contrasts with the arbitrary axes of a spatial representation, and can be extremely useful in many applications (e.g., Griffiths & Steyvers, 2004; Rosen-Zvi, Griffiths, Steyvers, & Smyth, 2004; Steyvers, Smyth, Rosen-Zvi, & Griffiths, 2004).

The plan of this chapter is as follows. First, it describes the key ideas behind topic models in more detail and outlines how it is possible to identify the topics that appear in a set of documents. It then discusses methods for answering two kinds of questions about similarities: assessing the similar-

Topic 247		Topic 5		Topic 43		Topic 56	
word	prob.	word	prob.	word	prob.	word	prob.
DRUGS	.069	RED	.202	MIND	.081	DOCTOR	.074
DRUG	.060	BLUE	.099	THOUGHT	.066	DR.	.063
MEDICINE	.027	GREEN	.096	REMEMBER	.064	PATIENT	.061
EFFECTS	.026	YELLOW	.073	MEMORY	.037	HOSPITAL	.049
BODY	.023	WHITE	.048	THINKING	.030	CARE	.046
MEDICINES	.019	COLOR	.048	PROFESSOR	.028	MEDICAL	.042
PAIN	.016	BRIGHT	.030	FELT	.025	NURSE	.031
PERSON	.016	COLORS	.029	REMEMBERED	.022	PATIENTS	.029
MARIJUANA	.014	ORANGE	.027	THOUGHTS	.020	DOCTORS	.028
LABEL	.012	BROWN	.027	FORGOTTEN	.020	HEALTH	.025
ALCOHOL	.012	PINK	.017	MOMENT	.020	MEDICINE	.017
DANGEROUS	.011	LOOK	.017	THINK	.019	NURSING	.017
ABUSE	.009	BLACK	.016	THING	.016	DENTAL	.015
EFFECT	.009	PURPLE	.015	WONDER	.014	NURSES	.013
KNOWN	.008	CROSS	.011	FORGET	.012	PHYSICIAN	.012
PILLS	.008	COLORED	.009	RECALL	.012	HOSPITALS	.011

Figure 21.1. An illustration of 4 (out of 300) topics extracted from the TASA corpus.

ity between two documents and assessing the associative similarity between two words. It closes by considering how generative models have the potential to provide further insight into human cognition.

GENERATIVE MODELS

A generative model for documents is based on simple probabilistic sampling rules that describe how words in documents might be generated on the basis of latent (random) variables. When fitting a generative model, the goal is to find the best set of latent variables that can explain the observed data (i.e., observed words in documents), assuming that the model actually generated the data. Figure 21.2 illustrates the topic modeling approach in two distinct ways: as a generative model and as a problem of statistical inference. On the left, the generative process is illustrated with two topics. Topics 1 and 2 are thematically related to money and rivers and are illustrated as bags containing different distributions over words. Different documents can be produced by picking words from a topic depending on the weight given to the topic. For example, documents 1 and 3 were generated by sampling only from topic 1 and 2, respectively, whereas document 2 was generated by an equal mixture of the two topics. Note that the superscript numbers associated with the words in documents indicate which topic was used to sample the word. The way that the model is defined, there is no notion of mutual exclusivity that restricts words to be part of one topic only. This allows topic models to capture polysemy, where the same word has multiple meanings. For example, both the money and river topic can give high probability to the word *bank*, which is sensible given the polysemous nature of the word.

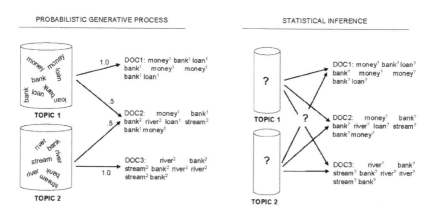

Figure 21.2.   Illustration of the generative process and the problem of statistical inference underlying topic models.

The generative process described here does not make any assumptions about the order of words as they appear in documents. The only information relevant to the model is the number of times words are produced. This is known as the *bag-of-words assumption*, and is common to many statistical models of language, including LSA. Of course, word-order information might contain important cues to the content of a document and this information is not utilized by the model. Griffiths, Steyvers, Blei, and Tenenbaum (2005) present an extension of the topic model that is sensitive to word-order and automatically learns the syntactic as well as semantic factors that guide word choice (see also Dennis, chap. 3 in this book for a different approach to this problem).

The right panel of Figure 21.2 illustrates the problem of statistical inference. Given the observed words in a set of documents, we would like to know what topic model is most likely to have generated the data. This involves inferring the probability distribution over words associated with each topic, the distribution over topics for each document, and often the topic responsible for generating each word.

PROBABILISTIC TOPIC MODELS

A variety of probabilistic topic models have been used to analyze the content of documents and the meaning of words (Blei et al., 2003; Griffiths & Steyvers, 2002, 2003, 2004; Hofmann, 1999, 2001; Ueda & Saito, 2003). These models all use the same fundamental idea—that a document is a mixture of topics—but make slightly different statistical assumptions. To introduce notation, we will write $P(z)$ for the distribution over topic z in a particular document and $P(w \mid z)$ for the probability distribution over words w given topic z. Several topic-word distributions $P(w \mid z)$ were illustrated in Figures 21.1 and 21.2, each giving different weight to thematically related words. Each word w_i in a document (where the index refers to the ith word token) is generated by first sampling a topic from the topic distribution, then choosing a word from the topic-word distribution. We write $P(z_i = j)$ as the probability that the jth topic was sampled for the ith word token and $P(w_i \mid z_i = j)$ as the probability of word w_i under topic j. The model specifies the following distribution over words within a document:

$$P(w_i) = \sum_{j=1}^{T} P(w_i \mid z_i = j) P(z_i = j) \qquad \textbf{21.1}$$

where T is the number of topics. To simplify notation, let $\phi^{(j)} = P(w \mid z = j)$ refer to the multinomial distribution over words for topic j and $\theta^{(d)} = P(z)$ refer to the multinomial distribution over topics for document d.

Furthermore, assume that the text collection consists of D documents and each document d consists of N_d word tokens. Let N be the total number of word tokens (i.e., $N = \Sigma\, N_d$). The parameters ϕ and θ indicate which words are important for which topic and which topics are important for a particular document, respectively.

Hofmann (1999, 2001) introduced the probabilistic topic approach to document modeling in his probabilistic latent semantic indexing method (pLSI; also known as the aspect model). The pLSI model does not make any assumptions about how the mixture weights θ are generated, making it difficult to test the generalizability of the model to new documents. Blei et al. (2003) extended this model by introducing a Dirichlet prior on θ, calling the resulting generative model latent Dirichlet allocation (LDA). As a conjugate prior for the multinomial, the Dirichlet distribution is a convenient choice as prior, simplifying the problem of statistical inference. The probability density of a T-dimensional Dirichlet distribution over the multinomial distribution $p = (p_1, \dots, p_T)$ is defined by:

$$Dir(\alpha_1, \dots, \alpha_T) = \frac{\Gamma(\sum_j \alpha_j)}{\prod_j \Gamma(\alpha_j)} \prod_{j=1}^{T} p_j^{\alpha_j - 1} \qquad \textbf{21.2}$$

The parameters of this distribution are specified by $\alpha_1 \dots \alpha_T$. Each hyperparameter α_j can be interpreted as a prior observation count for the number of times topic j is sampled in a document, before having observed any actual words from that document. It is convenient to use a symmetric Dirichlet distribution with a single hyperparameter α such that $\alpha_1 = \alpha_2 = \dots = \alpha_T = \alpha$. By placing a Dirichlet prior on the topic distribution θ, the result is a smoothed topic distribution, with the amount of smoothing determined by the α parameter. Figure 21.3 illustrates the Dirichlet distribution for three topics in a two-dimensional simplex. The simplex is a convenient coordinate system to express all possible probability distributions —for any point $p = (p_1, \dots, p_T)$ in the simplex, we have $\Sigma_j p_j = 1$. The Dirichlet prior on the topic distributions can be interpreted as forces on the topic combinations with higher α moving the topics away from the corners of the simplex, leading to more smoothing (compare the left and right panel). For $\alpha < 1$, the modes of the Dirichlet distribution are located at the corners of the simplex. In this regime (often used in practice), there is a bias toward sparsity, and the pressure is to pick topic distributions favoring just a few topics.

Griffiths and Steyvers (2002, 2003, 2004) explored a variant of this model, discussed by Blei et al. (2003), by placing a symmetric Dirichlet(β) prior on ϕ as well. The hyperparameter β can be interpreted as the prior observation count on the number of times words are sampled from a topic before any

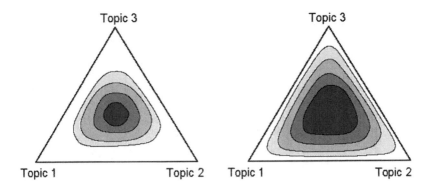

Figure 21.3.   Illustrating the symmetric Dirichlet distribution for three topics on a two-dimensional simplex. Darker colors indicate higher probability. Left: $\alpha = 4$. Right: $\alpha = 2$.

word from the corpus is observed. This smoothes the word distribution in every topic, with the amount of smoothing determined by β. Good choices for the hyperparameters α and β will depend on number of topics and vocabulary size. From previous research, we have found $\alpha = 50/T$ and $\beta = .01$ to work well with many different text collections.

Graphical Model

Probabilistic generative models with repeated sampling steps can be conveniently illustrated using plate notation (see Buntine, 1994, for an introduction). In this graphical notation, shaded and unshaded variables indicate observed and latent (i.e., unobserved) variables, respectively. The variables ϕ and θ, as well as z (the assignment of word tokens to topics) are the three sets of latent variables that we would like to infer. As discussed earlier, we treat the hyperparameters α and β as constants in the model. Figure 21.4 shows the graphical model of the topic model used in Griffiths and Steyvers (2002, 2003, 2004). Arrows indicate conditional dependencies between variables, whereas plates (the boxes in the figure) refer to repetitions of sampling steps with the variable in the lower right corner referring to the number of samples. For example, the inner plate over z and w illustrates the repeated sampling of topics and words until N_d words have been generated for document d. The plate surrounding $\theta^{(d)}$ illustrates the sampling of a distribution over topics for each document d for a total of D documents. The plate surrounding $\phi^{(z)}$ illustrates the repeated sampling of word distributions for each topic z until T topics have been generated.

Geometric Interpretation

The probabilistic topic model has an elegant geometric interpretation as shown in Figure 21.5 (following Hofmann, 1999). With a vocabulary containing W distinct word types, a W dimensional space can be constructed where each axis represents the probability of observing a particular word type. The $W - 1$ dimensional simplex represents all probability distributions over words. In Figure 21.5, the shaded region is the two-dimensional simplex that represents all probability distributions over three words. As a probability distribution over words, each document in the text collection

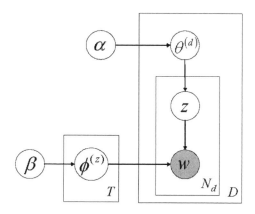

Figure 21.4.   The graphical model for the topic model using plate notation.

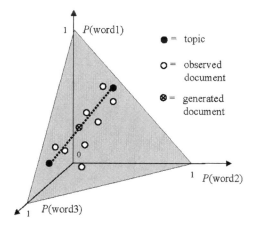

Figure 21.5.   A geometric interpretation of the topic model.

can be represented as a point on the simplex. Similarly, each topic can also be represented as a point on the simplex. Each document generated by the model is a convex combination of the T topics, which not only places all word distributions generated by the model as points on the $W - 1$ dimensional simplex, but also as points on the $T - 1$ dimensional simplex spanned by the topics. For example, in Figure 21.5, the two topics span a one-dimensional simplex and each generated document lies on the line segment between the two topic locations. The Dirichlet prior on the topic-word distributions can be interpreted as forces on the topic locations with higher β moving the topic locations away from the corners of the simplex.

When the number of topics is much smaller than the number of word types (i.e., $T << W$), the topics span a low-dimensional subsimplex and the projection of each document onto the low-dimensional subsimplex can be thought of as dimensionality reduction. This formulation of the model is similar to latent semantic analysis. Buntine (2002) has pointed out formal correspondences between topic models and principal component analysis, a procedure closely related to LSA.

Matrix Factorization Interpretation

In LSA, a word-document co-occurrence matrix can be decomposed by singular value decomposition into three matrices (see Martin & Berry, chap. 2 in this volume): a matrix of word vectors, a diagonal matrix with singular values, and a matrix with document vectors. Figure 21.6 illustrates this decomposition. The topic model can also be interpreted as matrix factorization, as pointed out by Hofmann (1999). In the model already de-

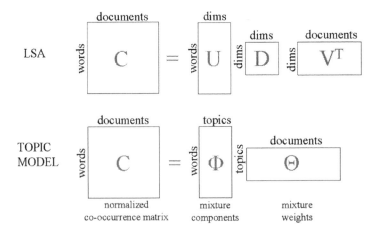

Figure 21.6. The matrix factorization of the LSA model compared to the matrix factorization of the topic model.

scribed, the word-document co-occurrence matrix is split into two parts: a topic matrix Φ and a document matrix Θ. Note that the diagonal matrix D in LSA can be absorbed in the matrix U or V, making the similarity between the two representations even clearer.

This factorization highlights a conceptual similarity between LSA and topic models, both of which find a low-dimensional representation for the content of a set of documents. However, it also shows several important differences between the two approaches. In topic models, the word- and document vectors of the two decomposed matrices are probability distributions with the accompanying constraint that the feature values are nonnegative and sum up to one. In the LDA model, additional a priori constraints are placed on the word and topic distributions. There is no such constraint on LSA vectors, although there are other matrix factorization techniques that require nonnegative feature values (Lee & Seung, 2001). Second, the LSA decomposition provides an orthonormal basis that is computationally convenient because one decomposition for T dimensions will simultaneously give all lower dimensional approximations as well. In the topic model, the topic-word distributions are independent but not orthogonal; model inference needs to be done separately for each dimensionality.

Other Applications

The statistical model underlying the topic modeling approach has been extended to include other sources of information about documents. For example, Cohn and Hofmann (2001) extended the pLSI model by integrating content and link information. In their model, the topics are associated not only with a probability distribution over terms, but also over hyperlinks or citations between documents. Recently, Steyvers et al. (2004) and Rosen-Zvi et al. (2004) proposed the author-topic model, an extension of the LDA model that integrates authorship information with content. Instead of associating each document with a distribution over topics, the author-topic model associates each author with a distribution over topics and assumes each multiauthored document expresses a mixture of the authors' topic mixtures. The statistical model underlying the topic model has also been applied to data other than text. The grade-of-membership (GoM) models developed by statisticians in the 1970s are of a similar form (Manton, Woodbury, & Tolley, 1994), and Erosheva (2002) considers a GoM model equivalent to a topic model. The same model has been used for data analysis in genetics (Pritchard, Stephens, & Donnelly, 2000).

ALGORITHM FOR EXTRACTING TOPICS

The main variables of interest in the model are the topic-word distributions ϕ and the topic distributions θ for each document. Hofmann (1999) used the expectation-maximization (EM) algorithm to obtain direct estimates of ϕ and θ. This approach suffers from problems involving local maxima of the likelihood function, which has motivated a search for better estimation algorithms (Blei et al., 2003; Buntine, 2002; Minka & Lafferty, 2002). Instead of directly estimating the topic-word distributions ϕ and the topic distributions θ for each document, another approach is to directly estimate the posterior distribution over z (the assignment of word tokens to topics), given the observed words w, while marginalizing out ϕ and θ. Each z_i gives an integer value [$1..T$] for the topic that word token i is assigned to. Because many text collections contain millions of word tokens, the estimation of the posterior over z requires efficient estimation procedures. We will describe an algorithm that uses Gibbs sampling, a form of Markov chain Monte Carlo, which is easy to implement and provides a relatively efficient method of extracting a set of topics from a large corpus (Griffiths & Steyvers, 2004; see also Buntine, 2004, Erosheva, 2002, and Pritchard et al., 2000). More information about other algorithms for extracting topics from a corpus can be obtained in the previous references.

Markov chain Monte Carlo (MCMC) refers to a set of approximate iterative techniques designed to sample values from complex (often high-dimensional) distributions (Gilks, Richardson, & Spiegelhalter, 1996). Gibbs sampling (also known as alternating conditional sampling), a specific form of MCMC, simulates a high-dimensional distribution by sampling on lower dimensional subsets of variables where each subset is conditioned on the value of all others. The sampling is done sequentially and proceeds until the sampled values approximate the target distribution. Although the Gibbs procedure we will describe does not provide direct estimates of ϕ and θ, we will show how ϕ and θ can be inferred from posterior estimates of z.

The Gibbs Sampling Algorithm

We represent the collection of documents by a set of word indices w_i and document indices d_i, for each word token i. The Gibbs sampling procedure considers each word token in the text collection in turn, and estimates the probability of assigning the current word token to each topic, conditioned on the topic assignments to all other word tokens. From this conditional distribution, a topic is sampled and stored as the new topic assignment for this word token. We write this conditional distribution as $P(z_i = j \mid z_{-i}, w_i, d_i, \_)$, where $z_i = j$ represents the topic assignment of token i to topic j, z_{-i} refers to the topic assignments of all other word tokens, and "$\_$" refers to all other known or observed information such as all other word and document indices w_{-i} and d_{-i}, and hyperparameters α and β. Griffiths and Steyvers (2004) showed how this can be calculated by:

$$P(z_i = j | z_{-i}, w_i, d_i, .) \propto \frac{C_{w_i j}^{WT} + \beta}{\sum\limits_{w=1}^{W} C_{w_i j}^{WT} + W\beta} \frac{C_{d_i j}^{DT} + \alpha}{\sum\limits_{t=1}^{T} C_{d_i t}^{DT} + T\alpha} \qquad 21.3$$

where $\mathbf{C}^{WT}$ and $\mathbf{C}^{DT}$ are matrices of counts with dimensions $W \times T$ and $D \times T$ respectively; C_{wj}^{WT} contains the number of times word w is assigned to topic j, not including the current instance i, and C_{dj}^{DT} contains the number of times topic j is assigned to some word token in document d, not including the current instance i. Note that Equation 21.3 gives the unnormalized probability. The actual probability of assigning a word token to topic j is calculated by dividing the quantity in Equation 21.3 for topic t by the sum over all topics T.

The factors affecting topic assignments for a particular word token can be understood by examining the two parts of Equation 21.3. The left part is the probability of word w under topic j, whereas the right part is the probability that topic j has under the current topic distribution for document d. Once many tokens of a word have been assigned to topic j (across documents), it will increase the probability of assigning any particular token of that word to topic j. At the same time, if topic j has been used multiple times in one document, it will increase the probability that any word from that document will be assigned to topic j. Therefore, words are assigned to topics depending on how likely the word is for a topic, as well as how dominant a topic is in a document.

The Gibbs sampling algorithm starts by assigning each word token to a random topic in [1..T]. For each word token, the count matrices $\mathbf{C}^{WT}$ and $\mathbf{C}^{DT}$ are first decremented by one for the entries that correspond to the current topic assignment. Then, a new topic is sampled from the distribution in Equation 21.3 and the count matrices $\mathbf{C}^{WT}$ and $\mathbf{C}^{DT}$ are incremented with the new topic assignment. Each Gibbs sample consists of the set of topic assignments to all N word tokens in the corpus, achieved by a single pass through all documents. During the initial stage of the sampling process (also known as the burnin period), the Gibbs samples have to be discarded because they are poor estimates of the posterior. After the burnin period, the successive Gibbs samples start to approximate the target distribution (i.e., the posterior distribution over topic assignments). At this point, to get a representative set of samples from this distribution, a number of Gibbs samples are saved at regularly spaced intervals, to prevent correlations between samples (see Gilks et al., 1996).

Estimating ϕ and θ

The sampling algorithm gives direct estimates of z for every word. However, many applications of the model require estimates ϕ' and θ' of the word-topic distributions and topic-document distributions respectively. These can be obtained from the count matrices as follows:

$$\varphi_i'^{(j)} = \frac{C_{ij}^{WT} + \beta}{\sum_{k=1}^{W} C_{kj}^{WT} + W\beta} \qquad \theta_j'^{(d)} = \frac{C_{dj}^{DT} + \alpha}{\sum_{k=1}^{T} C_{dk}^{DT} + T\alpha} \qquad \text{21.4}$$

These values correspond to the predictive distributions of sampling a new token of word i from topic j, and sampling a new token (as of yet unobserved) in document d from topic j, and are also the posterior means of these quantities conditioned on a particular sample z.

An Example

The Gibbs sampling algorithm can be illustrated by generating artificial data from a known topic model and applying the algorithm to check whether it is able to infer the original generative structure. We illustrate this by expanding on the example that was given in Figure 21.2. Suppose topic 1 gives equal probability to words *money*, *loan*, and *bank*, that is, $\phi_{MONEY}^{(1)} = \phi_{LOAN}^{(1)} = \phi_{BANK}^{(1)}$, and topic 2 gives equal probability to words *river*, *stream*, and *bank*, that is, $\phi_{RIVER}^{(2)} = \phi_{STREAM}^{(2)} = \phi_{BANK}^{(2)}$. Figure 21.7, top panel, shows how 16 documents can be generated by arbitrarily mixing the two topics. Each circle corresponds to a single word token and each row to a document (e.g., document 1 contains 4 times the word *bank*). In Figure 21.7, the color of the circles indicates the topic assignments (black = topic 1; white = topic 2). At the start of sampling (top panel), the assignments show no structure yet; these just reflect the random assignments to topics. The lower panel shows the state of the Gibbs sampler after 64 iterations. Based on these assignments, Equation 21.4 gives the following estimates for the distributions over words for topic 1 and 2: $\phi_{MONEY}^{(1)} = .32$, $\phi_{LOAN}^{(1)} = .29$, $\phi_{BANK}^{(1)} = .39$ and $\phi_{RIVER}^{(2)} = .25$, $\phi_{STREAM}^{(2)} = .4$, $\phi_{BANK}^{(2)} = .35$. Given the size of the dataset, these estimates are reasonable reconstructions of the parameters used to generate the data.

Exchangeability of Topics

There is no a priori ordering on the topics that will make the topics identifiable between or even within runs of the algorithm. Topic j in one Gibbs sample is theoretically not constrained to be similar to topic j in another sample, regardless of whether the samples come from the same or different Markov chains (i.e., samples spaced apart that started with the same random assignment or samples from different random assignments). Therefore, the different samples cannot be averaged at the level of topics. However, when

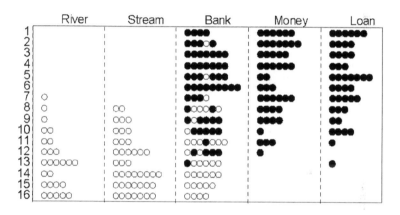

Figure 21.7.   An example of the Gibbs sampling procedure.

topics are used to calculate a statistic that is invariant to the ordering of the topics, it becomes possible and even important to average over different Gibbs samples (see Griffiths & Steyvers, 2004). Model averaging is likely to improve results because it allows sampling from multiple local modes of the posterior.

Stability of Topics

In some applications, it is desirable to focus on a single topic solution in order to interpret each individual topic. In that situation, it is important to know which topics are stable and will reappear across samples and which topics are idiosyncratic for a particular solution. In Figure 21.8, an analysis is shown of the degree to which two topic solutions can be aligned be-

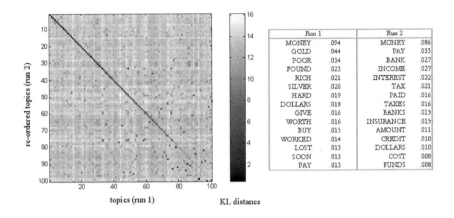

Figure 21.8.   Stability of topics between different runs.

tween samples from different Markov chains. The TASA corpus was taken as input ($W = 26, 414; D = 37, 651; N = 5, 628, 867; T = 100; \alpha = 50/T = .5; \beta = .01$) and a single Gibbs sample was taken after 2,000 iterations for two different random initializations. The left panel shows a similarity matrix of the two topic solutions. Dissimilarity between topics j_1 and j_2 was measured by the symmetrized Kullback Liebler (KL) distance between topic distributions:

$$KL(j_1, j_2) = \frac{1}{2} \sum_{k=1}^{W} \phi_k'^{(j_1)} \log_2 \phi_k'^{(j_2)} / \phi_k''^{(j_1)}$$
$$+ \frac{1}{2} \sum_{k=1}^{W} \phi_k''^{(j_2)} \log_2 \phi_k''^{(j_2)} / \phi_k'^{(j_1)}$$

21.5

where ϕ' and ϕ'' correspond to the estimated topic-word distributions from two different runs. The topics of the second run were reordered to correspond as best as possible (using a greedy algorithm) with the topics in the first run. Correspondence was measured by the (inverse) sum of KL distances on the diagonal. The similarity matrix in Figure 21.8 suggests that a large percentage of topics contain similar distributions over words. The right panel shows the *worst* pair of aligned topics with a *KL* distance of 9.4. Both topics seem related to money but stress different themes. Overall, these results suggest that in practice, the solutions from different samples will give different results but that many topics are stable across runs.

Determining the Number of Topics

The choice of the number of topics can affect the interpretability of the results. A solution with too few topics will generally result in very broad topics, whereas a solution with too many topics will result in uninterpretable topics that pick out idiosyncratic word combinations. There are a number of objective methods to choose the number of topics. Griffiths and Steyvers (2004) discussed a Bayesian model selection approach. The idea is to estimate the posterior probability of the model while integrating over all possible parameter settings (i.e., all ways to assign words to topics). The number of topics is then based on the model that leads to the highest posterior probability. Another approach is to choose the number of topics that lead to best generalization performance to new tasks. For example, a topic model estimated on a subset of documents should be able to predict word choice in the remaining set of documents. In computational linguistics, the measure of perplexity has been proposed to assess generalizability of text models across subsets of documents (e.g., see Blei et al. 2003; Rosen-Zvi et al., 2004). Recently, researchers have used methods from nonparametric Bayesian statistics to define models that automatically select the appropriate number of topics (Blei, Griffiths, Jordan, & Tenenbaum, 2004; Teh, Jordan, Beal, & Blei, 2004).

Topic 77		Topic 82		Topic 166	
word	prob.	word	prob.	word	prob.
MUSIC	.090	LITERATURE	.031	PLAY	.136
DANCE	.034	POEM	.028	BALL	.129
SONG	.033	POETRY	.027	GAME	.065
PLAY	.030	POET	.020	PLAYING	.042
SING	.026	PLAYS	.019	HIT	.032
SINGING	.026	POEMS	.019	PLAYED	.031
BAND	.026	PLAY	.015	BASEBALL	.027
PLAYED	.023	LITERARY	.013	GAMES	.025
SANG	.022	WRITERS	.013	BAT	.019
SONGS	.021	DRAMA	.012	RUN	.019
DANCING	.020	WROTE	.012	THROW	.016
PIANO	.017	POETS	.011	BALLS	.015
PLAYING	.016	WRITER	.011	TENNIS	.011
RHYTHM	.015	SHAKESPEARE	.010	HOME	.010
ALBERT	.013	WRITTEN	.009	CATCH	.010
MUSICAL	.013	STAGE	.009	FIELD	.010

Figure 21.9.   Three topics related to the word *play*.

POLYSEMY WITH TOPICS

Many words in natural language are polysemous, having multiple senses; their semantic ambiguity can only be resolved by other words in the context. Probabilistic topic models represent semantic ambiguity through uncertainty over topics. For example, Figure 21.9 shows 3 topics selected from a 300 topic solution for the TASA corpus (Fig. 21.1 showed 4 other topics from this solution). In each of these topics, the word *play* is given relatively high probability related to the different senses of the word (*playing* music, theater *play*, *playing* games).

In a new context, having only observed a single word *play*, there would be uncertainty over which of these topics could have generated this word. This uncertainty can be reduced by observing other less ambiguous words in context. The disambiguation process can be described by the process of iterative sampling as described in the previous section (Equation 21.4), where the assignment of each word token to a topic depends on the assignments of the other words in the context. In Figure 21.10, fragments of three documents are shown from TASA that use *play* in three different senses. The superscript numbers show the topic assignments for each word token. The gray words are stop words or very low-frequency words that were not used in the analysis. The sampling process assigns the word *play* to topics 77, 82, and 166 in the three document contexts. The presence of other less ambigu-

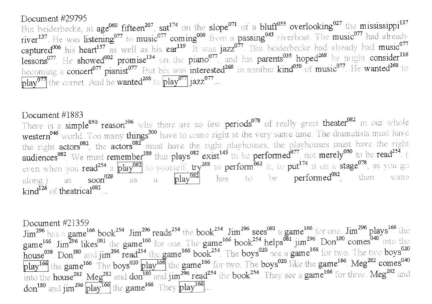

Figure 21.10.   Three TASA documents with the word *play*.

ous words (e.g., *music* in the first document) builds up evidence for a particular topic in the document. When a word has uncertainty over topics, the topic distribution developed for the document context is the primary factor for disambiguating the word.

COMPUTING SIMILARITIES

The set of topics derived from a corpus can be used to answer questions about the similarity of words and documents: Two words are similar to the extent that they appear in the same topics, and two documents are similar to the extent that the same topics appear in those documents.

Similarity Between Documents

The similarity between documents d_1 and d_2 can be measured by the similarity between their corresponding topic distributions $\theta^{(d_1)}$ and $\theta^{(d_2)}$. There are many choices for similarity functions between probability distributions (Lin, 1991). A standard function to measure the difference or *divergence* between two distributions p and q is the Kullback Leibler (KL) divergence,

$$D(p,q) = \sum_{j=1}^{T} p_j \log_2 \frac{p_j}{q_j}$$

21.6

This nonnegative function is equal to zero when for all j, $p_j = q_j$. The KL divergence is asymmetric and in many applications, it is convenient to apply a symmetric measure based on KL divergence:

$$KL(p,q) = \frac{1}{2}[D(p,q) + D(p,q)]$$

21.7

Another option is to apply the symmetrized Jensen-Shannon (JS) divergence:

$$JS(p,q) = \frac{1}{2}[D(p,(p+q)/2) + D(q,(p+q)/2)]$$

21.8

which measures similarity between p and q through the average of p and q—two distributions p and q will be similar if they are similar to their average $(p+q)/2$. Both the symmetrized KL and JS divergence functions seem to work well in practice. In addition, it is also possible to consider the topic distributions as vectors and apply geometrically motivated functions such as Euclidian distance, dot product, or cosine.

For information retrieval applications, document comparison is necessary to retrieve the most relevant documents to a query. The query can be a (new) set of words produced by a user or it can be an existing document from the collection. In the latter case, the task is to find similar documents to the given document. One approach to finding relevant documents is to assess the similarity between the topic distributions corresponding to the query and each candidate documents d_i, using one of the distributional similarity functions as discussed earlier. Another approach (e.g., Buntine et al., 2004) is to model information retrieval as a probabilistic query to the topic model—the most relevant documents are those that maximize the conditional probability of the query, given the candidate document. We write this as $P(q \mid d_i)$, where q is the set of words contained in the query. Using the assumptions of the topic model, this can be calculated by:

$$P(q|d_i) = \prod_{w_k \in q} P(w_k|d_i)$$

$$= \prod_{w_k \in q} \sum_{j=1}^{T} P(w_k|z=j) P(z=j|d_i)$$

21.9

Note that this approach also emphasizes similarity through topics, with relevant documents having topic distributions that are likely to have generated the set of words associated with the query.

Whatever similarity or relevance function is used, it is important to obtain stable estimates for the topic distributions. This is especially important for short documents. With a single Gibbs sample, the topic distribution might be influenced by idiosyncratic topic assignments to the few word tokens available. In that case, it becomes important to average the similarity function over multiple Gibbs samples.

Similarity Between Two Words

The similarity between two words w_1 and w_2 can be measured by the extent that they share the same topics. Using a probabilistic approach, the similarity between two words can be calculated based on the similarity between $\theta^{(1)}$ and $\theta^{(2)}$, the conditional topic distributions for words w_1 and w_2 where $\theta^{(1)} = P(z \mid w_i = w_1)$ and $\theta^{(2)} = P(z \mid w_i = w_2)$. Either the symmetrized KL or JS divergence would be appropriate to measure the distributional similarity between these distributions.

There is an alternative approach to express similarity between two words, emphasizing the associative relations between words. The association between two words can be expressed as a conditional distribution over potential response words w_2 for cue word w_1, that is, $P(w_2 \mid w_1)$—what are likely words that are generated as an associative response to another word? Much data has been collected on human word association. Typically, a cue word is presented and the subject writes down the first word that comes to mind. Nelson, McEvoy, and Schreiber (1998) have developed word association norms for over 5,000 words using hundreds of subjects per cue word. In Figure 21.11, left panel, the distribution of human responses is shown for the cue word *play*. The responses reveal that different subjects associate with the cue in the different senses of the word (e.g., *play* → *ball* and *play* → *actor*). In the topic model, word association corresponds to having observed a single word in a new context, and trying to predict new words that might appear in the same context, based on the topic interpretation for the observed word. For a particular subject who activates a single topic j, the predicted distribution for w_2 is just $P(w_2 \mid z = j)$. If it assumed that each subject activates only a single topic sampled from the distribution $P(z = j \mid w_1)$, then the predictive conditional distributions can be calculated by:

$$P(w_2 \mid w_1) = \sum_{j=1}^{T} P(w_2 \mid z = j) P(z = j \mid w_i) \qquad \textbf{21.10}$$

HUMANS		TOPICS	
FUN	.141	BALL	.036
BALL	.134	GAME	.024
GAME	.074	CHILDREN	.016
WORK	.067	TEAM	.011
GROUND	.060	WANT	.010
MATE	.027	MUSIC	.010
CHILD	.020	SHOW	.009
ENJOY	.020	HIT	.009
WIN	.020	CHILD	.008
ACTOR	.013	BASEBALL	.008
FIGHT	.013	GAMES	.007
HORSE	.013	FUN	.007
KID	.013	STAGE	.007
MUSIC	.013	FIELD	.006

Figure 21.11. Observed and predicted response distributions for the word *play*.

In human word association, high-frequency words are more likely to be used as response words than low-frequency words. The model captures this pattern because the left term $P(w_2 \mid z = j)$ will be influenced by the word frequency of w_2—high-frequency words (on average) have high probability conditioned on a topic.

The right panel of Figure 21.11 shows the predictions of the topic model for the cue word *play* using a 300 topic solution from the TASA corpus. Griffiths and Steyvers (2002, 2003) compared the topic model with LSA in predicting word association, finding that the balance between the influence of word frequency and semantic relatedness found by the topic model can result in better performance than LSA on this task.

CONCLUSIONS

Generative models for text, such as the topic model, have the potential to make important contributions to the statistical analysis of large document collections, and the development of a deeper understanding of human language learning and processing. These models make explicit assumptions about the causal process responsible for generating a document, and enable the use of sophisticated statistical methods to identify the latent structure that underlies a set of words. Consequently, it is easy to explore different representations of words and documents and to develop richer models capable of capturing more of the content of language. Topic models illustrate how using a different representation can provide new insights into the statistical modeling of language, incorporating many of the key assumptions behind LSA, but making it possible to identify a set of interpretable probabilistic topics rather than a semantic space. Topic models have also been extended to capture some interesting properties of language, such as the hierarchical semantic relations between words (Blei et al., 2004) and the interaction between syntax and semantics (Griffiths et al., 2004). The vast majority of generative models are yet to be defined, and investigating these models provides the opportunity to expand both the practical benefits and the theoretical understanding of statistical language learning.

ACKNOWLEDGMENTS

We would like to thank Simon Dennis and Sue Dumais for thoughtful comments that improved this chapter. Matlab implementations of a variety of probabilistic topic models are available at http://www.psiexp.ss.uci.edu/research/programs_data/toolbox.htm

REFERENCES

Blei, D. M., Griffiths, T. L., Jordan, M. I., & Tenenbaum, J. B. (2004). Hierarchical topic models and the nested Chinese restaurant process. In S. Thrun, L. K. Saul, & B. Schölkopf (Eds.), *Advances in neural information processing systems 16,* (pp. 17–24). Cambridge, MA: MIT Press.

Blei, D. M., Ng, A. Y., & Jordan, M. I. (2003). Latent Dirichlet allocation. *Journal of Machine Learning Research, 3,* 993–1022.

Buntine, W. (2002). Variational extensions to EM and multinomial PCA. In T. Elomaa et al. (Eds.), *ECML, LNAI 2430* (pp. 23–34). Berlin: Springer-Verlag.

Buntine, W. L. (1994). Operations for learning with graphical models. *Journal of Artificial Intelligence Research, 2,* 159–225.

Buntine, W., Löfström, J., Perkiö, J., Perttu, S., Poroshin, V., Silander, T., Tirri, H., Tuominen, A., & Tuulos, V. (2004). A scalable topic-based open source search engine. *Proceedings of the IEEE/WIC/ACM Conference on Web Intelligence,* 228–234.

Cohn, D., & Hofmann, T. (2001). The missing link: A probabilistic model of document content and hypertext connectivity. In *Advances in neural information processing systems 13* (pp. 430–436). Cambridge, MA: MIT Press.

Erosheva, E. A. (2002). *Grade of membership and latent structure models with applications to disability survey data.* Unpublished doctoral dissertation, Department of Statistics, Carnegie Mellon University.

Gilks, W. R., Richardson, S., & Spiegelhalter, D. J. (1996). *Markov chain Monte Carlo in practice.* London: Chapman & Hall.

Griffiths, T. L., & Steyvers, M. (2002). A probabilistic approach to semantic representation. In W. D. Gray & C. D. Schunn, (Eds.), *Proceedings of the 24th Annual Conference of the Cognitive Science Society,* (pp. 381–386). Hillsdale, NJ: Lawrence Erlbaum Associates.

Griffiths, T. L., & Steyvers, M. (2003). Prediction and semantic association. In S. Becker, S. Thrun, & K. Obermayer (Eds.), *Advances in neural information processing systems 15* (pp. 11–18). Cambridge, MA: MIT Press.

Griffiths, T. L., & Steyvers, M. (2004). Finding scientific topics. *Proceedings of the National Academy of Science, 101,* 5228–5235.

Griffiths, T. L., Steyvers, M., Blei, D. M., & Tenenbaum, J. B. (2005). Integrating topics and syntax. In L. K. Saul (Ed.), *Advances in neural information processing systems 17* (pp. 537–544). Cambridge, MA: MIT Press.

Hofmann, T. (1999). Probabilistic latent semantic indexing. *Proceedings of the 22nd Annual International SIGIR Conference on Research and Development in Information Retrieval,* 50–57.

Hofmann, T. (2001). Unsupervised learning by probabilistic latent semantic analysis. *Machine Learning Journal, 42*(1), 177–196.

Landauer, T. K., & Dumais, S. T. (1997). A solution to Plato's problem: The latent semantic analysis theory of acquisition, induction, and representation of knowledge. *Psychological Review, 104,* 211–240.

Landauer, T. K., Foltz, P. W., & Laham, D. (1998). Introduction to latent semantic analysis. *Discourse Processes, 25,* 259–284.

Lee, D. D., & Seung, H. S. (1999). Learning the parts of objects by non-negative matrix focalization. *Nature, 401,* 788–791.

Lin, J. (1991). Divergence measures based on Shannon entropy. *IEEE Transactions on Information Theory, 37*(14), 145–51.

Manton, K. G., Woodbury, M. A., & Tolley, H. D. (1994). *Statistical applications using fuzzy sets.* New York: Wiley.

Minka, T., & Lafferty, J. (2002). Expectation-propagation for the generative aspect model. *Proceedings of the 18th Conference on Uncertainty in Artificial Intelligence,* 352–359.

Nelson, D. L., McEvoy, C. L., & Schreiber, T. A. (1998). *The university of south Florida word association, rhyme, and word fragment norms.* Retrieved September 1, 1999, from http://www.usf.edu/FreeAssociation/

Pritchard, J. K., Stephens, M., & Donnelly, P. (2000). Inference of populationstructure using multilocus genotype data. *Genetics, 155,* 945–955.

Rosen-Zvi, M., Griffiths T., Steyvers, M., & Smyth, P. (2004). The author-topic model for authors and documents. *Proceedings of the 20th International Conference on Uncertainty in Artificial Intelligence,* 487–494.

Steyvers, M., Smyth, P., Rosen-Zvi, M., & Griffiths, T. (2004). *Probabilistic author-topic models for information discovery.* Paper presented at the 10th ACM SIGKDD International Conference on Knowledge Discovery and Data Mining, Seattle, WA.

Teh, Y. W., Jordan, M. I., Beal, M. J. & Blei, D. M. (2004). *Hierarchical Dirichlet processes* (Tech. Rep. No. 653). UC Berkeley Statistics.

Ueda, N., & Saito, K. (2003). Parametric mixture models for multi-labeled text. In S. Becker, S. Thrun, & K. Obermayer (Eds.), *Advances in neural information processing systems 15* (pp. 737–744). Cambridge, MA: MIT Press.

22

Introducing Word Order Within the LSA Framework

Simon Dennis
University of Adelaide

Latent semantic analysis (LSA) is a "bag of words" technique. A training corpus is represented as a word by document matrix. Weights are entered into the cells of the matrix based on the number of times a word appears in each document, but no attempt is made to capture the order in which the words appeared within the document. Furthermore, when constructing the meaning representation of a new document, the vectors representing each unique word in the document are added, so again no attempt is made to capture word order. This insensitivity to word order has been raised as an important limitation of LSA.

However, Landauer, Laham, Rehder, and Schreiner (1997) have argued that the success of LSA in capturing human semantic judgments provides evidence that word choice rather than word order plays a more important role in assigning meaning. Landauer (2002) attempted to quantify the relative contributions of word order and word choice, based on the potential information available given human-size vocabularies and typical sentence lengths. He estimates that about 80% of the information content of a message could be contained in the word choice. In addition, many languages rely little on word order to convey meaning. For instance, the Warlpiri language of central Australia is almost completely free order (Kashket, 1986).

Nonetheless, there is still a significant contribution to meaning that is made by word order, particularly in English. Kintsch (2001) has shown how LSA can be extended to capture some of the effects of word order specifically in the areas of metaphor interpretation, causal inference, similarity rating, and homophone discrimination. What remains to be explained, however, is how LSA style models can be made to capture the propositional information necessary to disambiguate who did what to whom, when, and where. The sentence "Mary loves John" does not express the same content as the sentence "John loves Mary." A complete understanding of the meaning of these sentences must make some distinction between "John" as a lover and "John" as a lovee and must explain how people are able to bind elements to these roles and extract them when necessary.

Furthermore, LSA representations focus on the lexical level and do not specify how words combine to form higher level units such as phrases and clauses. The evidence for such units is substantial (Radford, 1988) and role and sense assignments often apply to these constituents rather than individual words. Term extraction methods that chunk sequences of words so that they can be treated as units can be used as preprocessing stages to LSA. However, people are capable of forming constituents productively, so whereas term *extraction* may be practically useful it does not offer a complete explanation. That is, it does not provide an account of syntactic phenomena.

LSA can be thought of as a tool for analyzing language and a theory of meaning. In addition, however, LSA is an exemplar of a more general corpus-based approach to cognitive modeling. In this approach, simple statistical operations are applied to large naturally occurring corpora and no recourse is made to preexisting knowledge (e.g., linguistic knowledge). So the question arises concerning whether the limitations of LSA outlined earlier are just issues that have yet to be addressed versus stumbling blocks to the general framework.

The syntagmatic paradigmatic model (SP; Dennis, 2005, 2004) attempts to answer this question by addressing both the propositional and syntactic levels of analysis using the general approach of LSA. In this chapter, the model is described and work demonstrating its ability to capture propositional information is summarized. The model will then be modified to operate over the starts and ends of words, rather than over words themselves. This modification allows the model to have a genuine sense of constituent and to directly address syntactic structure. The modified model was used to predict the phrase structure trees from preparsed sentences drawn from the *Wall Street Journal* corpus in the Penn Treebank.

THE SYNTAGMATIC PARADIGMATIC MODEL

The SP model was designed as a model of verbal cognition. It is based on the distinction between syntagmatic associations that occur between words that appear together in utterances (e.g., run fast) and paradigmatic associations that occur between words that appear in similar contexts, but not necessarily in the same utterances (e.g., deep and shallow; cf. Ervin, 1961; Ervin-Tripp, 1970; McNeill, 1966). The model has been used to account for a number of phenomena, including long-term grammatical dependencies and systematicity (Dennis, 2005), the extraction of statistical lexical information (syntactic, semantic, and associative) from corpora (Dennis, 2003a), sentence priming (Harrington & Dennis, 2003), verbal categorization and property judgment tasks (Dennis, 2005), serial recall (Dennis, 2003b), and relational extraction and inference (Dennis, 2005, 2004). This section gives a brief overview of the SP model. More complete descriptions, including the mathematical foundations, are provided by Dennis (2005, 2004).

In the SP model, sentence processing is characterized as the retrieval of associative constraints from sequential and relational long-term memory and the resolution of these constraints in working memory. Sequential long-term memory contains the sentences from a corpus. Relational long-term memory contains the extensional representations of the same sentences (see Fig. 22.1).

Creating an interpretation of a sentence/utterance involves the following steps:

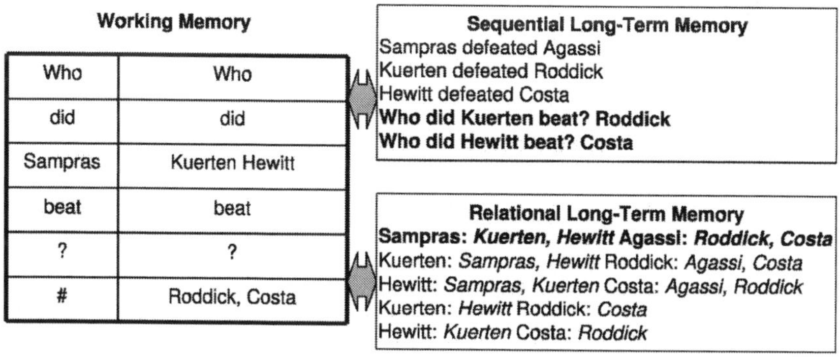

Figure 22.1. The syntagmatic paradigmatic (SP) architecture. The "#" symbol indicates an empty slot. Ultimately, it will contain the answer to the question.

Sequential Retrieval: The current sequence of input words is used to probe sequential memory for traces containing similar sequences of words. These traces are assumed to come from the corpus to which the model has been exposed. In the example, traces four and five—"Who did Kuerten beat? Roddick" and "Who did Hewitt beat? Costa"—are the closest matches to the target sentence "Who did Sampras beat? #" and are assigned high probabilities.

Sequential Resolution: The retrieved sequences are then aligned with the target sentence to determine the appropriate set of substitutions for each word. Note that the slot adjacent to the "#" symbol aligns with the pattern Costa, Roddick. This pattern represents the role that the answer to the question must fill (i.e., the answer is the loser).

Relational Retrieval: The bindings of input words to their corresponding role vectors (the relational representation of the target sentence) are then used to probe relational long-term memory. In this case, trace one is favored as it involves similar role filler bindings. That is, it contains a binding of Sampras onto the Kuerten, Hewitt pattern and it also contains the Roddick, Costa pattern. Despite the fact that "Sampras defeated Agassi" has a different surface form than "Who did Sampras beat ? #" it contains similar relational information and consequently has a high retrieval probability.

Relational Resolution: Finally, the paradigmatic associations in the retrieved relational traces are used to update working memory. In the relational trace for "Sampras defeated Agassi," "Agassi" is bound to the Roddick, Costa pattern. Consequently, there is a strong probability that "Agassi" should align with the "#" symbol, which as a consequence of sequential retrieval is also aligned with the Roddick, Costa pattern. Note that the model has now answered the question—it was Agassi who was beaten by Sampras.

One important point to note about the mechanism is that no transformation ever maps between sentences of different forms. In this example, there is never an explicit mapping from the active to the interrogative form. Rather, it is the fact that Sampras is associated with the same words in both forms that ensures that the relational cue that is created when processing the question retrieves the appropriate active sentence from relational memory.

That completes the description of the basic model. An outstanding question, however, is how one decides how similar two strings of words are during sequential retrieval and how they should align during sequential resolution. Fortunately, there is a significant literature on this problem known as string edit theory (SET). In the next section, a brief overview of SET is provided.

STRING EDIT THEORY

When similar sentences are of the same length, they can be aligned in a one-to-one fashion. If we are comparing "John loves Mary" and "Bert loves Ellen," then "John" aligns with "Bert," by virtue of the fact that "John" and "Bert" both fill the first slot of their respective sentences, and "Mary" aligns with "Ellen" because they both fill slot three.

However, in general this will not be the case. It is typical in natural languages for structure to be embedded. If we add a single adjective to our example, so that we are now comparing "Little John loves Mary" and "Bert loves Ellen," it becomes unclear how the sentences should align. What we require is a model of the alignment process.

One candidate for such a model is string edit theory. String edit theory was popularized by Sankoff and Kruskal (1983) and has been developed in both the fields of computer science and molecular biology (Allison, Wallace, & Yee, 1992; Levenshtein, 1965; Needleman & Wunsch, 1970; Sellers, 1974). As the name suggests, the purpose of string edit theory is to describe how one string, which could be composed of words, letters, amino acids, and so on, can be edited to form a second string. That is, what components must be inserted, deleted ,or changed to turn one string into another.

As an example, suppose we are trying to align the sentences "John loves Mary" and "Bert loves Ellen." The most obvious alignment is that which maps the two sentences to each other in a one to one fashion as suggested earlier:

John   loves   Mary

| | |

Bert   loves   Ellen

In this alignment, we have three edit operations. There is a change of "John" for "Bert," a match of "loves" and a change of "Mary" for "Ellen."

Now if we add "Little" to the first sentence, we can use a deletion to describe one way in which the sentences could be aligned:

Little   John   loves   Mary

| | | |

-     Bert   loves   Ellen

The "-" symbol is used to fill the slot left by a deletion (or an insertion) and can be thought of as the empty word. Whereas these alignments may be the most obvious ones, there are many other options.

For instance, in aligning "John loves Mary" and "Bert loves Ellen," we could start by deleting "John":

```
John   loves   Mary   -
 |      |       |      |
 -     Bert    loves   Ellen
```

Note that "Ellen" is now inserted at the end of the alignment. Alternatively, we could have deleted "John," and then inserted "Bert" to give:

```
John    -      loves   Mary
 |      |       |      |
 -     Bert    loves   Ellen
```

In total, there are 63 ways in which "John loves Mary" can be aligned with "Bert loves Ellen." Intuitively, the last alignment seems better than the one before because the word "loves" is matched. However, this alignment still seems worse than the first alignment because it requires "John" to be deleted and "Bert" to be inserted. A mechanism that produces alignments of sentences should favor those that have many matches and should penalize those that require many insertions and deletions. In probabilistic versions of SET, probabilities are assigned to the edit operations. Probabilities of alignments are then determined by multiplying the probabilities of the edit operations of which they are composed. Matches are assigned higher probabilities and so alignments that contain many matches are considered more likely. Strings that have high probability alignments with the input sentence become active during sequential retrieval. Similarly, the probabilities of alignments are used to determine which words should align during sequential resolution.

Only a cursory explanation of SET has been possible in this chapter. Interested readers are referred to Sankoff and Kruskal (1983) and Allison et al. (1992). In addition, Dennis (2005) provides a more complete mathematical treatment in the context of the SP model, including an explanation of how the edit model can be trained using the expectation maximization algorithm (Dempster, Laird, & Rubin, 1977), so that it does not rely on direct word overlap as is the case in the previous examples.

PROPOSITIONAL INFORMATION

The extraction of propositional information from text and speech is a key human ability that, although well established as an empirical phenomena (Kintsch, 1998), has yet to be satisfactorily explained (Dennis & Kintsch, in press). To illustrate the SP models ability to extract propositional information from natural texts, Dennis (2004) employed the model as a simple question answering system. The model was exposed to 69 articles taken from the Association of Tennis Professionals (ATP) Web site at http://www.atptennis.com/ and then was required to answer questions of the form "Who won the match between Sampras and Agassi?"

The tennis news domain was chosen primarily because choosing the winner of a tennis match cannot be solved by appealing to simple type heuristics. Relevant source sentences often contain the names of both the winner and the loser so that the correct answer must be selected from items of the same type. Consequently, successful completion of this task requires a propositional analysis.

The model was trained on the ATP corpus supplemented with a set of questions referring to the facts in the corpus. Then each question was presented with the final answer slot vacant (e.g., "Who won the match between Sampras and Agassi? #"). The SP model was invoked to complete the pattern. The word with the highest probability in the "#" slot was assumed to be the answer returned by the model. Following relational processing, on 67% of occasions the model correctly returned the winner of the match; 26% of the time it incorrectly produced the loser of the match; 5% of the time it responded with a player other than either the winner or loser of the match; and on 3% of occasions it committed a type error, responding with a word or punctuation symbol that was not a players name. Although this performance is far from perfect, it does demonstrate that the model is able to extract relational information from natural text at rates well above chance.

Another important aspect of the model is that it is often able to answer questions on the basis of sentences that imply the result, but do not directly state it, which is a property termed "inference by coincidence." To assess the contribution of this kind of inference, the sentence with maximal relational retrieval strength for each query was classified as either a literal statement of the result, a statement from which the result could be inferred (see Table 22.1) or some other statement that did not entail the result.

Of the 270 correct answers produced by the model, 79 fell into the literal category, 113 into the inference category, and 78 into the other category. So for those traces for which a categorization could be made (i.e., the literal and inference categories), 59% were in the inference category. Given that in each case a literal statement of the result existed in the corpus, it is significant that inference by coincidence seems to be playing such an important role in the performance of the model.

In summary, the ability of the SP model to isolate the combatants from arbitrary sentences and to successfully separate winners from losers demonstrates that it is capable of extracting propositional information from text. Unlike existing work in this domain (Blaheta & Charniak, 2000;

TABLE 22.1
Examples of Questions and the Statements That Were Classed as Examples
of Inference by Coincidence

Who won the match between Carlsen and Kiefer? Carlsen.

Kafelnikov now meets Kenneth Carlsen of Denmark in the second round.

Who won the match between Kiefer and Safin? Safin.

Safin, Kafelnikov surge toward hometown showdown.

Who won the match between Ljubicic and Kutsenko? Ljubicic.

Sixth seed Davide Sanguinetti of Italy and eighth seed Ivan Ljubicic of Croatia took different paths to their opening-round wins at the presidents cup in Tashkent.

Who won the match between Voltchkov and Haas? Voltchkov.

According to Haas, the injury first arose during Wednesdays match against Sargis Sargsian, and became progressively worse during practice and then the match against Voltchkov.

Who won the match between Srichaphan and Lapentti? Srichaphan.

Srichaphan has now won two titles in four finals this year.

Who won the match between Mamiit and Coria? Coria.

Kuerten, Coria withstand heat, set up fiery South American showdown.

Dumais, 2003; Gildea & Jurafsky, 2002; Palmer, Rosenzweig, & Cotton, 2001), it need make no a priori commitment to particular grammars, heuristics, or sets of semantic roles, and it does not require an annotated corpus on which to train. In this way, the model conforms to the general LSA framework. Furthermore, the large number of occasions on which the most probable relational trace was a sentence from which the result could be inferred, but not directly derived, suggests that "inference by coincidence" is a useful by-product of extracting propositional information in this way.

SYNTACTIC INFORMATION

In the work on proposition extraction described earlier, each question required only a single word answer. More generally, however, answers will be constituents—Pete Sampras, the President of the United States of America, the dolly with the hat on, and so on. The edit model described deals at the word level and is not well suited to capturing constituent information.

To illustrate the problem, consider aligning the target sentence "Bert who knows Ralph loves Ellen" against "John loves Mary."

```
Bert who knows Ralph loves Ellen
John --------------------loves Mary A1
--------------------John loves Mary A2
```

Alignments A1 and A2 are equally probable as they involve the same numbers of each type of edit operation, that is, three deletions, two changes, and one match. However, alignment A1 is preferable in terms of the propositional content being extracted. Furthermore, one might argue that it isn't just any Bert who loves Ellen, but rather it is the Bert who knows Ralph who loves Ellen. That is, the alignment could be considered to be:

```
| Bert who knows Ralph | loves | Ellen |
| --------John------------ | loves | Ellen |
```

Furthermore, if one were able to construct constituent alignments, it becomes possible to see how an exemplar-based approach of this kind could approximate the more familiar tree analyses of formal linguistics. Figure 22.2 shows the alignment of several possible exemplars against the target sentence "Bert who knows Ralph loves Ellen." The fact that John, Joe, Sofie,

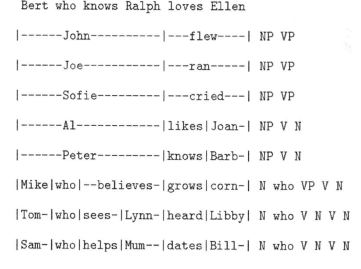

```
     Bert who knows Ralph loves Ellen

|------John----------|---flew----| NP VP

|------Joe-----------|---ran-----| NP VP

|------Sofie---------|---cried---| NP VP

|------Al------------|likes|Joan-| NP V N

|------Peter---------|knows|Barb-| NP V N

|Mike|who|--believes-|grows|corn-| N who VP V N

|Tom-|who|sees-|Lynn-|heard|Libby| N who V N V N

|Sam-|who|helps|Mum--|dates|Bill-| N who V N V N
```

Figure 22.2. Aligning multiple exemplars against a target sentence can approximate a traditional parse. N = Noun, V = Verb, NP = Noun Phrase, and VP = Verb Phrase.

Al, and Peter align with "Bert who knows Ralph" could be taken to indicate that this span is a constituent and perhaps a noun phrase given that these words are nouns. Likewise, the fact that flew, ran, and cried align with "loves Ellen" might indicate that this span is a verb phrase. Because there are multiple exemplars, all of which align (and possibly multiple alignments of a given exemplar), structure is induced. Although not constrained to be tree-like, this structure may tend to correspond to a tree for many structurally unambiguous cases.

One way in which the SP model can be modified to generate these sorts of alignments is by focusing on the gaps between the words (as characterized by the words on either side) rather than on the words themselves. That is, the sentence "Bert who knows Ralph loves Ellen" becomes:

S | Bert Bert | who who | knows knows | Ralph Ralph | loves loves | Ellen Ellen | E

where S is a start of sentence symbol and E is an end of sentence symbol. Now if we align the gaps in the same way that we aligned words, we get the following alignment:

S | Bert Bert | who who | knows knows | Ralph Ralph | loves loves | Ellen Ellen | E
S | John John | loves loves | Mary Mary | E

Note that in contrast to the case in which individual words were aligned, we now have an unambiguously preferred alignment: S—Bert should align with S—John and Ralph—loves should align with John—loves. Aligning the gaps in this way then generates the following alignment in the obvious way:

| Bert who knows Ralph | loves | Ellen |
| --------John-------------- | loves | Ellen |

Employing gap alignment requires that one construct a model of bigram substitutability. To calculate bigram change probabilities a version of Hofmann's (2001) aspect model of dyadic data was employed. Hoffmann's (2001) model was developed for extracting term and document meaning from large corpora as is done in LSA. However, rather than use the singular value decomposition as a dimension reduction technique, Hofmann defined a Bayesian forward model in which a latent aspect variable generated both a document index and a word index. He then employed the expectation maximization algorithm (EM; Dempster et al., 1977) to induce the document given latent class and word given latent class conditional probabilities. In the current application, the same forward model has been applied, however, now the data that are generated from the latent class are the first and second words, respectively, of a bigram. Furthermore, rather than training using the EM approach, a Markov Chain Monte Carlo method similar to that used by Griffiths and Steyvers (2002) was employed. This allowed the probability of each latent class given the words of a bigram to be calculated. To calculate a bigram substitution probability, the multinomial class distribution for each bigram was calculated and the probability of drawing the same class from both distributions (i.e., the dot-product of the distributions) was used.[1]

Evaluating the Modified Model

The task of unsupervised parsing provides a useful testbed with which to evaluate the ability of the modified model to identify constituents in sentences. Figure 22.3 shows a parse of the sentence "Bert who knows Ralph loves Ellen," which specifies four constituents:

- Bert who knows Ralph loves Ellen
- Bert who knows Ralph
- knows Ralph
- loves Ellen

The task of the model, then, is to identify these constituents and conversely to avoid identifying nonconstituent spans such as "knows Ralph loves."

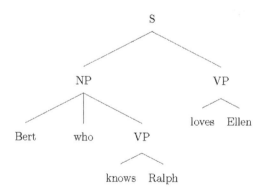

Figure 22.3. A parse of the sentence "Bert who knows Ralph loves Ellen."

---

[1]Note that strictly, the Markov Chain should be rerun for each similarity calculation and an expectation over the some similarity measure of the distributions, such as the square root of the Jenson-Shannon measure, should be calculated. However, such a procedure is computationally infeasible when employed in this circumstance, and the simpler dot product procedure retains the essential characteristics for the current purposes.

To allow the model to be compared against other unsupervised parsing methods (e.g., Klein & Manning, 2001), a binary parse was constructed by applying the modified model to exemplars taken from the *Wall Street Journal* section of the Penn Treebank (Marcus et al., 1993). Only sentences that were shorter than the target sentence were chosen. The 50 most probable sentences for each length less than that of the target were used. The number of times each span of words was identified by the model as a constituent was determined and normalized to give probabilities. For instance, the alignments presented in Figure 22.2 would give the following counts:

Span	Count	Probability
Bert who knows Ralph	5	.56
loves Ellen	3	.33
knows Ralph	1	.11

The most probable binary parse was then chosen. This procedure was applied to all of the sentences from the *Wall Street Journal* section of the treebank that were of length 10 or less.

Results

To assess performance the parses produced by the model were compared against the gold standard parses provided by the treebank. Four measures were calculated:

- Unlabeled Recall: The mean proportion of constituents in the gold standard that the model proposed.
- Unlabeled Precision: The mean proportion of constituents in the models answer that appear in the gold standard.
- Noncrossing Boundaries Precision: The proportion of constituents proposed by the model that do not cross constituent boundaries in the gold standard.
- $F1$: The harmonic mean of unlabeled recall and unlabeled precision.

Because the treebank provides parses that are not binary (in Chomsky normal form), but the procedure used makes this assumption, it is not possible to achieve perfect performance. Klein and Manning (2001) calculated that best possible $F1$ measure that can be achieved is 87%.

Figure 22.4 shows the performance of the model against chance selection of trees and against three versions of the constituent context model (CCM) proposed by Klein and Manning (2001). Clearly, all of these models are performing well above chance, although all are still well below the theoretically achievable maximum of 87%.

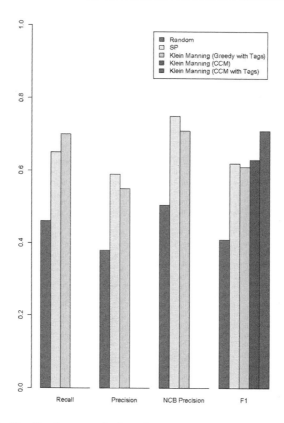

Figure 22.4. Results of unsupervised parsing experiment.

Note that the "greedy with tags" and "CCM with tags" models both employed part of speech tags, which provides a boost to performance. The use of tag information means that these models are no longer strictly unsupervised. As the modified SP model was not provided with tag information, the most appropriate comparison is against the straight CCM model. The performance of the modified SP model is approximately the same level as the CCM model with $F1$ measures around 62%–63%. Note, however, that unlike the context constituent model, the SP model provides insight into not only the problem of parsing, but also how propositional information can be extracted in an unsupervised manner.

GENERAL CONCLUSIONS

Latent semantic analysis (LSA) is a tool for analyzing text and a theory of how meaning is constructed. In addition, however, it exemplifies an approach to the modeling of cognition. In this approach, simple statistical operations are applied to large naturally occurring corpora. Structure is extracted from the environment rather than being specified a priori. This chapter has attempted to illustrate using the syntagmatic paradigmatic model how this same approach can be applied to extracting propositional and syntactic information—domains that standard LSA cannot address because of its insensitivity to word order.

The ability of the model to answer questions about tennis matches shows that the model is able to extract propositional knowledge. In addition, the model's reliance on "inference by coincidence," in many cases, suggests that it may prove more robust than existing inferential systems. Furthermore, a modified version of the model can be used to parse naturally occurring sentences at levels that are close to the state of the art for unsupervised parsers. In both cases, there remains significant room for improvement.

Nonetheless, success on these tasks demonstrates that it is possible to extract both propositional and syntactic information from corpora within the general constraints imposed by the LSA approach.

ACKNOWLEDGMENTS

I would like to acknowledge the many discussions that have influenced the current work. In particular, I would like to thank Walter Kintsch, Tom Landauer, and Jose Quesada for helpful comments and suggestions. This research was supported by Australian Research Foundation Grant A00106012, U.S. National Science Foundation Grant EIA-0121201, and U.S. Department of Education Grant R305G020027.

REFERENCES

Allison, L., Wallace, C. S., & Yee, C. N. (1992). Finite-state models in the alignment of macromolecules. *Journal of Molecular Evolution, 35*(1), 77–89.

Blaheta, D., & Charniak, E. (2000, May). Assigning function tags to parsed text. *Proceedings of the First Annual Meeting the North American Chapter of the ACL (NAACL)*, 234–240.

Dempster, A. P., Laird, N. M., & Rubin, D. B. (1977). Maximum liklelihood from incomplete data via the em algorithm (with discussion). *Journal of the Royal Statistical Society, series B, 39*, 1–38.

Dennis, S. (2003a). An alignment-based account of serial recall. In R. Alterman & D. Kirsh (Eds.), *Proceedings of the 25th Annual Conference of the Cognitive Science Society* (pp. 336–341). Mahwah, NJ: Lawrence Erlbaum Associates.

Dennis, S. (2003b). A comparison of statistical models for the extraction of lexical information from text corpora. In R. Alterman & D. Kirsh (Eds.), *Proceedings of the 25th Annual Conference of the Cognitive Science Society*. Mahwah, NJ: Lawrence Erlbaum Associates.

Dennis, S. (2004). An unsupervised method for the extraction of propositional information from text. *Proceedings of the National Academy of Sciences, 101*, 5206–5213.

Dennis, S. (2005). A memory-based theory of verbal cognition. *Cognitive Science, 29*(2), 145–193.

Dennis, S., & Kintsch, W. (in press). The text mapping and inference generation problems in text comprehension. In C. A. Perfetti & F. Schmalhofer (Eds.), *Higher level language processes in the brain: Inference and comprehension processes.*

Dumais, S. T. (2003). Data-driven approach to information access. *Cognitive Science, 27*, 491–524.

Ervin, S. M. (1961). Changes with age in the verbal determinants of word association. *American Journal of Psychology, 74*, 361–372.

Ervin-Tripp, S. M. (1970). Substitution, context and association. In L. Postman & G. Keppel (Eds.), *Norms of word association* (p. 383–467). New York: Academic Press.

Gildea, D., & Jurafsky, D. (2002). Automatic labeling of semantic roles. *Computational Linguistics, 28*(3), 245–288.

Griffiths, T. L., & Steyvers, M. (2003). Prediction and semantic association. In S. Becker, S. Thrun, & K. Obermayer (Eds.), *Advances in neural information proccessing 15* (pp. 11–18). Cambridge, MA: MIT Press.

Harrington, M., & Dennis, S. (2003). Structural priming in sentence comprehension. In R. Alterman & D. Kirsh (Eds.), *Proceedings of the 25th Annual Conference of the Cognitive Science Society* (pp. 510–515). Mahwah, NJ: Lawrence Erlbaum Associates.

Hofmann, T. (2001). Unsupervised learning by probabilistic latent semantic analysis. *Machine Learning, 42* (1–2), 177–196.

Kashket, M. (1986). Parsing a free-word order language: Warlpiri. *Proceedings of the 24th Conference on Association for Computational Linguistics,* 60–66.

Kintsch, W. (1998). *Comprehension: A paradigm for cognition.* Cambridge, England: Cambridge University Press.

Kintsch, W. (2001). Predication. *Cognitive Science, 25*, 173–202.

Klein, D., & Manning, C. D. (2001). Distributional phrase structure induction. In W. Daelemans & R. Zajac (Eds.), *Proceedings of the Fifth Conference on Computational Language Learning (CoNNL-2001)* (pp. 113–120). Morristown, NJ: Association for Computational Linguistics.

Landauer, T. K. (2002). On the computational basis of learning and cognition: Arguments from lsa. In N. Ross (Ed.), *The psychology of learning and motivation* (Vol. 41, pp. 43–84). New York: Academic Press.

Landauer, T. K., Laham, D., Rehder, B., & Schreiner, M. E. (1997). How well can passage meaning be derived without using word order? A comparison of latent semantic analysis and humans. In P. Langley (Ed.), *Proceedings of the 19th Annual Conference of the Cognitive Science Society* (p. 412–417). Mahwah, NJ: Lawrence Erlbaum Associates.

Levenshtein, V. I. (1965). Binary codes capable of correcting deletions, insertions and reversals. *Dokl. Akad. Nauk. SSSR, 163*, 845–848.

Marcus, M., Kim, G., Marcinkiewicz, M. A., MacIntyre, R., Bies, A., Ferguson, M., et al. (1993). Building a large annotated corpus of english: The penn treebank. *Computational Linguistics, 19*(2), 313–330.

McNeill, D. (1966). A study of word association. *Journal of Verbal Learning and Verbal Behavior, 2*, 250–262.

Needleman, S. B., & Wunsch, C. D. (1970). A general method applicable to the search for similarities in the amino acid sequence of two proteins. *Journal of Molecular Biology, 48*, 443–453.

Palmer, M., Rosenzweig, J., & Cotton, S. (2001). Automatic predicate argument analysis of the penn treebank. In J. Allan (Ed.), *Proceedings of hlt 2001, First International Conference on Human Language Technology Research.* San Francisco: Morgan Kaufmann.

Radford, A. (1988). *Transformational grammar: A first course.* Cambridge, England: Cambridge University Press.

Sankoff, D., & Kruskal, J. B. (1983). *Time warps, string edits and macromolecules: The theory and practise of sequence comparison.* Reading, MA: Addison Wesley.

Sellers, P. H. (1974). An algorithm for the distance between two finite sequences. *Journal of Combinatorial Theory, 16*, 253–258.

VI

Conclusion

23

LSA and Meaning: In Theory and Application

Walter Kintsch
Universtiy of Colorado

Danielle S. McNamara
University of Memphis

Simon Dennis
University of Adelaide

Thomas K Landauer
Pearson Knowledge Technologies and University of Colorado

Cognition depends on knowledge. High-level cognition, in particular, as in text and discourse comprehension and problem solving, is shaped in every respect by the nature and limitations of its knowledge base. Hence, models of high-level cognition must include a workable model of human knowledge. One could argue that such a model is a necessary prerequisite to the study of higher level cognition. However, we do not have such a model today—a model of human knowledge representation that does justice to the vast scale of human experiences and their intricate structure—and cognitive scientists cannot afford to wait with their work for such a model. Thus, cognitive scientists interested in building models of cognition have been forced to take shortcuts, supplying their models of cognitive processes with hand-coded, on-demand knowledge structures. This has been a general practice in cognitive psychology. For instance, models of text comprehension (including Kintsch, 1974, 1998) and models of analogy making (e.g., Forbus, Gentner, & Law, 1995; Holyoak & Thagard, 1989) have relied on hand-coded propositional representations and knowledge structures. This was a defensible practice because the alternative was not to attempt to model cognition at all. Moreover, the use of ad hoc knowledge structures in these models yielded many valuable insights about comprehension and analogy making, as it did in all of the other areas where such shortcuts were employed. But today, we are moving beyond hand-coding knowledge and toward actually modeling it. Among the first attempts to do so has been LSA. We judge it to have been highly successful at this point. We judge this success on the basis of its contribution to cognitive theory, as well as to real-world applications. But we also believe that LSA is just the beginning of a widespread surge of models of human knowledge that will revolutionize the study of higher level cognitive processes in the coming decades. We have attempted to communicate in this book what LSA has achieved already, but the goal was also to foreshadow the exciting possibilities for LSA-like systems in the future.

There are various ways to go about modeling human knowledge. One method is to try to hand-code all of human knowledge in some suitable formal language (e.g., CYC, Lenat, 1995) in all its complexity, with inference rules to account for its endless implications. Alternatively, one can try to build a system that acquires something akin to human knowledge. The human child is such a system. Landauer and Dumais (1997) proposed to simulate what the human child achieves with LSA. They took a well-known mathematical technique—singular value decomposition—that had been applied in many different areas, including information retrieval (Dumais, chap. 16 in this volume), and used it to model human language knowledge, or at least the associative basis of human knowledge.

The notion of using LSA to model semantic knowledge proved to open up rich new research possibilities for statistical models of language. LSA learns everything it knows from a large corpus of texts. Children live and act and feel and perceive, and language is only part of their experience. For LSA, language is everything, because computers can read ASCII code but have no life. Thus, what LSA knows will always be only one slice of what we know. But, in one very important respect, LSA learns as we do: It learns from experience, without explicit instruction. We take to be the essence of LSA that it learns what language means from a large linguistic corpus, without supervision. We emphasize the word "large": LSA is not a toy system, but it acquires knowledge on a scale comparable to human knowledge.

Just what is the knowledge that LSA acquires? Texts are represented in the LSA space as the sum of the words they contain, and words are represented as (roughly) 300-dimensional vectors. The 300 numbers that represent a word are meaningless by themselves, because readers can easily convince themselves by glancing at Table 23.1, which shows the meaning of "life" according to LSA. Obviously, LSA is even less informative than the usual homilies we know so well about the meaning of life. Nonetheless, although the numbers in an LSA vector by themselves do not mean anything, their relationship to other vectors is meaningful. Meaning in LSA is the totality of relationships between words and texts in a high-dimensional space. Meaning in LSA is neither defined in some formal language (e.g., as a combination of a set of semantic elements), nor is it tied to reference (meaning is what a word refers to in the world), but is strictly relational.

Thus, all one can do with meaning in LSA is to compute degrees of relationship—the semantic similarity between vectors representing words and texts, as a cosine, dot product, or other distance measures. We do not claim that a model of meaning that is restricted to computing similarity measures between words and texts makes for a complete theory of meaning, particularly one that neglects syntactic relations in its computations as LSA does. But we do claim that LSA approximates the associative basis of meaning on which a complete theory can be built. Just what all the components of a complete theory should be is not clear today. However, progress in that direction continues to be made, and in the present volume we have endeavored to tell how this work has progressed so far.

There is more to meaning than semantic similarity, but the first thing we should mention is the enormous usefulness of the LSA measures of semantic similarity for both theory and application. We shall describe the applications of LSA, but first we want to point out their significance. It is a sign of a mature science that it has practical applications that are in wide use and have entered the commercial marketplace; LSA is a poster child for cognitive science in that respect.

THEORETICAL CONTRIBUTIONS

The attempt to use LSA to build a psychological theory of meaning began with Landauer and Dumais (1997). A long-standing puzzle for developmental psychology has been the question of how children can acquire their vocabulary at the rate they actually do. From ages 2 to 20, people learn about 7–15 new words a day, almost all without explicit instruction. What sort of learning mechanism could make such an achievement possible? Landauer and Dumais estimated that about three quarters of LSA's word knowledge derives from "indirect induction, the effect of exposure to text not containing words used in the text"—that is, instead of learning separate word meanings, LSA constructs a semantic space. Landauer and Dumais proposed that children similarly generate a semantic space and showed that the observed rates of vocabulary ac-

TABLE 23.1
The Meaning of "Life": A Vector With 300 Numbers

1.30005e+00 –4.24608e–01 1.71412e–01 –2.80347e–02 –1.86302e–01 3.82443e–01
–6.46366e–01 –2.81268e–01 –1.95218e–01 3.29385e–01

–1.44783e–01 8.13897e–02 1.90094e–02 4.09875e–01 1.28020e–01 4.24867e–02 –7.72349e–02
1.15015e–01 1.95297e–02 –6.86995e–02

–1.24804e–01 4.80603e–02 –3.28658e–01 –8.34451e–03 1.83348e–01 2.27321e–02
–1.76595e–01 7.30420e–02 –9.70418e–03 1.83936e–01

–6.83673e–02 –9.36324e–02 –1.09831e–01 –2.21078e–01 2.06871e–01 6.64929e–02
2.14467e–01 –2.64663e–02 –5.96536e–02 4.00352e–02

–4.88043e–02 –1.19202e–01 9.16792e–02 4.04345e–03 4.03044e–01 1.10074e–02 9.76383e–02
–1.62073e–01 –1.37145e–01 –1.05125e–01

–1.07162e–01 1.78804e–02 –2.21964e–01 –2.44697e–01 –1.07126e–01 1.49053e–01
–1.39864e–01 3.69245e–02 1.25525e–02 –1.09803e–03

1.91197e–01 –8.34294e–02 –8.91210e–02 –9.40070e–02 5.58079e–02 –4.59393e–02
–3.95034e–02 6.57098e–03 1.50526e–01 –1.09730e–01

4.22467e–03 –1.59632e–02 1.40204e–01 1.39837e–01 1.19193e–01 –1.66848e–01 –9.52017e–02
8.58765e–02 –4.39967e–02 1.01935e–01

2.39166e–01 –6.00644e–02 7.76687e–02 –1.20613e–01 2.43552e–01 –6.64873e–02
–1.34709e–01 –7.38876e–02 –6.11585e–02 –2.65114e–02

–1.66603e–02 8.74497e–02 –4.60425e–02 7.45567e–02 2.37507e–02 –1.11651e–01
–1.01813e–01 –2.20171e–02 –3.66160e–03 –4.61425e–02

–2.23869e–01 2.99265e–02 8.36938e–02 1.49893e–01 –1.09973e–01 6.64440e–02 –2.03885e–01
–1.70184e–01 1.62782e–01 –6.16084e–02

8.06657e–02 2.51575e–02 5.32226e–02 –9.46372e–02 1.17950e–01 –3.52391e–01 –1.32552e–01
1.23505e–01 –3.48393e–02 3.42460e–02

6.93436e–02 –4.03613e–02 9.29355e–02 7.48137e–02 1.61383e–01 5.33447e–02 –6.73022e–02
–2.01878e–02 –2.61693e–02 –2.16201e–01

1.77294e–01 1.02963e–01 2.80082e–01 –2.20166e–01 –1.23996e–01 –8.22025e–02
–7.31311e–02 4.45074e–02 –3.29775e–01 4.64337e–02

1.86889e–01 1.26325e–01 –1.31999e–01 –1.35938e–01 5.53130e–02 –1.37053e–02
–3.92023e–02 –2.26752e–01 2.94359e–01 –1.44406e–01

–1.32999e–01 –1.64604e–01 –1.29910e–01 2.79384e–02 1.13993e–01 –1.99767e–01
–1.84919e–01 8.64867e–02 2.53541e–02 4.40151e–02

–1.84659e–01 –2.64037e–01 6.82079e–02 7.78948e–02 2.82499e–02 4.88331e–02 –1.26880e–01
–2.82237e–02 –1.07448e–01 –1.35152e–01

2.90096e–02 1.96244e–01 –1.53366e–01 4.16463e–02 2.20839e–01 1.21343e–01 –6.46179e–02
–1.86165e–01 1.55918e–01 2.10254e–01

–1.80290e–01 5.58804e–02 –9.93090e–02 2.63256e–02 –3.78750e–02 –6.03536e–02
1.01662e–02 2.02439e–01 2.61005e–01 1.34275e–02

–5.46672e–02 7.70258e–02 7.59846e–02 –6.50621e–02 –1.26441e–01 –1.04003e–01
7.63466e–03 6.87013e–02 7.05767e–02 2.37486e–01

–1.15609e–01 7.95852e–02 1.03509e–01 –4.59342e–02 –1.62234e–01 –1.40266e–02
–1.89387e–01 –1.44254e–01 –5.09304e–02 –1.26006e–02

470

2.25111e–01 –1.52292e–01 2.82736e–02 –8.71207e–02 –2.12974e–01 –1.24165e–01
–2.04582e–01 6.27359e–02 8.71273e–02 1.49151e–01

–9.03411e–02 2.22180e–01 –6.54227e–02 –3.73054e–02 2.61804e–02 –7.15970e–02
6.18082e–02 –9.06257e–02 –7.67701e–02 –1.63213e–01

1.39286e–01 –3.64138e–02 –2.62987e–01 6.21967e–02 –3.32768e–02 –1.49299e–01
7.61626e–02 2.79826e–02 9.89913e–02 5.12352e–02

–7.26299e–02 1.39969e–02 –8.43933e–02 2.40706e–02 –3.08347e–02 –7.20671e–02
2.76463e–01 3.30438e–01 3.80859e–02 9.14251e–02

1.16140e–01 6.60441e–02 –6.56658e–02 –3.24131e–02 1.24872e–01 –7.61784e–02
–2.32851e–01 –1.53873e–01 3.63699e–02 2.85644e–01

4.04029e–02 1.54646e–01 –2.68456e–02 3.36918e–02 –1.91935e–01 2.28271e–01 –1.93628e–01
3.86685e–02 1.02273e–01 4.11630e–02

1.34092e–01 2.10905e–02 –2.28208e–01 –1.41330e–01 –3.37850e–01 1.62136e–01
–2.53480e–01 2.93980e–02 –3.88667e–02 –1.10969e–01

–2.60985e–02 –1.29961e–01 –1.21331e–01 1.80849e–01 1.85689e–02 –3.01514e–02
–4.97732e–03 1.57721e–01 1.65492e–01 –2.01690e–02

–1.08547e–01 1.62958e–01 –4.97631e–02 1.55311e–01 2.41228e–01 1.22816e–01 –2.66239e–02
–8.23251e–02 –7.51498e–02 –7.93151e–02

quisition correspond to the rates expected on the basis of LSA theory, with no need to postulate language specific innate vocabulary knowledge.

There is, of course, a huge difference in the way semantic spaces are constructed in LSA and by people. The human semantic space is generated gradually and continues to evolve throughout life, whereas LSA does a single or a series of SVDs on larger and larger corpora of texts. Nevertheless, LSA can be used as a tool to explore human vocabulary acquisition, as Denhière, Lemaire, Bellissens, and Jhean-Larose (chap. 8 in this volume) have done. In related work, Jones and Mewhort (in press) uses an LSA-like holographic representation that is capable of modeling the gradual acquisition of vocabulary during childhood. We may anticipate that in the coming years the work of Denhière et al. and Jones will allow the modeling of human vocabulary acquisition on a scale that has not been possible previously.

LSA has also proven useful for the analysis of texts because it provides an automatic and objective method to compare texts in terms of their content. Much work has focused on the concept of coherence between the sentences or paragraphs of a text with the cosine as a convenient measure of semantic coherence (Foltz, chap. 9 in this volume; McNamara, Cai, & Louwerse, chap. 19 in this volume). Thus, the effects of linguistic signals in a text, which indicate cohesion, and semantic similarity, which accounts for coherence, can be distinguished in a principled way using LSA. Whereas coherence is concerned with the relationship between text units, it is also important to analyze the relation between a reader's prior knowledge and potential texts to be read. If a text is too close to what a student already knows, then little can be learned from it; if it is too distant, then little can be learned from it either, because there are no ways to link such a text with prior knowledge. Again, the cosine between relevant portions of prior knowledge and the text to be studied provides a measure of whether a text is too hard or too easy, or for whether it is at an intermediate distance that makes efficient learning possible (Wolfe et al., 1998). Indeed, the principle goal of the Coh-Metrix project (Graesser, McNamara, Louwerse, & Cai, 2004; McNamara, Cai, & Louwerse, chap. 19 in this volume) is to provide indices of both cohesion and coherence in to order to match readers to their optimal levels of difficulty in text. LSA laid the groundwork for this goal to be reached.

Although LSA in its original form has proven to be enormously useful, both theoretically and practically, a great deal of work in recent years has gone toward expanding the scope of LSA and exploring LSA-like alternative methods for the semantic representation of language. One line of research that remains squarely within LSA, but aims to extend the range of phenomena LSA can account for, has been the work on predication. The predication model (Kintsch, 2001; Kintsch, chap. 5 in this volume) is an algorithm that describes how a context sensitive meaning for a word can be generated from its context-free LSA representation as a vector in the semantic space. Thus, the predication model is really a model of contextualization and the term "predication" does not really do justice to the recent applications of the model. The heart of the model, as described in this volume, is a generative lexicon, a theory of how word meanings emerge in context, even though each word is represented by a single context-free vector. The claim is made that the predication algorithm describes not only the contextual generation of different word meanings (*bark* in the context of *tree* and *dog*) and word senses (*run* in the context of *horse* and *color*), but also nonliteral meaning, as in metaphors of the type noun-is-noun (*My surgeon is a butcher*). That does not mean that all metaphors are comprehended in this way. The comprehension of some involves analytic reasoning, not simple contextualization. To understand *She shot down my arguments*, it is necessary to reconstruct an underlying analogy to realize that my arguments were destroyed like a bird or plane that was shot down. Interestingly, LSA can model this sort of analogical reasoning too, using the predication algorithm to generate contextualized word senses, but then focusing on the relations that hold between words, rather than their content (Kintsch, in press; Mangalath, Quesada, & Kintsch, 2004).

LSA knowledge is purely symbolic (as opposed to embodied, e.g.), derived from written language only. Human knowledge and experience are richer, based on our interactions with the real world. It is not all book knowledge. Because computers have no bodies and cannot live and act as people do, this constitutes an inherent limitation of LSA-like knowledge representations. It is not a fatal one, however, because of the very nature of language. Human language is not an arbitrary symbol system, but has evolved as a tool of the mind to aid in its interaction with the world and other people. Talking (or writing) about perception, action, or emotion is not the same as perception, action,or emotion, but neither is it unrelated. If it were, language would be far less useful to us. Instead, language mirrors the world of perception and action, mapping it into the symbolic domain. This map is rather faithful, which means, for instance, that many perceptual relations are implicitly preserved in the multidimensional LSA space. Louwerse (chap. 6 in this volume) and Kintsch (chap. 5 in this volume) have explored these issues further. Their point is not that language has evolved and is used divorced from perception and action. Instead, language maps perception and action with great subtlety into the symbolic domain, so that a computer-based symbolic system like LSA is sensitive to perceptual distinctions reflected in the language. People, of course, can do better than that, because they can rely both on direct experience, as well as its reflection in the mirror of language.

Most people are surprised, to the point of disbelief, that LSA can do as well as it does when it disregards word order, not to mention syntax. Landauer (chap. 1 in this volume) has argued that they should not be so surprised, because there is a great deal of information carried by the words of a sentence, irrespective of their order. We do not need the word order to understand *The boy climbed the mountain*. Similarly, in *The boy saw the deer*, the words alone irrespective of their order, tell a great deal—although not all about that sentence. Syntax and word order are of obvious importance, and neglect is a major limitation of LSA. Whereas it is possible in principle to include word order information in an SVD, LSA is not well suited for that purpose. However, alternative approaches currently being explored that preserve the essence of LSA (unguided learning from a large corpus of text) appear to be very promising in overcoming this limitation. Two of these approaches, including the SP model of Dennis (chap. 3 in this volume; Dennis, 2005) and recent work by Jones and Mewhort (in press), should be mentioned. Jones is working with a semantic representation that differentiates between item and order information, thus permitting a separate assessment of their contribution.

These types of endeavors, combining semantic models with order information, are likely to make substantial contributions, both theoretically and practically. In the long run, more than that will be required, however. Philosophers, linguists, and psychologists (including one if us, Kintsch, 1974, 1998) have long argued that propositions, not single words, are the real units of cognition. Progress in that direction is much more difficult to achieve than merely including word order information in an LSA-like representation. Nevertheless, such progress does not appear to be impossible, and at least a beginning has been made with the SP model (Dennis, 2005; Dennis & Kintsch, in press). The crucial idea in the work of Dennis has been to abandon the traditional attempt to construct an intensional semantics, which has never gone beyond the stage of hand-coding, and to substitute for it an extensional semantics that can be derived by an unguided statistical learning mechanism. In an intensional semantics, such as the case grammar of Fillmore (1968), the propositional representation of a sentence like *The boy saw the dear* is coded in terms of a predicate SEE, and Agent BOY, and Object DEER, yielding *(SEE, Agent: BOY, Object: DEER)*, using the notation of Kintsch (1974). The trouble is that it has never been possible to construct an automatic parser that can take as input arbitrary English sentences and produce their propositional representation. The extensional semantics of the SP model circumvent this problem by automatically constructing for a verb such as *see*, a set of words that appear in the equivalent of an "Agent slot," and a set of words that appear in the "Object slot," thus defining Agent and Object by their extensions only. Just how far this approach can be pushed remains to be seen, but it certainly appears to be a promising way to deal with the problem of constructing propositional units.

Quesada's chapter on spaces for problem solving (Quesada, chap. 4 in this volume) takes the LSA methodology out of the realm of language altogether. LSA describes the latent structure of semantics as it is inferred from the way people use words; LPSA describes the latent structure of complex problems from the way people have attempted to solve them. Instead of words, LPSA observes actions and events, and problem-solving episodes correspond to documents. A latent problem structure is revealed from the way actual problem solvers interact with their environment. Simon (1969) used the metaphor of the ant on the beach: The path of the ant is determined not only by the nature of the ant, but to a large extent also by the nature of the beach—where the big pebbles are and where the going is smooth. LPSA maps how the beach looks to experienced problem solvers: What they do depends on how they perceive their environment. Gibson (1979) made a similar point about perception in general: To understand it, we need to study not only the perceptual mechanisms of people, but also the affordances of the environment. The LPSA generated problem spaces are maps of these affordances for particular problem-solving tasks. The LSA space is the map for how we deal with words.

PRACTICAL CONTRIBUTIONS

At the heart of learning or knowledge acquisition is, of course, knowledge. The process of helping a student or employee acquire new knowledge requires monitoring the state and quality of prior knowledge as well as changes in knowledge. Because LSA provided a means to efficiently gauge states of knowledge and understanding in automated systems, LSA essentially opened the door to many educational applications. AutoTutor is one of these applications (Graesser et al., chap. 13 in this volume). The beginning of AutoTutor, as with so many of these types of systems, was marked with a grant proposal in 1996. Funding (in relatively large amounts) is essential for projects to develop and test educational applications such as the ones discussed in this volume. Not only did the existence of LSA make it feasible to create AutoTutor, it also made it possible to convince funding agencies that the concept of engaging in a dialogue with an automated tutor was even a possibility. Indeed, the availability and success of LSA has led to the proposal and subsequent funding of an increasing number of educational applications based on using LSA or similar algorithms to assess learners' knowledge and understanding.

AutoTutor uses a pedagogical agent, or talking head, to converse with students about topics such as physics or computer technology. The goal is to engage the student in a dialog composed of questions, hints, and prompts such that the student improves their understanding of a specific content area. LSA is used to compare the student's answers to benchmarks or desired answers. When the answers reach a certain threshold indicating that the right answers have been given (Graesser et al., chap. 13 in this volume; Hu et al., chap. 20 in this volume), then the student is posed a different question. This continues until the tutoring session has been completed. LSA is essential to the success of AutoTutor for several reasons. First, LSA allows a rapid, automated assessment of the student answer to guide the dialog. Second, in such an open-ended learning environment, where the student can respond with just about anything, it is important that the system be capable of judging remote associations as related to the domain—this would not be possible in a purely word-based system.

Similar to AutoTutor, iSTART (McNamara, Boonthum et al., chap. 12 in this volume) also uses LSA to guide dialog between pedagogical agents (albeit full bodied) with students. Like AutoTutor, the first iSTART systems were based on the use of benchmarks—comparing the student's answer, or in this case explanation, to a set of ideal explanations (see Millis et al., chap. 11 in this volume). For iSTART, however, this approach couldn't work in the long run because it needs to be extendable to other texts with little manual preparation (e.g., so that it can be used with classroom texts). The use of the target text as the comparison was possible because, in contrast to AutoTutor, which is concerned with accuracy of content, iSTART is concerned only with the quality of the answer in terms of evidence of strategy use. That is, it assesses the quality of self-explanations in terms of whether high-level strategies, such as making bridging inferences or elaborations, are evident. Because the assessment of strategies is possible without assessing the accuracy of the content, ideal answer benchmarks could be dropped from the system with little loss of accuracy (McNamara, Boonthum et al., chap. 12 in this volume). Instead, the system now uses a combination of word-based and LSA algorithms that compare the explanations to benchmarks derived solely from the text itself. As discussed in the chapters by Millis et al. (chap. 11 in this volume) and McNamara, Boonthum, et al. (chap. 12 in this volume), this system works remarkably well, with a high correspondence to experts' judgments of explanations' quality.

Many of the educational applications use a combination of information sources, in addition to LSA, to judge students input. That is, LSA is often augmented with information from the explicit words or syntax. This is true of AutoTutor and iSTART, as well as the conceivably most successful educational applications that use LSA, the Intelligent Essay Assessor (Landauer, Foltz, & Laham, 2003) and Summary Street® (E. Kintsch et al., chap. 14 in this volume). These two systems have had marked success. The Intelligent Essay Assessor is widely used commercially, having, for example, instantly scored many millions of practice essays for important high-stakes exams with as high reliability as two human scorers (http://www.p-k-t.com). Summary Street® is currently used in over 300 schools and has been shown to not only help middle school students to write better summaries when they use the tool (Wade-Stein & Kintsch, 2004), but also when they no longer have access to it (Franzke et al., 2005). Summary Street® has produced highly significant gains on reading, writing, and related scores on large-scale high-stakes exams after only a few weeks of use.

Automated systems to grade essays and responses with LSA use several different methods. The Intelligent Essay Assessor compares the to-be-graded essay to a large set of hand-graded essays and assigns it a grade based on those of the essays most similar to it. AutoTutor compares the student's response to a question with ideal benchmark answers. ISTART and Summary Street® compare the student's explanation or summary directly with the target text. Which method is used depends on the system training time and effort to apply the system to a new target text or content area, in relation to how important it is that the system be quickly or immediately applicable to a wide range of texts or topics. There is also the question of feasibility—for an essay that integrates ideas from a variety of texts or sources, it is less feasible to use texts as a benchmark.

The success of LSA in educational applications is landmarked in the chapter by Streeter and colleagues (chap. 15 in this volume). Their use of LSA has moved from passive information retrieval in the late 1980s to its current use in online learning and discussion forums to actively monitor and assess individuals and groups. Knowledge Post is a prototype of success for LSA because it combines so many of its capabilities into one integrated system designed to support online learning and collaboration. Similar to other systems, it uses LSA to search for semantically similar notes and provide summaries of notes, and it incorporates the Intelligent Essay Assessor to grade essays in a class setting. Its more novel contributions are its functions to assess and promote the quality of group discussions. Online learning is clearly a direction that many universities are taking; however, the load on the instructor's time is excessive. A system such as Knowledge Post facilitates distance learning without sacrificing the learning activities so important to knowledge acquisition, interactive dialog, and writing.

CONCLUSIONS

We started out by claiming that LSA provides a basis for a computational theory of meaning. What can we conclude about the current status of this claim? At a minimum, the work presented here demonstrates that it is reasonable to persevere in pursuing this goal. The work reviewed in this book shows that it is possible to build computational models based on LSA for many semantic problems. Concrete progress has been made in several areas, but the task is quite far from done.

A good example of how much has been achieved versus what still needs to be achieved is given by the research on words versus propositions mentioned earlier. LSA itself is strictly word based and disregards syntax and word order. Recent work has made progress in incorporating word order information in LSA-like systems (Dennis, chap. 3 in this volume). That is a significant step forward, but it still leaves us far from the goal of propositional representation. Solving the word order problem does not by itself provide a propositional analysis. Word order information is important and useful, but it is not the same thing as information about the propositional structure of texts. Nonetheless, just as we have seen such substantial progress is so many other areas in the last decade, we have no doubt that progress will continue to be made along both of these fronts.

The theory of meaning that we aspire to is still incomplete. In the application domain, on the other hand, LSA has cashed the promissory notes, at least some of them. Mature and proven applications of LSA exist today, several of which are described in the present volume. More importantly, what has been done suggests a rich set of potential LSA-based projects that can be done and will be done in the years to come.

Whereas LSA has been tremendously successful both as a theory of cognition and as a practical tool for constructing representations of meaning, these are the most tangible contributions of LSA. Embedded within the LSA enterprise there is also a radical reconceptualization both of how one should go about producing cognitive theories and how one should test them—what we might call the corpus-based approach.

Prior to LSA (and still more often than not), models of cognitive process have focused on small-scale demonstrations that often required significant hand-coding. The LSA message is that scale matters—not just quantitatively, but qualitatively. The meaning representations produced by LSA rely on triangulation in a large corpus and many key properties simply do not occur until critical mass is reached. So, although models like the topics model (Griffiths & Steyvers, 2004; Griffiths, Steyvers, Blei, & Tanenbaum, 2005) and the SP model (Dennis, 2005) employ quite different mathematics, they retain an essential element of LSA—the application of very simple mathematical procedures to very large corpora—so that the burden of explanation lies in the corpus rather than in the method.This general approach aligns well with the rational approach of Anderson (1990). The basic tenet of this approach is that human cognition has been optimized to the structure of the environment, so to understand cognition one should first understand the environment and then build the regularities one finds into a model. The LSA approach removes the middle man. It says optimize directly to a corpus representing the environment using the simplest (and possibly a simpler) model that you can get away with. In this way, the LSA approach is similar to and can ride on the back of current developments in machine learning and computational linguistics.

In addition, the LSA approach rethinks what it means to test a theory. First, it starts by pointing out that a corpus is an empirical record of human behavior as surely as the results from laboratory experiments. By its very nature, LSA recapitulates important properties of the corpus on which it is trained and its ability to do so is a testament to its ability to do what people do. Furthermore, because the corpus contains behaviors roughly in proportion to the frequencies with which they actually occur, LSA is sure to recapitulate the important stuff first. Although laboratory studies remain the best way to illuminate certain issues, they have no mechanism that inherently indicates how crucial the issue being investigated is to the general behavior of the system.

Scale matters not only for theory, but also for applications. The development of LSA has progressed to a large extent through a series of demonstrations of practical usefulness. The ability to grade essays remains the paradigmatic confirmation of LSA's success. Scale is an important property of evaluation also. By focusing evaluation on applications, LSA has been tested on things people actually do at the scale that they actually do them.

REFERENCES

Anderson J. R. (1990). *The adaptive character of thought*. Mahwah, NJ: Lawrence Erlbaum Associates.

Dennis, S. (2005). A memory-based theory of verbal cognition. *Cognitive Science, 29*(2), 145–193.

Dennis, S. & Kintsch, W. (in press). Text mapping and inference rule generation problems in text comprehension: Evaluating a memory-based account. In F. Schmalhofer & C. Perfetti (Eds.), *Higher level language processes in the brain: Inference and comprehension*. Mahwah, NJ: Lawrence Erlbaum Associates.

Fillmore, C. J. (1968). *Lexical entries for verbs*. Dordrecht, Holland: D. Reidel.

Forbus, K., Gentner, D., & Law, K. (1995). MAC/FAC: A model of similarity-based retrieval. *Cognitive Science, 19*, 141–205.

Franzke, M., Kintsch, E., Caccamise, D., & Johnson, N. (2005). Summary Street®: Computer support for comprehension and writing. *Journal of Educational Computing Research, 33*, 53–80.

Gibson, J. J. (1979). *The ecological approach to visual perception*. Boston: Houghton Mifflin

Graesser, A. C., McNamara, D. S., Louwerse, M. M., & Cai, Z. (2004). Coh-Metrix: Analysis of text on cohesion and language. *Behavioral Research Methods, Instruments, and Computers, 36*, 193–202.

Griffiths, T. L., & Steyvers, M. (2004). Finding scientific topics. *Proceedings of the National Academy of Sciences, 101*, 5228–5235.

Griffiths, T. L., Steyvers, M., Blei, D. M., & Tenenbaum, J. B. (2005). Integrating topics and syntax. In L. K. Saul, Y. Weiss, & L. Bottou (Eds.), *Advances in neural information processing system 17* (pp. 537–544). Cambridge, MA: MIT Press.

Holyoak, K., & Thagard, P. (1989). Analogical mapping by constraint satisfaction. *Cognitive Science, 13*, 295–355.

Jones, M. N., & Mewhort, D. (in press). Representing semantic and syntactic information in a composite holographic lexicon. *Psychological Review*.

Kintsch, W. (1974). *The representation of meaning in memory*. Hillsdale, NJ: Lawrence Erlbaum Associates.

Kintsch, W. (1998). *Comprehension: A paradigm for cognition*. New York: Cambridge University Press.

Kintsch, W. (2001). Predication. *Cognitive Science, 25*, 173–202.

Kintsch, W. (in press). How the mind computes the meaning of metaphor: A simulation based on LSA. In R. Gibbs (Ed.), *Cambridge handbook of metaphor and thought*. New York: Cambridge University Press.

Landauer, T., & Dumais, S. (1997). A solution to Plato's problem: The latent semantic analysis theory of acquisition, induction, and representation of knowledge. *Psychological Review, 104*, 211–240.

Landauer, T. K., Laham, D., & Foltz, P. W. (2003). Automated essay assessment. *Assessment in Education: Principles, Policy and Practice, 10*, 295–308.

Lenat, D. B. (1995). Cyc: A large-scale investment in knowledge infrastructure. *Communications of the ACM, 38*, 33–38.

Mangalath, P., Quesada, J., & Kintsch, W. (2004). Analogy-making as predication using relational information and LSA vectors. In K. D. Forbus, D. Gentner, & T. Regier (Eds.), *Proceedings of the 26th Annual Meeting of the Cognitive Science Society*. Chicago: Lawrence Erlbaum Associates.

Simon, H. A. (1969) *The sciences of the artificial*. Cambridge, MA: MIT Press

Wade-Stein, D., & Kintsch, E. (2004). Summary Street: Interactive computer support for writing. *Cognition and Instruction, 22*, 333–362.

Wolfe, M. B. W., Schreiner, M. E., Rehder, B., Laham, D., Foltz, P. W., Kintsch, W., et al. (1998). Learning from text: Matching readers and text by latent semantic analysis. *Discourse Processes, 25*, 309–336.

Author Index

LSA-Based Subject Index

INDEXING METHOD

The indexing for this volume was performed with a novel experimental method used here for the first time. The goal was to help readers find pages of interest by semantic content rather than literal words.

The index was constructed as follows. First, for each page in the book, LSA was used to find a set of three terms such that the LSA representation of their combined meaning was as close as possible to that of the whole page. Call this an LSA "concept set." Each of these terms then became a potential main alphabetized entry. Next, every page that included the main entry term in *its* LSA concept set was given a subheading under the main entry; its cosine with the main entry term listed first. Note that subheaded pages do not necessarily contain the main entry word; rather they are all similar to the common concept that it represents. When the literal word of the main heading does not appear in a referenced page, the page number is italicized. Finally, for each of the subheadings, one or two additional high-cosine terms were chosen from *that page's* LSA concept set. When these terms do not appear literally on the referenced page, they are italicized.

A certain amount of manual pre- and postediting was used to reduce redundancy and other flaws. It is hoped that the need for human intervention can be reduced in future versions. The editors will welcome all comments from readers.

INTERPRETING THE INDEX ENTRIES

Alphabetized main entries are LSA-generated terms that have high similarity (cosine >= .2; ~2 sd above average) with one or more pages of the text. Subheadings list pages with cosines >= .20 with their main entries—plus a few added manually. Italicized subhead *page numbers* indicate pages that have high similarity to a term but do not contain the literal term; italicized *key words* are ones with above-threshold cosines with the page they index but do not appear in it.

Readers looking for literal word occurrences should ignore italicized references and keywords. Those looking for pages with particular semantic content should be guided by similarity to the main entry words modulated by their cosine similarities to the concepts they reference, and by the keyword tags for individual pages whether or not italicized. *The combination of similarity to main entry words and to keywords and phrases for particular pages should be the best guide to content of interest.*

Subject Index

See the first page of the index for an explanation of how to interpret the LSA-based entries.